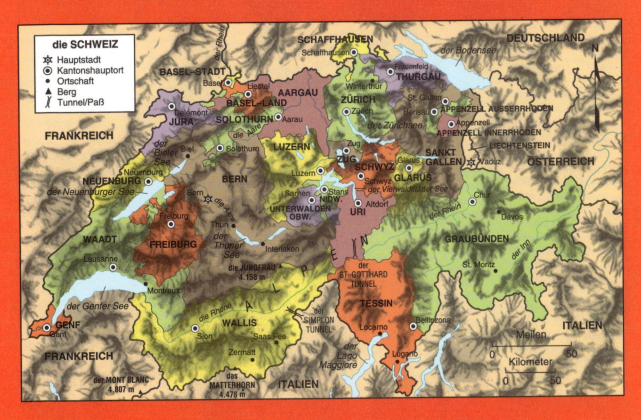

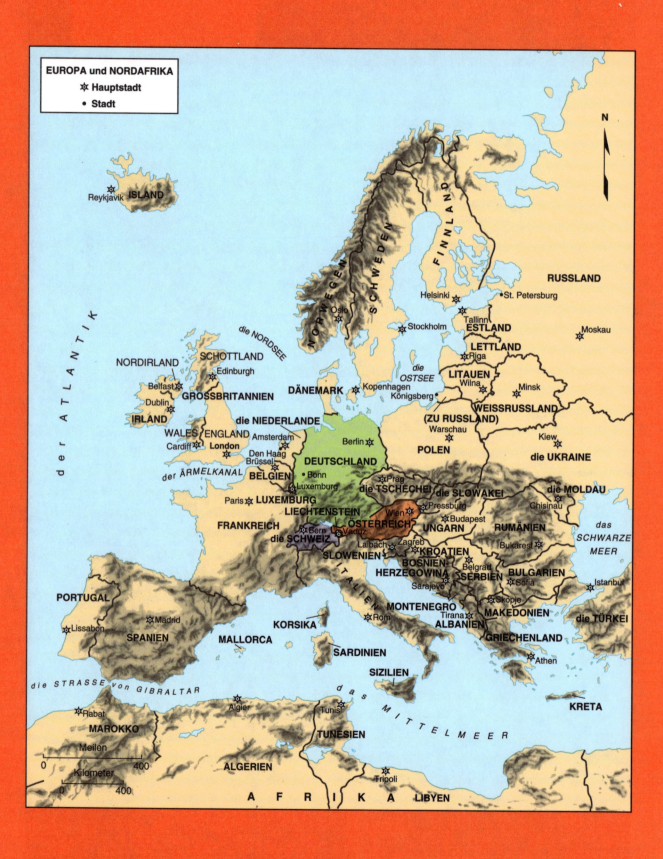

WIE GEHT'S?

An Introductory German Course

Fifth Edition

WIE GEHT'S?

An Introductory German Course

Fifth Edition

Dieter Sevin

Vanderbilt University

Ingrid Sevin   **Katrin T. Bean**

Holt, Rinehart and Winston
Harcourt Brace College Publishers

Fort Worth   Philadelphia   San Diego   New York   Orlando   Austin   San Antonio
Toronto   Montreal   London   Sydney   Tokyo

Publisher	Ted Buchholz
Senior Acquisitions Editor	Jim Harmon
Developmental Editor	John Baxter
Project Editor	Annelies Schlickenrieder
Production Manager	Debra A. Jenkin
Senior Art Director	David A. Day
Illustrations	Tom O'Sullivan
Photo Researcher	Judy Mason
Composition	Monotype

Cover Image: For permission to use "Bremer Stadtmusikanten" from the poster series ECHT DEUTSCH, the publisher is grateful to the Goethe-Institut Werbekommission in Munich.

ISBN: 0-15-501060-3

Library of Congress Catalog Card Number: 94-75563
Copyright © 1995, 1991, 1988, 1984, 1980 by Holt, Rinehart and Winston, Inc.

Photo and illustration credits appear on page 491.

Address for Editorial Correspondence
Harcourt Brace College Publishers, 301 Commerce Street, Suite 3700, Fort Worth, TX 76102.

Address for Orders
Harcourt Brace & Company, 6277 Sea Harbor Drive, Orlando, FL 32887.
1-800-782-4479, or 1-800-433-0001 (in Florida).

Printed in the United States of America

4 5 6 7 8 9 0 1 2 3   0 4 8   9 8 7 6 5 4 3 2 1

To the Student

The double meaning of *Wie geht's?* reflects the double goal of the book: to show the German language at work and to show how the language works. The main text is divided into six pre-units (*Schritte*), fifteen chapters (*Kapitel*), five review sections (*Rückblicke*), and an appendix.

The purpose of the pre-units is to acquaint you with the German language and the language learning process by focusing on listening and speaking. When you have completed the last pre-unit, you should be able to greet others, describe your classroom and your clothes, use numbers, discuss the weather, and tell time, all in German.

A summary of the learning objectives opens each chapter. It is followed by a cultural preview (*Vorschau*) that provides you with background information for the chapter topic. The first section of the learning materials is called *Gespräche*. It includes one or two dialogues that focus on the topic of the chapter and function as models for conversation. English translations for these dialogues can be found in the appendix, but use them only when you have exhausted all other means of trying to understand the German. Cultural notes (*Übrigens*) that follow the dialogues explain differences between life in the United States or Canada and countries where German is spoken.

Most of the new vocabulary is listed in *Wortschatz 1;* it is arranged thematically, and nouns are listed in alphabetical order according to gender. The vocabulary list is followed by exercises (*Zum Thema*) that foster communication and help you learn the new words. Here, and again after the reading text, you will find an exercise (*Hören Sie zu*) that will help improve your listening comprehension. To complete it, you will need to listen to the tape that accompanies the book.

Each chapter introduces two or three major points of grammar. A variety of exercises (*Übungen*) provides practice of the principles presented.

A reading passage (*Einblicke*) features one or more cultural aspects related to the chapter topic. It offers additional examples of the new grammar and a review of the chapter vocabulary. A list of cognates and other easily recognized words precedes the text (*Was ist das?*); other words that are not part of the active vocabulary are given in the margin. Those few additional words that must be mastered actively are listed in *Wortschatz 2;* they will recur in later chapters. The reading text is followed by exercises (*Zum Text*) that check comprehension and provide additional grammar, writing, and speaking practice. They are preceded and followed by additional cultural notes in English and a second listening exercise (*Hören Sie zu*).

The *Sprechsituationen* (Speaking Situations) at the end of the pre-units and each chapter list and practice expressions that are useful in social situations, such as extending, accepting, or declining invitations.

After the pre-units and Chapters 3, 7, 11, and 15, you will find review sections (*Rückblicke*) that deal with structures and vocabulary. Correct answers for the exercises that are marked with an asterisk can be found in the appendix. The appendix also includes information on predicting the gender of some nouns, a grammar summary in chart form, tables of all basic verb forms, lists of irregular verbs, translations of dialogues, a German–English and English–German vocabulary, and a grammar index.

The tape program and the lab manual/workbook provide additional practice in listening, speaking, and writing. On the tapes you will find the dialogues and reading texts, supplementary grammar exercises, listening-comprehension exercises, and pronunciation practice. The lab manual section of the workbook (*Im Sprachlabor*) contains instructions and examples for all the grammar and pronunciation exercises, and a worksheet which will let you check your progress. The following section (*Zu Hause*) focuses on vocabulary building, structure, and cultural enrichment. The workbook also includes a complete pronunciation guide with brief explanations of correct sound production and corresponding exercises that are available on a separate tape.

The computer diskettes let you practice and review most of the exercises in the book on your own; error analysis will guide you to correct answers.

We hope that you will find this course enjoyable. You will be surprised at the rapid progress you will make in just one year. Many students have been able to study abroad after only two years of studying German!

Acknowledgments

We would like to thank the following colleagues who reviewed the manuscript during its various stages of development for the fifth edition:

Renate Born, University of Georgia at Athens; Jonathan Clark, Rutgers University; Ingeborg Goessl, University of Missouri at St. Louis; Ronald K. Morgan, Western Carolina University; Solveig Olson, University of North Texas at Denton; Graeme Tytler, Southeastern Louisiana University; Cordelia Stroinigg, University of Cincinnati; Joe Wipf, Purdue University; and Robert Youngblood, Washington and Lee University.

We wish to extend special thanks to Joe Rea Phillips of the Blair School of Music at Vanderbilt University for his musical interludes in the tape program. Finally, we are grateful to the following of Holt, Rinehart and Winston: Jim Harmon, Senior Acquisitions Editor; John Baxter, Developmental Editor; Annelies Schlickenrieder, Project Editor; David Day, Senior Art Director; Debra Jenkin, Production Manager; and Elke Herbst, Ancillary Editor.

We also wish to thank the holder of copyright of „Immer schön fressen und nicht so viel nachdenken!" from *Frankfurter Rundschau,* reprinted by permission of Stefan Schüch.

About the Cover

Gerhard Marcks' sculpture of the Bremen Town Musicians (*Die Bremer Stadtmusikanten*) stands at one corner of the Bremen city hall in northern Germany, commemorating the characters of one of the best-known folktales collected by the nineteenth-century German philologists, Jacob and Wilhelm Grimm. The Grimm brothers discovered that the story of the would-be street musicians, who combined their talents and united as one to overcome a difficult situation, is in fact common to the folklores of the peoples speaking the languages now grouped together as the Indo-European family. Jacob and Wilhelm not only left a legacy of a collected body of entertaining and instructive tales, but also made important contributions to the field of historical linguistics.

Contents

WIE GEHT'S?

An Introductory German Course

Fifth Edition

Hallo, wie geht's?

LERNZIELE   *(Learning Objectives)*

The pre-units will help you take your first steps in German. You will learn to . . .

- introduce yourself and say hello and good-bye
- describe your classroom
- talk about articles of clothing and use adjectives to describe them
- use numbers
- discuss the calendar and the weather
- tell time.

Vorschau   *(Preview)*

- The German language

Sprechsituationen   *(Communication)*

- Greeting and saying good-bye
- Expressing incomprehension

The German Language

More than 100 million people speak German as their native tongue. It is the official language in Germany, Austria, Liechtenstein, and large areas of Switzerland. It is also spoken in parts of Luxembourg, Belgium, France (Alsace), and Italy (South Tyrol), and by some of the German minorities in Poland, Romania, and a few of the republics of the former Soviet Union.

German belongs to the Germanic branch of the Indo-European language family and is closely related to Dutch, English, the Scandinavian languages, Flemish, Frisian, Yiddish, and Afrikaans. For various political, literary, and linguistic reasons, we speak of Germans and the German language as dating from around the year 800. At that time at least six major dialects and numerous variations of them were spoken. Not until the twelfth and thirteenth centuries was an effort made to write a standardized form of German; the period from 1170–1254 was one of great literary achievement. Afterwards, however, this literary language declined and, with few exceptions, Latin was used in writing; it remained the sole language of instruction at German universities until the 1700s. Luther's translation of the Bible in the sixteenth century was a major influence on the development of a common written German language. Because of political fragmentation, a standard language was slow to develop in Germany. As late as the beginning of this century, most people spoke only in dialect. First, newspapers and magazines, then radio and television, fostered the use of standard German; but regional accents are still very common, even among the highly educated.

Because German and English are members of the same branch of the Indo-European language family, they share a considerable amount of vocabulary. Some of these related words, called cognates, are identical in spelling (e.g., **der Arm, die Hand, der Finger**), and others are similar (e.g., **der Vater, die Mutter, das Haus**). As the two languages developed, certain cognates acquired different meanings, such as **die Hose** *(pair of pants)* versus "hose" *(stockings)*. Differences between English and German cognates developed quite systematically; here are a few examples:

	English	German
t > z	*ten*	zehn
	salt	Salz
p > pf	*pound*	Pfund
	apple	Apfel
t > ss	*water*	Wasser
	white	weiß
p > f	*ship*	Schiff
	help	helfen
k > ch	*book*	Buch
	make	machen
d > t	*bed*	Bett
	dance	tanzen
th > d	*bath*	Bad
	thank	danken

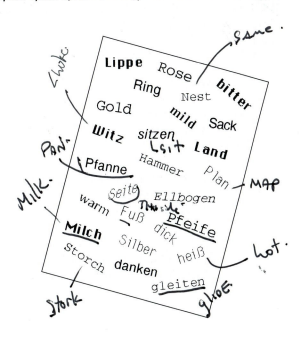

Guten Tag!

Wie geht's?

> Read the following dialogues aloud until you can do so fluently, and be prepared to answer questions about them. If necessary, you may consult the translations in the Appendix.

HERR SANDERS	Guten Tag!
FRAU LEHMANN	Guten Tag!
HERR SANDERS	Ich heiße Sanders, Willi Sanders. Und Sie, wie heißen Sie?
FRAU LEHMANN	Mein Name ist Erika Lehmann.
HERR SANDERS	Freut mich.

HERR MEIER	Guten Morgen, Frau Fiedler! Wie geht es Ihnen?
FRAU FIEDLER	Danke, gut. Und Ihnen?
HERR MEIER	Danke, es geht mir auch gut.

HEIDI	Hallo, Ute! Wie geht's?
UTE	Tag, Heidi. Ach, ich bin müde.
HEIDI	Ich auch. Zu viel Streß. Bis später!
UTE	Tschüß!

> You are responsible for knowing all the vocabulary in this section, including the headings. Be sure to learn the gender and plural forms of nouns. Words and phrases listed under *Zum Erkennen* are intended for comprehension only; you will not be asked to produce them actively.

lol24 Learn for next class

- In German, all nouns are capitalized.

- The pronoun **ich** *(I)* is NOT capitalized unless it occurs at the beginning of a sentence. The pronoun **Sie** *(you)* is always capitalized.

der Herr, die Herren *(pl.)*	*Mr.; gentleman*
das Fräulein, die Fräulein *(pl.)*✠	*young lady; Miss*
die Frau, die Frauen *(pl.)*	*Mrs., Ms.; woman; wife*

Guten Morgen! / Guten Abend!	*Good morning. / Good evening.*
Guten Tag!	*Hello.*
Tag!	*Hi! (informal)*

Wie heißen Sie?	*What's your name? (formal)*
Mein Name ist . . .	*My name is . . .*

heißen	*to be called*
ich heiße . . .	*my name is . . .*
Sie heißen . . .	*your name is . . . (formal)*

Freut mich.	*I'm glad to meet you.*
Wie geht es Ihnen?	*How are you? (formal)*
Wie geht's?	*How are you? (informal)*
wie?	*how?*
Es geht mir gut.*	*I'm fine.*
gut / schlecht	*good, fine / bad(ly)*
wunderbar	*wonderful(ly), great*
Ich bin müde.*	*I'm tired.*
ja / nein	*yes / no*
danke / bitte	*thank you / please*
auch	*also, too*
nicht	*not*
und	*and*
Auf Wiedersehen!	*Good-bye.*
Tschüß! *(colloquial)*	*Good-bye. Bye.*

Ich bin müde!

✠ In modern German usage the title **Fräulein** is being replaced by **Frau** for adult women, regardless of a woman's age or marital status. Only very young unmarried women are now addressed with **Fräulein.**

* Es **geht** mir gut (schlecht, wunderbar). BUT Ich **bin** müde.

ZUM ERKENNEN   *(For comprehension only):* Hallo! *(Hi! Hello!);* ach *(oh);* ich auch *(me too);* zu viel Streß *(too much stress);* Bis später! *(See you later!)*

Aussprache (*Pronunciation*): a, e, er, i, o, u

> The words listed below are either familiar words, cognates (words related to English), or proper names (**Erika, Amerika**). A simplified phonetic spelling for each sound is given in brackets. The colon (:) following a vowel means that the vowel is long. Pay particular attention to word stress as you hear it from your instructor or the tape. For a while, you may want to mark words for stress.

Hören Sie gut zu und wiederholen Sie!   *(Listen carefully and repeat.)*

[a:]   **A**dam, **A**bend, Kl**a**ra, D**a**vid, T**a**g, Ban**a**ne, N**a**me, j**a**
[a]   **A**nna, **A**lbert, H**a**ns, w**a**s, d**a**s, d**a**nke, H**a**nd
[e:]   **E**rika, L**e**hmann, **E**duard, P**e**ter, Am**e**rika, g**e**ht, T**ee**, S**ee**
[e]   **E**llen, H**e**rmann, **e**s, schl**e**cht
[ə]   (*unstressed* **e**) Ut**e**, dank**e**, heiß**e**, gut**e**n, Morg**e**n, Ihn**e**n
[ʌ]   (*final* **-er**) Diet**er**, Fiedl**er**, Rain**er**, Mei**er**, Wern**er**, Schneid**er**
[i:]   **I**hnen, Mar**i**a, Sab**i**ne, m**i**r, W**ie**dersehen, w**ie**, S**ie**
[i]   **I**ngrid, L**i**nda, **i**ch, b**i**n, b**i**tte, n**i**cht, Schr**i**tt
[o:]   **R**obert, M**o**nika, R**o**se, H**o**se, B**oo**t, s**o**, w**o**, Z**oo**
[o]   **O**lga, **O**skar, **O**liver, **o**ft, M**o**rgen, S**o**mmer, k**o**sten
[u:]   **U**te, **U**we, G**u**drun, H**u**go, g**u**t, N**u**del, Sch**u**h
[u]   **U**rsula, G**u**stav, **u**nd, w**u**nderbar, Ges**u**ndheit, H**u**nger, B**u**tter

- As you may have noticed, double vowels (**Tee**), vowels followed by **h** (**geht**), and the combination **ie** (**wie**) are long. Vowels followed by double consonants (two identical consonants as in **Sommer**) are short.

Mündliche Übungen
(Oral Exercises)

A.   Mustersätze   *(Patterns and cues)*

> These patterns give you a chance to practice phrases from the dialogues and the vocabulary of each *Schritt*. Listen carefully and repeat the sentences until you can say them fluently.

1. Willi Sanders: **Ich heiße** Willi Sanders.
    Hugo Schmidt, Helmut Rose, Gudrun Kleese, Anna Peters
2. Erika Lehmann: **Heißen Sie** Erika Lehmann?
    Monika Schulz, Brigitte Fischer, Wolfgang Friedrich, Hermann Ohler
3. Hugo Schmidt: **Ja, ich heiße** Hugo Schmidt.
    Helmut Rose, Hans Holbein, Brigitte Fischer, Gudrun Kleese
4. Oskar Meier: **Nein, ich heiße nicht** Oskar Meier.
    Gustav Mahler, Clara Schumann, Wolfgang Amadeus Mozart
5. Frau Fiedler: **Wie geht es Ihnen,** Frau Fiedler?
    Fräulein Lehmann, Herr Sanders, Frau Bauer, Herr Meier
6. gut: **Es geht mir** gut.
    auch gut, nicht gut, schlecht, nicht schlecht, wunderbar

B. Das Alphabet

1. **Lesen Sie laut!** *(Read aloud.)*

a	ah	**g**	geh	**m**	emm	**s**	ess	**y**	üppsilon
b	beh	**h**	hah	**n**	enn	**t**	teh	**z**	tsett
c	tseh	**i**	ih	**o**	oh	**u**	uh	**ā**	äh (a-umlaut)
d	deh	**j**	jot	**p**	peh	**v**	fau	**ō**	öh (o-umlaut)
e	eh	**k**	kah	**q**	kuh	**w**	weh	**ū**	üh (u-umlaut)
f	eff	**l**	ell	**r**	err	**x**	iks	**ß**	ess-tsett

For capital letters say **Großes A (B, C . . .)**. For further explanation of the **ß**-sound, see III A.6 in the pronunciation section of the Workbook.

2. **Buchstabieren Sie auf deutsch!** *(Spell in German.)*

BMW, VW, UPS, BRD, USA;
ja, gut, müde, danke, schlecht, heißen, Fräulein, Name, wunderbar

LERNTIP

What's it like to learn a language?

Learning another language is more like learning a musical instrument or a sport than studying philosophy or history. Just as you can't learn to play the piano or swim by reading about it, you can't learn a foreign language by thinking or reading about it. You must practice. Listen to your instructor, to tapes, to the answers of your fellow students. Speak German every chance you get. Whenever possible, read the language aloud and write it.

Remember also that you are still improving your English; therefore don't expect perfection in another language. You made mistakes while learning English; when you are learning a foreign language, mistakes are also inevitable. With daily practice, however, your fluency in German will rapidly increase.

Prepare all assignments so that you can answer fluently in class.

Aufgabe
(Assignment)

A. Buchstabieren Sie Ihren Namen auf deutsch! *(Spell your name in German.)*

B. Was sagen Sie? *(What do you say? Read the cue lines and prepare appropriate responses.)*

S1 Guten Tag!
S2 _____ .
S1 Ich heiße _____ . Und Sie, wie heißen Sie?
S2 Ich heiße _____ .
S1 Freut mich.
S2 Wie geht es Ihnen?
S1 _____ . Und Ihnen?
S2 _____ .
S1 Auf Wiedersehen!

Klassenzimmer und Farben

Was ist das?

DEUTSCHPROFESSOR	Hören Sie jetzt gut zu, und antworten Sie auf deutsch! Was ist das?
JIM MILLER	Das ist der Bleistift.
DEUTSCHPROFESSOR	Welche Farbe hat der Bleistift?
SUSAN SMITH	Gelb.
DEUTSCHPROFESSOR	Bilden Sie einen Satz, bitte!
SUSAN SMITH	Der Bleistift ist gelb.
DEUTSCHPROFESSOR	Ist das Heft auch gelb?
DAVID JENKINS	Nein das Heft ist nicht gelb. Das Heft ist hellblau.
DEUTSCHPROFESSOR	Gut!
SUSAN SMITH	Herr Professor, was bedeutet *hellblau?*
DEUTSCHPROFESSOR	*Hellblau* bedeutet *light blue* auf englisch.
SUSAN SMITH	Und wie sagt man *dark blue?*
DEUTSCHPROFESSOR	*Dunkelblau.*
SUSAN SMITH	Ah, der Kuli ist dunkelblau.
DEUTSCHPROFESSOR	Richtig! Das ist alles für heute. Für morgen lesen Sie bitte das Gespräch noch einmal, und lernen Sie auch die Wörter!

- In English the DEFINITE ARTICLE has just one form: *the*. The German singular definite article has three forms: **der, das, die.** Some nouns take **der** and are called MASCULINE; some take **das** and are called NEUTER; and some take **die** and are called FEMININE. This is a grammatical distinction and has little to do with biological sex, although it is true that most nouns referring to females are feminine and most referring to males are masculine.

  der Herr, **die** Frau, BUT **das** Fräulein

  Inanimate objects such as table, blackboard, and book can be of any gender.

  der Tisch, **das** Buch, **die** Tafel

  Because the gender of many nouns is unpredictable, you must always learn the article with the noun.

- In German the plural of nouns is formed in various ways that are often unpredictable. You must therefore learn the plural together with the article and the noun. Plurals are given in an abbreviated form in vocabulary lists. These are the most common plural forms and their abbreviations.

Abbreviation	Listing	Plural Form
-	das Fenster, -	die Fenster
¨	der Mantel, ¨	die Mäntel
-e	der Tisch, **-e**	die Tische
¨e	der Stuhl, ¨**e**	die Stühle
-er	das Bild, **-er**	die Bild**er**
¨er	das Buch, ¨**er**	die Büch**er**
-en	die Frau, **-en**	die Frau**en**
-n	die Farbe, **-n**	die Farb**en**
-s	der Kuli, **-s**	die Kuli**s**

NOTE: The plural article for all nouns is **die.** In this book, when the noun is not followed by one of the plural endings, either it does not have a plural or the plural is rarely used.

Die Farbe, -n *(color)*

blau   rot   orange   gelb

grün

braun   grau   rosa   schwarz   weiß

Das Zimmer, -   *(room)*

der	Bleistift, -e	*pencil*	das	Heft, -e	*notebook*
	Kuli, -s	*pen*		Papier, -e	*paper*
	Stuhl, ̈e	*chair*	die	Kreide	*chalk*
	Tisch, -e	*table*		Tafel, -n	*blackboard*
das	Bild, -er	*picture*		Tür, -en	*door*
	Buch, ̈er	*book*		Wand, ̈e	*wall*
	Fenster, -	*window*			

Weiteres   *(Additional words and phrases)*

auf deutsch / auf englisch	*in German / in English*
für morgen	*for tomorrow*
hier / da	*here / there*
noch einmal	*again, once more*
richtig / falsch	*correct, right / wrong, false*
Was ist das?	*What is that?*
Das ist (nicht) . . .	*That is (not) . . .*
Welche Farbe hat . . .?	*What color is . . .?*
Was bedeutet . . .?	*What does . . . mean?*
Wie sagt man . . .?	*How does one say . . . ?*
Wo ist . . .?	*Where is . . .?*
antworten	*to answer*
fragen	*to ask*
hören	*to hear*
lernen	*to learn; to study*
lesen	*to read*
wiederholen	*to repeat*

sein		*to be*
ich	bin	*I am*
es	ist	*it is*
sie	sind	*they are*
Sie	sind	*you (formal) are*

ZUM ERKENNEN *(For comprehension only):* Hören Sie gut zu! *(Listen carefully!);* jetzt *(now);* Bilden Sie einen Satz! *(Form a sentence.);* hell[grün] / dunkel[blau] *(light [green] / dark [blue]);* Das ist alles für heute. *(That's all for today.);* das Gespräch, -e *(dialogue);* das Wort, ˝er *(word);* der Artikel (von); das Beispiel, -e *(example);* zum Beispiel *(for example);* der Plural (von); Alle zusammen! *(All together!)*

Aussprache: ä, ö, ü, eu, äu, au, ei, ie

Hören Sie gut zu und wiederholen Sie!

[e:] Erika, Käthe, geht, lesen, Gespräch, Bär
[e]   Ellen Keller, Bäcker, Wände, Hände, hängen
[ö:] Öl, hören, Löwenbräu, Goethe, Österreich
[ö]   Ötker, Jörg, Pöppel, öffnen, Wörter
[ü:] Übung, Tür, Stühle, Bücher, für, müde, grün, typisch
[ü]   Jürgen Müller, Günter Hütter, müssen, küssen, Tschüß
[oi] deutsch, freut, Europa, Fräulein, Löwenbräu
[au] Frau Paula Bauer, Klaus Braun, auf, auch, blaugrau
[ai] Rainer, Heinz, Heidi, Kreide, weiß, heißen, nein

• Pay special attention to the pronunciation of **ei** and **ie** (as in *Einstein's niece*):

[ai]   eins, heißen, Heidi, Heinz, Meier
[i:]   Sie, wie, Wiedersehen, Dieter Fiedler
[ai / i:]   Heinz Fiedler, Beispiel, Heidi Thielemann

A. Mustersätze

**Mündliche
Übungen**

1. der Tisch: **Das ist** der Tisch.
    das Zimmer, die Tür, das Fenster, die Tafel, die Wand, das Bild, der Stuhl, das Papier, der Kuli, der Bleistift, die Kreide

2. das Papier: **Wo ist** das Papier? **Da ist** das Papier.
    der Kuli, die Kreide, die Tür, der Bleistift, das Buch, der Tisch, die Tafel, das Fenster, das Bild

3. das Buch: **Ist das** das Buch? **Ja, das ist** das Buch.
    der Bleistift, das Fenster, die Tür, der Kuli, die Kreide

4. die Tafel: **Ist das** die Tafel? **Nein, das ist nicht** die Tafel.
    der Tisch, das Papier, der Bleistift, der Kuli, der Stuhl

5. schwarz: **Das ist** schwarz.
    rot, gelb, grün, braun, orange, grau, rosa, blau, weiß

6. der Bleistift: **Welche Farbe hat** der Bleistift?
    der Kuli, das Papier, das Buch, die Tafel, die Kreide

7. lesen: Lesen **Sie bitte!**
    antworten, hören, fragen, lernen, wiederholen

B. Fragen und Antworten   *(Questions and answers)*

1. Ist das Papier weiß? **Ja, das Papier ist weiß.**
    Ist das Buch gelb? die Tafel grün? die Kreide weiß? der Kuli rot?

2. Ist die Kreide grün? **Nein, die Kreide ist nicht grün.**
    Ist die Tafel rot? der Bleistift weiß? das Buch rosa? das Papier braun?

3. Die Kreide ist weiß.   Ist das richtig?   **Ja, das ist richtig.**
   Die Tafel ist schwarz.   Ist das richtig?   **Nein, das ist nicht richtig.**

Das Papier ist weiß. Die Tür ist orange. Der Kuli ist blau. Das Buch ist rosa. Der Tisch ist braun.

C.   Wiederholung   *(Review)*

1.   **Was sagen sie?** *(What are they saying?)*

a.   b.   c.

2.   **Buchstabieren Sie auf deutsch!**

Elefant, Maus, Tiger, Löwe, Katze, Hund, Giraffe, Hamster, Ratte, Goldfisch, Dinosaurier

LERNTIP

How to get organized

Take a few minutes to get acquainted with your textbook. Read the table of contents, then find the index, the vocabulary lists, and the appendix. Find out how each chapter is organized. Familiarize yourself with the Workbook, too. See how the lab work and the supplementary exercises are arranged. Learn whether the language lab is set up to duplicate tapes, and what other support is available to you.

In addition, find out whether you have access to the text-specific software. It features the exercises in the book and can be particularly useful if you have not been able to attend class or if you want to review before a test. Make it a habit to divide your assignments into small units. Since it's almost impossible to cram in a foreign language course, don't fall behind. Study and review daily.

Aufgabe   **Fragen und Antworten**

1.   Was ist der Artikel? **Tür → die Tür**
     Zimmer, Bleistift, Bild, Kreide, Kuli, Stuhl, Tafel, Buch, Tisch, Fenster, Farbe, Papier, Wand, Heft, Wort, Herr, Frau, Fräulein

2.   Was ist der Plural? **Kuli → die Kulis**
     Tür, Bild, Bleistift, Buch, Heft, Tisch, Fenster, Tafel, Stuhl, Wort, Farbe

3.   Welche Farben hat das Deutschbuch?

Kleidungsartikel

Im Kleidungsgeschäft

VERKÄUFERIN	Na, wie ist die Hose?
CHRISTIAN	Zu groß und zu lang.
VERKÄUFERIN	Und der Pulli?
MAIKE	Zu teuer.
CHRISTIAN	Aber die Farben sind toll. Schade!
CHRISTIAN	Mensch, wo ist meine Jacke?
MAIKE	Ich weiß nicht.
VERKÄUFERIN	Welche Farbe hat denn die Jacke?
CHRISTIAN	Blau.
VERKÄUFERIN	Ist das die Jacke?
MAIKE	Ja, danke!

WORTSCHATZ

Die Kleidung *(clothing)*

das T-shirt, -s — der Mantel, ═ — das Hemd, -en — die Hose, -n ✠ — die Bluse, -n

der Schuh, -e

das Sweatshirt, -s — die Jacke, -n — das Kleid, -er — der Pullover, - / der Pulli, -s — der Rock, ═e

Das Gegenteil, -e *(opposite)*

dick / dünn	*thick, fat / thin, skinny*
groß / klein	*tall, big, large / short, small, little*
lang / kurz	*long / short*
langsam / schnell	*slow(ly) / fast, quick(ly)*
neu / alt	*new / old*
sauber / schmutzig	*clean, neat / dirty*
teuer / billig	*expensive / inexpensive, cheap*

Weiteres

aber	*but, however*
oder	*or*
zu	*too (+ adjective or adverb)*
gehen	*to go; to walk*
sagen	*to say, tell*
schreiben	*to write*
sprechen	*to speak*
verstehen	*to understand*
Gehen Sie an die Tafel!	*Go to the board.*
Ich weiß nicht.	*I don't know.*
Passen Sie auf!	*Pay attention.*
Sprechen Sie lauter!	*Speak louder.*
Wie bitte?	*What did you say, please?*

ZUM ERKENNEN: das Geschäft, -e *(store);* die Verkäuferin, -nen *(sales clerk, f.);* na *(well);* toll *(great, terrific);* Schade! *(Too bad!);* Mensch! *(Hey!);* denn *(flavoring particle to express curiosity)*

✠ Note that **die Hose** is singular in German.

Aussprache: l, s, st, sp, sch, x

Hören Sie gut zu und wiederholen Sie!

[l]   lernen, lesen, langsam, alle, Pullover, Kuli, klein, blau, alt, Stuhl, Tafel, Mantel, Beispiel, schnell

[z]   so, sagen, sauber, sie, sind, lesen, Bluse, Hose

[s]   Professor, passen, heißen, was, groß, weiß

[st]   ist, kosten, Fenster

[št]   Stephan, Stuhl, Stein, Bleistift, verstehen

[šp]   sprechen, Sport, Beispiel, Gespräch, Aussprache

[š]   schlecht, schnell, schmutzig, schwarz, schreiben, falsch, deutsch

[ks]   Axel, Max, Felix, Beatrix

A.   Mustersätze

Mündliche Übungen

1.   der Schuh: **Das ist** der Schuh.
     die Jacke, das Hemd, der Mantel, das Kleid, die Bluse, der Pullover, der Rock, die Hose

2.   alt / neu: **Das Gegenteil von** alt **ist** neu.
     groß / klein; lang / kurz; dick / dünn; langsam / schnell; sauber / schmutzig; richtig / falsch; ja / nein; hier / da

3.   der Mantel / alt: **Ist** der Mantel alt? **Nein,** der Mantel **ist nicht** alt.
     die Jacke / dick; das Kleid / lang; der Pullover / dünn; das Hemd / sauber; die Hose / billig

4.   Jacken / klein: **Sind die** Jacken **zu** klein? **Ja, die** Jacken **sind zu** klein.
     Hosen / lang; Röcke / kurz; Blusen / dünn; Pullover / dick; Kleider / groß; Schuhe / schmutzig; Hemden / teuer

5.   schreiben: Schreiben **Sie bitte schnell!**
     lesen, sprechen, gehen, wiederholen, antworten

6.   verstehen: Verstehen **Sie das? Ja, ich** verstehe **das.**
     sagen, hören, wiederholen, lernen, lesen

B.   Fragen und Antworten

1.   Ist der Rock rot? **Ja, der Rock ist rot.**
     Ist die Bluse rosa? die Jacke braun? der Kuli neu? das Papier dünn? der Bleistift kurz?

2.   Ist der Rock blau? **Nein, der Rock ist nicht blau.**
     Ist das Buch dick? das Wort kurz? das Fenster klein? der Pulli neu? Sind die Schuhe weiß? die Fenster groß? die Bücher billig?

C.   Wiederholung

1.   **Fragen**

     a.   Geht es Ihnen schlecht? Sind Sie müde?

     b.   Was ist rot? braun? blau? weiß? gelb? orange? rosa? schwarz? grau?

     c.   Ist der Tisch orange? die Tafel grün? das Buch rot? . . .

2. **Wie fragen Sie?**   *(What questions would elicit the following answers?)*

BEISPIEL: Ja, ich bin müde.
            Sind Sie müde?

a. Danke, gut.
b. Nein, ich heiße nicht Heinz Fiedler.
c. Das Buch ist blau.
d. Da ist die Tür.
e. Das ist das Bild.
f. Mein Name ist Schneider.
g. Ja, das ist richtig.
h. Ja, ich antworte auf deutsch.

3. **Was sagen Sie?**   *(Point to a familiar object in the room and ask your neighbor questions, using the left-hand column as a guideline.)*

S1 Ist das die Tafel?
S2 Nein, das ist nicht die Tafel.
    Das ist die Wand.
S1 Wo ist die Tafel?
S2 Da ist die Tafel.
S1 Welche Farbe hat die Tafel?
S2 Die Tafel ist grün.
S1 Was ist auch grün?
S2 Das Buch ist auch grün.

S1 Ist das _____?
S2 Nein, das ist nicht _____ .
    Das ist _____ .
S1 Wo ist _____?
S2 _____ .
S1 Welche Farbe hat _____?
S2 _____ ist _____ .
S1 Was ist auch _____?
S2 _____ ist auch _____ .

4. **Buchstabieren Sie auf deutsch!**

Mozart, Beethoven, Strauß, Schönberg, Dürer, Barlach, Kandinsky, Goethe, Nietzsche, Aichinger, Wohmann, Einstein, Röntgen, Zeppelin, Schwarzenegger

LERNTIP

Developing listening comprehension

Being able to understand spoken German is probably your most important skill. Without it, you can't learn to speak. Use class time well; listen carefully to the instructor and your classmates. Play the tape that comes with this book as often as you need in order to understand the dialogues and anecdotes and to complete the exercises correctly. Use the tape program in the lab, at home, or in the dormitory, and be sure to listen to the reading texts with the book closed. Take advantage of opportunities to hear German in the German Club or German House, if there is one on your campus. Watch plays or movies; listen to tapes and records. Even if you can't understand much of it in the beginning, you will be able to pick out key words and learn to "tune in" to German.

Aufgabe

A. **Fragen**

1. Was ist der Artikel von Mantel? Kleidung? Pulli? Bluse? Hemd? Rock? Hose? Kleid? Jacke? Schuh? T-Shirt?
2. Was ist der Plural von Schuh? Jacke? Rock? Kleid? Hose? Hemd? Bluse? Pullover? Mantel?
3. Sprechen Sie langsam oder schnell? Hören Sie gut oder schlecht? Sind Sie groß oder klein?

4. Was ist das Gegenteil von lang? dick? sauber? da? richtig? alt? schlecht? schnell? schmutzig? billig? nein? danke?

5. Welche Farbe hat das Buch? das Papier? die Hose? der Rock? die Bluse? . . .

B. Beschreiben Sie bitte!   *(Describe some of your clothing or one or two items you have with you.)*

BEISPIEL: Die Hose ist blau. Die Schuhe sind . . .

Zahlen und Preise

Was kostet das?

VERKÄUFER	Guten Tag! Was darf's sein?
SILVIA	Ich brauche ein paar Bleistifte, Kulis und Papier. Was kosten die Bleistifte?
VERKÄUFER	Fünfundneunzig Pfennig (0,95 DM).
SILVIA	Und der Kuli?
VERKÄUFER	Zwei Mark fünfundsiebzig (2,75 DM[1]).
SILVIA	Und was kostet das Papier da?
VERKÄUFER	Nur sechs Mark zwanzig (6,20 DM).
SILVIA	Gut. Ich nehme sechs Bleistifte, zwei Kulis und das Papier.
VERKÄUFER	Ist das alles?
SILVIA	Ja, danke.
VERKÄUFER	Siebzehn Mark vierzig (17,40 DM), bitte!

---

[1] Note the difference between English and German: *$2.75* BUT **2,75 DM**; *$1,600.00* BUT **1 600,00 DM** (or **1.600,00 DM**). Where German uses a period (or a space), English uses a comma, and vice versa.

As a memory aid, note these similarities between English and German:

| **-zehn** | = *-teen* | vierzehn | = *fourteen* |
| **-zig** | = *-ty* | vierzig | = *forty* |

- 21–29, 31–39, and so on to 91–99 follow the pattern of "four-and-twenty (**vierundzwanzig**) blackbirds baked in a pie."

- German numbers above twelve are seldom written out, except on checks. When they are written out, however, they are written as one word, no matter how long:

234 567
zweihundertvierunddreißigtausendfünfhundertsiebenundsechzig

Die Zahl, -en *(number)*

1	eins	11	elf	21	einundzwanzig	0	null
2	zwei	12	zwölf	22	zweiundzwanzig	10	zehn
3	drei	13	dreizehn	30	dreißig	100	hundert
4	vier	14	vierzehn	40	vierzig	101	hunderteins
5	fünf	15	fünfzehn	50	fünfzig	200	zweihundert
6	sechs	16	se**chz**ehn	60	se**chz**ig	1 000	tausend
7	sieben	17	sie**b**zehn	70	sie**b**zig	1 001	tausendeins
8	acht	18	achtzehn	80	achtzig	10 000	zehntausend
9	neun	19	neunzehn	90	neunzig	100 000	hunderttausend
10	zehn	20	zwanzig	100	hundert	1 000 000	eine Million
						1 000 000 000	eine Milliarde[✠]
						1 000 000 000 000	eine Billion[✠]

Weiteres

ein Pfennig (zehn Pfennig)	*one pfennig (ten pfennigs)*
eine Mark (zwei Mark)*	*one mark (two marks)*
auf Seite 2	*on / to page 2*
heute / morgen	*today / tomorrow*
nur	*only*
von . . . bis . . .	*from . . . to . . .*
Was kostet / kosten . . .?	*How much is / are . . .?*
Das kostet . . .	*That comes to . . .*
wie viele?	*how many?*
brauchen	*to need*
kosten	*to cost, come to (a certain amount)*
nehmen	*to take*
öffnen	*to open*
zählen	*to count*
ich zäh**le**	*I count*
wir ⎫	*we count*
sie ⎬ zähl**en**	*they count*
Sie ⎭	*you (formal) count*

[✠] Note: **eine Milliarde** = *(American) billion;* **eine Billion** = *(American) trillion.*
[*] **eins** BUT **eine Mark!**

ZUM ERKENNEN: der Verkäufer, - *(sales clerk, m.);* Was darf's sein? *(May I help you?);* ein paar *(a couple of);* der Preis, -e; plus / minus; und so weiter = usw. *(and so on = etc.)*

Aussprache: z, w, v, f, pf, qu

Hören Sie gut zu und wiederholen Sie!

[ts]	Fri**tz**, **Z**immer, **Z**ahl, **z**u, **z**usammen, **z**ählen, **z**wei, **z**ehn, **z**wölf, **z**wanzig, **z**weiund**z**wanzig, **z**weihundert**z**weiund**z**wanzig, je**tz**t
[z / ts]	se**ch**zehn, se**ch**zig, se**ch**sundse**ch**zig, se**chs**hundertse**ch**sundse**ch**zig, sieben, sieb**z**ig, sieben**un**dsieb**z**ig, siebenhundertsiebenundsiebzig, Sa**tz**
[v]	**W**illi, **W**olfgang, **W**and, **W**ort, **w**ie, **w**as, **w**o, **w**elche, **w**eiß, **w**iederholen, **V**olvo, **V**ase
[f]	**v**ier, **v**ierzehn, **v**ierzig, **v**ierund**v**ierzig, **v**ierhundert**v**ierund**v**ierzig, **v**iele, **v**erstehen, **V**olkswagen, **V**orschau
[f]	**f**ünf, **f**ünfzehn, **f**ünfzig, **f**ünfund**f**ünfzig, **f**ünfhundert**f**ünfund**f**ünfzig, **f**ür, **F**enster, öf**f**nen, Ta**f**el, au**f**, el**f**, zwöl**f**
[pf]	**Pf**ennig, **Pf**effer, **Pf**efferminz, Dummko**pf**, **pf**ui
[kv]	**Qu**alität, **Qu**antität, **Qu**artal, **Qu**artett, **Qu**intett, Ä**qu**ivalent

Mündliche Übungen

A.   **Hören Sie gut zu und wiederholen Sie!**

1. Wir zählen von eins bis zehn: eins, zwei, drei, vier, fünf, sechs, sieben, acht, neun, zehn.
2. Wir zählen von zehn bis zwanzig: zehn, elf, zwölf, dreizehn, vierzehn, fünfzehn, sechzehn, siebzehn, achtzehn, neunzehn, zwanzig.
3. Wir zählen von zwanzig bis dreißig: zwanzig, einundzwanzig, zweiundzwanzig, dreiundzwanzig, vierundzwanzig, fünfundzwanzig, sechsundzwanzig, siebenundzwanzig, achtundzwanzig, neunundzwanzig, dreißig.
4. Wir zählen von zehn bis hundert: zehn, zwanzig, dreißig, vierzig, fünfzig, sechzig, siebzig, achtzig, neunzig, hundert.
5. Wir zählen von hundert bis tausend: hundert, zweihundert, dreihundert, vierhundert, fünfhundert, sechshundert, siebenhundert, achthundert, neunhundert, tausend.

B.   **Lesen Sie laut auf deutsch!**

1. **Seitenzahlen**

    Seite 1, 5, 7, 8, 9, 11, 12, 17, 19, 22, 25, 31, 42, 57, 66, 89, 92, 101

2. **Plus und minus**

    BEISPIEL: $4 + 4 = 8$ **Vier plus vier ist acht.**
    $8 - 4 = 4$ **Acht minus vier ist vier.**

$3 + 2 = 5$	$8 + 1 = 9$	$8 - 2 = 6$
$7 + 3 = 10$	$10 - 2 = 8$	$7 - 6 = 1$
$1 + 1 = 2$	$9 - 4 = 5$	$5 - 5 = 0$

3. **Preise**

BEISPIEL: 0,10 DM   **zehn Pfennig**
                  1,20 DM   **eine Mark zwanzig**

0,25 DM   0,31 DM   0,44 DM   0,67 DM   0,72 DM   0,88 DM
2,50 DM   4,75 DM   8,90 DM   5,60 DM   10,40 DM   3,25 DM

4. **Inventar**   *(With an employee, played by a partner, you are taking the inventory of the items you have in stock in your store.)*

BEISPIEL: Jacke / 32
                  Wie viele Jacken?—Zweiunddreißig Jacken.

a.   Pullover / 42   f.   Jacke / 37
b.   Rock / 14   g.   Mantel / 12
c.   Hemd / 66   h.   Sweatshirt / 89
d.   Kleid / 19   i.   Schuh / 58
e.   Hose / 21   j.   Jeans / 102

C.   Mustersätze

1. das Papier: **Was kostet** das Papier?
   die Kreide, die Hose, der Mantel, die Jacke, der Pulli
2. Bleistifte: **Was kosten** die Bleistifte?
   Kulis, Bücher, Schuhe, Hemden, Bilder
3. brauchen: **Was** brauchen **Sie?**
   sagen, hören, schreiben, lesen, zählen, nehmen
4. brauchen: **Wir** brauchen **das.**
   lesen, nehmen, zählen, verstehen, wiederholen, öffnen
5. brauchen: Brauchen **Sie das? Nein, ich** brauche **das nicht.**
   hören, sagen, verstehen, zählen, wiederholen, öffnen

D.   Wiederholung

1. **Gegenteile**   *(Tell which adjectives best describe each pair.)*

a.   b.

c.   d.   e.

2. **Fragen und Antworten**

   a.   Wie geht's?
   b.   Heißen Sie Meier?
   c.   Wie heißen Sie? Wie heiße ich?
   d.   Was ist das? *(Point to items in the classroom.)*
   e.   Ist das Buch dick oder dünn? der Bleistift lang oder kurz? das Zimmer groß
        oder klein? die Tafel schwarz oder grün?
   f.   Welche Farbe hat das Buch? der Kuli? die Bluse? die Hose? die Jacke?

3. **Antworten Sie mit JA!**   *(Answer with YES.)*

   BEISPIEL: Wiederholen Sie das?
               Ja, ich wiederhole das.

   a.   Sprechen Sie langsam?
   b.   Verstehen Sie die Frage?
   c.   Nehmen Sie die Kreide?
   d.   Öffnen Sie das Fenster?
   e.   Lesen Sie das noch einmal?
   f.   Gehen Sie an die Tafel?
   g.   Lernen Sie das für morgen?

4. **Antworten Sie mit NEIN!**   *(Answer with NO.)*

   BEISPIEL: Sind die Schuhe neu?
               Nein, die Schuhe sind nicht neu.
               Nein, die Schuhe sind alt.

   a.   Sind die Fenster klein?
   b.   Sind die Bücher alt?
   c.   Sind die Jacken sauber?
   d.   Sind die Bleistifte dick?
   e.   Sind die Mäntel lang?

5. **Geben Sie Befehle!**   *(State as requests.)*

   BEISPIEL: antworten
               Antworten Sie bitte!

   fragen, wiederholen, gehen, lesen, schreiben, lernen

6. **Buchstabieren Sie auf deutsch!**

   Blume *(flower),* Rose, Tulpe, Narzisse, Gladiole, Nelke *(carnation),* Sonnen-
   blume, Dahlie, Iris

LERNTIP

Learning vocabulary

To remember vocabulary, you must use it. Name things as you see them in the course of your day. Label objects in your room or home, using 3 × 5 cards. Practice new words aloud—the use of your auditory and motor memory will quadruple your learning efficiency. Be sure to learn the gender and plural with each noun. For some, the gender and plural are predictable; study part 1 in the Appendix.

A.   Wieviel ist das?   *(How much is that?)*

15 + 9 = ?	20 − 1 = ?	72 + 8 = ?
28 + 4 = ?	12 + 48 = ?	114 − 16 = ?
22 − 8 = ?	60 − 5 = ?	1 000 − 25 = ?

B.   Wie geht's weiter?   *(What comes next?)*

100 − 10 = 90	90 − 10 = 80	80 − 10 = ?
70 − 7 = 63	63 − 7 = 56	56 − 7 = ?

C.   Was kostet das zusammen?

1.   Sechs Bleistifte kosten 2,40 DM, der Kuli kostet 1,60 DM, das Buch 24,55 DM und das Papier 3,– DM. Das kostet zusammen _____ .

2.   Die Jacke kostet 75,– DM, die Bluse 48,– DM und die Schuhe kosten 84,– DM. Das kostet zusammen _____ .

3.   Das Buch kostet 5,50 DM. Was kosten drei Bücher?

4.   Das Hemd kostet 28,50 DM und die Hose 125,– DM. Das kostet zusammen _____ .

D.   Was sagen Sie?

VERKÄUFER	Guten Tag! Wie geht es Ihnen?
SIE	_____ .
VERKÄUFER	Was darf's sein?
SIE	_____ ein paar _____ und ein paar _____ . Was kosten
	/ kostet _____?
VERKÄUFER	_____ DM.
SIE	Und was kostet _____?
VERKÄUFER	_____ DM.
SIE	Ich nehme zwei (drei . . .) _____ .
VERKÄUFER	Ist das alles?
SIE	_____ .
VERKÄUFER	_____ DM, bitte!

Viskose-Blusen verschiedene Formen, florale Röcke, Gr. 36 – 44

25,–

Hosenröcke Baumwolle oder Viskose, uni und bedruckt, Gr. S, M, L

18,–

adidas® Tennisschuh „Edberg Champ" „Graf Champ" Obermaterial Leder Gr. 37 – 45

75,–*

Das Jahr und das Wetter

Das Wetter im April

NORBERT	Es ist schön heute, nicht wahr?
JULIA	Ja, wirklich. Die Sonne scheint wieder!
RUDI	Aber der Wind ist kühl.
JULIA	Ach, das macht nichts.
NORBERT	Ich finde es toll.

DOROTHEA	Das Wetter ist furchtbar, nicht wahr?
MATTHIAS	Das finde ich auch. Es regnet und regnet!
SONJA	Und es ist wieder so kalt.
MATTHIAS	Ja, typisch April.

Das Jahr, -e   *(year)*

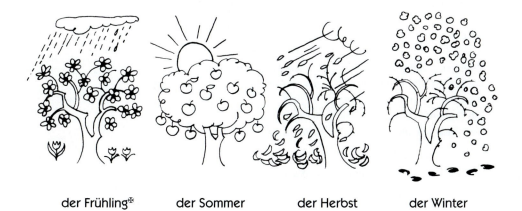

der Frühling✠   der Sommer   der Herbst   der Winter

Die Woche, -n   *(week)*
Der Tag, -e   *(day)*
Der Monat, -e   *(month)*✠

der			*der*		
Montag	*Monday*✠		Januar	*January*	
Dienstag	*Tuesday*		Februar	*February*	
Mittwoch	*Wednesday*		März	*March*	
Donnerstag	*Thursday*		April	*April*	
Freitag	*Friday*		Mai	*May*	
Samstag	*Saturday*		Juni	*June*	
Sonntag	*Sunday*		Juli	*July*	
			August	*August*	
			September	*September*	
			Oktober	*October*	
			November	*November*	
			Dezember	*December*	

Das Wetter   *(weather)*

Es ist . . .	*It's . . .*	heiß / kalt	*hot / cold*
Es regnet.	*It's raining.*	furchtbar	*awful, terrible*
Es schneit.	*It's snowing.*	prima	*great, wonderful*
Die Sonne scheint.	*The sun is shining.*	schön	*nice, beautiful, fine*
		super	*superb, super*
		toll	*great, terrific*
		warm / kühl	*warm / cool*

✠ Note that the days, months, and seasons are all masculine!

Weiteres

Die Woche hat [sieben Tage].	*The week has [seven days].*
nicht wahr?	*isn't it? isn't this true?*
sehr	*very*
wieder	*again*
wirklich	*really, indeed*
Wann sind Sie geboren?	*When were you born?*
Ich bin im Mai* geboren.	*I was born in May.*
finden	*to find*
Ich finde es . . .	*I think it's . . .*
Das finde ich auch.	*I think so, too.*

* **Im** is used with the names of the months and seasons: **im Mai, im Winter.**

ZUM ERKENNEN: der Wind; Das macht nichts *(It doesn't matter; That is OK.)*; typisch; die Jahreszeit, -en *(season)*

Aussprache: r; p, t, k; final b, d, g; j, h

Hören Sie gut zu und wiederholen Sie!

[r]   **r**ichtig, **r**egnet, **r**ot, **r**osa, **R**ock, b**r**aun, g**r**ün, d**r**ei, f**r**agen, F**r**au, F**r**eitag, P**r**eis, hö**r**en, gebo**r**en, o**r**ange

[ʌ]   wi**r**, vie**r**, ode**r**, abe**r**, nu**r**, seh**r**, fü**r**, teue**r**, wiede**r**, Fenste**r**, Papie**r**, Wette**r**, Somme**r**, Winte**r**, Oktobe**r**, Dezembe**r**
BUT [ʌ / r] Tü**r** / Tü**r**en; Jah**r** / Jah**r**e; Uh**r** / Uh**r**en

[p]   **P**eter **P**öppel, **P**apier, **P**ullover, **P**lural, **p**lus, ka**p**utt
AND [p] Herb**st**, Jako**b**, gel**b**, hal**b**
BUT [p / b] gel**b** / gel**b**e; hal**b** / hal**b**e

[t]   **Th**eo, **T**ür, **T**isch, **t**oll, Doro**th**ea, Ma**tth**ias, bi**tt**e
AND [t] un**d**, tausen**d**, Bil**d**, Klei**d**, Hem**d**, Wan**d**
BUT [t / d] Bil**d** / Bil**d**er; Klei**d** / Klei**d**er; Hem**d** / Hem**d**en; Wan**d** / Wän**d**e

[k]   **k**lein, **k**ühl, **k**urz, **K**uli, **K**leidung, dan**k**e, di**ck**
AND [k] sa**gt**, fra**gt**, Ta**g**
BUT [k / g] sa**gt** / sa**g**en; fra**gt** / fra**g**en; Ta**g** / Ta**g**e

[j]   **J**akob, **J**osef, **J**ulia, **j**a, **J**anuar, **J**uni, **J**uli

[h]   **H**err, **H**erbst, **H**emd, **H**ose, **h**ören, **h**eiß, **h**at, **h**undert, vier**h**undert

[:]   zä**h**len, ne**h**men, ge**h**en, verste**h**en, I**h**nen, Stu**h**l, Schu**h**

A. Hören Sie gut zu und wiederholen Sie!

1. Das Jahr hat vier Jahreszeiten. Die Jahreszeiten heißen Frühling, Sommer, Herbst und Winter.
2. Das Jahr hat zwölf Monate. Die Monate heißen Januar, Februar, März, April, Mai, Juni, Juli, August, September, Oktober, November und Dezember.
3. Die Woche hat sieben Tage. Die Tage heißen Montag, Dienstag, Mittwoch, Donnerstag, Freitag, Samstag und Sonntag.

B. Mustersätze

1. schön: **Es ist heute** schön.
   kalt, kühl, heiß, warm
2. sehr kalt: **Es ist** sehr kalt.
   sehr heiß, sehr schön, schön warm, furchtbar heiß, furchtbar kalt
3. toll: **Ich finde es** toll.
   schön, gut, wunderbar, schlecht, furchtbar, prima
4. Juli: **Ich bin im** Juli **geboren.**
   Januar, März, Mai, Juni, August, Sommer, Winter
5. 19: **Ich bin** neunzehn.
   16, 18, 20, 21, 27, 31

C. Wiederholung

1. **Antworten Sie mit JA!**

   BEISPIEL: Verstehen Sie das?
              Ja, wir verstehen das.

   a. Zählen Sie schnell?
   b. Fragen Sie auf deutsch?
   c. Hören Sie gut zu?
   d. Lernen Sie die Wörter?
   e. Lesen Sie auf Seite dreißig?
   f. Passen Sie auf?
   g. Sprechen Sie laut?

2. **Wie geht's weiter?**

   BEISPIEL: Wo ist _____?
              Wo ist die Frau?

   a. Ich heiße _____ .
   b. Ich bin _____ .
   c. Es geht mir _____ .
   d. Das Gegenteil von _____ .
   e. Der Artikel von _____ .
   f. Der Pulli _____ .
   g. Das kostet _____ .

3. **Zahlen, Preise und Telefonnummern**

   a. **Wieviel ist das?**

$3 + 6 = ?$	$65 + 15 = ?$	$50 - 20 = ?$
$9 + 9 = ?$	$75 + 25 = ?$	$33 - 11 = ?$
$23 + 10 = ?$	$100 - 60 = ?$	$16 - 6 = ?$
$40 + 50 = ?$	$80 - 15 = ?$	$12 - 11 = ?$

b. **Lesen Sie laut auf deutsch!**
101 / 315 / 463 / 555 / 1 110 / 20 000 / 88 888 / 267 315 / 987 654
100,10 DM / 212,25 DM / 667,75 DM / 1 920,– DM / 9 999,99 DM

c. **Wie ist Ihre Telefonnummer?** *(What's your phone number? Ask another student.)*

 BEISPIEL: Wie ist Ihre Telefonnummer?
      Meine Telefonnummer ist 646-0195
      (sechs vier sechs, null eins neun fünf).

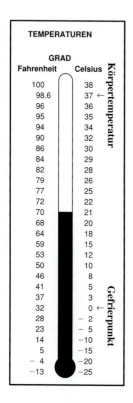

D. **Temperaturen**

> European thermometers use the Celsius scale. On that scale water freezes at 0°C and boils at 100°C. Normal body temperature is about 37°C, and fever starts at about 37.6°C. To convert Fahrenheit into Celsius, subtract 32, multiply by 5, divide by 9. To convert Celsius into Fahrenheit, multiply by 9, divide by 5, add 32. Another rule that works within a few degrees is:
> $F > C = \dfrac{temperature\ -32°}{2}$ BUT $C > F = (temperature \times 2) + 32°.$

1. **Wieviel Grad Celsius sind das?** *(How many degrees Celsius? Use the thermometer as a reference.)*

 BEISPIEL: 32°F = 0°C
      Zweiunddreißig Grad Fahrenheit sind null Grad Celsius.

 100°F, 96°F, 84°F, 68°F, 41°F, 23°F, −4°F, −13°F

2. **Wie ist das Wetter?** *(What's the weather like?)*

 BEISPIEL: 12°C (zwölf Grad Celsius)
      Es ist kühl.

 21°C, 0°C, 30°C, 38°C, −10°C, −25°C

Aufgabe

Fragen

1. Wie ist das Wetter hier im Winter? im Sommer? im Frühling? im Herbst?
2. Was ist der Artikel von Montag? September? Donnerstag? Herbst? Juni? Monat? Jahr? Woche?
3. Welcher Tag ist heute? morgen?
4. Wie viele Tage hat die Woche? Wie heißen die Tage?
5. Wie viele Tage hat der September? der Oktober? der Februar?
6. Wie viele Monate hat das Jahr? Wie heißen die Monate?
7. Wie viele Wochen hat das Jahr?
8. Wie viele Jahreszeiten hat das Jahr? Wie heißen die Jahreszeiten?
9. Wie heißen die Wintermonate? die Sommermonate? die Herbstmonate?
10. Wie ist das Wetter heute? Scheint die Sonne, oder regnet es?

Die Uhrzeit

Wie spät ist es?

RITA	Hallo, Axel! Wie spät ist es?
AXEL	Hallo, Rita! Es ist zehn vor acht.
RITA	Oje, in zehn Minuten habe ich Philosophie.
AXEL	Dann mach's gut! Tschüß!
RITA	Ja, Tschüß!

PHILLIP	Hallo, Steffi! Wieviel Uhr ist es denn?
STEFFI	Tag, Phillip! Es ist halb zwölf.
PHILLIP	Gehen wir jetzt essen?
STEFFI	OK, die Vorlesung beginnt erst um Viertel nach eins.

HERR RICHTER	Wann sind Sie heute fertig?
HERR HEROLD	Um zwei. Warum?
HERR RICHTER	Spielen wir heute Tennis?
HERR HEROLD	Ja, prima! Es ist jetzt halb eins. Um Viertel vor drei dann?
HERR RICHTER	Gut! Bis später!

WORTSCHATZ • German has a formal (see Chapter 7) and informal way of telling time. The informal system is used in everyday speech and varies somewhat from region to region. The system below is a compromise, but certain to be understood everywhere.

Wie spät ist es? *(How late is it ? What time is it?)*
Wieviel Uhr ist es?

die	Minute, -n	*minute*	morgens	*in the morning*
	Sekunde, -n	*second*	mittags	*at noon*
	Stunde, -n*	*hour*	nachmittags	*in the afternoon*
	Uhr, -en	*watch, clock; o'clock*	abends	*in the evening*
	Zeit, -en	*time*		

Es ist ein Uhr.
Es ist eins.

Es ist zwei Uhr.
Es ist zwei.

Es ist Viertel
nach zwei.

Es ist halb drei.

Es ist Viertel
vor drei.

Es ist drei.

Es ist fünf
nach vier.

Es ist zwanzig
nach sieben.

Es ist zehn
vor neun.

Es ist fünf
vor zwölf.

Es ist fünf
vor halb eins.

Es ist fünf
nach halb eins.

---

* **Stunde** refers to duration or a particular class: Die Deutsch**stunde** ist von acht bis neun. Eine **Stunde** hat 60 Minuten. **Uhr** refers to clock time. Es ist 9 **Uhr**.

Weiteres

der	Student, -en	*student (male)*
die	Studentin, -nen✻	*student (female)*
	Vorlesung, -en	*lecture, class (university)*

Es ist ein Uhr (zwei Uhr).✳	*It's one o'clock (two o'clock).*
Es ist eins (zwei).	*It's one (two).*
(um) eins✳	*(at) one o'clock*
(um) Viertel nach eins	*(at) quarter past one*
(um) halb zwei, 1.30❉	*(at) half past one, 1:30*
(um) Viertel vor zwei, 1.45	*(at) quarter to two, 1:45*
fertig	*finished, done*
jetzt	*now*
Bitte!	*here: You're welcome.*
beginnen	*to begin*
essen	*to eat*
Tennis spielen	*to play tennis*

haben	*to have*
ich habe	*I have*
es hat	*it has*
wir ⎫	*we have*
sie ⎬ haben	*they have*
Sie ⎭	*you (formal) have*

Ich habe eine Frage.	*I have a question.*
Ich habe keine Zeit.	*I don't have time.*
Bis später!	*See you later!*

✻ The plural of **Studentin** is **Studentinnen**.
✳ **um ein Uhr** BUT **um eins**.
❉ Note the difference in punctuation between English (*1:30*) and German (**1.30**).

ZUM ERKENNEN:　Hallo! *(Hi! Hello!);* Oje! *(Oh no! Oops!);* dann *(then);* Mach's gut! *(Take care!);* erst *(only, not until);* warum? *(why?);* die Uhrzeit *(time of day)*

Aussprache: ch, ig, ck, ng, gn, kn, ps

Hören Sie gut zu und wiederholen Sie!

[x]　a**ch**, a**ch**t, a**ch**thunderta**ch**tunda**ch**tzig, Joa**ch**im, ma**ch**t, au**ch**, brau**ch**en, Wo**ch**e, Mittwo**ch**, Bu**ch**

[ç]　i**ch**, mi**ch**, ni**ch**t, wirkli**ch**, Ri**ch**ard, Mi**ch**ael, wel**ch**e, schle**ch**t, spre**ch**en, Gesprä**ch**e, Bü**ch**er

[iç]　richt**ig**, fert**ig**, sech**zig**, fünf**zig**, vier**zig**, drei**ßig**, bill**ig**, Pfenn**ig**

[ks]　se**chs**, se**chs**undsechzig, se**chs**hundertse**chs**undsechzig, Da**chs**hund

[k]　**Ch**ristian, **Ch**ristine, **Ch**rista, **Ch**aos

[k]　Ja**ck**e, Ro**ck**, di**ck**, Pi**ck**ni**ck**

[ŋ]　I**ng**e La**ng**e, Wolfga**ng** E**ng**el, e**ng**lisch, si**ng**en, Fi**ng**er, Hu**ng**er

[gn]　**Gn**om, re**gn**et, resi**gn**ieren, Si**gn**al

[kn]　**Kn**irps, **Kn**ie, **Kn**oten, **Kn**ut **Kn**orr

[ps]　**Ps**ychologie, **Ps**ychiater, **Ps**ychoanalyse, **Ps**eudonym

Mündliche Übungen

A.   Wie spät ist es? Wieviel Uhr ist es?

1.   1.00: **Es ist** ein **Uhr.**
       3.00, 5.00, 7.00, 9.00, 11.00
2.   1.05: **Es ist** fünf **nach** eins.
       3.05, 5.05, 7.05, 9.10, 11.10, 1.10, 4.20, 6.20, 8.20
3.   1.15: **Es ist Viertel nach** eins.
       2.15, 4.15, 6.15, 8.15, 10.15
4.   1.30: **Es ist halb** zwei.
       2.30, 4.30, 6.30, 8.30, 10.30
5.   1.40: **Es ist** zwanzig **vor** zwei.
       3.40, 5.40, 7.40, 9.50, 11.50, 1.50, 12.55, 2.55, 4.55
6.   1.45: **Es ist Viertel vor** zwei.
       3.45, 5.45, 7.45, 9.45, 11.45, 12.45

B.   Wann ist die Vorlesung?   *(When is the lecture?)*

1.   9.00: **Die Vorlesung ist um** neun.
       3.00, 11.00, 1.00, 9.15, 12.15, 9.45, 12.45, 1.30, 3.30
2.   5: **Die Vorlesung beginnt in** fünf **Minuten.**
       2, 10, 12, 15, 20
3.   morgens: **Die Vorlesung ist** morgens.
       nachmittags, abends, um acht, um Viertel nach acht, um halb neun,
       um Viertel vor neun.

C.   Mustersätze

1.   essen: Essen **Sie jetzt? Ja, ich** esse **jetzt.**
       gehen, fragen, schreiben, lernen, antworten, beginnen
2.   heute: **Ich spiele** heute **Tennis.**
       jetzt, morgens, nachmittags, abends, wieder
3.   Sie: **Wann** sind Sie **heute fertig?**
       Horst, ich, Rolf und Maria, sie *(pl.)*
4.   ich: Ich habe **keine Zeit.**
       wir, Maria, Maria und Rita

D.   Wiederholung

1.   **Wie ist das Wetter?**

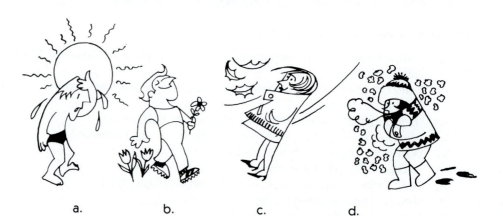

a.   b.   c.   d.

2. **Was sagen Sie?**   *(Talk about the weather with a classmate.)*

S1   Wie ist das Wetter heute?
S2   _____ .
S1   Wie finden Sie das Wetter?
S2   _____ .
S1   Typisch _____ , nicht wahr?
S2   _____ .

3. **Wie fragen Sie?**   *(Formulate the questions for these answers.)*

BEISPIEL: Das ist die Tafel.
            Was ist das?

a.   Da sind die Schuhe.   f.   Ich finde das nicht schön.
b.   Der Bleistift ist gelb.   g.   Fünf plus sechzehn ist einundzwanzig.
c.   Das Papier kostet 1,50 DM.   h.   Der Januar hat einunddreißig Tage.
d.   Ich brauche Zeit.   i.   Heute ist Dienstag.
e.   Heute ist es furchtbar heiß.

4. **Und Sie?**   *(Answer, then ask someone else.)*

a.   Wie alt sind Sie? **(Ich bin _____ . Und Sie?)**
b.   Wann sind Sie geboren? **(Ich bin im _____ geboren. Und Sie?)**

5. **Was tun Sie wann?**   *(What do you do when? Match months or seasons with the activities based on the drawings.)*

BEISPIEL: Was tun Sie im Sommer?
            Im Sommer spiele ich Tennis.

joggen

reiten

schwimmen

Golf spielen

Tennis spielen

Ski laufen

angeln

segeln

campen

Aufgabe

1. Wie viele Stunden hat der Tag? Wie viele Minuten hat die Stunde?
2. Wie viele Sekunden hat die Minute?
3. Wie spät ist es? (8.45, 9.30, 10.15, 11.30, 1.05, 2.20, 2.45, 6.59)
4. Was studieren Sie? *(What courses are you taking?)* **(Ich studiere . . .)**

   Biologie, Chemie, Deutsch, Englisch, Französisch *(French)*, Geographie, Geologie, Geschichte *(history)*, Informatik *(computer science)*, Kunst *(art)*, Latein, Mathe(matik), Musik, Philosophie, Physik, Politik, Psychologie, Soziologie, Spanisch, Sport

5. Welche Vorlesungen haben Sie heute? morgen? wann? **(Ich habe Deutsch um _____ und Englisch um _____ ·)**
6. Wie heißt der Deutschprofessor? Englischprofessor? . . .
7. Wann sind Sie heute fertig? **(Ich bin heute um _____ fertig.)**
8. Wann essen Sie morgens? mittags? abends?

SPRECHSITUATIONEN

These sections focus on practical language functions. In German as in English, there are many ways to say the same thing, but what you choose depends on the circumstances. Your instructor will indicate which expressions you will need to learn.

Greeting and Saying Good-bye

1. In formal situations or when meeting strangers, you can use these expressions:

> Guten Tag!
> Guten Morgen! *(until about 10:00 A.M.)*
> Guten Abend! *(from about 5:00 to 10:00 P.M.)*
> Wie geht es Ihnen?
> Auf Wiedersehen!

Speakers of German usually shake hands whenever they meet, not only when they meet for the first time—and they do so with a single up and down motion. **Wie geht es Ihnen?** is an inquiry, and an answer is expected.

2. Here is a list of greetings for informal situations or when meeting friends:

> Hallo!   Wiedersehen! Tschüß!
> Tag! Wie geht's?   Bis später!
> Morgen! Abend!

Other informal ways of saying *Hi!* are **Grüß dich! Servus!** (in Bavaria and Austria) and **Gruezi!** (in Switzerland). **Gute Nacht!** *(good night)* is normally used to wish someone who lives in the same house a good night's sleep.

3. Here are some responses to **Wie geht es Ihnen?** or **Wie geht's?**:

> Gut, danke.
> Sehr gut, danke.
> Prima! Super!
> Es geht mir gut / nicht gut.
> Es geht mir schlecht / nicht schlecht.

4. To introduce yourself, you should say:

> Mein Name ist . . .
> Ich heiße . . .

5. When meeting someone for the first time, you can use the following expressions:

> (Es) freut mich!   *(I'm) glad to meet you.*
> (Es) freut mich auch.   *Glad to meet you, too. Same here.*

Expressing Incomprehension

Especially when speaking a foreign language, you need to be able to say that you don't understand something or that you'd like to have something repeated.

Ich habe eine Frage.
Ich verstehe (das) nicht.
Wie bitte?
Sagen Sie das noch einmal, bitte!
Wiederholen Sie (das), bitte!
Was bedeutet . . .?
Wie sagt man . . .?
Sprechen Sie nicht so schnell, bitte!
Sprechen Sie langsam, bitte!
Sprechen Sie lauter!

A. **Was sagen sie?** *(What are they saying?)*   **Übungen**

1.   2.

3.   4.

B.   **Was sagen Sie?**   *(What would you say in response to these statements?)*

1.   Mein Name ist Taeger, Dr. Kai Taeger.
2.   Guten Morgen! Wie geht es Ihnen?
3.   Auf Wiedersehen!
4.   Sprechen Sie nicht so schnell, bitte!
5.   Dort drüben ist die Straßenbahnhaltestelle.
6.   Tag! Wie geht's?

C.   **Was sagen Sie?** *(What would you say in these situations?)*

1.   You got called on in class and didn't hear the question.
2.   You were unable to follow your instructor's explanation.
3.   You have to ask your instructor to repeat something.
4.   You want to say good-bye to the host after an evening party.
5.   You are staying with the family of a friend in Austria. What do you say as you go to bed?
6.   You have asked a native of Berlin for directions and she is speaking much too fast.
7.   In a conversation the word **Geschwindigkeitsbegrenzung** keeps coming up. You want to ask for clarification.
8.   You want to find out how one says *Excuse me* in German.

D.   **Kurzgespräche** *(With a partner, practice the following conversations in German until you are fluent in both parts. Eventually you want to include additional phrases of your own.)*

1.   S1   Hi! How are you?
     S2   Great!
     S1   That's wonderful. I'm glad.
     S2   And how are you?
     S1   Not bad, but I'm very tired.
     S2   See you later!
     S1   Bye!

2.   S1   Hello! My name is . . . What's yours?
     S2   My name is . . .
     S1   Glad to meet you.
     S2   Glad to meet you, too.

RÜCKBLICK *(Review)* SCHRITTE

By now you know quite a few German words and a number of idiomatic expressions. You have learned how to pronounce German and to say a few things about yourself. You also have learned a good deal about the structure of the German language.

I. Nouns

1. German has three genders: MASCULINE, NEUTER, and FEMININE. Nouns are distinguished by **der, das,** and **die** in the singular. In the plural there are no gender distinctions; the article **die** is used for all plural nouns:

der Herr, **der** Bleistift		Herren, Bleistifte
das Fräulein, **das** Bild	**die**	Fräulein, Bilder
die Frau, **die** Tafel		Frauen, Tafeln

2. There are several ways to form the plural of nouns. You have learned how to interpret the most common plural abbreviations found in dictionaries and vocabulary lists:

das Fenster, **-**		Fenster
der Mantel, **⸚**		**Mä**ntel
der Tag, **-e**		Ta**ge**
der Stuhl, **⸚e**		St**ü**h**le**
das Kleid, **-er**		Kleid**er**
das Buch, **⸚er**	die	B**ü**ch**er**
die Uhr, **-en**		Uhr**en**
die Sekunde, **-n**		Sekunde**n**
die Studentin, **-nen**		Studentin**nen**
der Kuli, **-s**		Kuli**s**

3. When you learn a noun, you must also learn its gender and plural form.

4. All nouns are capitalized.

   Ich brauche **B**leistifte, **K**ulis und **P**apier.

II. Pronouns

You have used the following pronouns:

ich	*I*	Ich heiße Sanders.
es	*it*	Es regnet.
wir	*we*	Wir zählen von eins bis zehn.
sie	*they*	Sind sie neu?
Sie	*you (formal)*	Wann sind Sie heute fertig?

- The pronoun **ich** is not capitalized unless it stands at the beginning of a sentence.

  Ja, **ich** finde das Wetter schön. BUT **Ich** finde das Wetter schön.

- The pronoun **Sie** *(you)*, which is always capitalized, is used in all formal relationships, and always when others are addressed with such titles as **Herr** and **Frau.** It is used to address one or more persons.

  Frau Thielemann, verstehen Sie das?
  Frau Thielemann und Herr Fiedler, verstehen Sie das?

III. Verbs

1. You have noticed that German verbs have different endings—that is, they are INFLECTED, or CONJUGATED. You have used the following verb endings:

ich	-e	Ich brauche Papier.
wir	-en	Wir brauchen Papier.
sie, Sie	-en	Sie brauchen Papier.

2. **Sein** *(to be)* and **haben** *(to have)* are two important verbs. As in English, their forms are not regular.

ich	bin	Ich bin groß.
es	ist	Es ist groß.
sie, Sie	sind	Sie sind groß.

ich	habe	Ich habe Zeit.
es	hat	Es hat Zeit.
sie, Sie	haben	Sie haben Zeit.

IV. Sentence Structure

You have encountered three basic sentence types: STATEMENTS, QUESTIONS, and IMPERATIVES. In all of them, verb position plays a significant role.

1. Statements

   One of the most important observations you will make is that the verb is always the second element in a statement. (As you see from the examples, a SENTENCE ELEMENT can consist of more than one word.)

Sie	**schreiben**	schön.
Mein Name	**ist**	Dieter Schneider.
Gerda und Dorothea	**sind**	fertig.
Der Rock und die Bluse	**kosten**	150,– DM.

2. Questions

   You have practiced two types of questions: INFORMATION QUESTIONS and QUESTIONS THAT ELICIT YES / NO ANSWERS.

   a. Information questions begin with a question word or phrase and ask for specific information: *what, where, how.* In information questions, too, the verb is the second element. You have learned the following question words and phrases. Note that all question words begin with **w**!

Wann	**haben**	Sie Deutsch?
Was	**kostet**	das?
Wo	**ist**	der Stuhl?
Wie	**geht**	es Ihnen?
Welche Farbe	**hat**	das Buch?
Wieviel Uhr	**ist**	es?
Wie viele Tage	**hat**	die Woche?

b.   Questions eliciting a yes / no response, on the other hand, begin with the verb.

Haben Sie Zeit?
Regnet es morgen?
Spielen wir heute Tennis?
Ist das richtig?

3. Imperatives

Imperatives (commands, requests, suggestions) also begin with the verb. Note that they usually conclude with an exclamation mark.

Antworten Sie bitte!
Nehmen Sie die Kreide!
Öffnen Sie das Buch!
Sagen Sie das noch einmal!
Zählen Sie von zwanzig bis dreißig!

Wiederholung   Hören Sie zu!

Twice in every chapter, you will find listening comprehension exercises like the one below for the audio-cassette that comes with the textbook. These exercises provide you with an opportunity to listen to conversations that are as close to native speech as possible. You may listen as often as necessary. It is not necessary to understand every word in order to comprehend the meaning of the dialogue. Occasionally a few vocabulary items are used that you have not yet learned; they are listed after the instructions and are intended for recognition only. Additional listening exercises are included in the tape program in the section called *Verstehen Sie?*

Das Klassenzimmer   *(Listen to the description of this class and classroom. Then select the correct response from those given below.)*

1. Das Klassenzimmer ist _____ .
    a. kühl   b. groß   c. schmutzig

2. Das Zimmer hat _____ Fenster.
    a. vier   b. fünf   c. sieben

3. Die Wände sind _____ .
   a. grau   b. blau   c. schwarz

4. Die _____ sind rot.
   a. Türen   b. Bücher   c. Stühle

5. Der Professor heißt _____ .
   a. Theo Seidl   b. Oskar Thieme   c. Otto Brockmann

6. Die Bilder sind _____ .
   a. alt   b. schön   c. klein

7. Die Studenten lernen _____ .
   a. Deutsch   b. Spanisch   c. Englisch

A.   Zahlen und Zeiten

1. **Wie geht's weiter?**   *(Add to or subtract from the previous sum. Continue from one person to another.)*

   BEISPIEL: $7 + 5 = 12 + 9 = 21 - ? = ? \ldots$

2. **Was kostet das?**   *(A student writes prices on the board for others to read aloud.)*

3. **Wie ist die Telefonnummer?**   *(Ask each other for the telephone number of persons listed below.)*

   BEISPIEL: Wie ist die Telefonnummer von *(of)* Karl-Heinz Kuckuck?
   Die Nummer ist 74 88.

Fischer Ulrich Berliner-1	71 29	**Harms Ralf** (Du) 18 93	**Jung Detlef** 73 35	**Kreissparkasse Alfeld Leine**
Fittje Herta Heinsen 4B	67 44	Alte Mühlen-8	Heinrich-Sohnrey-Weg 13	Geschäftsstellen
Flentje Isabella Alte-12	74 99	**Harstick Alfred** Landw. (Du) 5 98	—**Walter** 73 24	Duhnser-1 64 01
Flor Andrea Heinser-4	65 74	Deinsen	Heinrich-Sohnrey-Weg 11	Deilmissen 71 00
Forstverwaltung		—**Werner** Landw. (Du) 5 08	**Junge Kurt** Alte-1 65 00	Deinsen (Du) 5 28
o Staatl. Revierförsterei (Du) 5 92		Deinsen 14	—**Rolf** Betriebswirt Am Knick 78 76 45	**Krempig Dieter** Dunser-13 63 64
Deinsen		**Hartig Jürgen** KfzRep. Dorf-36 72 71	—**Wilhelm** RohrMstr. 61 36	**Kreth Erich** Am Knick 33 71 17
Freimut Ella Breslauer-1	71 45	**Hartmann Helene** 64 94	Am Knick 78	—**Harald** Kampweg 6 76 85
Freund Achim Im Küllfeld 6	62 40	Schachtweg 30	**Kahle Wolfgang** (Du) 12 86	—**Hugo** Königsberger-7 72 87
—**Friedrich** Haupt-49	61 39	**Haushaltswaren- und** 66 63	Lange-22	**Kreutz Kurt** Drogerie Haupt-1 66 08
—**Helga** Fußpflege Am Knick 32	65 97	**Geschenkartikel-Vertriebs**	**Kaiser Rolf** Bantelner-12 65 69	**Kreybohm Erich** (Du) 14 03
—**Klaus** Haupt-49	68 80	**GmbH** Haupt-17A	—**Siegfried** SparkassenOInsp. 66 82	Landw. Deinsen 23
Frie August Wassertor-18	76 54	**Hausmann Christian** 61 35	Breslauer-19	**Krieter Franz** (Du) 65 85
Friebe Martha Alte-10	74 17	Kampweg 5	—**Willi** Bantelner-29 68 91	Aschenkamp 3
—**Paul** Deilmissen Dorf-29	73 55	—**Heinz** Schachtweg 12 74 59	**Kalkof Carsten** Mühlen-3 68 35	**Krömer Alfred** 72 41
Friedrich Leo Berliner-19	72 60	**Hebisch Ernst** Haupt-5 62 09	—**Otto** Mühlen-3 73 59	Wilhelm-Raabe-4
—**Norbert** Wassertor-10	75 13	—**Heinrich** jun. Dunser-14 66 70	**Kanngießer Wolfgang** 63 40	**Krüger Horst** Neue-3 65 22
Friese Horst Heinser-2	70 84	—**Heinrich** sen. Dunser-16 68 27	Dunser-46	—**Selma** Dunser-56 73 19
Fritsche Herbert	62 24	—**Karl** Deilmissen Dorf-22 69 44	**Kasper Bernhard** 72 11	**Krumfuß Anna** Haupt-30 75 92
Unter den Tannen 9		—**Karl** Deilmissen Dorf-20A 71 52	Schachtweg 85	**Kube Klemens** (Du) 17 62
Frömming H.	72 06	**Hecht Friedrich W.** 62 84	**Kassebeer Horst** 65 66	Schlesierweg 102
Am Bahndamm 21		Bantelner-6	Im Küllfeld 2	**Kuchenbach Waldtraut** 73 37
Frohns Gustav Landw.	68 13	**Hehr W.** Gronauer-14 70 31	**Kassing Uwe** 69 88	Wassertor-9
Deilmisser-6		**Hein Alfred** Ing. Gastst. 66 50	Unter den Tannen 10	**Kuckuck Friedhelm** 66 57
Fromm Josef Berg-10	69 43	Haupt-41	**Katt Günter** Berg-30 61 76	Kampweg 6
		—**Günter** Neue-1 60 89	**Kaufmann Friedel** 62 55	—**Karl-Heinz** ElektroMstr. 74 88

B. **Buchstabieren Sie bitte!** *(Pronounce and spell these familiar words that English has borrowed from German.)*

Angst, Gesundheit, Poltergeist, Rucksack, Strudel, Zwieback

C. **Wann ist die Deutschstunde?** *(At the registration desk of your school, you are giving information about the schedule of next semester's classes. Use the suggested cues from both groups.)*

BEISPIEL: 9.00: **Die Deutschstunde ist um neun.**

Politik, Musik, Spanisch, Deutsch, Geologie, Kunst *(art),* Soziologie, Informatik *(computer science),* Psychologie, Geschichte *(history),* Sport, Physik, Philosophie, Biologie, Chemie

3.30, 4.00, 11.15, 10.45, 12.50, 8.30, 2.00, 5.45, 10.30

In Norwegen bringt stürmischer Wind Schnee/Regen und auch im Südosten Europas ist's winterlich. Viel Sonne steht dagegen von Warschau über Paris bis Malaga auf dem Programm – dazu in Südspanien 20°.

Although Germany lies between the 47th and 55th parallel north, roughly as far north as northern New England and southern Canada, its climate is generally far milder due to the effect of the Gulf Stream. Overall, Germany enjoys a temperate climate, plentiful rainfall throughout the year, and an absence of extreme heat and cold. In the northwest, summers tend to be cool and winters mild. Towards the east and south, the climate becomes more continental. Average daytime temperatures in Berlin are 30°F in January and 64°F in July; in Munich they are 33°F in January and 73°F in August. Autumns are usually mild, sunny, and dryer than other seasons. Between December and March it snows in the mountainous regions of Germany. At the Zugspitze, the highest point in the German Alps, snow can reach a depth of 13 to 16 feet, and in the Black Forest it averages five feet. Nevertheless it is at the outer slopes of the Black Forest and the Upper Rhine Valley where fruit trees are the first to bloom in spring.

Familie, Länder, Sprachen

Familie Schneider aus Hannover

LERNZIELE

Vorschau

- Focus on Germany

Gespräche und Wortschatz

- Your family, yourself, and the countries of Europe

Struktur

- Present tense of regular verbs
- Nominative case
- Sentence structure: position of subject; linking verbs and predicate adjectives
- Compound nouns

Einblicke

- The European Union and languages in Europe

Sprechsituationen

- Making small talk
- Asking for personal information

Focus on Germany

LAND.   Approximately 135,700 square miles, comparable to the combined size of New York, Pennsylvania, and Ohio.

PEOPLE.   About 81 million (including 5.6 million foreigners). Next to Russia, the most populous country of Europe, followed by Italy (58 million), the United Kingdom (57 million), and France (56 million). Major religions: 50% Protestant, 37% Catholic, about 13% other.

GEOGRAPHY.   From north to south divided into three major regions: the flat lowlands in the north, the central mountain region, and the southern highlands with the narrow band of the Alps that is part of Germany.

CURRENCY.   Deutsche Mark, 1 DM = 100 Pfennige.

PRINCIPAL CITIES.   Berlin (pop. 3.9 million, official capital); Bonn (pop. 300,000, current seat of government); Hamburg (pop. 1.6 million); München (pop. 1.3 million); Köln (pop. 914,000); Frankfurt am Main (pop. 670,000); Düsseldorf (pop. 590,000); Stuttgart (pop. 563,000); Leipzig (pop. 554,000); Dresden (519,000).

Germany's sometimes turbulent history spans nearly 2,000 years. Unlike many of its neighbors, Germany never became a centralized state but was always a federation. Initially there were various Germanic tribes; even now their heritage gives the various regions of Germany their particular identity. The "Holy Roman Empire of the German Nation," a loose federation of states under an emperor, lasted from 962 to 1806. During this time, the country further divided until there were almost 350 individual political entities, some of them tiny. Under Napoleon they were consolidated into thirty-two states. In 1871, under Prussian leadership, Germany became one state for the first time; this monarchy lasted until the end of World War I, when Germany became a republic.

After the Second World War, Germany was divided into two countries: the Federal Republic of Germany, or FRG (**Bundesrepublik = BRD**), in the west and the German Democratic Republic, or GDR (**Deutsche Demokratische Republik = DDR**), in the east. The line between the Communist World and the West, a heavily fortified border, ran through the middle of Germany, and the infamous Berlin Wall, built in 1961, right through its former capital. After the collapse of the former Soviet Union, the two Germanies were united again on October 3, 1990. More than forty years of separation and the differences between two diametrically opposed social and economic systems are not easily overcome despite a common language and history. The cost of unification, both socially and economically, has been much higher than anticipated. In the East, the closing of obsolete plants and high unemployment, and, in the West, higher taxes, were the most obvious immediate results. Germany still has the most powerful economy in Europe, but the internationally competitive industries are located primarily in the eleven western states (**Länder**), while industry in the five new states is struggling. Great efforts are being made to help the eastern states deal with their economic problems, but the real question is how long it will take to overcome the psychological impact of the division—the "wall in the minds" of people. Only when that wall finally falls will the unification process be complete.

NOCH 'NE MAUER

Gespräche Am Goethe Institut[1]

SHARON	Roberto, woher kommst du[2]?
ROBERTO	Ich bin aus Rom. Und du?
SHARON	Ich komme aus Sacramento, aber jetzt wohnt meine Familie in Seattle.
ROBERTO	Hast du Geschwister?
SHARON	Ja, ich habe zwei Schwestern und zwei Brüder. Und du?
ROBERTO	Ich habe nur eine Schwester. Sie wohnt in Montreal, in Kanada.
SHARON	Wirklich? So ein Zufall! Mein Onkel wohnt auch da.

Später

ROBERTO	Sharon, wann ist die Prüfung?
SHARON	In zehn Minuten. Du, wie heißen ein paar Flüsse in Deutschland?
ROBERTO	Im Norden ist die Elbe, im Osten die Oder, im Süden . . .
SHARON	Die Donau?
ROBERTO	Richtig! Und im Westen der Rhein. Wo liegt Düsseldorf[3]?
SHARON	Düsseldorf? Hm. Wo ist eine Landkarte?
ROBERTO	O hier. Im Westen von Deutschland, nördlich von Bonn, am Rhein.
SHARON	Ach ja, richtig! Na, viel Glück!

> Superscript numbers in the dialogue texts refer to cultural information in the *Übrigens*-section below.

Fragen

1. Woher kommt Roberto?   2. Woher kommt Sharon?   3. Wo wohnt Sharons Familie?
4. Wie groß ist Sharons Familie?   5. Wann ist die Prüfung?   6. Was sind die Elbe, die Oder, die Donau und der Rhein?   7. Wo ist die Elbe? die Oder? die Donau? der Rhein?
8. Wo liegt Düsseldorf?

Übrigens (By the way)

1. The Goethe Institute supports the study of the German language and culture through study centers for students and teachers of German throughout the world.

2. There is now no equivalent form of address in English for **du,** but its cognate *thou* is still in poetic and religious use. Although it has become customary for university students to address each other with the **du-**form, it might be prudent for an American visitor to wait until the familiar **du** is offered by the German-speaking person. All adults must be addressed with **Sie** unless they are relatives or close friends (see also p. 48).

3. Düsseldorf is the capital of North Rhine-Westphalia and the administrative center for the state's heavy industry. An affluent city, it is also a university town, an art and fashion center, and the site of numerous conventions and trade fairs.

Düsseldorf am Rhein

Die Familie, -n   *(family)*

der	Bruder, ⁝	*brother*	*die*	Frau, -en	*woman; wife*
	Junge, -n	*boy*		Kusine, -n	*cousin*
	Onkel, -	*uncle*		Mutter, ⁝	*mother*
	Mann, ⁝er	*man; husband*		Großmutter, ⁝	*grandmother*
	Sohn, ⁝e	*son*		Schwester, -n	*sister*
	Vater, ⁝	*father*		Tante, -n	*aunt*
	Großvater, ⁝	*grandfather*		Tochter, ⁝	*daughter*
	Vetter, -n	*cousin*			
das	Kind, -er	*child*	*die*	Eltern (pl.)	*parents*
	Mädchen, -	*girl*		Großeltern (pl.)	*grandparents*

Weiteres

der	Satz, ⁝e	*sentence*	*die*	Frage, -n	*question*
	Berg, -e	*mountain*		Prüfung, -en	*test, exam*
	Fluß, ⁝sse	*river*		Landkarte, -n	*map*
	See, -n	*lake*		Stadt, ⁝e	*city*
				Hauptstadt, ⁝e	*capital city*

amerikanisch	*American*
kanadisch	*Canadian*

Das Land, ⁝er[1] **Die Leute (pl.)**[2]		**Die Sprache, -n**[3]
(country, state) *(people)*		*(language)*
Deutschland	der Deutsche, -n/die Deutsche, -n	Deutsch
Frankreich	der Franzose, -n/die Französin, -nen	Französisch
Österreich	der Österreicher, -/die Österreicherin, -nen	Deutsch
die Schweiz	der Schweizer, -/die Schweizerin, -nen	Deutsch, Französisch, Italienisch
Italien	der Italiener, -/die Italienerin, -nen	Italienisch
Spanien	der Spanier, -/die Spanierin, -nen	Spanisch
England	der Engländer, -/die Engländerin, -nen	Englisch
Amerika	der Amerikaner, -/die Amerikanerin, -nen	Englisch
Kanada	der Kanadier, -/die Kanadierin, -nen	Englisch, Französisch

[1] All countries and cities are neuter unless indicated otherwise **(die Schweiz).**

[2] Many feminine nouns can be derived from masculine nouns by adding **-in,** in which case their plurals end in **-nen (der Schweizer > die Schweizerin, -nen).** BUT: **der Deutsche > die Deutsche, -n; der Franzose > die Französin, -nen!**

[3] Adjectives denoting nationality are not capitalized: Typisch **deutsch!** *(Typically German!),* Antworten Sie **auf deutsch!** *(Answer in German!)* BUT: Ich spreche **Deutsch** *(the German language).*

Weiteres *(cont.)*

kommen	*to come*
liegen	*to lie (be located)*
wohnen	*to live, reside*
woher?	*from where?*
Ich bin / komme aus . . .	*I'm from . . . (a native of)*
im Norden / Süden / Osten / Westen[4]	*in the north / south / east / west*
nördlich / südlich / östlich / westlich von . . .	*north / south / east / west of . . .*
mein(e)[5]	*my*
dein(e) / Ihr(e)[5]	*your (informal / formal)*

[4] **im** is used with months, seasons, and points of the compass (**im** Mai, **im** Winter, **im** Norden); **in** is used with names of cities, countries, and continents (**in** Berlin, **in** Deutschland, **in** Europa).

[5] **mein, dein,** and **Ihr** have no ending when used before masculine and neuter nouns that are sentence subjects: mein Vater, dein Bruder, Ihr Kind. Before feminine and plural nouns, **meine, deine,** and **Ihre** are used (see p. 52): meine Mutter, deine Schwester, Ihre Eltern.

ZUM ERKENNEN: die Geschwister *(pl.) (siblings, brothers and / or sisters);* So ein Zufall! *(What a coincidence!);* Na, viel Glück! *(Well, good luck!)*

Zum Thema

A.   Mustersätze

1. Ihre Familie: **Woher kommt** Ihre Familie?
   Ihr Vater, Ihre Mutter, Ihr Onkel, Ihre Tante
2. Rom: **Ich bin aus** Rom.
   Frankfurt, Österreich, Amerika, Berlin
3. Hamburg / Norden: Hamburg **liegt im** Norden.
   Leipzig / Osten; München / Süden; Düsseldorf / Westen; Rostock / Norden
4. die Schweiz / südlich: Die Schweiz **liegt** südlich **von Deutschland.**
   Dänemark / nördlich; Polen / östlich; Österreich / südlich; Luxemburg / westlich
5. Österreich / Deutsch: **In** Österreich **sprechen die Leute** Deutsch.
   Frankreich / Französisch; England / Englisch; Italien / Italienisch; Spanien / Spanisch.

B.   Was sind sie?

NOTE: Unlike English, German does not use an indefinite article before nationalities or references to membership in a group: Sie ist **Amerikanerin** *(an American).* Sie ist **Studentin** *(a student).* Er ist **Berliner** *(a Berliner).*

1. BEISPIEL: Juan ist Spanier. Und Juanita?
   Juanita ist Spanierin.

   a. Antonio ist Italiener. Und Luisa?
   b. Hugo ist Österreicher. Und Lilo?
   c. Walter ist Schweizer. Und Helga?
   d. Pierre ist Franzose. Und Monique?

2. BEISPIEL: Uwe und Monika sind aus Frankfurt.
      Uwe ist Frankfurter, und Monika ist Frankfurterin.

   a. Robert und Evi sind aus Berlin.
   b. Klaus und Inge sind aus Hamburg.
   c. Rolf und Katrin sind aus Wien.
   d. Ulrich und Romy sind aus Zürich.

C. **Was paßt?**   *(For each question or statement on the left, select one or more appropriate responses from the right-hand column, or give your own.)*

_____ 1. Woher kommst du?	a. Sehr klein. Ich habe keine Brüder und Schwestern.
_____ 2. Wie groß ist deine Familie?	b. Am Rhein.
_____ 3. Meine Schwester wohnt in Seattle.	c. Mein Onkel wohnt auch da.
_____ 4. Wann ist die Prüfung?	d. Aus Seattle, und du?
_____ 5. Wo liegt Weimar?	e. Um Viertel nach zehn.
	f. Im Osten von Deutschland.
	g. In zwanzig Minuten.
	h. Östlich von Erfurt.
	i. Ich bin aus Rom.
	j. Wir sind sechs.
	k. Wirklich?
	l. Ich weiß nicht.

Stadtzentrum von Erfurt

D. Familien

1. **Elkes Stammbaum** *(Look at Elke's family tree and explain who each person is.)*

    BEISPIEL: Elke ist die Tochter von Jens und Ute.
    Elke ist Arndts Schwester.

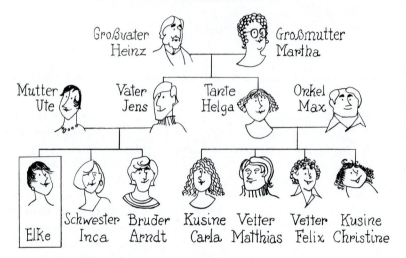

2. **Meine Familie** *(Draw your own family tree modeled on the one above and name all the people on it. Then describe your family to a classmate. Take turns; don't hesitate to ask questions.)*

    BEISPIEL: Meine Mutter heißt . . . und ist . . . Jahre alt. Sie wohnt . . .

E.   Fragen   *(Ask another student the following questions, then answer them in your turn.)*

1.   Woher kommst du? deine Eltern? deine Großeltern?

2.   Wo wohnt deine Familie?

     BEISPIEL: Meine Familie wohnt in Santa Barbara.

3.   Wo liegt _____ *(name of city)?*

     BEISPIEL: Santa Barbara liegt in Kalifornien.

4.   Wo liegt _____ *(name of state or province)?*

     BEISPIEL: Kalifornien liegt südlich von Oregon.

5.   Wie heißt die Hauptstadt von _____ *(name of state)?*

     BEISPIEL: Die Hauptstadt von Kalifornien heißt Sacramento.

6.   Welche Stadt liegt im Norden und im Süden von _____ *(name of your city)?*

     BEISPIEL: Im Norden von Santa Barbara liegt San Francisco und im Süden Los Angeles.

7.   Ist _____ *(name of your city)* groß oder klein? Wie viele Leute wohnen da?

8.   Ist da ein Fluß, ein See oder der Ozean *(ocean)?* Wenn ja *(if so),* wie heißt der Fluß, der See oder der Ozean? Ist der Fluß (der See, der Ozean) schön? sauber?

9.   Sind da Berge? Wenn ja, wie heißen sie? Wenn nein, wo sind Berge?

10.   Wie ist das Wetter da im Frühling? im Sommer? im Herbst? im Winter?

F. **Aussprache: i, a, u**   *(See also section II. 1, 3–4, 11–13, 17, 19–20 in the pronunciation section of the Workbook.)*

1. [i:]   **I**hnen, l**ie**gen, w**ie**der, W**ie**n, Berl**i**n
2. [i]   **i**ch b**i**n, b**i**tte, K**i**nd, r**i**chtig
3. [a:]   Fr**a**ge, Spr**a**che, Amerik**a**ner, Sp**a**nier, V**a**ter
4. [a]   St**a**dt, L**a**ndkarte, K**a**nada, S**a**tz, T**a**nte
5. [u:]   g**u**t, Br**u**der, K**u**li, Min**u**te, d**u**
6. [u]   **u**nd, St**u**nde, J**u**nge, M**u**tter, Fl**u**ß
7. Wortpaare
    a. still / Stil   c. Kamm / komm   e. Rum / Ruhm
    b. Stadt / Staat   d. Schiff / schief   f. Ratte / rate

Hören Sie zu!

Guten Morgen!   *(Listen to the conversation between Hugo Schmidt and Monika Müller. Then decide whether the statements below are true or false according to the dialogue. Remember that you may listen as often as you wish.)*

ZUM ERKENNEN: die Assistentin; die Arbeit *(work)*

_____ 1. Hugo Schmidt ist Professor.
_____ 2. Monika Müller ist Professorin.
_____ 3. Monika spricht *(speaks)* Deutsch, Englisch und Spanisch.
_____ 4. Monika ist aus Spanien.
_____ 5. Monikas Mutter ist aus Deutschland.
_____ 6. Monika ist 23.
_____ 7. Der Professor braucht Monika von 2 Uhr bis 6 Uhr.
_____ 8. Monika braucht Arbeit.
_____ 9. Monika ist zwei Monate da.

LERNTIP

Studying grammar

Don't let the idea of grammar scare you. It's a shortcut to learning, providing you with the patterns native speakers follow when they use the language. The fact that German and English are closely related will be both a help and a hindrance: note well the instances when German functions differently from English. As a bonus, your study of German will make you more aware of the fine points of English grammar.

Hamburger Hafen
(harbor)

STRUKTUR

I. The Present Tense

1. You are already familiar with some of the PERSONAL PRONOUNS; there are four others: **du, er, sie,** and **ihr.**

	singular	plural	singular / plural
1st person	ich *(I)*	wir *(we)*	
2nd person	**du** *(you, fam.)*	**ihr** *(you, fam.)*	Sie *(you, formal)*
3rd person	**er** / es / **sie** *(he, it, she)*	sie *(they)*	

    • **du** and **ihr** are intimate forms of address used with family members, close friends, children up to the age of fourteen, and animals.

    • **Sie,** which is always capitalized when it means *you,* is used in formal relationships and with titles such as **Herr** and **Frau.** It is used to address one or more persons. **Sie** *(you)* and **sie** *(they,* not capitalized) can be distinguished in conversation only through context.

    Herr Schmidt, wo wohnen **Sie?** Und Ihre Eltern, wo wohnen **sie?**
    Mr. Schmidt, where do you live? And your parents, where do they live?

    • The pronouns **sie** *(she, it)* and **sie** *(they)* can be distinguished through the personal endings of the verb.

    Sie komm**t** im Mai, und **sie** komm**en** im Juni.
    She comes in May, and they come in June.

2. The INFINITIVE is the form of the verb that has no subject and takes no personal ending (e.g., *to learn*). Almost every German infinitive ends in **-en: lernen, antworten.** The stem of the verb is the part that precedes the infinitive ending **-en.** Thus the stem of **lernen** is **lern-,** and that of **antworten** is **antwort-.**

    English verbs have at most one personal ending in the present tense, *-s: I (you, we, they) learn,* BUT *he (it, she) learns.* In German, endings are added to the verb stem for all persons.

    > stem + personal ending = present tense verb form

    German verb endings vary, depending on whether the subject is in the FIRST, SECOND, or THIRD PERSON, and in the SINGULAR or PLURAL. The verb must agree with the subject. You have already learned the endings used for some persons.

Here is the complete list of endings:

	singular	plural	formal (sg. / pl.)
1st person	ich lerne	wir lernen	
2nd person	du lernst	ihr lernt	Sie lernen
3rd person	er / es / sie lernt	sie lernen	

NOTE: The verb forms for formal *you* (**Sie**) and plural *they* (**sie**) are identical. The same holds true for **er / es / sie.** For that reason **Sie** and **es / sie** will not be repeated in future chapters.

These verbs, which you already know from the *Schritte* and from this chapter, follow the model of **lernen.** Be sure to review them.

beginnen	*to begin*	sagen	*to say, tell*
brauchen	*to need*	schreiben	*to write*
fragen	*to ask*	spielen	*to play*
gehen	*to go*	verstehen	*to understand*
hören	*to hear*	wiederholen	*to repeat, review*
kommen	*to come*	wohnen	*to live, reside*
liegen	*to be (located)*	zählen	*to count*

3. When a verb stem ends in **-d** or **-t** (**antwort-**), or in certain consonant combinations (**öffn-, regn-**), an **-e** is inserted between the stem and the **-st** and **-t** endings to make these endings clearly audible.

	singular	plural	formal (sg. / pl.)
1st person	ich antworte	wir antworten	
2nd person	du antwortest	ihr antwortet	Sie antworten
3rd person	er / es / sie antwortet	sie antworten	

These familiar verbs follow the model of **antworten:**

finden	*to find*	öffnen	*to open*
kosten	*to cost*	regnen	*to rain*

4. The **du**-form of verbs with a stem ending in any **s**-sound (**-s, -ss, -ß, -tz, -z**) adds only a **-t** instead of **-st: ich heiße, du heißt.** Thus, the **du**-form is identical with the **er**-form of these verbs: **du heißt, er heißt.**

5. German has only one verb form to express what can be said in English in several ways.

Ich **wohne** in Köln.
$\begin{cases} I\ live\ in\ Cologne. \\ I'm\ living\ in\ Cologne. \\ I\ do\ live\ in\ \text{Cologne.} \end{cases}$

Wohnst du in Köln?
$\begin{cases} Are\ you\ living\ in\ Cologne? \\ Do\ you\ live\ in\ Cologne? \end{cases}$

6. In both languages the present tense is very frequently used to express future time, particularly when a time expression clearly indicates the future.

In dreißig Minuten **gehe** ich in die Stadt.   *I'm going downtown in thirty minutes.*
Er **kommt** im Sommer.   *He's coming in the summer.*

Übungen

A.   Du, ihr oder Sie?   *(How would you address these people? Explain why.)*

1. your father   **2.** members of your family   **3.** your German professor   **4.** a store clerk   **5.** two police officers   **6.** your roommate   **7.** friends of your three-year-old niece   **8.** your classmates   **9.** a group of strangers who are older than you

B.   Ersetzen Sie das Subjekt!   *(Replace the subject by using the words in parentheses.)*

BEISPIEL: Ich sage das noch einmal. (wir, Maria)
Wir sagen das noch einmal.
Maria sagt das noch einmal.

1.   Wir antworten auf deutsch. (Roberto, du, ich, die Mutter)
2.   Ich wiederhole die Frage. (er, wir, ihr, Sie)
3.   Ihr lernt die Wörter. (ich, du, die Kinder, wir)
4.   Du öffnest das Buch auf Seite 3. (der Franzose, ich, ihr, sie / *sg.*)
5.   Heidi Bauer geht an die Tafel. (ihr, sie / *pl.,* ich, du)
6.   Brauchst du Papier und Bleistifte? (wir, ich, Sie, ihr)
7.   Wie finden Sie das? (ihr, du, Ihre Familie, die Leute)

C.   Kombinieren Sie!   *(Create sentences by combining items from each column.)*

BEISPIEL: Er kommt aus Kanada.

1	2	3
ich	beginnen	auf deutsch
du	brauchen	auf englisch
er	hören	aus . . .
es	kommen	(das) nicht
sie	kosten	Deutsch
das	lernen	heute
die Deutschvorlesung	regnen	in . . .
das Mädchen	schreiben	jetzt
wir	spielen	morgen
ihr	wohnen	(nicht) gut
Sie	zählen	Tennis
sie		um . . . Uhr
		vier Mark
		von zehn bis zwanzig

D.   Was fehlt?   *(What's missing? Fill in the missing verb forms.)*

JENS   Inge und Heidi, woher _____ ihr? (kommen)
HEIDI   Ich _____ aus Heidelberg. (kommen)
INGE   Und ich _____ aus Berlin. (sein)
JENS   Wirklich? Meine Großmutter _____ auch aus Berlin. (kommen)
         Aber sie _____ jetzt in Hamburg. (wohnen) Wie _____
         ihr es hier? (finden)
HEIDI   Wir _____ es hier prima. (finden)
INGE   Ich _____ die Berge wunderbar. (finden)
JENS   Ich auch!

E. **Auf deutsch bitte!**

1. We're learning German.
2. I'm counting slowly.
3. Where do you *(pl. fam.)* come from?
4. They come from Canada.
5. I'm from America.
6. Do you *(sg. fam.)* answer in English?
7. No, I'll speak German.
8. She's opening the book.
9. I do need the book.
10. What does she say?
11. Do you *(sg. fam.)* understand that (**das**)?
12. Is she repeating that?
13. Her name is Sabine.
14. They do live in Wittenberg.

II. The Nominative Case

To show the function of nouns or pronouns in a sentence, German uses a system called CASE. There are four cases in German: nominative, accusative, dative, and genitive. The nominative case is the case of the subject and of the predicate noun. (The latter is discussed in Section III.2, p. 54).

In the English sentence *The boy asks the father,* the SUBJECT of the sentence is *the boy;* he does the asking. We know that the boy is the subject of the sentence because in English the subject precedes the verb. This is not always true in German, where one frequently knows the function of a word or phrase from its form rather than from its position. In the sentence **Der Junge fragt den Vater,** the phrase **der Junge** tells us we are dealing with the subject, whereas **den Vater** tells us we are dealing with a direct object (more about this in Chapter 2). In dictionaries and vocabulary lists, nouns are given in the nominative. The nominative answers the questions *who?* for persons or *what?* for objects and ideas.

Der Junge fragt den Vater.	*The boy asks the father.*
Der See ist schön.	*The lake is beautiful.*

1. The nominative forms of the INTERROGATIVE PRONOUNS are **wer** *(who)* and **was** *(what).*

	persons	things and ideas
nom.	wer	was

Wer fragt den Vater? → **Der Junge.**
Who is asking the father? → The boy.

Was ist schön? → **Der See.**
What is beautiful? → The lake.

2. The nominative forms of the DEFINITE ARTICLE **der** *(the)* and the INDEFINITE ARTICLE **ein** *(a, an)* are already familiar. Note that the indefinite article is the same for masculine and neuter nouns; it has no ending. It also has no plural: *I have a pencil,* BUT *I have pencils.*

	\begin singular			plural	
	masc.	**neut.**	**fem.**		
nom.	der	das	die	die	*the*
	ein	ein	eine	—	*a, an*
	kein	kein	keine	keine	*no, not a, not any*

The POSSESSIVE ADJECTIVES **mein** *(my),* **dein** *(your),* and **Ihr** *(your)* follow the pattern of **ein** and **kein.**

Die Frau, der Junge und das Mädchen sind aus Österreich.
Mein Onkel und meine Tante wohnen auch da. Wo wohnen deine Eltern?

3.   Nouns can be replaced by PERSONAL PRONOUNS. In English we replace persons with *he, she,* or *they,* and objects and ideas with *it* or *they.* In German the pronoun used depends on the gender of the noun.

Wer ist **der** Mann?	**Er** heißt Max.	*He's called Max.*
Wie heißt **das** Kind?	**Es** heißt Susi.	*She's called Susi.*
Wer ist **die** Frau?	**Sie** heißt Ute.	*She's called Ute.*
Wie ist **der** See?	**Er** ist groß.	*It's big.*
Wie ist **das** Land?	**Es** ist klein.	*It's small.*
Wie heißt **die** Stadt?	**Sie** heißt Ulm.	*It's called Ulm.*

•   Note that German uses three pronouns (**er, es, sie**) for objects where English uses only one *(it).*

•   Note also how similar these pronouns are to the forms of the articles:

der → er *(he, it);* das → es *(it, he, she);* die → sie *(she, it)*

•   In the plural there are no gender distinctions, as the definite article for all plural nouns is **die.** The pronoun for all plural nouns is **sie.**

die Männer ⎫
die Kinder ⎬ **sie** *(they)*
die Frauen ⎭

die Seen ⎫
die Länder ⎬ **sie** *(they)*
die Städte ⎭

Übungen

F.   **Ersetzen Sie die Wörter mit Pronomen!**   *(Replace the nouns with pronouns.)*

BEISPIEL: Fritz   **er**
            die Landkarte   **sie**

der Vater, der Berg, das Land, die Großmutter, der Junge, die Stadt, der Bleistift, der Pulli, Österreich, der Österreicher, die Schweiz, die Schweizerin, Deutschland, das Kind

G.   **Die Geographiestunde**

1.   **Was ist das?**   *(As the instructor of a geography course, describe some features of Europe to your class. Use the appropriate form of **ein**.)*

BEISPIEL: Frankfurt / Stadt
            Frankfurt ist eine Stadt.

Österreich / Land; die Donau / Fluß; Italienisch / Sprache; Berlin / Stadt; der Main / Fluß; das Matterhorn / Berg; Französisch / Sprache; Kanada / Land; der Bodensee / See; Bremen / Stadt

2. **Ist das richtig?** *(Now test your students to see what they do and don't know about Europe. Use the appropriate form of kein.)*

BEISPIEL: die Donau / Land?
Ist die Donau ein Land?
Nein, die Donau ist kein Land. Die Donau ist ein Fluß.

Frankfurt / Fluß; Frankreich / Sprache; Heidelberg / Berg; der Rhein / Stadt; die Schweiz / See; Spanien / Sprache; Bonn / Land

3. **Ethnisches Mosaik** *(Working in pairs, find out the ethnic background of your classmate. Use the appropriate form of mein and dein.)*

BEISPIEL: Woher kommt dein Vater?
Mein Vater kommt aus Salzburg.

Woher kommt dein Vater oder dein Stiefvater *(stepfather)?* deine Mutter oder deine Stiefmutter *(stepmother)?* dein Großvater? deine Großmutter? dein Urgroß-vater *(great-grandfather)?* deine Urgroßmutter?

1200 JAHRE '94
FRANKFURT

H. Ersetzen Sie das Subjekt!

1. **Antworten Sie mit JA!** *(A curious neighbor asks you questions about the new family in the neighborhood. Answer positively, using pronouns.)*

BEISPIEL: Die Eltern kommen aus Italien, nicht wahr?
Ja, sie kommen aus Italien.

a. Der Sohn antwortet auf italienisch, nicht wahr? **b.** Die Tochter versteht Deutsch, nicht wahr? **c.** Das Kind ist fünf Jahre alt, nicht wahr? **d.** Die Großmutter heißt Maria, nicht wahr? **e.** Der Großvater wohnt auch da, nicht wahr? **f.** Die Familie kommt aus Rom, nicht wahr?

2. **Antworten Sie bitte!** *(Ask another student the following questions. He or she answers, using pronouns. Then change roles.)*

BEISPIEL: Wann beginnt dein Tag?
Er beginnt morgens um sechs.

a. Wann beginnt die Deutschvorlesung? **b.** Ist das Vorlesungszimmer groß? **c.** Wie heißt das Deutschbuch? **d.** Ist dein Kuli schwarz? **e.** Welche Farbe hat dein Heft? **f.** Welche Farbe hat deine Jacke? **g.** Wo ist das Fenster? **h.** Wie ist das Fenster? **i.** Wie viele Monate hat das Jahr? **j.** Wie viele Wochen hat der Monat? **k.** Wie viele Tage hat die Woche? **l.** Wie viele Stunden hat der Tag? **m.** Wie viele Minuten hat die Stunde?

III. Sentence Structure

1.   In English the subject usually precedes the verb, and more than one element may do so.

They **are learning** German at the Goethe Institute.
*At the Goethe Institute they **are learning** German.*

As you know, in German statements and information questions the <u>verb</u> is always the second sentence element.

1   2   3   4

Sie **lernen** Deutsch am Goethe Institut.

In contrast to English, however, only ONE sentence element may precede the verb, and this element is not necessarily the subject. If an element other than the subject precedes the verb, the *verb stays* in the second position and *the subject follows* the verb. This pattern is called INVERTED WORD ORDER.

1   2   3   4

Am Goethe Institut **lernen** sie Deutsch.
Deutsch **lernen** sie am Goethe Institut.

2.   The verbs **sein** *(to be)* and **heißen** *(to be called)* are LINKING VERBS. They normally link two words referring to the same person or thing, both of which are in the nominative: the first is the subject, the other a PREDICATE NOUN.

subject   predicate noun

Der Herr **ist**   Schweizer.
Er **heißt** Stefan Wolf.

The verb **sein** can be complemented not only by a predicate noun, but also by a PREDI-CATE ADJECTIVE. Both are considered part of the verb phrase. This is an example of a typical and important feature of German sentence structure: when the verb consists of more than one part, the inflected part (V1)—that is, the part of the verb that takes a personal ending—is the second element in the sentence. The uninflected part (V2) stands at the very end of the sentence.

Stefan Wolf **ist** auch **Schweizer.**
Er <u>ist</u> heute <u>**sehr müde.**</u>
V1   V2

REMEMBER: In German no indefinite article is used before nationalities. **Er ist Stuttgarter** *(an inhabitant of Stuttgart).*

I.   **Sagen Sie es anders!**   *(Say it differently. Begin each sentence with the word or phrase in boldface.)*

BEISPIEL: Mein Vetter kommt **morgen.**
              Morgen kommt mein Vetter.

1. Ich bin **jetzt** am Goethe Institut.
2. Die Leute sprechen **hier** nur Deutsch.
3. Wir haben **in zehn Minuten** eine Prüfung in Geographie.
4. Du findest die Landkarte **auf Seite 162.**
5. Die Donau ist **im Süden.**
6. Düsseldorf liegt **nördlich von Bonn.**
7. Es geht **mir** gut.
8. Wir spielen **um halb drei** Tennis.
9. Es regnet oft **im April.**
10. Es schneit aber **im Winter** nicht.
11. Es ist **schön** heute.
12. Die Sonne scheint **jetzt** wieder.
13. Ich finde es hier **toll.**
14. Die Berge sind **wirklich wunderschön.**

J.   **Welche Nationalität?**   *(Professor Händel of the Goethe Institute is determining the nationality of his summer-school students. Follow the model.)*

BEISPIEL: Pierre kommt aus Frankreich.
              Er ist Franzose.

1. Roberto kommt aus Italien.
2. Sam kommt aus Amerika.
3. Carla kommt aus Spanien.
4. James kommt aus England.
5. Helen kommt aus Kanada.
6. Maria und Caroline kommen aus Amerika.
7. Marie und Simone kommen aus Frankreich.
8. Evita und Pia kommen aus Spanien.

IV. Compound Nouns

In German, two or three simple words are frequently combined to create one new one, like **Fingerhut** (a "hat" that protects your finger = *thimble*), **Menschenfreund** (a friend of human beings = *philanthropist*), or **Stinktier** (an animal that stinks = *skunk*). The last component determines the gender and the plural form.

$$\text{das Land } + \text{ die Karte } = \text{ die Landkarte, -n}$$
$$\text{der Arm } + \text{ das Band } + \text{ die Uhr } = \text{ die Armbanduhr, -en}$$
$$\text{schreiben } + \text{ der Tisch } = \text{ der Schreibtisch, -e}$$
$$\text{klein } + \text{ die Stadt } = \text{ die Kleinstadt, ¨e}$$

Übung

K. Was sind die Artikel? Was bedeuten die Wörter?   *(Determine the gender and meaning of the following words.)*

BEISPIEL: Schokoladentafel
die Schokoladentafel; *chocolate bar*

Wochentag, Neujahr, Sommerbluse, Frühlingswetter, Altstadt, Bergsee, Wörterbuch, Sprechübung, Familienvater, Jungenname, Zimmertür, Hosenrock, Hemdbluse, Hausschuh, Handschuh, Deutschstunde, Wanduhr, Uhrzeit

---

Zusammen-fassung

These sentences include the material introduced in this chapter and in the *Schritte*. Watch carefully for differences between English and German patterns.

L.   Sprachstudenten.   Auf deutsch, bitte!

1. Tomorrow my parents are coming.
2. My father is (a) French(man), and my mother is (an) Austrian.   **3.** In France they (the people) speak French, and in Austria they speak German.
4. France is west of Germany, and Austria is south of Germany.   **5.** I do understand French and German, but I answer in English.   **6.** Where are you *(fam.)* from?   **7.** I'm from Texas.
8. There's Thomas. Thomas is (an) American.   **9.** He's learning Spanish.
10. I think it's beautiful here, but I am very tired.

LERNTIP

Reading German texts

First read for general content without worrying about unfamiliar words and phrases. Then reread carefully and always finish a paragraph, or at least a sentence, before looking up an unfamiliar word or phrase. Look up as little as possible. Underline and pronounce the words in question, but do not scribble the English translation into the text. It will only distract you from the German.

Read the text a third time after having guessed or looked up all the underlined words. See how many of them you remember. Try to learn them now, at least passively, so as to avoid looking them up repeatedly. If a word or phrase still remains unclear, circle it and ask your instructor instead of spending more time on it.

EINBLICKE

The European Community, or EC (**Europäische Gemeinschaft = EG**)—now called European Union, or EU (*Europäische Union*)—is an economic association of Western European nations dedicated to the unrestricted movement of goods, capital, services, and people among member countries. Created in 1957 by the Treaty of Rome, the six original Community members—Belgium, France, Italy, the Netherlands, Luxembourg, and West Germany—have been joined by Denmark, Great Britain, Greece, Ireland, Portugal, and Spain. East Germany had indirect access to the EC by virtue of special trade arrangements with West Germany. Upon unification, East Germany automatically became a part of the EC. In February 1993 negotiations on EU membership started with Austria, Finland, Norway, and Sweden.

For the 345 million residents of the EU, January 1, 1993, marked the culmination of drawn-out, intense efforts towards a single market. Most trade barriers between member nations were eliminated and travel across Europe became even easier. All EU citizens, including students and retirees, can now live in the country of their choice, provided they can support themselves. European integration is planned to take place in two stages. The first goal, the creation of one single market, was realized to some extent in 1993. The second phase, political and economic unity as set forth in the Maastricht Treaty, would create a single European currency and a tight-knit "United States of Europe" by the end of the decade. Popular opposition to the treaty remains strong, however. Moreover, there are signs that many EU countries would have trouble meeting Maastricht's stiff economic standards for monetary union. Only time will tell whether plans continue on track.

WORTSCHATZ 2

These reading texts expand on the chapter topic. All vocabulary that is to become active is listed under *Wortschatz 2*. Learn these words well; they will recur in future exercises and activities. Each reading selection is introduced by *Was ist das?*, a short set of cognates and compounds that you should be able to pronounce and recognize but do not have to master actively. Superscript numbers in the reading texts refer to additional cultural information in the *Übrigens*-section at the end of most chapters.

der	Mensch, -en	*human being, person; pl. people*
	Nachbar, -n / die Nachbarin, -nen	*neighbor*
	Teil, -e	*part*
	schon	*already*
	so . . . wie . . .	*as . . . as . . .*
	ungefähr	*about, approximately*
	wichtig	*important*

WAS IST DAS?   der Bankier, Europäer, Großteil, Tourismus; (das) Europa, Sprachenlernen; die Muttersprache, Politik; die USA (pl.); Dänisch, Finnisch, Griechisch, Holländisch, Norwegisch, Polnisch, Portugiesisch, Schwedisch, Tschechisch; studieren; europäisch, interessant

Viele Länder, viele Sprachen

of course   Europa hat viele Länder und viele Sprachen. In Deutschland hören Sie natürlich° Deutsch. Aber die Nachbarn im Norden sprechen Dänisch, Schwedisch, Norwegisch und Finnisch. Die Nachbarn im Osten sprechen Polnisch und Tschechisch, und im Westen sprechen sie Holländisch und Französisch. Im Süden von Europa sprechen die Menschen Italienisch,

by far not   Spanisch, Portugiesisch und Griechisch; und das sind noch lange nicht° alle Sprachen!   5

as   Deutsch ist sehr wichtig. Ungefähr 90 Millionen Europäer sprechen Deutsch als° Mut-
of the   tersprache: die Deutschen, die Österreicher, die Liechtensteiner und ein Großteil der°
foreigners / work   Schweizer. Viele Ausländer° arbeiten° oder studieren in Deutschland, Österreich und in
in / this way   der° Schweiz und lernen so° auch Deutsch. Sehr viele Menschen in Europa sprechen zwei
trade   oder drei Sprachen. Sie finden das interessant und auch wichtig für Tourismus, Handel°   10
und Politik.

In Westeuropa wohnen ungefähr 350 Millionen Menschen; das sind mehr Menschen
more than / in the / most / of   als° in den° USA und in Kanada zusammen. Die meisten° Länder sind ein Teil der° Eu-
the / abroad   ropäischen Union (EU). Viele Europäer wohnen und arbeiten im Ausland°. Ein Beispiel ist
says, tells   Familie Bruegel. Marcel Bruegel erzählt°: „Ich bin aus Brüssel, und meine Frau Nicole ist   15
Französin. Wir sind Bankiers. Wir wohnen schon zwei Jahre in Frankfurt [1]. Wir finden es
at home   hier sehr schön. Wir haben zwei Kinder, Maude und Dominique. Sie sprechen zu Hause°
in school   Französisch, aber in der Schule° sprechen sie Deutsch. Das finde ich toll. Das Sprachenler-
as never before   nen ist heute so wichtig wie nie zuvor°."

Zum Text

A.   Richtig oder falsch?

_____   1.   In Europa hören Sie viele Sprachen.
_____   2.   Alle Europäer sprechen Schwedisch.
_____   3.   Ungefähr 900 000 Europäer sprechen Deutsch.
_____   4.   Die Liechtensteiner sprechen Deutsch als Muttersprache.
_____   5.   In Westeuropa wohnen so viele Menschen wie in Kanada und in den USA zusammen.

_____   6.   Alle Länder in Europa sind ein Teil der EU.
_____   7.   In Deutschland wohnen keine Ausländer.
_____   8.   Herr und Frau Bruegel sind Bankiers.
_____   9.   Herr Bruegel ist Franzose.
_____ 10.   Familie Bruegel wohnt schon fünf Jahre in Frankfurt.
_____ 11.   Sie finden es da sehr schön.
_____ 12.   Die Eltern und die Kinder sprechen zu Hause Deutsch.

B.   Interview   _(Imagine yourself to be Mr. or Mrs. Bruegel. Respond to the reporter's questions.)_

1. Guten Tag! Woher kommen Sie?   **2.** Warum sind Sie hier in Frankfurt?   **3.** Wie heißt Ihre Frau / Ihr Mann?   **4.** Haben Sie Kinder?   **5.** Sind die Kinder auch hier?   **6.** Was sprechen Sie zu Hause, Deutsch oder Französisch?   **7.** Sprechen die Kinder noch andere Sprachen?   **8.** Wie finden Sie es hier in Frankfurt?

C.   Etwas Geographie   _(Look at the maps of Europe and of Germany on the inside cover of the book. Then, together with a classmate, work out the answers to the questions below.)_

1.   **Sehen Sie auf die Landkarte von Europa!**

   a.   Wie viele Nachbarn hat Deutschland? Wie heißen sie?
   b.   Wo liegt Dänemark? Belgien? Spanien? Frankreich? Italien? Schweden? . . .
   c.   Wie heißt die Hauptstadt von Deutschland? Dänemark? Belgien? Frankreich? Spanien? Italien? Finnland? Norwegen? Schweden? England? Polen?
   d.   Welche Sprache sprechen die Leute wo?

2.   **Sehen Sie auf die Landkarte von Deutschland!**

   a.   Welche Flüsse, Seen und Berge gibt es in Deutschland?
   b.   Wo liegt die Nordsee? die Ostsee? die Insel _(island)_ Rügen? die Insel Helgoland? Wo liegen die Nord- / Ostfriesischen Inseln?
   c.   Wo liegt . . .? _(Ask each other about the location of various towns in Germany.)_

Hören Sie zu!

Europäer in Deutschland   _(Many foreigners live in Germany. Listen to the four speakers, and then circle the letter of the response which correctly completes the statement.)_

ZUM ERKENNEN: zuerst _(first of all)_; komisch _(strange)_

Vittorio: 1.   Vittorio ist _____ .
                 a. 20   b. 29   c. 21
            2.   Seine Eltern sind aus _____ .
                 a. Portugal   b. Italien   c. Spanien
            3.   Seine Eltern sind schon _____ Jahre in Deutschland.
                 a. 25   b. 34   c. 24
            4.   Vittorio und seine Großeltern sprechen _____ .
                 a. Deutsch   b. Italienisch   c. Spanisch
            5.   Vittorio studiert _____ .
                 a. Physik   b. Musik   c. Politik

Manuel: 6.   Manuel ist aus _____ .
              a.   Spanien   b.   Portugal   c.   Italien
           7.   Er wohnt schon _____ Jahre in Deutschland.
              a.   34   b.   33   c.   23
           8.   Er ist _____ .
              a.   Wiener   b.   Frankfurter   c.   Hamburger

Maria: 9.   Maria wohnt in _____ .
              a.   Frankfurt   b.   Dresden   c.   Düsseldorf
          10.   Maria hat _____ Brüder.
              a.   vier   b.   zwei   c.   drei
          11.   Sie und ihre Familie sind _____ .
              a.   Griechen   b.   Italiener   c.   Deutsche

José: 12.   José wohnt schon _____ Jahre in Deutschland.
              a.   34   b.   24   c.   14
          13.   Er ist Professor in _____ .
              a.   Frankfurt   b.   Bonn   c.   Düsseldorf
          14.   Seine Frau ist aus _____ .
              a.   Berlin   b.   Erfurt   c.   Köln
          15.   Sie haben _____ Kinder.
              a.   zwei   b.   drei   c.   vier

Übrigens

1. Frankfurt am Main (pop. 670,000) is Germany's principal transportation hub with the largest train station in the country and an airport that handles every major international airline and more freight than any other in Europe. Nicknamed "Mainhattan" or "Bankfurt," it is the financial center of Germany: some 430 banks have headquarters or branch offices there, and the Frankfurt stock exchange is the third largest in Germany. Frankfurt will also play a major role as a financial center of the EU. In 1993 the city was selected as the location of the central European Bank (**Eurobank**) that will develop a single European currency by the end of the century. With more than 2,450 factories, it is a significant industrial city, and it has been hosting Germany's most important trade fairs since the Middle Ages. Because of its strategic geographical location, Frankfurt has been prominent since Roman times. Beginning in 1356 emperors of the Holy Roman Empire were crowned there. The poet Johann Wolfgang von Goethe (1749–1832), for whom the city's university is named, was born in Frankfurt, and the first German national assembly met there in the Paulskirche in 1848.

SPRECHSITUATIONEN

Making Small Talk

When you meet someone for the first time, it is useful to be able to make small talk. The weather is a typical point of departure.

Es ist wirklich schön heute, nicht wahr?   Heute ist es heiß!
Furchtbares Wetter heute, nicht wahr?   Jetzt regnet es schon wieder!

Asking for Personal Information

You have already learned many words that make it possible for you to ask questions, e.g., **was? wo? woher? wer? wann? wie? wieviel? wie viele?** Here is a list of expressions you can use to elicit personal information.

Ich bin aus . . . . Woher sind Sie / bist du?   Wo wohnt Ihre / deine Familie?
Ach, Sie sind / du bist (auch) aus . . .!   Wie finden Sie / findest du es hier / da?
Sind Sie / bist du auch Student(in) . . .?   Wie alt sind Sie / bist du?
Was studieren Sie / studierst du?   Haben Sie / hast du Geschwister?
Wo wohnen Sie / wohnst du?

The confirmation tag **nicht wahr?**—abbreviated to **nicht** in informal speech—is used to get someone to agree with the speaker.

Sie lernen auch Deutsch, nicht wahr?—Ja, natürlich.
Sie sind auch Amerikanerin, nicht?—Ja!

Kurzgespräche

1. As you wait for a class to start, you begin a conversation with the student next to you by commenting on the weather. First you introduce yourself. You then ask what the other student is studying and learn that he / she is also taking German. Respond appropriately.

2. You have been asked to prepare a brief background report on one of your classmates for a radio broadcast. Find a classmate you don't know well, and ask where the person comes from, about his or her family, what he or she is studying, etc. Prepare and present your report.

> The *Kurzgespräche* are intended to give you an opportunity to practice conversational German. The situations presented in the book will give you a start, but you are free to elaborate on or embellish the basic structure in any way you see fit. Make use of your sense of humor, too. Take turns with your partner(s) in playing the roles suggested until you are quite fluent.

Lebensmittel und Geschäfte

Einkaufszentrum in Hamburg

LERNZIELE

Vorschau
- Shopping and store hours

Gespräche and Wortschatz
- Food and shopping

Struktur
- Present tense of *sein* and *haben*
- Accusative case
- Sentence structure: verb complements, negation, and coordinating conjunctions

Einblicke
- Pedestrian zones and shopping

Sprechsituationen
- Making a purchase

Shopping and Store Hours

While the development of American-style supermarket chains and warehouse stores has changed the way Europeans shop, customs are still quite different from those in the United States and Canada. Many people continue to shop daily or at least several times a week, frequently going on foot rather than by car. In some neighborhoods shoppers still enjoy the convenience of small grocery stores (**Tante-Emma-Läden**), but the competition from supermarkets and mega-stores, even though they are located farther away, has caused many of these small shops to disappear. Specialty stores, however, such as butcher shops and bakeries, continue to thrive.

In supermarkets, shopping carts can be obtained from a rack by inserting a coin, which is refunded when the cart is returned. Customers usually bring their own shopping bags (**Einkaufstaschen**) with them, or they buy plastic bags (**Plastik-tüten**) at the check-out counter. They also bag their purchases themselves. Grocery store clerks sit rather than stand when checking out customers. People generally pay cash for their purchases rather than by check or credit card. There are no separate sales taxes; the value-added taxes common to most Central European countries are included in the price of all goods.

Recent changes in recycling laws require stores to take back all packaging materials; products that are completely recyclable are marked with a green dot.

Store hours are strictly regulated by comparatively rigid laws. In Germany, stores are generally open Monday through Friday from 9:00 A.M. to 6:30 P.M., and on Saturday normally from 9:00 A.M. to 2:00 P.M.—some stay open on Thursdays until 8:30 P.M. Exceptions are the first Saturday in the month, when shops may remain open until 4 P.M. (**langer Samstag**), and the four Saturdays before Christmas, when stores don't close until 6:00 P.M. Especially in smaller towns, neighborhood stores and shops close for lunch from 1:00 to 3:00 P.M. With the exception of some flower shops and stores in airports and railroad stations, all stores are closed on Sundays.

Efforts have repeatedly been made by business owners and consumers to change the laws regulating store hours, since working people find it difficult to fit shopping into their schedules. Unions representing store personnel have so far resisted change, however, maintaining that employees need regular work schedules and free time on weekends to spend with their families.

In Deutschland gibt es nicht mehr viele Tante-Emma-Läden.

Gespräche   Im Lebensmittelgeschäft

VERKÄUFER   Guten Tag! Was darf's sein?

OLIVER   Ich hätte gern etwas Obst. Haben Sie
denn keine Bananen?

VERKÄUFER   Doch, da drüben.

OLIVER   Was kosten sie?

VERKÄUFER   1,80 DM das Pfund.[1]

OLIVER   Und die Orangen?

VERKÄUFER   90 Pfennig das Stück.

OLIVER   Gut, zwei Pfund Bananen und sechs Orangen bitte!

VERKÄUFER   Sonst noch etwas?

OLIVER   Ja, zwei Kilo[1] Äpfel bitte!

VERKÄUFER   16,20 DM, bitte! Danke! Auf Wiedersehen!

In der Bäckerei

VERKÄUFER   Guten Morgen! Was darf's sein?

SIMONE   Guten Morgen! Ein Schwarzbrot[2] und sechs Brötchen, bitte!

VERKÄUFER   Sonst noch etwas?

SIMONE   Ja, ich brauche etwas Kuchen. Ist der Apfelstrudel frisch?

VERKÄUFER   Natürlich, ganz frisch.

SIMONE   Gut, dann nehme ich vier Stück.

VERKÄUFER   Ist das alles?

SIMONE   Ich möchte auch ein paar Plätzchen. Was für Plätzchen haben Sie heute?

VERKÄUFER   Zitronenplätzchen, Schokoladenplätzchen, Butterplätzchen . . .

SIMONE   Hm . . . Ich nehme 250 Gramm[1] Schokoladenplätzchen.

VERKÄUFER   Noch etwas?

SIMONE   Nein, danke. Das ist alles.

VERKÄUFER   Das macht dann 18,90 DM, bitte.

Fragen

1. Was braucht Oliver?   2. Was kosten die Bananen? die Orangen?   3. Wie viele Bananen und wie viele Orangen kauft er?   4. Was kauft er noch?   5. Was kostet alles zusammen?   6. Wie viele Brötchen möchte Simone?   7. Was ist frisch?   8. Wieviel Apfelstrudel kauft sie?   9. Was für Plätzchen kauft sie?   10. Kauft sie sonst noch etwas?

Übrigens

1.   In Europe the metric system is used to measure distances and weights. Exception: the older measurement **Pfund** is still used with some foods. A shopper may ask for various amounts: **100 Gramm Leberwurst, ein Pfund Kaffee,** or **ein Kilo (2 Pfund) Äpfel.**

German				
	1 g	=	Gramm	
	125 g	=	1 Viertelpfund	
	250 g	=	1 halbes Pfund	
	500 g	=	1 Pfund	
	1000 g	=	1 Kilo(gramm)	

U.S.: 1 oz = 28.3 g

1 lb = 454 g

2.   When Germans think of **Brot,** they probably think first of a firm, heavy loaf of rye bread (**Schwarzbrot**) and not of the soft white bread so common in America. White loaves and rolls are prized for their crisp crust. There are over two hundred varieties of bread available in Central Europe, including bread made from a mixture of wheat and rye (**Graubrot**) or of cracked rye-and-wheat grains (**Vollkornbrot**), and bread with linseed (**Leinsamenbrot**) or sunflower seeds (**Sonnenblumenbrot**). For Germans, bread is the most important food—on the average they eat four slices of bread and one roll a day.

Die Deutschen essen gern Brot.

Die Lebensmittel *(pl.) (groceries)*

der	Apfel, ¨	*apple*	*die*	Banane, -n	*banana*
	Fisch, -e	*fish*		Bohne, -n	*bean*
	Kaffee	*coffee*		Butter	*butter*
	Käse	*cheese*		Cola	*coke*
	Kuchen, -	*cake*		Erbse, -n	*pea*
	Saft, ¨e	*juice*		Erdbeere, -n	*strawberry*
	Salat, -e	*lettuce, salad*		Gurke, -n	*cucumber*
	Tee	*tea*		Karotte, -n	*carrot*
	Wein, -e	*wine*		Limonade, -n	*soft drink, lemonade*
das	Bier, -e	*beer*			
	Brot, -e	*bread*		Marmelade, -n	*jam*
	Brötchen, -	*roll*		Milch	*milk*
	Ei, -er	*egg*		Orange, -n	*orange*
	Fleisch	*meat*		Tomate, -n	*tomato*
	Gemüse, -	*vegetable(s)*		Wurst, ¨e	*sausage*
	Obst	*fruit*		Zitrone, -n	*lemon*
	Plätzchen,-	*cookie*			
	Wasser	*water*			

Weiteres

der	Markt, ⸚e	*(farmers') market*
	Supermarkt, ⸚e	*supermarket*
das	(Lebensmittel)geschäft, -e	*(grocery) store*
	Kaufhaus, ⸚er	*department store*
	Pfund; ein Pfund[1]	*pound; one pound (of)*
	Stück, -e; ein Stück[1]	*piece; one piece (of)*
die	Bäckerei, -en	*bakery*
	Buchhandlung, -en	*bookstore*

alles	*everything, all*
Das ist alles.	*That's all. That's it.*
dann	*then*
doch	*yes, sure, certainly, of course*
es gibt[2]	*there is, there are*
etwas . . .	*a little, some . . . (used with sg. collective nouns)*
frisch	*fresh*
gern	*gladly*
Ich esse (trinke) gern . . .	*I like to eat (drink) . . .*
Ich hätte gern . . .[3]	*I would like (to have) . . .*
Ich möchte . . .[3]	*I would like (to have) . . .*
glauben	*to believe, think*
kaufen / verkaufen	*to buy / to sell*
machen	*to make, do*
suchen	*to look for*
natürlich	*of course*
was für (ein) . . . ?[4]	*what kind of (a) . . . ?*
zusammen	*together*

[1] One says **ein Pfund Fleisch, zwei Pfund Fleisch; ein Stück Kuchen, zwei Stück Kuchen.** Remember also **eine Mark, zwei Mark.**

[2] See Struktur II, 1 d.

[3] **möcht-** and **hätt-** are subjunctive verb forms that will be explained later: ich möchte, du möchtest, er möchte, wir möchten, ihr möchtet, sie möchten; ich hätte, du hättest, er hätte, wir hätten, ihr hättet, sie hätten.

[4] Treat this phrase as you would treat **ein** by itself: Das ist **ein** Kuchen. Was für **ein** Kuchen? Das ist **eine** Wurst. Was für **eine** Wurst? There's no **ein** in the plural: Das sind Plätzchen. Was für Plätzchen? Don't use **für** in answers to a **was für** question: Was für Obst essen Sie gern? Ich esse gern Bananen.

ZUM ERKENNEN: Was darf's sein? *(May I help you?)*; da drüben *(over there)*; Sonst noch etwas? *(Anything else?)*; das Kilo / zwei Kilo; der Apfelstrudel; das Gramm / 250 Gramm

A. Mustersätze

1. Bananen: **Ich esse gern** Bananen.
   Äpfel, Erdbeeren, Orangen, Gurken, Plätzchen
2. Fisch: **Die Kinder essen nicht gern** Fisch.
   Salat, Tomaten, Karotten, Gemüse, Eier
3. Cola: **Wir trinken gern** Cola.
   Limonade, Kaffee, Tee, Bier, Wein
4. Obst: **Ich hätte gern etwas** Obst.
   Brot, Fleisch, Marmelade, Käse, Wurst
5. Bananen: **Haben Sie keine** Bananen?
   Erdbeeren, Bohnen, Erbsen, Zitronen, Brötchen

B. Was paßt nicht?   *(Which item does not belong in each list?)*

1. die Butter, der Käse, die Wurst, die Bohne
2. das Brötchen, die Zitrone, das Plätzchen, der Kuchen
3. die Tomate, die Erdbeere, die Gurke, der Salat
4. das Gemüse, der Apfel, die Orange, die Banane
5. das Obst, das Gemüse, der Salat, der Tee
6. der Wein, das Bier, die Zitrone, die Milch
7. das Geschäft, die Lebensmittel, die Bäckerei, das Kaufhaus

C. Was bedeuten die Wörter, und was sind die Artikel?

Bohnensalat, Buttermilch, Delikatessengeschäft, Erdbeermarmelade, Fischbrötchen, Kaffeemilch, Milchkaffee, Obstsalat, Orangenlimonade, Schreibwarengeschäft, Teewasser, Wurstbrot, Zitronensaft

D. Was paßt?

_____ 1. Ich glaube, der Fisch ist nicht frisch.
_____ 2. Möchten Sie etwas Obst?
_____ 3. Die Bäckerei verkauft Wurst, nicht wahr?
_____ 4. Wir kaufen auch Kuchen.
_____ 5. Ich trinke morgens gern Cola.

a. Wirklich?
b. Wie bitte?
c. Ich nicht.
d. Ja, gern.
e. Ja, bitte.
f. Natürlich nicht.
g. Prima!
h. Wir auch.
i. Richtig.
j. Nein, danke.
k. Doch.
l. Nein, das ist alles.

E. Und Sie?   *(Interview a classmate to find out what foods he / she likes and what his / her eating habits are.)*

1. Was für Obst essen Sie (nicht) gern?   2. Was für Gemüse essen Sie (nicht) gern?
3. Was für Kuchen, Plätzchen, Salat essen Sie gern?   4. Was trinken Sie (nicht) gern?   5. Was essen Sie morgens / mittags / abends?

F.   Aussprache: e, o   *(See also section II. 2, 5, 14–16, 18, and 21 in the pronunciation section of the Workbook.)*

1. [e:]   g**eh**en, K**ä**se, M**äd**chen, Apoth**eke**, Am**e**rika, n**eh**men, T**ee**, S**ee**
2. [e]   **es**, **e**twas, spr**e**chen, M**e**nsch, Gesch**ä**ft, **e**ssen, H**e**md
3. [o:]   **oh**ne, **o**der, **O**bst, w**oh**nen, Br**o**t, B**oh**ne, M**o**ntag, s**o**
4. [o]   **O**sten, k**o**mmen, N**o**rden, Kar**o**tte, d**o**ch, S**o**nne, t**o**ll
5. Wortpaare

    a. *gate* / geht   c. zähle / Zelle   e. Ofen / offen
    b. den / denn   d. *shown* / schon   f. Bonn / Bann

Hören Sie zu!

Was essen und trinken sie gern, was nicht?   *(Listen to three students tell what they like and don't like to eat and drink. Then note which foods and beverages each student mentions; write H for Hanjo, M for Martina, and D for Dirk. Not all the available slots will be filled.)*

ZUM ERKENNEN: also *(well);* und so weiter *(etc.);* manchmal *(sometimes);* Kartoffeln *(potatoes);* der Kakao *(hot chocolate)*

<table>
<tr><th colspan="2" align="center">Essen</th><th colspan="2" align="center">Trinken</th></tr>
<tr><td>*Gern*</td><td>*Nicht gern*</td><td>*Gern*</td><td>*Nicht gern*</td></tr>
<tr><td>—— Äpfel</td><td>—— Gemüse</td><td>—— Tee</td><td>—— Kaffee</td></tr>
<tr><td>—— Bananen</td><td>—— Gurken</td><td>—— Kaffee</td><td>—— Bier</td></tr>
<tr><td>—— Kartoffeln</td><td>—— Karotten</td><td>—— Milch</td><td>—— Milch</td></tr>
<tr><td>—— Kuchen</td><td>—— Erbsen</td><td>—— Saft</td><td>—— Cola</td></tr>
<tr><td>—— Erdbeeren</td><td>—— Fisch</td><td>—— Bier</td><td>—— Wasser</td></tr>
<tr><td>—— Gemüse</td><td>—— Bananen</td><td>—— Cola</td><td>—— Tee</td></tr>
<tr><td>—— Fisch</td><td>—— Pizza</td><td>—— Mineralwasser</td><td>—— Kakao</td></tr>
<tr><td>—— Fleisch</td><td>—— Käsebrot</td><td>—— Limonade</td><td>—— Eiswasser</td></tr>
</table>

Eine Metzgerei (*butcher shop*). Hier gibt es Fleisch und Wurst.

STRUKTUR

I. The Present Tense of *sein* (to be) and *haben* (to have)

	sein		haben	
1st person	ich bin	wir sind	ich habe	wir haben
2nd person	du bist	ihr seid	du hast	ihr habt
3rd person	er ist	sie sind	er hat	sie haben

A.   Ersetzen Sie das Subjekt!

Übungen

BEISPIEL: Haben Sie Zeit? (du)
            Hast du Zeit?

1.   Ich bin schon fertig. (er, wir, sie / *sg.*)
2.   Sind Sie müde? (du, ihr, sie / *pl.*)
3.   Sie hat die Landkarte. (ich, er, wir)
4.   Haben Sie Papier? (sie / *sg.,* ihr, du)
5.   Wir sind Amerikaner. (er, sie / *pl.,* ich)
6.   Er hat eine Frage. (ich, wir, Sie)
7.   Seid ihr aus Wien? (Sie, du, sie / *sg.*)
8.   Er hat Orangensaft. (sie / *pl.,* ich, ihr)
9.   Sie suchen eine Bäckerei. (wir, ich, ihr)
10. Ich glaube das nicht. (du, Sie, er)

II. The Accusative Case

The accusative case has two major functions: it is the case of the direct object, and it follows certain prepositions.

1.   In the English sentence *The boy asks the father,* the DIRECT OBJECT of the sentence is *the father.* He is being asked; he is the target of the verb's action. One determines what the direct object is by asking *who* or *what* is directly affected by the verb's action. In other words, the person you see, hear, or ask, or the thing you have, buy, or eat is the direct object.

Der Junge fragt **den Vater.**   *The boy asks the father.*
Ich kaufe **den Kuchen.**   *I buy the cake.*

a.   The accusative forms of the INTERROGATIVE PRONOUN are **wen** *(whom)* and **was** *(what).* You now know two cases for this pronoun.

	persons	things and ideas
nom.	wer	was
acc.	**wen**	**was**

Wen fragt der Junge? → **Den Vater.**
Whom does the boy ask? → *The father.*

Was kaufe ich? → **Den Kuchen.**
What am I buying? → *The cake.*

b.   Of the ARTICLES, only those for masculine nouns have special forms for the accusative. In the other genders, the nominative and accusative are identical in form.

	singular			plural
	masc.	**neut.**	**fem.**	
nom.	der	das	die	die
	ein	ein	eine	—
	kein	kein	keine	keine
acc.	**den**	**das**	**die**	**die**
	einen	**ein**	**eine**	**—**
	keinen	**kein**	**keine**	**keine**

PETER   Der Käse, das Obst, die Wurst und die Brötchen sind frisch.
PETRA   Dann kaufe ich den Käse, das Obst, die Wurst und die Brötchen.
PETER   Aber wir brauchen keinen Käse, kein Obst, keine Wurst und keine Brötchen.

The POSSESSIVE ADJECTIVES **mein, dein,** and **Ihr** follow the pattern of **ein** and **kein:**

Brauchen Sie mein**en** Bleistift?
Nein danke, ich brauche Ihr**en** Bleistift nicht.

c.   German has a few masculine nouns that have an **-n** or **-en** ending in all cases (singular and plural) except in the nominative singular. They are called N-NOUNS. Note how they are listed in vocabularies and dictionaries: the first ending refers to the singular for cases other than the nominative, the second one to the plural. You are already familiar with all of the n-nouns below.

der   Franzose, **-n,** -n   *Frenchman*
     Herr, **-n,** -en   *gentleman*
     Junge, **-n,** -n   *boy*
     Mensch, **-en,** -en   *human being, person*
     Nachbar, **-n,** -n   *neighbor*
     Student, **-en,** -en   *student*

	singular	plural
nom.	der Student	die Studenten
acc.	**den Studenten**	die Studenten

Der Herr heißt Müller. Fragen Sie Herr**n** Müller!
Da kommt ein Student. Fragen Sie den Student**en**!

d. Verbs that can take accusative objects are called TRANSITIVE. (Some verbs are INTRANSITIVE, i.e., they cannot take a direct object: **gehen** *to go.*) Here are some familiar transitive verbs.

brauchen	*to need*	möcht-	*would like*
es gibt	*there is, there are*	nehmen	*to take*
essen	*to eat*	öffnen	*to open*
finden	*to find*	sagen	*to say*
fragen	*to ask*	schreiben	*to write*
haben	*to have*	sprechen	*to speak, talk*
hören	*to hear*	suchen	*to look for*
kaufen	*to buy*	trinken	*to drink*
lernen	*to learn*	verkaufen	*to sell*
lesen	*to read*	verstehen	*to understand*
machen	*to make, do*		

Sie kauft den Rock und die Bluse.
Schreiben Sie den Satz!
Ich esse einen Apfel und eine Banane.
Wir haben einen Supermarkt und ein Kaufhaus.
Das Geschäft verkauft keinen Fisch und kein Fleisch.

• The idiom **es gibt** is always followed by the accusative case in the singular or in the plural.

Es gibt hier einen Markt.	*There's a market here.*
Es gibt auch Lebensmittelgeschäfte.	*There are also grocery stores.*

The pronoun **es** is the subject of the sentence. What "there is," is in the accusative. **Es gibt** implies a general, unspecified existence, unlike **hier ist** or **da ist,** which points to a specific item.

Gibt es hier einen Markt?	*Is there a market here (in town)?*
Ja, **es gibt** einen Markt.	*Yes, there's a market.*

Wo ist ein Markt?	*Where is a market?*
Da ist ein Markt.	*There's a market. (There it is.)*

2. ACCUSATIVE PREPOSITIONS are always followed by the accusative case. Here are those used most frequently:

durch	through	Britta kommt **durch die Tür.**
für	for	Das Obst ist **für den Kuchen.**
gegen	against	Was hast du **gegen den Kaffee?**
ohne	without	Wir essen das Brötchen **ohne den Käse.**
um	around	Die Kinder laufen **um den Tisch.**
	at	Wir kommen **um 12 Uhr.**

• Some prepositions may be contracted with the definite article. These forms are especially common in everyday speech.

durch	+	das	=	**durchs**
für	+	das	=	**fürs**
um	+	das	=	**ums**

Note: A sentence can contain two accusatives, one the direct object and the other the object of a preposition.

Sie kauft den Fisch für den Fischsalat.

Übungen

B.   Wiederholen Sie die Sätze noch einmal mit *ein* und *kein*!

BEISPIEL: Er kauft den Bleistift, das Buch und die Landkarte.
              Er kauft einen Bleistift, ein Buch und eine Landkarte.
              Er kauft keinen Bleistift, kein Buch und keine Landkarte.

1. Sie möchte den Rock, das Kleid und die Bluse.
2. Du brauchst das Hemd, die Hose und den Pullover.
3. Ich esse das Brötchen, die Orange und den Apfel.
4. Wir fragen den Herrn, die Frau und das Mädchen.
5. Öffnen Sie bitte die Tür und das Fenster!
6. Kauft ihr den Kuchen, das Brot und die Brezel *(pretzel)*?

C.   Einkaufen   *(Make small talk while you are shopping with some friends. Substitute the nouns in parentheses.)*

BEISPIEL: Wir kaufen den Saft. (Salat)
              Wir kaufen den Salat.

1. Möchtest du das Fleisch? (Gemüse, Obst, Schwarzbrot)
2. Die Wurst essen wir nicht. (Marmelade, Tomate, Gurke)
3. Meine Schwester trinkt keinen Saft. (Limonade, Cola, Wasser)
4. Hast du den Tee? (Saft, Milch, Käse)
5. Gibt es hier eine Buchhandlung? (Markt, Delikatessengeschäft, Kaufhäuser)
6. Fragen Sie den Herrn! (Junge, Mensch, Student, Studenten / *pl.*)
7. Den Verkäufer verstehe ich nicht! (Verkäuferin, Nachbar, Fräulein)
8. Ich hätte gern eine Hose. (Mantel, Hemd, Jeansjacke)
9. Haben Sie kein Obst? (Saft, Eier, Limonade)
10. Machst du einen Salat? (Obstkuchen, Butterbrot)

D.   **Umzug**   *(Moving. You are giving instructions to the movers who are bringing your belongings into your new apartment. Use the cues.)*

BEISPIEL: durch / Zimmer
                 Durch das Zimmer bitte!

1. gegen / Wand
2. um / Tisch
3. ohne / Bücher

4. durch / Tür
5. ohne / Tisch
6. für / Kinderzimmer *(pl.)*

7. gegen / Fenster *(sg.)*
8. um / Ecke *(f., corner)*

E.   **Sagen Sie es noch einmal!**   *(Replace the noun following the preposition with another noun.)*

BEISPIEL: Ich suche etwas für meinen Vater. (Mutter, Kind)
                 Ich suche etwas für meine Mutter.
                 Ich suche etwas für mein Kind.

1. Wir gehen durch die Geschäfte. (Supermarkt, Kaufhaus, Bäckerei)
2. Er kommt ohne das Bier. (Wein, Cola, Kaffee, Käsebrot, Salat)
3. Was haben Sie gegen den Herrn? (Frau, Mädchen, Junge, Nachbarin)
4. Wiederholen Sie das für Ihren Großvater! (Bruder, Schwester, Nachbar, Eltern)

F.   **Kombinieren Sie!**   *(You are a salesperson in a clothing store. Ask your customers what kind of items they need. Also indicate how you would address your customers if they were: (a) a friend, (b) a stranger, (c) two of your relatives.)*

BEISPIEL: **Was für einen Pullover möchten Sie?**

1	2	3	4
was für (ein)	Rock	brauchen	du
	Hemd	möchten	ihr
	Jacke		Sie
	Schuhe		
	usw.		

Aus der Käsetheke:
Galbani Mozzarella
italienischer Weichkäse,
45 % Fett i. Tr.
100 g
1.99

Aus der Käsetheke:
Galbani Gorgonzola
50 % Fett i. Tr., 100 g
1.99

G. Was kaufen Sie? *(Answer each question with four to six items, drawing on all the vocabulary you have had so far. Use articles whenever necessary.)*

BEISPIEL: Sie sind im Supermarkt. Was kaufen Sie?
Ich kaufe einen Kuchen, eine Cola, ein Pfund Butter, ein Stück Käse, etwas Obst . . .

1. Sie sind in der Bäckerei. Was kaufen Sie?
2. Sie sind im Lebensmittelgeschäft. Was kaufen Sie?
3. Sie sind im Kaufhaus. Was kaufen Sie?
4. Sie sind in der Buchhandlung. Was kaufen Sie?

H. Wie bitte? *(Your grandfather, who is hard of hearing and forgets quickly, always asks you to repeat whatever you say.)*

BEISPIEL: Rudi hat heute eine Prüfung.
Wer hat eine Prüfung?
Was hat Rudi?

1. Vater hört den Nachbarn.
2. Matthias fragt Tante Martha.
3. Die Mutter kauft Obst.
4. Die Kinder möchten einen Apfel.
5. Helga und Britta verstehen die Engländer nicht.
6. Wir lernen Deutsch.
7. Ich suche eine Landkarte.

I. Im Kaufhaus. Sagen Sie es auf deutsch!

S1   Good morning! May I help you?
S2   Hi! I need a sweater for my son.
S1   The sweater here is from England. Would you like a sweater in blue (**in Blau**)?
S2   No. Don't you have any sweater in red?
S1   Of course we do—here.
S2   Fine. I think the color is very beautiful. (**finden**)
S1   Do you also need a shirt or (a pair of) slacks *(sg.)*?
S2   No, he doesn't need any shirt or (any) slacks. (He needs no shirt and no slacks.)

III. Sentence Structure

1. Objects and Verbs as Verb Complements (V2)

As you know from Chapter 1, predicate nouns and predicate adjectives are VERB COMPLEMENTS (V2). Sometimes objects or another verb also become part of the verb phrase, i.e., verb complements, and in that combination they complete the meaning of the main verb (V1).

Sie **sprechen Deutsch.**
Sie **sprechen** gut **Deutsch.**
Sie **sprechen** wirklich gut **Deutsch.**
      V1   V2

Wir **spielen Tennis.**
Wir **spielen** gern **Tennis.**
Wir **spielen** morgens gern **Tennis.**
      V1   V2

Er **geht essen.**
Er **geht** hier **essen.**
Er **geht** mittags hier **essen.**
      V1   V2

2. Negation

    a. **kein**

        The negative article **kein** *(no, not a, not any)* negates nouns that in an affirmative sentence would be preceded by the indefinite article **ein** or by no article at all.

        preceded by **ein:**   Ist das **ein** Kuli?
        Nein, das ist **kein** Kuli.
        No, that's no (not a) pen.

        Brauchen sie **eine** Landkarte?
        Nein, ich brauche **keine** Landkarte.
        No, I don't need a map.

        unpreceded: Haben Sie Zeit?
        Nein, ich habe **keine** Zeit.
        No, I don't have (any) time.

        Sind Sie Kanadier?
        Nein, ich bin **kein** Kanadier.
        No, I'm not a Canadian.

        Haben Sie Kinder?
        Nein, ich habe **keine** Kinder.
        No, I do not have (don't have any) children.

    b. **nicht**

        nicht *(not)* usually negates an entire sentence (actually the predicate). Its position is determined as follows:

        *   **nicht** <u>always comes after</u> the subject and verb:

            Sie schreiben nicht.

        *   **nicht** <u>usually comes after</u> all noun and pronoun objects and expressions of definite time. It stands at the end of many sentences.

noun object:	Ich brauche die Landkarte **nicht.**
pronoun object:	Ich brauche sie **nicht.**
definite time:	Ich brauche sie heute **nicht.**

        *   **nicht** <u>usually comes before</u> adverbs of manner *(how?)*, place *(where?)*, or general time, before prepositional phrases, and before verb complements (V2).

adverb of manner:	Ich kaufe das **nicht** gern.
adverb of place:	Ich kaufe das **nicht** hier.
general time:	Ich kaufe das **nicht** oft *(often).*
prepositional phrase:	Ich kaufe das **nicht** im Geschäft.
verb complements:	Ich gehe heute **nicht** essen.
	Das Buch ist **nicht** neu.
	Das ist **nicht** mein Buch.
	Ich heiße **nicht** Gerda.

        *   The following chart shows the pattern for the placement of **nicht:**

            S   V1   0   time expression ↑ other adverbs or adverbial phrases   V2.
                                    nicht

c. **kein** vs. **nicht**

COMPARE: Ich kaufe ein Brot.   Ich kaufe Brot.
Ich kaufe **kein** Brot.   Ich kaufe **kein** Brot.

Ich kaufe das Brot.
Ich kaufe das Brot **nicht.**

d. **ja, nein, doch**

COMPARE: Hast du das Buch?   **Ja!**   *Yes.*
Nein!   *No.*
Hast du das Buch **nicht?**   **Doch!**   *Of course I do.*

- **doch** is an affirmative response to a negative question.

Wohnt Erika Schwarz **nicht** in Salzburg?—**Doch!**
Haben Sie **keine** Swatch-Uhren?—**Doch,** hier sind sie.

3. Joining Sentences

Two independent clauses can be joined into one sentence by means of COORDINATING
CONJUNCTIONS. Each of the two clauses keeps the original word order.

aber	*but*	Wir essen Fisch, aber sie essen Fleisch.
denn	*because, for*	Sie kauft Obst, denn es ist frisch.
oder	*or*	Nehmen Sie Brot, oder möchten Sie Brötchen?
und	*and*	Ich kaufe Wurst, und er kauft Käse.

Übungen

J. Die Nachbarin   *(Every time you visit your elderly neighbor, she insists that you eat
or drink something. Use the negative **kein**.)*

BEISPIEL: Möchten Sie eine Banane?
Möchten Sie keine Banane?

1. Nehmen Sie Erdbeeren?   **2.** Essen Sie Gurkensalat?   **3.** Trinken Sie Limonade?   **4.** Essen Sie Käsekuchen?   **5.** Möchten Sie ein Stück Brot?   **6.** Möchten
Sie eine Cola?   **7.** Nehmen Sie ein Wurstbrötchen?   **8.** Essen Sie Tomaten?
9. Trinken Sie ein Glas Milch?   **10.** Möchten Sie einen Apfel?

K. Das stimmt nicht!   *(That's not true. Correct some misconceptions about you, using
nicht. You may use the cues in brackets or your own.)*

BEISPIEL: Ist Ihr Name [Fiedler]?
Nein, mein Name ist nicht [Fiedler]. Mein Name ist [Fiede].

1. Heißen Sie [Watzlik]?   **2.** Kommen Sie aus [Polen]?   **3.** Sind Ihre Großeltern
aus [Polen]?   **4.** Wohnt Ihre Familie in [Mecklenburg]?   **5.** Sprechen Ihr Onkel
und Ihre Tante [Mecklenburgisch]?   **6.** Wohnt Ihr Bruder in [Thüringen]?
7. Sehen Sie Ihre [Geschwister] oft?   **8.** Studieren Sie [Musik]?   **9.** Trinken Sie
gern [Tomatensaft]?   **10.** Essen Sie gern [Fleischsalat]?

L.   **Nein!**   *(To get your attention, your little brother negates everything you say. Use either **nicht** or **kein**.)*

1. Heute ist es heiß.   **2.** Die Sonne scheint.   **3.** Da drüben *(over there)* ist ein Geschäft.   **4.** Das Geschäft verkauft Limonade und Eistee.   **5.** Die Cola ist teuer.   **6.** Ich möchte ein Käsebrötchen.   **7.** Ich esse das Käsebrötchen!   **8.** Ich bin Vegetarier *(vegetarian)*.   **9.** Ich esse gern Käse.   **10.** Käse ist gesund *(healthy)*.   **11.** Wir gehen jetzt in eine Buchhandlung.   **12.** Vater braucht eine Landkarte und einen Stadtplan *(city map)*.   **13.** Er braucht die Landkarte!   **14.** Ich finde das Amerikabuch schön.   **15.** Wir haben Zeit.   **16.** Ich lese gern Bücher.   **17.** Das ist ein Spanischbuch.   **18.** Heinz lernt Spanisch.   **19.** Er studiert in Madrid.   **20.** Ich brauche einen Kalender *(calendar)*.   **21.** Ich finde den Städtekalender toll.   **22.** Ich möchte den Kalender!   **23.** Wir brauchen Bleistifte und Kulis.

M.   **Ja, nein oder doch!**   *(You are the instructor of your German class. Ask your students the following questions to check how much they know about German-speaking countries.)*

BEISPIEL: Ist der Rhein im Westen von Deutschland?   **Ja!**
Ist der Rhein im Osten von Deutschland?   **Nein!**
Ist der Rhein nicht im Westen von Deutschland?   **Doch!**

1.   Sprechen die Österreicher nicht Deutsch?
2.   Hat Deutschland viele Nachbarn?
3.   Ist Bonn die Hauptstadt von Deutschland?
4.   Ist Wien nicht die Hauptstadt von Österreich?
5.   Hamburg liegt in Norddeutschland, nicht wahr?
6.   Gibt es in Deutschland keine Supermärkte?
7.   Sind 600 Gramm ein Pfund?
8.   Ein Viertelpfund ist nicht 125 Gramm?
9.   Ein Kilogramm ist ein halbes Pfund, nicht wahr?

N.   **Eine Postkarte**   *(After your first week in Bremen, write a brief postcard home. Join the two sentences with the conjunctions indicated.)*

Liebe *(dear)* Mutter, lieber Vater!
1.   Ich schreibe nicht viel. Ich habe keine Zeit. *(because)*
2.   Ich finde es hier schön. Ich lerne auch sehr viel. *(and)*
3.   Meine Zimmerkolleginnen / Zimmerkollegen *(roommates)* kommen aus Kanada. Sie sind 21 Jahre alt. *(and)*
4.   Sie sprechen Französisch. Sie verstehen nicht viel Deutsch. *(but)*
5.   Sonntag spielen wir zusammen Minigolf. Wir gehen in die Stadt. *(or)*

O.   **Im Lebensmittelgeschäft.** Auf deutsch, bitte!

Zusammen-fassung

1. What would you like?   **2.** What kind of vegetables do you have today?   **3.** I think I'll take two pounds of beans.   **4.** The eggs are fresh, aren't they?—Of course.   **5.** We don't need (any) eggs.   **6.** But we need some fish and lettuce.   **7.** I'm not eating any fish.   **8.** Do you have any carrot juice (**Karottensaft**)?   **9.** Don't you like (to drink) carrot juice?—No!   **10.** Do you have any coke? I like to drink coke.   **11.** She's buying a coke and some orange juice.   **12.** Is that all?—No, I'd also like two pieces of strawberry cake.

EINBLICKE

Fußgängerzone in
Heidelberg.

Most European cities have developed pedestrian areas (**Fußgängerzonen**), usually in the center of town. Since no motor vehicles or streetcars are allowed,
these areas are free of traffic noise and exhaust fumes. In warm weather people
sit on benches or have refreshments in sidewalk cafés. Although merchants initially feared a decrease in business from closing streets to traffic, there has been
an increase instead. Establishing these areas provided an incentive for property
owners to refurbish older buildings, which typically combine apartments in the
upper stories and retail businesses on the first and second floors. These shopping areas attract not only people who live downtown, but also those living in
the suburbs and surrounding areas.

der	Durst	*thirst*
	Hunger	*hunger*
das	Glas, ⸚er; ein Glas[1]	*glass; a glass (of)*
	Würstchen, -[2]	*wiener, hot dog*
die	Apotheke, -n[3]	*pharmacy*
	Blume, -n	*flower*
	Drogerie, -n[3]	*drugstore*
	Tasse, -n; eine Tasse[1]	*cup; a cup (of)*

Ach du liebes bißchen!	*Good grief! My goodness! Oh dear!*
Bitte, bitte!	*You're welcome.*
ein paar[4]	*a few, some (used with plural nouns)*
montags (dienstags usw.)	*on Mondays (Tuesdays, etc.)*
offen / zu	*open / closed*
oft	*often*
warum?	*why?*
Ich gehe . . . einkaufen.	*I go shopping . . .*
Ich habe Hunger / Durst.	*I'm hungry / thirsty.*

---

[1] Möchten Sie **ein Glas Milch** *(a glass of milk)* oder **eine Tasse Kaffee** *(a cup of coffee)*?

[2] All nouns ending in **-chen** are neuter. The suffix makes diminutives of nouns, i.e., it makes them smaller. They often have an umlaut, but there is no special plural ending: der Bruder, das Brüder**chen**; die Schwester, das Schwester**chen**.

[3] A **Drogerie** sells over-the-counter drugs, cosmetics, and toiletries. An **Apotheke** sells prescription and non-prescription drugs.

[4] **Ein paar** Tomaten, **ein paar** Äpfel *(pl.)* BUT **etwas** Kaffee, **etwas** Butter *(sg. collective noun)*

WAS IST DAS?   das Auto, Café, Sauerkraut, Spezialgeschäft; die Boutique, Medizin; romantisch

Sonntags sind die Geschäfte zu

Carolyn ist Studentin. Sie studiert ein Jahr in Regensburg.[1] In der Studentenheimküche°   *dorm kitchen*
findet sie zwei Regensburger Studenten, Ursula und Peter.

	CAROLYN	Guten Morgen! Mein Name ist Carolyn.	
5	URSULA	Freut mich. Das ist Peter, und ich heiße Ursula.	
	PETER	Guten Morgen, Carolyn! Woher kommst du?	
	CAROLYN	Ich komme aus Colorado.	
	PETER	Du, wir essen gerade° Frühstück°. Möchtest du eine Tasse Kaffee?	*just now / breakfast*
	CAROLYN	Ja, gern. Ich habe wirklich Hunger.	
10	URSULA	Hier hast du ein Stück Brot, etwas Butter und Marmelade.	
	CAROLYN	Danke!	
	PETER	Etwas Milch für den Kaffee?	
	CAROLYN	Ja, bitte.	
	PETER	Auch ein Ei?	
15	CAROLYN	Nein, danke.—Mm, das Brot ist gut!—Wo gibt es hier Geschäfte?	
	URSULA	Um die Ecke° gibt es ein Lebensmittelgeschäft, eine Metzgerei°[2] und auch eine Drogerie.	*corner / butcher shop*
	CAROLYN	Prima! Ich brauche auch etwas Medizin.	
	URSULA	Da findest du auch eine Apotheke.	
20	CAROLYN	Ist das Lebensmittelgeschäft sehr teuer?	

	PETER	Billig ist es nicht. Wir gehen oft in die Stadt, denn da findest du alles. Da gibt es Spezialgeschäfte, Supermärkte und auch Kaufhäuser.	
cathedral	URSULA	Regensburg ist wirklich sehr schön. Es ist alt und romantisch, und um den Dom° gibt es viele Boutiquen.	
pedestrian area	PETER	Ich finde die Fußgängerzone° prima, denn da gibt es keine Autos, nur Fußgänger. Da beobachte° ich gern die Leute.	25
watch			
mean	URSULA	Du meinst° die Mädchen.	
So what!	PETER	Na und°!	
	URSULA	Wir gehen auch oft in ein Café³ und essen ein Stück Kuchen.	
to the	PETER	Oder wir gehen an die Donau zur° „Wurstküche", essen ein paar Würstchen und trinken ein Glas Bier.	30
farmers	URSULA	Samstags ist Markt. Da verkaufen die Bauern° Obst, Gemüse, Eier und Blumen⁴. Alles ist sehr frisch.	
	CAROLYN	Und wann sind die Geschäfte offen?	
	URSULA	Die Kaufhäuser sind von morgens um neun bis abends um halb sieben offen, donnerstags bis abends um halb neun. Aber hier draußen° ist mittags von halb eins bis zwei alles zu.	35
out here			
	CAROLYN	Gut, dann gehe ich heute nachmittag einkaufen.	
That won't work	PETER	Das geht nicht°.	
	CAROLYN	Warum nicht?	40
	PETER	Heute ist Samstag. Samstags sind die Geschäfte nur bis um zwei offen, und sonntags ist alles zu.	
	CAROLYN	Aber nicht die Kaufhäuser, oder?	
once a month	URSULA	Doch! Nur einmal im Monat° sind sie samstags bis um vier offen.	
	CAROLYN	Ach du liebes bißchen! Dann gehe ich jetzt einkaufen. Danke fürs Frühstück!	45
	PETER	Bitte, bitte!	

LANGER
Diese Woche
SAMSTAG

Zum Text

A.   Was paßt wo?   *(Find the correct places for the listed words.)*

Apotheke, einkaufen, Hunger, Kaffee, Kuchen, Kaufhäuser, Lebensmittelgeschäft, samstags, Studenten, Studentin

1. Carolyn ist _____ .   **2.** Peter und Ursula sind auch _____ .   **3.** Carolyn hat wirklich _____ .   **4.** Um die Ecke gibt es ein _____ und eine _____ .   **5.** Die Leute im Café essen _____ und trinken _____ .
6. Donnerstags sind die _____ bis abends um halb neun offen.   **7.** _____ sind die Geschäfte nur bis um zwei offen.   **8.** Carolyn geht jetzt _____ .

B.   Verstehen Sie?   *(Answer according to the reading. Use **ja, nein,** or **doch.**)*

1. Essen Peter und Ursula zum Frühstück Wurst und Käse?
2. Gibt es um die Ecke eine Apotheke?
3. Regensburg ist nicht sehr alt, nicht wahr?
4. Ist samstags Markt?
5. Verkaufen die Bauern da Kuchen und Kaffee?
6. Sind die Geschäfte samstags nicht offen?
7. Ich glaube, die Geschäfte sind heute nicht zu, oder?

C. **Verneinen Sie die Sätze!** *(Negate the sentences.)*

1. Sie möchte ein Ei.
2. Sie möchte Milch für den Kaffee.
3. Die Kaufhäuser sind samstags zu.
4. Verkauft die Drogerie Medizin?
5. Das Lebensmittelgeschäft ist billig.
6. Gibt es da Autos?
7. Das glaube ich.
8. Die Blumen sind frisch.
9. Mittags sind die Geschäfte offen.

D. **Was bedeuten die Wörter, und was sind die Artikel?**

Söhnchen, Töchterlein, Stühlchen, Tischlein, Büchlein, Heftchen, Flüßchen, Mäntelchen, Höschen, Stündchen, Teilchen

E. **Carolyns Einkaufsliste** *(Consult Carolyn's shopping list where she has checked what she needs. Then complete the sentences below.)*

1. **Was hat sie, und was braucht sie nicht?**

   a. Carolyn hat noch etwas _____ , ein paar _____ und ein Stück _____ .

   b. Sie braucht kein(e / en) _____ .

2. **Was hat sie nicht, und was kauft sie?**

   a. Carolyn hat kein(e / en) _____ .
   b. Sie kauft ein paar _____ , ein Pfund _____ und etwas _____ .

F. **Interviews**

1. **Einkaufen hier** *(Ask a partner about the stores in his / her native town and his / her shopping habits.)*

    a. Welche Geschäfte sind billig? teuer?
    b. Gibt es eine Fußgängerzone? Wo? Was für Kaufhäuser gibt es da?
    c. Gibt es einen Markt? Was kaufen die Leute da?
    d. Wann sind die Geschäfte offen? Sind sonntags alle Geschäfte zu?
    e. Gehst du gern einkaufen? Was kaufst du oft? Kaufst du oft Blumen?

2. **Einkaufen in Regensburg** *(On your first day in Regensburg, you find out about shopping from a fellow student who answers your questions.)*

    You want to know . . .
    a. where stores are. **b.** when they are open. **c.** if the grocery store is expensive. **d.** where the drugstore is. **e.** if the department store is closed on Sundays. **f.** if there is a pedestrian area. **g.** if the city is very beautiful. **h.** if there is a (farmers') market and when.

Hören Sie zu!

Neu in Regensburg *(Listen to the conversation between two students. Then decide whether the statements below are true or false according to the information in the dialogue.)*

ZUM ERKENNEN: Sag mal! *(Say)*; nachher *(afterwards)*

_____ 1. Ursula wohnt schon zwanzig Jahre in Regensburg.
_____ 2. Claudia ist aus Passau.
_____ 3. Claudia braucht Schuhe.
_____ 4. Ursula geht heute nachmittag einkaufen.
_____ 5. Sie geht um drei Uhr.
_____ 6. Ursula braucht Jeans und ein Sweatshirt.
_____ 7. Dann gehen sie ein paar Würstchen essen.

Regensburg an der Donau. Die Steinerne Brücke *(stone bridge)* ist 800 Jahre alt.

Übrigens

1. Regensburg dates back to Roman times. Since this city is one of the few in Germany that was not seriously damaged during World War II, a variety of architecture spanning the centuries has survived. A tour through the old section of town reveals Romanesque, Gothic, and baroque buildings, many of which have been restored.

2. There are still many regional differences in the German language: In Hamburg a butcher is a **Schlachter,** in Berlin a **Schlächter,** in central Germany a **Fleischer,** and in the south a **Metzger.**

3. **Cafés** and **Konditoreien** are favorite places for conversation or for breaks in shopping excursions. They serve coffee, tea, and hot chocolate, along with a great variety of delicious cakes and pastries.

4. Germans are very fond of having fresh flowers in their homes. It is customary for coffee or dinner guests to bring their hosts a small gift, usually flowers. They have to be carefully chosen, though: red roses, for example, carry the message of love, while white chrysanthemums are considered funeral flowers. The gift of flowers eliminates the need for a thank-you note, but a follow-up telephone call is very much appreciated.

Blumenmarkt in Freiburg

SPRECHSITUATIONEN

Making a Purchase

Here are some useful phrases for shopping.

1. Salesclerks offer assistance, saying:

> Was darf's sein? *(May I help you?)*
> Ja, bitte?

You may respond with:

Ich brauche . . .	Haben Sie . . .?
Ich möchte . . .	Gibt es . . .?
Ich hätte gern . . .	Was kosten / kostet . . .?
Ich suche . . .	Ich nehme . . .

2. After you have made a selection, you may hear the following and respond accordingly:

Sonst noch (et)was? *(Anything else?)*	Ja, ich brauche (auch) noch . . .
	Nein, danke! (Das ist alles.)
Ist das alles?	Ja, danke! (Das ist alles)
	Nein, ich brauche (auch) noch . . .

After adding up the bill, the salesclerk might say:

> Das macht (zusammen) . . .

When you get your change back, you may hear:

> Und . . . Mark zurück *(back).*

Übungen

A. **Wir kaufen ein Buch.** *(Organize the sentences below in proper sequence.)*

_____ Ist das alles?
_____ 35,– DM.
_____ Ich suche ein Bilderbuch von Österreich für meinen Großvater.
_____ Auf Wiedersehen!
_____ Ach, es ist wirklich sehr schön!
_____ Das macht dann 35 Mark.
_____ Guten Tag! Was darf's sein?
_____ Was kostet es?
_____ Hier, wie finden Sie dieses *(this)* Buch?
_____ Gut, ich nehme es.
_____ Vielen Dank! Auf Wiedersehen!
_____ Ja, danke.

B.   **Im Lebensmittelgeschäft**

S1   Guten Tag! Was darf's sein?

S2   Ich brauche _____ und _____ . Was kosten / kostet _____?

S1   _____ .

S2   Und was kosten / kostet _____?

S1   _____ .

S2   Gut, dann nehme ich _____ und _____ .

S1   Sonst noch etwas?

S2   _____ .

S1   _____ DM, bitte!

C.   **Kurzgespräche**

1. You want to buy an item of clothing in a department store. Describe to the salesclerk what you are looking for. After viewing and commenting on several items the clerk has shown you (e.g., one is too small, one too big, one too expensive, etc.), decide whether or not to buy one. If you do not buy it, explain your reasons. If you do buy it, of course you must pay before you leave!

2. You stop at a refreshment stand in a railway station. The vendor asks what you'd like. You purchase some food for your seven-hour trip. The vendor inquires whether that is all and then tells you what the total comes to. You pay with two fives and are told you are getting back DM _____ . (Some prices in DM: apples and bananas 0,70; sandwiches 2,00; chocolate and potato chips 2,00; beverages 2,00.)

3. At the beginning of the semester you want to organize a welcome party for your new roommate. At the grocery store buy cookies, the ingredients for a fruit salad, soft drinks, etc. Always ask the clerk for the price of each item to make sure that anything you are buying is within your limited budget. Try to include phrases like *half a pound, a quarter of a pound, a kilo,* and *a dozen* (**ein halbes Pfund, ein Viertelpfund, ein Kilo, ein Dutzend**).

Im Restaurant

Das Stuttgarter Teehaus ist „in".

LERNZIELE

Vorschau
- Eating in and out

Gespräche and Wortschatz
- Meals and restaurants

Struktur
- Verbs with vowel changes
- Dative case

Einblicke
- Eating habits in German-speaking countries

Sprechsituationen
- Choosing and ordering a meal
- Expressing likes and dislikes

F.   Persönliche Fragen   *(At the exit of your cafeteria a marketing specialist, who is studying what college students eat and drink, asks you to answer some questions. Work in pairs.)*

1.   Was essen Sie zum Frühstück? zum Mittagessen? zum Abendessen?
2.   Trinken Sie morgens Kaffee, Tee, Milch oder Kakao? Trinken Sie Ihren Kaffee schwarz oder mit *(with)* Milch? mit oder ohne Zucker?
3.   Was essen Sie gern zum Nachtisch? Essen Sie oft Nachtisch? Wann?
4.   Trinken Sie Wein oder Bier? Wenn *(if)* ja, wann? Wenn nicht, was trinken Sie auf *(at)* Parties?

G.   Aussprache: ü   *(See also II. 22–28 in the pronunciation section of the Workbook.)*

1.   [ü:]   über, Tür, für, Frühling, Prüfung, Gemüse, südlich, grün, natürlich, müde
2.   [ü]   Flüsse, Würste, Stück, Müller, München, fünf, fünfundfünfzig, dünn
3.   Wortpaare
    a.   vier / für   c.   Stuhle / Stühle   e.   fühle / fülle
    b.   missen / müssen   d.   Mutter / Mütter   f.   Goethe / Güte

Hören Sie zu!

Im Gasthaus   *(Find out what Jürgen, Helga, and Michael are ordering for dinner. Put their initials by the foods and beverages they order, then add up their total bill to see whether the waitress calculated it correctly.)*

ZUM ERKENNEN: früh *(early)*; das Getränk, -e *(beverages)*; einmal *(one order of)*

Getränke	*Essen*	*Nachtisch*
__ Limonade	__ Schnitzel	__ Apfelkuchen
__ Apfelsaft	__ Rindsrouladen	__ Vanilleeis
__ Bier	__ Pizza	__ Reispudding
__ Mineralwasser	__ Würstchen	__ Schokoladenpudding
__ Cola	__ Fisch	__ Käsekuchen
Das kostet:		
_____	_____	_____
_____	_____	_____
_____		_____
	Alles zusammen:	_____ DM

Milka Schokolade
versch. Sorten, 300-g-Tafel
2.99

STRUKTUR

1. Verbs with Vowel Changes

Some very common verbs have a STEM-VOWEL CHANGE in the SECOND and THIRD PERSON SINGULAR. These changes will be clearly noted in all vocabulary lists like this: **sprechen (spricht).**

	e > i **sprechen** *to speak*	e > ie **sehen** *to see*	a > ä **fahren** *to drive*	au > äu **laufen** *to walk, run*
ich	spreche	sehe	fahre	laufe
du	**sprichst**	**siehst**	**fährst**	**läufst**
er	**spricht**	**sieht**	**fährt**	**läuft**
wir	sprechen	sehen	fahren	laufen
ihr	sprecht	seht	fahrt	lauft
sie	sprechen	sehen	fahren	laufen

Siehst du Eisenach auf der Landkarte?
Dieter **fährt** nach Eisenach.

A few verbs in this group have additional, consonant changes:

	nehmen *to take*	**werden** *to become, get*	**essen** *to eat*	**lesen** *to read*
ich	nehme	werde	esse	lese
du	**nimmst**	**wirst**	**ißt**	**liest**
er	**nimmt**	**wird**	**ißt**	**liest**

Note that the second and third person singular forms of **essen** and **lesen** are identical (**du liest, er liest**). As you know from Chapter 1, the **du**-form of verbs with a stem ending in any s-sound (**-s, -ß, -tz, -z**) adds only a **t**-ending instead of an **-st**: lesen > du lies**t**.

 You need to know the following common verbs with stem-vowel changes.

essen	**ißt**	*to eat*		lesen	**liest**	*to read*
empfehlen	**empfiehlt**	*to recommend*		nehmen	**nimmt**	*to take;*
fahren	**fährt**	*to drive*				*to have (food)*
geben	**gibt**	*to give*		**sehen**	**sieht**	*to see*
gefallen	**gefällt**	*to please,*		sprechen	**spricht**	*to speak*
		be pleasing		**tragen**	**trägt**	*to carry;*
helfen	**hilft**	*to help*				*to wear*
laufen	**läuft**	*to run; to walk*		**werden**	**wird**	*to become, get*

NOTE: The pointing finger signals that a vocabulary list includes some new words. Those are always in boldface type; learn them before you do the exercises that follow. The other words are included for review.

A.   Ersetzen Sie das Subjekt!

BEISPIEL: Der Ober trägt die Teller. (ich)
            Ich trage die Teller.

1.   Fahren Sie zum Kaufhaus? (wir, er, ihr, du)
2.   Wir nehmen Nudelsuppe. (er, ich, sie / *pl.*, du)
3.   Ich werde müde. (das Kind, wir, sie / *sg.*, sie / *pl.*)
4.   Sie empfehlen das Schnitzel. (der Ober, ich, du, das Fräulein)
5.   Sehen Sie die Apotheke nicht? (du, ihr, er, die Leute)
6.   Ich esse Käsekuchen. (wir, sie / *pl.*, er, du)
7.   Sprechen Sie Deutsch? (er, du, sie / *pl.*)
8.   Hilfst du heute nicht? (ihr, Sie, sie / *sg.*)
9.   Lesen Sie gern Bücher? (du, ihr, er, sie / *pl.*)

B.   Was tun sie?   *(Answer logically, telling what others do. Use pronouns and stem-changing verbs.)*

BEISPIEL: Ich esse schnell. Und Ihr Großvater?
            Er ißt sehr langsam.

1.   Ich spreche Englisch. Und Ihre Großmutter?
2.   Ich helfe gern. Und Ihr Nachbar?
3.   Ich nehme Apfelstrudel. Und Gabi?
4.   Ich empfehle den Schweinebraten. Und der Ober?
5.   Ich laufe langsam. Und Ihr Bruder oder Ihre Schwester?
6.   Ich lese gern. Und Ihre Mutter?
7.   Ich fahre im Sommer nach Deutschland. Und Ihre Familie?
8.   Ich sehe alles. Und Ihre Nachbarin?
9.   Ich trage gern blau. Und Ihr Bruder oder Ihre Schwester?
10. Ich gebe gern Hausaufgaben. Und Ihr [Englisch]professor?
11. Ich esse Käsekuchen. Und Axel?
12. Ich werde müde. Und Erika?

II. The Dative Case

The dative case has three major functions in German: it is the case of the INDIRECT OBJECT, it follows certain verbs, and it follows certain prepositions.

1.   In English the INDIRECT OBJECT is indicated in two ways:

   •   through word order: *The boy gives **the father** the plate.*

   •   with a preposition: *The boy gives the plate **to the father.***

In German this function is expressed through case and word order. One finds the indirect object by asking for whom or in reference to whom (or occasionally what) the action of the verb is taking place.

Der Junge gibt **dem Vater** den Teller.   *The boy gives the father the plate.*

a.   The dative form of the INTERROGATIVE PRONOUN is **wem** *(to whom).*

	persons	things and ideas
nom.	wer	was
acc.	wen	was
dat.	**wem**	—

Wem gibt der Junge den Teller? → **Dem Vater.**
To whom does the boy give the plate? → *To the father.*

b.   The dative forms of the DEFINITE and INDEFINITE ARTICLES are as follows:

	singular masc.	singular neut.	singular fem.	plural
nom.	der ein kein	das ein kein	die eine keine	die — keine
acc.	den einen keinen	das ein kein	die eine keine	die — keine
dat.	**dem einem keinem**	**dem einem keinem**	**der einer keiner**	**den — keinen**

Der Ober empfiehlt **dem** Vater, **der** Mutter und **den** Kindern das Schnitzel. Er bringt **dem** Kind einen Löffel, aber er gibt **einem** Kind kein Messer und keine Gabel.

- The POSSESSIVE ADJECTIVES **mein, dein,** and **Ihr** follow the pattern of **ein** and **kein:**

  Was empfiehlt er Ihr**em** Vater und Ihr**er** Mutter?
  Er empfiehlt mein**em** Vater und mein**er** Mutter den Fleischsalat.

- In the dative plural all nouns add an **-n** ending, unless the plural form already ends in **-n** or **-s.**

  die Väter / den Väter**n**   BUT   die Eltern / den Eltern
  die Kinder / den Kinder**n**   die Mädchen / den Mädchen
  die Äpfel / den Äpfel**n**   die Kulis / den Kulis

- N-nouns also have an **-n** or **-en** ending in the dative singular, as they do in the accusative singular: Das Eis schmeckt dem Student**en.**

c. Many verbs can have both accusative and dative objects. Note that the direct object is usually a thing and the indirect object a person.

Der Ober bringt dem Kind den Kuchen.
The waiter brings the child the cake.

Er empfiehlt der Studentin den Fisch.
He recommends the fish to the student.

Note the difference in meaning:

Der Onkel trägt der Tante die Lebensmittel. BUT Der Onkel trägt die Tante.

d. In sentences with two objects, the direct object, <u>if it is a noun,</u> generally follows the indirect object.

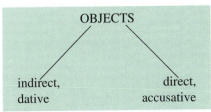

OBJECTS

indirect,
dative

direct,
accusative

Die Kellnerin bringt dem Herrn den Tee.

2. Dative Verbs

Some verbs take only dative objects; a few such verbs are:

antworten	*to answer*	**gehören**	*to belong to*
danken	*to thank*	helfen	*to help*
gefallen	*to please*		

Der Bruder antwortet der Kusine.	*The brother answers (gives an answer to) the cousin.*
Alex dankt dem Kellner.	*Alex thanks (gives thanks to) the waiter.*
Die Mensa gefällt den Studenten.	*The students like the cafeteria (the cafeteria pleases the students).*
Der Mantel gehört dem Mädchen.	*The coat belongs to the girl.*
Ich helfe dem Nachbarn.	*I'm helping (giving help to) the neighbor.*

3.   Dative Prepositions

These prepositions are always followed by the dative case:

aus	*out of* *from (a place of origin)*	Sie kommt **aus** dem Geschäft. Er ist **aus** Berlin.
außer	*besides*	**Außer** dem Café ist alles zu.
bei	*at (for)* *near, by* *at the home of*	Sie arbeitet **bei** VW. Die Drogerie ist **bei** der Buchhandlung. Er wohnt **bei** Familie Angerer.
mit	*with* *together with*	Ich schreibe **mit** einem Kuli. Alex kommt **mit** Gabi.
nach	*after (time)* *to (cities, countries, continents)* *to (used idiomatically)*	Kommst du **nach** dem Mittagessen? Fahrt ihr auch **nach** Österreich? Gehen Sie **nach** Hause!
seit	*since* *for (time)*	Sie wohnen **seit** Mai in Bonn. Sie wohnen **seit** drei Tagen da.[1]
von	*of* *from* *by*	Das Gegenteil **von** billig ist teuer. Wir fahren **von** Berlin nach Hamburg. Das Bild ist **von** Albrecht Dürer.
zu	*to (in the direction of)* *at (used idiomatically)* *for (purpose)*	Sie fährt **zum** Supermarkt. Sie sind **zu** Hause. Was gibt es **zum** Nachtisch?

- In everyday speech, some of the dative prepositions are usually contracted with the definite article.

bei + dem = **beim**	zu + dem = **zum**
von + dem = **vom**	zu + der = **zur**

- Pay particular attention to the contrasting use of these pairs of prepositions:

Sie fährt **zum** *(to the)* Supermarkt.
Fahrt ihr **nach** *(to)* Deutschland?

Wir fahren **von** *(from)* Salzburg nach München.
Er kommt **aus** *(from)* Salzburg.

Gehen Sie **nach Hause** *(home)!*
Sie sind nicht **zu Hause** *([at] home).*

---

[1] **seit** translates as *for* in English when it expresses duration of time (three minutes, one year) that began in the past and still continues in the present: *They have been living there for three days.*

C. **Sagen Sie die Sätze im Plural!** *(Restate in the plural the phrases in boldface.)*

BEISPIEL: Wir sprechen mit **dem Kanadier.**
Wir sprechen mit den Kanadiern.

1. Er lernt seit **einem Jahr** Deutsch. (drei)
2. Das Restaurant gehört **dem Schweizer.**
3. Sie kommen aus **dem Geschäft.**
4. Der Bleistift liegt bei **dem Buch.**
5. Nach **einem Monat** bezahlt er die Rechnung. (zwei)
6. Ich gehe nur mit **dem Kind.**
7. Die Stadt gefällt **dem Amerikaner.**
8. Sie gibt **dem Engländer** eine Landkarte.
9. Die Löffel liegen bei **dem Teller.**
10. Die Kellnerin kommt mit **der Serviette.**
11. Wir sprechen mit **dem Nachbarn.**
12. Das Geschäft ist bei **dem Restaurant.**
13. Der Kuchen schmeckt **dem Studenten.**
14. Der Ober kommt mit **der Tasse.**

D. **Ersetzen Sie das Dativobjekt!**

BEISPIEL: Der Kellner bringt dem Kind ein Eis. (Großvater)
Der Kellner bringt dem Großvater ein Eis.

1. Die Kellnerin empfiehlt dem Vater die Rouladen. (Bruder, Spanier, Schweizer)
2. Der Junge gibt der Mutter ein Bild. (Schwester, Studentin, Frau)
3. Der Ober bringt den Eltern das Essen. (Leute, Amerikaner / *pl.*, Studenten / *pl.*)
4. Die Drogerie gehört meiner Großmutter. (Großvater, Eltern, Familie)
5. Axel dankt dem Bruder. (Schwester, Vater, Leute)
6. Meine Großmutter hilft meinem Vater. (Mutter, Kusinen, Vettern)

E. **Sagen Sie es noch einmal!** *(Replace the nouns following the prepositions with the words suggested.)*

BEISPIEL: Eva geht zum Lebensmittelgeschäft. (Apotheke)
Eva geht zur Apotheke.

1. Paula kommt aus dem Kaufhaus. (Drogerie, Café, Mensa)
2. Seit Sonntag ist er wieder hier. (zwei Tage, eine Stunde, ein Monat)
3. Wir sprechen mit dem Großvater. (Frau, Mädchen, Großeltern)
4. Ich wohne bei meinen Eltern. (Bruder, Schwester, Familie)
5. Er möchte etwas Salat zu den Rouladen. (Schnitzel, Suppe, Würstchen / *pl.*, Fleisch)
6. Das Café ist bei der Apotheke. (Kaufhaus, Lebensmittelgeschäft, Drogerie)
7. Nach dem Mittagessen spielen sie Tennis. (Frühstück, Kaffee, Deutschstunde)
8. Außer meinem Bruder sind alle hier. (Vater, Mutter, Nachbar, Studentin)
9. Tante Liesl bleibt bei den Kindern. (Vetter, Kusine, Töchter)

F.   Wer, wem oder was?   *(At your son's graduation party you are talking to a friend. Because of the loud music, he / she can't hear what you are saying.)*

BEISPIEL: Oskar gibt dem Bruder die Bücher.
  Wer gibt dem Bruder die Bücher?—Oskar!
  Wem gibt Oskar die Bücher?—Dem Bruder!
  Was gibt Oskar dem Bruder?—Die Bücher!

1.   Der Nachbar verkauft Onkel Willi den BMW.
2.   Onkel Willi gibt dem Jungen den BMW.
3.   Großmutter empfiehlt Irene ein paar Tage Ferien *(vacation)*.
4.   Die Kinder zahlen der Mutter die Hotelrechnung.

G.   Was gehört wem?   *(You and some friends are unpacking your family's boxes after a move. Tell what belongs to whom.)*

BEISPIEL: Wem gehört die Jeansjacke?
  Sie gehört meinem Bruder.

1	2	3
das Familienbild	gehört	mein Bruder
die Kochbücher *(cook . . .)*	gehören	meine Schwester
das Taschenmesser *(pocket . . .)*		mein Vetter
die Teller und Tassen		meine Kusine
das Sporthemd		meine Mutter
die Hausschuhe		mein Vater
die Tennishose		mein Großvater
die Winterpullover		meine Eltern
die Krawatte *(tie)*		meine Großmutter
die Golduhr		
die Ringe *(pl., rings)*		
die Landkarten		
das Bilderbuch		
die Jacken		
die Gläser		
der Mantel		
das Deutschbuch		

Übung macht den Meister.
(Practice makes perfect.)

H.   Was gefällt wem?

1.   **Ersetzen Sie das Dativobjekt!**

   a.   Das Restaurant gefällt dem Onkel. (Tante, Großmutter, Kinder, Student, Studentin, Studenten)
   b.   Aber die Preise gefallen der Familie nicht. (Frau, Leute, Nachbar, Herren)

2. **Auf deutsch, bitte!**

BEISPIEL: **Meinem Vetter gefällt Hamburg.**

a. Ms. Bayer likes the country. **b.** My father likes the city. **c.** My mother likes the South. **d.** My sister likes the lakes. **e.** My brothers like the mountains. **f.** My grandparents like the student. **g.** The student likes my grandparents. **h.** I like German (**mir**).

I. **Was kaufen wir wem?** *(The Christmas season is approaching, and you and your roommate are coming up with ideas for presents. Working with a classmate, form sentences using one word from each list. Follow the model.)*

BEISPIEL: Mutter / das Kochbuch, ¨er
           Meiner Mutter gefallen Kochbücher.
           Prima! Ich kaufe meiner Mutter ein Kochbuch.

1. Bruder, Schwester, Mutter, Vater, Großeltern, Onkel, Tante, Freund *(friend)*, Freundin

2. die Blumenvase, -n   die Krawatte, -n *(tie)*
    die Bluse, -n   das Portemonnaie, -s *(wallet)*
    das Buch, ¨er   der Pullover, -
    der Kalender, -   der Ring, -e
    die Kassette, -n   die Tasche, -n *(handbag)*
    die Kette, -n *(necklace)*   das Taschenmesser, - *(pocket . . .)*

J. **Was fehlt?**

1. **Nach Hause oder zu Hause?**

    a. Heute essen wir —————— .
    b. Jürgen ist nicht —————— .
    c. Er kommt oft spät —————— .
    d. Morgen bleibt er —————— .
    e. Wir arbeiten gern —————— .
    f. Geht ihr um sechs —————— ?
    g. Bringst du die Großeltern —————— ?

2. **Die Präpositionen mit, bei, aus, von, nach und zu**   *(Use contractions when appropriate.)*

    a. Gehst du ————— Buchhandlung? — Nein, ich gehe —————
        Kaufhaus. *(to the / to the)*
    b. Kaufhaus Horten ist ————— Café Kranzler. *(by)*
    c. Christl arbeitet ————— Horten. *(at)*
    d. Julia fährt heute ————— Leipzig und Philipp ————— Dresden. *(to)*
    e. Sind Sie auch ————— Norddeutschland? *(from)*
    f. Antonio kommt ————— Rom und wohnt ————— Familie
        Dinkelacker. *(from / at the home of)*
    g. Herr Dinkelacker fährt morgen ————— Frankfurt ————— Stuttgart.
        (from / to)
    h. Er fährt ————— der Familie. *(together with)*
    i. Der Hund *(dog)* bleibt ————— den Nachbarn. *(at the home of)*

Zusammen-fassung

K. Bilden Sie Sätze!

BEISPIEL: das / sein / für / Onkel
Das ist für den Onkel.

1. Ober / kommen / mit / Speisekarte
2. Mutter / kaufen / Kind / Apfelsaft
3. Fräulein / empfehlen / Studentin / Apfelkuchen
4. er / sehen / Großvater / nicht
5. kommen / du / von / Mensa?
6. Familie / fahren / nicht / nach Berlin
7. arbeiten / du / auch / bei / Delikatessengeschäft Dallmayr?

L. Guten Appetit! Was fehlt?

1. Zu_____ Essen braucht man ein_____ Messer und ein_____ Gabel. **2.** Suppe ißt man mit ein_____ Eßlöffel *(tablespoon),* und für d_____ Kaffee braucht man ein_____ Kaffeelöffel. **3.** Wir haben kein_____ Messer, kein_____ Gabel und kein_____ Löffel *(sg.).* **4.** Gibt es hier kein_____ Salz und kein_____ Pfeffer? **5.** Doch, d_____ Salz steht bei d_____ Pfeffer. **6.** Jetzt habe ich alles außer ein_____ Speisekarte. **7.** Der Ober empfiehlt d_____ Studentin d_____ Schweine-braten *(pork roast, m.).* **8.** Nach d_____ Essen bringt er ein_____ Eis und ein_____ Kaffee. **9.** D_____ Restaurant gefällt d_____ Studenten *(pl.).* **10.** Aber sie haben etwas gegen d_____ Preise *(pl.).* **11.** Wir sprechen von d_____ Professor und von d_____ Prüfung. **12.** Ich bestelle noch ein_____ Cola. **13.** Hier trinke ich d_____ Cola aus ein_____ Glas, aber zu Hause aus ein_____ Flasche *(f., bottle).* **14.** Da kommt der Ober mit d_____ Rechnung. **15.** Ohne d_____ Rechnung geht's nicht. **16.** Danke für d_____ Mittagessen!

M. In der Mensa. Auf deutsch, bitte!

1. We're going through the cafeteria with the students. **2.** They're from Hamburg. They're Hamburgers. **3.** Paul lives with (at the home of) a family, and Helga lives at home. **4.** Helga, what are you having? **5.** I think I'll take the roast (**der Braten**), peas and carrots, and a glass of juice. **6.** Would you *(formal)* like a piece of cake for dessert? **7.** No, I'm not eating any cake because it's fattening (**dick machen**). **8.** I have no knife, no fork, and no spoon. **9.** Paul brings the student *(f.)* a knife, a fork, a spoon, and (some) ice cream. **10.** Whose ice cream is that? (To whom does the ice cream belong?) **11.** Would you *(fam.)* like some ice cream with a cookie? **12.** She thanks the student. **13.** Who's paying for (the) lunch?

Reviewing for Tests

If you have taken full advantage of all class sessions, kept up with your work, and reviewed regularly, you should not have to spend much time preparing for tests. Concentrate on the areas that give you the most trouble. Use the "Rückblicke" for efficient reviewing. Go over the vocabulary lists of the chapters that will be covered by the test; make sure you know genders and plurals of nouns. Mark any words you seem to have trouble remembering; review them again. Begin your review early enough so that you can clear up any questions with your instructor.

EINBLICKE

Mittagessen in der
Würzburger Mensa

"Food and drink are the glue that holds body and soul together," claims an old Viennese saying. The sentiment is popular in all of the German-speaking countries.

German cooking has many regional specialties. In addition to excellent hams and sausages, there are numerous fish dishes, such as Helgoland lobster, **Hamburger Matjestopf** *(pickled herring with sliced apples and onion rings in a sour cream sauce)*, Berlin eel soup, or Black Forest trout. Some regional dishes include **Sauerbraten** *(marinated pot roast)* from the Rhineland, **Kasseler Rippchen** *(smoked loin of pork)*, or Bavarian **Leberkäse** *(meat loaf made from minced pork)*. In the South dumplings and pasta dishes (e.g., **Spätzle**) are popular. Germany also boasts a large variety of pastries, such as **Schwarzwälder Kirschtorte, Frankfurter Kranz** *(a rich cake ring decorated with whipped cream and nuts)*, or **Thüringer Mohnkuchen** *(poppy-seed cake)*. A favorite summer dessert is **Rote Grütze** *(berries and their juices thickened with cornstarch and served with vanilla sauce or cream)*.

Most famous among Austrian dishes are **Schnitzel, Gulasch,** and a variety of salted and smoked meats, as well as dumplings. But desserts like **Strudel, Palatschinken** *(dessert crêpes)*, or **Sachertorte** delight visitors even more. Swiss cooking has also developed many specialties of its own, such as **Geschnetzeltes** *(minced veal in a cream sauce)*, **Berner Platte** *(dish with a variety of hams and sausages)*, or **Röschti** *(fried potatoes with bacon cubes)*. The most famous Swiss dish is probably the cheese fondue (**Käsefondue**), a reminder that Switzerland produces a great variety of excellent cheeses (e.g., **Schweizer Käse, Gruyère, Emmentaler, Appenzeller**).

WORTSCHATZ 2

der	Freund, -e	*(a close) friend; boyfriend*
die	Freundin, -nen	*(a close) friend; girlfriend*
	Flasche, -n; eine Flasche . . .	*bottle; a bottle of . . .*
	Hand, ¨-e	*hand*

besonders	*especially*
gewöhnlich	*usual(ly)*
man	*one (they, people), you*
manchmal	*sometimes*
nicht nur . . . sondern auch	*not only . . . but also*
überall	*everywhere*
vielleicht	*perhaps*
schlafen (schläft)	*to sleep*

WAS IST DAS? der Kaffeeklatsch; das Joghurt, Omelett; die Bratwurst, Großstadt, Schule, Spezialität, Kartoffelchips *(pl.);* lokal, relativ, voll

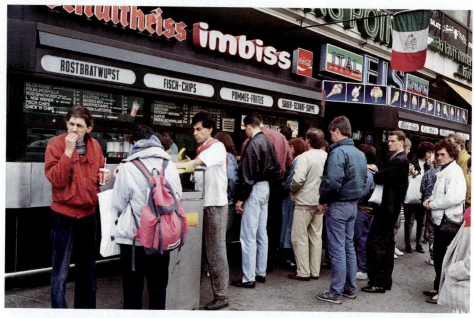

Guten Appetit!

Man ist, was man ißt

Die Deutschen, Österreicher und Schweizer beginnen den Tag gewöhnlich mit einem guten Frühstück. Zum Frühstück gibt es Brot oder Brötchen, Butter, Marmelade, vielleicht auch ein Ei, etwas Wurst oder Käse und manchmal auch etwas Joghurt oder Müsli°. Dazu° trinkt man Kaffee, Milch, Obstsaft, Tee oder Kakao.

Mittags ißt man warm. Um die Zeit sind die Schulen aus[1], und die Kinder kommen 5 zum Mittagessen nach Hause. Manche° Geschäfte und Büros° machen mittags zu. Viele Leute essen mittags zu Hause. Andere° gehen nicht nach Hause, sondern in die Kantine° oder in ein Restaurant.

whole-grain granola / with it

some / offices
others / company cafeteria

Im Restaurant gibt es gewöhnlich ein Tagesmenü. Das ist oft besonders gut und billig.
10 Außer Bratwurst, Omelett oder Hühnchen° findet man natürlich auch lokale Spezialitäten,
wie zum Beispiel Berliner Aal grün° oder in Bayern Schweinshax'n° mit Knödeln°. Zum
Mittagessen trinkt man gern Saft, Mineralwasser, Bier oder Wein, aber kein Leitungs-
wasser° und auch keinen Kaffee. Kaffee trinkt man manchmal nach dem Essen. Egal° wo,
überall findet man etwas Besonderes°. Wenn° Sie in Europa sind, probieren Sie mal° so
15 eine Spezialität! Nehmen Sie auch das Messer in die rechte° Hand und die Gabel in die
linke° Hand[2], und dann Guten Appetit! Noch etwas: Manchmal sitzen° auch andere Leute
bei Ihnen am° Tisch. So° gibt es hier und da interessante Gespräche. Fürs Mittagessen
braucht man gewöhnlich Zeit. Leute mit wenig° Zeit gehen gern zu einer Imbißbude°. Da
gibt es Bratwurst, Fischbrötchen, Pizza oder Schaschlik°. In Großstädten finden Sie mei-
20 stens° auch McDonald's oder Burger King. Schnell essen ist manchmal besser als° nichts,
aber ein Mittagessen ist das für die meisten° Leute nicht.

Nachmittags sieht man viele Menschen in Cafés[3]. Sie sitzen gemütlich° bei einer Tasse
Kaffee und reden°. Kaffeeklatsch gibt es aber nicht nur im Café, sondern auch zu Hause.
Besonders sonntags kommt man oft mit Freunden zusammen zu einer Tasse Kaffee und
25 einem Stück Kuchen.

Abends ißt man gewöhnlich kalt und nicht so viel wie mittags. Man sagt: Mit einem
vollen Bauch° schläft man schlecht. Was man abends ißt, macht dick. So gibt es nur etwas
Brot mit Käse, Wurst oder Fisch, ein paar Tomaten oder saure Gurken°. Dazu gibt es vielleicht eine Tasse Tee oder ein Bier. Abends öffnet man auch gern eine Flasche Wein[4] für
30 Freunde[5]. Dazu gibt es Salzstangen° oder Kartoffelchips.

Den meisten Deutschen, Österreichern und Schweizern ist wichtig, was sie essen. Wie
bei uns° essen sie relativ viel Obst, Salat und Gemüse. Auch haben sie etwas gegen Farb-
stoffe° und Konservierungsmittel°. Sie glauben: „Man ist, was man ißt."

chicken
fresh eel in herb sauce /
pig's knuckles / dumplings

tap water / no matter
special / when / do try
right
left / sit
at your / this way
little / snack bar
shish kebabs
usually / better than
most

comfortably
chat

stomach

pickles

pretzel sticks

as we do here
artificial colors / preserva-
tives

DAS GIFT IN UNSERER NAHRUNG IST UNSICHTBAR.

ALTERNATIVE: DIE GRÜNEN

CHEMIE GEHÖRT NICHT AUF DEN SPEISEPLAN!

④ **CURRYWURST-BUDE RATHAUS SCHÖNEBERG**
30 Schöneberg, John-F.-Kennedy-Platz, U: Rathaus Schöneberg. Geöffnet Di. und Fr. vormittags.

⑤ **DÖNER-KEBAB KREUZBERG**
36 Kreuzberg, Oranienstraße, U: Kottbusser Tor.

⑥ **FALAFEL-IMBISS**
30 Schöneberg, Potsdamer Straße 110, U: Kurfürstenstraße.

Zum Text

A.   Welche Antwort paßt?   *(Indicate the correct answer according to the text.)*

1. Zum Frühstück gibt es _____ .
    a. Sauerbraten
    b. Kuchen und Plätzchen
    c. viel Obst und Gemüse
    d. Brot, Butter und Marmelade
2. Mittags essen die Schulkinder _____ .
    a. in der Schule
    b. zu Hause
    c. im Restaurant
    d. etwas Besonderes
3. Zum Mittagessen trinkt man gern _____ .
    a. Kaffee, Milch oder Tee
    b. Eiswasser
    c. Mineralwasser, Bier oder Wein
    d. Cola
4. Zum Abendessen ißt man gewöhnlich _____ .
    a. Kaffee und Kuchen
    b. Brot, Wurst, Käse und Fisch
    c. Suppe, Fleisch und Gemüse
    d. Salzstangen und Kartoffelchips
5. Die Deutschen, Österreicher und Schweizer essen _____ Obst und Gemüse.
    a. wenig
    b. kein
    c. nur
    d. viel

B.   Guten Appetit! Was fehlt?

1. Ich beginne den Tag gewöhnlich mit ein_____ guten Frühstück: mit ein_____ Brötchen, ein_____ Ei und ein_____ Tasse Tee.   **2.** Gehst du mittags _____ Hause? **3.** Ja, _____ Hause ist es nicht so teuer.   **4.** Bei d_____ Preisen *(pl.)* esse ich gern Hause.   **5.** Warum gehst du nicht zu_____ Mensa?   **6.** D_____ Essen schmeckt nicht.   **7.** Manchmal gehe ich zu ein_____ Imbißbude *(f.)*.   **8.** Dann esse ich nichts außer ein_____ Bratwurst, und die Cola trinke ich schnell aus d_____ Flasche. **9.** Oft habe ich kein_____ Hunger.   **10.** Dann esse ich nur ein_____ Apfel oder ein_____ Banane.   **11.** Möchtest du etwas Brot mit ein_____ Stück Käse? **12.** Es ist von d_____ Reformhaus *(n., health-food store)* und hat kein_____ Konservierungsmittel *(pl.)*!

C.   Vergleichen Sie!   *(With a classmate make two lists that compare German and North American food and drink preferences.)*

ZUM ERKENNEN: der Speck *(bacon)*; die Cornflakes; der Krapfen, - *(doughnut)*; ein gekochtes Ei *(a boiled egg)*; das Spiegelei, -er *(fried egg)*; Rühreier *(scrambled eggs)*; der Schinken *(ham)*; der Hamburger, -; der Honig *(honey)*; der Senf *(mustard)*; ein belegtes Brot / Brötchen *(an open-faced sandwich)*; der Pfannkuchen, - *(pancake)*; der Toast, -s; die Waffel, -n; das Müsli *(whole-grain granola)*

	in den deutschsprachigen Ländern	in Nordamerika
zum Frühstück		
ißt man		
trinkt man		
zum Mittagessen		
ißt man		
trinkt man		
zum Abendessen		
ißt man		
trinkt man		

D.   Schreiben Sie!   *(Write eight to ten sentences, describing your eating habits, i.e., when you eat, what you eat and drink at various meals, and what you like and dislike.)*

E.   Käsefondue für vier bis sechs Personen   *(Read the recipe and summarize briefly in English how a cheese fondue is prepared.)*

500 g° geriebener° Gruyère und Emmentaler Käse	*4 cups / grated*
etwas Knoblauch°	*garlic*
½ 1° leichter° Weißwein	*2 cups / light*
2 Teelöffel Kartoffelmehl°	*potato starch*
2 Teelöffel Kirsch°	*cherry brandy*
etwas Salz, Pfeffer und Muskat°	*nutmeg*
Weißbrotwürfel°	*. . . bite-size pieces*

Den Fonduetopf° mit Knoblauch ausreiben°. Den Wein hineingeben° und langsam er-
wärmen°. Den Käse dazugeben° und unter Rühren° schmelzen lassen° und zum
Kochen° bringen (ungefähr 5 Minuten). Das Kartoffelmehl mit dem Kirsch kom-
biniert daruntermischen°. Das Fondue ist jetzt cremig° dick. Mit Salz, Pfeffer und
Muskat würzen°. Das Fondue zusammen mit den Brotwürfeln servieren. Beim Essen
Würfel mit der Gabel in das Fondue tauchen°. Guten Appetit!

. . . pot / rub / pour in
heat / add / stirring / let melt
boil
blend in / creamy
season
dip into

Hören Sie zu!

Gäste zum Wochenende   *(Listen to Kai and Gerda's plans for their weekend guests, Ruth and Uwe. Then read the questions below and select the correct response.)*

ZUM ERKENNEN: gegen *(around)*; genug *(enough)*; Forelle *(trout)*

1.   Ruth und Uwe kommen am _____ .
     a.   Sonntag um vier   b.   Samstag nachmittag   c.   Sonntag zum Kaffee

2.   Gerda macht einen _____ .
     a.   Käsekuchen   b.   Apfelkuchen   c.   Erdbeerkuchen

3.   Zum Abendessen gibt es _____ .
     a.   Kartoffelsalat und Würstchen   b.   Fondue, Brot und Wein   c.   Eier,
     Wurst und Käse

4.   Uwe ißt gern _____ .
     a.   Joghurt   b.   Schwarzbrot   c.   Erdbeerkuchen

5.   Zum Mittagessen machen sie _____ .
     a.   eine Nudelsuppe   b.   Fleisch und Gemüse   c.   Fisch mit Kartoffelsalat

6.   Zum Nachtisch gibt's _____ .
     a.   Äpfel und Orangen   b.   Obst   c.   Obstsalat

7.   Kai fährt _____ .
     a.   zum Supermarkt   b.   zum Markt   c.   zur Bäckerei

8.   Gerda kauft Eier, _____ .
     a.   Joghurt und Kaffee   b.   Obstsalat und Plätzchen   c.   Gemüse und Blumen

Ein Café in Wien. Hier gibt's Eis und Kuchen.

Übrigens

1.   In Germany and Austria schools generally let out between 12 noon and 1:30 P.M.; children usually eat their main meal at home after school. The afternoons are for homework and play. In Switzerland children attend school from 8 to 12 and from 2 to 4, but Wednesday and Saturday afternoons are free.

2.   Whenever Europeans eat something that needs to be cut, they hold the knife in the right hand and the fork in the left throughout the meal, rather than shifting the fork to the right hand. If no knife is needed, the left hand is put on the table next to the plate, not into the lap. To signal that one is finished eating, the knife and fork are placed parallel and diagonally on the plate.

3.   In Austria, many people have a favorite café (**das Kaffeehaus**), where they can relax over such items as **Kaffee mit Schlag** (*coffee with whipped cream*) or a piece of **Linzertorte.** The tradition of the coffee house goes back to the early 1700s, when it was the preferred meeting place not only of the literati, reformers, artists, and philosophers, but also of middle-class society.

4.   German wines are produced mainly in western and southwestern Germany. The Rhine and Moselle (**Mosel**) rivers have given their names to two great wines famous throughout the world. The Swiss, too, love wine, which is for them what beer is to a Bavarian. Out of 23 cantons, 18 grow wine. In Austria there are excellent vineyards along the Danube around Vienna. Wines are classified as **Tafelwein** (*table or ordinary wine),* **Qualitätswein** (*quality wine),* and **Qualitätswein mit Prädikat** (*superior wine).* A wine's classification and vintage year reflect its quality.

5.   Germans consciously distinguish between friends (**Freunde**) and acquaintances (**Bekannte**), in the belief that one can have only few real friends among the many people one knows. Genuine friendships are considered special and often last for a lifetime.

SPRECHSITUATIONEN

Choosing and Ordering a Meal

To order a meal, you can use the following expressions:

> Herr Ober, die (Speise)karte, bitte!
> Ich möchte bestellen.
> Was empfehlen Sie?
> Was ist heute besonders gut?

> (Ich glaube,) ich nehme . . .
> Ich möchte . . .
> Ich hätte gern . . .
> Bringen Sie mir bitte . . .! *(Please, bring me . . .)*

To request the bill, you should say:

> Herr Ober, ich möchte (be)zahlen!
> Zahlen, bitte!
> Die Rechnung, bitte!

Expressing Likes and Dislikes

1. Likes

   > Ich esse / trinke gern . . .
   > Ich finde . . . gut.
   > . . . schmeckt wunderbar.
   > . . . ist prima.
   > . . . gefällt mir. *(I like . . .)*
   > Wie gefällt Ihnen / dir . . . ? *(How do you like . . .?)*

2. Dislikes

   > Ich esse / trinke nicht gern . . .
   > Ich finde . . . nicht gut.
   > . . . schmeckt nicht gut (furchtbar).
   > . . . ist zu heiß / kalt, teuer, usw.
   > . . . gefällt mir nicht.

NOTE: **Gefallen** is usually not used to talk about food, but rather when you want to say that a city, a picture, an item of clothing, or a person is pleasing to you. **Schmecken** is used with food and beverages.

Übungen

A.　**Im Ratskeller**

Ratskeller

Tagesmenü:	I Nudelsuppe, Schnitzel und Kartoffelsalat, Eis　DM	24,20
	II Gemüsesuppe, Rindsrouladen mit	
	Kartoffelklößen, Eis	27,60

Tagesspezialitäten:

Bratwurst und Sauerkraut	12,50
Omelett mit Schinken°, Salat	14,00
Kalbsleber°, Erbsen und Karotten, Pommes Frites	18,75
Hühnchen° mit Weinsoße°, Reis, Salat	21,00
Schweinebraten°, Kartoffelbrei°, Salat	22,40
Sauerbraten°, Kartoffelbrei°, Salat	23,75
Gemischte Fischplatte, Kartoffeln, Salat	26,25

Suppen:

Tomatensuppe, Erbsensuppe, Bohnensuppe, Kartoffelsuppe	4,50

Salate:

Grüner Salat, Tomatensalat, Gurkensalat°, Bohnensalat	4,80

Getränke°:

Apfelsaft	2,75	Bier (0,2 l)[1]	2,40
Limonade	2,75	Wein (0,2 l)	3,20
Tee	3,00	Mineralwasser	1,80
Kaffee	3,50		

Zum Nachtisch:

Schokoladenpudding	2,80	Käsekuchen	4,55
Vanilleeis	4,75	Apfelstrudel	4,80
Frische Erdbeeren	5,00	Erdbeertorte°	5,60
Schlagsahne°	1,50	Kirschtorte	6,00

Glossary (left margin):

ham
calves' liver
chicken / . . . sauce
pork roast
marinated pot roast / mashed potatoes

cucumber . . .

beverages

strawberry cake
whipped cream

1. **Wir möchten bestellen!**　*(In groups of two to five students, take turns ordering from the menu.)*

2. **Zahlen, bitte!**　*(Ask for the check. Tell the server what you had, e.g.,* **einmal Bratwurst . . .,** *and let him / her figure out what you owe. Round up your bill to include an appropriate tip.)*

---

[1] A liter is a little more than a quart. 0,2 l therefore is approximately three-fourths of a cup.

B.   Wie gefällt dir das?   *(In pairs, ask each other about three likes and three dislikes, using various expressions, e.g.,* **gern** + *verb,* **gefallen, schmecken, finden.** *You might ask about people, places, restaurants, food and beverages, clothing, books, and so on.)*

BEISPIEL: Wie gefällt es dir hier? Was schmeckt dir besonders gut? Was für Obst ißt du gern? Wie findest du Fisch? usw.

C.   Kurzgespräche

1.   You have just met another student in the cafeteria for the first time and inquire how he / she likes it here. Very much, he / she answers. The other student then asks you whether the soup tastes good. You reply that it is not bad, but too hot. You ask how your fellow student likes the chicken. He / she replies that it doesn't taste particularly good and is cold. You say the food is usually cold.

2.   You and a friend are in a German restaurant. The server asks what you would like, and you ask what he / she recommends. He / she mentions a particular dish. Both you and your friend order, each choosing a soup, a main dish, and a salad. The server asks what you would like to drink, and you order beverages. Use the menu on the previous page.

Schweizer Fondue
schmeckt besonders gut.

RÜCKBLICK   KAPITEL 1–3

I. Verbs

1. Forms: PRESENT TENSE

    a.   Most verbs inflect like **danken:**

singular	plural
ich dank**e**	wir dank**en**
du dank**st**	ihr dank**t**
er dank**t**	sie dank**en**

    b.   Verbs whose stem ends in **-d, -t,** or certain consonant combinations inflect like **antworten,** e.g., arbeiten, finden, kosten, öffnen, regnen.

p. 49

singular	plural
ich antwort**e**	wir antwort**en**
du antwort**est**	ihr antwort**et**
er antwort**et**	sie antwort**en**

p. 92

    c.   Some verbs have vowel changes in the second and third person singular, e.g., gefallen, tragen; essen, geben, helfen, nehmen, werden; empfehlen, lesen.

	a > ä **fahren**	au > äu **laufen**	e > i **sprechen**	e > ie **sehen**
ich	fahre	laufe	spreche	sehe
du	**fährst**	**läufst**	**sprichst**	**siehst**
er	**fährt**	**läuft**	**spricht**	**sieht**

pp. 69, 92

    d.   Some verbs are irregular in form:

	haben	sein	werden	essen	nehmen
ich	habe	**bin**	werde	esse	nehme
du	**hast**	**bist**	**wirst**	**ißt**	**nimmst**
er	**hat**	**ist**	**wird**	**ißt**	**nimmt**
wir	haben	**sind**	werden	essen	nehmen
ihr	habt	**seid**	werdet	**eßt**	nehmt
sie	haben	**sind**	werden	essen	nehmen

2. Usage

    a. German has only one verb to express what English says with several forms:

Er antwortet meinem Vater.
$\begin{cases} \textit{He answers my father.} \\ \textit{He's answering my father.} \\ \textit{He does answer my father.} \end{cases}$

p. 49

    b. The present tense occasionally expresses future time.

Im Mai fährt sie nach Aachen.
$\begin{cases} \textit{She's going to Aachen in May.} \\ \textit{She'll be going to Aachen in May.} \end{cases}$

II. Nouns and Pronouns

1. You have learned three of the four German cases.

    a. The NOMINATIVE is the case of the subject: pp. 51–52, 54

Da kommt **der Ober. Er** bringt das Essen.

It is also used for PREDICATE NOUNS following the linking verbs **heißen, sein,** and **werden.**

Der Herr	**heißt**	Oskar Meyer.
Er	**ist**	Wiener.
Er	**wird**	Vater.

    b. The ACCUSATIVE is the case of the direct object: pp. 69–72

Wir fragen **den Freund.** Wir fragen **ihn.**

It follows these prepositions: durch, für, gegen, ohne, um

    c. The DATIVE is the case of the indirect object: pp. 93–96

Rotkäppchen bringt **der Großmutter** den Wein.
Es bringt **ihr** den Wein.

It follows these prepositions: aus, außer, bei, mit, nach, seit, von, zu

It also follows these verbs: antworten, danken, gefallen, gehören, helfen.

Nouns in the dative plural have an **-n** ending unless the plural ends in **-s:**

die Freunde / den Freunde**n**   BUT   die Kulis / den Kulis

    d. N-NOUNS. Some masculine nouns have an **-n** or **-en** ending in all cases (singular and plural) except in the nominative singular. pp. 70–71, 94

der Franzose, **-n,** -n	der Mensch, **-en,** -en
der Herr, **-n,** -en	der Nachbar, **-n,** -n
der Junge, **-n,** -n	der Student, **-en,** -en

Der Junge fragt den Nachbar**n.** Der Nachbar antwortet dem Junge**n.**

RÜCKBLICK
KAPITEL 1–3

pp. 51, 70, 94

2. These are the case forms of the DEFINITE and INDEFINITE ARTICLES.

	singular			plural
	masc.	**neut.**	**fem.**	
nom.	der ein kein	das ein kein	die eine keine	die — keine
acc.	den einen keinen			
dat.	dem einem keinem	dem einem keinem	der einer keiner	den — keinen

Mein, dein, and **Ihr** follow the pattern of **ein** and **kein.**

pp. 51, 70, 94

3. These are the case forms of the INTERROGATIVE PRONOUN.

	persons	**things and ideas**
nom.	wer	was
acc.	wen	was
dat.	wem	—

III. Sentence Structure

1. Verb position

pp. 36, 54

a. In a German statement the verb must be the second GRAMMATICAL ELEMENT. The element before the verb is not necessarily the subject.

$$1 \qquad 2$$

Ich **sehe** meinen Vater morgen.
Morgen **sehe** ich meinen Vater.
Meinen Vater **sehe** ich morgen.

pp. 54, 74

b. A verb phrase consists of an INFLECTED VERB and a COMPLEMENT that completes its meaning. Such complements include predicate nouns, predicate adjectives, some accusatives, and other verbs. When the verb consists of more than one part, the inflected part (V1) is the second element in a statement, and the other part (V2) stands at the very end of the sentence.

Das	**ist**		meine Schwester.
Du	**bist**		prima.
Er	**spielt**	sehr gut	Tennis.
Jetzt	**gehen**	wir schnell	**essen.**
	V1		V2

2. Negation

a.

> nicht + (ein) = kein

| Möchten Sie **ein** Eis? | Nein, ich möchte **kein** Eis. |
| Möchten Sie Erdbeeren? | Nein, ich möchte **keine** Erdbeeren. |

pp. 75–76

b.

> S   V1   0   time expression ↑ other adverbs or adverbial phrases   V2.
> **nicht**

Wir spielen heute **nicht** mit den Kindern Tennis.

3. Clauses

Coordinate clauses are introduced by COORDINATING CONJUNCTIONS.

> aber, denn, oder, und

Coordinating conjunctions do not affect the original word order of the two sentences.   p. 76

Ich bezahle den Kaffee, **und** du bezahlst das Eis.

Wortschatzwiederholung

A. **Welches Wort kommt Ihnen in den Sinn?** *(What word comes to mind?)*

BEISPIEL: Winter
            kalt

Sprache, Fluß, Gemüse, Glas, Bäckerei, Frühstück, Suppe, Rechnung, trinken, Restaurant, Geschäft, schlafen, Sommer, Tasse, Schokoladenkuchen, Mensa, Messer, Nachtisch

B. **Geben Sie das Gegenteil!**

kaufen, fragen, kommen, nördlich, im Westen, offen, alles, toll

C. **Geben Sie den Artikel!**

Buttermilch, Bananeneis, Gurkensalat, Kartoffelsalat, Obstkuchen, Lebensmittelrechnung, Marmeladenbrot, Salatkartoffel, Weinglas, Zitronenpudding

D. **Was fehlt?**

1. Vater, Mutter und Kinder sind zusammen eine _____ .
2. In Deutschland ißt man Brot mit Wurst, Käse oder Fisch zum _____ .
3. Für Suppe, Pudding oder Eis braucht man einen _____ .
4. Orangen, Bananen, Erdbeeren und Äpfel sind _____ .
5. Karotten, Erbsen und Bohnen sind _____ .
6. Der Vater von meiner Mutter ist mein _____ , aber der Bruder von meiner Mutter ist mein _____ .
7. Zum Schreiben braucht man einen _____ oder einen _____ und ein Stück _____ .

8. Im Winter braucht man einen _____ oder eine _____ .
9. Hier essen die Studenten: _____ .
10. Hier essen die Leute Kuchen, und sie trinken Kaffee oder Tee: _____ .
11. Hier kauft man Röcke und Blusen, Jacken und Hosen, auch Schuhe:
    _____ .

Strukturwiederholung

* **E.** **Verben. Variieren Sie die Sätze!** *(Vary the German base sentence as suggested.)*

1. **Ich trinke Saft.**
   We drink juice. Do you drink juice? She doesn't drink juice.

2. **Sie antwortet den Leuten.**
   I'm answering the people. They answer the people. Does she answer the people? Answer the people. Don't answer the people. Why aren't you answering the people?

3. **Er fährt nach Berlin.**
   They're driving to Berlin. Why is she driving to Berlin? I'm not going to drive to Berlin. Are you driving to Berlin? Drive to Berlin. Don't drive to Berlin.

4. **Wir essen Fisch.**
   Who's eating fish? Are you eating fish? They don't eat fish. Eat fish.

5. **Sie werden müde.**
   I'm getting tired. She's not getting tired. Don't get tired. Who's getting tired? We're getting tired, too.

6. **Er hat Hunger.**
   I'm hungry. Are you hungry? Who's hungry? They're hungry. They're not hungry. We're hungry.

7. **Sie ist sehr groß.**
   You're very tall. They're not very tall. I'm very tall. Isn't he tall?

* **F.** **Nominativ, Akkusativ und Dativ.** Variieren Sie die Sätze!

1. **Herr Díaz ist Spanier.**
   Mr. Schmidt is (an) Austrian. No, he's from Switzerland. Is Ms. Bayer an Austrian? She's not an Austrian either. (She's also not an Austrian.) They say Ms. Klein is an American. Joe is an American, too.

2. **Hier gibt es einen Supermarkt.**
   There's a river here (a restaurant, no cafeteria, no lake). There are mountains here (bakeries, lakes, no stores, no cafés).

3. **Das Geschäft gehört den Großeltern.**
   Who does the store belong to? (To whom does the store belong?) What belongs to the grandfather? She says it doesn't belong to the brother. It doesn't belong to the aunt.

4. **Der Herr bringt der Freundin Blumen.**
   What is he bringing to the girlfriend? Who's he bringing flowers to? (To whom is he bringing flowers?) Who's bringing the flowers? Why is he bringing flowers? Isn't he bringing flowers to the girlfriend? They're bringing the children some cookies. Is she bringing the friends a bottle of wine? He's bringing the neighbors apples. I'm bringing the sisters some books.

G. **Präposition.** Kombinieren Sie die Präpositionen mit den Wörtern!

BEISPIEL: durch / Land
            durch das (durchs) Land

durch: Stadt, Zimmer / *pl.,* Kaufhaus, Supermarkt
für: Kuchen, Vater, Junge, Eltern, Familie
gegen: Leute, Restaurant, Kinder, Ober, Mensch
ohne: Essen, Speisekarte, Pudding, Herr, Freunde
um: Geschäft, Markt, Mensa, Tisch

aus: Flasche, Gläser, Supermarkt, Bäckerei, Café
außer: Bruder, Eltern, Schwester, Leute, Student
bei: Supermarkt, Familie Schmidt, Apotheke, Nachbar
mit: Herr, Freundin, Leute, Messer, Gabel
nach: Frühstück, Mittagessen, Vorlesung, Kaffee
seit: Abendessen, Frühling, Zeit
von: Ober, Tante, Kinder, Mutter, Studentin
zu: Restaurant, Mensa, Markt, Apotheke

*
H. **Verneinen Sie die Sätze mit kein oder nicht!**

1. Heute gibt es Schokoladenpudding.
2. Der Junge hilft dem Vater.
3. Sehen Sie den Ober?
4. Ich habe ein Messer.
5. Wir brauchen heute Milch.
6. Geht ihr nach Hause?
7. Haben Sie Rindsrouladen?
8. Er trinkt Kaffee.
9. Sie ißt gern Eis.
10. Joachim ist mein Freund.
11. Hast du Durst?
12. Heute ist es sehr kalt.

Feste und Daten

Renaissancefest in Augsburg

LERNZIELE

Vorschau

- Holidays and vacations

Gespräche and Wortschatz

- Celebrations and the calendar

Struktur

- Present perfect with *haben*
- Present perfect with *sein*
- Subordinate clauses

Einblicke

- German festivities and celebrations

Sprechsituationen

- Offering congratulations and best wishes
- Expressing surprise and gratitude

Holidays and Vacations

One of the most pleasant aspects of life in Germany, Switzerland, and Austria is the large number of secular and religious holidays (**Feiertage**) that are celebrated. There are, for example, two holidays each on Christmas, Easter, and Pentecost. In combination with a weekend and a couple of vacation days, these holidays make it easy to visit family in other parts of the country, to go skiing, or to go south for a few days in the sun.

Secular holidays include New Year's Eve and New Year's Day (**Silvester** and **Neujahr**), May Day or Labor Day (**Maifeiertag** or **Tag der Arbeit**), and national holidays, marked by parades, speeches, and fireworks. On October 3 (**Tag der deutschen Einheit**), Germany commemorates its reunification in 1990, and on October 26 (**Nationalfeiertag**) Austria celebrates its independence from the Allied occupation in 1955. Switzerland's **Bundesfeiertag** on August 1 is based on the country's founding in 1291. Besides Christmas (**Weihnachten**), Good Friday and Easter (**Karfreitag, Ostern**), religious holidays include Ascension Day (**Himmelfahrt**) and Pentecost (**Pfingsten**) throughout Germany, Austria, and Switzerland. Additional religious holidays, such as Epiphany (**Heilige Drei Könige**), Corpus Christi (**Fronleichnam**), and All Saints' Day (**Allerheiligen**), are observed only in those states and areas where the majority of the population is Catholic.

The combination of very generous vacations (**Urlaub**)—up to six weeks for wage earners—and of the many holidays has reduced the average number of working days in Germany to about 180 per year, compared with 230 in the United States and 260 in Japan. Germans feel that frequent holidays and generous vacations improve efficiency and productivity, but recently some concerns have arisen about the competitiveness of German workers in the global economy.

German enthusiasm for vacation travel has created some problems, such as overcrowding on highways when school vacations (**Ferien**) begin and end. To alleviate this situation, a system of rotating and staggered school vacations was developed in the various federal states, so that no state—with the exception of Bavaria—always has very late or very early vacations.

Feuerwerk *(fireworks)* zu Silvester in Berlin

Gespräche   Am Telefon

CHRISTA   Hallo, Michael!
MICHAEL   Hallo, Christa! Wie geht's dir denn?
CHRISTA   Nicht schlecht, danke. Was machst du
    am Wochenende?
MICHAEL   Nichts Besonderes. Warum?
CHRISTA   Klaus hat übermorgen Geburtstag, und wir geben eine Party.
MICHAEL   Super! Aber bist du sicher, daß Klaus übermorgen Geburtstag hat? Ich glaube,
    sein Geburtstag ist schon gewesen.
CHRISTA   Quatsch! Klaus hat am dritten Mai Geburtstag. Und Samstag ist der dritte.
MICHAEL   Na gut! Wann und wo ist die Party?
CHRISTA   Samstag um sieben bei mir.[1] Aber nichts sagen! Es ist eine Überraschung.
MICHAEL   OK! Also, bis dann!
CHRISTA   Tschüß! Mach's gut!

Klaus klingelt bei Christa

CHRISTA   Tag, Klaus! Herzlichen Glückwunsch zum Geburtstag![2]
KLAUS   Grüß dich! Danke!
MICHAEL   Ich wünsche dir alles Gute zum Geburtstag.
KLAUS   Tag, Michael! . . . Hallo, Gerda! Kurt und Sabine, ihr auch? Was macht ihr denn
    alle hier?
ALLE   Wir gratulieren dir zum Geburtstag!
KLAUS   Danke! So eine Überraschung!

Richtig oder falsch?

_____   1.   Michael hat Geburtstag.
_____   2.   Klaus hat vor einem Monat Geburtstag gehabt.
_____   3.   Am 3. Mai gibt es eine Party.
_____   4.   Die Party ist bei Christa.
_____   5.   Gerda, Kurt und Sabine kommen auch.
_____   6.   Zum Geburtstag sagt man „Grüß dich!"
_____   7.   Klaus gratuliert zum Geburtstag.
_____   8.   Die Party ist eine Überraschung für Christa.
_____   9.   Alle gratulieren.

Übrigens

1.   The Swiss, as well as most Germans, consider punctuality a great virtue. Dinner guests are expected to arrive on time, neither too early nor more than ten to fifteen minutes late.

2.   **Herzlichen Glückwunsch zum Geburtstag!** is the most accepted and popular way of saying *Happy birthday!* The first two words (or the plural, **Herzliche Glückwünsche**) suit almost any occasion, be it a birthday, an engagement, a wedding, the birth or christening of a baby, church confirmation or communion, or an anniversary. Germans make more fuss over the celebration of birthdays than do Americans. Instead of having a party given for them, they are usually expected to throw their own party for family and friends, which may be anything from just coffee and cake to an elaborate dinner party. Coming of age and special birthdays (25, 30, 40, 50, etc.) are considered particularly important—the older you get, the more so.

Das Fest, -e *(celebration, festival)*

der	Feiertag, -e	*holiday*	*die*	Ferien *(pl.)*	*vacation*
	Geburtstag, -e	*birthday*		Party, -s	*party*
	Sekt	*champagne*		Überraschung, -en	*surprise*
das	Geschenk, -e	*present*			

bekommen	*to get, receive*		singen	*to sing*
dauern	*to last (duration), take*		tanzen	*to dance*
denken	*to think*		tun[1]	*to do*
feiern	*to celebrate, party*		überraschen	*to surprise*
schenken	*to give (a present)*			

Das Datum, die Daten   *(calendar date)*

Den wievielten haben wir heute?	*What's the date today?*
Heute ist der erste Mai (1.5.).[2]	*Today is the first of May (5/1).*
Ich habe am ersten Mai (1.5.) Geburtstag.[2]	*My birthday is on the first of May.*
Die Ferien sind vom . . . bis zum . . .	*The vacation is from . . . until . . .*

1.	**erste**[3]	9.	neunte	17.	**siebzehnte**
2.	zweite	10.	zehnte	18.	achtzehnte
3.	**dritte**	11.	elfte	19.	neunzehnte
4.	vierte	12.	zwölfte	20.	zwanzigste
5.	fünfte	13.	dreizehnte	21.	einundzwanzigste
6.	sechste	14.	vierzehnte	22.	zweiundzwanzigste
7.	**siebte**	15.	fünfzehnte	30.	dreißigste
8.	**achte**	16.	**sechzehnte**		

Weiteres

am Wochenende	*on the weekend*
gerade	*just, right now*
noch	*still; else*
sicher	*sure(ly), certain(ly)*
vor einer Woche[4]	*a week ago*
vorgestern	*the day before yesterday*
gestern / morgen	*yesterday / tomorrow*
übermorgen	*the day after tomorrow*
Wie lange?	*How long?*
Mach's gut!	*Take care.*

---

[1] The present tense forms of **tun** are: **ich tue, du tust, er tut, wir tun, ihr tut, sie tun.**

[2] In writing dates, Americans give the month and then the day: *5/1 (May 1), 1/5 (January 5).* In German one usually gives the day first and then the month. The ordinal number is followed by a period: **1.5. (1. Mai), 5.1. (5. Januar).** Thus **1.5.** reads **der erste Mai,** and **5.1.** reads **der fünfte Januar.** Note the **-en** after **am, vom,** and **zum: am ersten Mai, vom neunten Juli bis zum achtzehnten August.**

[3] From 1 to 19, the ordinal numbers have a **-te(n)** ending. Starting with 20, they end in **-ste(n).** Note the irregularities within the numbers.

[4] **vor** meaning *ago* is PREpositional rather than POSTpositional as it is in English: **vor einem Monat** *(a month ago),* **vor zwei Tagen** *(two days ago).*

(zu) Ostern	*(at / for) Easter*
(zu) Weihnachten	*(at / for) Christmas*
(zu) Silvester	*(at / for) New Year's Eve*
zum Geburtstag	*(on / for) the birthday*
Herzlichen Glückwunsch zum Geburtstag!	*Happy birthday!*
Ich gratuliere dir / Ihnen zum Geburtstag!	*Congratulations on your birthday.*
Ich wünsche dir / Ihnen alles Gute!	*I wish you all the best.*

ZUM ERKENNEN: Wie geht's dir denn? *(How are you? [sg. fam.]);* nichts Besonderes *(nothing special);* Quatsch! *(Nonsense!);* na gut *(all right);* also *(well);* klingeln *(here: to ring the doorbell);* Grüß dich! *(Hi! Hello!);* So eine Überraschung! *(What a surprise!)*

Zum Thema

A. Sagen Sie das Datum!

1. **Den wievielten haben wir?** *(Chain reaction. Start with any date, then name the next two.)*

    BEISPIEL: Heute ist der 2. Juli.
    Morgen ist der 3. Juli, und übermorgen ist der 4. Juli.

2. **Nationalfeiertage in Europa** *(Say when these European countries celebrate their national holidays.)*

    BEISPIEL: Irland (3.3.)
    Der Nationalfeiertag in Irland ist am dritten März.

    a. Griechenland (25.3.) **b.** England (23.4.) **c.** Italien (2.6.) **d.** Dänemark (5.6.)
    e. Portugal (10.6.) **f.** Luxemburg (23.6.) **g.** Frankreich (14.7.) **h.** Belgien (21.7.) **i.** Deutschland (3.10.) **j.** Spanien (12.10.)

B. Was spielt wann? *(You work at the box office of the Berlin Ensemble. Give patrons information about dates and times of the upcoming performances. Read aloud.)*

BEISPIEL: Am ersten spielt *Vor Sonnenaufgang* von Hauptmann.

1. Mi.	19.30	Hauptmann Vor Sonnenaufgang
2. Do.	19.30–22.45	Brecht Der kaukasische Kreidekreis
3. Fr.	19.30–22.30	Brecht/Weill Die Dreigroschenoper
4. Sa.	19.30	Hauptmann Vor Sonnenaufgang
5. So.	19.30–22.30	Brecht Galileo Galilei
6. Mo.	19.30–22.30	Brecht Der gute Mensch von Sezuan
7. Di.	19.30–22.00	Labiche Florentiner Strohhut
8. Mi.	19.30–22.15	Zuckmayer Der Hauptmann von Köpenick
9. Do.	19.30–22.00	Brecht Baal
10. Fr.	19.30–22.15	Brecht Schweyk
11. Sa.	19.30–22.30	Brecht/Weill Die Dreigroschenoper
12. So.	19.30–22.30	Brecht/Weill Die Dreigroschenoper

C.   Tierkreiszeichen   *(Signs of the zodiac. Ask each other your birthdays, and find out what sign of the zodiac you are.)*

BEISPIEL: Wann hast du Geburtstag, und was bist du?
Ich habe am 2. Februar Geburtstag. Ich bin Wassermann.

Schütze
23.11.-21.12.

Steinbock
22.12-20.1.

Skorpion
24.10.-22.11.

Wassermann
21.1.-19.2.

Waage
24.9.-23.10.

Fisch(e)
20.2.-20.3.

Jungfrau
24.8.--23.9.

Widder
21.3.-20.4.

Löwe
23.7.-23.8.

Stier
21.4.-20.5.

Krebs
22.6.-22.7.

Zwilling(e)
21.5.-21.6.

D.   Fragen   *(Ask a classmate the following questions.)*

1.   Wie alt bist du?
2.   Was für Geschenke bekommst du gewöhnlich zum Geburtstag? Was möchtest du gern?
3.   Was für Geschenke schenkst du zum Muttertag? zum Vatertag?
4.   Welcher Feiertag gefällt dir besonders gut? Welcher Feiertag ist bald *(soon)?*

E.   Ferienkalender für deutsche Schulen

1.   Wie viele Länder gibt es in Deutschland? Wie heißen sie?
2.   Was für Ferien gibt es? Wie lange sind sie ungefähr?
3.   Wo gibt es keine Herbstferien? keine Pfingstferien?
4.   Von wann bis wann sind die Osterferien in Bayern? die Pfingstferien in Baden-Württemberg? die Sommerferien in Berlin und in Schleswig-Holstein? die Herbstferien in Niedersachsen? die Weihnachtsferien in Hessen? usw.
5.   Was für Ferien gibt es hier? Wann sind sie? Wie lange dauern sie?
6.   Wann beginnen die nächsten *(next)* Ferien? Wann enden sie? Was tun Sie dann?

Schulferien

Land	Sommer	Herbst	Weihnachten	Ostern	Pfingsten
Baden-Württemberg	11.7.-24.8.	25.10.-30.10.	23.12.- 4.1.	13.4.-25.4.	1.6.-5.6.
Bayern	25.7.- 9.9.	28.10.- 2.11.	23.12.- 7.1.	13.4.-25.4.	9.6.-20.6.
Berlin	4.7.-17.8.	26.10.- 2.11.	23.12.- 6.1.	4.4.-25.4.	6.6.- 9.6.
Brandenburg		21.10.-25.10.	23.12.- 3.1.	14.4.-16.4.	5.6.- 9.6.
Bremen	4.7.-17.8.	14.10.-19.10.	23.12.- 6.1.	1.4.-21.-4	–
Hamburg	1.7.-10.8.	7.10.-19.10.	23.12.- 4.1.	9.3.- 21.3. 16.4.-21.4.	29.5.
Hessen	1.7.-10.8.	7.10.-18.10.	23.12.-11.1.	3.4.-22.4.	–
Mecklenburg-Vorpommern		21.10.-25.10.	23.12.- 3.1.	15.4.-21.4.	5.6.- 9.6.
Niedersachsen	4.7.-14.8.	10.10.-19.10.	21.12.- 6.1.	1.4.-21.4.	6.6.- 9.6.
Nordrhein-Westfalen	18.7.-31.8.	21.10.-26.10.	23.12.- 6.1.	6.4.-25.4.	9.6.
Rheinland-Pfalz	20.6.-31.7.	21.10.-26.10.	23.12.- 8.1.	6.4.-25.4.	9.6.
Saarland	18.6.-31.7.	7.10.-19.10.	23.12.- 6.1.	13.4.-27.4.	–
Sachsen		14.10.-18.10.	23.12.- 3.1.	16.4.-24.4.	4.6.- 9.6.
Sachsen-Anhalt		21.10.-25.10.	23.12.- 6.1.	13.4.-21.4.	4.6.-10.6.
Schleswig-Holstein	28.6.-10.8.	14.10.-26.10.	23.12.- 6.1.	9.4.-25.4.	–
Thüringen		21.10.-25.10.	23.12.- 3.1.	13.4.-16.4.	5.6.- 9.6.

F. Aussprache: ch, ck *(See also III.13–15 in the pronunciation section of the Workbook.)*

1. [ç] i**ch**, di**ch**, ni**ch**t, ni**ch**ts, si**ch**er, fur**ch**tbar, viellei**ch**t, man**ch**mal, mö**ch**ten, spre**ch**en, Re**ch**nung, Mäd**ch**en, Mil**ch**, dur**ch**, gewöhnli**ch**, ri**ch**tig, wi**ch**tig, se**ch**zig

2. [x] a**ch**, a**ch**t, ma**ch**en, na**ch**, Weihna**ch**ten, Spra**ch**e, au**ch**, brau**ch**en, Wo**ch**e, no**ch**, do**ch**, Bu**ch**, Ku**ch**en

3. [ks] se**chs**, se**chs**te, Da**chs**hund

4. [k] di**ck**, Zu**ck**er, Bä**ck**er, Ro**ck**, Ja**ck**e, Frühstü**ck**, Glü**ck**wunsch, schme**ck**en

5. Wortpaare

   a. mich / misch   c. nickt / nicht   e. Nacht / nackt

   b. Kirche / Kirsche   d. lochen / locken   f. möchte / mochte

Hören Sie zu!

Die Geburtstagsparty *(Listen to the conversation between Anke and Paul. Then answer the questions below by jotting down key words.)*

ZUM ERKENNEN: Gute Idee! *(That's a good idea!);* geht's sicher *(it's probably all right)*

1. Wer hat am 10. Oktober Geburtstag? _____
   Wer hat am 12. Oktober Geburtstag? _____
2. Was möchte Paul machen? _____
3. Was tut Claire samstags bis um drei? _____
4. Wo wollen sie feiern? _____
5. Was bringt Paul? _____ und _____
   Was bringt Klaus? _____
6. Wer telefoniert mit Peter und Claire? _____
7. Wann beginnt die Party? _____

STRUKTUR

I. The Present Perfect with *haben*

1. The PRESENT PERFECT corresponds closely in form to the English present perfect. In both languages it consists of an inflected auxiliary verb (or "helping verb") and an unchanging past participle.

   *You **have learned** that well.*   Du **hast** das gut **gelernt.**
   *She **has brought** the books.*   Sie **hat** die Bücher **gebracht.**
   *We **haven't spoken** any English.*   Wir **haben** kein Englisch **gesprochen.**

2. In the USE of this tense, however, there is a considerable difference between German and English. In everyday conversation English makes more use of the simple past, whereas German prefers the present perfect.

   Du **hast** das gut **gelernt.**   *You **learned** that well.*
   Sie **hat** die Bücher **gebracht.**   *She **brought** the books.*
   Wir **haben** kein Englisch **gesprochen.**   *We **didn't speak** any English.*

   The German present perfect corresponds to four past-tense forms in English.

   Wir haben das gelernt.
   $\begin{cases} \textit{We have learned that.} \\ \textit{We learned that.} \\ \textit{We did learn that.} \\ \textit{We were learning that.} \end{cases}$

3. Most German verbs FORM the present perfect by using the present tense of **haben** (V1) with the past participle (V2). The past participle is placed at the end of the sentence or clause.

ich	**habe**	. . . gelernt	wir	**haben**	. . . gelernt
du	**hast**	. . . gelernt	ihr	**habt**	. . . gelernt
er	**hat**	. . . gelernt	sie	**haben**	. . . gelernt

4. German has two groups of verbs that form their past participles in different ways: T-VERBS (also called "weak verbs") with the participle ending in **-t** (**gelernt**), and N-VERBS (also called "strong verbs") with the participle ending in **-en** (**gesprochen**). Any verb not specifically identified as an irregular t-verb or as an n-verb can be assumed to be a regular t-verb.

   a. The majority of German verbs are regular t-verbs. They form their past participles with the prefix **ge-** and the ending **-t**. They correspond to such English verbs as *learn, learned,* and *ask, asked.*

ge + stem + t	lernen →	ge lern t

      Verbs that follow this pattern include: brauchen, danken, dauern, feiern, fragen, glauben, hören, kaufen, machen, sagen, schenken, spielen, suchen, tanzen, wohnen, zählen.

- Verbs with stems ending in **-d, -t,** or certain consonant combinations make the final **-t** audible by inserting an **-e-.**

$$\boxed{\text{ge} + \text{stem} + \text{et}} \qquad \text{kosten} \rightarrow \boxed{\text{ge kost et}}$$

Other verbs that follow this pattern include: antworten, arbeiten, öffnen, regnen.

- A few t-verbs are irregular (MIXED VERBS), i.e., they usually change their stem. They can be compared to such English verbs as *bring, brought,* and *think, thought.*

$$\boxed{\text{ge} + \text{stem (change)} + \text{t}} \qquad \text{bringen} \rightarrow \boxed{\text{ge brach t}}$$

Here are the participles of familiar irregular t-verbs:

bringen	**gebracht**	haben	**gehabt**
denken	**gedacht**		

b. A smaller but extremely important group of verbs, the N-VERBS, form their past participles with the prefix **ge-** and the ending **-en.** They correspond to such English verbs as *write, written,* and *speak, spoken.* The n-verbs frequently have a stem change in the past participle; their forms are not predictable. (Many of them also have a stem change in the second and third person singular of the present tense: **sprechen, du sprichst, er spricht.** Note: those that do have this change are always n-verbs.)

$$\boxed{\text{ge} + \text{stem (change)} + \text{en}} \qquad \begin{array}{l} \text{geben} \rightarrow \boxed{\text{ge geb en}} \\ \text{finden} \rightarrow \boxed{\text{ge fund en}} \end{array}$$

You need to learn the past participles of these n-verbs:

essen	**gegessen**	schlafen	**geschlafen**
finden	**gefunden**	schreiben	**geschrieben**
geben	**gegeben**	sehen	**gesehen**
heißen	**geheißen**	singen	**gesungen**
helfen	**geholfen**	sprechen	**gesprochen**
lesen	**gelesen**	tragen	**getragen**
liegen	**gelegen**	trinken	**getrunken**
nehmen	**genommen**	tun	**getan**
scheinen	**geschienen**		

5. Two groups of verbs have no **ge-**prefix.

a. Inseparable-prefix verbs

In English as in German, many verbs have been formed by the use of inseparable prefixes, e.g., *to belong, to impress, to proceed.* In both languages the stress is on the verb, not on the prefix. The German inseparable prefixes are **be-, emp-, ent-, er-, ge-, ver-,** and **zer-.**

$$\boxed{\begin{array}{l} \text{bestellen} \rightarrow \text{be stell t} \\ \text{verstehen} \rightarrow \text{ver stand en} \end{array}}$$

Familiar t-verbs that also follow this pattern include: bezahlen, gehören, verkaufen, überraschen, wiederholen (**über-** and **wieder-** are not always inseparable prefixes).

You will need to learn the past participles of these familiar n-verbs:

beginnen	**begonnen**	gefallen	**gefallen**
bekommen	**bekommen**	verstehen	**verstanden**
empfehlen	**empfohlen**		

b.   Verbs ending in **-ieren** (all of which are t-verbs): gratulieren, gratuliert; studieren, studiert.

Übungen

A.   Geben Sie das Partizip!

BEISPIEL: fragen   **gefragt**

1.   dauern, feiern, danken, wohnen, tanzen, antworten, kosten, öffnen, regnen, verkaufen, bezahlen, gratulieren, denken, bringen, studieren
2.   essen, finden, tun, helfen, lesen, heißen, trinken, schlafen, scheinen, singen, bekommen, empfehlen, beginnen, gefallen, verstehen

B.   Geben Sie den Infinitiv!

BEISPIEL: gebracht   **bringen**

begonnen, bekommen, bezahlt, empfohlen, geantwortet, gedacht, gefallen, gefeiert, gefunden, gegessen, geglaubt, gehabt, geholfen, gelegen, genommen, geschienen, geschrieben, gesprochen, gesucht, gesungen, getan, getrunken, gratuliert, überrascht, verkauft, verstanden

C.   Ersetzen Sie das Subjekt!

BEISPIEL: Ich habe eine Flasche Sekt gekauft. (er)
            Er hat eine Flasche Sekt gekauft.

1.   Du hast nichts gesagt. (ihr, man, ich)
2.   Ich habe auf englisch geantwortet. (wir, du, er)
3.   Er hat Klaus Geschenke gebracht. (ihr, sie / *pl.,* ich)
4.   Sie haben nur Deutsch gesprochen. (du, ihr, Robert und Silvia)

D.   Was habt ihr gemacht?   *(Tell your roommate what happened at Klaus' party.)*

BEISPIEL: Ich habe Klaus ein Buch gegeben. (schenken)
            Ich habe Klaus ein Buch geschenkt.

1.   Wir haben viel gefeiert. (tanzen, spielen, essen, tun, servieren)
2.   Christa und Joachim haben Kuchen gekauft. (bestellen, nehmen)
3.   Susanne hat Klaus gratuliert. (danken, glauben, helfen, überraschen, suchen)
4.   Klaus hat viel gegessen. (arbeiten, trinken, singen, bekommen)
5.   Wie gewöhnlich hat Peter nur gelesen. (schlafen, lernen, sprechen)
6.   Sabine hat Helmut nicht gesehen. (fragen, antworten, schreiben)

E.   Auf deutsch, bitte!

1.   She was still sleeping.
2.   They helped, too.
3.   Have you (3×) already eaten?
4.   Did you (*formal*) find it?
5.   I didn't understand that.
6.   Have you (*sg. fam.*) read that?
7.   I repeated the question.
8.   Who took it?
9.   They bought winter coats.
10.   My aunt recommended the store.
11.   Did you (*pl. fam.*) sell the books?
12.   I was paying the bills.

II. Present Perfect with *sein*

Whereas most German verbs use **haben** as the auxiliary in the perfect tenses, a few common verbs use **sein.** You will probably find it easiest to memorize **sein** together with the past participles of those verbs requiring it. However, you can also determine which verbs take **sein** by remembering that they must fulfill two conditions:

- They are INTRANSITIVE, i.e., they cannot take an accusative (direct) object. Examples of such verbs are: **gehen, kommen, laufen,** and **fahren.**

- They express a CHANGE OF PLACE OR CONDITION. **Sein** and **bleiben** are exceptions to this rule.

Wir **sind** nach Hause **gegangen**.	*We went home.*
Er **ist** müde **geworden**.	*He got tired.*
Ich **bin** zu Hause **geblieben**.	*I stayed home.*

Caution: A change in prefix may cause a change in auxiliary because the meaning of the verb changes.

Ich **bin** nach Hause **gekommen.**	*I came home.*
Ich **habe** ein Geschenk **bekommen.**	*I received a present.*

The present perfect of the following verbs is formed with the present tense of **sein** (V1) and the past participle (V2).

ich	**bin** . . . gekommen	wir	**sind** . . . gekommen
du	**bist** . . . gekommen	ihr	**seid** . . . gekommen
er	**ist** . . . gekommen	sie	**sind** . . . gekommen

The following verbs form the present perfect with **sein.** They are all n-verbs, although some t-verbs also take **sein.**

sein	**ist gewesen**	kommen	**ist gekommen**
bleiben	**ist geblieben**	laufen	**ist gelaufen**
gehen	**ist gegangen**	werden	**ist geworden**
fahren	**ist gefahren**		

Occasionally **fahren** takes an object. In that case the auxiliary **haben** is used:

Sie **sind** nach Hause **gefahren.**	*They drove home.*
Sie **haben** mein Auto nach Hause **gefahren.**	*They drove my car home.*

Übungen

F. Sein oder haben? Geben Sie das Partizip!

BEISPIEL: empfehlen   **hat empfohlen**
             gehen   **ist gegangen**

essen, bringen, werden, sein, gefallen, bleiben, liegen, sprechen, laufen, helfen

G. Ersetzen Sie das Subjekt!

BEISPIEL: Sie ist gerade gegangen. (sie / *pl.*)
             Sie sind gerade gegangen.

1. Ihr seid zu lange auf der Party geblieben. (du, ich, wir, er)
2. Er ist spät nach Hause gekommen. (ich, Sie, du, ihr)
3. Wir sind mit Reinhold gefahren. (ich, ihr, du, er)
4. Sie sind müde gewesen. (ihr, sie / *sg.,* du, ich)

H. Auf deutsch, bitte!

1. Have you (*pl. fam.*) eaten?—No, we haven't had time till now.
2. Did you like the restaurant, Uncle Georg?—Yes, the food tasted good.
3. Where have you been, Andrea?—I drove to the supermarket.
4. Did you buy the book, Mom (**Mutti**)?—No, the bookstore was closed.
5. What did you get for your birthday, Kirsten?—My parents gave me a watch.
6. When did you (*pl. fam.*) get home?—I don't know. It got very late.

I. Sommerferien   (*Michael is explaining what he did during his last summer vacation. Use the present perfect. In each case decide whether to use the auxiliary* **haben** *or* **sein.***)

BEISPIEL: Im August habe ich Ferien.
             Im August habe ich Ferien gehabt.

1. In den Ferien fahre ich nach Zell.
2. Ich nehme zwei Wochen frei.
3. Ich wohne bei Familie Huber.
4. Das Haus liegt direkt am See.
5. Zell gefällt mir gut.
6. Nachmittags laufe ich in die Stadt.
7. Manchmal gehen wir auch ins Café.
8. Das Café gehört Familie Huber.
9. Mittwochs hilft Renate da.
10. Renate bringt mir (*me*) oft Kuchen.
11. Ich bekomme alles frei.
12. Sie empfiehlt die Sahnetorte.
13. Die schmeckt wirklich gut.
14. Den Apfelstrudel finde ich besonders gut.
15. Renate ist in den Sommerferien bei uns.
16. Wir werden gute Freunde.
17. Leider regnet es viel.
18. Wir lesen viel und hören Musik.

J. Interview   (*Find out the following information from your classmate and then tell the class what he / she said.*)

1. wann er / sie gestern ins Bett (*to bed*) gegangen ist
2. ob er / sie viel für die Deutschstunde gelernt hat
3. wie er / sie geschlafen hat und wie lange
4. was er / sie heute zum Frühstück gegessen und getrunken hat
5. wie er / sie zur Uni(versität) gekommen ist, ob er / sie gelaufen oder gefahren ist
6. wie viele Vorlesungen er / sie heute schon gehabt hat und welche

III. Subordinate Clauses

You already know how to join sentences with a coordinating conjunction. Clauses can also be joined with SUBORDINATING CONJUNCTIONS. Subordinating conjunctions introduce a subordinate or dependent clause, i.e., a statement with a subject and a verb that cannot stand alone as a complete sentence.

because it's his birthday
that they have left already

While coordinating conjunctions do not affect word order, subordinating conjunctions do. German subordinate clauses are always set off by a COMMA, and the inflected verb (V1) stands at the very end.

1. Six common subordinating conjunctions are:

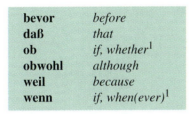

bevor	*before*
daß	*that*
ob	*if, whether*[1]
obwohl	*although*
weil	*because*
wenn	*if, when(ever)*[1]

Ich ⎡kaufe⎤ ein Geschenk.
Ich frage Helga, **bevor** ich ein Geschenk **kaufe.**
I'll ask Helga before I buy a present.

Klaus ⎡hat⎤ Geburtstag.
Sie sagt, **daß** Klaus morgen Geburtstag **hat.**
She says that Klaus has a birthday tomorrow.

⎡Ist⎤ sie sicher?
Ich frage, **ob** sie sicher **ist.**
I ask whether she is sure.

Sie ⎡hat⎤ nicht viel Zeit.
Sie kommt zur Party, **obwohl** sie nicht viel Zeit **hat.**
She's coming to the party although she doesn't have much time.

Er ⎡trinkt⎤ gern Sekt.
Wir bringen eine Flasche Sekt, **weil** er gern Sekt **trinkt.**
We are bringing a bottle of champagne because he loves to drink champagne.

Ich ⎡habe⎤ Zeit.
Ich komme auch, **wenn** ich Zeit **habe.**
I'll come, too, if I have time.

Note that the subject of the dependent clause almost always follows the subordinating conjunction. When a sentence with inverted word order becomes a dependent clause, the subject moves to the position immediately after the conjunction.

Morgen hat **Klaus** Geburtstag.
Ich glaube, daß **Klaus morgen** Geburtstag hat.

---

[1]When it is possible to replace *if* with *whether,* use **ob;** otherwise use **wenn.**

2. Information questions can become subordinate clauses by using the question word (**wer? was? wie? wo?** etc.) as a conjunction and putting the verb last.

Wie [schmeckt] der Salat? ▼
Sie fragt, **wie** der Salat **schmeckt.**
She asks how the salad tastes.

Wo [sind] die Brötchen? ▼
Sie fragt, **wo** die Brötchen **sind.**
She asks where the rolls are.

Note the similarity with English:

Where [are] the rolls? ▼
*She asks **where** the rolls **are.***

3. Yes / no questions require **ob** as a conjunction.

Schmeckt der Salat gut?
Sie fragt, **ob** der Salat gut schmeckt.
She asks whether the salad tastes good.

Sind die Würstchen heiß?
Sie fragt, **ob** die Würstchen heiß sind.
She asks whether the franks are hot.

4. Subordinate Clauses as the First Sentence Element

If the subordinate clause precedes the main clause, the inflected verb of the main clause—the second sentence element—comes right after the comma. In that case, the subordinate clause is the first sentence element.

1   2

Ich **komme,** wenn ich Zeit habe.
Wenn ich Zeit habe, **komme** ich.

5. The Present Perfect in Subordinate Clauses

In subordinate clauses in the present perfect, the inflected verb **haben** or **sein** (V1) stands at the end of the sentence.

Er hat ein Radio bekommen.
Er sagt, **daß** er ein Radio bekommen **hat.**

Er ist überrascht gewesen.
Er sagt, **daß** er überrascht gewesen **ist.**

When listening or reading, pay special attention to the end of the sentence, which often contains crucial sentence elements. As Mark Twain said in *A Connecticut Yankee in King Arthur's Court,* "Whenever the literary German dives into a sentence, that is the last we are going to see of him till he emerges on the other side of his Atlantic with his verb in his mouth."

K.   Verbinden Sie die Sätze!

BEISPIEL: Eva geht zur Bäckerei. Sie braucht noch etwas Brot. *(because)*
Eva geht zur Bäckerei, weil sie noch etwas Brot braucht.

1.   Der Herr fragt die Studentin. Kommt sie aus Amerika? *(whether)*
2.   Die Stadt gefällt den Amerikanern. Sie ist alt und romantisch. *(because)*
3.   Eine Tasse Kaffee tut gut. Man ist müde. *(when)*
4.   Zählen Sie alles! Sie bezahlen die Rechnung. *(before)*
5.   Wir spielen nicht Tennis. Das Wetter ist schlecht. *(if)*
6.   Sie hat geschrieben. Sie ist in Österreich gewesen. *(that)*
7.   Ich habe Hunger. Ich habe gerade ein Eis gegessen. *(although)*
8.   Ich arbeite bei Tengelmann. Ich brauche Geld. *(because)*

L.   Sagen Sie die Sätze noch einmal!

1.   **Er sagt, daß ...**   *(A friend has just come back from Luxembourg. Tell the class what he has observed. Follow the model.)*

BEISPIEL: Luxemburg ist wirklich schön.
Er sagt, daß Luxemburg wirklich schön ist.

a. Die Luxemburger sprechen Französisch, Deutsch und Letzeburgisch.
b. Letzeburgisch ist der Luxemburger Dialekt.   **c.** Er hat den Geburtstag auf einer Burg *(in a castle)* gefeiert.   **d.** Das ist einfach toll gewesen.   **e.** In Luxemburg gibt es viele Banken.   **f.** Den Leuten geht es wirklich sehr gut.
g. Überall sieht man BMWs und Citroëns.

2.   **Sie fragt, ...**   *(Your mother wants to know about Carla's graduation party. Follow the model.)*

BEISPIEL: Wer ist Carla?
Sie fragt, wer Carla ist.

a. Wo wohnt Carla?   **b.** Wie viele Leute sind da gewesen?   **c.** Wie lange hat die Party gedauert?   **d.** Was habt ihr gegessen und getrunken?   **e.** Mit wem hast du getanzt?   **f.** Wie bist du nach Hause gekommen?

3.   **Er fragt, ob ...**   *(Your parents are celebrating their 30th anniversary and your sister is in charge of the party. Now she asks whether you and your brothers have completed the tasks she assigned a week ago.)*

BEISPIEL: Hast du Servietten gekauft?
Sie fragt, ob du Servietten gekauft hast.

a. Seid ihr gestern einkaufen gegangen?   **b.** Hat Alfred Sekt gekauft?
c. Haben wir jetzt alle Geschenke?   **d.** Habt ihr den Kuchen beim Bäcker *(baker)* bestellt?   **e.** Hat Peter mit den Nachbarn gesprochen?   **f.** Hat Alfred die Kamera gefunden?

M. Beginnen Sie mit dem Nebensatz! *(Begin with the subordinate clause.)*

BEISPIEL: Ich trinke Wasser, wenn ich Durst habe.
Wenn ich Durst habe, trinke ich Wasser.

1. Ich habe ein Stück Käse gegessen, weil ich Hunger gehabt habe.
2. Ich verstehe nicht, warum die Lebensmittel Farbstoffe brauchen.
3. Ihr habt eine Party gegeben, weil ich 21 geworden bin.
4. Ich finde (es) prima, daß ihr nichts gesagt habt.
5. Ich bin nicht müde, obwohl wir bis morgens um sechs gefeiert haben.

Zusammen-fassung

N.   Was haben Sie gestern gemacht? Schreiben Sie acht Sätze im Perfekt!

BEISPIEL: Ich habe bis 10 Uhr geschlafen. Dann . . .

O.   Die Party

1. **Wir planen eine Party.** *(With one or several partners, work out a plan for your cousin's graduation party. Be prepared to outline your ideas.)*

   Sagen Sie, . . . !

   a. wann und wo die Party ist   **b.** wie lange sie dauert   **c.** wer kommt
   d. was Sie trinken und essen   **e.** was Sie noch brauchen

2. **Wie ist die Party gewesen?** *(Describe what happened at the party.)*

P.   Die Geburtstagsparty. Auf deutsch, bitte!

1. The day before yesterday I gave a birthday party.   **2.** Did Volker and Bettina come?   **3.** Yes, they came, too.   **4.** Everybody (**alle**) brought presents.   **5.** My father opened a bottle of champagne.   **6.** How long did you *(pl. fam.)* celebrate?   **7.** Until three o'clock. We danced, ate well, and drank a lot of Coke.   **8.** The neighbors said that the music was too loud (**laut**).   **9.** Did you *(sg. fam.)* hear that?   **10.** Yesterday a neighbor came and spoke with my parents.   **11.** I liked the party.

Studying Verbs

The main difference between verbs in English and in German is the personal endings. The best way to master them is through frequent practice, such as pattern drills. It may also help to write out some charts on cards (see Appendix pp. 437–440) that you can review easily.

When it comes to learning the principal parts of n-verbs, memorization and frequent review are necessary. Use the lists of principal parts in the Appendix, checking off verbs as they are presented in the text.

Festzug in Bad Ems

EINBLICKE

Karnevalumzug
(. . . *parade*) in Köln

Germany is a thoroughly modern industrial society, no less so than the United States or Canada. It is also a country with a long history and many traditions with roots in various historical periods and events. Some of these are carried on, no doubt, not only out of reverence for tradition, but also to foster tourism, which accounts for a considerable part of the healthy trade balance.

The **Oktoberfest** in Munich, the world's biggest beer festival, is attended by several million visitors each year. It started with a royal wedding more than 150 years ago. Similar events on a much smaller scale take place elsewhere, with carrousels and game booths for children and young adults. In late summer and early fall, wine festivals (**Winzerfeste**) are celebrated in wine-growing regions, especially along the Rhine, Main, and Moselle rivers. Wine production, too, is economically significant.

Some towns attract visitors by recreating historical events in their carefully preserved surroundings: The **Meistertrunk** in Rothenburg ob der Tauber recalls an event from the Thirty Years' War (1618–1648); Landshut involves many of its citizens in the reenactment of the 1475 wedding of the son of Duke Ludwig to a Polish princess (**Fürstenhochzeit**); and the *Play of the Pied Piper* in Hameln commemorates the Children's Crusade of 1284 when 130 children of the city mysteriously vanished.

Carnival time, which starts in January and ends with Ash Wednesday, has its roots in the pre-Christian era. Its purpose was to exorcise the demons of winter. Celebrated in the South as **Fasching** and along the Rhine as **Karneval**, it ends just before Lent with parades and merry-making in the streets. Such picturesque events have parallels in other cultures and are but one aspect of life in Germany.

das	Lied, -er	*song*
die	Kerze, -n	*candle*

dort	*(over) there*
eigentlich	*actual(ly)*
ein bißchen	*some, a little bit*
immer	*always*
laut	*loud, noisy*
lustig	*funny, amusing*
(noch) nie	*never, never before*
verrückt	*crazy*
fallen (fällt), ist gefallen	*to fall*
Glück (Pech) haben, gehabt	*to be (un)lucky*
Spaß machen[1]	*to be fun*
studieren[2]	*to study a particular field, be a student at a university*

WORTSCHATZ 2

»Ich tue, was mir Spaß macht«

[1] Das **macht Spaß.** *(It's fun.)* Tanzen **macht Spaß.** *(Dancing is fun.)*
[2] Ich **studiere** *(I am a student)* in Heidelberg. Ich **studiere** Philosophie. BUT Ich **lerne** *(I'm learning / studying)* Vokabeln.

WAS IST DAS?   der Prinz, Studentenball, Vampir; das Kostüm, Musikinstrument, Weihnachtsessen, Weihnachtslied; die Adventszeit, Brezel, Kontaktlinse, Konversationsstunde, Prinzessin, Weihnachtsdekoration, Weihnachtszeit; Ende Juli; ins Bett fallen; authentisch, enorm, erst, exakt, historisch, Hunderte von, wunderschön

Deutsche Feste

(Carolyn berichtet° für die Konversationsstunde.)   *reports*

Wie ihr gehört habt, habe ich gerade ein Jahr in Deutschland studiert. Ich bin erst° vor   *only*
einem Monat wieder nach Hause gekommen, weil ich dort mit der Uni erst Ende Juli fertig
5   geworden bin. Es ist wunderschön gewesen. Ich habe viel gesehen und viel gelernt. Heute
habe ich ein paar Bilder gebracht.

Im September bin ich mit Freunden beim Winzerfest° in Bacharach am Rhein gewe-   *vintage festival*
sen[1]. Da haben wir Wein getrunken, gesungen und getanzt. Ich habe immer gedacht, daß
die Deutschen etwas steif° sind. Aber nicht, wenn sie feiern! So lustig und verrückt habe   *stiff*
10   ich sie° noch nie gesehen. Zwei Wochen später sind wir zum Oktoberfest nach München   *them*
gefahren. Im Bierzelt° haben wir Brezeln gegessen und natürlich auch Bier getrunken. Die   *... tent*
Musik ist mir ein bißchen zu laut gewesen. Was mir aber besonders gefallen hat, war° der   *was*
Trachtenzug°[2] zur Wies'n°.   *parade in traditional costumes / (festival) grounds*

Halloween gibt es in Deutschland nicht, aber dafür° gibt es im Februar den Fasching.   *instead*
15   Das ist so etwas wie° Mardi Gras in New Orleans, mit Umzügen° und Kostümen. Ich bin   *like / parades*
als Vampir zu einem Studentenball gegangen. Wir haben lange getanzt, und morgens bin
ich dann todmüde° ins Bett gefallen.   *dead-tired*

Außer diesen° Festen gibt es natürlich noch viele Feiertage.[3] Weihnachten war° beson-   *these / was*
ders schön. Beim Christkindlmarkt in Nürnberg[4] gibt es Hunderte von Buden° mit Weih-   *booths*
20   nachtsdekorationen, Spielzeug°, Lebkuchen° und auch Buden mit Glühwein°. Den Weih-   *toys / gingerbread / mulled wine*
nachtsengel° habe ich dort gekauft, und der Nußknacker° und die Weihnachtspyramide   *... angel / nutcracker*
kommen aus dem Erzgebirge. In der Adventszeit hat man nur einen Adventskranz°. Den   *... wreath*

Beim Münchner Oktoberfest

. . . tree Weihnachtsbaum° sehen die Kinder erst am 24. Dezember, am Heiligabend. Aber dann bleibt er bis zum 6. Januar im Zimmer.

their Zu Weihnachten bin ich bei Familie Fuchs gewesen. Die Kerzen auf ihrem° Baum sind 25
real / dangerous / festive echt° gewesen. Ich habe das etwas gefährlich° gefunden, aber es ist sehr festlich°. Bevor das Christkind[5] die Geschenke gebracht hat, haben wir Weihnachtslieder gesungen. Am 25. und 26. Dezember sind alle Geschäfte zu. Die zwei Feiertage sind nur für Familie und Freunde. Das finde ich eigentlich gut. Zum Weihnachtsessen hat es übrigens Gans° mit
goose
red cabbage / dumplings Rotkraut° und Knödeln° gegeben. Die Weihnachtsplätzchen und der Stollen[5] haben mir 30 besonders gut geschmeckt.

at midnight / church bells Silvester habe ich mit Freunden gefeiert. Um Mitternacht° haben alle Kirchenglocken°
rang / Happy New Year! geläutet°, und wir haben mit Sekt und „Prost Neujahr!"° das neue Jahr begonnen.

Das Bild hier ist von der Fürstenhochzeit in Landshut. Da bin ich im Juni gewesen.
forget / medieval Das vergesse° ich nie. Viele Landshuter haben mittelalterliche° Kleidung getragen, und 35
really authentic / knights alles ist ganz echt° gewesen: die Ritter°, Prinzen und Prinzessinnen, die Musikinstrumente

Christkindlmarkt in Nürnberg

Landshuter
Fürstenhochzeit

und Turniere°. Man ist historisch so exakt, daß Leute mit Brillen° Kontaktlinsen tragen,   *tournaments / glasses*
weil es im Mittelalter° noch keine Brillen gegeben hat. Übrigens habe ich Glück gehabt,   *Middle Ages*
weil man das Fest nur alle° vier Jahre feiert.   *every*

40   Ich habe immer gedacht, daß die Deutschen viel arbeiten. Das tun sie, aber sie haben
auch enorm viele Feiertage[3], viel mehr als° wir. Und Feiern in Deutschland macht Spaß.   *more than*

A.   Was hat Carolyn gesagt?   *(Match the sentence fragments from the two groups.)*   **Zum Text**

_____ 1. Wie ihr gehört habt,

_____ 2. Ich bin erst vor einem
            Monat wieder nach
            Hause gekommen,

_____ 3. Ich habe immer gedacht,

_____ 4. Im Bierzelt haben wir

_____ 5. Der Weihnachtsbaum
            bleibt

_____ 6. Bevor das Christkind die
            Geschenke gebracht hat,

_____ 7. Was mir besonders gut
            gefallen hat,

_____ 8. Man ist historisch so
            exakt,

a. haben wir Weihnachtslieder gesungen.

b. war der Trachtenzug.

c. Brezeln gegessen.

d. bis zum 6. Januar im Zimmer.

e. weil ich dort mit der Uni erst Ende
    Juli fertig geworden bin.

f. daß Leute mit Brillen Kontaktlinsen
    tragen.

g. habe ich gerade ein Jahr in Deutsch-
    land studiert.

h. daß die Deutschen etwas steif sind.

B.   Feiern in Deutschland   *(Complete these sentences with the appropriate verb in the present perfect.)*

bringen, fahren, feiern, gefallen, gehen, haben, kaufen, kommen, sein, studieren

1. Carolyn _____ vor einem Monat nach Hause _____ . **2.** Sie _____ ein Jahr in Deutschland _____ . **3.** Es _____ wunderbar _____ . **4.** Sie _____ ein paar Bilder in die Deutschstunde _____ . **5.** Im September _____ sie mit Freunden zum Winzerfest nach Bacharach _____ . **6.** Im Fasching _____ sie als Vampir zu einem Studentenball _____ . **7.** Die Weihnachtszeit _____ Carolyn besonders gut _____ . **8.** In Nürnberg _____ sie einen Weihnachtsengel _____ . **9.** Sie _____ Weihnachten bei der Familie Fuchs _____ . **10.** Mit der Landshuter Fürstenhochzeit _____ sie Glück, _____ , weil man das Fest nur alle vier Jahre feiert.

C.   Interview.   Fragen Sie einen Nachbarn / eine Nachbarin, . . .!

1.   wie und wo er / sie das (Ernte)dankfest *(Thanksgiving)* feiert
2.   wie er / sie gewöhnlich Weihnachten (oder Hannukah) feiert
3.   wie und wo er / sie das letzte Silvester gefeiert hat
4.   ob er / sie zum 4. Juli auch Kracher *(firecrackers)* gehabt oder ein Feuerwerk gesehen hat

D.   Schriftliche Übung   *(Jot down some key words about two of the holidays Carolyn mentions, then write three to five sentences about each.)*

BEISPIEL: Winzerfest
            Bacharach am Rhein, September, Wein, singen

Carolyn ist zum Winzerfest nach Bacharach gefahren. Bacharach liegt am Rhein. Das Winzerfest ist im September. Die Leute haben Wein getrunken, gesungen und getanzt. Es ist sehr lustig gewesen.

E.   Plätzchen für die Feiertage: Spritzgebäck

1.   **Lesen Sie das Rezept!**

175 g° Butter oder Margarine	1 Eigelb
100 g° Zucker	300 g° Mehl°
1 Teelöffel Vanille	¼ Teelöffel Salz

¾ cup
½ cup / 2 cups / flour

350°F / preheat / cream until fluffy
add / sift / mix
dough / cookie press / put / different
greased / cookie sheet / press

Erst Ofen auf 175–190 Grad° wärmen°. Butter schaumig rühren°, Zucker, Vanille und Eigelb dazu geben°. Mehl und Salz sieben° und in die Masse geben, gut mischen°. Den Teig° in eine Teigspritze° füllen° und verschiedene° Formen auf ein gefettetes° Backblech° spritzen°. Acht bis zehn Minuten backen, oder bis die Plätzchen braun werden.

Guten Appetit!

2.   **Wie haben Sie die Plätzchen gemacht?**   *(Tell your classmates how you made these cookies. Except for **backen / gebacken**, all new verbs in this recipe are t-verbs.)*

BEISPIEL: Erst habe ich den Ofen auf 175 Grad gewärmt. Dann habe ich . . .

Hören Sie zu!

Straßenfest *(Listen to what Bibi tells Matthias about their local street fair. Then select the correct response from those given below.)*

ZUM ERKENNEN: Was gibt's? *(What's up?)*; niemand *(nobody)*; Krimskrams *(this and that)*; Spiele *(games)*; jung *(young)*

1. Matthias ist bei Bibi gewesen, aber niemand hat ____ geöffnet.
   a. das Fenster   b. die Garage   c. die Tür

2. Bei Bibi hat es am ____ ein Straßenfest gegeben.
   a. Freitag   b. Samstag   c. Sonntag

3. Bibi findet das eigentlich ____ ganz gut.
   a. nie   b. immer   c. noch

4. Bibi hat mit ____ beim Straßenfest geholfen.
   a. Matthias   b. den Eltern   c. dem Bruder

5. Der Vater hat ____ .
   a. Würstchen verkauft   b. mit den Kindern gespielt
   c. mit den Tischen und Stühlen geholfen

6. Abends haben die Leute ein bißchen ____ .
   a. Pech gehabt   b. getanzt   c. geschlafen

There are two types of street festivals: the more professional ones held in downtown districts where during business hours local merchants join together to stage a festival in their immediate vicinity, and the do-it-yourself festivals in smaller neighborhoods where the party keeps hopping until way past midnight. In this case, the municipal authorities will establish a curfew to protect the peace and quiet of those neighbors who don't take part.

Übrigens

1. Germany's largest wine festival, the Sausage Fair **(Wurstmarkt)** in Bad Dürkheim—between Mannheim and Kaiserslautern—dates back to the year 1442 and attracts more than 500,000 visitors annually. Aside from Bacharach, big wine festivals are also held in Koblenz, Mainz, Assmannshausen, Trier, and Bingen.

2. The old folk costumes **(Trachten)** are still worn in rural areas of Germany, Austria, and Switzerland, but only on church holidays, for weddings, and on similar occasions. Special clubs **(Trachtenvereine)** try to keep the tradition alive.

3. Germans don't have a Thanksgiving Holiday with traditional foods like cranberry sauce and pumpkin pie. Instead, churches and rural communities celebrate Harvest Thanksgiving **(Erntedankfest)** with special services and harvest wreaths.

4. Nuremberg's outdoor **Christkindlmarkt** is the largest German Christmas market. Over two million people visit it during the four weeks before Christmas. Booths offer Christmas decorations, candy, toys, etc. The smell of hot punch, burnt almonds, and roasted chestnuts is in the air, and there are performances by choirs and instrumentalists. Nuremberg is also the source of the fancy gingerbread called **Nürnberger Lebkuchen.**

5. In Germany, Christmas includes a late afternoon or midnight church service on Christmas Eve **(Heiligabend)**. Presents, usually not wrapped but displayed on tables, are exchanged on Christmas Eve. In southern Germany the **Christbaum** and gifts are brought by the **Christkind;** in northern Germany the **Weihnachtsbaum** is brought by the **Weihnachtsmann.** No Christmas is complete without the traditional **Weihnachtsplätzchen** and especially **Stollen,** a fragrant buttery yeast bread filled with almonds, currants, raisins, and candied citrus peel.

SPRECHSITUATIONEN

Offering Congratulations and Best Wishes

What do you say to wish someone well on a birthday or a similar occasion, or a special holiday? Here are some useful expressions.

Ich gratuliere dir / Ihnen zum Geburtstag.
Alles Gute zum Geburtstag!
Herzlichen Glückwunsch zum Geburtstag!
Herzliche Glückwünsche! *(Best wishes.)*

Ich wünsche dir / Ihnen . . .
Fröhliche Weihnachten!
Frohe Ostern!
Ein gutes neues Jahr!
Ein schönes Wochenende!
Alles Gute!
Viel Glück (und Gesundheit)!
Gute Besserung! *(Get well soon.)*

365 Tage Gesundheit und Glück

♥ 52 Wochen Lebensfreude und Liebe

12 Monate reichlich Geld und Erfolg

Expressing Surprise

Here are a few ways to express surprise.

So eine Überraschung!
Das ist aber eine Überraschung!
Toll!
Wirklich?
Das ist ja unglaublich! *(That's unbelievable.)*
Das gibt's doch nicht! *(I don't believe it!)*

Zum Geburtstag
herzliche Glückwünsche

Expressing Gratitude

There are many ways to express your gratitude:

Danke! / Danke sehr! / Danke schön!
Vielen Dank! / Herzlichen Dank!

Appropriate responses include:

Bitte! / Bitte bitte! / Bitte sehr! / Bitte schön!
Nichts zu danken! *(My pleasure.)*
Gern geschehen! *(Glad to . . .)*

A.   **Was sagen Sie?**   *(Use the appropriate expression for each of the following situations.)*

1. Ein Freund oder eine Freundin hat heute Geburtstag.
2. Sie haben Geburtstag. Ein Freund oder eine Freundin aus der Oberschule *(high school)* telefoniert und gratuliert Ihnen.
3. Sie schreiben Ihrer Großmutter zu Weihnachten.
4. Sie haben einen Aufsatz *(paper)* geschrieben. Sie haben nicht viel Zeit gebraucht und doch ein „A" bekommen.
5. Sie haben mit einer Freundin in einem Restaurant gegessen. Die Freundin zahlt fürs Essen.
6. Sie sind im Supermarkt gewesen und haben viel gekauft. Die Tür zu Ihrem Studentenheim ist zu. Ein Student öffnet Ihnen die Tür.
7. Ihre Eltern haben Ihnen etwas Schönes zu Weihnachten geschenkt.
8. Sie haben eine Million Dollar gewonnen.
9. Sie danken Ihrem Zimmernachbarn, weil er Ihnen geholfen hat. Was antwortet der Nachbar?
10. Ein Freund fragt, ob Sie zu einer Party kommen möchten.
11. Ihre beste Freundin sagt, daß sie im Herbst ein Jahr nach Deutschland geht.
12. Sie studieren in Deutschland. Ein deutscher Student fragt, ob Sie Weihnachten bei seiner *(his)* Familie feiern möchten.
13. Sie haben Weihnachten bei Familie Schmidt gefeiert. Sie fahren wieder nach Hause. Was sagen Sie zu Herrn und Frau Schmidt?
14. Ihr Vetter hat die Grippe *(flu).*

B.   **Kurzgespräche**

1. One of your very best friends has been quite sick. You stop by to visit. Your friend expresses his / her surprise. You have also brought a little present (a book, flowers, cookies, for example). Your friend is very pleased and thanks you. You respond appropriately and wish him / her a speedy recovery.

2. Your parents call you up and ask whether you have plans for the weekend. They are driving through the town where you are studying and would like to see you (**dich**). You are surprised and pleased. It is your mother's birthday, and you wish her a happy birthday. Tell her you have bought a present and that she'll get it when they come. You conclude the conversation.

KAPITEL 5

In der Stadt

Blick auf *(view of)* Wien vom Schloß Belvedere

LERNZIELE

Vorschau
- Focus on Austria

Gespräche and Wortschatz
- City life and asking for directions

Struktur
- Personal pronouns
- Modal auxiliary verbs
- *Sondern* vs. *aber*

Einblicke
- A trip to Vienna

Sprechsituationen
- Getting someone's attention
- Asking for directions
- Understanding directions

Focus on Austria

LAND.   Approximately 32,400 square miles, about the size of Maine.

PEOPLE.   About 7.6 million. 98% German-speaking; ethnic minorities include some 50,000 Croats in the Burgenland, 20,000 Slovenes in southern Carinthia, and small groups of Hungarians, Czechs, Slovaks, and Italians. Major religions: 84% Catholic, 6% Protestant, 4% other.

GEOGRAPHY.   The Alps are the dominant physical feature, covering all of the narrow western part of the country and much of its central region and the South. The Danube Valley and the open Vienna Basin lie in the northeastern part of Austria.

CURRENCY.   Schilling, 1 ÖS = 100 Groschen.

PRINCIPAL CITIES.   Vienna (pop. 1.6 million, capital); Graz (pop. 243,000), Linz (pop. 200,000); Salzburg (pop. 140,000); Innsbruck (pop. 120,000).

The history of Austria and that of the Habsburg family were closely linked for nearly 650 years. In 1273 Rudolf von Habsburg was the first of the dynasty to be elected the head of the Holy Roman Empire (962–1806). Over the course of several centuries, the Habsburg empire grew to include Flanders, Burgundy, Bohemia, Hungary, and large areas of the Balkans. These acquisitions were made not only through wars but also through shrewd marriages (**Heiratspolitik**). The Holy Roman Empire ended with the Napoleonic wars, but members of the Habsburg family ruled the Austro-Hungarian empire until 1918, when Austria was declared a republic (**Republik Österreich**).

Present-day Austria is but a fraction of the multi-national empire it was before World War I: in 1918 Czechoslovakia, Hungary, Yugoslavia, and Rumania achieved their independence. Austria now extends only about 350 miles from east to west. In 1938, after several political and economic crises, Austria was annexed into Hitler's Third Reich. After World War II it was occupied by the allies, but it regained its sovereignty in 1955, pledged to armed neutrality—during the Cold War it was neither a member of the Warsaw Pact nor of NATO.

Since the end of World War II, Austria has been deeply involved in international humanitarian relief efforts, granting temporary or permanent asylum to two million people from more than thirty countries. Its decision to allow East German refugees to enter through its border with Hungary was a contributing factor in the fall of the East German government. Austria spends more on cultural subsidies than on its military. In addition, it is an active member of the United Nations and the site of numerous international conferences. In 1995 it is expected to join the European Union (EU).

In der Altstadt von Wien

Gespräche   Entschuldigen Sie! Wo ist . . . ?

TOURIST   Entschuldigen Sie! Können Sie mir sagen,
           wo das Hotel Sacher[1] ist?
WIENER   Erste Straße links hinter der Staatsoper[2].
TOURIST   Und wie komme ich von da zum
           Stephansdom[3]?
WIENER   Geradeaus, die Kärntnerstraße entlang.
TOURIST   Wie weit ist es zum Dom?
WIENER   Nicht weit. Sie können zu Fuß gehen!
TOURIST   Danke!
WIENER   Bitte schön!

Da drüben!

TOURIST   Entschuldigung! Wo ist das Burgtheater[4]?
HERR   Es tut mir leid. Ich bin nicht aus Wien.
TOURIST   Verzeihung! Ist das das Burgtheater?
DAME   Nein, das ist nicht das Burgtheater, sondern die Staatsoper. Fahren Sie mit der
           Straßenbahn zum Rathaus! Gegenüber vom Rathaus ist das Burgtheater.
TOURIST   Und wo hält die Straßenbahn?
DAME   Da drüben links!
TOURIST   Vielen Dank!
DAME   Bitte sehr!

Fragen

1. Wo ist das Hotel Sacher?   2. Wie kommt man von der Staatsoper zum Stephansdom?
3. Wen fragt der Tourist im zweiten Gespräch?   4. Ist der Herr Wiener?   5. Wie kommt
der Tourist zum Burgtheater?   6. Wo ist die Haltestelle?   7. Was ist gegenüber vom
Burgtheater?

Übrigens

1.   **Hotel Sacher** is probably the best-known hotel in Vienna. One of the reasons for its
popularity is its famous café, for which a rich, delicious cake (**Sachertorte**) has been
named.

2.   Vienna's Opera (**Staatsoper**), inaugurated in 1869, was built in the style of the early
French Renaissance and is one of the foremost European opera houses.

3.   St. Stephen's (**Stephansdom**) is a masterpiece of Gothic architecture dating from the
twelfth century. Its roof of colored tile and its 450-foot-high spire make it the landmark of
Vienna.

4.   Vienna's **Burgtheater** was declared Austria's national theater in 1776 by Emperor
Joseph II. The Burgtheater has always been devoted to classical drama and has developed a
stylized mode of diction, giving it an aura of conservatism. Most of the ensemble, number-
ing more than a hundred, have lifetime contracts.

Das Wiener Burgtheater

Der Stadtplan, ⁼e *(city map)*

der	Bahnhof, ⁼e	*train station*	*die*	Bank, -en	*bank*
	Bus, -se	*bus*		Bibliothek, -en	*library*
	Dom, -e	*cathedral*		Brücke, -n	*bridge*
	Park, -s	*park*		Haltestelle, -n	*(bus etc.) stop*
	Platz, ⁼e	*place; square*		Kirche, -n	*church*
	Weg, -e	*way; trail*		Post	*post office*
das	Auto, -s	*car*		Schule, -n	*school*
	Hotel, -s	*hotel*		Straße, -n	*street*
	Kino, -s	*movie theater*		Straßenbahn, -en	*streetcar*
	Museum, Museen	*museum*		U-Bahn	*subway*
	Rathaus, ⁼er	*city hall*		Universität, -en ⎫	*university*
	Schloß, ⁼sser	*palace*		Uni, -s ⎭	
	Taxi, -s	*taxi*			
	Theater, -	*theater*			

Weiteres

der	Tourist, -en, -en	*tourist*
die	Dame, -n	*lady*
	Touristin, -nen	*tourist*

da drüben	*over there*
Entschuldigen Sie! ⎫	*Excuse me!*
Entschuldigung! / Verzeihung! ⎭	
Es tut mir leid.	*I'm sorry.*
Fahren Sie mit dem Bus!	*Go by bus.*
gegenüber von (+ *dat.*)	*across from*
(immer) geradeaus	*(keep) straight ahead*
in der Nähe von (+ *dat.*)	*near (in the vicinity of)*
links / rechts	*on the left / on the right*
nah / weit	*near / far*
schade	*too bad*

sondern	*but (on the contrary)*
Vielen Dank!	*Thank you very much.*
besichtigen	*to visit (palace, etc.), tour*
halten (hält), gehalten[1]	*to stop; to hold*
zeigen	*to show*
zu Fuß gehen, ist zu Fuß gegangen	*to walk*

[1] When **halten** is intransitive (i.e., without an accusative object), it means *to come to a stop:* Der Bus **hält** hier. When it is transitive, it means *to hold:* **Halten** Sie mir bitte das Buch!

ZUM ERKENNEN: hinter *(behind);* die Oper, -n *(opera house);* entlang *(along)*

Zum Thema

A.   Mustersätze

1. das Theater / die Oper: **Das ist nicht** das Theater, **sondern** die Oper.
   das Rathaus / die Universität; das Museum / die Bibliothek; die Bank / die Post; die Bushaltestelle / die Straßenbahnhaltestelle
2. zur Universität: **Können Sie mir sagen, wie ich** zur Universität **komme?**
   zum Rathaus, zur Bibliothek, zum Museum, zur Schulstraße
3. erste / links: **Die** erste **Straße** links.
   zweite / rechts; dritte / links; vierte / rechts
4. Straßenbahn: **Fahren Sie mit** der Straßenbahn!
   Bus, Auto, U-Bahn, Taxi
5. da drüben: **Die Straßenbahn hält** da drüben.
   da drüben rechts, beim Bahnhof, in der Nähe vom Park, gegenüber vom Theater

Hier hält die Straßenbahn.

B.   Was bedeuten die Wörter, und was sind die Artikel?

Domplatz, Fußgängerweg, Schloßhotel, Postbus, Touristenstadt, Kirchenfest, Schulferien, Studentenkino, Bahnhofsdrogerie, Universitätsparkplatz, Parkuhr

C.   Was paßt nicht?

1. der Bus, das Taxi, die Straßenbahn, das Kino
2. das Theater, der Weg, das Museum, die Bibliothek
3. die U-Bahn, die Bank, die Post, das Rathaus
4. die Straße, die Brücke, der Stadtplan, der Platz
5. da drüben, gegenüber von, in der Nähe von, schade
6. fahren, zu Fuß gehen, halten, laufen

D.   Wo ist . . . ?   *(Working with a classmate, practice asking for and giving directions to various places on campus or in town.)*

S1	Entschuldigen Sie! Ist das ＿＿＿＿＿＿＿ ?
S2	Nein, das ist nicht ＿＿＿＿＿＿ , sondern ＿＿＿＿＿＿＿ .
S1	Wo ist ＿＿＿＿＿＿ ?
S2	＿＿＿＿＿＿ ist in der Nähe von ＿＿＿＿＿＿ .
S1	Und wie komme ich von hier zu ＿＿＿＿＿＿ ?
S2	＿＿＿＿＿＿ .
S1	Wie weit ist es zu ＿＿＿＿＿＿ ?
S2	＿＿＿＿＿＿ .
S1	Vielen Dank!
S2	＿＿＿＿＿＿ !

E.   **Aussprache: ö**   *(See also II.29–36 in the pronunciation section of the Workbook.)*

1. [ö:]   Österreich, Brötchen, Bahnhöfe, Klöße, Goethe, schön, gewöhnlich,
    französisch, hören
2. [ö]   öffnen, östlich, können, Löffel, zwölf, nördlich, möchten, Wörter, Röcke
3. Wortpaare
    a. kennen / können   c.   große / Größe   e.   Sühne / Söhne
    b. Sehne / Söhne   d.   schon / schön   f.   Höhle / Hölle

Hören Sie zu!

Touristen in Innsbruck   *(Listen to this conversation between two tourists and a woman from Innsbruck. Then complete the sentences below with the correct information from the dialogue.)*

ZUM ERKENNEN: uns *(us);* das Goldene Dachl *(The Golden Roof, a 15th-century burgher house);* das Konzert *(concert);* erst *(only);* Viel Spaß! *(Have fun!)*

1. Die Touristen fragen, wo _____ ist.
2. Es ist _____ sehr weit. Sie können _____ gehen.
3. Bei der Brücke _____ die Fußgängerzone.
4. Da geht man _____ , bis man links zum Dachl kommt.
5. Der Dom ist _____ Dachl.
6. Das Konzert beginnt _____ .
7. Vor dem Konzert möchten die Touristen _____ .
8. Von der Maria-Theresia-Straße sieht man wunderbar _____ .
9. Sie sollen nicht *(are not supposed to)* zu spät zum Dom gehen, weil _____ .

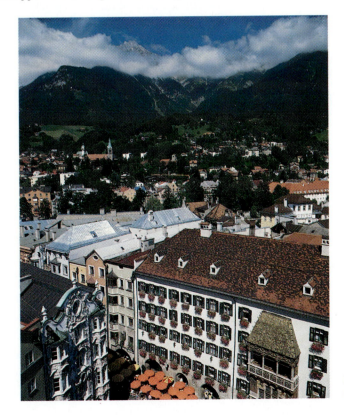

Das Goldene Dachl in
Innsbruck

STRUKTUR

I. Personal Pronouns

1. In English the PERSONAL PRONOUNS are *I, me, you, he, him, she, her, it, we, us, they,* and *them.* Some of these pronouns are used as subjects, others as direct or indirect objects, or objects of prepositions.

SUBJECT:	***He** is coming.*
DIRECT OBJECT:	*I see **him.***
INDIRECT OBJECT:	*I give **him** the book.*
OBJECT OF A PREPOSITION:	*We'll go without **him.***

The German personal pronouns are likewise used as subjects, direct or indirect objects, or objects of prepositions. Like the definite and indefinite articles, personal pronouns have special forms in the various cases. You already know the nominative case of these pronouns. Here are the nominative, accusative, and dative cases together.

	singular					plural			sg. / pl.
nom.	ich	du	er	es	sie	wir	ihr	sie	Sie
acc.	**mich**	**dich**	**ihn**	**es**	**sie**	**uns**	**euch**	**sie**	**Sie**
dat.	**mir**	**dir**	**ihm**	**ihm**	**ihr**	**uns**	**euch**	**ihnen**	**Ihnen**

SUBJECT:	**Er** kommt.
DIRECT OBJECT:	Ich sehe **ihn.**
INDIRECT OBJECT:	Ich gebe **ihm** das Buch.
OBJECT OF A PREPOSITION:	Wir gehen **ohne ihn.**

• Note the similarities between the definite article of the noun and the pronoun that replaces it.

	masc.	neut.	fem.	pl.
nom.	**der** Mann = er	**das** Kind = es	**die** Frau = sie	**die** Leute = sie
acc.	**den** Mann = ihn	**das** Kind = es	**die** Frau = sie	**die** Leute = sie
dat.	**dem** Mann = ihm	**dem** Kind = ihm	**der** Frau = ihr	**den** Leuten = ihnen

2. As in English, the dative object usually precedes the accusative object, unless the accusative object is a pronoun. If that is the case, the accusative object pronoun comes first.

Ich gebe **dem Studenten**	den Kuli.	*I'm giving the student the pen.*
Ich gebe **ihm**	den Kuli.	*I'm giving him the pen.*
Ich gebe ihn	**dem Studenten.**	*I'm giving it to the student.*
Ich gebe ihn	**ihm.**	*I'm giving it to him.*

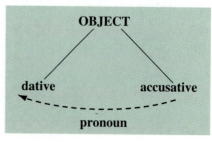

A.   **Ersetzen Sie die Hauptwörter durch Pronomen!**   *(Replace each noun with a pronoun in the appropriate case.)*

BEISPIEL: den Bruder   **ihn**

1. der Vater, dem Mann, den Großvater, dem Freund, den Ober
2. die Freundin, der Großmutter, der Dame, die Frau, der Familie
3. die Eltern, den Herren, den Frauen, die Freundinnen, den Schweizern
4. für die Mutter, mit den Freunden, gegen die Studenten, außer dem Großvater, ohne den Ober, von den Eltern, zu dem Mädchen, bei der Großmutter

B.   **Kombinieren Sie mit den Präpositionen!** Was sind die Akkusativ- und Dativformen?

BEISPIEL: ich (ohne, mit)
                ohne mich, mit mir

1. er (für, mit)   5. ihr (für, außer)
2. wir (durch, von)   6. sie / *sg.* (um, nach)
3. Sie (gegen, zu)   7. sie / *pl.* (für, aus)
4. du (ohne, bei)   8. es (ohne, außer)

C.   **Antworten Sie!** Ersetzen Sie die Hauptwörter durch neue Hauptwörter und Pronomen!

BEISPIEL: Wo ist das Hotel?   Es ist da drüben. (Bank)
              Wo ist die Bank?   **Sie ist da drüben.**

1. Wo ist die Post? Da ist sie. (Dom, Rathaus, Apotheke)
2. Ist das Museum weit von hier? Nein, es ist nicht weit von hier. (Kirche, Geschäft, Platz)
3. Zeigen Sie der Dame den Weg? Ja, ich zeige ihr den Weg. (Mann, Leute, Touristin)
4. Helfen Sie dem Herrn? Ja, ich helfe ihm. (Kind, Damen, Touristin)
5. Haben Sie die Straßenbahn genommen? Ja, ich habe sie genommen. (Bus, U-Bahn, Taxi)
6. Wie hat dir die Stadt gefallen? Sie hat mir gut gefallen. (Hotel, Universität, Park)

D.   **Was fehlt?**

1. **Geben Sie die Pronomen!**   *(Complete the sentences with the appropriate German case forms of the suggested pronouns.)*

    BEISPIEL: Sie kauft _____ das Buch. *(me)*
                Sie kauft mir das Buch.

    a. Siehst du _____ ? *(them, him, her, me, us)*
    b. Geben Sie es _____ ! *(him, me, her, us, them)*
    c. Sie braucht _____ . *(you / sg. fam., you / pl. fam., you / formal, me, him, them, us)*
    d. Wie geht es _____ ? *(he, they, you / formal, she, you / sg. fam., you / pl. fam.)*
    e. Das Fräulein hat _____ das Eis gebracht. *(you / sg. fam., you / pl. fam., us, him, her, me, you / formal)*
    f. Hat die Party _____ überrascht? *(you / formal, me, you / sg. fam., us, her, him, you / pl. fam.)*

2. **Fragen und Antworten**   *(Working with a partner, complete the following sentences.)*

S1   Siehst du _____ ? *(them)*
S2   Nein, aber sie sehen _____ . *(us)*
S1   Gehört das Buch _____ ? *(you / sg. fam.)*
S2   Nein, es gehört _____ . *(him)*
S1   Glaubst du _____ ? *(him)*
S2   Nein, ich glaube _____ . *(you / pl. fam.)*
S1   Sie sucht _____ . *(you / sg. fam.)*
S2   Ich suche _____ . *(her)*
S1   Hilft er _____ ? *(us)*
S2   Nein, er hilft _____ . *(them)*
S1   Zeigst du _____ die Kirche? *(us)*
S2   Ja, ich zeige sie _____ . *(you / pl. fam.)*

E.   **Auf deutsch, bitte!**

1.   Did you *(sg. fam.)* thank him?
2.   We congratulated her.
3.   I surprised them.
4.   We'll show you *(pl. fam.)* the palace.
5.   Did they answer you *(pl. fam.)*?
6.   I was writing (to) you *(sg. fam.)*.
7.   Are you *(sg. fam.)* going to give him the present?

F.   **Variieren Sie die Sätze!**

1.   **Es tut mir leid.**
   a. He's sorry.   **b.** She's sorry.   **c.** They're sorry.   **d.** Are you *(3×)* sorry?
   e. We aren't sorry.   **f.** Why are you *(sg. fam.)* sorry?   **g.** I was sorry.   **h.** We weren't sorry.   **i.** Who was sorry?

2.   **Wien gefällt mir.**
   a. They like Vienna.   **b.** Do you *(3×)* like Vienna?   **c.** He doesn't like Vienna.   **d.** We like Vienna.   **e.** I liked Vienna.   **f.** How did you *(sg. fam.)* like Vienna?   **g.** Who didn't like Vienna?   **h.** She didn't like Vienna.

G.   **Wem gibt sie was?**   *(Carolyn has just cleaned out her closet and is going to give away all the souvenirs from her European trip. Explain to whom she is going to give them.)*

BEISPIEL: ihrer Schwester / die Bilder
   Sie gibt ihrer Schwester die Bilder.
   Sie gibt ihr die Bilder.
   Sie gibt sie ihrer Schwester.
   Sie gibt sie ihr.

1. ihrem Vater / den Stadtplan   **2.** ihren Großeltern / die Landkarte   **3.** ihrer Mutter / den Zuckerlöffel   **4.** ihrer Schwester / das Kleingeld *(small change)*   **5.** Eva / die Kassette von Udo Lindenberg   **6.** Markus und Charlotte / die Posters   **7.** dir / das T-Shirt

II. Modal Auxiliary Verbs

1. Both English and German have a small group of MODAL AUXILIARY VERBS that modify the meaning of another verb. Modal verbs express such ideas as the permission, ability, necessity, obligation, or desire to do something.

dürfen	*to be allowed to, may*	**sollen**	*to be supposed to*
können	*to be able to, can*	**wollen**	*to want to*
müssen	*to have to, must*	**mögen**	*to like*

*   The German modals are irregular in the singular of the present tense:

	dürfen	können	müssen	sollen	wollen	mögen / möchten	
ich	darf	kann	muß	soll	will	mag	möchte
du	darfst	kannst	mußt	sollst	willst	magst	möchtest
er	darf	kann	muß	soll	will	mag	möchte
wir	dürfen	können	müssen	sollen	wollen	mögen	möchten
ihr	dürft	könnt	müßt	sollt	wollt	mögt	möchtet
sie	dürfen	können	müssen	sollen	wollen	mögen	möchten

*   The **möchte**-forms of **mögen** occur more frequently than the **mag**-forms. **Mögen** is usually used in a negative sentence.

    Ich **möchte** eine Tasse Tee.   *I would like (to have) a cup of tea.*
    Ich **mag** Kaffee nicht.   *I don't like coffee.*

2. Modals are another example of the two-part verb phrase. In statements and information questions, the modal is the inflected second element of the sentence (V1). The modified verb (V2) appears at the very end of the sentence in its infinitive form.

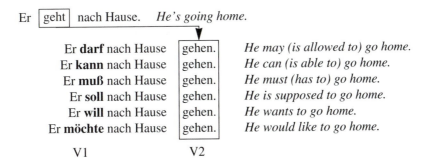

Er geht nach Hause.   *He's going home.*

Er **darf** nach Hause gehen.   *He may (is allowed to) go home.*
Er **kann** nach Hause gehen.   *He can (is able to) go home.*
Er **muß** nach Hause gehen.   *He must (has to) go home.*
Er **soll** nach Hause gehen.   *He is supposed to go home.*
Er **will** nach Hause gehen.   *He wants to go home.*
Er **möchte** nach Hause gehen.   *He would like to go home.*
     V1   V2

CAUTION:

*   The English set of modals is frequently supplemented by such forms as *is allowed to, is able to, has to, is supposed to.* The German modals, however, do not use such supplements. They follow the pattern of *may, can,* and *must:* **Ich muß gehen.** *(I must go.)*

- The subject of the modal and of the infinitive are always the same: **Er will nach Hause gehen.** *(He wants to go home.)* The English *He wants you (to go home)* cannot be imitated in German. The correct way to express this idea is **Er will, daß du (nach Hause gehst).**

3. Modals can be used without an infinitive, provided the modified verb is clearly understood. This structure is common with verbs of motion.

   Mußt du jetzt nach Hause?—Ja, ich **muß.**
   Willst du zum Supermarkt?—Ja, ich **will,** aber ich **kann** nicht.

4. Watch these important differences in meaning:

   a. **gern** vs. **möchten**

   Ich **esse gern** Kuchen. BUT Ich **möchte** ein Stück Kuchen (**haben**).

   The first sentence says that I am generally fond of cake *(I like to eat cake)*. The second sentence implies a desire for a piece of cake at this particular moment *(I'd like a piece of cake)*.

   b. **wollen** vs. **möchten**

   Notice the difference in tone and politeness between these two sentences:

   Ich **will** Kuchen. BUT Ich **möchte** Kuchen.

   The first might be said by a spoiled child *(I want cake),* the second by a polite adult *(I would like cake).*

5. Modals in Subordinate Clauses

   a. Remember that the inflected verb stands at the very end of clauses introduced by subordinate conjunctions such as **bevor, daß, ob, obwohl, wenn,** and **weil.**

   Sie sagt, **daß** du nach Hause gehen **kannst.**
   Du kannst nach Hause gehen, **wenn** du **möchtest.**

   b. If the sentence starts with the subordinate clause, then the inflected verb of the main sentence (the modal) follows right after the comma.

   Du **kannst** nach Hause gehen, wenn du möchtest.
   Wenn du möchtest, **kannst** du nach Hause gehen.

»Wenn du dein ganzes Leben lang glücklich sein willst, mußt du gute Freunde haben«

H. **Ersetzen Sie das Subjekt!**

BEISPIEL: Wir sollen zum Markt fahren. (ich)   **Ich soll zum Markt fahren.**

1. Wir wollen zu Hause bleiben. (er, sie / *pl.,* du, ich)
2. Sie müssen noch die Rechnung bezahlen. (ich, ihr, du, Vater)
3. Du darfst zum Bahnhof kommen. (er, ihr, die Kinder, ich)
4. Möchtet ihr ein Eis haben? (sie / *pl.,* du, er, das Fräulein)
5. Können Sie mir sagen, wo das ist? (du, ihr, er, die Damen)

I. **Am Sonntag**   *(Say what these people will do on Sunday.)*

BEISPIEL: Carolyn spricht nur Deutsch. (wollen)
   Carolyn will nur Deutsch sprechen.

1. Volker und Silvia spielen Tennis. (wollen)
2. Paul fährt mit ein paar Freunden in die Berge. (möchten)
3. Friederike bezahlt Rechnungen. (müssen)
4. Helmut hilft Vater zu Hause. (sollen)
5. Herr und Frau Ahrendt besichtigen Schloß Schönbrunn. (können)
6. Die Kinder gehen in den Zoo. (dürfen)

J. **Besucher**   *(Visitors)*

1. **Stadtbesichtigung**   *(Sightseeing in town. Mitzi and Sepp are visiting their friends Heike and Dirk in Quedlinburg. Dirk tells Mitzi and Sepp what Heike wants to know.)*

   Beginnen Sie mit **Heike fragt, ob . . . !**

   a. Könnt ihr den Weg in die Stadt allein finden?
   b. Wollt ihr einen Stadtplan haben?
   c. Möchtet ihr zu Fuß gehen?
   d. Soll ich euch mit dem Auto zum Stadtzentrum bringen?
   e. Müßt ihr noch zur Bank?

2. **Fragen**   *(Mitzi has several questions. Tell us what she asks.)*

   a. Wo kann man hier in der Nähe Blumen kaufen?
   b. Was für ein Geschenk sollen wir für den Vater kaufen?
   c. Wie lange dürfen wir hier bleiben?
   d. Wann müssen wir abends wieder hier sein?
   e. Wer will mit in die Stadt?

K. **In Wien**   *(You and your friends have been in Vienna for a couple of days, but there are many more things to do.)*

BEISPIEL: Wir haben noch nicht den Stephansdom besichtigt. (wollen)
   Wir wollen noch den Stephansdom besichtigen.

1. Ich habe noch nicht Sachertorte gegessen. (mögen)
2. Thomas hat die Uni noch nicht gesehen. (wollen)
3. Kevin und ich sind noch nicht zum Burgtheater gegangen. (sollen)
4. Du hast noch kein Geschenk gefunden. (müssen)
5. Mareike hat noch keine Bilder gemacht. (können)
6. Frank und Margit sind noch nicht durch die Kärntnerstraße gelaufen. (mögen)

L. Auf deutsch, bitte!

1. He wants to see the cathedral.
2. They have to go to the post office.
3. I can't read that.
4. You *(pl. fam.)* are supposed to speak German.
5. You *(sg. fam.)* may order a piece of cake.
6. She's supposed to study (**lernen**).
7. We have to find the way.
8. Can't you *(3×)* help me?
9. We'd like to drive to Vienna.
10. Are we allowed to see the palace?

M. Welches Modalverb paßt?

UWE   Till, ＿＿＿＿＿＿＿ du mit mir gehen? Ich ＿＿＿＿＿＿＿ einen Stadtplan kaufen.

TILL   Wo ＿＿＿＿＿＿＿ wir einen Stadtplan bekommen?

UWE   Die Buchhandlung ＿＿＿＿＿＿＿ Stadtpläne haben.

TILL   Gut. Ich ＿＿＿＿＿＿＿ zwei Bücher für meinen Bruder kaufen. Ich gehe mit dir.

UWE   ＿＿＿＿＿＿＿ wir zu Fuß gehen, oder ＿＿＿＿＿＿＿ wir mit dem Fahrrad *(bicycle)* fahren?

TILL   Ich ＿＿＿＿＿＿＿ mit dem Fahrrad fahren. Dann ＿＿＿＿＿＿＿ wir noch zur Bank. Die Bücher sind bestimmt nicht billig. ＿＿＿＿＿＿ du nicht auch zur Bank?

UWE   Ja, richtig. Ich ＿＿＿＿＿＿＿ diese Rechnung bezahlen.

N. Was machst du morgen?   *(Using the modals, ask your partner what he / she wants to, has to, is supposed to, would like to do tomorrow. In the responses you may use some of the phrases below or choose your own expressions.)*

BEISPIEL: Was möchtest du morgen tun?
   Ich möchte morgen Tennis spielen.

einen Pulli kaufen	ein Geschenk für . . . kaufen
Pizza essen gehen	meine Eltern überraschen
viel studieren	nach . . . fahren
ein Buch lesen	zu Hause bleiben
einkaufen gehen	das Schloß besichtigen
Rechnungen bezahlen	

III. Contrasting *sondern* and *aber*

German has two coordinating conjunctions corresponding to the English *but*.

aber	*but, however*
sondern	*but on the contrary, but rather*

• **sondern** must be used when the first clause is negated AND the meaning *but on the contrary* is implied (frequently with opposites).

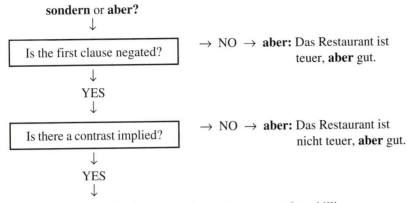

sondern or **aber?**
↓
| Is the first clause negated? | → NO → | **aber:** Das Restaurant ist teuer, **aber** gut. |

↓
YES
↓

| Is there a contrast implied? | → NO → | **aber:** Das Restaurant ist nicht teuer, **aber** gut. |

↓
YES
↓

sondern: Das Restaurant ist nicht teuer, **sondern** billig.

- **nicht nur ... sondern auch ...**

Das Restaurant ist **nicht nur** gut, **sondern auch** billig.
The restaurant is not only good, but also inexpensive.

O. Sondern oder aber? *(Insert the appropriate conjunction.)*

1. Wien ist sehr schön, —————— Salzburg gefällt mir besser *(better)*.
2. Die Straßenbahn hält nicht hier, —————— gegenüber von der Post.
3. Gehen Sie beim Theater nicht rechts, —————— geradeaus!
4. Die Kirche ist nicht alt, —————— neu.
5. Das Rathaus ist nicht besonders schön, —————— sehr alt.
6. Das ist kein Museum, —————— eine Bibliothek.
7. Die Mensa ist billig, —————— nicht gut.

P. Können Sie mir sagen, ... ? *(Ask for directions.)*

BEISPIEL: können / Sie / sagen / mir / / wo / sein / Universität?
Können Sie mir sagen, wo die Universität ist?

1. können / du / sagen / ihm / / wie / heißen / Straße?
2. können / er / sagen / uns / / wie / weit / es / sein / zu / Bahnhof?
3. können / sie *(pl.)* / sagen / euch / / ob / es / geben / hier / Straßenbahn oder Bus?
4. können / Sie / sagen / ihr / / wo / Bus / halten?
5. können / ihr / sagen / mir / / wie / lange / Geschäfte / sein / offen?

Q. Wie geht's weiter?

BEISPIEL: Ich esse nicht gern Karotten, aber ...
Ich esse nicht gern Karotten, aber Bohnen finde ich gut.

1. Ich trinke nicht gern Cola, aber ...
2. Wir besichtigen nicht das Museum, sondern ...
3. Die Straßenbahn hält nicht hier, sondern ...
4. Es gibt keinen Bus, aber ...
5. Er kann uns heute die Stadt nicht zeigen, aber ...
6. Ich bin nicht in Wien geblieben, sondern ...
7. Ihr lernt nicht Spanisch, sondern ...

R. Wo ist eine Bank? Auf deutsch, bitte!

1. Excuse me *(formal),* can you tell me where there's a bank?   **2.** I'm sorry, but I'm not from Vienna.   **3.** Whom can I ask?   **4.** Who can help me?   **5.** May I help you?   **6.** I'd like to find a bank.   **7.** Near the cathedral (there) is a bank.   **8.** Can you tell me whether that's far from here?   **9.** You can walk (there), but the banks close (are closed) in twenty minutes.   **10.** Take the subway or a taxi!

ST.-STEPHANS-DOM

T U R M

Eintrittskarte für Studenten

INKLUSIVE 8% MEHRWERTSTEUER

S 8.—   № 43524

Die Altstadt von Passau zwischen der Donau (links) und dem Inn (rechts)

EINBLICKE

Der Stephans-dom ist das Wahrzeichen *(landmark)* von Wien.

Originally Vienna was a Roman settlement. The city's fate was linked to its geographical location on the Danube and at the gateway to the plains of eastern Europe. Here merchants met where ancient trade routes crossed; crusaders passed through on their way to the Holy Land; and in 1683 at the walls and gates of this city the Turks had to abandon their hope of conquering the heart of Europe.

The center of Vienna (the **Innenstadt**) dates from medieval times. As late as the 1850s, it was surrounded by horseshoe-shaped walls. The city reached its zenith of power and wealth as the capital of the Austro-Hungarian Empire during the reign of Emperor Franz Josef (1848–1916), when it developed into one of Europe's most important cultural centers. Composers such as Haydn, Mozart, Beethoven, Schubert, Brahms, Bruckner, Johann and Richard Strauß, Mahler, and Schönberg have left a lasting imprint on the city's cultural life. The psychoanalyst Freud, the writers Schnitzler, Zweig, and von Hofmannsthal, and the painters Klimt and Kokoschka laid the intellectual and artistic foundation of the 20th century. Today Vienna ranks among the leading convention cities in the world and is headquarters for the International Atomic Energy Agency, the Organization of Petroleum Exporting Countries (OPEC), and the United Nations Industrial Development Organization.

WORTSCHATZ 2

bekannt	*well-known*
Das macht nichts.	*That doesn't matter.*
einmal	*once, (at) one time*
gemütlich	*pleasant, cozy, convivial*
genug	*enough*
interessant	*interesting*
leider	*unfortunately*
lieb*	*dear*
stundenlang	*for hours*
bummeln, ist gebummelt	*to stroll*

WAS IST DAS?   der Sport, Stop, Walzer; das Gästehaus, Schiff; die Innenstadt, Studentengruppe, Winterresidenz; kunsthistorisch, zentral

Grüße° aus Österreich

greetings

Liebe Eltern!

Jetzt muß ich Euch[†] aber wirklich wieder einmal schreiben! Ich habe so viel gesehen, daß ich gar nicht weiß, wo ich beginnen soll. Vor einer Woche war° unsere Studentengruppe noch in Passau[1]. Von dort sind wir mit dem Schiff die Donau hinuntergefahren°. 5 Wir haben einen Stop in Linz[2] gemacht und haben die Stadt, das Schloß und den Dom besichtigt. Dann sind wir mit dem Schiff weiter bis nach Wien gefahren. Die Weinberge°, Burgen° und besonders Kloster° Melk[3] haben mir sehr gut gefallen. Das Wetter ist auch sehr schön gewesen.

was
traveled down

vineyards
castles / monastery

Kloster Melk an der Donau

---

* liebe Eltern, lieber Michael, liebe Elisabeth
† In letters, it is customary to capitalize pronouns (**Du, Dir, Dich; Ihr, Euch**) and possessive adjectives (**Dein, Euer, Ihr**) that refer to the addressee.

10   Jetzt sind wir schon ein paar Tage in Wien. Ich finde es toll hier! Unser Gästehaus liegt sehr zentral, und wir können alles zu Fuß oder mit der U-Bahn erreichen°. So viel bin ich noch nie gelaufen! Am Freitag sind wir stundenlang durch die Innenstadt gebummelt. Die Geschäfte in der° Kärntnerstraße sind sehr teuer, aber man muß ja° nichts kaufen. Wir haben natürlich auch den Stephansdom besichtigt und sind mit dem Aufzug° im Turm hin-
15 aufgefahren°. Von dort kann man ganz° Wien sehen. Am Abend haben wir Mozarts *Zauberflöte*° in der Staatsoper gehört.

      Am Samstag haben wir die Hofburg[4] besichtigt. Das ist einmal die Winterresidenz der° Habsburger Kaiser° gewesen. Dort ist auch die Spanische Reitschule°, und man kann die Lipizzaner° beim Training sehen. Das haben wir auch getan. Wirklich prima! Da ist das
20 Reiten° kein Sport, sondern Kunst.° Am Abend sind wir mit der Straßenbahn nach Grin-zing[5] gefahren und haben dort Marks Geburtstag mit Musik und Wein gefeiert. Die Wein-stube° war sehr gemütlich.

reach

in the / flavoring particle
elevator
went to the top of the tower /
all of / Magic Flute

of the
emperors / riding academy
white horses
riding / art

small restaurant

In der Spanischen
Reitschule

      Heute besichtigen wir das Museum für Völkerkunde,° und später wollen ein paar von uns noch zum Prater[6]. Das Riesenrad° dort soll toll sein. Das muß man doch gesehen
25 haben! Morgen früh wollen wir noch zum Schloß Schönbrunn[7], der Sommerresidenz der Habsburger; und dann ist unsere Zeit in Wien auch schon fast um°.

ethnology
ferris wheel

almost over

MUSEUM FÜR VÖLKERKUNDE

A-1014 WIEN, NEUE HOFBURG
TELEFON (0222) 93 45 41

monuments

traffic

simply

we get going again

Wien ist wirklich interessant. Überall findet man Denkmäler° oder Straßen mit bekannten Namen wie Mozart, Beethoven, Johann Strauß, usw. Aber Ihr dürft nicht denken, daß
man hier nur Walzer hört und alles romantisch ist. Wien ist auch eine Großstadt mit vielen
Menschen und viel Verkehr°. Es gefällt mir hier so gut, daß ich gern noch ein paar Tage 30
bleiben möchte. Das geht leider nicht, weil wir noch nach Salzburg[8] und Innsbruck[9]
wollen. Eine Woche ist einfach° nicht lang genug für so eine Reise. Nach Budapest können
wir leider auch nicht. Nun, das macht nichts. Das muß ich dann im Frühling machen.

So, jetzt muß ich schnell frühstücken, und dann geht's wieder los°! Tschüß und viele
liebe Grüße!
                                                                                        35

Euer Michael

Schloß Schönbrunn, die
Sommerresidenz der
Habsburger Kaiser

Zum Text

A. Wer, was oder wo ist das?   *(Match the descriptions with the places or people in
the list below.)*

die Donau, Grinzing, die Hofburg, die Kärntnerstraße, Linz, Melk, Passau, der Prater,
Schloß Schönbrunn, die Spanische Reitschule, die Staatsoper, der Turm vom Stephansdom

1. Hier hat die Flußfahrt nach Wien begonnen.
2. Auf diesem *(on this)* Fluß kann man mit dem Schiff bis nach Wien fahren.
3. Hier haben die Habsburger Kaiser im Sommer gelebt.
4. Hier gibt es ein Barockkloster. Es ist sehr bekannt.

5. Da haben die Studenten einen Stop gemacht und die Stadt besichtigt.
6. Hier kann man schön bummeln, aber die Geschäfte sind sehr teuer.
7. Von hier kann man ganz Wien sehen.
8. Das ist einmal die Winterresidenz der *(of the)* Habsburger Kaiser gewesen.
9. Hier kann man die Lipizzaner trainieren sehen.
10. Hier kann man Mozarts *Zauberflöte* hören.
11. Hier gibt es ein Riesenrad.
12. Dort kann man gemütlich essen und Wein trinken.

B. Sondern oder aber?   *(Insert the appropriate conjunction.)*

1. Das Gästehaus ist nicht sehr elegant, _____ es liegt zentral.
2. Wir sind nicht viel mit dem Bus gefahren, _____ gelaufen.
3. Bei der Spanischen Reitschule ist das Reiten kein Sport, _____ Kunst.
4. Die Geschäfte in der Kärntnerstraße sind teuer, _____ sie gefallen mir.

C. Fahrt *(trip)* **nach Österreich**   *(Mr. Schubach tells about his travel plans. Use modal verbs.)*

BEISPIEL: Ihr fahrt mit uns mit dem Schiff bis nach Wien. (müssen)
Ihr müßt mit uns mit dem Schiff bis nach Wien fahren.

1. Unsere Fahrt beginnt in Passau. (sollen)
2. In Linz machen wir einen Stop. (wollen)
3. Meine Frau besichtigt Kloster Melk. (möchten)
4. Vom Schiff sieht man viele Weinberge und Burgen. (können)
5. Wir bleiben fünf Tage in Wien. (wollen)
6. Dort gibt es viel zu sehen. (sollen)
7. Man hat natürlich gute Schuhe dabei *(along)*. (müssen)
8. Ich laufe aber nicht so viel. (dürfen)
9. Meine Frau bummelt gemütlich durch die Kärntnerstraße. (möchten)
10. Ich sehe viele Museen. (wollen)

D. Interview. Fragen Sie einen Nachbarn / eine Nachbarin, . . . !

1. ob er / sie schon einmal in Wien gewesen ist
2. wenn ja, was ihm / ihr in Wien besonders gut gefallen hat (**Was hat dir . . . ?**) wenn nein, was er / sie sehen möchte, wenn er / sie einmal nach Wien fährt
3. ob er / sie in einer Großstadt oder Kleinstadt wohnt
4. ob die Stadt eine Altstadt hat, und ob sie schön ist
5. ob es dort auch eine Straßenbahn, eine U-Bahn oder Busse gibt
6. was ihm / ihr dort besonders gefällt, und was nicht
7. ob er / sie schon einmal in einem Schloß gewesen ist; wenn ja, wo; wenn nein, welches Schloß er / sie einmal sehen möchte
8. was für Denkmäler und Straßen mit bekannten Namen es hier gibt

E. Etwas Geographie. Sehen Sie auf die Landkarte von Österreich, und beantworten Sie die Fragen! Arbeiten Sie mit einem Partner!

1. Wie viele Nachbarländer hat Österreich? Wie heißen sie, und wo liegen sie?
2. Wie heißt die Hauptstadt von Österreich? Wie heißen ein paar Städte in Österreich?
3. Welcher Fluß fließt (*flows*) durch Wien? Salzburg? Innsbruck? Linz? Graz?
4. Welcher See liegt nicht nur in Österreich, sondern auch in Deutschland und in der Schweiz? Welcher See liegt zum Teil in Österreich und zum Teil in Ungarn? An welchem See liegt Klagenfurt?
5. Wo liegt der Brenner-Paß? der Großglockner? der Tauern-Tunnel?

Hören Sie zu!

Schon lange nicht mehr gesehen!   (*Listen to the conversation between Uwe and Erika, then answer the questions. You do not need to write complete sentences.*)

ZUM ERKENNEN: schon lange nicht mehr (*not for a long time*); Bergwanderungen (*mountain hikes*); die Burg (*castle*)

1. Wo ist Uwe gewesen? _____
2. Mit wem ist er gefahren? _____
3. Wie ist das Wetter gewesen? _____
4. Wo ist Maria Alm? _____
5. Was haben sie dort gemacht? _____
6. Wo sind sie noch gewesen? _____
7. Was haben sie dort besichtigt? _____
8. Wann will Uwe nach Wien? _____
9. Warum muß Erika gehen? _____

Übrigens

1. The German city of Passau (pop. 51,000), not far from the border with Austria and the Czech Republic, is known as the "town of the three rivers" since it lies at the confluence of the Danube, Inn, and Ilz rivers. It is the starting point for regular steamer service down the Danube to Vienna and the Black Sea.

2. Linz is the capital of Upper Austria and, after Vienna and Graz, Austria's third largest city. Located on the Danube river, it is a large port and commercial center.

3. The Benedictine Abbey of Melk, built between 1702 and 1783, is one of Austria's most splendid monasteries. Its twin-towered chapel ranks as one of the finest examples of the baroque north of the Alps.

4. The **Hofburg** is almost a self-contained city within the city of Vienna. For two and a half centuries (until 1918) it was the residence of the Austrian emperors. It now houses a museum of art and ethnography, the portrait collection of the National Library, the treasury, the Spanish Riding Academy, and the federal chancellor's residence.

5. Grinzing, on the outskirts of Vienna, is probably the best-known **Heurigen** wine village, where the young, fresh wine (**der Heurige**) is sold by wine-growers in their courtyards or houses, some of which they have turned into restaurants (**Weinstuben** or **Heurigenschänken**).

6. The **Prater** is a large amusement park with a giant ferris wheel and many modern rides, a stadium, fairgrounds, race tracks, bridle paths, pools, and ponds.

7. **Schönbrunn** was the favorite summer residence of the Empress Maria Theresa (**Maria Theresia**), who ruled Austria, Hungary, and Bohemia from 1740–1780. Her daughter Marie Antoinette, who was beheaded during the French Revolution, spent her childhood there. It was Schönbrunn where Mozart dazzled the empress with his talents. Napoleon used it as his headquarters during the wars of 1805 and 1809. Francis Joseph I (**Franz Josef I.**), Emperor of Austria from 1848 to 1916, was born and died at Schönbrunn, and the last of the Habsburgs, Charles I (**Karl I.**), abdicated here in 1918, when Austria became a republic. Schönbrunn's park is one of the best preserved French-style baroque gardens.

8. Salzburg is a very beautiful city. Its narrow streets, tall medieval houses, arcaded courtyards, and the palaces and cathedral of the prince-bishops are all dominated by the massive Hohensalzburg Castle. Salzburg's most famous son is undoubtedly Mozart, who is commemorated at the music academy and the annual summer music festival.

9. Innsbruck, the capital of Tyrol, lies on the Inn River. Everywhere in the city one has a beautiful view of the surrounding mountains. The 1964 and 1976 Winter Olympics took place there, and its sports facilities attract tourists and winter-sports enthusiasts from all over the world.

SPRECHSITUATIONEN

When traveling or living abroad, it is very important to be able to ask for and understand directions, but first you must get someone's attention.

Getting Someone's Attention

Entschuldigen Sie, bitte!
Entschuldigung! / Verzeihung!

Asking for Directions

Bitte, wo ist . . . ?
Können Sie mir (bitte) sagen, wo . . . ist?
Ich möchte zum / zur . . .
Ich kann . . . nicht finden.
Wie kommt man (von hier) zum / zur . . . ?
Ist hier in der Nähe . . . ?
Wo gibt es hier . . . ?
Wie weit ist es . . . ?

Understanding Directions

Gehen Sie / Fahren Sie . . . !
(immer) geradeaus   bis Sie zum / zur . . . kommen
die erste Straße links / rechts   bis Sie . . . sehen
die Hauptstraße entlang

Fahren Sie mit dem Auto / der Straßenbahn!
Nehmen Sie den Bus / die U-Bahn / ein Taxi!
Sie können zu Fuß gehen.
Kommen Sie! Ich kann Ihnen . . . zeigen.
Fragen Sie dort noch einmal!

Übungen   **A.**   **Fragen zum Stadtplan von Wien**

1. **Wie fragt man?**   *(Ask for directions to several of the buildings in Vienna, e.g., the university or the Hofburg. Use as many different ways of asking as you can.)*

2. **Wie komme ich dorthin?**   *(In groups of two or three, practice asking and giving directions from one place in Vienna to another.)*

   BEISPIEL: vom Stephansdom zur Oper
   Entschuldigen Sie bitte! Können Sie mir sagen, wie ich von hier zur Oper komme?—Gern. Gehen Sie immer geradeaus die Kärntner Straße entlang! Sie sehen dann die Oper rechts.

   a. von der Oper zur Hofburg   d. vom Parlament zum Schwarzenbergplatz
   b. von der Hofburg zur Uni   e. vom Schwarzenbergplatz zum Donaukanal
   c. von der Uni zum Parlament   f. vom Donaukanal zum Stephansdom

B. **Kurzgespräche**

1. You are new in town or on campus, and you're looking for a particular building. Ask someone, beginning *Pardon me, is that . . . ?* The stranger tells you that that's not what you're looking for but rather something else. Ask for directions, and inquire whether the building is close by or far away. Thank the person for the information.

2. You and a friend are in a Viennese coffee house. Your friend suggests visiting the *Museum für Völkerkunde.* You ask someone at the table next to yours where the museum is located. You find out that it is not too far away, but that unfortunately it is closed today. You respond politely. Your friend suggests an alternative activity (strolling along the *Kärntner Straße,* visiting the Lipizzaner *Reitschule* or the *Stephansdom,* etc.). Discuss how to reach your destination. Then consider what you might want to do in the evening (**heute abend**): go to Grinzing or the Prater, etc.

KAPITEL

Wohnen

Moderne Wohnungen können sehr schön sein.

LERNZIELE

Vorschau
- Housing

Gespräche and Wortschatz
- Housing and furniture

Struktur
- Two-way prepositions
- Imperative
- *Wissen* vs. *kennen*

Einblicke
- Public transportation and city life

Sprechsituationen
- Describing locations
- Offering apologies
- Expressing forgiveness

6

Housing

After World War II West Germany suffered an acute housing shortage, not only because so many buildings had been destroyed, but also because of the large number of refugees who moved west. Highrise apartment clusters (**Wohnsilos**) mushroomed around the old cities, often contrasting sharply with the traditional architecture. Fortunately people have rediscovered the beauty of older buildings, and subsidies and tax incentives have made it possible to restore and modernize them. More recently, new housing developments have been designed to fit better into the landscape and to conform to local building styles. Strict zoning laws prevent the loss of open space and agricultural land, but they also make it more difficult to add housing.

With the end of the Cold War and the collapse of the eastern economies, another wave of people moved west, which again created a housing crisis. Students, young couples, large families, and foreigners have great difficulties finding affordable accommodations.

In the former GDR two-thirds of the housing units date back to the time before World War II, and they often lack modern sanitary facilities and heating systems. Because the Communist regime kept rents extremely low, there was little money for maintenance and modernization. In the West, on the other hand, homes are often priced out of reach for the average person. Nine out of ten Germans would prefer to own a house or condominium (**Eigentumswohnung**), but only every third family reaches that goal.

Apartments are advertised by the number of rooms. Those who want to rent a three-bedroom apartment with a living room and a dining room need a **5-Zimmer-Wohnung**; bathroom and kitchen are excluded from the room count. Furnished apartments are relatively rare. "Unfurnished" is usually to be taken literally. There are no built-in closets, kitchen cabinets, appliances, light fixtures, etc. Tenants are responsible for furnishing and maintaining their apartments, including interior painting and decorating. In some buildings they are even expected to clean the stairs between floors.

Das Haus hat man sehr schön restauriert.

Gespräche   Wohnung zu vermieten

INGE	Hallo, mein Name ist Inge Moser. Ich habe gehört, daß Sie eine Zwei-Zimmer-Wohnung zu vermieten haben. Stimmt das?
VERMIETER	Ja, in der Nähe vom Dom.
INGE	Wie alt ist die Wohnung?
VERMIETER	Ziemlich alt, aber sie ist renoviert und schön groß und hell. Sie hat sogar einen Balkon.
INGE	In welchem Stock liegt sie?
VERMIETER	Im dritten Stock[1].
INGE	Ist sie möbliert oder unmöbliert?
VERMIETER	Unmöbliert.
INGE	Und was kostet die Wohnung?
VERMIETER	1100 DM.
INGE	Ist das kalt oder warm?
VERMIETER	Kalt.
INGE	O, das ist ein bißchen zu teuer. Vielen Dank! Auf Wiederhören!
VERMIETER	Auf Wiederhören!

In der Wohngemeinschaft[2]

INGE	Euer Haus gefällt mir!
HORST	Wir haben noch Platz für dich! Komm, ich zeige es dir! . . . Hier links ist unsere Küche. Sie ist klein, aber praktisch.
INGE	Wer kocht?
HORST	Wir alle: Jens, Gisela, Renate und ich.
INGE	Und das ist das Wohnzimmer?
HORST	Ja. Es ist ein bißchen dunkel, aber das ist OK.
INGE	Eure Sessel gefallen mir.
HORST	Sie sind alt, aber echt bequem. Oben sind dann vier Schlafzimmer und das Bad.
INGE	Nur ein Bad?
HORST	Ja, leider! Aber hier unten ist noch eine Toilette.
INGE	Was bezahlt ihr im Monat?
HORST	Jeder 400 Mark.
INGE	Nicht schlecht! Und wie kommst du zur Uni?
HORST	Zu Fuß natürlich! Es ist ja nicht weit.
INGE	Klingt gut!

Richtig oder falsch?

——— 1. In der Nähe vom Dom gibt es eine Wohnung zu vermieten.
——— 2. Die Wohnung hat vier Zimmer.
——— 3. Die Wohnung soll etwas dunkel sein.
——— 4. Sie liegt im Parterre.
——— 5. Horst wohnt in einer Wohngemeinschaft.
——— 6. Von da ist es nicht weit zum Dom.
——— 7. Sie fahren mit der U-Bahn zur Uni.
——— 8. Für das Haus bezahlen die Studenten 200 DM pro Person.
——— 9. Horst möchte, daß Inge auch dort wohnt.
——— 10. Aber das gefällt Inge nicht.

Übrigens

1. For German-speakers the first floor (ground floor) is **das Parterre** or **das Erdge-schoß.** Only the floors above the ground floor are numbered. When we say *on the second floor,* they say **im ersten Stock.** Homes and apartments usually have a foyer, or hallway (**der Flur**), with doors leading into the various rooms. The doors are usually kept closed, however, since many Germans feel uncomfortably exposed when doors are open, whereas Americans prefer open doors.

2. **Wohngemeinschaften,** where several students share an apartment or a house, are quite common because rooms in dormitories are scarce and waiting lists long.

WORTSCHATZ 1

Das Haus, ¨er   *(house)*
Das Studentenheim, -e   *(dorm)*
Die Wohnung, -en   *(apartment)*

---

der	Balkon, -s	*balcony*	die	Ecke, -n	*corner*
	Baum, ¨e	*tree*		Garage, -n	*garage*
	Flur	*hallway, foyer*		Küche, -n	*kitchen*
	Garten, ¨	*garden, yard*		Toilette, -n	*toilet*
das	Bad, ¨er	*bathroom*			
	Arbeitszimmer,-	*study*			
	Eßzimmer, -	*dining room*			
	Schlafzimmer, -	*bedroom*			
	Wohnzimmer, -	*living room*			

Die Möbel   *(pl.) (furniture)*

---

der	Fernseher, -	*TV set*	das	Bett, -en	*bed*
	Kühlschrank, ¨e	*refrigerator*		Radio, -s	*radio*
	Schrank, ¨e	*closet, cupboard*		Regal, -e	*shelf, bookcase*
	Schreibtisch, -e	*desk*		Sofa, -s	*sofa*
	Sessel, -	*armchair*		Telefon, -e	*telephone*
	Stuhl, ¨e	*chair*	die	Kommode, -n	*dresser*
	Teppich, -e	*carpet*		Lampe, -n	*lamp*
	Tisch, -e	*table*			
	Vorhang, ¨e	*curtain*			

Weiteres

---

hell / dunkel	*bright, light / dark*
im Parterre	*on the first floor (ground level)*
im ersten Stock	*on the second floor*
im Monat	*per month*
oben / unten	*up(stairs) / down(stairs)*
praktisch	*practical(ly)*
sogar	*even*
(un)bequem	*(un)comfortable; (in)convenient*
ziemlich	*quite, rather*
baden	*to take a bath; to swim*
duschen	*to take a shower*

Weiteres *(cont.)*

hängen, gehängt	*to hang (up)*
hängen, gehangen	*to hang (be hanging)*
kochen	*to cook*
legen	*to lay, put (flat)*
liegen, gelegen	*to lie (be lying flat)*
mieten / vermieten	*to rent / to rent out*
setzen	*to set, put*
sitzen, gesessen	*to sit (be sitting)*
stehen, gestanden	*to stand (be standing)*
stellen	*to stand, put (upright)*
waschen (wäscht), gewaschen	*to wash*
(Das) klingt gut.	*(That) sounds good.*
(Das) stimmt.	*(That's) true. / (That's) right.*
Auf Wiederhören!	*Good-bye! (on the phone)*

ZUM ERKENNEN: renoviert *(renovated);* (un)möbliert *([un]furnished);* kalt oder warm? *(here: with or without heat);* die Wohngemeinschaft, -en *(group sharing a place);* echt *(really);* jeder *(each one)*

Zum Thema

A.   Mustersätze

1. das Haus: Das Haus **gefällt mir.**
   das Wohnzimmer, die Küche, das Bad, der Garten
2. der Sessel: **Wie gefällt dir** der Sessel?
   das Sofa, der Teppich, das Regal, das Radio
3. die Möbel: Die Möbel **gefallen mir.**
   Sessel, Stühle, Vorhänge, Schränke
4. sehr praktisch: **Die Wohnung ist** sehr praktisch.
   schön hell, ziemlich dunkel, zu klein, sehr gemütlich, wirklich bequem
5. unten: **Die Wohnung ist** unten.
   oben, im Parterre, im ersten Stock, im zweiten Stock, im dritten Stock

Hildesheim mit Blick
auf die Michaeliskirche

B. Beschreiben Sie die Wohnung! *(Tell what furniture is in what room. You may need the optional vocabulary below.)*

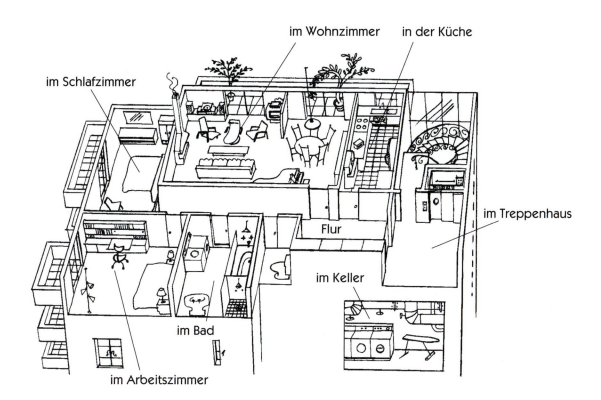

im Wohnzimmer   in der Küche

im Schlafzimmer

im Treppenhaus

Flur

im Keller

im Bad

im Arbeitszimmer

ZUM ERKENNEN: *basement* (der Keller), *bathtub* (die Badewanne), *closet* (der Kleiderschrank), *dining room cabinet* (das Büfett), *dishwasher* (die Spülmaschine), *dryer* (der Trockner), *elevator* (der Aufzug), *fireplace* (der Kamin), *kitchen cabinet* (der Küchenschrank), *microwave oven* (der Mikrowellenherd), *mirror* (der Spiegel), *nightstand* (der Nachttisch), *oven* (der Ofen), *piano* (das Klavier), *range* (der Herd), *shower* (die Dusche), *sink* (das Waschbecken), *staircase* (das Treppenhaus), *stereo set* (die Stereoanlage), *terrace* (die Terrasse), (der Videorecorder), *washing machine* (die Waschmaschine)

C. Was bedeutet das, und was ist der Plural?

Balkontür, Bücherregal, Duschvorhang, Elternschlafzimmer, Kinderbad, Farbfernseher, Garagentür, Gartenmöbel, Kinderzimmer, Küchenfenster, Kleiderschrank, Kochecke, Nachttisch, Schreibtischlampe, Sitzecke, Waschecke, Wohnzimmerteppich

D. Interview. Fragen Sie einen Nachbarn / eine Nachbarin, . . . !

1. ob er / sie eine Wohnung hat, oder zu Hause oder im Studentenheim wohnt
2. wie lange er / sie schon da wohnt
3. ob er / sie eine Küche hat; wenn ja, was es in der Küche gibt und wer kocht
4. was für Möbel er / sie im Zimmer hat
5. was man vom Zimmerfenster sehen kann

E. Eine Wohnung zu vermieten *(Complete the dialogue with a classmate.)*

S1   Ich habe gelesen, daß Sie ein Haus zu vermieten haben. Wo ist das Haus?

S2   _____ .

S1   Können Sie mir das Haus etwas beschreiben *(describe)?*

S2   Ja, gern. Es hat _____ .

S1   Gibt es auch _____ (eine Terrasse, einen Balkon, einen Pool . . .)?

S2   _____ .

S1   Wie weit ist es zu _____ ?

S2   _____ .

S1   Und was kostet das Haus?

S2   _____ .

S1   _____ . *(Make a final comment.)*

F. Aussprache: ei, au, eu, äu   *(See also II.37–39 in the pronunciation section of the Workbook.)*

1. [ai]   **Ei, Hei**zung, w**ei**t, w**ei**l, l**ei**der, **ei**gentlich, **ei**nmal, z**ei**gen, f**ei**ern, bl**ei**ben
2. [au]   **au**f, **au**ch, br**au**n, bl**au**gr**au**, K**au**fh**au**s, B**au**m, br**au**chen, l**au**fen, d**au**ern
3. [oi]   **eu**ch, n**eu**, h**eu**te, t**eu**er, d**eu**tsch, L**eu**te, Fr**eu**nde, H**äu**ser, B**äu**me, Fr**äu**lein
4. Wortpaare
    a. *by* / bei   c. *mouse* / Maus   e. aus / Eis
    b. *Troy* / treu   d. Haus / Häuser   f. euer / Eier

Hören Sie zu!

Hier Müller   *(Listen to the conversation between Inge and Mrs. Müller. Then decide whether the statements below are true or false according to the dialogue.)*

ZUM ERKENNEN: Mutti *(Mom)*; nett *(nice)*; teilen *(to share)*; mit dem Fahrrad *(by bike)*; na gut *(well, good)*; Bis bald! *(See you soon!)*

_____   1.   Inge ist Frau Müllers Tochter.

_____   2.   Frau Müller hat ein Zimmer gefunden.

_____   3.   Das Zimmer ist in der Schillerstraße.

_____   4.   Inges Telefonnummer ist 91 68.

_____   5.   Wohnungen sind sehr teuer.

_____   6.   Inge hat Horst vor ein paar Tagen gesehen.

_____   7.   Sie teilt jetzt ein Zimmer mit Horst.

_____   8.   Inge zahlt 280 Mark im Monat.

_____   9.   Sie kann mit dem Fahrrad zur Uni fahren.

_____ 10.   Am Wochenende kommt sie nach Hause.

TRAUMHAUS IM GRÜNEN: auch in Zukunft die Sehnsucht der Deutschen

Wohnen 2000: das Haus im Grünen ist Favorit

STRUKTUR

I. Two-Way Prepositions

You have learned some prepositions that are always followed by the dative and some that are always followed by the accusative. You will now learn a set of prepositions that sometimes take the dative and sometimes the accusative.

1. The basic meanings of the nine TWO-WAY PREPOSITIONS are:

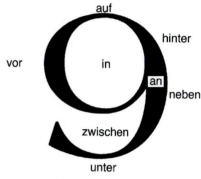

an	*to, up to, at (the side of), on (vertical surface)*
auf	*on (top of, horizontal surface), onto*
hinter	*behind*
in	*in, into, inside of*
neben	*beside, next to*
über	*over, above*
unter	*under, below*
vor	*before, in front of*
zwischen	*between*

Most of these prepositions may be contracted with articles. The most common contractions are:

an das = **ans**	in das = **ins**
an dem = **am**	in dem = **im**
auf das = **aufs**	

In colloquial speech you will also hear: hinter**s**, hinter**m**, über**s**, über**m**, unter**s**, unter**m**, vor**s**, vor**m**.

CAUTION: The preposition **vor** precedes a noun (**vor dem Haus**). The conjunction **bevor** introduces a clause (**. . . , bevor du das Haus mietest**).

2. **Wo? Wohin?**

    a. German has two words to ask *where:* **wo?** *(in what place?)* and **wohin?** *(to what place?).* **Wo** asks about location, where something is, or an activity within a place. **Wohin** asks about destination or a change of place.

    LOCATION: **Wo** ist Horst?   *Where's Horst? (in what place)*
    DESTINATION: **Wohin** geht Horst?   *Where's Horst going? (to what place)*

    b. The difference between location and destination also plays a role in determining the case following two-way prepositions. If the question is **wo?**, the <u>dative</u> is used. If the question is **wohin?**, the <u>accusative</u> is used.

    Wo ist Horst? → **In der** Bibliothek.   *Where's Horst? → In the library.*
    Wohin geht Horst? → **In die** Bibliothek. *Where's Horst going? → To the library.*

wo?	LOCATION	→	<u>dative</u>
wohin?	DESTINATION	→	<u>accusative</u>

3.   The difference lies entirely in the verb!

- Some verbs denoting LOCATION or activity within a place (**wo?** → <u>dative</u>) are: hängen, kaufen, kochen, lesen, liegen, schlafen, schreiben, sein, sitzen, spielen, stehen, studieren, tanzen, trinken, wohnen

- Typical verbs implying DESTINATION or a change of place or motion towards one (**wohin?** → <u>accusative</u>) are: bringen, fahren, gehen, hängen, kommen, laufen, legen, setzen, stellen, tragen

4.   Some important verb pairs

N-VERBS / LOCATION → <u>dative</u>	T-VERBS / CHANGE OF PLACE → <u>accusative</u>
hängen, gehangen *(to be hanging)*	hängen, gehängt *(to hang up)*
liegen, gelegen *(to be lying [flat])*	legen, gelegt *(to lay down, put [flat])*
sitzen, gesessen *(to be sitting)*	setzen, gesetzt *(to set down)*
stehen, gestanden *(to be standing)*	stellen, gestellt *(to put [upright])*

- Note that these four n-verbs are all intransitive, i.e., they do not take a direct object: **Der Mantel hängt im Schrank.**

- The four t-verbs are transitive, i.e., they do take a direct object: **Ich hänge den Mantel in den Schrank.**

CAUTION: Although **legen, setzen,** and **stellen** are all sometimes translated as *to put,* they are <u>not</u> interchangeable.

Sie **stellt** den Stuhl an die Wand. *(upright position)*
Sie **legt** das Heft auf den Tisch. *(flat position)*
Er **setzt** das Kind auf den Stuhl. *(sitting position)*

5.   Summary

4. Wo können die Kinder spielen? (hinter / Haus; unter / Baum; auf / Spielplatz)
5. Wohin gehen sie gern? (in / Park; an / Fluß; in / Kino)
6. Wohin soll ich den Hund (*dog*) tun? (vor / Tür; in / Garten; auf / Balkon)

F. Wir bekommen Besuch   (*Tell what you still have to do by filling in the blanks.*)

1. Die Gläser sind in _____ Küche.   **2.** Ich muß die Gläser in _____
Wohnzimmer bringen und sie auf _____ Tisch stellen.   **3.** Der Wein ist noch
in _____ Kühlschrank.   **4.** Wir müssen die Teller neben _____ Gläser
stellen.   **5.** Ich muß in _____ Küche gehen und die Wurst und den Käse auf
_____ Teller legen.   **6.** Haben wir Blumen in _____ Garten?   **7.** Wir
stellen die Blumen auf _____ Tischchen (*sg.*) vor _____ Sofa.   **8.** Sind
die Kerzen in _____ Schrank?   **9.** Nein, sie sind in _____ Kommode
in _____ Flur.

G. Im Wohnzimmer

1. **Wohin sollen wir das stellen?**   (*Tell where the movers are supposed to put things.*)

    BEISPIEL: Kommode / an / Wand
    Stellen Sie die Kommode an die Wand!

    a. Regal / auf / Kommode
    b. Radio / in / Regal
    c. Fernseher / neben / Radio
    d. kleine Regal / unter / Fenster
    e. Blumen / an / Fenster
    f. Glasschrank / zwischen / Kommode (*pl.*)
    g. Bücher / auf / Kommode
    h. Tisch / vor / Sessel
    i. Bild / in / Regal

2. **Was ist wo?**   (*As you check the picture below, make ten statements telling where things are standing, lying, or hanging.*)

    BEISPIEL: Das Glas steht auf dem Fernseher.

3. **Mein Zimmer**   (*Describe your room in eight to ten sentences. Use a two-way preposition in each sentence.*)

II. The Imperative

You are already familiar with the FORMAL IMPERATIVE, which addresses one individual or several people. You know that the verb is followed by the pronoun **Sie:**

Herr Schmidt, **lesen Sie** das bitte!
Frau Müller und Fräulein Schulz, **kommen Sie** später wieder!

1. The FAMILIAR IMPERATIVE has two forms: one for the plural and one for the singular.

    a. The plural corresponds to the **ihr**-form of the verb WITHOUT the pronoun **ihr.**

ihr schreibt	ihr tut	ihr antwortet	ihr nehmt	ihr lest	ihr eßt
Schreibt!	**Tut!**	**Antwortet!**	**Nehmt!**	**Lest!**	**Eßt!**

    b. The singular usually corresponds to the **du**-form of the verb WITHOUT the pronoun **du** and WITHOUT the -st ending:

du schreibst	du tust	du antwortest	du nimmst	du liest	du ißt
Schreib!	**Tu!**	**Antworte!**	**Nimm!**	**Lies!**	**Iß!**

    NOTE: **lesen** and **essen** retain the **s** or **ss** of the verb stem. **Lies! Iß!**

    •   There is an OPTIONAL **-e** ending in the **du**-form. However, the more informal the situation, the less likely its use.

        Schreib(e) mir! **Sag(e)** das noch einmal!

    •   Verbs ending in **-d, -t, -ig,** or in certain other consonant combinations USUALLY have an **-e** ending in the **du**-form.

        Finde das! **Antworte** ihm! **Entschuldige** bitte! **Öffne** die Tür!

    •   Verbs with vowel changes from **e** > **i(e)** in the present singular NEVER have an **-e** ending in the **du**-form.

        Sprich Deutsch! **Sieh** mal!

    •   Verbs with vowel changes from **a** > **ä** in the present singular DO NOT MAKE THIS CHANGE in the imperative.

        Fahr langsam! **Lauf** nicht so schnell!

2. English imperatives beginning with *Let's . . .* are expressed in German as follows:

Sprechen wir Deutsch!	*Let's speak German.*
Gehen wir nach Hause!	*Let's go home.*

3. Here is a summary chart of the imperative.

Schreiben Sie!	Schreibt!	Schreib(e)!	Schreiben wir!
Antworten Sie!	Antwortet!	Antworte!	Antworten wir!
Fahren Sie!	Fahrt!	**Fahr(e)!**	Fahren wir!
Nehmen Sie!	Nehmt!	**Nimm!**	Nehmen wir!
Lesen Sie!	Lest!	**Lies!**	Lesen wir!
Essen Sie!	Eßt!	**Iß!**	Essen wir!

Frau Schmidt, **schreiben Sie** mir!

Kinder, **schreibt** mir!

Helga, **schreib(e)** mir!

Schreiben wir Lisa!

NOTE: The German imperative is usually followed by an EXCLAMATION MARK.

H. Geben Sie den Imperativ! *(First form the plural familiar and then the singular familiar.)*

BEISPIEL: Bleiben Sie bitte!
Bleibt bitte! Bleib bitte!

1. Fragen Sie ihn!
2. Entschuldigen Sie bitte!
3. Bitte helfen Sie uns!
4. Zeigen Sie uns den Weg!
5. Geben Sie mir die Landkarte!
6. Fahren Sie immer geradeaus!
7. Wiederholen Sie das bitte!
8. Halten Sie da drüben!
9. Hören Sie mal!
10. Schlafen Sie nicht!
11. Essen Sie einen Apfel!
12. Trinken Sie eine Cola!

I. Geben Sie Befehle! *(Form formal and familiar commands, using the phrases below.)*

BEISPIEL: an die Tafel gehen   **Gehen Sie an die Tafel!**
Geht an die Tafel!
Geh an die Tafel!

1. die Kreide nehmen   **2.** ein Wort auf deutsch schreiben   **3.** von 1 bis 10 zählen
4. wieder an den Platz gehen   **5.** das Deutschbuch öffnen   **6.** auf Seite 150 lesen
7. mit dem Nachbarn auf deutsch sprechen   **8.** mir einen Kuli geben   **9.** nach
Hause gehen   **10.** das nicht tun

J. Was tun? *(Decide with your friend what to do with the rest of the day.)*

BEISPIEL: zu Hause bleiben   **Bleiben wir zu Hause!**

1. in die Stadt gehen   **2.** mit der Straßenbahn fahren   **3.** durch die Geschäfte bummeln   **4.** eine Pizza essen   **5.** das Schloß besichtigen   **6.** ins Kino gehen

K. **Geben Sie Befehle an** *(to)* **. . . !**   *(Address three commands to each.)*

BEISPIEL: **Fahren Sie mit dem Bus!**
Hilf mir!
Fallt nicht!

1.   einen Touristen oder einen Angestellten *(employee at work)*
2.   einen Freund oder eine Freundin
3.   zwei kleine Kinder

III. *wissen vs. kennen*

In German two verbs correspond to the English *to know:*

> **kennen, gekannt**   *to know (to be acquainted with a person or thing)*
> **wissen, gewußt**   *to know a fact (the fact is often expressed in a subordinate clause)*

Whereas **kennen** is regular in the present tense, the forms of **wissen** are very similar to the forms of the modals.

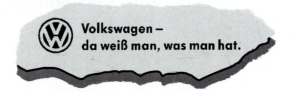

ich	weiß
du	weißt
er	weiß
wir	wissen
ihr	wißt
sie	wissen

Ich **kenne** das Buch.   BUT Ich **weiß, daß** es gut ist.
Ich **kenne** den Lehrer.   BUT Ich **weiß, daß** er aus Wien ist.

Übungen

L. **Kennen oder wissen?**   *(Fill in the appropriate forms.)*

ANGELIKA   Entschuldigen Sie! _____ Sie, wo die Wipplinger Straße ist?

DAME   Nein. Ich _____ Wien gut, aber das _____ ich leider nicht.

MICHAEL   Danke! Du, Angelika, _____ du, wie spät es ist?

ANGELIKA   Nein, aber ich _____ , daß ich Hunger habe.

MICHAEL   Hallo, Holger und Sabine! Sagt mal, _____ ihr Angelika?

SABINE   Ja, natürlich.

MICHAEL   Wir haben Hunger. _____ ihr, wo es hier ein Restaurant gibt?

HOLGER   Ja, da drüben ist das Bastei Beisl. Wir _____ es nicht, aber wir _____ , daß es gut sein soll.

MICHAEL   _____ ihr was? Gehen wir essen!

M. Bilden Sie Sätze!   *(Add suitable subjects and verbs.)*

BEISPIEL: über dem Tisch
      Die Lampe hängt über dem Tisch.

1.	in den Schrank	7.	neben dem Telefon
2.	unter dem Bett	8.	zwischen der Schulstraße und dem Domplatz
3.	über dem Sofa	9.	auf den Schreibtisch
4.	hinter der Staatsoper	10.	unter dem Baum
5.	in die Bank	11.	ins Regal
6.	vor das Haus	12.	ans Fenster

N. An der Uni. Auf deutsch, bitte!

1. Hello, Hans! Where have you been?   **2.** I've been in the dorm.   **3.** Where are you going?—To the library.   **4.** I'd like to live in a dorm, too.   **5.** Where do you live now?   **6.** In an apartment. Unfortunately it's over a disco (**die Disko**) and next to a restaurant.   **7.** Tell me, are the rooms in the dorms nice?   **8.** I like my room, but I don't like the furniture.   **9.** On which floor do you live?—On the third floor. **10.** Do you know how much it costs?—350 marks a month.   **11.** There's Reinhart. **12.** Who's that? From where am I supposed to know him? (Where am I supposed to know him from?)   **13.** I didn't know that you don't know him.   **14.** Let's say hello.

Einfamilienhäuser mit Garten

EINBLICKE

There are many excellent public transportation systems in Germany. Those in Berlin, Hamburg, and Munich are typical. Munich, for example, has an extensive subway system that is linked with suburban commuter trains. During rush hour, trains arrive precisely every two minutes. Trains and stations are clean and safe, and commuters cancel their own tickets—those who fail to do so (**schwarzfahren**) and are caught during one of the periodic checks pay heavy fines. Streetcars and buses supplement the subway system. Users often reach the suburban train stations by bicycle.

All cities have some form of public transportation, usually heavily subsidized in an effort to limit the driving and parking of private cars in the often narrow streets. Public transportation is also considered environmentally sounder and allows those who can't afford cars to reach their work places. Discount rates are available for regular commuters, students, senior citizens, and weekend travelers.

der	Wald, ⸚er	*forest, woods*
das	(Fahr)rad, ⸚er	*bicycle*

am Abend	*in the evening*
am Tag	*during the day*
aufs Land	*in(to) the country(side)*
auf dem Land	*in the country*
ausgezeichnet	*excellent*
außerdem	*besides (adverb)*
mitten in	*in the middle of*
noch nicht	*not yet*
trotzdem	*nevertheless, in spite of that*
bauen	*to build*
leben	*to live*
lieben	*to love*
sparen	*to save (money, time)*

WAS IST DAS?   der Biergarten, Clown, Dialekt, Fahrradweg, Münchner, Musiker, Spielplatz, Stadtpark, Wanderweg; das Bauland, Feld, Leben, Konsulat, Zentrum; die Arbeit, Bar, Energie, Wirklichkeit; frei, idyllisch; Ball spielen, eine Pause machen, formulieren, picknicken

Schaffen°, sparen, Häuschen° bauen

work hard / little house

Dieser Spruch° aus Schwaben° (im Dialekt[1] heißt es „Schaffe, spare, Häusle baue") ist nicht nur typisch für die Schwaben, sondern für die meisten° Deutschen, Österreicher und Schweizer.

this saying / Swabia
most

5   In den drei Ländern leben viele Menschen, aber es gibt nur wenig° Land. Die meisten wohnen in Wohnungen und träumen von° einem Haus mit Garten. Für viele bleibt das aber nur ein Traum°, denn in den Städten ist Bauland sehr teuer. Es gibt auch nicht genug Bauland, weil man nicht überall bauen darf.

little
dream of
dream

Viele Menschen leben gern in der Stadt, besonders in München.

edge of . . . / move
out(side)
commute back and forth /
  money / easily

necessarily
sidewalks / public
  transportation / on time
commuter train / with them
right through

goes window-shopping
there's a lot going on /
  sidewalk artists
any time
dependent
ocean
almost / therefore
restaurant

out into nature

benches / meadows
rowboats
condominium
by renting

hard

Oft muß man an den Stadtrand° oder aufs Land ziehen°, wo mehr Platz ist und wo Land noch nicht so teuer ist. Aber nicht alle möchten so weit draußen° wohnen und stundenlang hin und her pendeln°. Das kostet Energie, Zeit und Geld°. Abends kommt man 10 auch nicht leicht° ins Kino oder ins Theater. Das Leben zwischen Wäldern und Feldern ist oft idyllisch, aber nicht immer sehr bequem.

In der Stadt kann man eigentlich sehr gut leben. Die Wohnungen sind oft groß und schön. Man braucht nicht unbedingt° ein Auto, weil alles in der Nähe liegt. Überall gibt es Bürgersteige° und Fahrradwege, und die öffentlichen Verkehrsmittel° sind ausgezeich- 15 net. Die Busse kommen relativ oft und pünktlich°. In Großstädten gibt es auch Straßenbahnen, eine U-Bahn und eine S-Bahn°. Damit° können Sie nicht nur aus der Stadt oder quer durch° die Stadt, sondern auch mitten ins Zentrum, in die Fußgängerzonen fahren, wo die Leute am Tag einkaufen und am Abend gern bummeln gehen. Man sieht ein bißchen in die Schaufenster° und geht vielleicht in eine Bar oder ein Café. Auf den Straßen ist im Sommer 20 oft viel los°: Es gibt Straßenkünstler°, Musiker und Clowns.

Wenn man in der Stadt wohnt, kann man aber auch jederzeit° leicht aufs Land fahren. Viele tun das gern und oft. Wenn man nicht jeden Tag vom Auto abhängig° ist, fährt man am Wochenende gern einmal an die See° oder in die Berge. Überall findet man Wanderwege und oft auch Fahrradwege. Fast° alle Wege sind öffentlich, und deshalb° kann man 25 überall spazierengehen. Unterwegs findet man oft auch einen Gasthof°, wo man gemütlich Pause machen kann.

Man muß aber nicht unbedingt aufs Land fahren, wenn man ins Grüne° will. Fast alle Städte, ob groß oder klein, haben Stadtparks. Die Münchner z.B. lieben ihren Englischen Garten (in der Nähe vom amerikanischen Konsulat). Dort gibt es nicht nur Wanderwege, 30 sondern auch Spielplätze und Bänke°, Biergärten, Wiesen° zum Picknicken und zum Ball spielen und einen See mit Ruderbooten°.

Die meisten leben eigentlich gern in der Stadt, entweder in einer Eigentumswohnung° oder zur Miete°. In der Stadt gibt es viel zu sehen und zu tun. Alles ist ziemlich nah, nicht nur der Arbeitsplatz, die Geschäfte und die Schulen, sondern auch die Theater, Kinos, 35 Museen und Parks. Viele träumen trotzdem von einem Haus mit Garten. Sie wissen, daß sie schwer° arbeiten und sparen müssen, wenn der Traum Wirklichkeit werden soll. Und das tun auch viele.[2]

Laufen und
Fahrradfahren ist gesund
und kostet nichts.

A.   Richtig oder falsch? Wenn falsch, sagen Sie warum!

_____   1.   In Deutschland, in Österreich und in der Schweiz gibt es nicht viel Bauland, besonders nicht in den Städten.

_____   2.   Die meisten Leute dort wohnen in einem Haus mit Garten.

_____   3.   Auf dem Land ist Bauland nicht so teuer wie in der Stadt.

_____   4.   Das Leben zwischen Wäldern und Feldern _(fields)_ ist sehr bequem.

_____   5.   In allen Städten gibt es Straßenbahnen, eine U-Bahn und eine S-Bahn.

_____   6.   Mit öffentlichen Verkehrsmitteln kann man quer durch die Stadt fahren.

_____   7.   Überall in Wäldern und Feldern gibt es Fahrradwege und Fuß-gängerzonen.

_____   8.   In der Fußgängerzone kann man am Tag einkaufen, am Abend bummeln und manchmal Musik hören.

_____   9.   Im amerikanischen Konsulat in München kann man picknicken.

_____ 10.   Wenn man ein Haus kaufen oder bauen möchte, muß man schwer arbeiten und sparen.

B.   Haus oder Wohnung?   _(Fill in the appropriate form.)_

1. Die meisten wohnen in ein_____ Wohnung.   **2.** In d_____ Städten ist Bauland sehr teuer.   **3.** Der Traum vom Häuschen mit Garten hat viele an d_____ Stadtrand _(m.)_ oder auf d_____ Land gebracht.   **4.** Zwischen d_____ Wäldern und auf d_____ Feldern stehen Reihenhäuser _(town houses)._   **5.** Die Reihenhäuser stehen manch-mal direkt an d_____ Straße.   **6.** Morgens fahren viele in d_____ Stadt.   **7.** Das Leben auf d_____ Land kann unbequem sein.   **8.** Viele bleiben in d_____ Stadt, weil dort alles in d_____ Nähe liegt.   **9.** Nach d_____ Arbeit fahren viele noch ein-mal in d_____ Innenstadt.   **10.** Mitten in d_____ Zentrum _(n.)_ ist immer etwas los.

C.   In der Großstadt   _(You have never been to Munich before. Ask questions about the city, using **wo** or **wohin**.)_

BEISPIEL: In Großstädten gibt es eine U-Bahn.
             Wo gibt es eine U-Bahn?

1.   Mit der U-Bahn kann man mitten in die Fußgängerzone fahren.
2.   Dort kann man immer schön bummeln.
3.   Abends kann man ins Kino gehen.
4.   Man geht in den Park, wenn man ins Grüne will.
5.   Dort gibt es überall Wege und Bänke.

D.   Kennen oder wissen?

1.   _____ Sie den Spruch „Schaffen, sparen, Häuschen bauen"?
2.   _____ Sie, wie viele Leute in Deutschland auf dem Land leben?
3.   _____ Sie den Englischen Garten? _____ Sie, wo er ist?
4.   _____ ihr, daß es überall Fahrradwege gibt?
5.   Ich habe auch nicht _____ , daß es in der Stadt so viele Fußgängerwege gibt.
6.   _____ du Herrn Jakob? Nein, aber Hans hat ihn _____ .
7.   _____ du, daß er mit seinen 80 Jahren immer noch viel wandert?

„Der arme Poet" von
Carl Spitzweg. So kann
man auch wohnen.

E.   Fragen

1. Leben die meisten Leute hier in Wohnungen oder in Häusern mit Garten?
2. Wo ist Bauland teuer? Wo ist es nicht so teuer?
3. Was für öffentliche Verkehrsmittel gibt es hier?
4. Wie kommen die meisten Leute zur Arbeit? Wie kommen Sie zur Universität?
    Braucht man hier unbedingt *(necessarily)* ein Auto?
5. Gibt es hier Schlafstädte *(bedroom communities),* von wo die Leute morgens in
    die Stadt pendeln? Geben Sie Beispiele!
6. Wohin gehen oder fahren die Leute hier, wenn sie ins Grüne wollen?

F.   Wo möchten Sie wohnen, und warum?   *(Write three to four sentences describing where you would like to live and why. Include one phrase or word from each group below. After you have completed the exercise, your instructor polls the entire class to determine what choices others have made.)*

BEISPIEL: Ich möchte in einem Reihenhaus mitten in San Francisco wohnen. Da
komme ich schnell zur Arbeit und zum Ozean. Man braucht nicht
unbedingt ein Auto.

1	2
in einer Wohngemeinschaft	mitten in . . .
in einer Wohnung	in der Nähe von . . .
in einer Eigentumswohnung	am Stadtrand von . . .
in einem Reihenhaus	auf dem Land . . .
in einem Haus mit Garten	

Hören Sie zu!

Die Großeltern kommen   *(Listen to the message that Mrs. Schmidt has left for her children on the answering machine. Then indicate which chores each child has been asked to do; write S for Sebastian, M for Mareike, and J for Julia. Finally, note briefly what the children are* not *supposed to do.)*

ZUM ERKENNEN: Vati *(Dad);* nämlich *(you know)*

1. **Wer soll was tun?**

   —— zum Supermarkt fahren

   —— einen Schokoladenpudding machen

   —— Bratwurst und Käse kaufen

   —— den Großeltern zeigen, wo sie schlafen

   —— zum Blumengeschäft fahren

   —— Kartoffeln kochen

   —— Blumen ins Eßzimmer stellen

   —— dreißig Mark aus dem Schreibtisch nehmen

   —— Mineralwasserflaschen zum Supermarkt bringen

   —— die Kleidung der *(of the)* Großeltern in den Schrank hängen

   —— Wein in den Kühlschrank stellen

2. **Was sollen die Kinder nicht tun?**

   a. _____

   b. _____

Übrigens

1. Germany has numerous dialects (**Dialekte**) that are, in fact, much older than the standard German used today; and movements are alive to cultivate regional languages. North German Radio, for instance, broadcasts short daily sermons in Low German (**Plattdeutsch**); some Bavarian newspapers include a regular feature in Bavarian; and dialects are staging a comeback in song, poetry, literature, and the theater. Children frequently learn to speak dialect first, but they need to master standard German (**Hochdeutsch**) in order not to have a distinct disadvantage in school, a handicap that also carries over into the job market.

2. In the German-speaking countries, the per capita savings rate is unusually high—employees put aside approximately 15% of their income. Generous tax incentives encourage people to save in special savings institutions for the building of private homes and condominiums. Thrift is also reflected in the relatively low consumption of energy in spite of a high standard of living and industrial output.

SPRECHSITUATIONEN

Describing Locations

You have already learned many ways of describing the location of something, including the two-way prepositions in this chapter. Here are a few reminders:

im Norden / nördlich von	an der Ecke
bei	Ecke Schillerstraße
in der Nähe von	in der Schillerstraße
nicht weit von	da drüben
mitten in	hier / da / dort
rechts / links von	im Parterre / im ersten Stock
gegenüber von	am [Rhein] / an der [Donau]

Offering Apologies

Entschuldigung! / Verzeihung!
Entschuldige! / Entschuldigen Sie!
Es tut mir (furchtbar) leid!
Leider . . .

Expressing Forgiveness

(Das) macht nichts.
(Das ist) kein Problem.
(Es ist) schon gut. *(It's OK.)*

Übungen

 A. **Wo ist was?** *(Working with a classmate, look at the map of Germany inside the front cover of the book and write at least ten different statements about the location of various cities in the former GDR.)*

BEISPIEL: Halle liegt an der Saale, nordöstlich von Leipzig.

B. **Was sagen Sie?** *(Use the appropriate expression for each of the following situations.)*

1. Sie haben den Pullover von einem Freund getragen. Der Pullover ist schmutzig geworden.
2. Sie und ihr Zimmerkollege / ihre Zimmerkollegin haben am Samstag Plätzchen gekauft. Am Sonntag haben Sie alle Plätzchen gegessen. Ihr Zimmerkollege / Ihre Zimmerkollegin kann kein Plätzchen mehr finden.
3. Sie haben bei einem Professor gegessen. Ihr Glas ist vom Tisch gefallen.
4. Ihre Zimmerkollegin hat Ihre Cola getrunken.
5. Ein Freund hat Ihnen nicht zum Geburtstag geschrieben, weil er zu viel zu tun hatte.

C. **Wo genau ist das?**   *(Describe the location of ten places shown on this map of Rostock.)*

BEISPIEL: Die Post ist beim Rathaus, gegenüber vom Haus Sonne.

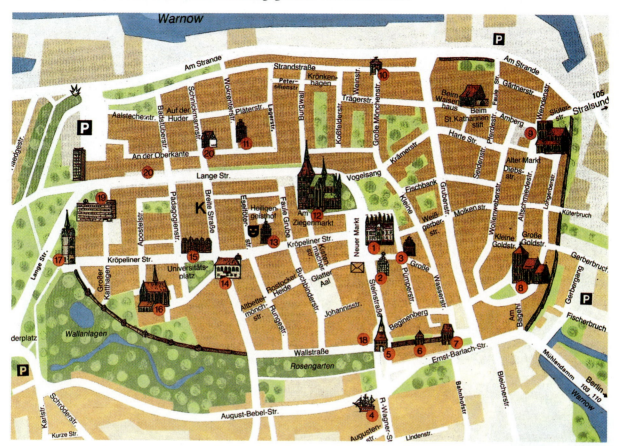

1. das Rathaus 2. Haus Sonne 3. das Stadtarchiv 4. das Schiffahrtsmuseum 5. das Steintor (*. . . gate*) 6. der Lagebuschturm (*. . . tower*) 7. das Kuhtor 8. die Nikolaikirche 9. die Petrikirche 10. das Mönchentor 11. das Hausbaumhaus 12. die Marienkirche 13. das Heiligen-Geist-Hospital 14. der Barocksaal (*festival hall*) 15. das Fünfgiebelhaus 16. Klostermuseum 17. das Kröpeliner Tor 18. das Ständehaus (*guild hall*) 19. Hotel Warnow 20. die Information

D.   **Kurzgespräche**

1.   You are visiting Hildesheim and want to see the well-known *Knochenhauer Amtshaus* (a 16th-century guildhouse). You stop a Hildesheimer and ask where the building is. He / she replies that it is at the *Marktplatz,* across from city hall. Your informant asks whether you see the pedestrian area (**Fußgängerzone**) over there; he / she directs you to walk along that street and turn right at the pharmacy. The *Marktplatz* is nearby (**ganz in der Nähe**). You thank the stranger and say good-bye.

2.   You have been invited to a classmate's house for dinner, but you are quite late. You introduce yourself to his / her mother, who asks you to come in (**herein**). You apologize repeatedly for being so late, while she maintains it doesn't matter. When you hand her the flowers you have brought, she thanks you and says that dinner is ready.

Auf der Bank und im Hotel

Schweizer Geld

LERNZIELE

Vorschau

- Money and banking

Gespräche and Wortschatz

- Banking and hotel accommodations

Struktur

- *Der-* and *ein-*words
- Separable-prefix verbs
- Flavoring particles

Einblicke

- Hotels, youth hostels, and other lodgings for travelers

Sprechsituationen

- Telling time
- Expressing disbelief
- Giving a warning

Money and Banking

Despite the strength of the German economy from the 1950s until 1991, economic policies were and are shaped by a concern about inflation that goes back to the early twenties, when Germany experienced what was probably the worst inflation of any modern industrialized country. At that time the mark had so little value that people needed pushcarts to carry the money to buy groceries, and billions of marks bought just one loaf of bread.

After the Second World War, in order to control inflation, reduce the enormous German war debt, and instill economic confidence, the Western Allies replaced the **Reichsmark (RM)** with the **Deutsche Mark (DM)** in June of 1948. The Soviet Union followed suit in the eastern zone with a new currency, the **Mark (M)**, which accentuated the division of Germany. While the West German economy, aided by the Marshall Plan, experienced dramatic growth, East Germany was stripped of anything that could be moved. Nevertheless, its economy eventually became one of the strongest of the eastern block countries.

On July 2, 1990, after reunification, GDR residents were allowed to exchange between M 2,000 and M 6,000, depending on age, at a ratio of 1 : 1; savings above those rates were exchanged at a ratio of 1 : 2. That meant, for example, that after the exchange (**Umtausch**), the average savings of a three-family household were reduced from M 27,000 to DM 19,500. The introduction of the strong western currency had a devastating economic impact on East Germany by making its industries noncompetitive overnight and throwing large numbers of workers out of work. This situation required huge infusions of cash into the new states, increasing inflationary pressures in all of Germany. The independent German central bank (**Bundesbank**), charged with ensuring monetary stability, raised interest rates to the highest point in decades and only reluctantly reduced them after Germany, in the early 1990s, plunged into the worst recession since World War II. The desire for a stable currency and low inflation still supersedes all other economic concerns in the eyes of the German people and their government.

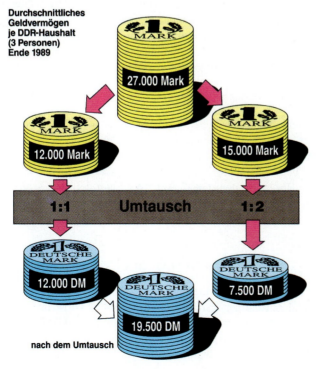

Gespräche   Auf der Bank[1]

TOURISTIN	Guten Tag! Können Sie mir sagen, wo ich Geld umtauschen kann?[2]
ANGESTELLTE	Am Schalter 1.
TOURISTIN	Vielen Dank! *(Sie geht zum Schalter 1.)* Guten Tag! Ich möchte Dollar in Schillinge umtauschen. Hier sind meine Reiseschecks.[3]
ANGESTELLTE	Darf ich bitte Ihren Paß sehen?
TOURISTIN	Hier.
ANGESTELLTE	Unterschreiben Sie bitte hier! Gehen Sie dort zur Kasse! Da bekommen Sie Ihr Geld.
TOURISTIN	Danke! *(Sie geht zur Kasse.)*
KASSIERER	324 Schilling 63: einhundert, zweihundert, dreihundert, zehn, zwanzig, vierundzwanzig Schilling und dreiundsechzig Groschen.
TOURISTIN	Danke! Auf Wiedersehen!

An der Rezeption im Hotel

EMPFANGSDAME	Guten Abend!
GAST	Guten Abend! Haben Sie ein Einzelzimmer frei?
EMPFANGSDAME	Für wie lange?
GAST	Für zwei oder drei Nächte; wenn möglich ruhig und mit Bad.
EMPFANGSDAME	Leider haben wir heute nur noch ein Doppelzimmer, und das nur für eine Nacht. Aber morgen wird ein Einzelzimmer frei. Wollen Sie das Doppelzimmer sehen?
GAST	Ja, gern.
EMPFANGSDAME	Zimmer Nummer 12, im ersten Stock rechts. Hier ist der Schlüssel.
GAST	Sagen Sie, kann ich meinen Koffer einen Moment hier lassen?
EMPFANGSDAME	Ja, natürlich. Stellen Sie ihn da drüben in die Ecke!
GAST	Danke! Noch etwas, wann machen Sie abends zu?
EMPFANGSDAME	Um 24.00 Uhr. Wenn Sie später kommen, müssen Sie klingeln.

Fragen

1. Wer möchte Geld umtauschen?   2. Wo ist sie?   3. Wohin muß sie gehen?   4. Was muß die Touristin der Angestellten zeigen?   5. Wo bekommt sie ihr Geld?   6. Wieviel Schilling bekommt sie?   7. Was für ein Zimmer möchte der Gast?   8. Für wie lange braucht er es?   9. Was für ein Zimmer nimmt er, und wo liegt es?   10. Was gibt die Dame an der Rezeption dem Gast?   11. Wo kann der Gast seinen Koffer lassen?   12. Wann macht das Hotel zu?

Übrigens

1.   Between 1990 and 1992, the German central bank issued new bank notes that are more difficult to counterfeit. Pictured on these notes are the poet Bettina von Arnim (5 DM), the mathematician and astronomer Carl Friedrich Gauß (10 DM), the writer Annette von Droste-Hülshoff (20 DM), the architect Balthasar Neumann (50 DM), the pianist and composer Clara Schumann (100 DM), the physician Paul Ehrlich (200 DM), the artist Anna Maria Merian (500 DM), and the Grimm Brothers (1 000 DM).

2.   Currency can be exchanged and travelers' checks can be cashed in banks and post of-fices. Exchange offices (**Wechselstuben**) are open daily at all major railroad stations, air-ports, and border crossings.

3.   While credit cards (**Kreditkarten**) are becoming more accepted in Europe, eu-rocheques continue to be very popular. Used in conjunction with a special eurocheque card, these checks can be used to obtain cash from banks and to pay bills in shops, restaurants, and hotels throughout Europe.

Die Uhrzeit   *(time of the day)*

• The formal (official) time system is like the one used by the military. The hours are counted from 0 to 24, with 0 to 11 referring to A.M. and 12 to 24 referring to P.M. The system is commonly used in timetables for trains, buses, planes, etc., on radio and TV, and to state business hours of stores and banks.

16.05 Uhr	=	**sechzehn Uhr fünf**	*4:05* P.M.
16.15 Uhr	=	**sechzehn Uhr fünfzehn**	*4:15* P.M.
16.30 Uhr	=	**sechzehn Uhr dreißig**	*4:30* P.M.
16.45 Uhr	=	**sechzehn Uhr fünfundvierzig**	*4:45* P.M.
17.00 Uhr	=	**siebzehn Uhr**	*5:00* P.M.

Hallo Pizza ist für Sie geöffnet:
Täglich
von 17.00 - 23.00 Uhr
Mindestbestellwert DM 15,- (ohne Getränke)

Die Bank, -en   *(bank)*

---

der	Ausweis, -e	*identification card*	*das*	Geld	*money*
	Dollar, -	*dollar*		Bargeld	*cash*
	Paß, Pässe	*passport*		Kleingeld	*change*
	Schalter, -	*counter, ticket window*	*die*	Kasse, -n	*cashier's window*
	Scheck, -s	*check*			*(lit. cash register)*
	Reisescheck, -s	*traveler's check*			

Das Hotel, -s   *(hotel)*

der	Ausgang, ⸚e	*exit*	das	Einzelzimmer, -	*single room*
	Eingang, ⸚e	*entrance*		Doppelzimmer, -	*double room*
	Gast, ⸚e	*guest*		Gepäck	*baggage, luggage*
	Koffer, -	*suitcase*	die	Nacht, ⸚e	*night*
	Schlüssel, -	*key*		Nummer, -n	*number*
				Tasche, -n	*bag; pocket*

Weiteres

bald	*soon*
frei	*free, available*
geöffnet / geschlossen	*open / closed*
möglich	*possible*
ruhig	*quiet(ly)*
einen Moment	*(for) just a minute*
Wann machen Sie auf / zu?	*When do you open / close?*
Wie steht . . . ?	*What's the exchange rate of . . . ?*
einen Scheck einlösen	*to cash a check*
umtauschen	*to exchange*
wechseln	*to change; to exchange*
lassen (läßt), gelassen	*to leave (behind)*
unterschreiben, unterschrieben	*to sign*

ZUM ERKENNEN: die Angestellte,-n *(clerk, employee, f.)*; die Empfangsdame, -n *(receptionist);* klingeln *(here: to ring the doorbell)*

Zum Thema

A.   Mustersätze

1. Geld wechseln: **Wo kann ich hier** Geld wechseln?
   Dollar umtauschen, einen Scheck einlösen, Reiseschecks einlösen
2. Paß: **Darf ich bitte Ihren** Paß **sehen?**
   Scheck, Reisescheck, Ausweis
3. Dollar: **Können Sie mir das in** Dollar **geben?**
   D-Mark, Franken, Schilling, Kleingeld, Bargeld
4. mein Auto: **Wo kann ich** mein Auto **lassen?**
   meinen Schlüssel, mein Gepäck, meinen Koffer, meine Tasche
5. 24.00 Uhr: **Wir machen um** 24.00 Uhr **zu.**
   22.00 Uhr, 22.15 Uhr, 22.30 Uhr, 22.45 Uhr, 23.00 Uhr

B.   Was bedeuten die Wörter, und was ist der Artikel?

Ausgangstür, Gästeausweis, Geldwechsel, Gepäckstück, Handtasche, Hoteleingang, Kofferschlüssel, Nachtapotheke, Nachthemd, Nachtmensch, Paßnummer, Scheckbuch, Sparbuch, Taschengeld, Taschenlampe, Theaterkasse

C. Ich brauche Kleingeld.   *(With a partner, practice asking for a place where you can get change. Take turns, and vary your responses.)*

S1   Ich habe kein Kleingeld. Kannst du mir ＿＿＿＿＿＿ Mark wechseln?

S2   Nein, ＿＿＿＿＿＿ .

S1   Schade!

S2   Aber du kannst ＿＿＿＿＿＿ .

S1   Wo ist ＿＿＿＿＿＿ ?

S2   ＿＿＿＿＿＿ .

S1   Danke schön!

S2   ＿＿＿＿＿＿ !

D. Im Hotel   *(With a partner, practice inquiring about a hotel room. Take turns, and be sure to vary your responses.)*

S1   Guten ＿＿＿＿＿ ! Haben Sie ein ＿＿＿＿＿＿ mit ＿＿＿＿＿＿ frei?

S2   Wie lange wollen Sie bleiben?

S1   ＿＿＿＿＿＿ .

S2   Ja, wir haben ein Zimmer im ＿＿＿＿＿＿ Stock.

S1   Was kostet es?

S2   ＿＿＿＿＿＿ .

S1   Kann ich es sehen?

S2   ＿＿＿＿＿＿ . Hier ist der Schlüssel. Zimmer Nummer ＿＿＿＿＿＿ .

S1   Sagen Sie, wo kann ich ＿＿＿＿＿＿ lassen?

S2   ＿＿＿＿＿＿ .

S1   Und wann machen Sie abends zu?

S2   ＿＿＿＿＿＿ .

Dieser Bankautomat
ist immer offen.

E.   Wie spät ist es?   *(Ralf loves his new digital watch. Kurt prefers his old-fashioned one with hands. As Ralf says what time it is, Kurt confirms it in a more casual way. Work with a classmate. Take turns.)*

BEISPIEL: 14.15   Auf meiner Uhr ist es vierzehn Uhr fünfzehn.
Ich habe Viertel nach zwei.

1. 8.05	4. 13.25	7. 19.40	10. 23.59
2. 11.10	5. 14.30	8. 20.45	11. 00.01
3. 12.30	6. 17.37	9. 22.50	12. 02.15

F.   Interview.   Fragen Sie einen Nachbarn / eine Nachbarin, . . . !

1. wo man hier Bargeld oder Kleingeld bekommt
2. wie er / sie bezahlt, wenn er / sie einkaufen geht: bar, mit einem Scheck oder mit einer Kreditkarte
3. wie er / sie bezahlt, wenn er / sie reist *(travels)*
4. wo man hier D-Mark, Schillinge oder Franken *(Swiss currency)* bekommen kann
5. ob er / sie weiß, wie viele Mark (Schillinge, Franken) man für einen Dollar bekommt
6. was er / sie tut, wenn er / sie kein Geld mehr hat

G.   Aussprache: ei, ie   *(See also 11.37, 40–41 in the pronunciation section of the Workbook.)*

1. [ei]   **wei**l, **wei**t, **sei**t, **sei**n, **wei**ßt, **blei**bst, **lei**der, **bei**, **frei**, **Mey**er, **Bay**ern
2. [ie]   **wie**, **wie**viel, **nie**, **lie**ben, **lie**gen, **mie**ten, **lie**st, **sie**hst, **Die**nstag
3. **Bei**spiel, viel**lei**cht, **Wie**n / **Wei**n, **Bei**ne / **Bie**ne, **blei**ben / **blie**ben, **Lie**der / **lei**der, **zei**gen / **Zie**gen, **hie**ßen / **hei**ßen
4. Wortpaare

a. See / Sie	c. biete / bitte	e. leider / Lieder
b. beten / bieten	d. Miete / Mitte	f. Mais / mies

Hören Sie zu!

Eine Busfahrt   *(Listen to the discussion between these American exchange students in Tübingen and their professor before taking a bus trip early in their stay. Then complete the statements below according to the dialogue.)*

ZUM ERKENNEN: abfahren *(to depart);* das Konto *(account);* die Jugendherberge *(youth hostel);* also *(in other words);* Briefmarken *(stamps)*

1. Der Professor und die Studenten wollen am _____ um _____ abfahren.
2. Sie sind von _____ bis _____ in der Schweiz.
3. Sie sind von _____ bis _____ in Österreich.
4. Sie sollen heute noch _____ gehen.
5. Die Jugendherbergen und _____ sind schon bezahlt.
6. Sie brauchen Franken und Schilling nur, wenn sie _____ oder _____ kaufen wollen.
7. _____ und _____ sind auch schon bezahlt.
8. Manchmal braucht man Kleingeld für _____ .
9. Die Banken sind nur bis _____ offen.

STRUKTUR

I. *der-* and *ein-*words

1. **der**-words

This small but important group of limiting words is called DER-words because their case endings are the same as those of the definite articles **der, das, die.**

der, das, die	*the, that (when stressed)*
dieser, -es, -e	*this, these*
jeder, -es, -e	*each, every (sg. only, pl. **alle**)*
mancher, -es, -e	*many a (sg.); several, some (usually pl.)*
solcher, -es, -e	*such (usually pl.)*
welcher, -es, -e	*which*

Caution: The singular of **solcher** usually is **so ein,** which is not a **der**-word but an **ein**-word: **so ein Hotel** *(such a hotel)* BUT **solche Hotels** *(such hotels).*

COMPARE the endings of the definite article and the **der**-words!

	masc.	neut.	fem.	pl.
nom.	der dieser welcher	das dieses welches	die diese welche	die diese welche
acc.	den diesen welchen			
dat.	dem diesem welchem	dem diesem welchem	der dieser welcher	den diesen welchen

nom.   Wo ist **der** Schlüssel?—**Welcher** Schlüssel? **Dieser** Schlüssel?
acc.   Hast du **den** Kofferschlüssel gesehen?—Wie soll ich **jeden** Schlüssel kennen?
dat.   Kannst du ihn mit **dem** Schlüssel öffnen?—Mit **welchem** Schlüssel?
pl.   Gib mir **die** Schlüssel!—Hier sind **alle** Schlüssel. **Manche** Schlüssel sind vom Haus, **solche** Schlüssel zum Beispiel.
BUT   **Der** Kofferschlüssel ist **so ein** Schlüssel. Hast du **so einen** Schlüssel?

2. **ein**-words

POSSESSIVE ADJECTIVES are called **ein**-words because their case endings are the same as those of the indefinite article **ein** and the negative **kein.**

mein	*my*	**unser**	*our*
dein	*your (sg. fam.)*	**euer**	*your (pl. fam.)*
sein	*his / its*	**ihr**	*their*
ihr	*her / its*	**Ihr**	*your (sg. / pl. formal)*

COMPARE the endings of the indefinite article and the **ein**-words.

	masc.	neut.	fem.	pl.
nom.	ein mein unser	ein mein unser	eine meine unsere	keine meine unsere
acc.	einen meinen unseren			
dat.	einem meinem unserem	einem meinem unserem	einer meiner unserer	keinen meinen unseren

NOTE: The **-er** of uns**er** and eu**er** is not an ending!

• **Ein**-words have no endings in the masc. sing. nominative and in the neut. sing. nominative and accusative.

nom.   Hier ist **ein** Paß. Ist das **mein** Paß oder **dein** Paß?

acc.   Braucht er **keine** Kreditkarte?—Wo ist **seine** Kreditkarte?
Hat sie **einen** Ausweis?—Natürlich hat sie **ihren** Ausweis.
Haben Sie **Ihren** Ausweis?

dat.   In **welcher** Tasche sind die Schlüssel?—Sie sind in **meiner** Tasche.
Oder sind die Schlüssel in **einem** Koffer?—Sie sind in **Ihrem** Koffer.

pl.   Wo sind **die** Schecks?—Hier sind **unsere** Schecks, und da sind **euere** Schecks.

Übungen

A. Ersetzen Sie die Artikel!

1. **der-Wörter**

BEISPIEL: die Tasche *(this)*
              diese Tasche

a. das Gepäck *(every, which, this)*   **b.** der Ausweis *(this, every, which)*   **c.** die Nummer *(which, every, this)*   **d.** die Nächte *(some, such, these)*   **e.** an dem Schalter *(this, which, each)*   **f.** an der Kasse *(this, every, which)*   **g.** mit den Schecks *(these, some, all)*

2. **ein-Wörter**

BEISPIEL: die Gäste *(your / 3×)*
   deine / euere / Ihre Gäste

a. der Paß *(my, her, no, his)*   **b.** das Bargeld *(our, her, their)*   **c.** die Wohnung *(my, our, your / 3×)*   **d.** neben den Koffer *(your / 3×, our, their)*   **e.** in dem Doppelzimmer *(no, his, your / 3×)*   **f.** mit den Schlüsseln *(your / 3×, my, her)*

3. **der- und ein-Wörter**

BEISPIEL: **Das** Bad ist klein. *(our)*
   Unser Bad ist klein.

a.   **Das** Zimmer hat einen Fernseher. *(each, my, his, our)*
b.   Bitte bringen Sie **den** Koffer zum Auto! *(this, her, our, my)*
c.   Ich kann **die** Schlüssel nicht finden. *(your / 3×, our, some, my)*
d.   Darf ich **das** Gepäck hier lassen? *(her, his, this, our)*
e.   Der Ober kennt **den** Gast. *(each, our, this, your / 3×)*
f.   **Die** Taschen sind schon vor dem Ausgang. *(our, all, some, my)*
g.   **Den** Leuten gefällt das Hotel nicht. *(these, some, such)*
h.   Du kannst **den** Scheck auf der Bank einlösen. *(this, my, every, such a, your / sg. fam.)*

B.   Dias *(slides)* **von einer Deutschlandreise**

1. Auf _____ Bild seht ihr _____ Freunde aus Holland.   **2.** Das sind
this   *my*

_____ Sohn Heiko und _____ Tochter Anke.   **3.** In _____
their   *their*   *which*

Stadt ist _____ Kirche?   **4.** _____ Kirchen gibt es in Norddeutsch-
this   *such*

land.   **5.** _____ Haus ist sehr alt, aber nicht _____ Haus in Neubran-
this   *every*

denburg ist so alt.   **6.** Ich finde _____ Häuser sehr schön; Müllers wohnen
such

in _____ Haus.   **7.** Und hier sind _____ Onkel Thomas und
such a   *my*

_____ Tante Hilde.   **8.** Ist das nicht _____ Auto da vor _____
my   *your*   *this*

Hotel?

HOTEL VIER TORE

NEUBRANDENBURG

Treptower Straße 1   O - 2000 NEUBRANDENBURG
Telefon 5141 - Fax 41015   **Parkplatz direkt am Hotel**

II. Separable-Prefix Verbs

1. English has a number of two-part verbs that consist of a verb and a preposition or an adverb.

   Watch out! Get up! Buzz off!

   In German such verbs are called SEPARABLE-PREFIX verbs. You are already familiar with two of them:

   Passen Sie auf! Hören Sie zu!

   Their infinitives are **aufpassen** and **zuhören.** The prefixes **auf** and **zu** carry the main stress: **auf′passen, zu′hören.** From now on we will identify such separable-prefix verbs by placing a raised dot (·) between the prefix and the verb in vocabulary lists: **auf·passen, zu·hören.**

   • These verbs are SEPARATED from the prefixes when the inflected part of the verb is the first or second sentence element: in imperatives, questions, and statements.

   Hören Sie bitte **zu!**
   Hören Sie jetzt **zu?**
   .rum **hören** Sie nicht **zu?**
   Wir **hören** immer gut **zu.**
   　　V1　　　　　　　　　V2

   • These verbs are NOT SEPARATED from the prefix when the verb stands at the end of a sentence or clause: with modals, in the present perfect, and in subordinate clauses. Note, however, that in the present perfect the **-ge-** of the past participle is inserted BETWEEN the stressed prefix and the participle.

   Ich soll immer gut **zuhören.**
   Ich habe immer gut **zugehört.**
   Ich weiß, daß ich immer gut **zuhöre.**
   Ich weiß, daß ich immer gut **zuhören** soll.
   Ich weiß, daß ich immer gut **zugehört** habe.

2. Knowing the basic meanings of some of the most frequent separable prefixes will help you derive the meanings of some of the separable-prefix verbs.

ab-	*away, off*	**mit-**	*together with, along with*
an-	*to, up to*	**nach-**	*after, behind*
auf-	*up, open*	**vor-**	*ahead, before*
aus-	*out, out of*	**vorbei-**	*past, by*
ein-	*into*	**zu-**	*closed*
her-	*toward (the speaker)*	**zurück-**	*back*
hin-	*away from (the speaker)*		

BEISPIEL:	**an**·kommen	*to arrive (come to)*
	her·kommen	*to come (toward the speaker)*
	herein·kommen	*to come in (toward the speaker)*
	heraus·kommen	*to come out (toward the speaker)*
	hin·kommen	*to get there (away from the point of reference)*
	mit·kommen	*to come along*
	nach·kommen	*to follow (come after)*
	vorbei·kommen	*to come by*
	zurück·kommen	*to come back*

You will need to learn these common separable-prefix verbs.

an·**rufen, angerufen**	*to call, phone*
auf·**machen**	*to open*
auf·**passen**	*to pay attention, watch out*
auf·**schreiben, aufgeschrieben**	*to write down*
auf·**stehen, ist aufgestanden**	*to get up*
aus·**gehen, ist ausgegangen**	*to go out*
ein·**kaufen**	*to shop*
ein·**lösen**	*to cash (in)*
mit·**bringen, mitgebracht**	*to bring along*
mit·**gehen, ist mitgegangen**	*to go along*
mit·**kommen, ist mitgekommen**	*to come along*
mit·**nehmen, mitgenommen**	*to take along*
um·**tauschen**	*to exchange*
vorbei·**gehen, ist vorbeigegangen (an, bei)**	*to pass by*
zu·**hören** (+ dat.)	*to listen*
zu·**machen**	*to close*
zurück·**kommen, ist zurückgekommen**	*to come back*

Caution: Not all verbs with prefixes are separable, e.g., **unterschreiben, wiederholen.** Here the main stress is on the verb, not on the prefix: **unterschrei′ben, wiederho′len.** Remember also the inseparable prefixes **be-, ent-, er-, ge-, ver-,** etc. (Chapter 4, Struktur I). They never stand alone.

C. Was bedeuten diese Verben? *(Knowing the meanings of the basic verbs and the prefixes, can you tell what these separable-prefix verbs mean?)*

abgeben, abnehmen
ansprechen
aufbauen, aufgeben, aufstehen, aufstellen
ausarbeiten, aushelfen, aus(be)zahlen
heraufkommen, herauskommen, herüberkommen, herunterkommen
hinaufgehen, hinausgehen, hineingehen, hinuntergehen
mitgehen, mitfahren, mitfeiern, mitsingen, mitspielen
nachkommen, nachlaufen
vorbeibringen, vorbeifahren, vorbeikommen
zuhalten
zurückbekommen, zurückbleiben, zurückbringen, zurückgeben, zurücknehmen,
  zurücksehen

D.   Noch einmal. Wiederholen Sie die Sätze ohne Modalverb!

BEISPIEL: Sie soll ihm zuhören.
             Sie hört ihm zu.

1. Wir dürfen am Wochenende ausgehen.   **2.** Wann mußt du morgens aufstehen?
3. Wollt ihr mit mir einkaufen?   **4.** Ich soll Wein mitbringen.   **5.** Er will morgen
zurückkommen.   **6.** Ich möchte dich gern mitnehmen.   **7.** Du kannst das Geld umtauschen.   **8.** Er will an der Universität vorbeigehen.   **9.** Können Sie bitte die Fenster aufmachen!   **10.** Ihr sollt gut aufpassen.

E.   Am Telefon   *(Report to a brother what your mother is telling or asking you about tomorrow's family reunion.)*

BEISPIEL: Sie möchte wissen, ob Rainer und Wolfgang die Kinder mitbringen.
             Bringen Rainer und Wolfgang die Kinder mit?

1.   Sie sagt, daß wir abends alle zusammen ausgehen.
2.   Sie möchte wissen, ob du deine Kamera mitbringst.
3.   Sie sagt, daß sie morgen noch ein paar Geschenke einkauft.
4.   Sie möchte wissen, wann die Bank aufmacht.
5.   Sie sagt, daß sie noch etwas Geld umtauscht.
6.   Sie sagt, daß sie dann hier vorbeikommt.

F.   Das tut man.   *(Say what things one needs to do before checking out of a hotel.)*

BEISPIEL: früh aufstehen
             Man steht früh auf.

1. die Koffer zumachen   **2.** das Gepäck zur Rezeption mitnehmen   **3.** den Schlüssel zurückgeben   **4.** vielleicht ein Taxi anrufen   **5.** einen Reisescheck einlösen

G.   Vor der Reise   *(Before leaving for your trip, make sure that everything is under control.)*

BEISPIEL: Macht ihr die Fenster zu?
             Habt ihr die Fenster zugemacht?

1. Machst du die Garagentür wieder zu?   **2.** Macht ihr das Licht aus *(turn off the
light)*?   **3.** Geht Anke bei der Post vorbei?   **4.** Tauscht Kurt Dollar in Schillinge
um?   **5.** Nehmen wir genug Geld mit?   **6.** Bringt ihr euere Pässe mit?   **7.** Rufst
du die Pension noch an?   **8.** Schreibst du die Telefonnummer auf?   **9.** Nimmst du
ein paar Bücher mit?   **10.** Kaufen wir etwas zu essen ein?

H.   Auf deutsch, bitte!

1. You *(sg. fam.)* didn't close your book.   **2.** Listen! *(formal)*   **3.** They came back on the weekend.   **4.** Are you *(pl. fam.)* going out soon?   **5.** I don't know if he's coming along.   **6.** Do you *(sg. fam.)* know when she went out?   **7.** I exchanged our money.   **8.** Whom did you *(formal)* bring along?

I.   Geben Sie alle vier Imperative!

BEISPIEL: Die Tür aufmachen
Machen Sie die Tür auf!
Macht die Tür auf!
Mach die Tür auf!
Machen wir die Tür auf!

1. jetzt aufstehen
2. in der Stadt einkaufen
3. den Scheck noch nicht einlösen
4. genug Bargeld mitbringen
5. das Gepäck mitnehmen
6. mit ihnen mitgehen
7. bei der Bank vorbeigehen
8. trotzdem zuhören
9. wieder zurückkommen

J.   Interview. Fragen Sie einen Nachbarn / eine Nachbarin, . . . !

1. wann er / sie heute aufgestanden ist
2. wann er / sie gewöhnlich am Wochenende aufsteht
3. wohin er / sie gern geht, wenn er / sie ausgeht
4. wo er / sie einkauft
5. was er / sie heute mitgebracht hat (drei Beispiele, bitte!)

III. Flavoring Particles

In everyday speech, German uses many flavoring words (or intensifiers) to convey what English often expresses through gestures or intonation, e.g., surprise, admiration, or curiosity. When used in these contexts, flavoring particles have no exact English equivalent. Here are some examples:

aber	*expresses admiration, or intensifies a statement*
denn	*expresses curiosity, interest (usually in a question)*
doch	*expresses concern, impatience, assurance*
ja	*adds emphasis*

Euer Haus gefällt mir **aber**!	*I <u>do</u> like your house.*
Die Möbel sind **aber** hübsch!	*Isn't <u>this furniture</u> beautiful!*
Was ist **denn** das?	*What (on earth) is that?*
Wieviel kostet **denn** so etwas?	*(Just) how much <u>does</u> something like that cost?*
Das weiß ich **doch** nicht.	*That I <u>don't</u> know.*
Frag **doch** Julia!	*Why don't you ask Julia!*
Du kennst **doch** Julia?	*You <u>do</u> know Julia, don't you?*
Euer Garten ist **ja** super!	*(Wow,) your garden is great!*
Ihr habt **ja** sogar einen Pool!	*(Hey,) you even have a pool!*

Übungen

K.   Im Hotel. Auf englisch, bitte!

BEISPIEL: Haben Sie denn kein Einzelzimmer mehr frei?
Don't you have any single room available?

1.   Hier ist ja der Schlüssel!
2.   Das Zimmer ist aber schön!
3.   Es hat ja sogar einen Balkon!
4.   Hat es denn keine Dusche?
5.   Wir gehen doch noch aus?
6.   Hast du denn keinen Hunger?
7.   Komm doch mit!
8.   Ich komme ja schon!
9.   Laß doch den Mantel hier!
10.   Wohin gehen wir denn?

**Zusammen-
fassung**

L.   Bilden Sie Sätze!   *(Use the tenses suggested.)*

BEISPIEL: Eva / gestern / ausgehen / mit Willi *(present perfect)*
Eva ist gestern mit Willi ausgegangen.

1.   man / umtauschen / Geld / auf / eine Bank *(present tense)*
2.   welch- / Koffer *(sg.)* / du / mitnehmen? *(present tense)*
3.   einkaufen / ihr / gern / in / euer / Supermarkt? *(present tense)*
4.   unser / Nachbarn *(pl.)* / zurückkommen / vor einer Woche *(present perfect)*
5.   wann / ihr / aufstehen / am Sonntag? *(present perfect)*
6.   ich / mitbringen / dir / mein / Stadtplan *(present perfect)*
7.   vorbeigehen / noch / schnell / bei / Apotheke! *(imperative / sg. fam.)*
8.   zumachen / Schalter / um 17.30 Uhr! *(imperative / formal)*
9.   umtauschen / alles / in Schilling! *(imperative / pl. fam.)*

M.   An der Rezeption. Auf deutsch, bitte!

1. All (the) hotels are full (**voll**).   **2.** Look, there's another hotel.   **3.** Let's ask once more.   **4.** Do you *(formal)* still have a room available?   **5.** Yes, one room without (a) bath on the first floor and one room with (a) shower (**Dusche**) on the second floor.   **6.** Excellent! Which room would you *(sg. fam.)* like?   **7.** Give *(formal)* us the room on the second floor.   **8.** Where can I leave these suitcases?   **9.** Over there. But don't go yet.   **10.** May I see your ID, please?   **11.** Yes. Do you cash traveler's checks?—Of course.   **12.** Did you see our restaurant?—Which restaurant?   **13.** This restaurant. From each table you can see the sea.   **14.** You don't find a restaurant like this (such a restaurant) everywhere.   **15.** That's true.

GOTHIA HOTEL
WISMAR

EINBLICKE

Gasthof zur Post in
Kochel am See

Names of small hotels (**Gasthöfe** or **Gasthäuser**), which first sprang up
around monasteries toward the end of the Middle Ages, often referred to
the Bible: **Gasthof Engel** *(angel)*, **Gasthof Drei Könige** (the Kings were sym-
bols of travel), **Gasthof Rose** or **Lilie** (both flowers representing the Virgin
Mary), and **Gasthof Lamm** (the Lamb of God). In the 1400s, when a postal
system was developing, names like **Gasthof Goldenes Posthorn, Alte Post,
Neue Post,** and **Zur Post** appeared.

WORTSCHATZ 2

der	Gasthof, ⸚e	*small hotel*
die	Jugendherberge, -n	*youth hostel*
	Pension, -en	*boarding house; hotel*
	Reise, -n	*trip*

einfach	*simple, simply*
fast	*almost*
meistens	*mostly, usually*
an·kommen, ist angekommen[1]	*to arrive*
an·nehmen, angenommen	*to accept*
kennen·lernen[2]	*to get to know, meet*
packen	*to pack*
reisen, ist gereist	*to travel*
reservieren	*to reserve*
übernachten	*to spend the night*
Vorsicht!	*Careful!*
Das kommt darauf an.	*That depends.*

[1] Two-way prepositions take the dative with **an·kommen:** Er ist am Bahnhof (in der Stadt) angekommen.

[2] The verb **kennen** functions as a separable prefix in this combination: Er hat sie hier kennengelernt. *(He met her here.)*

WAS IST DAS?   der Campingplatz, Evangelist; das Symbol; die Adresse, Bibel, Möglichkeit, Übernachtung, Übernachtungsmöglichkeit, Touristeninformation; ausfüllen, campen, diskutieren, Karten spielen; extra, international, luxuriös, modern, privat

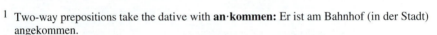

Übernachtungsmöglichkeiten

well

farther out / castle

same / . . . chain

are alike inside / on the contrary / different Middle Ages / about / location / other / lion / eagle bull

Wo kann man gut übernachten? Nun°, das kommt darauf an, ob das Hotel elegant oder einfach, international oder typisch deutsch sein soll, ob es zentral liegen muß, oder ob es weiter draußen° sein darf. Wer will, kann auch Gast in einem Schloß oder auf einer Burg° sein.

In Amerika gibt es viele Hotels mit gleichen° Namen, weil sie zu einer Hotelkette° 5 gehören, z.B. „Holiday Inn" oder „Hilton". Bei diesen Hotels weiß man immer, was man findet, wenn man hineingeht. In Deutschland gibt es auch Hotels mit gleichen Namen, z.B. „Hotel zur Sonne" oder „Gasthof Post". Aber das bedeutet nicht, daß solche Hotels innen gleich sind.° Im Gegenteil°, sie sind meistens sehr verschieden°, weil sie privat sind. Ihre Namen gehen oft bis ins Mittelalter° zurück. Oft sagen sie etwas über° ihre Lage°, z.B. 10 Berghotel, Pension Waldsee. Andere° Namen, wie z.B. Gasthof zum Löwen°, zum Adler° oder zum Stier° sind aus der Bibel genommen. Sie sind Symbole für die Evangelisten Markus, Johannes und Lukas.

Manche Hotels sind sehr luxuriös und teuer, andere sind einfach und billig. Sprechen
wir von einem normalen Hotel, einem Gasthof oder Gasthaus! Wenn Sie ankommen, gehen
Sie zur Rezeption! Dort müssen Sie meistens ein Formular° ausfüllen[1] und bekommen
dann Ihr Zimmer: ein Einzelzimmer oder Doppelzimmer, ein Zimmer mit oder ohne Bad.
Für Zimmer ohne Bad gibt es auf dem Flur eine Toilette und meistens auch eine Dusche.[2]
Das Frühstück ist gewöhnlich im Preis inbegriffen°. Übrigens hat jeder Gasthof seinen
Ruhetag°. Dann ist das Restaurant geschlossen, und man nimmt keine neuen Gäste an. Der
Herr oder die Dame an der Rezeption kann Ihnen auch Geschäfte und Sehenswürdigkeiten°
empfehlen, manchmal auch Geld umtauschen. Aber Vorsicht! Auf der Bank ist der Wech-
selkurs° fast immer besser°.

Wenn Sie nicht vorher reservieren können, dann finden Sie auch Übernachtungsmöglichkeiten durch die Touristeninformation am Hauptbahnhof.[3] Hier finden Sie
Adressen von Privatfamilien und Pensionen. So eine Übernachtung ist gewöhnlich nicht
sehr teuer, aber sauber und gut.

Haben Sie schon einmal in einer Jugendherberge[4] oder einem Jugendgästehaus übernachtet? Wenn nicht, tun Sie es einmal! Sie brauchen dafür° einen Jugendherbergsausweis.
So einen Ausweis können Sie aber schon vorher° in Amerika oder Kanada bekommen. Fast
jede Stadt hat eine Jugendherberge, manchmal in einem modernen Gebäude°, manchmal in
einer Burg oder in einem Schloß. Jugendherbergen und Jugendgästehäuser sind in den Ferien meistens schnell voll, denn alle Gruppen reservieren schon vorher. Das Übernachten in
einer Jugendherberge kann ein Erlebnis° sein, weil man immer wieder° interessante Leute
kennenlernt. Jugendherbergen haben nur einen Nachteil°: Sie machen gewöhnlich abends
um 23.00 Uhr zu. Wenn Sie später zurückkommen, haben Sie Pech gehabt. In fast allen
Großstädten gibt es Jugendgästehäuser. Wenn Sie schon vorher wissen, daß Sie fast jeden
Abend ausgehen und spät nach Hause kommen, dann übernachten Sie lieber° in so einem
Jugendgästehaus, denn diese machen erst° um 24.00 oder 1.00 Uhr zu, und in manchen
Gästehäusern kann man sogar einen Hausschlüssel bekommen.

Man kann natürlich auch anders° übernachten, z.B. auf dem Campingplatz, aber da
braucht man ein Zelt° oder einen Wohnwagen°. Campen gefällt aber nicht jedem°. Ob im
Hotel oder auf dem Campingplatz, in einer Pension oder Jugendherberge, überall wünschen wir Ihnen viel Spaß auf Ihrer Reise durch Europa.

form

included
day off
attractions

exchange rate / better

for that
in advance
building

experience / again and
again / disadvantage

rather
not until

in other ways
tent / camper / everybody

Jugendherberge in
Nürnberg. Haben Sie
noch Platz für zwei
Leute?

Zum Text

A.   Was paßt?   *(Indicate the correct answer.)*

1.   Deutsche Hotels mit gleichen Namen sind . . .
     a.   immer alle gleich
     b.   innen meistens nicht gleich
     c.   alle aus dem Mittelalter
     d.   Symbole

2.   Wenn Sie in einem Gasthof ankommen, gehen Sie erst . . .
     a.   ins Bad
     b.   ins Restaurant
     c.   zur Rezeption
     d.   in Ihr Zimmer

3.   Im Hotel kann man Geld umtauschen, aber . . .
     a.   nur an der Rezeption
     b.   nicht an der Rezeption
     c.   der Wechselkurs ist meistens nicht sehr gut
     d.   der Wechselkurs ist oft eine Sehenswürdigkeit

4.   Wenn Sie jung sind, können Sie auch in . . . übernachten.
     a.   einem Luxushotel billig
     b.   einer Jugendherberge oder einem Jugendgästehaus
     c.   einem Café
     d.   einem Schloß

5.   Das Übernachten in einer Jugendherberge kann sehr interessant sein, weil . . .
     a.   Jugendherbergen in den Ferien schnell voll sind
     b.   sie gewöhnlich abends um 22.00 Uhr zumachen
     c.   man oft interessante Leute kennenlernt
     d.   sie immer auf einer Burg sind

6.   Übernachten Sie in einem Jugendgästehaus, wenn Sie . . . !
     a.   spät nach Hause kommen wollen
     b.   Pech gehabt haben
     c.   es gern primitiv haben wollen
     d.   Karten spielen wollen

7.   Auf dem Campingplatz . . .
     a.   gibt es eine Toilette auf dem Flur
     b.   ist das Frühstück im Preis inbegriffen
     c.   gibt es viele Zelte und Wohnwagen
     d.   darf man nicht früh ankommen

B.   Wo sollen wir übernachten?   *(Match each lodging with the corresponding description.)*

Campingplatz, Gasthof, Jugendgästehaus, Jugendherberge, Luxushotel, Pension

1.   Diese Übernachtungsmöglichkeit ist meistens nicht teuer, aber doch gut. Man kann sie z.B. durch die Touristeninformation am Bahnhof finden.
2.   Hier ist es besonders billig, aber wenn es viel regnet, kann es sehr ungemütlich sein.
3.   Wenn man viel Geld hat, ist es hier natürlich wunderbar.
4.   Diese Möglichkeit ist für junge Leute. Sie ist nicht teuer, und man kann abends spät zurückkommen oder einen Schlüssel bekommen.

5. Das Übernachten kann hier sehr bequem und gemütlich sein; das Frühstück kostet nichts extra. Am Ruhetag kann man dort nicht essen.

6. Hier können Leute mit Ausweis billig übernachten, aber man darf abends nicht nach elf zurückkommen.

C. Übernachtungsmöglichkeiten. Was fehlt?

1. In _____ Hotel kann man gut übernachten, aber das kann man nicht von _____ Hotel sagen. *(this, every)*

2. Bei _____ Hotel wissen Sie immer, wie es innen aussieht. *(such a)*

3. _____ Hotels sind sehr luxuriös und teuer, _____ Hotel zum Beispiel. *(some, this)*

4. _____ Hotel ist sehr schön gewesen. *(our)*

5. Hast du schon einmal von _____ Pension gehört? *(this)*

6. Wie gefällt es euch in _____ Jugendherberge? *(your)*

7. _____ Jugendherberge ist in einer Burg. *(our)*

8. In _____ Jugendherberge gibt es noch Platz. *(this)*

9. Wollen wir auf _____ Campingplatz übernachten? *(this)*

10. _____ Campingplatz meinst du *(do you mean)*? *(which)*

D. Kofferpacken

1. **Europareise.** Was packen Sie in den Koffer, wenn Sie einen Monat unterwegs sind?

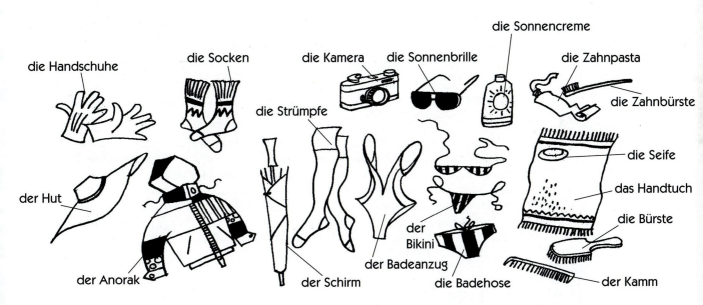

Und was noch? Machen Sie eine Liste!

2. **Was haben Sie mitgenommen?** *(Tell what you took along. One student starts, the next one repeats and adds to it, etc. When your memory fails, you're out.)*

BEISPIEL: Ich habe eine Sonnenbrille mitgenommen.
Ich habe eine Sonnenbrille und meine Kamera mitgenommen.

E.   In der Jugendherberge. Sagen Sie die Sätze noch einmal ohne Modalverb, (a) im Präsens und (b) im Perfekt!

> BEISPIEL: Du kannst in den Ferien vorbeikommen.
> **Du kommst in den Ferien vorbei.**
> **Du bist in den Ferien vorbeigekommen.**

1.   Wann möchtet ihr ankommen?
2.   In der Jugendherberge könnt ihr Leute kennenlernen.
3.   Du mußt natürlich einen Jugendherbergsausweis mitbringen.
4.   Wollt ihr abends spät ausgehen?
5.   Die Jugendherberge soll um elf zumachen.
6.   Wer spät zurückkommen möchte, kann Pech haben.

F.   Ruck, zuck! Wem gehört das?   *(One person claims to own everything. Quickly correct him / her and tell whose property it is.)*

> BEISPIEL: Das ist mein Buch.
> **Quatsch! Das ist nicht dein Buch; das ist mein (ihr, sein) Buch.**

G.   Schriftliche Übung   *(Using the questions as a guideline, write a brief paragraph.)*

1.   Wohin geht Ihre nächste *(next)* Reise? Wann? Wo übernachten Sie dann, und warum dort?
2.   Wo sind Sie das letzte Mal *(the last time)* gewesen? Wann? Wo haben Sie übernachtet, und wie hat es Ihnen gefallen?

Hören Sie zu!

Hotel Lindenhof   *(Mr. Baumann calls the reception of Hotel Lindenhof on Lake Constance. Listen to their conversations. Then complete the sentences below with the correct information from the dialogue.)*

ZUM ERKENNEN: die Person, -en; das Frühstücksbüfett; schwimmen; das Schwimmbad; Minigolf; der Blick auf *(view of)*

1. Herr Baumann und seine Familie fahren im Sommer an den _____ . **2.** Sie wollen am _____ Juli ankommen und _____ bleiben. **3.** Sie brauchen Zimmer für _____ Personen, also _____ Zimmer. **4.** Die Zimmer kosten _____ pro Tag. **5.** Das Frühstücksbüfett kostet _____ extra. **6.** Herr Baumann findet das nicht _____ . **7.** Die Kinder können dort _____ und in der Nähe auch _____ und _____ spielen. **8.** Zum See ist es auch nicht _____ . **9.** Vom Balkon hat man einen Blick auf den _____ und die _____ . **10.** Er _____ die Zimmer.

Übrigens

1.   When registering in a hotel, all guests are required by law to fill out forms providing home address, date of birth, nationality, etc., in the interest of public safety.

2.   If you intend to stay in a moderately priced hotel, take your own soap and shampoo. All hotels supply towels, but only the more expensive ones supply soap.

3.   The Tourist Information Office has a room-referral service (**Zimmernachweis**). It usually charges a small fee for locating a room in the price range you indicate. **Pensionen** usually have no rooms with bath. **Fremdenzimmer** are rooms in private homes.

4.   Youth hostels (**Jugendherbergen**) can be found in almost every city and many small towns throughout Europe. They are particularly popular with students.

SPRECHSITUATIONEN

Telling and Asking About Time

You have now learned both the formal and the informal (see *Schritt 6*) ways of telling time.

Es ist drei.

Es ist Viertel nach eins.

Meine Vorlesung beginnt um Viertel nach eins.
Meine Vorlesung beginnt um 13.15 Uhr.

Sie dauert von Viertel nach eins bis um drei.
Sie dauert von 13.15 Uhr bis 15.00 Uhr.

Wie spät ist es?
Wieviel Uhr ist es?
Wann beginnt . . . ?
Können Sie mir sagen, wie spät / wieviel Uhr es ist?

Expressing Disbelief

What can you say when someone tells you something that is hard to believe?

Stimmt das?
Wirklich?
Das glaube ich nicht.
Das kann ich nicht glauben.
Das ist doch nicht möglich!
Das kann doch nicht wahr *(true)* sein!
Das gibt's doch nicht! *(That's not possible.)*

Ach du liebes bißchen! *(Good grief!)*
Das ist ja Wahnsinn! *(That's crazy!)*
Du spinnst (wohl)! *(You're crazy!)*
Mach keine Witze! *(Stop joking!)*
Quatsch! *(Nonsense.)*

Giving a Warning

Here are a few ways to caution someone:

Vorsicht!
Paß auf! / Paßt auf! / Passen Sie auf!
Warte! / Wartet! / Warten Sie! *(Wait!)*
Halt!

Öffnungszeiten. Wann sind diese Restaurants und Kunstgalerien offen?

Gasthaus BAUER
1., Schottenbastei 4, Tel.:533 6128
Mo-Fr 9-24 Uhr, warme Küche bis 21 Uhr,
Café MUSEUM 1., Friedrichstraße 6,
Tel.: 56 52 02
tgl. 7-23 Uhr; Alt-Wiener Kaffeehaus

ZUR WEINPERLE
9., Alserbachstraße 2, Tel.: 34 32 52
Mo-Fr 9-21.30 Uhr, Sa 9-14.30 Uhr.
Café CENTRAL, 1., Herrengasse 14 (im
inside Palais Ferstel), Tel.: 535 41 76
Mo-Sa 10-22 Uhr.

SCHNITZELWIRT
7., Neubaugasse 52, Tel.: 93 37 71
Mo-Sa 10-22 Uhr, warme Küche 11.30-
14.30 Uhr und 17.30-22 Uhr.
SCHWEIZERHAUS 2., Prater, Straße des
1. Mai 116, Tel.: 218 01 52
tgl. 10-24 Uhr, mitten im Wurstelprater.

GALERIE NÄCHST ST. STEPHAN
1., Grünangergasse 1, Tel.: 512 12 66
Mo-Fr 10-18 Uhr, Sa 11-14 Uhr,
GALERIE HUMMEL
1., Bäckerstraße 14, Tel.: 512 12 96
Di-Fr 15-18 Uhr, Sa 10-13 Uhr.

GALERIE PETER PAKESCH
1., Ballgasse 6, Tel.: 52 48 14 und
3., Ungargasse 27, Tel.: 713 74 56
Di-Fr 14-19 Uhr, So 11-14 Uhr,
GALERIE STEINEK
1., Himmelpfortgasse 22, Tel: 512 87 59
Di-Fr 13-18 Uhr, Sa 10-12 Uhr.

B.   **Was sagen Sie?**   *(Use the appropriate expression for each of the following situations.)*

1.   Hier kostet ein Hotelzimmer 225 Mark.
2.   Ich habe ein Zimmer für 200 Mark im Monat gefunden.
3.   Du, die Vorlesung beginnt um 14.15 Uhr, und es ist schon 14.05 Uhr!
4.   Sie bummeln mit einem Freund in der Stadt. Ihr Freund will bei Rot *(at a red light)* über die Straße laufen.
5.   Sie sind auf einer Party, und es macht Ihnen viel Spaß. Aber morgen ist eine Prüfung, und Sie hören, daß es schon zwei Uhr ist.
6.   Sie lernen auf einer Party einen Studenten kennen. Sie hören, daß sein Vater und Ihr Vater als Studenten Freunde gewesen sind.
7.   Sie stehen mit einer Tasse Kaffee an der Tür. Die Tür ist zu. Ein Freund möchte hereinkommen.
8.   Ein Freund aus Deutschland will die Kerzen auf seinem Weihnachtsbaum anzünden *(light)*. Sie sind sehr nervös.

C.   **Kurzgespräche**

1.   You are visiting your aunt in Heidelberg. As you tour the castle, you see a German student whom you got to know while you both stayed at a youth hostel in Aachen. Call out to the German student. Both of you express your disbelief that you have met again. Your friend is studying in Heidelberg; you explain why you are there. You ask whether your friend would like to go for a Coke, and he / she agrees.

2.   You and a friend are in Stralsund and are looking for a hotel room. You have both inquired in several places. All the hotels you saw had no available rooms at all; in desperation your friend has taken a double room that will cost you 185 DM for one night. You both express your disbelief at your bad luck.

RÜCKBLICK KAPITEL 4–7

I. Verbs

1. **wissen**

p. 180

wissen, like the modals below, is irregular in the singular of the present tense. It means *to know a fact,* as opposed to **kennen** which means *to be acquainted with a person or thing.*

singular	plural
ich weiß	wir wissen
du weißt	ihr wißt
er weiß	sie wissen

2. Modals

pp. 151–52

	dürfen	können	müssen	sollen	wollen	mögen/möchten	
ich	darf	kann	muß	soll	will	mag	möchte
du	darfst	kannst	mußt	sollst	willst	magst	möchtest
er	darf	kann	muß	soll	will	mag	möchte
wir	dürfen	können	müssen	sollen	wollen	mögen	möchten
ihr	dürft	könnt	müßt	sollt	wollt	mögt	möchtet
sie	dürfen	können	müssen	sollen	wollen	mögen	möchten

The modal is the second sentence element (V1); the infinitive of the main verb (V2) stands at the end of the sentence.

Sie **sollen** ihr den Kaffee **bringen.**   *You're supposed to bring her the coffee.*
   V1   V2

3. The Imperative

pp. 178–79

The forms of the familiar imperative have no pronouns; the singular familiar imperative has no **-st** ending.

Formal sg. + pl.	Fam. pl. (ihr)	Fam. sg. (du)	3rd pers. pl. *(let's . . .)*
Schreiben Sie!	Schreibt!	Schreib(e)!	Schreiben wir!
Antworten Sie!	Antwortet!	Antworte!	Antworten wir!
Fahren Sie!	Fahrt!	**Fahr(e)!**	Fahren wir!
Nehmen Sie!	Nehmt!	**Nimm!**	Nehmen wir!

4. The Present Perfect

a. Past Participles

pp. 124–27

t-verbs (weak and mixed verbs)	n-verbs (strong verbs)
(ge) + stem (change) + (e)t	(ge) + stem (change) + en
gekauft	geschrieben
gearbeitet	
gebracht	
eingekauft	mitgeschrieben
verkauft	unterschrieben
reserviert	

b. Most verbs use **haben** as the auxiliary. Those that use **sein** are intransitive (take no object) and imply a change of place or condition. (**bleiben** and **sein** are exceptions to the rule.)

Wir haben Wien gesehen.
Wir sind viel gelaufen.
Abends sind wir müde gewesen.

pp. 125–26

5. Verbs with Inseparable and Separable Prefixes

a. Inseparable-prefix verbs (verbs with the unstressed prefixes **be-, emp-, ent-, er-, ge-, ver-,** and **zer-**) are never separated.

Was bedeutet das?
Das verstehe ich nicht.
Was empfehlen Sie?
Wer bezahlt das Mittagessen?

über-, unter-, and **wieder-** can be used as separable or inseparable prefixes, depending on the particular verb and meaning.

Übernach'tet ihr in der Jugendherberge?
Unterschrei'ben Sie bitte hier!
Wiederho'len Sie, bitte!

pp. 200–01

b. Separable-prefix verbs (verbs where the prefix is stressed) are separated in statements, questions, and imperatives.

Du **bringst** deine Schwester **mit.**
Bringst du deine Schwester **mit?**
Bring doch deine Schwester **mit!**

They are not separated when used with modals, in the present perfect, or in dependent clauses.

Du sollst deine Schwester **mitbringen.**
Hast du deine Schwester **mitgebracht?**
Sie will wissen, ob du deine Schwester **mitbringst.**

II. Cases

1. Two-Way Prepositions: Accusative or Dative?

> an, auf, hinter, in, neben, über, unter, vor, zwischen

The nine two-way prepositions take either the dative or the accusative, depending on the verb.

pp. 173–75

wo?	LOCATION, activity within a place → <u>dative</u>
wohin?	DESTINATION, motion to a place → <u>accusative</u>

Remember the difference between these two sets of verbs:

to put (upright)	Er **stellt** den Koffer neben den Ausgang.
to stand	Der Koffer **steht** neben dem Ausgang.
to put (flat), lay	**Legen** Sie den Ausweis auf den Tisch!
to lie (flat)	Der Ausweis **liegt** auf dem Tisch.

2. **der**-words and **ein**-words

    a. **der**-words have the same endings as the definite article **der.**

    p. 197

dieser	solcher (so ein)
jeder	welcher
mancher	alle

    b. **ein**-words (or possessive adjectives) have the same endings as **ein** and **kein.**

    p. 198

mein	unser
dein	euer
sein, sein, ihr	ihr, Ihr

3. Pronouns

    a. Personal Pronouns

    p. 148

	singular					plural			sg. / pl.
nom.	ich	du	er	es	sie	wir	ihr	sie	Sie
acc.	**mich**	**dich**	**ihn**	**es**	**sie**	**uns**	**euch**	**sie**	**Sie**
dat.	**mir**	**dir**	**ihm**	**ihm**	**ihr**	**uns**	**euch**	**ihnen**	**Ihnen**

    Don't confuse these pronouns with the **ein**-words (or possessive adjectives, see 2b above), which are always followed by a noun.

    b. Interrogative Pronouns

nom.	wer	was
acc.	wen	was
dat.	wem	—

4. Summary of the Three Cases

	use	follows . . .	masc.	neut.	fem.	pl.
nom.	Subject, Predicate noun	**heißen, sein, werden**	der dieser ein mein	das dieses ein mein	die diese eine meine	die diese keine meine
acc.	Direct object	**durch, für, gegen, ohne, um**	den diesen einen meinen			
		an, auf, hinter, in, neben, über, unter, vor, zwischen				
dat.	Indirect object	**aus, außer, bei, mit, nach, seit, von, zu**	dem diesem einem meinem	dem diesem einem meinem	der dieser einer meiner	den diesen keinen meinen
		antworten, danken, gefallen, gehören, helfen, zuhören				

III. Sentence Structure

1. Verb Position

pp. 36–37, 74

    a. V1—V2

In declarative sentences, yes / no questions, and imperatives, two-part verb phrases are split: the inflected part (V1) is the first or second sentence element; the other part (V2) appears at the end of the clause.

> Er **ist** hier an der Uni **Student.**
> Er **ist** wirklich sehr **interessant.**
> **Hast** du ihn schon **kennengelernt?**
> Ich **kann** jetzt nicht lange **sprechen.**
> **Komm** doch später bei uns **vorbei!**
> V1   V2

pp. 129–30

    b. Subordinate Clauses

• Subordinate clauses are introduced by subordinating conjunctions or interrogatives:

> **bevor, daß, ob, obwohl, weil, wenn, etc.**

> **wer? wen? wem? was? was für ein(e)? wohin? woher? wo? wann? warum? wie? wie lange? wieviel? wie viele?**

- In subordinate clauses the subject usually comes right after the conjunction, and the inflected verb (V1) is at the end of the clause.

Sie sagt, **daß** sie das Einzelzimmer **nimmt.**
Er sagt, **daß** er den Zimmerschlüssel **mitbringt.**

- Two-part verb phrases appear in the order V2 V1.

Sie sagt, **daß** er den Koffer **mitbringen soll.**

- If a subordinate clause is the first sentence element, then the inflected part of the verb in the main clause comes right after the comma, retaining second position in the overall sentence.

Ich habe den Schlüssel mitgenommen, **weil** das Hotel um 24.00 Uhr zumacht.
Weil das Hotel um 24.00 Uhr zumacht, **habe ich** den Schlüssel mitgenommen.

2. Sequence of Objects p. 95

The indirect object usually precedes the direct object unless the direct object is a pronoun.

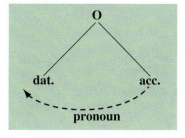

Sie gibt **dem Herrn** den Reisescheck.
Sie gibt **ihm** den Reisescheck.
Sie gibt ihn **dem Herrn.**
Sie gibt ihn **ihm.**

3. **sondern** vs. **aber** pp. 154–55

sondern must be used when the first clause is negated AND the meaning *but on the contrary* is implied.

Er wohnt hier, **aber** er ist gerade nicht zu Hause.
Heinz ist nicht hier, **aber** er kommt in zehn Minuten zurück.
Heinz ist nicht hier, **sondern** bei Freunden.

RÜCKBLICK KAPITEL 4–7

Wortschatzwiederholung

A. Geben Sie das Gegenteil von . . . !

Ausgang, Tag, antworten, fahren, Glück haben, mieten, zumachen, bequem, furchtbar, geöffnet, hier, immer, links, ruhig, unten, weit

B. Was ist der Artikel und der Plural?

Ausweis, Bank, Bibliothek, Fest, Garten, Gast, Gasthof, Haus, Hotel, Jugendherberge, Koffer, Lied, Mann, Nacht, Radio, Regal, Reise, Schlüssel, Sessel, Tasche, Taxi, Universität, Wald, Weg

C. Welche Wörter kommen Ihnen in den Sinn?

BEISPIEL: aufmachen
die Tür, das Fenster, der Schlüssel

baden, bekommen, bummeln, einkaufen, feiern, halten, kochen, packen, singen, sitzen, sparen, Spaß machen, übernachten, wechseln

D. Was für Wortkombinationen gibt es?

BEISPIEL: Telefon
Telefonnummer, Telefonbuch

1. Ausweis
2. Eingang
3. Ferien
4. Flasche
5. Gast
6. Geld
7. Haltestelle
8. Scheck
9. Schrank

E. Was paßt?

_____ 1. Können Sie mir sagen, wo das Hotel ist?
_____ 2. Wie komme ich dorthin *(to it)*?
_____ 3. Wie lange dauert das?
_____ 4. Wo kann ich das Gepäck lassen?
_____ 5. Einen Moment! Das gehört mir!
_____ 6. Wann machen Sie zu?
_____ 7. Wo ist das Zimmer?
_____ 8. Haben Sie kein Zimmer mit Bad?
_____ 9. Das Zimmer ist zu klein.
_____ 10. Nehmen Sie Reiseschecks an?

a. An der Rezeption.
b. Da drüben.
c. Das macht nichts.
d. Das tut mir leid.
e. Doch!
f. Ein paar Minuten.
g. Entschuldigen Sie!
h. Fahren Sie immer geradeaus!
i. Ich weiß nicht.
j. Im Parterre.
k. In ein paar Minuten.
l. Ja, gern.
m. Ja, natürlich.
n. Leider nicht.
o. Mit dem Bus.
p. Neben dem Rathaus.
q. Sind Sie sicher?
r. Um 23.00 Uhr.
s. Wirklich?
t. Zu Fuß!
u. Das stimmt nicht.

Strukturwiederholung

F. **Verben**

*1. **wissen oder kennen?**

a. Ich möchte _____ , für wen das Geschenk ist.

b. _____ du einen Herrn Mayerhofer?

c. _____ ihr eure Nachbarn nicht?

d. Nein, ich _____ sie nicht, aber ich _____ , daß sie aus Österreich sind.

e. _____ du, wann sie zurückkommen sollen?

2. **Geben Sie alle Imperative!**

BEISPIEL: Überraschen wir ihn!
Überraschen Sie ihn!
Überrascht ihn!
Überrasch(e) ihn!

a. Tun wir die Milch in den Kühlschrank! **b.** Stellen wir die Teller auf den Tisch! **c.** Gehen wir ins Wohnzimmer! **d.** Sprechen wir ein bißchen! **e.** Lassen wir alles liegen und stehen! **f.** Nehmen wir ein paar Gläser mit! **g.** Essen wir ein paar Kartoffelchips! **h.** Bleiben wir noch ein bißchen! **i.** Fahren wir später!

3. **Sagen Sie es im Perfekt!**

a. Wohin geht ihr?—Wir fahren zum Museum.

b. Was machst du heute?—Ich packe meinen Koffer.

c. Wie feiert ihr seinen Geburtstag?—Wir überraschen ihn mit einer Party.

d. Wie gefällt Ihnen die Landshuter Fürstenhochzeit?—Sie macht mir viel Spaß.

e. Vermieten Sie die Wohnung?—Ja, eine Studentin nimmt sie.

f. Weißt du, wo der Scheck ist?—Ja, er liegt auf dem Schreibtisch.

g. Wie lange dauert die Party?—Sie ist um 12.00 Uhr vorbei.

h. Wo sind Paula und Robert?—Sie kaufen ein.

*4. **Variieren Sie die Sätze!**

a. **Ihr dürft das Geschenk aufmachen.**

May we open the present? We want to open it. I can't open it. He has to open it. Why am I not supposed to open it? Wouldn't you *(3×)* like to open it?

b. **Wir kommen morgen an.**

I arrived yesterday. She's arriving today. When are they arriving? When did he arrive? Is he arriving, too? I know that they're not arriving tomorrow. They're supposed to arrive the day after tomorrow. Has she arrived yet **(schon)**?

*G. **Personalpronomen.** Variieren Sie die Sätze!

1. **Ich frage sie.**

   He's asking you *(formal)*. She's asking him. Are they asking us? Yes, they are asking you *(sg. fam.)*. We're asking you *(pl. fam.)*. Don't *(pl. fam.)* ask them! Did you *(sg. fam.)* ask them? Weren't they asking you *(sg. fam.)*? Have you *(pl. fam.)* asked me?

2. **Mir gefällt dieses Museum.**

   He likes our museum. Do you *(formal)* like this museum? They don't like their museum. Which museum do you *(sg. fam.)* like? I like such a museum. Don't you *(pl. fam.)* like any museum (Do you like no museum)? I don't like museums. I never liked such museums. He likes every museum.

3. **Das tut mir leid.**

   She's sorry. He isn't sorry. Are you *(3×)* sorry? I was sorry. They were sorry.

H. **Präpositionen.** Bilden Sie Sätze wie in den Beispielen!

1. BEISPIEL: Wo ist der Koffer?   **Der Koffer steht an der Tür.**
              Wohin soll ich den Koffer   **Stellen Sie ihn an die Tür!**
              stellen?

   vor / Haus; in / Gästezimmer; neben / Sofa; hinter / Sessel; unter / Tisch; zwischen / Stuhl / und / Bett

2. BEISPIEL: Wohin soll ich das Messer legen? **Legen Sie es auf den Tisch!**
              Wo liegt das Messer?   **Es liegt auf dem Tisch.**

   neben / Gabel; auf / Teller; zwischen / Butter / und / Käse; in / Küche; in / Eßzimmer

I. **Konjunktionen**

1. **Verbinden Sie die Sätze!** *(Note that both coordinating and subordinating conjunctions are used.)*

   a. Ich lerne Deutsch. Meine Großeltern sind aus Deutschland. *(because)*
   b. Sie möchte wissen. Bist du schon einmal in Deutschland gewesen? *(whether)*
   c. Ich sage (es) ihr. Ich bin im Sommer dort gewesen. *(that)*
   d. Ich möchte auch gern wieder einmal nach Deutschland. So eine Reise ist nicht billig. *(but)*
   e. Braucht man Hotelreservierungen? Man fährt nach Deutschland. *(when)*
   f. *(although)* Man braucht keine Reservierung. Es hat manchmal lange gedauert, bis ich ein Zimmer gefunden habe.
   g. Einmal habe ich bei einer Kusine übernachtet. Eine Nacht habe ich im Zug *(train)* geschlafen. *(and)*
   h. Man muß alles gut planen. Man möchte nach Deutschland fahren. *(if)*

*2. **Sondern oder aber?**

    a.   Momentan habe ich kein Kleingeld, —————— später gehe ich zur Bank.

    b.   Die Bank ist um diese Zeit geschlossen, —————— sie macht in einer Stunde wieder auf.

    c.   Wir möchten nicht in die Stadt gehen, —————— hier bleiben.

    d.   In der Stadt kann man viel sehen, —————— wir haben schon alles gesehen.

    e.   Das bedeutet nicht, daß die Stadt mir nicht gefällt, —————— es bedeutet nur, daß ich müde bin.

Post und Reisen

In Europa sind Züge bequem, pünktlich und schnell.

LERNZIELE

Vorschau

- Focus on Switzerland

Gespräche and Wortschatz

- Postal service and travel

Struktur

- Genitive case
- Time expressions
- Sentence structure: types and sequence of adverbs, and the position of *nicht*

Einblicke

- Tourists' views of Switzerland

Sprechsituationen

- Expressing sympathy and lack of sympathy
- Expressing empathy
- Expressing relief

Focus on Switzerland

LAND.   Approximately 16,000 square miles, about half the size of Indiana.

PEOPLE.   About 6.7 million. Major religions: 48% Catholic, 44% Protestant.

GEOGRAPHY.   A landlocked country that is clearly defined by three natural regions: the *Alpine ranges* that stretch from the French border south of Lake Geneva diagonally across the southern half of Switzerland and include the world-renowned resorts of the Bernese Oberland, Zermatt, and St. Moritz in the Inn River valley; the plateaus and valleys of the *midland* between Lake Geneva and Lake Constance; and the mountains of the *Jura* in the northernmost section of the Alps.

CURRENCY.   Schweizer Franken, 1 sfr = 100 Rappen or Centimes.

PRINCIPAL CITIES.   Capital Berne (**Bern**, pop. 141,000), Zurich (**Zürich**, pop. 370,000), Basel (pop. 180,000), Geneva (**Genf**, pop. 159,900), Lausanne (pop. 126,200).

Isolated and protected by its relative inaccessibility, Switzerland was able to develop without major hindrance after its founding in 1291 from a tiny confederation of three regions, called cantons (Uri, Schwyz, and Unterwalden), to a nation of 26 cantons, three of which are subdivided into half-cantons. These cantons maintain considerable autonomy, possessing their own constitutions and legislatures. In 1848 a new constitution merged the old confederation into a single state, eliminating all commercial barriers and establishing a common postal service, army, legislature, and judiciary.

In spite of its small size, meager supply of natural resources, and considerable ethnic diversity, Switzerland is politically and socially one of the most stable nations in the world. Its stability can be attributed to its high standard of living, the conservative character of its people, and the country's noninvolvement in Europe's major 20th-century wars. Switzerland has adhered to its principle of neutrality, even to the extent of staying out of the United Nations and the European Union. On the other hand, the country's involvement in world affairs is shown by its membership in the Council of Europe and several specialized agencies of the United Nations. The home of the League of Nations after World War I, Switzerland is now the permanent base of the UN's Economic and Social Council, the International Labor Organization and the World Health Organization, seat of the World Council of Churches, and headquarters of the International Red Cross.

Markt in Basel

Gespräche   Auf der Post[1] am Bahnhof

UTA   Ich möchte dieses Paket nach
Amerika schicken.

POSTBEAMTER   Normal oder per Luftpost?

UTA   Per Luftpost. Wie lange dauert das denn?

POSTBEAMTER   Ungefähr zehn Tage. Füllen Sie bitte
diese Paketkarte aus! . . . Moment,
hier fehlt noch Ihr Absender.

UTA   Ach ja! . . . Noch etwas. Ich brauche eine Telefonkarte.[2]

POSTBEAMTER   Für sechs, zwölf oder fünfzig Mark?

UTA   Für zwölf Mark. Vielen Dank!

Das Postpaket Schnell und sicher

Am Fahrkartenschalter

ANNEMARIE   Wann fährt der nächste Zug nach Interlaken[3]?

BEAMTIN   In zehn Minuten. Abfahrt um 11.28 Uhr, Gleis 2.

ANNEMARIE   Ach du meine Güte! Und wann kommt er dort an?

BEAMTIN   Ankunft in Interlaken um 14.16 Uhr.

ANNEMARIE   Muß ich umsteigen?

BEAMTIN   Ja, in Bern[4], aber Sie haben Anschluß zum InterCity[5] mit nur vierundzwanzig
Minuten Aufenthalt.

ANNEMARIE   Gut. Geben Sie mir bitte eine Hin- und Rückfahrkarte nach Interlaken!

BEAMTIN   Erster oder zweiter Klasse?

ANNEMARIE   Zweiter Klasse.

Fragen

1. Wo ist die Post?   2. Wohin will Uta ihr Paket schicken?   3. Wie schickt sie es?
4. Wie lange soll das dauern?   5. Was muß man bei einem Paket ins Ausland *(abroad)*
ausfüllen?   6. Was fehlt auf der Paketkarte?   7. Was braucht Uta noch?   8. Was
kosten Telefonkarten?   9. Wohin will Annemarie fahren?   10. Wann fährt der Zug ab,
und wann kommt er in Interlaken an?   11. Wo muß Annemarie umsteigen?   12. Was
für eine Karte kauft sie?

Zug		118	518	1720		120	1520	1822	
Zürich HB		10 03	10 07	10 28	11 03	11 07	11 28		
Baden				10 45			11 45		
Brugg (Aargau)				10 53			11 53		
Aarau			10 35	11 07		11 35	12 07		
Olten	24016 O		10 44	11 15		11 44	12 15		
Olten	24000		10 47			11 47			
Biel/Bienne	O		11 33			12 33			
Lausanne	O					13 48			
Genève	O		13 05						
Zug		721	2521		73	1866		725	
					7	4			
Basel SBB		10 00	10 11	10 29	11 00		11 29	12 00	
Liestal			10 21	10 46			11 46		
Olten	O	10 26	10 43	11 11	11 26		12 11	12 26	
Olten		10 28	10 48	11 17	11 28		12 17	12 28	
Langenthal			11 00	11 29			12 29		
Herzogenbuchsee			11 06	11 35			12 35		
Burgdorf			11 18	11 47			12 47		
Bern	O	11 10	11 14	11 35	12 04	12 10	12 14	13 04	13 10
Bern	24004	11 28			12 28	12 28		13 28	
Interlaken West	O	12 16			13 16	13 16		14 16	

Übrigens

1.   Post offices in Germany provide a far greater range of services than in the United States or Canada. You can, for example, open a checking or savings account, get traveler's checks, arrange for money transfers, or send a telegram. Post offices usually have several booths from which long-distance calls can be made and then paid for at the counter. This service is useful if you stay in a hotel, since many hotels impose a considerable surcharge on long-distance calls. Until recently, the post office had a monopoly on telephone and postal services. In 1989 the postal service was divided into three separate enterprises, administered by the **Bundesministerium für Post und Telekommunikation,** one for each function: telecommunications (**Telekom**), banking (**Postbank**), and postal service (**Post-dienst**). The post office no longer has a monopoly on mail delivery services. UPS and FedEx trucks have become a familiar sight in Europe.

2.   Compared with the United States and Canada, telephoning in the German-speaking countries is expensive. One pays for every call and, in some cases, even for unanswered ringing, according to the length of time and the distance. Most calls from public booths **(Telefonzellen)** are paid for with coins, but calling with a phone card **(Telefonkarte)** is becoming popular. These cards can be bought at any post office and allow you to make calls up to a certain prepaid value.

3.   Interlaken (pop. 13,000), located between lakes Thun and Brienz, is one of the oldest and most popular summer resorts in Switzerland. Tourists enjoy hiking, mountain climbing, and other excursions, especially into the mountains of the Bernese Oberland (**Berner Oberland**), accessible also by mountain railroads and cablecars.

Telephone cards are also used for extensive advertising. This card promotes the **Operettenhaus** in Hamburg and includes the box office telephone number.

4.   Berne is the capital of Switzerland. Founded in 1191, the old section of Berne sits one hundred feet above a bend in the Aare River, which surrounds the city on three sides. Gray stone buildings, red-tiled roofs, scenic paths, and fountains preserve the medieval charm of old Berne, which is linked by several bridges to its modern counterpart on the opposite side of the river.

5.   Train travel in Europe is very popular. An extensive network of rail lines serves commuters as well as long-distance travelers. Trains are comfortable, clean, punctual, and fast. The **IC** *(InterCity)* and **EC** *(EuroCity)* trains connect all major European cities. In 1991 new high-speed services were introduced between Hanover and Würzburg, Mannheim and Stuttgart; and other high-speed routes are planned. The **ICE** *(InterCityExpress),* traveling up to 250 km/h, makes the railroad even more attractive, especially to business people who can make or receive telephone calls on the train and even rent conference rooms equipped with fax machines. Non-European travelers can buy a Eurailpass that permits unlimited train and some bus and boat travel in Germany and most other European countries.

WORTSCHATZ 1

Die Post   *(post office, mail)*

der	Absender, -	*return address*
	Brief, -e	*letter*
	Briefkasten, ⁝	*mailbox*
das	Paket, -e	*package, parcel*
	Postfach, ⁝er	*P.O. box*
die	Adresse, -n	*address*
	(Ansichts)karte, -n	*(picture) postcard*
	Briefmarke, -n	*stamp*
	Telefonkarte, -n	*telephone card*
	Telefonnummer, -n	*telephone number*

Die Reise, -n   *(trip)*

der	Aufenthalt, -e	*stopover, stay*	das	Flugzeug, -e	*plane*
	Bahnsteig, -e	*platform*		Gleis, -e	*track*
	Fahrplan, ⁝e	*schedule*	die	Abfahrt, -en	*departure*
	Flug, ⁝e	*flight*		Ankunft, ⁝e	*arrival*
	Flughafen, ⁝	*airport*		Bahn, -en	*railway, train*
	Wagen, -	*car; railroad car*		Fahrt, -en	*trip, drive*
	Zug, ⁝e	*train*		Fahrkarte, -n	*ticket*
				(Hin- und) Rück-	*round-trip ticket*
				fahrkarte, -n	

Weiteres

Ach du meine Güte!	*My goodness!*
in einer Viertelstunde	*in a quarter of an hour*
in einer halben Stunde	*in half an hour*
in einer Dreiviertelstunde	*in three-quarters of an hour*
ab·fahren (fährt ab), ist abgefahren (von)	*to leave (from), depart*
ab·fliegen, ist abgeflogen (von)	*to take off, fly (from)*
aus·steigen, ist ausgestiegen	*to get off*
ein·steigen, ist eingestiegen	*to get on (in)*
um·steigen, ist umgestiegen	*to change (trains etc.)*
aus·füllen	*to fill out*
besuchen	*to visit*
fliegen, ist geflogen	*to fly, go by plane*
landen, ist gelandet	*to land*
schicken	*to send*
telefonieren	*to call up, phone*
mit dem Zug / der Bahn fahren	*to go by train*

ZUM ERKENNEN: normal *(regular);* per Luftpost *(by airmail);* die Paketkarte, -n *(parcel form);* noch etwas *(one more thing, something else);* der nächste Zug nach *(the next train to);* der Anschluß, ⁝sse *(connection);* die Klasse, -n

Im Hauptbahnhof von
Luzern

A. Was paßt nicht?

1. der Absender, der Briefkasten, die Adresse, die Briefmarke
2. der Bahnhof, der Bahnsteig, das Gleis, der Flugkartenschalter
3. die Luftpost, die Ankunft, die Abfahrt, der Fahrplan
4. fliegen, fahren, schicken, fehlen
5. abfahren, abfliegen, ausfüllen, ankommen
6. hinaufsteigen, aussteigen, einsteigen, umsteigen

B. Was bedeutet das, und was ist der Artikel?

Adressbuch, Abfahrtszeit, Ankunftsfahrplan, Bahnhofseingang, Busbahnhof, Busfahrt, Flugkarte, Flugschalter, Flugsteig, Gepäckkarte, Landung, Zwischenlandung,
Mietwagen, Nachtzug, Paketschalter, Postfachnummer, Speisewagen, Telefonrech-
nung

C. Fragen

1. Was kostet es, wenn man einen Brief innerhalb *(inside)* von Amerika oder
    Kanada schicken will? Wie lange braucht ein Brief innerhalb der Stadt? nach
    Europa?
2. Was muß man auf alle Briefe, Ansichtskarten und Pakete schreiben? Schreiben
    Sie oft Briefe? Wem?
3. In Deutschland sind die Briefkästen gelb. Welche Farbe haben die Briefkästen
    hier?
4. Wo kann man hier telefonieren? Kann man hier auch auf der Post anrufen? Gibt
    es Telefonkarten?
5. Wie kann man reisen? Wie reisen Sie gern? Warum?
6. Wo sind Sie das letzte Mal *(the last time)* gewesen? Sind Sie geflogen oder mit
    dem Wagen gefahren?
7. Wie heißt der Ort *(place)*, wo Züge abfahren und ankommen? wo Flugzeuge
    abfliegen und landen? wo Busse halten?
8. Was ist das Gegenteil von abfahren? abfliegen? einsteigen? Abfahrt? Abflug?

D.   Am Flugschalter. Was sagen Sie?

S1   Wann gehen Flüge nach _____ ?
S2   Zu welcher Tageszeit möchten Sie denn fliegen?
S1   Ich muß um _____ in _____ sein.
S2   Es gibt einen Flug um _____ .
S1   Hat er eine Zwischenlandung?
S2   Ja, in _____ . Dort haben Sie _____ Aufenthalt.
S1   Muß ich umsteigen?
S2   _____ .
S1   _____ . Dann geben Sie mir eine Hin- und Rückflugkarte nach
      _____ !

S2   Erster oder zweiter Klasse?
S1   _____ .

E.   Fragen über den Fahrplan

NOTE: 1 km = 0.62 miles. Here is an easy way to convert kilometers to miles: divide the km figure in half, and add a quarter of that to the half. Thus 80 km ÷ 2 = 40 + 10 = 50 miles.

km	Stuttgart–Zürich		E 3504	D 83	D 381	D 383			D 85	D 389		D 87	D 385	E 3309	D 387
0	**Stuttgart** Hbf	740		6 48	7 31	9 34			12 44	14 26		17 32	18 26	20 06	
26	Böblingen				7 53	9 56			13 06	14 48		17 55	18 48	20 29	
67	Horb			7 34	8 20	10 24			13 33	15 15		18 21	19 15	21 00	
110	Rottweil			8 05	8 59	10 54			14 02	15 52		18 51	19 45	21 36	
138	Tuttlingen			8 26	9 17	11 13			14 21	16 11		19 09	20 11	21 55	
172	Singen (Hohentwiel)	O		8 49	9 42	11 37			14 45	16 35		19 32	20 35	22 22	
192	Singen (Hohentwiel)	730	6 31	8 55	9 49	11 44	D 2162		14 51	16 44		19 37	20 44		22 44
	Schaffhausen	O	6 49	9 10	10 05	12 00	12 43		15 07	17 00		19 52	21 00		23 00
238	**Schaffhausen**	24032	7 02	9 12	10 09	12 09	13 09		15 09	17 09		19 55	21 09		23 09
	Zürich HB	O	7 47	9 47	10 47	12 47	13 47		15 47	17 47		20 31	21 47		23 47

1. Wie viele Kilometer sind es von Stuttgart nach Zürich?
2. Wann fährt der erste Zug morgens? der letzte *(last)* Zug abends?
3. In welchem Zug kann man Speisen und Getränke *(food and beverages)* kaufen? Welcher Zug hat einen Gepäckwagen oder Liegewagen?
4. Welcher Zug ist ab Schaffhausen ein EC-Zug? ein IC-Zug?
5. Wann ist man in Zürich, wenn man um 6.48 Uhr von Stuttgart abfährt? Wie lange dauert die Fahrt ungefähr?

F.   Aussprache: e, er   *(See also II.8–10 in the pronunciation section of the Workbook.)*

1. [ə] Adresse, Briefe, Pakete, Flüge, Züge, Wagen, Ecke, Haltestelle, bekommen, besuchen, eine halbe Stunde
2. [ʌ] aber, sauber, euer, unser, Zimmer, Absender, Koffer, Nummer, Uhr, wir, vier, vor, nur, unter, über, hinter, außer, feiern, wiederholen, verkaufen
3. Wortpaare

    a. Studenten / Studentin   d. arbeiten / Arbeitern
    b. Touristen / Touristin   e. lese / Leser
    c. diese / dieser   f. mieten / Mietern

Hören Sie zu!

Hilfe mit der Post   *(Bill, an American student who is studying in Germany for a year, needs help from Claudia, a German student living in the same dormitory.)*

ZUM ERKENNEN: Na klar! *(Sure!);* endlich mal *(finally);* das Papierwarengeschäft, -e *(office supply store);* zuerst *(first);* Laß sie wiegen! *(Have them weighed!);* Luftpostleicht-brief, -e *(aerogram)*

Richtig oder falsch?

_____   1.   Bill muß endlich mal an Claudias Eltern schreiben.
_____   2.   Claudia möchte wissen, wo man Papier, Ansichtskarten und Briefmarken
            bekommt.
_____   3.   Bei Schlegel in der Beethovenstraße gibt es Briefpapier.
_____   4.   Postkarten findet man nur in Drogerien.
_____   5.   Gegenüber vom Stadttheater ist die Post.
_____   6.   Bill kauft heute Briefmarken und geht morgen zum Bahnhof.
_____   7.   Er soll zur Post gehen und Claudia Briefmarken mitbringen.

Vor der Post

STRUKTUR

I. The Genitive Case

The genitive case has two major functions: it expresses possession or another close relationship between two nouns, and it follows certain prepositions.

1. The English phrases *the son's letter* and *the date of the letter* are expressed in German by phrases in the genitive.

    Das ist **der Brief des Sohnes.**   *That's the son's letter.*
    Was ist **das Datum des Briefes?**   *What's the date of the letter?*

    a. The genitive form of the INTERROGATIVE PRONOUN **wer** is **wessen** *(whose).* The chart below shows all four cases of the interrogative pronouns.

	persons	things and ideas
nom.	wer	was
acc.	wen	was
dat.	wem	—
gen.	wessen	—

    Wessen Brief ist das?   *Whose letter is that?*
    Der Brief des Sohnes.   *The son's letter.*

    b. The genitive forms of the DEFINITE and INDEFINITE ARTICLES complete this chart of articles:

	singular masc.	singular neut.	singular fem.	plural
nom.	der ein kein	das ein kein	die eine keine	die — keine
acc.	den einen keinen	das ein kein	die eine keine	die — keine
dat.	dem einem keinem	dem einem keinem	der einer keiner	den — keinen
gen.	des eines keines	des eines keines	der einer keiner	der — keiner

c. The genitive case is signaled not only by the forms of the articles but also by a special ending for MASCULINE and NEUTER nouns in the singular.

- Most one-syllable nouns and nouns ending in **-s, -ß, -z, -tz,** or **-zt,** add **-es:**

der Zug	das Geld	der Ausweis	der Paß	der Platz
des Zug**es**	**des** Geld**es**	**des** Ausweis**es**	**des** Pass**es**	**des** Platz**es**

- Proper names and nouns with more than one syllable add an **-s:**

Annemarie**s** Flug	*Annemarie's flight*
Frau Strobel**s** Fahrt	*Ms. Strobel's trip*
Wien**s** Flughafen	*Vienna's airport*
des Flughafen**s**	*of the airport, the airport's*

Note that German uses NO apostrophe (') for the genitive. In colloquial speech **von** is frequently used instead of the genitive of a name: **die Adresse von Hans.**

- N-nouns have an **-n** or **-en** ending in ALL CASES except in the nominative singular. A very few n-nouns have a genitive **-s** as well.

der	Franzose, **-n,** -n	des	Franzose**n**
	Herr, **-n,** -en		Herr**n**
	Junge, **-n,** -n		Junge**n**
	Mensch, **-en,** -en		Mensch**en**
	Nachbar, **-n,** -n		Nachbar**n**
	Student, **-en,** -en		Student**en**
	Tourist, **-en,** -en		Tourist**en**
	Name, **-n(s),** -n		Name**ns**

Note how n-nouns are listed in vocabularies and dictionaries: the first ending usually refers to the accusative, dative, and genitive singular; the second one to the plural.

d. FEMININE NOUNS and PLURAL nouns have no special endings in the genitive.

die Reise	**der** Reise
die Reisen	**der** Reisen

e. Nouns in the genitive NORMALLY FOLLOW the nouns they modify, while PROPER NAMES PRECEDE them.

Er liest **den Brief der Tante.**
Er liest **Annemaries Brief.**
Er liest **Herrn Müllers Brief.**

Caution: Don't confuse the use of the possessive adjectives **mein, dein,** etc., with that of the genitive case.

Das ist **mein** Onkel.	*That's my uncle.*
Das ist der Koffer **meines Onkels.**	*That's my uncle's suitcase (the suitcase of my uncle).*
Er ist der Bruder **meiner Mutter.**	*He's my mother's brother (the brother of my mother).*

2. These prepositions are followed by the genitive case:

(an)statt	*instead of*	Ich nehme oft den Bus **(an)statt der Straßenbahn.**
trotz	*in spite of*	**Trotz des Wetters** bummele ich gern durch die Stadt.
während	*during*	**Während der Mittagspause** gehe ich in den Park.
wegen	*because of*	Heute bleibe ich **wegen des Regens** (*rain*) hier.

Den Fahrer während der Fahrt nicht ansprechen

Übungen

A. Wissen Sie, wer das ist?

BEISPIEL: Wer ist der Vater Ihrer Mutter?
    Das ist mein Großvater.

1. Wer ist der Sohn Ihres Vaters?   **2.** Wer ist die Mutter Ihrer Mutter?   **3.** Wer ist die Tochter Ihrer Mutter?   **4.** Wer ist der Großvater Ihrer Mutter?   **5.** Wer ist die Schwester Ihrer Mutter?   **6.** Wer ist der Mann Ihrer Tante?   **7.** Wer ist die Tochter Ihres Großvaters?   **8.** Wer ist der Sohn Ihres Urgroßvaters?

B. Im Reisebüro   *(At the travel agency. Make sure that your assistant followed all the necessary steps to organize the tour leaving for Berne tomorrow.)*

BEISPIEL: Wo ist die Liste der Touristen? (Hotel / *pl.*)
    Wo ist die Liste der Hotels?

1. Wie ist der Name des Reiseführers *(tour guide)*? (Schloß, Dom, Museum, Straße, Platz, Tourist, Touristin, Franzose, Französin)
2. Wo ist die Adresse der Jugendherberge? (Theater, Studentenheim, Universität, Restaurant)
3. Wo ist die Telefonnummer des Hotels? (Gästehaus, Pension, Gasthof, Jugendherberge)
4. Wo ist die Adresse dieser Dame? (Gast, Mädchen, Junge, Herr, Herren, Student, Studenten / *pl.*)
5. Wann ist die Ankunft unserer Gruppe? (Bus, Zug, Flugzeug, Reiseführerin, Gäste)
6. Haben Sie wegen der Reservierung *(reservation)* angerufen? (Zimmer, Schlüssel, Gepäck, Adresse, Theaterkarten / *pl.*)
7. Wir fahren trotz des Gewitters *(thunderstorm)*. (Wetter, Regen *[m.]*, Eis, Feiertag, Ferien)
8. Christiane Binder kommt statt ihrer Mutter mit. (Vater, Bruder, Onkel, Nachbar, Nachbarin, Großeltern)

C. Wem gehört das?

BEISPIEL: Gehört die Jacke Ihrem Freund?
    Nein, das ist nicht die Jacke meines Freundes.
    Das ist meine Jacke.

Gehört das Hemd Ihrem Bruder? die Uhr Ihrer Mutter? das Buch Ihrem Professor? die Tasche Ihrer Freundin? die Post Ihrem Nachbarn? der Kuli Frau _____ *(name a student)*? das Heft Herrn _____ *(name a student)*? der Platz _____ *(add a name)*?

D. Bilden Sie Sätze mit dem Genitiv!

BEISPIEL: Die Abfahrt des Zuges ist um 19.05 Uhr.

1	2	3		4	5
die Farbe	d-	Auto	Gasthof	ist	_____
der Name	dies-	Bus	Ausweis	gefällt	
die Adresse	mein-	Zug	Paß		
die Nummer	unser-	Bahnsteig	Reisescheck		
das Zimmer		Koffer	Flug		
das Gepäck		Tasche	Frau		
die Abfahrt		Haus	Herr		
der Preis		Wohnung	Freund(in)		
die Lage *(location)*		Hotel	Tourist(in)		
		Pension	Gäste		
		Berge			
		Postfach			

E. Bahnfahrt. Auf deutsch, bitte!

1. Is that Eva's train?   **2.** Do you know the number of the platform?   **3.** No. Where's the train schedule (schedule of the trains)?   **4.** Her train leaves in a few minutes. (The departure of her train is in a few minutes).   **5.** Take along Kurt's package.   **6.** Kurt is a student and a friend of my friend *(f.)*.   **7.** Eva, do you have the student's *(m.)* address?   **8.** No, but I know the name of the dorm.   **9.** I'll take it to him during the holidays.   **10.** Because of the exams I don't have time now. **11.** I'll send you a postcard instead of a letter.

II. Time Expressions

1.   Adverbs of Time

a.   To refer to SPECIFIC TIMES, such as *yesterday evening* or *Monday morning,* combine one word from group A with another from group B. The words in group A can be used alone, while those in group B must be used in combinations: **gestern abend, Montag morgen, Sonntag nachmittag.**

A

vorgestern	*the day before yesterday*
gestern	*yesterday*
heute	*today*
morgen	*tomorrow*
übermorgen	*the day after tomorrow*

B

Montag	**früh, morgen**[2]	*early, morning*
Dienstag	**vormittag**	*midmorning (9 to 12 A.M.)*[4]
Mittwoch	**mittag**	*noon (12 to 2 P.M.)*
Donnerstag	**nachmittag**	*afternoon (2 to 6 P.M.)*
Freitag	**abend**[3]	*evening (6 to 10 P.M.)*
Samstag[1]	**nacht**[3]	*night (after 10 P.M.)*
Sonntag		

Heute fliege ich von New York ab.
Dann bin ich **morgen früh** in Frankfurt.
Übermorgen fahre ich nach Bonn.
Montag abend besuche ich Krauses.
Dann fahre ich **Dienstag nachmittag** mit dem Zug zurück.

b.   Such familiar adverbs as **montags** and **morgens** don't refer to specific time (a specific *Monday* or *morning*), but rather imply that events OCCUR USUALLY (more or less regularly), for example, *on Mondays* or *in the morning, most mornings:*

montags, dienstags, mittwochs, donnerstags, freitags, samstags, sonntags; morgens, vormittags, mittags, nachmittags, abends, nachts

Sonntags tue ich nichts, aber **montags** arbeite ich schwer.
Morgens und **nachmittags** gehe ich zur Universität.
Mittags spiele ich eine Stunde Tennis.

---

[1] People in northern Germany and in the former East Germany prefer **Sonnabend,** those in southern Germany **Samstag** (derived from the Hebrew word *Sabbat*).

[2] **Heute morgen** is used in northern Germany, **heute früh** in southern Germany; both mean *this morning. Tomorrow morning* is always **morgen früh.**

[3] German distinguishes clearly between **abend** and **nacht**: Wir sind **gestern abend** ins Kino gegangen. Ich habe **gestern nacht** schlecht geschlafen. **Heute nacht** can mean *last night* or *tonight* (whichever is closer), depending on context.

[4] The times may vary somewhat, but these are reasonable guidelines.

2.   Other Time Expressions

a.   The Accusative of Time

To refer to a DEFINITE point in time (**wann**?) or length of time (**wie lange**?), German often uses time phrases in the accusative, without any prepositions. Here are some of the most common expressions:

wann?		wie lange?	
jeden Tag	*every day*	zwei Wochen	*for two weeks*
diese Woche	*this week*	einen Monat	*for one month*

Haben Sie diese Woche Zeit?   *Do you have time this week?*
Die Fahrt dauert zwei Stunden.   *The trip takes two hours.*
Ich bleibe zwei Tage in Zürich.   *I'll be in Zurich for two days.*

b.   The Genitive of Time

To refer to an INDEFINITE point in time (in the past or future), German uses the genitive:

eines Tages   *one day, some day*

Eines Tages ist ein Brief gekommen.   *One day a letter came.*
Eines Tages fahre ich in die Schweiz.   *Some day I'll go to Switzerland.*

c.   Prepositional Time Phrases

You are already familiar with the phrases below:

an   am Abend, am Wochenende, am Montag, am 1. April
bis   bis morgen, bis 2.30 Uhr, bis (zum) Freitag, bis (zum) Januar
für   für morgen, für Freitag, für eine Nacht
in   im Juli, im Sommer, im Monat; in zehn Minuten, in einer
                 Viertelstunde, in einer Woche, in einem Jahr
nach   nach dem Essen, nach einer Stunde
seit   seit einem Jahr, seit September
um   um fünf (Uhr)
von ... bis vom 1. Juni bis (zum) 25. August; von Juli bis August
vor   vor einem Monat, vor ein paar Tagen
während   während des Sommers, während des Tages

- Two-way prepositions usually use the <u>dative</u> in time expressions: Wir fahren **in einer Woche** in die Berge. **Am Freitag** fahren wir ab.

- German uses **seit** plus the present tense to describe an action or condition that began in the past and is still continuing in the present. English uses the present perfect progressive to express the same thing: **Er wohnt seit zwei Jahren hier.** (*He has been living here for two years.*)

Übungen

F.   Ein Besuch. Was fehlt?

1. Erich ist _____ angekommen. *(one week ago)*
2. Wir sind _____ abgefahren. *(Thursday evening at 7 o'clock)*
3. Er ist _____ geflogen. *(for nine hours)*
4. Ich habe ihn schon _____ nicht mehr gesehen. *(for one year)*
5. Er schläft _____ gewöhnlich nicht lange. *(in the morning)*
6. Aber er hat _____ geschlafen. *(Friday morning until 11 A.M.)*
7. Er bleibt noch ungefähr _____ bei uns. *(for one week)*
8. _____ sind wir bei meiner Tante gewesen. *(the day before yesterday)*
9. _____ gehen wir ins Kino. *(this evening)*
10. _____ kommen Erika und Uwe vorbei. *(tomorrow morning)*
11. _____ gehen wir alle essen. *(tomorrow at noon)*
12. _____ bummeln wir etwas durch die Stadt. *(in the afternoon)*
13. Was wir _____ tun, weiß ich noch nicht. *(the day after tomorrow)*
14. _____ machen wir etwas Besonderes. *(every day)*
15. _____ wollen wir an den See fahren. *(on the weekend)*
16. Was machst du _____ ? *(this weekend)*
17. Komm doch _____ mit! *(Friday afternoon)*
18. Du tust doch _____ und _____ nichts. *(on Saturdays / Sundays)*
19. _____ fahren wir ab. *(on Saturday morning)*
20. Wir bleiben _____ dort. *(for two days)*
21. _____ ist der See wunderbar. *(in the summer)*
22. Schade, daß Erich _____ schon wieder zu Hause sein muß. *(in one week)*

G.   Was hat er / sie gemacht?   *(You've been asked to escort a visiting politician / musician / professor who will lecture on your campus. The dean asks you to report, indicating what he / she did.)*

BEISPIEL: Morgens um acht ist er / sie am Flughafen angekommen. Wir sind zuerst zum Hotel gefahren, und dann . . .

III. Sentence Structure

1. Types of Adverbs

You have already encountered various adverbs and adverbial phrases. They are usually divided into three major groups.

a.   ADVERBS OF TIME, answering the questions **wann? wie lange?**

am Abend, am 1. April, eines Tages, heute, im Juni, immer, jetzt, manchmal, meistens, montags, morgens, nie, oft, um zwölf, vor einer Woche, während des Winters, bis Mai, eine Woche, stundenlang, ein paar Minuten, usw.

b.   ADVERBS OF MANNER, answering the question **wie?**

gemütlich, langsam, laut, mit der Bahn, ohne Geld, schnell, zu Fuß, zusammen, usw.

c.   ADVERBS OF PLACE, answering the questions **wo? wohin? woher?**

auf der Post, bei uns, da, dort, hier, im Norden, zu Hause, mitten in der Stadt, über-all, nach Berlin, nach Hause, auf die Post, zur Uni, aus Kanada, von Amerika, aus dem Flugzeug, usw.

2. Sequence of Adverbs

If two or more adverbs or adverbial phrases occur in one sentence, they usually follow the sequence TIME, MANNER, PLACE.

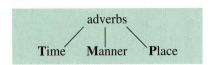

Er kann das Paket **morgen mit dem Auto zur Post** bringen.
    T   M   P

- If there is more than one time expression, general time references precede specific time references:

    Er bringt das Paket **morgen um neun Uhr** zur Post.

- Like other sentence elements, adverbs and adverbial phrases may precede the verb.

    Morgen kann er das Paket mit dem Auto zur Post bringen.
    Mit dem Auto kann er das Paket morgen zur Post bringen.
    Zur Post kann er das Paket morgen mit dem Auto bringen.

3. Position of **nicht**

As you already know from Chapter 2, section III, **nicht** usually comes <u>after adverbs of time</u> but <u>before adverbs of manner</u>.

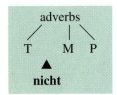

Er bringt das Paket ▲.
Er bringt das Paket ▲ mit.
Er kann das Paket   ▲ mitbringen.

Er kann das Paket **morgen** ▲ mitbringen.
Er kann das Paket **morgen** ▲ **mit dem Auto** mitbringen.
Er kann das Paket **morgen** ▲ **mit dem Auto zur Post** bringen.

Übungen

H. Sagen Sie das noch einmal!   *(Use the adverbial expressions in the proper order.)*

BEISPIEL: Ich kaufe die Briefmarken. (auf der Post, morgen)
Ich kaufe die Briefmarken morgen auf der Post.

1. Er kommt an. (heute abend, in Wien, mit dem Bus)
2. Sie reist. (nach Deutschland, ohne ihre Familie)
3. Deine Jeans liegt auf dem Sofa. (seit drei Tagen)
4. Wir fahren. (zu meiner Tante, am Sonntag, mit der Bahn)
5. Gehst du? (zu Fuß, in die Stadt, heute nachmittag)
6. Ich kaufe die Eier. (samstags, auf dem Markt, billig)
7. Wir wollen ins Kino gehen. (zusammen, morgen abend)
8. Ihr müßt umsteigen. (in einer Viertelstunde, in den Zug nach Nürnberg)
9. Sie läßt die Kinder in Salzburg. (bei den Großeltern, ein paar Tage)

I.   Ferienwünsche. Verneinen Sie die Sätze mit **nicht!**

GISELA	Ich möchte diesen Winter in die Berge fahren.
OTTO	Gefallen dir die Berge?
GISELA	Das habe ich gesagt. Warum fliegen wir diesen Winter nach Spanien? 479,–DM ist sehr teuer.
OTTO	Ich weiß.
GISELA	Im Flugzeug wird man so müde.
OTTO	Ich fliege gern.
GISELA	Ich möchte mit dem Auto fahren.
OTTO	Mittags kannst du lange in der Sonne liegen.
GISELA	Morgens und nachmittags ist die Sonne so heiß.
OTTO	In den Bergen ist es so langweilig.
GISELA	Gut. Wenn wir nach Spanien fliegen, komme ich mit.

J. **So kann man's auch sagen.** *(Start each sentence with the expression in boldface. How does this change affect the meaning?)*

BEISPIEL: Wir bleiben **während der Ferien** gewöhnlich zu Hause.
Während der Ferien bleiben wir gewöhnlich zu Hause.
During vacations we usually stay home.

1. Wir geben nicht viel Geld **für Reisen** aus.
2. Manfred hat **gerade** mit seiner Schwester in Holland gesprochen.
3. Sie ist **seit einer Woche** bei ihrem Bruder in Florida.
4. Wir wollen sie alle **am Wochenende** besuchen *(visit)*.
5. Das finde ich **schön.**

K. **Frau Köchli.** Bilden Sie Sätze!

BEISPIEL: Hauptstadt / Schweiz / sein / Bern
Die Hauptstadt der Schweiz ist Bern.

1. Tante / unsere Freunde / leben / hier in Bern
2. leider / ich / nicht / wissen / die / Adresse / diese Tante
3. Name / Dame / sein / Köchli
4. wegen / dieser Name / ich / nicht / können / finden / Frau Köchli
5. statt / ein Köchli *(m.)* / da / sein / viele Köchlis
6. du / nicht / wissen / Telefonnummer / euere Freunde?
7. Nummer / stehen / in / Adressbuch / meine Frau
8. ich / nicht / können / finden / Inge / Adressbuch
9. ein Tag / Inge / es / sicher / wieder / finden
10. können / ihr / mir / empfehlen / Name / ein Hotel?
11. trotz / Preise *(pl.)* / wir / brauchen / Hotelzimmer
12. während / Feiertage / du / haben / Probleme *(pl.)* / wegen / Touristen

Zusammen-fassung

L. **Schriftliche Übung** *(Write eight to ten sentences describing a typical week, i.e., when you get up; when you eat; when you leave for class; what classes you have when; what you do in the evening and on the weekend. Use as many time expressions as possible.)*

BEISPIEL: Ich bin fast jeden Tag an der Uni. Morgens stehe ich um sechs auf . . .

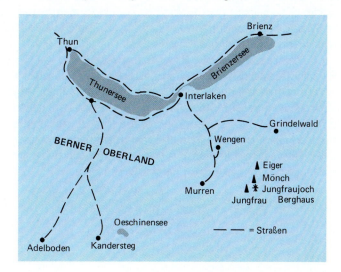

Viele Touristen besuchen das Berner Oberland.

EINBLICKE

Zürich, Blick auf den Limmat und das Rathaus

European cars usually carry a small sign indicating the country of origin: D stands for Germany, A for Austria, and CH for Switzerland. The CH comes from the Latin name of Switzerland, *Confoederatio Helvetica*. The Celtic tribe of the Helvetii settled in the territory of modern Switzerland when Julius Caesar prevented them from moving on to Gaul (today's France).

Switzerland has four official languages. In a population of about 6.7 million, 70 percent speak German (**Schweizerdeutsch / Schwyzerdütsch**, the spoken dialect, as well as standard German), 20 percent speak French, and 9 percent Italian. A small minority (1 percent) speaks Romansh (**Rätoromanisch**). Most Swiss people understand two or three, some even all four of these languages. This quadrilingualism goes back to the time of the Romans who colonized the area. Eventually, tribes from present-day Italy, France, and Germany migrated to this territory and established themselves there.

Romansh is a romance language that has evolved little from Vulgar Latin and is spoken mainly in the remote valleys of the Grisons (the canton of **Graubünden**). Since 1938 it has been one of the four official languages, but it comes under constant pressure from the major language groups in surrounding areas. The fact that Romansh is not one language but a group of dialects (including **Ladin**) makes it even harder to preserve.

das	Dorf, -̈er	*village*
die	Gegend, -en	*area, region*
	Geschichte, -n	*history; story*
	sofort	*immediately, right away*
	Geld aus·geben (gibt aus), ausgegeben	*to spend money*
	erzählen	*to tell*
	hinauf·fahren (fährt hinauf), ist hinaufgefahren	*to go or drive up (to)*
	weiter·fahren (fährt weiter), ist weitergefahren	*to drive on, keep on driving*
	1291 (zwölfhunderteinundneunzig)[1]	*(in) 1291*
	im Jahre . . .	*in the year . .*

---

[1] German does not use a preposition when simply naming a year: **Er ist 1972 geboren.** *(He was born in 1972.)*

WAS IST DAS?   der Film, Hollywoodstar, Kanton, Kurzkommentar, Meter, Sessellift, Wintersport; das Ferienhaus, Uhrengeschäft; die Alpenblume, Arkade, Bergbahn, Konferenz, Nation, Rückseite; bergsteigen, faszinieren, filmen, interessieren, restaurieren, wandern, Ski laufen; autofrei, intakt, phantastisch

Reise in die Schweiz

(Kurzinterviews mit Touristen in der Schweiz)

Felix

5

10

Wegen ihrer Geschichte finde ich die Gegend hier um den Vierwaldstätter See so interessant. Gestern bin ich in Luzern gewesen und über die bekannte Holzbrücke° gelaufen. Wie Sie wissen, ist die Brücke 1993 abgebrannt, aber man hat sie inzwischen° wieder restauriert. Heute früh bin ich mit dem Schiff von Luzern zum Rütli[1] gefahren, wo 1291 die drei Kantone Uri, Schwyz und Unterwalden ihren Bund° gemacht haben und die Schweiz als eine Nation begonnen hat. Dann bin ich weitergefahren nach Altdorf.

wooden bridge
in the meantime

confederation

Luzern am Vierwaldstätter See

Bern, die Hauptstadt der Schweiz

monument
outdoor performances /
national holiday
parades / fireworks

Hier in Altdorf steht ja Wilhelm Tells Denkmal°2. Heute abend gehe ich zu den Wilhelm
Tell Freilichtspielen°. Dieses Wochenende ist außerdem noch Bundesfeier° mit Umzü-
gen° und Feuerwerk°. Das möchte ich einmal sehen.

narrow streets / fountains
Middle Ages

last

view of
snow scenes

Yvonne

Bern, die Hauptstadt der Schweiz, gefällt mir besonders gut
wegen seiner alten Gassen°, Arkaden und Brunnen°, viele noch aus   15
dem Mittelalter°. Meine Freundin und ich fahren fast jedes Jahr
zum Wintersport in die Schweiz. Auf unserer Fahrt kommen wir
gewöhnlich durch Bern und bleiben dort einen Tag. Letztes° Jahr
sind wir ins Berner Oberland gefahren, nach Wengen. Wir sind
auch mit der Bergbahn zum Jungfraujoch3 hinaufgefahren. Von   20
dort oben ist der Blick auf° die Berge wirklich phantastisch. Haben
Sie übrigens gewußt, daß man fast alle Schneeszenen° der James Bond Filme im Berner
Oberland gefilmt hat und daß viele Hollywoodstars im Berner Oberland Ferienhäuser
haben, zum Beispiel Zsa Zsa Gabor und Sean Connery? Was ich aber besonders toll finde,
ist die Natur. Trotz der vielen Touristen ist alles relativ intakt geblieben. Eines Tages   25

better

möchte ich die Gegend um Kandersteg und Adelboden besser° kennenlernen.

glaciers
altitude
mountain goats / directions
cable cars
Alpine metro / underground
/ altitude

Hansruedi

Ich fahre gern nach Saas Fee, weil das Dorf autofrei ist und
man auf den Bergen und Gletschern° schön wandern und bergsteigen kann. Wegen der Höhenlage° gibt es hier viele Alpenblu-
men und Gemsen°. In alle Richtungen° gehen Sessellifte und Seil-   30
bahnen°. Und wenn ich im Juli Ski laufen möchte, fahre ich mit der
Metro Alpin° unterirdisch° bis auf eine Höhe° von 3500 Metern4.
Dort oben auf dem Gletscher kann man auch während des Sommers wunderbar Ski laufen.

numbered bank accounts

easily
this time / longer
carnival

Frau Weber

Mein Mann hat oft in Zürich5 und Basel6 mit den Schweizer   35
Banken zu tun. Zürich ist eine schöne Stadt am See mit einer Bank
neben der anderen. Viele Ausländer haben hier Nummernkonten°.
Während der Konferenzen meines Mannes bummle ich gern durch
die Bahnhofstraße mit ihren eleganten Uhrengeschäften und Boutiquen. Hier kann man leicht° viel Geld ausgeben. Auf der Rück-   40
reise bleiben wir dieses Mal° vielleicht ein paar Tage länger° in
Basel wegen der Basler Fasnacht°.

Zum Text

A. Richtig oder falsch? Wenn falsch, sagen Sie warum!

_____ 1. Felix findet die Gegend um den Bodensee so interessant wegen ihrer
Geschichte.

_____ 2. Die Schweiz hat 1691 als Nation begonnen.

_____ 3. Felix ist wegen des Wilhelm-Tell-Denkmals und der Freilichtspiele in
Altdorf.

_____ 4. Yvonne und ihre Freundin fahren jeden Sommer zum Sport in die
Schweiz.

_____ 5. Während ihrer Reise bleiben sie gewöhnlich einen Tag in Bern, weil
ihnen die Stadt so gut gefällt.

_____ 6. Hansruedi besucht Saas Fee so gern, weil er sein Auto mitbringen
kann.

_____ 7. Oben auf den Gletschern kann man auch während des Sommers Ski
laufen.

_____ 8. Frau Webers Mann muß oft nach Zürich oder Basel, weil er viel mit Schweizer Banken zu tun hat.

_____ 9. Zürich ist eine schöne Stadt am Genfer See.

_____ 10. Nummernkonten gibt es heute in der Schweiz nicht mehr.

B. Etwas Geschichte. Lesen Sie laut!

1. 1291 machten Uri, Schwyz, und Unterwalden am Rütli einen Bund.   **2.** Luzern ist 1332 dazu *(to it)* gekommen und Zürich 1351.   **3.** 1513 hat es dreizehn Kantone gegeben.   **4.** Heute, 19___ *(add current year)*, sind es sechsundzwanzig Kantone. **5.** 1848 ist die Schweiz ein Bundesstaat geworden.   **6.** Im 1. Weltkrieg (1914–1918) und im 2. Weltkrieg (1939–1945) ist die Schweiz neutral geblieben.

C. Die Eidgenossenschaft   *(The Swiss Confederacy. Restate these sentences, using the suggested expressions. There may be more than one appropriate place for the expressions.)*

BEISPIEL: Viele Touristen fahren in die Schweiz. (jedes Jahr)
Viele Touristen fahren jedes Jahr in die Schweiz.
Jedes Jahr fahren viele Touristen in die Schweiz.

1. Felix findet die Gegend um den Vierwaldstätter See interessant. (wegen ihrer Geschichte)
2. Die Luzerner Holzbrücke mit Bildern aus der Geschichte der Eidgenossenschaft ist abgebrannt. (1993)
3. Felix ist mit einem Schiff zum Rütli gefahren. (von Luzern)
4. Wilhelm Tell soll aus Altdorf gewesen sein. (wie Sie wissen)
5. Viele Touristen wollen Wilhelm Tells Denkmal sehen. (natürlich)
6. In der Schweiz feiert man die Bundesfeier. (jedes Jahr am 1. August)
7. Felix ist noch einen Tag geblieben. (wegen dieses Festes)

D. Welche Frage gehört zu welcher Antwort?   *(Working in groups, find the correct question for each of the responses below.)*

_____ 1. Geschichte ist mein Hobby.

_____ 2. Hier haben die drei Kantone Uri, Schwyz und Unterwalden ihren Bund gemacht, das heißt, hier hat die Schweiz als Nation begonnen.

_____ 3. Die Stadt gefällt uns so gut wegen ihrer alten Gassen, Arkaden und Brunnen.

_____ 4. Es ist trotzdem alles noch relativ intakt geblieben.

_____ 5. Man kann hier wunderbar wandern, bergsteigen und Ski laufen.

_____ 6. Dort oben auf dem Gletscher gibt es auch während des Sommers Schnee *(snow).*

_____ 7. Hier gibt es Nummernkonten.

_____ 8. Mir gefallen die Uhrengeschäfte und Boutiquen.

a. Warum bleiben Sie immer einen Tag in Bern?

b. Warum haben so viele Ausländer ein Bankkonto in der Schweiz?

c. Warum kommen Sie so gern nach Saas Fee?

d. Warum finden Sie die Gegend um den Vierwaldstätter See so interessant?

e. Finden Sie die vielen Touristen nicht furchtbar?

f. Warum bummeln Sie gern auf der Bahnhofstraße in Zürich?

g. Warum haben Sie jetzt, im Juli, Skier *(skis)* mitgebracht?

h. Warum sind Sie mit dem Schiff zum Rütli gefahren?

E.   Etwas Geographie   *(Answer the following questions, then write a paragraph about Switzerland, using the questions as guidelines).*

1.   Wie heißen die Nachbarländer der Schweiz? Wo liegen sie?
2.   Wie heißt die Hauptstadt der Schweiz?
3.   Nennen Sie ein paar Schweizer Flüsse, Seen und Berge! Welcher Fluß fließt weiter *(flows on)* nach Deutschland? nach Frankreich? Welcher See liegt zwischen der Schweiz und (a) Deutschland? (b) Italien? (c) Frankreich?
4.   Wo liegt Bern? Basel? Zürich? Luzern? Genf? Zermatt? Locarno? St. Moritz? Davos? Saas Fee?
5.   Wo spricht man Deutsch? Französisch? Italienisch? Rätoromanisch?

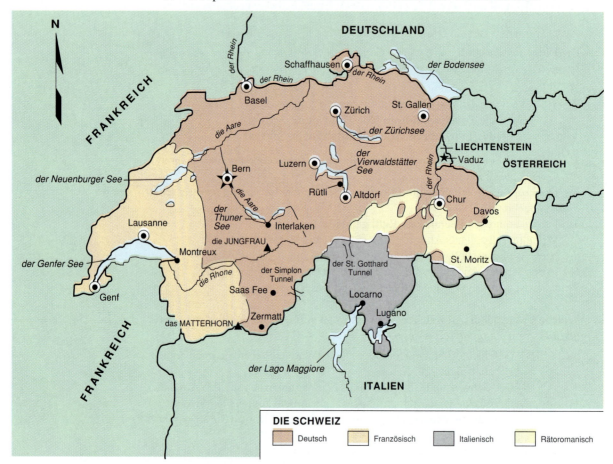

Hören Sie zu!

Im Reisebüro   *(Ulrike Schneider is in a travel agency to arrange a vacation trip for herself and her friend Steffi.)*

ZUM ERKENNEN: Skilift inbegriffen *(ski lift included);* die Broschüre, -n *(brochure);* ab·holen *(to pick up)*

Was stimmt?

1.   Ulrike und Steffi möchten im _____ reisen.
     a.   August   b.   März   c.   Januar

2. Sie wollen _____ .
   a. wandern   b. bergsteigen   c. Ski laufen

3. Ulrike reserviert ein Hotelzimmer in _____ .
   a. Grindelwald   b. Adelboden   c. Wengen

4. Ulrike und Steffi fahren mit der Bahn bis _____ .
   a. Bern   b. Interlaken   c. Grindelwald

5. Sie kommen um _____ Uhr an ihrem Ziel *(at their destination)* an.
   a. 12.16   b. 12.30   c. 1.00

6. Sie fahren am _____ um _____ nach Hause zurück.
   a. 15. / zwei   b. 14. / drei   c. 16. / sechs

Übrigens

1. The House of Habsburg dates back to the 10th century with holdings in Switzerland and Alsace. It first came into prominence when Count Rudolf was elected German king (**Rudolf I.**) in 1273. Members of the dynasty later came to rule Austria, the Holy Roman Empire, and Spain. On August 1, 1291, representatives of the three original Swiss cantons met on the Rütli meadow at the southern tip of Lake Lucerne (**Vierwaldstätter See**) and swore an oath of alliance against the Habsburgs, marking the birth of modern Switzerland. Each year on August 1, the Swiss national holiday (**Bundesfeier**) is celebrated with bonfires, parades, and fireworks.

2. William Tell (**Wilhelm Tell**) is a legendary Swiss folk hero and a universal symbol of resistance to oppression. In 1307, he supposedly refused to obey the commands of the tyrannical Austrian bailiff, Geßler, who then forced him to shoot an arrow through an apple on his son's head. Tell did, but later took revenge by killing Bailiff Geßler. That event was the beginning of a general uprising of the Swiss against the Habsburgs. In 1439, when the Habsburgs tried to bring Switzerland back under Austrian rule, the Confederation broke free of the Empire.

3. Besides the **Matterhorn** (14,692 feet above sea level), the most famous Swiss peaks are the **Jungfrau, Mönch,** and **Eiger,** all around 13,000 feet high. A tunnel, almost four and a half miles long, leads steeply up to the **Jungfraujoch** terminus (11,333 feet). Its observation deck offers a superb view of the surrounding mountains and the lakes of central Switzerland, and on a very clear day even of the Black Forest in Germany.

4. One meter equals 3.281 feet.

5. Zurich, Switzerland's industrial heart and its largest city, is built around the northern tip of Lake Zurich and is characterized by its many bridges over the Limmat River. The city is a center of international banking. Although banking is an old tradition in Switzerland, it expanded enormously after World War II. Even during the war, Switzerland had a stable government and a sound, freely convertible currency. These circumstances, along with a bank-secrecy law that allows numbered accounts without names (**Nummernkonten**), continue to attract capital from all over the world.

6. Basel, Switzerland's "northern gateway" to the Rhine, is the country's second-largest city. Basel is known not only as a center for international banking and insurance, but also for its pharmaceutical and chemical industry.

SPRECHSITUATIONEN

There are times when you want to sympathize or empathize with a friend. You may also feel the need to express relief when something turned out better than expected. Here are appropriate expressions.

Expressing Sympathy

(Ach, das ist aber) schade!
Das ist ja furchtbar!
So ein Pech!
Das tut mir (furchtbar) leid.
Ach du liebes bißchen!
Ach du meine Güte!
Um Gottes willen! *(For heaven's sake.)*
Das ist wirklich zu dumm! *(That's really too bad.)*

Expressing a Lack of Sympathy

Das ist doch nicht wichtig.
Das macht doch nichts.
Das ist doch egal. *(That doesn't matter. It's all the same to me.)*
Na und! *(So what?)*
Pech (gehabt)! *(Tough luck.)*
Das geschieht dir recht. *(That serves you right.)*
Das sieht dir ähnlich. *(That's typical of you.)*

Expressing Empathy

Das ist ja prima (wunderbar, toll)!
Das freut mich (für dich). *(I'm happy [for you].)*
Du Glückspilz! *(You lucky thing [literally: mushroom].)*

Expressing Relief

Gut / prima / toll / super!	
(Na,) endlich!	*(Well,) finally.*
Gott sei Dank!	*Thank God.*
Ich bin wirklich froh.	*I'm really glad.*
(Da haben wir aber) Glück gehabt!	*We were really lucky!*
(Da haben wir aber) Schwein gehabt!	*(We were really) lucky!*
Das ist noch mal gut gegangen.	*Things just worked out all right.*

A. **Was sagen Sie?** *(Your friend Daniel has his ups and downs. Respond appropriately to these events in his life.)*

1. Daniel hat von seinen Eltern zum Geburtstag ein Auto bekommen.
2. Das Auto ist nicht ganz neu.
3. Aber es fährt so schön ruhig und schnell, daß er gleich am ersten Tag einen Strafzettel *(ticket)* bekommen hat.
4. Am Wochenende ist er in die Berge gefahren, aber es hat immer nur geregnet.
5. Es hat ihm trotzdem viel Spaß gemacht, weil er dort eine nette *(nice)* Studentin kennengelernt hat.
6. Auf dem Weg zurück ist ihm jemand hinten in sein Auto gefahren. Totalschaden *(total wreck)!*
7. Daniel hat aber nur ein paar Kratzer *(scratches)* bekommen.
8. Er hat übrigens seit ein paar Tagen eine Wohnung mitten in der Stadt. Sie ist gar nicht teuer.
9. Er möchte das Mädchen aus den Bergen wiedersehen, aber er kann sein Adressbuch mit ihrer Telefonnummer nicht finden.
10. Momentan läuft alles falsch. Er kann sein Portemonnaie *(wallet)* auch nicht finden.
11. Noch etwas. Die Katze *(cat)* des Nachbarn hat seine Goldfische gefressen *(ate).*
12. Sein Bruder hat übrigens eine Operation gehabt. Aber jetzt geht es ihm wieder gut, und er ist wieder zu Hause.

B. **Jeder hat Probleme.** *(Form small groups, and have each person name at least one problem he or she has. Take turns expressing sympathy or lack of it.)*

C. **Kurzgespräche** *(Your classmate expresses his / her feelings after each statement you make.)*

1. Trip home: The weather was awful. Your plane arrived two hours late (**mit zwei Stunden Verspätung**) and departed five hours late. You arrived at two o'clock in the morning. Your suitcase wasn't there. There were no buses into town. You didn't have enough cash for a cab. You phoned your father. You got home at 4 A.M. You were very tired.

2. Staying overnight: You and your friend arrived in Unterschönau. You inquired at three hotels but they had no rooms available. They sent you to the *Gasthof zum Löwen.* There they had some rooms. Since you were very tired, you went to bed early (**ins Bett**). There was a party in the hotel until midnight. Then cars drove by. It was very loud. At 2 A.M. you heard a train, too. You got up early and left. What a night!

Hobbys

Ausflug *(excursion)* mit dem Fahrrad

INHALT

Vorschau

- Sports in Germany

Gespräche and Wortschatz

- Physical fitness and leisure time

Struktur

- Endings of preceded adjectives
- Reflexive verbs
- Infinitive with *zu*

Einblicke

- Leisure time in the German-speaking countries

Sprechsituationen

- Making a phone call
- Extending, accepting, and declining an invitation

Sports in Germany

Sports are very popular in Germany, not only with spectators, but also with participants. Soccer is as important in Europe as football, baseball, and basketball are in the United States and Canada. Of course, only a few play and large crowds watch, in the stadium as well as on television. On the other hand, one out of three Germans belongs to a sports club. The German Athletic Association (**Deutscher Sportbund** or **DSB**) has more than 75,000 sports clubs (**Sportvereine**) as affiliates. It sponsors such programs as **Trimm dich** and **Sport für alle** with competitions in running, swimming, cycling, and skiing in which millions of people participate every year. Also popular are **Volksmärsche**, group hiking events for anyone who wants to join. The success of such professional athletes as Steffi Graf, Boris Becker, and Michael Stich has given tennis a tremendous boost. While not as popular as in the U.S., golf is becoming more common.

High schools and universities are not involved in competitive sports. Sports organizations in Germany are basically autonomous and self-governing, but the government provides some support for those with insufficient funds. This applies particularly to the former GDR, where an effort has been made to set up independent clubs and organizations. In the seventies and eighties, the East German government spent a great deal of money not only on making sports activities accessible to every citizen, but especially on boosting the image of the GDR through victories in the Olympic Games and other international sports competitions. For years the GDR had a disproportionately high number of medal winners—in Seoul (1988), the GDR won 37 gold medals, the FRG 11. Young talents were sought out early and trained in special boarding schools, provided with equipment, and given numerous privileges.

In addition to sports clubs, there are associations promoting all kinds of leisure activities, ranging from dog breeding and pigeon racing to gardening, crafts, music, dancing, hiking, and mountain climbing (the **Alpenverein**). Clubs devoted to regional traditions and costumes (**Trachtenvereine**) and centuries-old rifle associations (**Schützenvereine**), with their own banners, badges, uniforms, and ceremonial meetings, keep some of the old traditions alive and draw thousands to their annual fairs and festivities.

Familie auf dem Trimm-dich-Pfad
(exercise trail).

 **Am Telefon**

FRAU SCHMIDT	Hier Schmidt.[1]
BÄRBEL	Guten Tag, Frau Schmidt. Ich bin's, Bärbel. Ist Karl-Heinz da?
FRAU SCHMIDT	Nein, tut mir leid. Er ist gerade zur Post gegangen.
BÄRBEL	Ach so. Können Sie ihm sagen, daß ich heute abend nicht mit ihm ausgehen kann?
FRAU SCHMIDT	Natürlich. Was ist denn los?
BÄRBEL	Ich bin krank. Mir tut der Hals weh, und ich habe Kopfschmerzen.
FRAU SCHMIDT	Das tut mir leid. Gute Besserung!
BÄRBEL	Danke. Auf Wiederhören!
FRAU SCHMIDT	Wiederhören!

Bis gleich!

YVONNE	Bei Mayer.
DANIELA	Hallo, Yvonne! Ich bin's, Daniela.
YVONNE	Tag, Daniela! Was gibt's?
DANIELA	Nichts Besonderes. Hast du Lust, Squash zu spielen oder schwimmen zu gehen?
YVONNE	Squash? Nein, danke. Ich habe noch Muskelkater von vorgestern. Ich kann mich kaum rühren. Mir tut alles weh.
DANIELA	Lahme Ente![2] Wie wär's mit Schach?
YVONNE	OK, das klingt gut. Kommst du zu mir?
DANIELA	Ja, bis gleich!

Wie geht's weiter?

1. Bärbels Freund heißt . . .   2. Bärbel spricht mit . . .   3. Karl-Heinz ist nicht zu Hause, weil . . .   4. Bärbel kann nicht mit ihm . . .   5. Bärbels Hals . . .   6. Sie hat auch . . .   7. Am Ende eines Telefongesprächs sagt man . . .   8. Danielas Freundin heißt . . .   9. Yvonne will nicht Squash spielen, weil . . .   10. Sie hat aber Lust, . . .

 ## Übrigens

1.   If Mrs. Schmidt answers her own phone, she says **Hier Schmidt.** If someone else answers, he / she would say **Hier bei Schmidt** (*Schmidt residence*).

2.   As in the case of **lahme Ente** (*lit. lame duck*), names of animals are frequently used in everyday speech to characterize people, usually in a derogatory way: **Du Esel! Du Affe!** (*donkey, monkey*) for someone who made a mistake or behaves in a silly manner; **Du hast einen Vogel! Bei dir piept's!** (*You're cuckoo*) for someone acting crazy; **Fauler Hund!** (*dog*) for someone lazy; **So ein Brummbär!** (*bear*) for someone grumpy; **(Das ist) alles für die Katz'!** (*That's all for nothing, i.e., useless*); **Du Schwein!** (*pig*) for someone messy

or for a scoundrel. **Schwein haben,** however, has quite a different meaning: *to be lucky.* In addition, names of food are used in special expressions: **Das ist Käse!** *(That's nonsense)* or **(Das) ist doch Wurst!** *(It doesn't matter).*

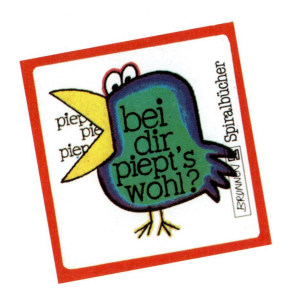

Das Hobby, -s   *(hobby)*

der	Fußball	*soccer*		*die*	CD, -s	*CD*
	Sport	*sport(s), athletics*			Gitarre, -n	*guitar*
das	Klavier, -e	*piano*			Karte, -n	*card*
	Spiel, -e	*game*			Kassette, -n	*cassette*

fern·sehen (sieht fern), ferngesehen	*to watch TV*
photographieren	*to take pictures*
sammeln[1]	*to collect*
schwimmen, geschwommen	*to swim*
schwimmen gehen, ist schwimmen gegangen[2]	*to go swimming*
Ski laufen gehen, ist Ski laufen gegangen[2]	*to go skiing*
spazieren·gehen, ist spazierengegangen	*to go for a walk*
(Dame, Schach) spielen[2]	*to play (checkers, chess)*
Sport treiben, getrieben[2]	*to engage in sports*
wandern, ist gewandert	*to hike*

---

[1] Like **bummeln: ich samm(e)le, du sammelst, er sammelt, wir sammeln, ihr sammelt, sie sammeln.**

[2] In each of these combinations, **gehen, spielen,** and **treiben** function as V1, while the other word, the verb complement, functions as V2: Ich **gehe** heute **schwimmen.** Wir **spielen** manchmal **Schach.** Sie **treiben** viel **Sport.**

Der Körper, - *(body)*

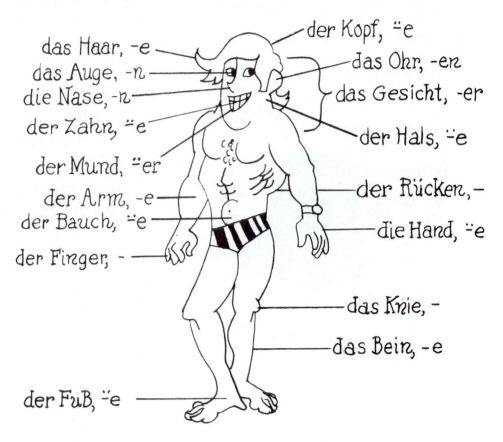

das Haar, -e

das Auge, -n

die Nase, -n

der Zahn, ̈e

der Mund, ̈er

der Arm, -e

der Bauch, ̈e

der Finger, -

der Fuß, ̈e

der Kopf, ̈e

das Ohr, -en

das Gesicht, -er

der Hals, ̈e

der Rücken, -

die Hand, ̈e

das Knie, -

das Bein, -e

Weiteres

die	Freizeit	*leisure time*
	Idee, -n	*idea*

gesund / krank	*healthy / sick, ill*
phantastisch	*fantastic, great, super*
Ich habe (Kopf)schmerzen.	*I have a (head)ache.*
Ich habe (keine) Lust, Tennis zu spielen.	*I (don't) feel like playing tennis.*
Mir tut der Hals weh.	*My throat hurts. I have a sore throat.*
Was gibt's (Neues)?[3]	*What's up? What's new?*
Was ist los?	*What's the matter? What's going on?*
nichts Besonderes[3]	*nothing special*
Ach so.	*I see.*
Bis gleich!	*See you in a few minutes.*

ZUM ERKENNEN: Ich bin's. *(It's me.)*; Gute Besserung! *(I hope you get better.)*; Ich habe Muskelkater. *(My muscles are sore. I have a charley horse.)*; Ich kann mich kaum rühren. *(I can hardly move.)*; Wie wär's mit . . . ? *(How about . . . ?)*; zu mir *(to my place)*

---

[3] Similarly **etwas B**esonderes, **etwas I**nteressants, **etwas S**chönes; **nichts N**eues, **nichts G**utes, **nichts S**chlechtes.

A. Mustersätze

1. Hals: **Mir tut** der Hals **weh.**
   Kopf, Zahn, Bauch, Fuß, Knie, Hand
2. Hände: **Mir tun die** Hände **weh.**
   Füße, Finger, Ohren, Beine, Augen
3. Kopf: **Ich habe** Kopf**schmerzen.**
   Hals, Zahn, Bauch, Ohren
4. Squash: **Hast du Lust,** Squash **zu spielen?**
   Tennis, Fußball, Klavier, CDs, Karten, Schach

B. Was tust du gern in deiner Freizeit? *(Read through the list below. Then ask classmates what they like to do during their leisure time. Poll the class to see which activities are most popular.)*

BEISPIEL: Ich lese gern, und du?
              Ich spiele gern Klavier.

angeln, backen, campen, joggen / laufen, kochen *(to cook),* lesen, malen *(to paint),* nähen *(to sew),* reiten *(to go horseback riding),* Rollschuh laufen *(to go roller skating),* Schlittschuh laufen *(to go ice-skating),* Ski laufen, Wasserski laufen, segeln *(to go sailing),* Sport treiben, wandern . . .

spielen: Basketball, Federball *(badminton),* Fußball, Volleyball, Golf, Hockey, Squash, Tennis, Tischtennis; Karten, Monopoly, Dame, Schach; Cello, Gitarre, Flöte *(flute),* Blockflöte *(recorder),* Trommel, Trompete . . .

C. Interview. Fragen Sie einen Nachbarn / eine Nachbarin, . . . !

1. ob er / sie als Kind ein Instrument gelernt hat, und wenn ja, welches Instrument; seit wann er / sie spielt und ob er / sie das heute noch spielt
2. ob er / sie gern singt, und wenn ja, was und wo (in der Dusche oder Badewanne *[bathtub],* im Auto, im Chor . . .)
3. was für Musik er / sie schön findet (klassische Musik, moderne Musik, Jazz, Rock-, Pop-, Country-, Volksmusik . . .)
4. ob er / sie viel fernsieht, und wenn ja, wie lange pro Tag; was er / sie gestern abend gesehen hat
5. ob er / sie oft lange am Telefon spricht, und wenn ja, mit wem

D. Mir tut 'was weh. *(Working with a partner, complete each sentence with one of the responses supplied or with one of your own.)*

_____ 1. Wenn ich Kopfschmerzen habe, . . .	a. mache ich die Augen zu.
_____ 2. Wenn mir die Füße weh tun, . . .	b. gurgele *(gargle)* ich.
_____ 3. Wenn mir der Bauch weh tut, . . .	c. sehe ich nicht fern.
_____ 4. Wenn ich Halsschmerzen habe, . . .	d. nehme ich Aspirin.
_____ 5. Wenn ich Augenschmerzen habe, . . .	e. trinke ich Cola.
_____ 6. Wenn ich krank bin, . . .	f. esse ich nichts.
	g. rufe ich einen Arzt *(doctor)* an.
	h. gehe ich ins Bett.
	i. gehe ich nicht spazieren.
	j. trinke ich Tee.

E. **Während der Freizeit.** Was sagen Sie?

S1   Hallo, _____ ! Hast du Lust, _____ ?
S2   Nein, ich kann nicht mit dir _____ .
S1   Warum? Was ist los?
S2   Ich bin krank. Mir tut / tun _____ weh.
S1   _____ . Wie lange hast du schon _____ schmerzen?
S2   Seit _____ .
S1   _____ . Ich wünsche dir gute Besserung.
S2   _____ .

F. **Aussprache: l, z**   *(See also III. 8–10 in the pronunciation section of the Workbook.)*

1. [l]   laut, lustig, leben, liegen, leider, Lampe, Luft, Hals, Geld, Platte, malen, spielen, fliegen, stellen, schnell, Schlüssel; Teil, Ball, hell

2. [ts]   zählen; zeigen, zwischen, ziemlich, zurück, Zug, Zahn, Schmerzen, Kerzen, Einzelzimmer, Pizza, bezahlen, erzählen, tanzen, ausgezeichnet, jetzt, schmutzig, trotz, kurz, schwarz, Salz, Schweiz, Sitzplatz

3. Wortpaare
    a. *felt* / Feld   c. *plots* / Platz   e. seit / Zeit
    b. *hotel* / Hotel   d. Schweiß / Schweiz   f. so / Zoo

Hören Sie zu!

Bei der Ärztin   *(Andreas Heller is at the doctor's office. Listen to their conversation.)*

ZUM ERKENNEN: passieren *(to happen);* war *(was);* der Ellbogen, - *(elbow);* hoch·legen *(to put up);* (Schmerz)tabletten *([pain] pills)*

Was fehlt?

1. Andreas geht zur Ärztin, weil ihm _____ wehtut.

2. Er ist mit seinem Freund zum _____ im Harz gewesen.

3. Am letzten Tag ist er _____ .

4. Er darf ein paar Tage nicht _____ .

5. Er soll das Bein _____ .

6. Die Ärztin gibt ihm ein paar _____ mit.

7. Andreas kann bald wieder _____ oder _____ .

8. Wenn Andreas in einer Woche immer noch Schmerzen hat, soll er _____ .

Im Schrebergarten

STRUKTUR

I. Endings of Adjectives Preceded by *der-* and *ein*-words

1. PREDICATE ADJECTIVES and ADVERBS do not have endings.

Willi fährt schnell.	*Willi drives fast.*
Willi ist schnell.	*Willi is quick.*

2. ATTRIBUTIVE ADJECTIVES—that is, adjectives used before nouns—do have endings. Before learning what these endings are, you need to distinguish between two forms of the article (definite as well as indefinite).

   a. Definitions

   • The STANDARD FORM is the form of the definite (and the corresponding indefinite) article that you learn with every noun: **der (ein)** Vater, **die (eine)** Mutter, **das (ein)** Kind. They are all nominative singular forms. Since **das, die,** and **eine** do not change in the accusative singular, they are also considered standard forms in that usage. This definition applies to all **der**-words (**dies-, jed-, welch-,** etc.) and **ein**-words (**mein, dein, sein, kein,** etc.) that correspond to these forms (**der, das, die, ein, eine**).

   • All other forms of the definite and indefinite articles, **der**-words, and **ein**-words are ALTERED FORMS: the accusative masculine singular **den (einen)**, all datives and genitives. Plural forms are also considered altered forms.

   b. Rules

   • In an adjective / noun combination involving a STANDARD FORM, gender must be shown. Certain forms of the article show gender readily: **der, das, die,** and **eine.** Thus the adjective takes only the "minimal ending" **-e**; das klein**e** Kind. **ein,** however, does not show gender; it is used with both masculine <u>and</u> neuter nouns. Thus the adjective must show gender. To do so, the ending **-er** is added to an adjective that precedes a masculine noun and **-es** to an adjective that precedes a neuter noun: mein lieb**er** Vater, ein klein**es** Kind.

Compare: der neue Wagen	ein neu**er** Wagen
das rote Auto	ein rot**es** Auto

   • After any ALTERED FORM, add **-en** to an adjective: mit unserem klein**en** Auto, für seine nett**en** Eltern.

   Here are some examples:

N	der	neue	Wagen	[standard form, shows gender, add minimal **-e**]
A	den	neuen	Wagen	[altered form, add **-en**]
D	dem	neuen	Wagen	[altered form, add **-en**]
G	des	neuen	Wagens	[altered form, add **-en**]

N	ein	rotes	Auto	[standard form, shows no gender, indicate gender by adding **-es**]
A	ein	rotes	Auto	[standard form, same as nominative]
D	einem	roten	Auto	[altered form, add **-en**]
G	eines	roten	Autos	[altered form, add **-en**]

N	die	schnellen	Fahrer	[altered form, add **-en**]
A	die	schnellen	Fahrer	[altered form, add **-en**]
D	den	schnellen	Fahrern	[altered form, add **-en**]
G	der	schnellen	Fahrer	[altered form, add **-en**]

Summary

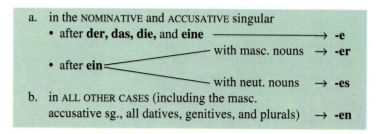

a. in the NOMINATIVE and ACCUSATIVE singular
 • after **der, das, die,** and **eine** ⟶ **-e**
 • after **ein** ⟨ with masc. nouns → **-er**
       with neut. nouns → **-es**
b. in ALL OTHER CASES (including the masc. accusative sg., all datives, genitives, and plurals) → **-en**

3. If two or more adjectives precede a noun, all have the same ending: Er hat ein klein**es**, schnell**es** und teur**es** Auto.

Übungen

A. Das Jubiläum   *(The anniversary. Comment on each photo you took at your grandparents' 50th anniversary.)*

BEISPIEL: Das ist mein Onkel Max mit seinen drei Kindern. (wild, klein)
   Das ist mein Onkel Max mit seinen drei wilden Kindern.
   Das ist mein Onkel Max mit seinen drei kleinen Kindern.

1. Das ist Tante Jutta mit ihrem Freund aus London. (verrückt, englisch)
2. Hier sitzen wir alle an einem Tisch und spielen Monopoly. (groß, rund)
3. Das ist Oma *(grandma)* mit ihrem Porsche *(m.)*. (teuer, rot)
4. Die Farbe dieses Autos gefällt mir. (toll, schnell)
5. Das ist wirklich ein Geschenk! (wunderbar, phantastisch)
6. Opa *(grandpa)* hat ein Fahrrad bekommen. (schön, neu)
7. Jetzt kann er mit seinen Freunden Fahrrad fahren. (viel, alt)
8. Das hier ist unser Hund *(dog, m.)*. (klein, braun)
9. Das ist wirklich ein Hündchen *(n.)*. (lieb, klein)
10. Wegen des Wetters haben wir nicht im Garten gefeiert. (schlecht, kalt)

B. Die neue Wohnung. Lesen Sie den Dialog mit den Adjektiven!

BEISPIEL: Ist der Schrank neu? (groß)
   Ist der große Schrank neu?

S1   Ist dieser Sessel bequem? (braun)
S2   Ja, und das Sofa auch. (lang)
S1   Die Lampe gefällt mir. (klein)
   Woher hast du diesen Teppich? (phantastisch)
   Und wo hast du dieses Bild gefunden? (supermodern)
S2   In einem Geschäft. (alt)
   Wenn du willst, kann ich dir das Geschäft mal zeigen. (interessant)

S1 Ist es in der Müllergasse *(f.)*? (klein)
S2 Ja, auf der Seite. (link-)
S1 Während der Woche habe ich keine Zeit. (nächst-)
    Sind diese Möbel teuer gewesen? (schön)
S2 Natürlich nicht. Für solche Möbel gebe ich nicht viel Geld aus. (alt)

C. Inge zeigt Jens ihr Zimmer. Jens stellt Fragen und macht Kommentare *(comments).*
Bilden Sie aus zwei Sätzen einen Satz!

BEISPIEL: Woher kommt dieses Schachspiel? Es ist interessant.
Woher kommt dieses interessante Schachspiel?

1. Weißt du, was so ein Schachspiel kostet? Es ist chinesisch *(Chinese).*
2. Bist du Schachspielerin? Spielst du gut? *(add **ein**!)*
3. Ich bin kein Schachspieler *(m.).* Ich spiele nicht gut.
4. Woher hast du diese Briefmarkensammlung? Sie ist alt.
5. Mein Vater hat auch eine Sammlung. Sie ist groß.
6. Sammelst du solche Briefmarken auch? Sie sind normal *(regular).*
7. Was machst du mit so einer Briefmarke? Sie ist doppelt *(double).*
8. Darf ich diese Briefmarke haben? Sie ist ja doppelt!
9. Hast du diese Bilder gemacht? Sie sind groß.
10. Wer ist der Junge? Er ist klein.
11. Ich habe nicht gewußt, daß du einen Bruder hast. Er ist noch so klein!
12. Was für ein Gesicht! Es ist phantastisch!
13. Die Augen gefallen mir! Sie sind dunkel.
14. Mit meiner Kamera ist das nicht möglich. Sie ist billig.
15. Und das hier ist ein Tennisspieler, nicht wahr? Er ist bekannt und kommt aus
    Deutschland.
16. Weißt du, daß wir gestern trotz des Wetters Fußball gespielt haben? Das Wetter
    ist schlecht gewesen.
17. Leider kann ich wegen meines Knies nicht mehr mitspielen. Das Knie ist
    kaputt.

Mercedes-Benz
Ihr guter Stern auf allen Straßen.

D. Ist das nicht schön? *(Your friend Alex is very indecisive and continuously needs*
reassurance. Show agreement and ask a question according to the model.)

1. BEISPIEL: Ist der Pullover nicht warm?
    Ja, das ist ein warmer Pullover.
    Woher hast du den warmen Pullover?

    a. Ist das Hemd nicht elegant?
    b. Ist die Uhr nicht phantastisch?
    c. Ist der Hut *(hat)* nicht verrückt?

2. BEISPIEL: Ist das Hotel nicht gut?
    Ja, das ist ein gutes Hotel.
    Wo hast du von diesem guten Hotel gehört?

    a. Ist die Pension nicht wunderbar?
    b. Ist der Gasthof nicht billig?
    c. Ist das Restaurant nicht gemütlich?

3. BEISPIEL: Ist das alte Schloß nicht schön?
                Ja, das ist ein altes, schönes Schloß.
                Ich gehe gern in solche alten, schönen Schlösser.

    a. Ist der neue Supermarkt nicht modern?
    b. Ist das kleine Café nicht gemütlich?
    c. Sind die alten Kirchen nicht interessant?

E. Beschreibung *(description)* **einer Wohnung**

1. **Petras Wohnung**   *(Fill in the missing adjective endings where needed.)*

Petra wohnt in einem toll_____ Haus im neu_____ Teil unserer schön_____
Stadt. Ihre klein_____ Wohnung liegt im neunt_____ Stock eines modern_____
Hochhauses *(high-rise)*. Sie hat eine praktisch_____ Küche und ein gemüt-
lich_____ Wohnzimmer. Von dem groß_____ Wohnzimmerfenster kann sie unsere ganz_____ Stadt und die viel_____ Brücken über dem breit_____ *(wide)*
Fluß sehen. Petra liebt ihre Wohnung wegen des schön_____ Blickes *(view, m.)*
und der billig_____ Miete. In ihrem hell_____ Schlafzimmer stehen ein einfach9
Bett und ein klein_____ Nachttisch mit einer klein_____ Nachttischlampe. An
der Wand steht ein braun_____ Schreibtisch, und über dem braun_____ Schreibtisch hängt ein groß_____ Regal mit ihren viel_____ Büchern. Petra findet ihre
Wohnung schön_____ .

2. **Ihre Wohnung**   *(Write a paragraph about your own place. Use at least one
adjective with an ending in each sentence.)*

II. Reflexive Verbs

If the subject and one of the objects of a sentence are the same person or thing, a reflexive
pronoun must be used for the object. In the English sentence, *I see myself in the picture,* the
reflexive pronoun *myself* is the accusative object. *(Whom do I see?—Myself.)* In the sentence, *I am buying myself a CD,* the pronoun *myself* is the dative object. *(For whom am I
buying the CD?—For myself.)*

In German only the third person singular and plural have a special reflexive pronoun: **sich.**
The other persons use the accusative and dative forms of the personal pronouns, which you
already know.

COMPARE: Ich sehe meinen Bruder auf dem Bild.
             Ich sehe **mich** auf dem Bild.

             Ich kaufe meinem Bruder eine CD.
             Ich kaufe **mir** eine CD.

nom.	ich	du	er / es / sie	wir	ihr	sie	Sie
acc.	mich	dich	**sich**	uns	euch	**sich**	**sich**
dat.	mir	dir					

1. Many verbs you have already learned CAN BE USED REFLEXIVELY. (Note that the English equivalent may not include a reflexive pronoun.)

   - The reflexive pronoun used as the direct object (ACCUSATIVE): sich fragen *(to wonder),* sich legen *(to lie down),* sich sehen *(to see oneself),* etc.

Ich frage **mich,** ob das richtig ist.	*I wonder (ask myself) whether that's right.*
Ich lege **mich** aufs Sofa.	*I lie down on the sofa.*
Ich sehe **mich** im Spiegel.	*I see myself in the mirror.*

   - The reflexive pronoun used as the indirect object (DATIVE): sich bestellen, sich kaufen, sich kochen, sich nehmen, sich wünschen *(to wish),* etc.

Ich bestelle **mir** ein Eis.	*I order an ice cream (for myself).*
Ich koche **mir** ein Ei.	*I'm cooking an egg (for myself).*
Ich wünsche **mir** ein Auto.	*I'm wishing for a car (for myself).*

2. Some verbs are ALWAYS REFLEXIVE, or are reflexive when they express a certain meaning. Here are some important verbs that you need to know.

sich an·hören	*to listen to*
sich an·sehen, angesehen	*to look at*
sich an·ziehen, angezogen	*to put on (clothing), get dressed*
sich aus·ziehen, ausgezogen	*to take off (clothing), get undressed*
sich um·ziehen, umgezogen	*to change (clothing), get changed*
sich baden	*to take a bath*
sich beeilen	*to hurry*
sich duschen	*to take a shower*
sich erkälten	*to catch a cold*
sich (wohl) fühlen	*to feel (well)*
sich (hin·)legen	*to lie down*
sich kämmen	*to comb one's hair*
sich (die Zähne / Nase) putzen	*to clean (brush one's teeth / blow one's nose)*
sich rasieren	*to shave*
sich (hin·)setzen	*to sit down*
sich waschen (wäscht), gewaschen	*to wash (oneself)*

Setz dich (hin)!	*Sit down.*
Warum müßt ihr euch beeilen?	*Why do you have to hurry?*
Ich fühle mich nicht wohl.	*I don't feel well.*
Sie hat sich erkältet.	*She caught a cold.*

   - With some of these verbs, the reflexive pronoun may be EITHER THE ACCUSATIVE OR THE DATIVE OBJECT. If there are two objects, then the person (the reflexive pronoun) is in the dative and the thing is in the accusative.

Ich wasche **mich.**	*I wash myself.*
Ich wasche **mir** die Haare.	*I wash my hair.*
Ich ziehe **mich** an.	*I'm getting dressed.*
Ich ziehe **mir** einen Pulli an.	*I'm putting on a sweater.*

3. In English possessive adjectives are used to refer to parts of the body: *I'm washing my hands.* In German the definite article is frequently used together with the reflexive pronoun in the dative.

Ich wasche **mir die** Hände.	*I'm washing **my** hands.*
Sie kämmt **sich die** Haare.	*She's combing **her** hair.*
Putz **dir die** Zähne!	*Brush **your** teeth.*

- Remember that when there are two object pronouns, the accusative precedes the dative!

Ich wasche mir **die Hände.**	Ich wasche **sie** mir.
Du kämmst dir **die Haare.**	Du kämmst **sie** dir.
acc.	acc.

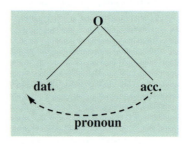

Übungen

F.   Antworten Sie mit JA!

1. **Singular** *(formal and familiar)*

   BEISPIEL: Soll ich mir die Hände waschen?
   Ja, waschen Sie sich die Hände!
   Ja, wasch dir die Hände!

   a.   Soll ich mich noch umziehen?
   b.   Soll ich mir die Haare kämmen?
   c.   Soll ich mir ein Auto kaufen?
   d.   Soll ich mich jetzt setzen?
   e.   Soll ich mir die Bilder ansehen?

2. **Plural** *(formal and familiar)*

   BEISPIEL: Sollen wir uns die Hände waschen?
   Ja, waschen Sie sich die Hände!
   Ja, wascht euch die Hände!

   a.   Sollen wir uns ein Zimmer mieten?
   b.   Sollen wir uns ein Haus bauen?
   c.   Sollen wir uns in den Garten setzen?
   d.   Sollen wir uns die Kassetten anhören?
   e.   Sollen wir uns die Briefmarken ansehen?

G. Antworten Sie mit JA!

BEISPIEL: Fühlen Sie sich wohl?
   Ja, ich fühle mich wohl.

1. Legen Sie sich aufs Sofa?
2. Möchten Sie sich die Jacke ausziehen?
3. Haben Sie sich wieder erkältet?
4. Haben Sie sich zu elegant angezogen?
5. Haben Sie sich die Bilder angesehen?
6. Haben Sie sich auf dem Bild gefunden?

H. Was fehlt?

1. Kinder, zieht _____ schnell an!
2. Ich muß _____ noch die Haare kämmen.
3. Wir haben _____ ein Klavier gekauft.
4. Setzen Sie _____ bitte!
5. Peter, putz _____ die Nase!
6. Kinder, erkältet _____ nicht!
7. Karin hat _____ einen Fernseher gewünscht.
8. Ich will _____ etwas im Radio anhören.
9. Fühlst du _____ nicht wohl, Dieter?
10. Möchten Sie _____ die Hände waschen?

I. Was machst du den ganzen Tag?   *(In pairs, ask each other what you do at certain hours of the day, using reflexive verbs whenever possible. Take notes and then report back to the class.)*

BEISPIEL: Was machst du abends um zehn?
   Ich höre mir die Nachrichten *(news)* **an. Und du?**
   Um diese Zeit lege ich mich ins Bett.

1.	6.00 Uhr	7.	13.00 Uhr
2.	6.30 Uhr	8.	13.30 Uhr
3.	9.00 Uhr	9.	16.00 Uhr
4.	9.30 Uhr	10.	17.30 Uhr
5.	11.00 Uhr	11.	20.00 Uhr
6.	11.30 Uhr	12.	22.00 Uhr

J. Auf deutsch, bitte!   *(Mrs. Brockmann is a health nut. She's determined to get her whole family up early and out on the exercise trail, but they aren't too eager.)*

1. Otto, get dressed.   **2.** Christian, hurry.   **3.** Lotte and Ulle, are you putting on a sweater?   **4.** We still have to brush our teeth.   **5.** Peter, comb your hair.   **6.** I don't feel well.   **7.** Then lie down.   **8.** Otto, have you shaved?   **9.** Yes, but I've caught a cold.   **10.** Nonsense (**Quatsch**)! Today we're all going jogging.

III. The Infinitive with *zu*

English and German use infinitives with **zu** *(to)* in much the same way.

Es ist interessant **zu** reisen.   *It's interesting to travel.*
Ich habe keine Zeit gehabt **zu** essen.   *I didn't have time to eat.*

1. In German, if the infinitive is combined with other sentence elements, such as a direct object or an adverbial phrase, a COMMA separates the infinitive phrase from the main clause.

   Haben Sie Zeit, eine Reise **zu machen?** *Do you have time to take a trip?*

   Note that in German the infinitive comes at the end of the phrase.

2. If a separable-prefix verb is used, the **-zu-** is inserted between the prefix and the verb.

   prefix + **zu** + verb

   Es ist Zeit ab**zu**fahren. *It's time to leave.*

Caution: No **zu** after modals! **Wir müssen jetzt abfahren.** See Caution on p. 151.

3. Infinitive phrases beginning with **um** explain the purpose of the action described in the main clause.

   Wir fahren nach Hessen, **um** unsere Oma **zu** besuchen.   *(in order to visit)*
   Rudi geht ins Badezimmer, **um** sich **zu** duschen.   *(in order to take a shower)*

Übungen

K.   Wie geht's weiter?

BEISPIEL: Hast du Lust . . . ? (sich Kassetten anhören)
            Hast du Lust, dir Kassetten anzuhören?

1. Dort gibt es viel . . . (sehen, tun, photographieren, zeigen, essen)
2. Habt ihr Zeit . . . ? (vorbeikommen, die Nachbarn kennenlernen, ein Glas Apfelsaft trinken, euch ein paar Bilder ansehen)
3. Es ist wichtig . . . (aufpassen, Sprachen lernen, einmal etwas anderes tun, Freunde haben, Sport treiben)
4. Es ist interessant . . . (ihm zuhören, Briefmarken sammeln, mit der Bahn fahren, mit dem Flugzeug fliegen)
5. Es hat Spaß gemacht . . . (reisen, wandern, singen, spazierengehen, aufs Land fahren, Freunde anrufen)

L.   Bilden Sie Sätze!

1. heute / wir / haben / nicht viel / tun
2. es / machen / ihm / Spaß / / Fußball spielen
3. sie *(sg.)* / müssen / einlösen / Scheck
4. ich / haben / keine Zeit / / Geschichte / fertig / erzählen *(pres. perf.)*
5. du / haben / keine Lust / / mit uns / spazierengehen *(pres. perf.)*
6. möchten / du / fernsehen / bei uns?
7. wir / wollen / kaufen / neu / Auto

8. es / sein / sehr bequem / / hier / sitzen

9. ich / sein / zu müde / / Tennis spielen

10. du / sollen / anrufen / dein- / Kusine

M. So bin ich. *(That's the way I am. Working in groups, tell each other about your hobbies and leisure time preferences.)*

1. Ich habe keine Lust . . .

2. Ich habe nie Zeit . . .

3. Mir macht es Spaß . . .

4. Ich finde es wichtig . . .

5. Ich finde es langweilig *(boring)* . . .

6. Als *(as)* Kind hat es mir Spaß gemacht . . .

7. Ich brauche das Wochenende gewöhnlich, um . . .

8. Ich lerne Deutsch, um . . .

„Die Menschen haben gelernt, zu schwimmen wie die Fische und zu fliegen wie die Vögel, aber wie Brüder zusammenzuleben haben sie nicht gelernt"
M. L. King

Zusammen-fassung

N. Rotkäppchen und der Wolf. Was fehlt?

1. Es hat einmal eine gut____ Mutter mit ihrem klein____ Mädchen in einem ruhig____ Dorf gewohnt. **2.** Sie hat zu ihrer klein____ Tochter gesagt: „Geh zu deiner alt____ Großmutter, und bring ihr diese gut____ Flasche Wein und diesen frisch____ Kuchen! **3.** Aber du mußt in dem dunkl____ Wald aufpassen, weil dort der bös____ *(bad)* Wolf *(m.)* wohnt." **4.** Das klein____ Mädchen ist mit seiner groß____ Tasche in den grün____ Wald gegangen. **5.** Auf dem dunkl____ Weg ist der bös____ Wolf gekommen und hat das klein____ Mädchen gefragt, wo seine alt____ Großmutter lebt. **6.** Er hat dem gut____ Kind auch die wunderbar____ Blumen am Weg gezeigt. **7.** Dann hat der furchtbar____ Wolf die arm____ *(poor)* Großmutter gefressen *(devoured)* und hat sich in das bequem____ Bett der alt____ Frau gelegt. **8.** Das müd____ Rotkäppchen ist in das klein____ Haus gekommen und hat gefragt: „Großmutter, warum hast du solche groß____ Ohren? Warum hast du solche groß____ Augen? Warum hast du so einen groß____ Mund?" **9.** Da hat der bös____ Wolf geantwortet: „Daß ich dich besser fressen *(eat)* kann!" **10.** Nun *(well)*, Sie kennen ja das Ende dieser bekannt____ Geschichte *(story, f.)*! **11.** Der Jäger *(hunter)* hat den dick____ Wolf getötet *(killed)* und dem klein____ Mädchen und seiner alt____ Großmutter aus dem Bauch des tot____ *(dead)* Wolfes geholfen.

O. Hallo, Max! Auf deutsch, bitte!

1. What have you been doing today? **2.** Oh, nothing special. I listened to my old cassettes. **3.** Do you feel like going swimming? **4.** No, thanks. I don't feel well. I have a headache and I have a sore throat. Call Stephan. **5.** Hello, Stephan! Do you have time to go swimming? **6.** No, I have to go to town (**in die Stadt**) in order to buy (myself) a new pair of slacks and a warm coat. Do you feel like coming along? **7.** No, I already went shopping this morning. I bought (myself) a blue sweater and a white shirt. **8.** Too bad. I've got to hurry. I want to put on my trunks (**die Badehose**) and go swimming. Bye!

Sie sollen sich bei uns wohl fühlen TWA

EINBLICKE

Drachenflieger
(hang-gliders)
vor dem Abflug

Whereas many Americans take their vacation days in short breaks, perhaps combined with a holiday and one or two weekends, Germans are more likely to view their annual vacation as the year's major event. Vacation planning and saving generally starts in September, just after people go back to work. With relatively high incomes and a minimum of three weeks paid vacation (**Urlaub**) each year, Germans have a wide range of interesting options to choose from. Many head south, to the beaches of Spain, France, Italy, Greece, and Turkey. Others opt for educational experiences, such as language courses abroad, adventure travel to exotic places, or, for city-dwellers, life on a farm (**auf dem Bauernhof**). The important thing is that a vacation be interesting.

das	Leben[1]	*life*	
die	Musik	*music*	

ander- *(adj.)*	*other, different*
anders *(adv.)*	*different(ly)*
etwas anderes	*something different*
ganz	*whole, entire(ly), all*
(genauso) wie . . .	*(just) like . . .*
sich aus·ruhen	*to relax, rest*
sich fit halten (hält), gehalten	*to keep in shape*
sich langweilen	*to get (or be) bored*
vor·ziehen, vorgezogen	*to prefer*

[1] In German, **Leben** is used only in the singular: Sport ist wichtig in **ihrem Leben** (*in her life, in their lives*).

WAS IST DAS?   der Arbeiter, Fernseher, Ferientag, Freizeitboom, Musikclub, National-sport; das Fernsehen, Gartenhäuschen, Gartenstück, Industrieland, Musikfest, Privileg, Problem, Windsurfen, Zusehen; die Aktivität, Autobahn, Disco, Kulturreise, Stadtwoh-nung; planen; aktiv, deutschsprachig, frustriert, nämlich, populär, täglich, überfüllt

Freizeit: Lust° oder Frust°?

fun / frustration

Vor hundert Jahren war° es das Privileg der reichen° Leute, nicht arbeiten zu müssen. Die Arbeiter in den deutschsprachigen Ländern haben zu der Zeit aber oft noch 75 Stunden pro Woche gearbeitet. Urlaub° für Arbeiter gibt es erst seit 1919: zuerst° nur drei Tage im Jahr! Heute ist das anders. Die Deutschen arbeiten nur ungefähr 180 Tage im Jahr, weniger als°
5 die Menschen in fast allen anderen Industrieländern. Außer den vielen Feiertagen haben sehr viele Leute fünf oder sechs Wochen Urlaub im Jahr. So ist die Freizeit ein sehr wichtiger Teil des Lebens und mehr als° nur Zeit, sich vom täglichen Streß auszuruhen.

was / rich

[paid] vacation / first

less than

more than

   Was tut man mit der vielen Freizeit? Natürlich ist Fernsehen sehr wichtig: Viele sitzen mehr als zwei Stunden pro Tag vor dem Fernseher. Auch Sport ist sehr populär, und nicht
10 nur das Zusehen, sondern auch das aktive Mitmachen°, um sich fit zu halten. Heute sind solche neuen Sportarten° wie Aerobik, Squash oder Windsurfen „in", genauso wie Tennis und Golf. Fußball ist besonders bei den Deutschen und Österreichern Nationalsport, aber auch Handball und Volleyball sind in den deutschsprachigen Ländern sehr beliebt°.

participation

. . . types

popular

   Die Leute sind gern draußen°. An Wochenenden fahren sie oft mit dem Zug oder mit
15 dem Auto aufs Land und gehen spazieren, fahren Rad oder wandern. Dann setzt man sich in ein schönes Gartenrestaurant und ruht sich aus. Im Sommer gehen sie oft ins öffentliche Schwimmbad oder fahren an einen schönen See. Sie sind auch viel im Garten. Wenn sie in einer Stadtwohnung leben, können sie sich ein kleines Gartenstück pachten°[1] und dort Blu-men und Gemüse ziehen°. Viele bauen sich dort auch ein Gartenhäuschen, wo sie sich
20 duschen, umziehen oder ausruhen können.

outdoors

lease

raise

   Die Deutschen sind besonders reiselustig°[2]. Sie geben fast ein Sechstel° des Touri-stikumsatzes° der ganzen Welt aus! Manche machen Kulturreisen, um Land und Leute ken-nenzulernen, in Museen zu gehen oder sich auf einem der vielen Festspiele Musik anzu-hören. Andere° reisen, um Sprachen zu lernen oder einmal etwas ganz anderes zu tun. Viele
25 fahren in den warmen Süden, um sich in die Sonne zu legen und schön braun wieder nach Hause zu kommen.

travel-happy / one-sixth

here: travel dollars

others

Windsurfen und
Bergsteigen ist nicht für
jeden.

above-mentioned
pubs

Und die jungen Leute? Außer den oben genannten° Aktivitäten macht es ihnen besonders Spaß, mit Freunden in Kneipen°, Discos, Cafés, Musikclubs oder ins Kino zu gehen.
Auch gehen sie gern bummeln oder einkaufen.

Dieser ganze Freizeitboom bringt aber auch Probleme mit sich: Manche langweilen   30
sich, weil sie nicht wissen, was sie mit ihrer Freizeit machen sollen. Andere sind frustriert,

traffic jams
just / last / on the road
peace and quiet / high sea-
son / ... spots / otherwise

wenn sie auf der Autobahn in lange Staus° kommen oder die Züge überfüllt sind. Manchmal
muß man eben° etwas planen. Man muß ja nicht am ersten oder letzten° Ferientag unterwegs°
sein. Und wenn man seine Ruhe° haben will, darf man nicht in der Hauptsaison° zu den
bekannten Ferienorten° fahren. Sonst° wird Freizeitlust zum Freizeitfrust.   35

Zum Text

A. Was paßt? *(Complete the sentences with one of the words or phrases from the list below.)*

a. im Garten
b. vorm Fernseher
c. Staus auf den Autobahnen
d. den vielen Feiertagen
e. mit ihrer Freizeit
f. sich da richtig wohl fühlen

g. sich ein kleines Gartenstück zu pachten
h. auszuruhen
i. anzuhören
j. arbeiten zu müssen
k. schön braun zurückzukommen
l. in Discos

———   1. Vor hundert Jahren war es das Privileg der reichen Leute, nicht . . .

———   2. Heute haben sehr viele Leute außer . . . auch noch fünf oder sechs
Wochen Urlaub im Jahr.

_____ 3. Die Freizeit ist mehr als nur Zeit, sich von der Arbeit . . . und sich hinzulegen.

_____ 4. Viele Leute sitzen über zwei Stunden am Tag . . .

_____ 5. Man arbeitet auch gern . . .

_____ 6. Wer keinen Garten hat, hat die Möglichkeit, . . .

_____ 7. Wenn das Wetter schön ist, kann man . . .

_____ 8. Manche machen Kulturreisen, um sich zum Beispiel auf einem der vielen Musikfeste Musik . . .

_____ 9. Andere fahren in den warmen Süden, um . . .

_____ 10. Junge Leute gehen gern . . .

_____ 11. Weil zu viele Leute zur gleichen _(same)_ Zeit in die Ferien fahren, ist oft alles überfüllt, und es gibt . . .

_____ 12. Für manche Leute ist Freizeit ein Problem, weil sie nicht wissen, was sie . . . tun sollen.

B. **Ich ziehe es vor . . .** _(You and your roommate can never agree on anything, especially when it comes to leisure activities. Follow the model.)_

BEISPIEL: Ich habe Lust, . . . (baden gehen // hier bleiben)
   Ich habe Lust, baden zu gehen. Und du?
   Ich ziehe es vor, hier zu bleiben.

1. Nach der Vorlesung habe ich Zeit, . . . (Tennis spielen // mein Buch lesen)
2. Mir gefällt es, . . . (durch Geschäfte bummeln und einkaufen // nichts ausgeben)
3. Ich habe Lust, diesen Sommer . . . (in den Süden fahren // nach Norwegen reisen)
4. Ich finde es schön, abends . . . (in einen Musikclub gehen // sich Musik im Radio anhören)
5. Meine Freunde und ich haben immer Lust, . . . (Windsurfen gehen // in den Bergen wandern)
6. Mir ist es wichtig, . . . (viel reisen und Leute kennenlernen // sich mit Freunden gemütlich hinsetzen)

C. **Welches Hobby hast du?** Geben Sie die Adjektivendungen!

1. Du fragst mich, was ich in meiner frei_____ Zeit mache. **2.** Ich gehe gern mit meinen gut_____ Freunden ins Kino und sehe mir einen neu_____ Film an, oder wir gehen in eine toll_____ Disco und tanzen. **3.** Manchmal gehen wir auch in das gemütlich_____ Café neben dem alt_____ Dom und essen ein gut_____ Stück Kuchen. **4.** Wenn es heiß ist, setzen wir uns gern in ein schön_____ Gartenrestaurant und trinken eine kalt_____ Limo(nade). **5.** Im Sommer fahren wir oft zusammen an einen schön_____ See und baden. **6.** Mein Freund Manfred ist ein fanatisch_____ Fußballspieler. **7.** Er sieht sich jedes wichtig_____ Fußballspiel an, und wir müssen uns immer die neu_____ Fußballresultate anhören. **8.** Wenn ich allein bin, lese ich gern ein interessant_____ Buch oder höre mir eine neu_____ CD an. **9.** Wenn ich Zeit habe, gehe ich in unser ausgezeichnet_____ Fitness-Center _(n.)._ **10.** Und du, welches interessant_____ Hobby hast du?

D. Mal etwas anderes in den Ferien!

1. Wo gibt es Sprachkurse in Französisch? Wie viele Stunden sind Sie da in der Klasse, und wie viele Stunden Praxis *(practice)* bekommen Sie in der Woche?
2. Was kann man in der Südschweiz in den Ferien machen?
3. Wohin kann man in den Osterferien fliegen? Wo fliegt man ab? Wie viele Tage braucht man für die Rundreise, und was kann man nach der Rundreise tun?
4. Wo kann man Segelfliegen lernen? Wie lange braucht ein Anfänger *(beginner)*, bevor er / sie allein fliegen kann? Von wann bis wann gibt es Intensivkurse?
5. Was für eine Farm ist Hotel Tannenhof? Was kann man da wohl *(probably)* tun?
6. Welche Ferienidee finden Sie besonders interessant? Warum?
7. Kostet es immer Geld, Spaß in den Ferien zu haben?

Hören Sie zu!

Eine tolle Radtour *(Listen to what Sabrina has to tell about her bike trip along Lake Constance.)*

ZUM ERKENNEN: im Büro *(at the office);* das Mietfahrrad, ¨er *(rent-a-bike);* abholen *(to pick up);* die Zahnradbahn *(cogwheel-railway);* das Panorama; bergab *(downhill);* die Fähre, -n *(ferry)*

1. Weil Sabrina _____ arbeitet, möchte sie in den Ferien etwas ganz anderes tun.
   a. im Krankenhaus   b. im Büro   c. bei der Post

2. Im _____ hat sie eine Fahrradtour um den Bodensee gemacht.
   a. Frühling   b. Sommer   c. Herbst

3. Sie hat diese Tour _____ gemacht.
   a. mit ihrer Familie   b. allein   c. mit ein paar Freunden

4. In _____ haben sie ihre Fahrräder abgeholt.
   a. St. Gallen   b. Romanshorn   c. Appenzell

5. Am ersten Tag sind sie bis nach _____ gekommen.
   a. Rorschach   b. Heiden   c. Bregenz

6. Am zweiten Tag haben sie eine schnelle Fahrt bergab _____ gehabt.
   a. bis an den See   b. durchs Rheindelta   c. zurück nach Heiden

7. Die zweite Nacht haben sie in _____ übernachtet.
   a. Bregenz   b. Lindau   c. Friedrichshafen

8. Am dritten Tag hat sie _____ zurück nach Romanshorn gebracht.
   a. ein Bus   b. ein Zug   c. eine Fähre

9. Im ganzen sind sie in _____ Ländern gewesen.
   a. zwei   b. drei   c. vier

10. Die Tour hat mit Übernachtungen (*overnight stays*) _____ Franken gekostet.
    a. 322   b. 233   c. 350

11. Zum Mittagessen haben sie meistens _____ .
    a. nichts gegessen b. im Hotel gegessen   c. gepicknickt

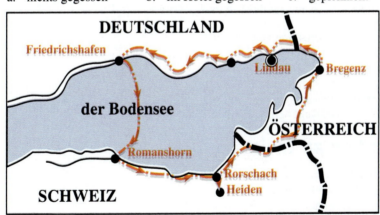

Übrigens

1. People who don't have a garden of their own can lease one from the city. These small gardens, called **Schrebergärten**—named after the orthopedist Daniel Schreber (1808–1861) from Leipzig who started them—not only supplement the family menu with fresh fruit and vegetables, but also provide outdoor recreation for many apartment dwellers.

2. Before the Berlin Wall was opened on November 9, 1989, the inability to travel freely, especially to the West, was among the most important causes of frustration and restlessness among the people of East Germany. The restrictions were especially irritating since East Germans were well informed via television about West Germans' extensive travel opportunities.

SPRECHSITUATIONEN

Speaking on the Telephone

Speaking on the telephone in a foreign language may seem scary, but with a little practice it is no more difficult than conversing in person.

When answering the phone, Germans identify themselves.

> Hier Schmidt. *(This is [Mr. / Mrs. / Ms.] Schmidt.)*
> (Hier) bei Schmidt. *(Schmidt residence.)*

When calling a business, you may hear:

> Guten Tag! Photo Albrecht, Margit *(Margit speaking).* Wen möchten Sie sprechen?

To ask for your party, say:

> Kann ich mit . . . sprechen?
> Ich möchte gern mit . . . sprechen.
> Ist . . . zu sprechen? *(May I speak to . . . ?)*

The answer might be:

> Einen Moment, bitte!
> . . . . ist nicht da. Kann ich ihm / ihr etwas ausrichten *(take a message)*?

At the end of a conversation you often hear:

> Auf Wiederhören!
> Mach's gut! *(sg. familiar)*
> Tschüß! *(colloquial)*
> Bis später! / Bis bald! / Bis gleich!

Extending an Invitation[1]

> Wir möchten euch am . . . zu einer Party einladen.
> Darf ich Sie zum Essen einladen?
> Möchtest du mit uns . . . (ins Kino) gehen?
> Wir gehen . . . Willst / kannst du mitkommen?
> Wir gehen . . . Komm doch mit!
> Wir gehen . . . Wir nehmen Sie gern mit.
> Habt ihr Lust, mit uns . . . zu gehen?

Accepting an Invitation

> Danke für die Einladung *(invitation)*!
> Das ist aber nett *(nice)*. Vielen Dank!
> Ja, gern.
> Prima! Wann denn?
> Sicher *(sure)*!
> Das klingt gut.

---

[1] The forms of the pronouns and verbs depend, of course, on who the addressed person is.

Declining an Invitation

Nein, danke. Heute kann ich nicht.
Nein, das geht (heute) nicht. *(No, that won't work [today].)*
Nein, ich kann leider nicht.
Ach, es tut mir leid . . .
Schade, aber ich habe schon etwas vor *(planned).*
Nein, ich habe keine Zeit / Lust.
Nein, ich bin zu müde.
Nein, ich fühle mich nicht wohl.
Nein, ich habe Kopfschmerzen.

A.   **Hast du Lust . . . ?**   *(Working with a classmate, take turns extending invitations.*   **Übungen**
Decline or accept them, depending on how they appeal to you. Use as many differ-
ent expressions as you can.)

1. ins Kino gehen
2. eine Vorlesung über deutsche Literatur anhören
3. ein Ballett ansehen
4. in ein Kunstmuseum gehen
5. am Wochenende mit dem Zug aufs Land fahren und wandern
6. während der Semesterferien eine Reise in die Schweiz machen
7. Ski laufen gehen
8. zu einem Fußballspiel gehen
9. in ein Restaurant gehen
10. eine Party für ein paar Freunde geben
11. Tennis oder Squash spielen
12. in den Park gehen und sich in die Sonne legen, usw.

B.   **Was tue ich gern?**

The class divides into two teams. One team thinks of a hobby, the other may ask ten
(or fifteen) questions to determine what the hobby might be. The teams alternate
roles.

C.   **Kurzgespräche**

1. Your aunt Elizabeth, who lives in Zurich, calls. You answer the phone, greet
her, and ask how she and Uncle Hans are doing. She says how they are and asks
about you. You tell her you've caught a cold and aren't feeling very well. She
expresses her sympathy and asks whether you'd like to visit them during
[spring break]. Do you want to accept? If so, your aunt says that she's glad, and
she reminds you to tell her when you are going to arrive. You both say good-
bye.

2. You call a travel agency, *Reisebüro Eckhardt.* An employee answers the phone
and connects you with an agent. You ask the agent about trains to Zurich. He /
she wants to know when you want to go. You tell him / her on [March 17]. He /
she says that you need to reserve a seat (**einen Platz reservieren**). Since you
will be departing for Zurich from Stuttgart, the travel agent will use the schedule on p. 228 to tell you about your options, depending on what time of day you
would like to travel. You also ask him / her about the return schedule and the
cost of a round-trip ticket. He / she says it costs [210 DM]; you tell him / her to
reserve a seat. The agent asks when you want the tickets, and you reply that
you'll come by on [Wednesday]. You both say good-bye.

KAPITEL

10

Szene aus *Mutter Courage* von Bertolt Brecht

LERNZIELE

Vorschau

- The German theater

Gespräche and Wortschatz

- Entertainment

Struktur

- Verbs with prepositional objects
- *Da-* and *wo*-compounds
- Endings of unpreceded adjectives

Einblicke

- German television

Sprechsituationen

- Expressing satisfaction and dissatisfaction
- Expressing anger

The German Theater

Germany, Austria, and Switzerland have a large number of theaters, the majority of them heavily subsidized by public funding. Some leading theater centers in Germany are Berlin, Munich, and Hamburg. Not only major cities possess their own theaters, however, but medium-sized and even small ones have them as well. Some date back to the 17th and 18th centuries when many of the sovereign princes established magnificent court theaters, and some to the 19th century when towns and cities established theaters as public institutions. Theaters were, after all, a major source of entertainment in those days.

Most are repertory theaters with resident actors who present a number of different plays each season. Municipal theaters in medium-sized cities usually also offer ballet, musicals, and operas.

Subsidies from public coffers come to more than two billion marks per year or roughly 100 marks per ticket. Most of this money goes to state or municipal theaters, but private ensembles also receive some support. Without it, only a few of the 420 German theater companies could survive. Public funding, however, is meeting with more and more criticism, at least in part because of the huge expense of rebuilding the economy of eastern Germany.

Most of the 67 theaters in the former GDR are struggling for survival. Many producers have been forced to seek alternative sources of funding. While art and commerce were strictly separated in the past, theater directors in both parts of the country are, for the first time, looking for industrial sponsors, perhaps following the example of the United States.

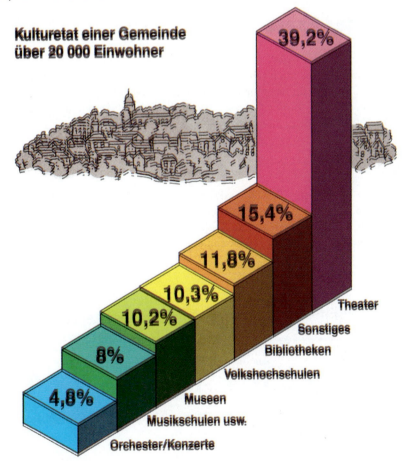

Kulturetat einer Gemeinde über 20 000 Einwohner

- 39,2% Theater
- 15,4% Sonstiges
- 11,8% Bibliotheken
- 10,3% Volkshochschulen
- 10,2% Museen
- 8% Musikschulen usw.
- 4,8% Orchester/Konzerte

Gespräche   Blick in die Zeitung

SONJA   Du, was gibt's denn heute abend im Fernsehen?
STEPHAN   Keine Ahnung. Sicher nichts Besonderes.
SONJA   Mal sehen! *Raumschiff Enterprise,* einen
         Dokumentarfilm und einen Krimi.
STEPHAN   Dazu habe ich keine Lust.
SONJA   Vielleicht gibt's was im Kino?[1]
STEPHAN   Ja, *Die Firma* und *Schlaflos in Seattle.*
SONJA   Hab' ich beide schon gesehen.
STEPHAN   Im Theater gibt's *Mutter Courage.*[2]
SONJA   Nicht schlecht. Hast du Lust?
STEPHAN   Ja, das klingt gut. Gehen wir!

An der Theaterkasse[3]

STEPHAN   Haben Sie noch Karten für heute abend?
FRÄULEIN   Ja, erste Reihe erster Rang links und Parkett rechts.
STEPHAN   Zwei Plätze im Parkett! Hier sind unsere Studentenausweise.
FRÄULEIN   28, 00 DM, bitte!
SONJA   Wann fängt die Vorstellung an?
FRÄULEIN   Um 20.15 Uhr.

Während der Pause

STEPHAN   Möchtest du eine Cola?
SONJA   Ja, gern. Aber laß mich zahlen! Du hast schon die Programme gekauft.
STEPHAN   Na gut. Wie hat dir der erste Akt gefallen?
SONJA   Prima. Ich habe *Mutter Courage* mal in der Schule gelesen, aber noch nie auf
         der Bühne gesehen.
STEPHAN   Ich auch nicht.

Fragen

1. Was gibt's im Fernsehen?   2. Gefällt das Stephan?   3. Hat Stephan Lust, sich einen
der Filme im Kino anzusehen?   4. Was gibt's im Theater?   5. Gibt es noch Karten für
dieses Stück?   6. Wo sind Stephans und Sonjas Plätze?   7. Wann fängt die Vorstellung
an?   8. Was tun Stephan und Sonja während der Pause?   9. Wer bezahlt dafür *(for it)*?
10. Woher kennt Sonja das Stück schon?

Übrigens

1. Although Germany produced many outstanding films in the 1920s and 1930s, it was long after World War II before German filmmaking again reached its prewar level of excellence. During the early 1970s, many German films won praise from critics and prizes at film festivals, but most of them were considered difficult or obscure and lacked popular appeal. Since the late seventies, however, many excellent films have reached the domestic and international markets. Television has helped by making money available to beginning and experienced directors for experimentation in the film medium. Some directors and representative films now known internationally are: Doris Dörrie, *Männer;* Rainer Werner Fassbinder, *Die Ehe der Maria Braun;* Hans W. Geissendörfer, *Der Zauberberg (The Magic Mountain);* Werner Herzog, *Fitzcarraldo;* Alexander Kluge, *Krieg und Frieden (War and Peace);* Wolfgang Peterson, *Das Boot* and *Die unendliche Geschichte;* Margarethe von Trotta, *Rosa Luxemburg;* Volker Schlöndorff, *Die Blechtrommel (The Tin Drum);* and Wim Wenders, *Der amerikanische Freund, Paris Texas, Der Himmel über Berlin (Wings of Desire),* and *Far Away, So Close.*

2. Bertolt Brecht (1898–1956) was one of the most important German playwrights of the 20th century. His theory of "epic theater" has had a considerable impact on German as well as non-German drama. By using various visual techniques and stylized acting, such as letting performers read their lines in a deliberately expressionless way, he tried to prevent the audience from identifying with the characters and increase the awareness of the play's moral and political message. Brecht's works include *Die Dreigroschenoper, Mutter Courage und ihre Kinder,* and *Der kaukasische Kreidekreis (The Caucasian Chalk Circle).*

3. Students and senior citizens are usually able to purchase tickets at a discount. This is also true for museums and galleries, so be sure to take your student ID along when you go to Europe.

WORTSCHATZ 1

Die Unterhaltung   *(entertainment)*

der	Anfang, -̈e	*beginning, start*
	Autor, -en	*author*
	Chor, -̈e	*choir*
	Film, -e	*film*
	Komponist, -en, -en	*composer*
	Krimi, -s	*detective story (book or film)*
	Roman, -e	*novel*
	Schauspieler, -	*actor*
das	Ende	*end*
	Konzert, -e	*concert*
	Orchester, -	*orchestra*
	Programm, -e	*program; channel*
	Stück, -e	*play*
die	Oper, -n	*opera*
	Pause, -n	*intermission, break*
	Vorstellung, -en	*performance*
	Werbung	*advertisement*
	Zeitschrift, -en	*magazine*
	Zeitung, -en	*newspaper*

dumm	*stupid, silly*
komisch	*funny (strange, comical)*
langweilig	*boring*
spannend	*exciting, suspenseful*
traurig	*sad*
an·fangen (fängt an), angefangen	*to start, begin*
an·machen / aus·machen	*to turn on / to turn off*
klatschen	*to clap, applaud*
lachen / weinen	*to laugh / to cry*

Konzert in der Berliner
Philharmonie

Weiteres

am Anfang / am Ende	*in the beginning / at the end*
letzt-	*last*
Was gibt's im Fernsehen?	*What's (playing) on TV?*
Keine Ahnung!	*I've no idea.*

ZUM ERKENNEN: der Blick *(glance);* Dazu habe ich keine Lust. *(I don't feel like [doing] that.);* beide *(both);* die Reihe, -n *(row);* im Rang *(in the balcony);* im Parkett *(in the orchestra);* der Akt, -e

Zum Thema

Mittelbayerische ZEITUNG

Zu einem guten
Frühstück gehört

natürlich
die
Mittelbayerische
Zeitung

A. Was sagen Sie? *(Inquire about tonight's movies.)*

S1	Was gibt's heute abend im Kino?
S2	——————— .
S1	Hast du Lust, ins Kino zu gehen?
S2	Ja / nein, ——————— .
S1	Hast du schon ——————— *(name of a movie)* gesehen?
S2	Ja / nein, ——————— , aber ——————— .
S1	Das ist ein ——————— Film!
S2	Wieso *(how come)*?
S1	——————— .
S2	Wo läuft dieser Film?
S1	——————— .

B. Wie geht's weiter?

1. Auf diesem Bild gehört zu einem guten Frühstück die ————— Zeitung.
2. Das ist natürlich ————— für diese Zeitung.   **3.** Ich kenne diese Zeitung
————— .   **4.** Auf dem Frühstückstisch stehen ————— .   **5.** Ich esse morgens gern ————— und trinke ————— .   **6.** Wenn ich Zeit habe, lese ich
————— .   **7.** Diese Woche liest man in den Zeitungen viel über *(about)*
————— .   **8.** Ich interessiere mich besonders für *(am interested in)* —————
9. Am ————— ist die Zeitung immer sehr dick.

C. Allerlei Fragen *(All sorts of questions)*

1. Lesen Sie gern die Zeitung oder Zeitschriften? Wenn ja, welche? Wie heißen ein paar gute amerikanische Zeitungen und ein paar interessante Zeitschriften?
2. Sind Sie ein Bücherwurm *(bookworm)*? Wenn ja, was für Bücher lesen Sie gern? Können Sie einen guten Roman empfehlen? Wie dick ist er (wie viele Seiten hat er)? Wie oft haben Sie das Buch schon gelesen? Welche Autoren finden Sie besonders gut?
3. Kann man hier Theaterstücke sehen? Wenn ja, wo? Haben Sie dieses Jahr ein interessantes Stück gesehen? Welches? Wie heißen ein paar Autoren von guten Theaterstücken?
4. Kann man hier Opern sehen / hören? Wenn ja, wo? Welche Opern haben Sie schon gesehen?
5. Gehen Sie manchmal in ein Rock-, Jazz- oder Popkonzert? Mögen Sie klassische Musik? Welche Komponisten hören Sie gern?
6. Wer von Ihnen singt gern? Wer singt im Chor? Wer spielt im Orchester oder in einer Band? Welches Instrument spielen Sie?
7. Wer hat schon einmal eine Rolle *(role, part)* in einem Theaterstück gespielt? Was für eine Rolle?
8. Was kann man hier noch zur *(for)* Unterhaltung tun?

D.   Ein toller (furchtbarer) Film   *(In small groups, talk about a movie that you've seen recently and discuss how you liked it.)*

E.   Mein Lieblingsplatz   *(My favorite place. Tell where you like best to relax and why. Choose from the options below or add your own.)*

1.   im Billardsalon oder Café
2.   unter einem Baum im Wald
3.   am Strand *(beach)* von . . .
4.   in meinem Zimmer
5.   bei uns im Keller
6.   im Fitness-Studio
7.   in der Bibliothek
8.   in unserer Garage
9.   _____

F.   Aussprache: r, er   *(See also II.9 and III.11 in the pronounciation section of the Workbook.)*

1.   [r]   **r**ot, **r**osa, **r**uhig, **r**echts, **R**adio, **R**egal, **R**eklame, **R**oman, P**r**og**r**amm, A**r**m, Ame**r**ika, Do**r**f, Konze**r**t, Fah**r**t, Gita**rr**e, t**r**au**r**ig, k**r**ank, wäh**r**end, mo**r**gens, He**rr**.
2.   [ʌ]   Absend**er**, Fing**er**, Koff**er**, Orchest**er**, Tocht**er**, Theat**er**, Mess**er**, Tell**er**, v**er**rückt, ab**er**, hint**er**, unt**er**, üb**er**, wied**er**, weit**er**
3.   [ʌ / r]   **U**hr / **U**hren; **O**hr / **O**hren; **T**ür / **T**üren; **C**hor / **C**höre; Aut**or** / Aut**or**en; Klavi**er** / Klavi**er**e; saub**er** / saub**er**e
4.   Wortpaare
     a.   *ring* / Ring
     b.   *Rhine* / Rhein
     c.   *fry* / frei
     d.   *brown* / braun
     e.   *tear* / Tier
     f.   *tour* / Tour

Hören Sie zu!

Biedermann und die Brandstifter   *(Christian Kolb has tickets to a play by Max Frisch, The Firebugs.)*

ZUM ERKENNEN: mal eben *(just for a minute);* die Inszenierung *(production);* na klar *(sure);* die Hauptrolle, -n *(leading role);* sich treffen *(to meet);* die Einladung, -en *(invitation)*

Richtig oder falsch?

_____   1.   Christians Vater hat ihm zwei Thea-
              terkarten gegeben.
_____   2.   Christian fragt seinen Freund
              Daniel, ob er mitkommen möchte.
_____   3.   Die Plätze sind in der dritten Reihe
              vom ersten Rang.
_____   4.   Die Vorstellung beginnt um halb
              sieben.
_____   5.   Christian muß sich noch rasieren
              und duschen.
_____   6.   Wenn Daniel sich beeilt, können sie
              noch schnell zusammen essen.
_____   7.   Sie treffen sich an der Straßenbahn-
              haltestelle in der Breslauerstraße.

An einer Litfaßsäule kann man Information über Konzerte und dergleichen *(the like)* finden.

STRUKTUR

I. Verbs with Prepositional Objects

In both English and German a number of verbs are used together with certain prepositions. These combinations often have special idiomatic meanings.

I'm thinking of my vacation. I'm waiting for my flight.

Since the German combinations differ from English, they must be memorized.

denken an (+ acc.)	*to think of (or about)*
schreiben an (+ acc.)	*to write to*
warten auf (+ acc.)	*to wait for*
sich freuen auf (+ acc.)	*to look forward to*
sich ärgern über (+ acc.)	*to get annoyed (upset) about*
sich interessieren für	*to be interested in*
erzählen von	*to tell about*
halten von	*to think of, be of an opinion*
sprechen von	*to talk about*

NOTE: In these idiomatic combinations, two-way prepositions most frequently take the accusative.

Er denkt an seine Reise.	*He's thinking about his trip.*
Sie schreibt an ihre Eltern.	*She's writing to her parents.*
Ich warte auf ein Telefongespräch.	*I'm waiting for a phone call.*
Freut ihr euch aufs Wochenende?	*Are you looking forward to the weekend?*
Ich ärgere mich über den Brief.	*I'm upset about the letter.*
Interessierst du dich für Sport?	*Are you interested in sports?*
Erzählt von euerem Flug!	*Tell about your flight.*
Was hältst du denn von dem Film?	*What do you think of the movie?*
Sprecht ihr vom *Raumschiff Enterprise?*	*Are you talking about Spaceship Enterprise?*

Caution: In these idiomatic combinations, **an, auf, über,** etc., are not separable prefixes, but prepositions followed by nouns or pronouns in the appropriate cases:

Ich **rufe** dich morgen **an.** BUT	Ich **denke an** dich.
I'll call you tomorrow.	*I'm thinking of you.*

Note also these two different uses of **auf:**

Ich warte **auf den** Zug. BUT	Ich warte **auf dem** Zug.
For what? For the train.	*Where? On (top of) the train.*

Übungen

A. Sagen Sie es noch einmal! *(Replace the nouns following the prepositions with the words suggested.)*

BEISPIEL: Sie warten auf den Zug. (Telefongespräch)
Sie warten auf das Telefongespräch.

1. Wir interessieren uns für Kunst. (Sport, Musik)
2. Er spricht von seinen Ferien. (Bruder, Hobbys)
3. Sie erzählt von ihrem Flug. (Familie, Geburtstag)
4. Ich denke an seinen Brief. (Ansichtskarte, Name)
5. Wartest du auf deine Familie? (Gäste, Freundin)
6. Freut ihr euch auf das Volksfest? (Vorstellung, Konzert)
7. Ich habe mich über das Wetter geärgert. (Junge, Kinder)
8. Haben Sie an Ihre Freunde geschrieben? (Frau, Vater)
9. Was haltet ihr von der Idee? (Krimi, Leute)

B. Afrikareise. Was fehlt?

1. Meine Tante hat _____ mein_____ Vater geschrieben.   **2.** Sie will uns _____ ihr_____ Reise durch Afrika erzählen.   **3.** Wir freuen uns _____ ihr_____ Besuch *(m.)*.   **4.** Meine Tante interessiert sich sehr _____ Afrika. **5.** Sie spricht hier im Museum _____ ihr_____ Fahrten.   **6.** Sie denkt nie _____ ihr_____ Gesundheit *(f.)*.   **7.** Wir halten sehr viel _____ ihr.

C. Was tun Sie? *(Working in groups of two or three, complete each sentence. Then ask your partners "Und du?" until everyone has had a chance to answer each question.)*

1. Ich denke oft _____ .   **2.** Ich warte _____ .   **3.** Ich schreibe gern _____ .   **4.** Ich interessiere mich _____ .   **5.** Ich freue mich _____ . **6.** Ich ärgere mich manchmal _____ .   **7.** Ich spreche gern _____ .   **8.** Ich halte nicht viel _____ .

D. Auf deutsch, bitte!

1. Don't wait for me *(pl. fam.)*   **2.** I'm writing to the newspaper.   **3.** He didn't think of the family.   **4.** Why do you *(sg. fam.)* always get upset about every performance?   **5.** I'm looking forward to the concert.   **6.** He isn't interested in such music.   **7.** We don't think much of his letter.

II. *da*- and *wo*-Compounds

1. **da**-Compounds

In English, pronouns following prepositions can refer to people, things, or ideas:

I'm coming with him.
I'm coming with it.

In German, this is not the case; pronouns following prepositions refer only to people:

Ich komme **mit ihm (mit meinem Freund).**

If you wish to refer to a thing or an idea, you must use a **da**-COMPOUND.

Ich komme **damit (mit unserem Auto).**

Most accusative and dative prepositions (except **außer, ohne,** and **seit**) can be made into **da**-compounds. If the preposition begins with a vowel (**an, auf, in,** etc.), it is used with **dar-:**

dafür	*for it (them)*	**darauf**	*on it (them)*
dagegen	*against it (them)*	**darin**	*in it (them)*
damit	*with it (them)*	**darüber**	*above it (them)*
danach	*after it (them)*	usw.	

Können Sie mir sagen, wo ein Briefkasten ist?—Ja, sehen Sie die Kirche dort? **Daneben** ist eine Apotheke, **dahinter** ist die Post, und **davor** ist ein Briefkasten.

2. **wo**-Compounds

The interrogative pronouns **wer, wen,** and **wem** refer to people.

Von wem sprichst du?	*About whom are you talking?*
	(Who are you talking about?)
Auf wen wartet ihr?	*For whom are you waiting?*
	(Who are you waiting for?)

In questions about things or ideas, **was** is used. If a preposition is involved, however, a **wo**-compound is required. Again, if the preposition begins with a vowel, it is combined with **wor-.**

wofür?	*for what?*	**worauf?**	*on what?*
wogegen?	*against what?*	**worüber?**	*above what?*
womit?	*with what?*	usw.	

Wovon sprichst du?	*About what are you talking?*
	(What are you talking about?)
Worauf wartet ihr?	*For what are you waiting?*
	(What are you waiting for?)

REMEMBER: To ask where something is located, use the question word **wo,** regardless of the answer expected: **Wo ist Peter?** To ask where someone is going, use **wohin** (NOT <u>wo</u> combined with <u>nach</u> or <u>zu</u>!): **Wohin ist Peter gegangen?** To ask where a person is coming from, use **woher** (NOT <u>wo</u> combined with <u>aus</u> or <u>von</u>!): **Woher kommt Peter?**

Wer weiß schon genau, woraus ein Hamburger besteht?

Übungen

E. **Wo ist die Brille?**   *(Remind your roommate, who is very careless, where he / she can find his / her glasses. Use a **da**-compound.)*

BEISPIEL: auf dem Sofa
             Sie liegt darauf.

neben dem Bett, vor dem Telefon, hinter der Lampe, auf dem Kassettenrecorder, in der Tasche, unter den Photos, zwischen den Zeitungen und Zeitschriften, . . .

F. Noch einmal, bitte! *(Replace the phrases in boldface with a preposition and a pronoun or with a **da**-compound. Always consider whether the sentence deals with a person or with an object or idea.)*

BEISPIEL: Hans steht **neben Christa.**
                Hans steht neben ihr.

                Die Lampe steht **neben dem Klavier.**
                Die Lampe steht daneben.

1. Was machst du **nach den Ferien**?
2. Bist du auch **mit dem Bus** gefahren?
3. Er hat die Gitarre **für seine Freundin** gekauft.
4. Was hast du **gegen Skilaufen?**
5. Das Paket ist **von meinen Eltern** gewesen.
6. Die Karten liegen **auf dem Tisch.**
7. Die Kinder haben **hinter der Garage** gespielt.
8. Anja hat **zwischen Herrn Fiedler und seiner Frau** gesessen.
9. Was halten Sie von **dem Haus?**
10. Ist die Nummer **im Telefonbuch?**
11. Er hat sich furchtbar **über diese Idee** geärgert.
12. Wir denken oft **an unseren kranken Freund.**
13. Freust du dich auch so **auf unsere Fahrt?**
14. Der Koffer ist **auf dem Schrank.**
15. Ich habe diese Theaterkarten **für meine Großeltern** gekauft.

G. Das Klassentreffen *(The class reunion. You were not able to attend the last high school reunion, but you are dying to know what has become of your ex-classmates. Ask one of the participants by referring to the phrases in boldface.)*

BEISPIEL: Horst interessiert sich **für Sport.**
                Wofür interessiert er sich?

                Horst interessiert sich **für eine junge Lehrerin.**
                Für wen interessiert er sich?

1. Jutta hat **von ihrem Mann** erzählt.
2. Gerd und Martina interessieren sich immer noch **für Politik.**
3. Ernst hält nicht viel **von Politik.**
4. Er ärgert sich oft **über die Politiker.**
5. Sebastian und Nicole sind **mit ihrem neuen Mercedes** gekommen.
6. Natürlich hat Sebastian **von seinen Hobbys** gesprochen.
7. Daniel wohnt jetzt in Kanada, aber er schreibt jede Woche **an seine Familie.**
8. Toni und Evelyn freuen sich **auf ihr erstes Baby.**
9. Wir haben oft **an die Vergangenheit** *(past)* gedacht.

H. Auf deutsch, bitte!

1. **a.** She's sitting next to them (i.e., their friends). **b.** They have two presents, one (**eins**) for her and one for him. **c.** Do you see the chair? The presents are lying on it. **d.** What's in them? **e.** Is this for me? **f.** What does one do with it? **g.** What do you *(sg. fam.)* think of it? **h.** Don't *(sg. fam.)* sit down on it.

2. **a.** Who is he coming with (With whom . . .)? **b.** What are they talking about? **c.** What are you *(sg. fam.)* thinking of? **d.** Who is he waiting for (For whom . . .)? **e.** What are you *(pl. fam.)* annoyed about?

f. What is she interested in?   **g.** Who are you writing to (To whom . . .)?   **h.** Who is this present for (For whom . . .)?

III. Endings of Unpreceded Adjectives

You already know how to deal with adjectives preceded by either **der-** or **ein-** words. Occasionally, however, adjectives are preceded by neither; they are then called UNPRECEDED ADJECTIVES. The equivalent in English would be adjectives preceded by neither *the* nor *a(n)*:

We bought fresh fish and fresh eggs.

1. Unpreceded adjectives take the endings that the definite article would have if it were used:

	der frische Fisch frischer Fisch	das frische Obst frisches Obst	die frische Wurst frische Wurst	die frischen Eier frische Eier
nom.	frischer Fisch	frisches Obst	frische Wurst	frische Eier
acc.	frischen Fisch	frisches Obst	frische Wurst	frische Eier
dat.	frischem Fisch	frischem Obst	frischer Wurst	frischen Eiern
gen.[1]	(frischen Fisches)	(frischen Obstes)	(frischer Wurst)	frischer Eier

Heute abend gibt es heiße Suppe, holländischen Käse, frische Brötchen und verschiedenes Obst.

*   If there are several unpreceded adjectives, all have the same ending.

    Ich wünsche dir schöne, interessante Ferien.

2. Several important words are often used as unpreceded adjectives in the plural:

andere	*other*
einige	*some, a few (pl. only)*
mehrere	*several (pl. only)*
viele	*many*
wenige	*few*

Wir haben uns mehrere neue Filme angesehen.
Sie haben einigen jungen Leuten gefallen, aber mir nicht.

*   Usually neither **viel** *(much)* nor **wenig** *(little, not much)* has an ending in the singular, but these words are often used as unpreceded adjectives in the plural.

    Viele Studenten haben **wenig** Geld, aber nur **wenige** Studenten haben **viel** Zeit.

*   Numerals, **mehr,** and **ein paar** have no endings. The same holds true for a few colors, such as purple and pink **(lila, rosa),** and adjectives like **Frankfurter, Berliner,** etc.

    Da sind **drei** junge **Wiener** Studenten mit **ein paar** kurzen Fragen.
    Haben Sie noch **mehr** graues oder blaues Papier?
    Was mache ich mit diesem alten **rosa** Pullover?

---

[1] The genitive singular forms are relatively rare, and the masculine and neuter forms of the genitive are irregular.

Übungen

I.   Ersetzen Sie die Adjektive!

BEISPIEL: Das sind nette Leute. (verrückt)
        Das sind verrückte Leute.

1.   Ich trinke gern schwarzen Kaffee. (heiß, frisch)
2.   Sie braucht dünnes Papier. (billig, weiß)
3.   Er schreibt tolle Bücher. (spannend, lustig)
4.   Heute haben wir wunderbares Wetter. (ausgezeichnet, furchtbar)
5.   Dort gibt es gutes Essen. (einfach, gesund)
6.   Hier bekommen wir frischen Fisch. (wunderbar, gebacken)
7.   Er hat oft verrückte Ideen. (dumm, phantastisch)

J.   Sagen Sie es noch einmal!   *(Omit the **der-** or **ein-**word preceding the adjective.)*

BEISPIEL: Der holländische Käse ist ausgezeichnet.
        Holländischer Käse ist ausgezeichnet.

1.   Die deutschen Zeitungen haben auch viel Werbung.
2.   Der Mann will mit dem falschen Geld bezahlen.
3.   Sie hat das frische Brot gekauft.
4.   Er hat den schwarzen Kaffee getrunken.
5.   Wir haben die braunen Eier genommen.
6.   Er ist mit seinen alten Tennisschuhen auf die Party gegangen.
7.   Sie trinken gern das dunkle Bier.
8.   Auf der Party haben sie diese laute Musik gespielt.
9.   Er erzählt gern solche traurigen Geschichten.
10.   Sie hat Bilder der bekannten Schauspieler.

K.   Was fehlt?

1.   Wir haben einig_____ bekannt_____ Autoren kennengelernt.
2.   Ich habe nur wenig_____ amerikanisch_____ Geld.
3.   Viel_____ neu_____ Studenten sind heute gekommen.
4.   Trinkst du gern warm_____ Milch?
5.   Wir wünschen Ihnen schön_____ und interessant_____ Ferien.
6.   Sie haben mit mehrer_____ ander_____ Ausländern an einem Tisch gesessen.
7.   Regensburg und Landshut sind zwei hübsch_____ alt_____ Städte.
8.   In der Prüfung habe ich ein paar_____ dumm_____ Fehler *(mistakes)* gemacht.
9.   Trink nicht so viel_____ kalt_____ Bier!
10.   Lieb_____ Bettina, lieb_____ Hans, lieb_____ Freunde!

L.   Was ich gern mache   *(Working in small groups, complete the sentences. Be sure to include an unpreceded adjective. Then ask "Und du?".)*

BEISPIEL: Ich singe gern . . .
        Ich singe gern alte Lieder.

1.   Ich esse gern . . .   4.   Ich lese gern . . .   7.   Ich finde . . . prima.
2.   Ich trinke gern . . .   5.   Ich trage gern . . .   8.   Ich möchte . . .
3.   Ich sammle gern . . .   6.   Ich sehe gern . . .

M. Bilden Sie ganze Sätze!

1. wie lange / du / warten / — / ich? *(pres. perf.)*
2. ich / sich freuen / — / Reise nach Spanien *(pres.)*
3. er / sich ärgern / — / Film *(pres. perf.)*
4. wo- / ihr / sich interessieren? *(pres.)*
5. wollen / sich kaufen / du / einig- / deutsch / Zeitschriften? *(pres.)*
6. in London / wir / sehen / mehrer- / interessant / Stücke *(pres. perf.)*
7. während / Pause / wir / trinken / billig / Sekt *(pres. perf.)*
8. Renate / schon / lesen / ein paar / spannend / Krimi *(pres. perf.)*
9. am Ende / viel / modern / Stücke / Leute / nicht / klatschen / lange *(pres.)*

N. Ein interessanter Mensch. Auf deutsch, bitte!

1. Two weeks ago an old friend of my father's visited us.   **2.** He is the author of several plays.   **3.** I'm very interested in the theater.   **4.** He knows many important people, also several well-known actors.   **5.** Our friend knows many other authors.
6. He spoke about them.   **7.** He also told us some exciting stories.   **8.** He has just been to (**in**) Vienna.   **9.** He saw several performances of his new play and he bought a few expensive books.   **10.** He's coming back in the summer.   **11.** We all are looking forward to that.   **12.** We have also bought him a few new novels.

EINBLICKE

German public radio and television are run by independent public corporations. The main nationwide television channels are ARD (or **1. Programm**) and ZDF (or **2. Programm**); together they produce a third regional channel (**3. Programm**) that concentrates on regional affairs and educational programming. Since 1985 the public corporations have been participating in additional ventures, e.g., 3-SAT (a joint venture of the German ZDF, the Austrian broadcasting corporation ORF, and the Swiss corporation SRG) and 1-PLUS. The public broadcasting corporations get most of their funds from fees that every owner of a radio or television set has to pay, but revenues from advertising are increasingly important.

The two major private German television networks are RTL and SAT-1, which present mainly sports, entertainment, and feature films, but also good political programs. Other private broadcasters include 1-PLUS, TELE-5, PRO-7, FAB, ARTE, VOX, the KABELKANAL, and the all-news channel N-TV. Their programs are transmitted by satellite and cable but can also be received through regular frequencies. These companies are operated by consortia—most of which are publishing companies—and advertising is their sole source of revenue.

der	Ausländer, -	*foreigner*
	Bürger, -	*citizen*
	Zuschauer, -	*viewer, spectator*
das	Fernsehen	*television (the medium)*
die	Nachricht, -en	*news (usually pl. in radio and TV)*
	Sendung, -en[1]	*(particular) program*

leicht / schwer	*light, easy / heavy, difficult*
monatlich (täglich, wöchentlich)	*monthly (daily, weekly)*
öffentlich / privat	*public / private*
verschieden	*different (kinds of), various*
vor allem	*mainly, especially, above all*
weder . . . noch	*neither . . . nor*

[1] Note the difference between **das Programm** and **die Sendung** as they refer to television: **das Programm** generally refers to *a channel* (Es gibt auch private Programme). **Die Sendung** refers to *a particular program* (Ich sehe mir gern diese Sportsendung an).

WAS IST DAS? der Haushalt, Kritiker, Regen, Sex; das Hauptprogramm, Kabelprogramm, Nachbarland, Satellitenprogramm; die Diskussion, Droge, Fernsehsendung, Interessengruppe, Kolonialisierung, Kreativität, Kultursendung, Serie; *(pl.)* die Kommunikationsmedien, Massenmedien, Statistiken; etwas Positives; finanzieren, ignorieren, registrieren, warnen; experimentell, finanziell, informativ, kritisch, kulturell, passiv, politisch, staatlich kontrolliert

Die Macht° des Fernsehens

power

Wie überall spielen die Massenmedien, vor allem das Fernsehen, auch in Deutschland eine wichtige Rolle. Ungefähr fünf Stunden jeden Tag nutzen° die Deutschen im Durchschnitt° Fernsehen, Radio, Zeitungen und Zeitschriften. Fast jeder Haushalt hat heute mindestens° einen Fernseher. Die Auswahl an° Fernsehsendungen ist groß und wird jedes Jahr größer°.
5 Zu den Hauptprogrammen kommen Programme aus Nachbarländern und auch privates Fernsehen, Kabel- und Satellitenprogramme.

use / on the average
at least
selection of / bigger

   Die privaten Sender° leben natürlich von der Werbung. Aber um das öffentliche Fernsehen zu finanzieren, müssen die Deutschen ihre Fernseher und Radios bei der Post registrieren und monatliche Gebühren° zahlen. Werbung gibt es da auch, aber nicht nach
10 acht Uhr abends und nie während einer Sendung.

stations

fees

   Das öffentliche Fernsehen ist weder staatlich noch privat kontrolliert, sondern finanziell und politisch unabhängig°. Darum° kann es auch leicht Sendungen für kleine Interessengruppen bringen, z.B. Nachrichten[1] in verschiedenen Sprachen, Sprachunterricht° für Ausländer[2], experimentelle Musik, politische Diskussionen und lokales Kabarett[3]. Das
15 deutsche Fernsehen bietet° eigentlich eine gute Mischung° von aktuellem° Sport und leichter Unterhaltung, von informativen Reiseberichten°, internationalen Filmen und kulturellen Sendungen (z.B. Theaterstücke, Opern und Konzerte).

independent / therefore
. . . instruction

offers / mixture / current
. . . reports

   Manche Kritiker halten nicht viel vom Fernsehen. Sie ärgern sich zum Beispiel darüber, daß so viele amerikanische Filme und Seifenopern° laufen, obwohl die Statistiken
20 zeigen, daß sich die Zuschauer dafür interessieren. Sie wollen nicht nur gute und informative Kultursendungen, sondern auch viel Sex und Gewalt°. Aber nicht nur darin sehen die Kritiker Probleme, sondern auch in der passiven Rolle der Zuschauer. Manche Menschen, vor allem Kinder, lassen sich täglich stundenlang vom Fernsehen berieseln°. Sie werden

soap operas

violence

let themselves be showered

dadurch passiv und verlieren an° Kreativität. Zeitungen und Zeitschriften warnen heute vor° der „Kolonialisierung der Köpfe" durch Fernsehen und Radio, und man spricht von 25 der Musik als Droge: „Was der saure° Regen in den Wäldern angerichtet° hat, ist sichtbar° geworden. Was die Massenmedien in unseren Köpfen anrichten, ist nicht sichtbar, aber trotzdem nicht weniger gefährlich°!"

Auf der anderen Seite darf man nicht ignorieren, was für eine wichtige Rolle Radio und Fernsehen bei den politischen Entwicklungen° in Osteuropa gespielt haben. In der 30 DDR° zum Beispiel konnte° man fast überall Fernsehsendungen aus der Bundesrepublik sehen; und die Bürger haben sich meistens mehr° für westliche Nachrichten, Filme und auch Werbung interessiert als° für die Sendungen ihres staatlich kontrollierten Fernsehens. So sind Radio und Fernsehen auch wichtige Kommunikationsmedien, weil sie Menschen verschiedener Nationen miteinander verbinden°. Man muß nur kritisch beurteilen°, was 35 man sieht.

Marginal glosses:
- *lose (in)* — an°
- *against* — vor°
- *acid / damaged / visible* — saure° / angerichtet° / sichtbar°
- *less dangerous* — weniger gefährlich°
- *developments* — Entwicklungen°
- *East Germany / could* — DDR° / konnte°
- *more* — mehr°
- *than* — als°
- *bring closer / evaluate* — verbinden° / beurteilen°

Zum Thema

A.   Richtig oder falsch? Wenn falsch, erklären Sie *(explain)* warum!

——   1.   In Deutschland spielt das Fernsehen keine wichtige Rolle.

——   2.   Die Menschen dort sehen sich ungefähr fünf Stunden am Tag Fernsehen an.

——   3.   In Deutschland gibt es auch privates Fernsehen.

——   4.   Weil die Deutschen monatliche Gebühren zahlen, gibt es im öffentlichen Fernsehen keine Werbung.

——   5.   Werbung läuft im öffentlichen Fernsehen nie nach sechs Uhr abends.

——   6.   Manche Kritiker finden es nicht gut, daß im deutschen Fernsehen so viele amerikanische Filme und Serien laufen.

——   7.   Aber die passive Rolle der Zuschauer findet mancher Kritiker gut.

——   8.   Ein paar Kritiker denken, daß die Massenmedien in unseren Köpfen tun, was der saure Regen in den Wäldern tut.

——   9.   Das westliche Fernsehen hat im Osten keine wichtige Rolle gespielt.

——   10.   Radio und Fernsehen können Nationen miteinander verbinden.

B.   Was fehlt? Geben Sie die fehlenden *(missing)* Präpositionen!

1. Der Artikel spricht _____ deutschen Fernsehen.   **2.** Viele denken bei Qualitätssendungen _____ internationale Nachrichten.   **3.** Manche Kritiker ärgern sich _____ die vielen amerikanischen Filme.   **4.** Sie interessieren sich nicht _____ amerikanische Serien.   **5.** Andere warten jede Woche _____ diese Serien.   **6.** Sie freuen sich schon _____ die nächste Woche.   **7.** Die Kritiker sprechen _____ einer Kolonialisierung der Köpfe durch die Massenmedien.   **8.** Wenn Sie das Quatsch finden, schreiben Sie bitte _____ die *Frankfurter Rundschau!*

C.   Womit? Damit! Stellen Sie Fragen mit einem wo-Wort, und antworten Sie mit einem da-Wort!

BEISPIEL: Das deutsche Fernsehen ist unabhängig **von der Werbung.**
            Wovon ist das deutsche Fernsehen unabhängig?
            Davon! Von der Werbung!

1. Einige Kritiker halten nicht viel **vom Fernsehen.**   **2.** Vor allem ärgern sie sich **über die vielen amerikanischen Serien.**   **3.** Manche Zuschauer lassen sich täglich stundenlang **vom Fernsehen oder von moderner Musik** berieseln.   **4. Durch zu viel Fernsehen und zu viel Musik** verlieren sie an Kreativität.   **5. Fürs Hobby** haben sie oft keine Zeit.

D.   Deutsches Fernsehen. Geben Sie die Adjektivendungen, wo nötig *(necessary)*!

1. Das deutsch——— Fernsehen ist eine gut——— Mischung von kulturell——— Sendungen und leicht——— Unterhaltung.   **2.** Man bekommt auch viel——— interessant——— Sendungen *(pl.)* aus verschieden——— Nachbarländern.   **3.** Das öffentlich——— Fernsehen finanziert man durch monatlich——— Gebühren.   **4.** Öffentlich——— Sender *(pl.)* haben natürlich auch öffentlich——— Aufgaben.   **5.** Sie können leicht verschieden——— Sendungen für klein——— Interessengruppen bringen, z.B. international——— Nachrichten in verschieden——— Sprachen oder auch lokal——— Kabarett *(n.)*.   **6.** Privat——— Fernsehen gibt es noch nicht lange. **7.** Diese klein——— Sender sind natürlich abhängig von viel——— Werbung, und sie bringen sie oft noch zu spät——— Stunde.   **8.** Beim privat——— Fernsehen kann man auch viel——— amerikanisch——— Filme sehen.   **9.** Kritiker sprechen von schlecht——— Qualität beim privat——— Fernsehen.   **10.** Sie ärgern sich auch über das Berieseln durch populär——— Musik.   **11.** Sie denken, daß das schwer——— Konsequenzen *(consequences)* bringt.   **12.** Wie wir in der letzt——— Zeit in Osteuropa gesehen haben, haben Fernsehen und Radio auch eine sehr positiv——— Seite.   **13.** Sie sind nämlich ein wichtig——— Kommunikationsmittel *(n.)*. **14.** Sie verbinden die Menschen verschieden——— Nationen miteinander.

Die Leipziger Mädler Passage lädt zum Einkaufen ein.

1. PROGRAMM   # 2. PROGRAMM   10. April DI

1. PROGRAMM

tagsüber

Das gemeinsame Programm von ARD und ZDF bis 13.45 Uhr:

9.00 Tagesschau

9.03 Unter der Sonne Kaliforniens
Eine neue Familie (Wh. v. 1989)

9.45 Sport treiben – fit bleiben

10.00 Tagesschau

10.03 Gesundheitsmagazin Praxis
Zum Weltgesundheitstag: „Handeln Sie jetzt!" Wo denn, wie denn, was denn? / Der unnötige Schmerz. Von Marlene Linke (Wh. vom 5. April)

10.50 Mosaik-Ratschläge
Ostereier aus aller Welt – Färbemittel / Hasentreffen in Stuttgart

11.00 Tagesschau

11.03 Fantomas
2. Teil: Tödliche Umarmung (Wh.) Ist Doktor Chaleck der geheimnisumwitterte Serienmörder Fantomas? Inspektor Juve findet im Haus des Arztes die Leiche einer Frau.
3. Teil: nächsten Dienstag

12.30 Umschau

12.55 Presseschau

13.00 Tagesschau

13.05 ARD-Mittagsmagazin

3. PROGRAMM

9.50 Tele-Gymnastik (27)

10.00 News of the week

10.15 Actualités

10.30 Avanti! Avanti!
Italienisch-Kurs (16)

11.00 Wer hat Angst vorm kleinen Chip?
Mikroelektronik: Verwandelt

11.30 Computerclub (5)

12.15 Reiseführer Die Borinage: Auf den Spuren des niederländischen Malers Vincent van Gogh

13.00 Telekolleg II
Deutsch (31): Das Buch des Lebens – Der Roman

13.30 Telekolleg II
Mathematik, Trigonometrie

17.00 Ferntourismus am Beispiel Kenias
Bericht. Letzter Teil: Hakuna Matata: Schönes Kenia – Keine Probleme?

17.30 Schüler machen Filme

RTL PLUS

16.25 Snoopy Zeichentrickfilm

17.45 Kunst und Botschaft Rembrandt »Josephs Traum im Stall« (1645)

17.50 Dirty Dancing Serie
Gefährliche Gefühle

18.15 Dr. Who Serie
Delta und die Bannermänner

18.45 RTL aktuell Nachrichten, Sport

19.00 Airwolf Serie
Dem Wolf eine Falle stellen

19.50 Der Hammer Serie

SAT 1

21.00 Der junge Löwe
Die Lebensgeschichte des Politikers Winston Churchill (1874–1965)

23.15 SAT 1-blick Berichte vom Tage

23.25 Grimms Märchen von lüsternen Pärchen
Spielfilm, Bundesrepublik 1969

2. PROGRAMM

13.00 Tennis:
Grand-Prix-Turniere
Grand-Prix der Damen in Hamburg. Reporter: Hans-Jürgen Pohmann

18.00 Sesamstraße
Für Kinder im Vorschulalter

18.30 flicflac
Magazin für Freizeit

abends

19.00 heute

19.30 Doppelpunkt ⊙
„Baby oder Beruf?"
Junge Frauen diskutieren über ihre Entscheidungen und Erfahrungen Moderation: Barbara Stöckl
▶ Siehe auch rechts

20.15 Und das am Montagmorgen ⊡
Deutsche Filmkomödie von 1959
Nach dem Bühnenstück von John Boynton Priestley
Alois Kessel . . . . . O. W. Fischer
Delia Mond . . . . Ulla Jacobsson
Herbert Acker . . . Robert Graf
Monika . . . . . Vera Tschechowa
Professor Gross . . Werner Finck
Müller . . . . Reinhard Kolldehoff
Frau Mutz . . . . . Lotte Stein
Frau Präfke . . Blandine Ebinger
v. Schmitz . Siegfried Schürenberg
Wegeleben . . Herbert Weissbach
Regie: Luigi Comencini (Wh. v. 83)
„Der englische Romancier, Buch- und Bühnenautor John Boynton Priestley lieferte den Stoff zu dieser reizenden Komödie, einem Brevier für Managerkranke. Wenn O. W. Fischer bisweilen auch reichlich theatralisch wird, so ist das Stück doch ein einziges Schmunzelvergnügen." (Hamburger Abendblatt)
▶ Siehe auch rechts

21.45 Magnum US-Serie
Hinter Gittern
Thomas Magnum . . Tom Selleck
Jonathan Higgins . John Hillerman
Rick . . . . Larry Manetti
TC . . . . Roger E. Mosley
Carol . . . . . . Kathleen Lloyd
Darryl Jacobs . . . Asher Brauner
Jack Damon . . . . . Matt Clark
Becky Damon . . . Linda Grovenor
Regie: Bernie Kowalski

22.40 Gottes eigenes Land
US-Dokumentarfilm von 1979/85
Kamera, Buch, Regie: Louis Malle
Der zweite Dokumentarfilm „. . . und das Streben nach Glück" folgt am 24. Mai.
▶ Siehe auch rechts

0.05 Europas Jugend musiziert ⊙
Auszüge aus dem fünften internationalen Konzert junger Solisten Ha Young Soul (Schweden), Klavier; Emer McDonough (Irland), Flöte; Koh Gabriel Kameda (Deutschland), Violine; Velgko Klenkovski (Jugoslawien), Klarinette
Werke von Haydn, Pergolesi und Weber. Das Orchester des belgischen Rundfunks und Fernsehens Leitung: Aleksander Rahbari

0.50 heute

Nachbarn: nächste Seiten

17.45 Hotel Paradies
Lisa bekommt ihr Traumhaus

Vor dem Glück der Lindemanns gibt's erst mal Streß: Max hat Magenbeschwerden und ohrfeigt seinen Sohn Michael. Lisa bekommt einen Schwächeanfall. Das ist zuviel für Max: Er will das Hotel aufgeben! Zwischen Renate und ihrem Freund, dem Schiffsmakler Rowalt, gibt es Spannungen.

Max (Klaus Wildbolz) macht seine Frau (Grit Boettcher) überglücklich: Er hat ihr heimlich das Traumhaus gekauft

19.30 Doppelpunkt
Junge Frauen diskutieren: Baby oder Beruf?

Wie sie es macht, ist's verkehrt: Entscheidet sich eine junge Frau für die Familie, gilt sie als „naives Dummchen", räumt sie dem Beruf Vorrang ein, muß sie mit dem Vorwurf „Karrierefrau" leben. Beides unter einen Hut bringen kann nur eine „Rabenmutter". Gibt es Auswege aus dem Dilemma? Barbara Stöckl diskutiert heute live mit Betroffenen.

20.15 Und das am Montagmorgen
Filmkomödie mit O. W. Fischer als „Aussteiger"

Korrekt und pflichtbewußt bis in die Knochen – Bankdirektor Kessel ist ohne Tadel. Das einzige Vergnügen, das sich der Junggeselle gönnt, ist die Mitarbeit in einem Kunstverein. Zwar findet er das hübsche Mitglied Dr. Delia Mond reizend, aber schließlich ist sie verlobt . . . An einem trüben Morgen reitet den Direktor offenbar der Teufel. Er will nicht mehr zur Bank gehen, sondern nur noch tun, was ihm Spaß macht! **88 Min.**

Verliebt schmiegt sich Delia (Ulla Jacobsson) an Bankdirektor Kessel (O. W. Fischer)

21.45 Magnum
. . . als Häftling auf einer Gefängnisfarm

Diese Art von Aufträgen haßt Magnum besonders: das Aufspüren durchgebrannter Teenager. Doch als seine Freundin Carol ihn bittet, ihre vermißte Cousine Becky zu suchen, muß er ran. Er findet heraus, daß Becky mit einem gewissen Darryl zusammen war. Der ist inzwischen auf einer Gefängnisfarm gelandet. Um mehr zu erfahren, läßt Magnum sich dort einschleusen.

Undankbarer Auftrag für Magnum (Tom Selleck)

E.   Was gibt's im Fernsehen? Sehen Sie aufs Programm auf Seite 290, und beantworten Sie die Fragen darüber!

1.   Wann beginnt das gemeinsame *(joint)* Vormittagsprogramm von ARD und
ZDF? Bis wann läuft es?

2.   Wann gibt es Nachrichten im ersten Programm *(die Tagesschau)*? im 2. Programm *(Heute)*? Wie lange sind diese Nachrichten? In welchen anderen
Sprachen gibt es Nachrichten im 3. Programm?

3.   Wo und wann gibt es eine Sendung über Sport oder Freizeit? über Kunst oder
Musik?

4.   Was ist vor allem für Kinder? für Schüler und Studenten?

5.   Worüber diskutieren Frauen in der Sendung um halb acht im 2. Programm? (**der
Beruf** *profession, work*)

6.   Worüber ist die Sendung um elf Uhr im 3. Programm? Um Viertel vor sechs im
RTL plus?

7.   Womit beginnt das Tagesprogramm von SAT 1? Was für ein Film ist das
bestimmt?

8.   Was für amerikanische Filme und Serien finden Sie auf dem Programm? Wann
und wo laufen sie?

F.   Wofür interessieren Sie sich im Fernsehen?   *(Together as a class, create a rat-
ings chart on various types of television programs. Use: 1 = sehr interessant; 2 =
manchmal interessant; 3 = uninteressant.)*

❑ Nachrichten	❑ Konzerte	❑ Seifenopern
❑ Politik	❑ Opern	❑ Horrorfilme
❑ Reisen	❑ Krimis	❑ Dokumentarfilme
❑ Hobbys	❑ Western	❑ Geschichtsfilme
❑ Sport	❑ Theaterstücke	❑ Liebesfilme *(love…)*
❑ Sprachen	❑ Fernsehspiele	❑ Science-Fiction-Filme
❑ Ballett	❑ Fernsehquizze	❑ Zeichentrickfilme *(cartoons)*

G.   Schriftliche Übung   *(Compare the German and American / Canadian TV systems
by writing brief statements of two to four sentences for each of the points below. Use
the reading text and the TV program as references.)*

1.   Popularität
2.   Anzahl *(number)* der Programme
3.   Art *(type)* der Programme
4.   Werbung und Fernsehgebühren
5.   Qualität
6.   Rolle von Radio und Fernsehen im politischen Leben

Hören Sie zu!

Pläne für den Abend   *(Three students in Berlin are making plans for the evening. Listen to their conversation.)*

ZUM ERKENNEN: Hätten Sie noch . . . ? *(Would you still have . . . ?);* die Anzeige, -n *(advertisement)*

1. Monika möchte gern ——— gehen.
   a.   ins Kino   b.   ins Kabarett   c.   ins Theater

2. Felix und Stefan finden das ——— .
   a.   eine gute Idee   b.   furchtbar langweilig   c.   komisch

3. Monika ruft an, um ——— .
   a.   Karten zu bestellen   b.   zu fragen, ob es noch   c.   zu fragen, wie man
                                    Karten gibt   zum Theater kommt

4. Sie wollen zum KARTOON gehen, weil ——— .
   a.   das Programm sehr   b.   sie dort essen können   c.   Monika Gutes dar-
        interessant ist   über gehört hat

5. Sie wollen um ——— Uhr essen.
   a.   18.30   b.   19.30   c.   21.00

6. Zum KARTOON kommt man ——— .
   a.   zu Fuß   b.   mit der U-Bahn   c.   das wissen wir nicht

Übrigens

1.   News reports are quite frequent throughout the day. The ARD calls them **Tagesschau,** and the ZDF calls them **Heute.** They are generally much shorter and have much less on-the-spot reporting than in the United States.

2.   During the fifties and sixties, West Germany experienced an economic boom (**Wirtschaftswunder**) that led to a labor shortage and the recruitment of foreign workers to fill job vacancies. By the late sixties and early seventies, about 2.6 million "guest workers" (**Gastarbeiter**) were living in the Federal Republic. The oil crisis in 1973 ended the recruitment of foreigners, most of whom came from countries around the Mediterranean. Today Turks form the largest single group among the more than 6 million foreigners living in Germany. These workers contributed greatly to Germany's flourishing economy and high standard of living, and continue to do so today.

   East Germans, too, had foreigners living and working among them, but in much smaller numbers. They came primarily from Poland, Hungary, Vietnam, Cuba, and Africa.

   Because of its very liberal asylum law, West Germany also attracted an ever increasing stream of refugees from totalitarian countries in Eastern Europe, Asia, and Africa. After the collapse of the Eastern bloc, "economic refugees" entered Germany in such large numbers that it became impossible to provide all of them with social services, housing, and jobs, especially after reunification. In 1993 Germany reluctantly amended its constitution to reduce the number of asylum seekers from neighboring countries.

3.   The term cabaret (**Kabarett**) describes both a form of theatrical entertainment and the dance halls and taverns in which the genre emerged at the turn of the century. Performers satirized contemporary culture and politics through skits, pantomimes, poems, and songs (chansons). This type of variety show flourished during the Weimar Republic but was banned during the last years of the Nazi regime because of the political satire. Since the end of World War II cabaret has reemerged as a popular form of entertainment. Some of Germany's most popular cabarets are the *Lach- und Schießgesellschaft* in Munich, the *Floh de Cologne* in Cologne, the *Mausefalle* in Hamburg, and in Berlin the *Stachelschweine,* the *Distel,* and the *Sündikat.* The *Kabarett der Komiker* was one of Berlin's most popular cabarets during the 1920s.

1. bis 5. Dezember, jew. 20 Uhr, URANIA-THEATER
Münchner Lach- und Schiessgesellschaft
Das neue Programm: "Altes oder nichts"
Mit Renate Küster, Rainer Basedow, Jochen Busse, Henning Venske

SPRECHSITUATIONEN

There are times when you want or need to express satisfaction or dissatisfaction with something. You may even be pushed to the point of anger. Here are phrases to deal with such situations.

Expressing Satisfaction

Das ist gut (prima, toll, wunderbar, phantastisch, super, ausgezeichnet).
Das ist praktisch (bequem, interessant, spannend, nicht schlecht).
Das ist genau das Richtige *(exactly the right thing)*.
Das gefällt mir (gut).
Das schmeckt (gut).
Das finde ich . . .

Expressing Dissatisfaction

Das ist schlecht (furchtbar, unpraktisch, unbequem, langweilig).
Das finde ich (nicht) . . .
Das ist zu . . .
Das ist nicht . . . genug.
Das gefällt mir nicht.
Das schmeckt mir nicht.

Expressing Anger

Das ist doch unglaublich!	*That's hard to believe.*
Das ist doch ärgerlich!	*That's annoying.*
Das ärgert mich wirklich.	*That really makes me mad.*
Jetzt habe ich aber genug.	*That's enough. I've had it.*
Ich habe die Nase voll.	*I'm fed up (with it).*
Das hängt mir zum Hals heraus.	*I'm fed up (with it).*
(So eine) Frechheit!	*Such impertinence.*

Übungen

 A.   **Weißt du . . .**   *(Working with a classmate, describe three situations that caused you satisfaction, dissatisfaction, or anger. Describe very briefly the cause, and then state your reaction.)*

BEISPIEL: Weißt du, das Autohaus hat mein Auto schon dreimal repariert. Ich habe über 400 Dollar dafür bezahlt, und es läuft immer noch nicht richtig. Jetzt habe ich aber die Nase voll!

B. **Was, wo und wann?** *(Telephone the cinema information, ask what films are showing in which theaters, and when the shows begin. Talk to your friend(s) and decide what you want to see and why.)*

C. **Kurzgespräche**

1. You are in a department store. As the clerk approaches you, tell him / her you need a new coat. He / she shows you one that he / she says is very nice. You try it on but soon realize that it is too big and the color is not practical. The next one doesn't fit either (**paßt auch nicht**) and it's too expensive. The third one is just right: it fits, you like it, it's practical and comfortable, and the price is right. You take it.

2. You've lent your notebook with class notes (**Notizen**) to a classmate [give him / her a name] who has failed to return it when promised—again. Not only that, but this classmate has passed the notebook on to a third person who is supposed to return it to you. You have called there and didn't get an answer. You are trying to prepare for a test. Tell your roommate your tale of woe and vent your anger about the situation.

Persönliche Eigenschaften

Junges Paar *(couple)* auf der Straße

LERNZIELE

Vorschau

- Women in Germany

Gespräche and Wortschatz

- Love and character traits

Struktur

- Simple past
- Conjunctions *als, wann,* and *wenn*
- Past perfect

Einblicke

- Fairy tale: *Rumpelstilzchen*

Sprechsituationen

- Expressing admiration
- Telling a story
- Encouraging a speaker

Women in Germany

The stereotype of German women—the concept that their lives revolve around children, kitchen, and church (**Kinder, Küche, Kirche**)—has changed a good deal in the last twenty years. Nevertheless, the role of women is still evolving. Until unification, West German women, especially those over 30, were far less likely to work full-time outside the home than their counterparts in the former GDR—50 percent vs. over 90 percent. Women living in the GDR were able to combine motherhood with full-time employment because state-run day care facilities and other services were readily available. Staying home with a sick child was taken for granted, and mothers could take as much as a year of maternity leave (**Mutterschaftsurlaub**) with full pay and a guarantee of their job when they returned to work. The loss of those facilities and privileges, combined with a high unemployment rate since unification, has caused a drastic and nearly unparalleled reduction—by roughly 60%—in the number of marriages and births and has been accompanied by a startling rise in death rates, especially among people between the ages of 25 and 45.

German attitudes and laws regarding pregnancy and childbirth reflect the conviction that women who bear and raise children are performing a task that is vital to the entire society. Thus, working women are entitled to maternity leave and maternity pay (**Mutterschaftsgeld**) six weeks before childbirth; eight weeks of paid leave after child birth is mandated. An extended leave of up to thirty-six months is also available, during which jobs are guaranteed, with a monthly government stipend for child care (**Erziehungsgeld**). Only since 1976 have women had equal rights (**Gleichberechtigung**) with men according to the Constitution (**Grundgesetz**) of the Federal Republic. The clause stipulating that women could work outside the home only if the job was compatible with their obligations toward marriage and family was eliminated at that time.

Women have had equal access to schools, universities, and other training facilities for many years, and they have increasingly taken advantage of these opportunities. On the whole, however, men still have higher incomes, while women tend to work in areas that are undervalued and therefore pay less. Although women won voting rights in 1918, the number of women in upper levels of business, government, and politics is very small.

Wir freuen uns über die Geburt unseres Sohnes

Jan

* 12. 9. 93 · 3740 g · 54 cm

Die glücklichen Eltern

Claudia und Dirk Haesloop

Anzeigen   Heiratswünsche[1]   ♂

♀

Gesucht wird[2]: charmanter, un-ternehmungslustiger, zärtlicher ADAM. Belohnung: hübsche, tem-peramentvolle EVA, Mitte 20, mag Antiquitäten, alte Häuser, schnelle Wagen, Tiere, Kinder.

Millionär bin ich nicht! Will mir ja auch kein Glück kaufen, sondern verdienen. Ich, 28 / 170[3], suche keine Modepuppe oder Disco-Queen, sondern ein nettes, natür-liches Mädchen, das auch hübsch sein darf.

Es gibt, was ich suche. Aber wie finden? Akademikerin, Ende 20 / 153[3], schlank, musikalisch, sucht sympathischen, gebildeten, ehr-lichen Mann mit Humor.

Tanzen, Segeln und Reisen sind meine drei großen Leidenschaften. Welche sympathische Frau mit Phantasie will mitmachen? Ich bin Journalist (Wassermann), opti-mistisch und unkonventionell.

Welcher Mann mit Herz, bis 45 Jahre jung, mag reisen, tanzen, schwimmen, Ski laufen und mich? Ich: Attraktiv, dunkelhaarig, unter-nehmungslustig und schick. Ge-schieden, Anfang 30, zwei nette Jungen.

Liebe gemeinsam erleben…zu Hause, im Konzert, beim Tanzen, in den Bergen, auf dem Tennis- oder Golfplatz, im und auf dem Wasser, wo auch immer, dazu wünsche ich mir eine gutaussehende, berufstätige Dreißigerin mit viel Charme und Esprit, die auch gern liest und schreibt.

Fragen   *(Read the personal ads above, and answer the following questions.)*

1. Wie soll der Partner / die Partnerin sein? Machen Sie eine Liste der gesuchten Qua-litäten!   2. Wie sehen die Leute sich selbst *(themselves)*? Was betonen *(emphasize)* sie? Machen Sie eine Liste!   3. Was sagen sie nicht?   4. Finden Sie Beispiele mit Adjek-tivendungen! Gruppieren Sie sie: a) mit Artikel; b) ohne Artikel!

Übrigens

1.   The assertiveness of women in Germany today is reflected and supported by changing traditions and laws. For example, when marrying, women no longer automatically take the name of the husband. Each partner may now keep his or her own name or choose to adopt the one of the partner.

2.   Advertising for marriage partners is generally accepted and not at all unusual in the German-speaking countries. Many newspapers and magazines carry such ads.

3.   In Europe the metric system is standard. Is someone who has a height of 180 cm short or tall? Figure it out yourself. Since 1 inch = 2.54 cm, divide the height by 2.54 to get the number of inches. How tall are you in metric terms? Multiply your height in inches by 2.54.

Die Liebe *(love)*

der	Partner, -	*partner*		
	Wunsch, ⸚e	*wish*		
die	Ehe, -n	*marriage*	ledig	*single*
	Hochzeit, -en	*wedding*	geschieden	*divorced*
	Scheidung, -en	*divorce*	verliebt	*in love (with)*
			(in + *acc.*)	

sich verlieben (in + *acc.*)	*to fall in love (with)*	verlobt (mit)	*engaged (to)*
sich verloben (mit)	*to get engaged (to)*	(un)verheiratet	*(un)married*
heiraten	*to marry, get married (to)*		

Die Eigenschaft, -en *(attribute, characteristic)*

attraktiv	*attractive*	schick	*chic, neat*
charmant	*charming*	schlank	*slim*
(un)ehrlich	*(dis)honest*	selbständig /	*independent /*
fleißig / faul	*industrious / lazy*	unselbständig	*dependent*
(un)freundlich	*(un)friendly*	selbstbewußt	*self-confident*
(un)gebildet	*(un)educated*	(un)sportlich	*(un)athletic*
(un)geduldig	*(im)patient*	(un)sympathisch	*(un)congenial, (un)likable*
(un)glücklich	*(un)happy*		
gutaussehend	*good-looking*	(un)talentiert	*(un)talented*
hübsch / häßlich	*pretty / ugly*	temperamentvoll	*dynamic*
intelligent / dumm	*intelligent / stupid*	unternehmungslustig	*enterprising*
jung	*young*	verständnisvoll	*understanding*
(un)musikalisch	*(un)musical*	vielseitig	*versatile*
nett	*nice*	zärtlich	*affectionate*
reich / arm	*rich / poor*		

Weiteres

auf diese Weise	*in this way*
beid-	*both*
bestimmt	*surely, for sure; certain(ly)*
Du hast recht / unrecht.	*You're right / wrong.*
jemand	*someone, somebody*
einladen (lädt ein), lud ein, eingeladen	*to invite*
träumen (von)	*to dream (of)*
vergessen (vergißt), vergessen	*to forget*
verlieren, verloren	*to lose*
versuchen	*to try*

ZUM ERKENNEN: die Anzeige, -n *(ad);* gesucht wird *(wanted);* die Belohnung *(reward);* Mitte . . . *(mid . . .);* die Antiquität, -en *(antique);* das Tier, -e *(animal);* die Akademikerin, -nen *(woman with university degree);* mit Humor *(with a sense of humor);* mit Herz *(with feelings);* der Millionär, -e; verdienen *(to earn);* die Modepuppe, -n *(fashion doll);* die Leidenschaft, -en *(passion);* mit Phantasie *(with imagination);* der Wassermann *(Aquarius);* optimistisch; unkonventionell; gemeinsam erleben *(to experience together);* die Dreißigerin, -nen *(woman in her 30s);* der Charme; der Esprit

Zum Thema

A. **Wie Sie jetzt Ihren Partner finden können!** *(Take this test. Which situation is most appealing to you? Label the picture you like best with a "1" and the one you like the least with a "0.")*

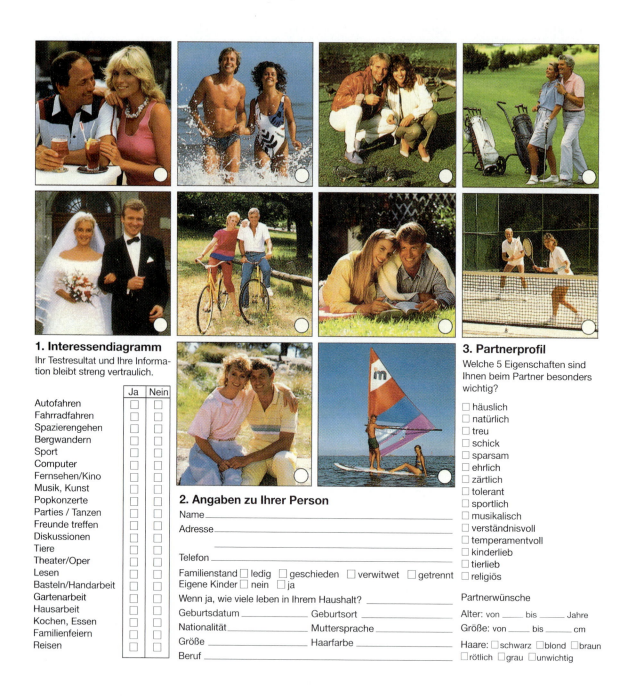

1. Interessendiagramm

Ihr Testresultat und Ihre Information bleibt streng vertraulich.

	Ja	Nein
Autofahren	☐	☐
Fahrradfahren	☐	☐
Spazierengehen	☐	☐
Bergwandern	☐	☐
Sport	☐	☐
Computer	☐	☐
Fernsehen/Kino	☐	☐
Musik, Kunst	☐	☐
Popkonzerte	☐	☐
Parties / Tanzen	☐	☐
Freunde treffen	☐	☐
Diskussionen	☐	☐
Tiere	☐	☐
Theater/Oper	☐	☐
Lesen	☐	☐
Basteln/Handarbeit	☐	☐
Gartenarbeit	☐	☐
Hausarbeit	☐	☐
Kochen, Essen	☐	☐
Familienfeiern	☐	☐
Reisen	☐	☐

2. Angaben zu Ihrer Person

Name _____

Adresse _____

_____

Telefon _____

Familienstand ☐ ledig ☐ geschieden ☐ verwitwet ☐ getrennt
Eigene Kinder ☐ nein ☐ ja

Wenn ja, wie viele leben in Ihrem Haushalt? _____

Geburtsdatum _____ Geburtsort _____

Nationalität _____ Muttersprache _____

Größe _____ Haarfarbe _____

Beruf _____

3. Partnerprofil

Welche 5 Eigenschaften sind Ihnen beim Partner besonders wichtig?

☐ häuslich
☐ natürlich
☐ treu
☐ schick
☐ sparsam
☐ ehrlich
☐ zärtlich
☐ tolerant
☐ sportlich
☐ musikalisch
☐ verständnisvoll
☐ temperamentvoll
☐ kinderlieb
☐ tierlieb
☐ religiös

Partnerwünsche

Alter: von ____ bis ____ Jahre

Größe: von ____ bis ____ cm

Haare: ☐ schwarz ☐ blond ☐ braun
☐ rötlich ☐ grau ☐ unwichtig

ZUM ERKENNEN: bleibt streng vertraulich *(remains strictly confidential);* treffen *(to meet);* Basteln *(crafts);* Handarbeit *(needlework);* Angaben *(information);* verwitwet *(widowed);* getrennt *(separated);* eigen- *(own);* der Geburtsort *(place of birth);* die Größe, -n *(size);* der Beruf, -e *(profession);* häuslich *(home-loving, domestic);* treu *(loyal, faithful);* sparsam *(thrifty);* kinderlieb *(loves children);* tierlieb *(loves animals);* Alter *(age)*

B.   Was ist das Adjektiv dazu?

der Charme, Freund, Optimismus, Reichtum, Sport, Verstand;
das Glück, Temperament, Unternehmen;
die Attraktion, Bildung, Dummheit, Ehrlichkeit, Faulheit, Gemütlichkeit, Intelligenz,
    Natur, Musik, Scheidung, Selbständigkeit, Sympathie, Zärtlichkeit;
sich verlieben, sich verloben, heiraten

C.   Fragen
1.   Was machen Sie und Ihre Freunde in der Freizeit? Worüber sprechen Sie?
2.   Was für Eigenschaften finden Sie bei Freunden wichtig? Wie dürfen sie nicht sein?
3.   Waren Sie schon einmal in einen Schauspieler / eine Schauspielerin verliebt? In
    wen?
4.   Was halten Sie vom Zusammenleben vor dem Heiraten?
5.   Was halten Sie vom Heiraten? Wie alt sollen Leute wenigstens *(at least)* sein,
    wenn sie heiraten? Finden Sie eine lange Verlobung wichtig? Warum *(nicht)*?

D.   Gesucht wird. Schreiben Sie Ihre eigene *(own)* Anzeige!

E.   Charakterisierung *(characterization).* Schreiben Sie 8 bis 10 Sätze!
1.   So bin ich.
2.   Ein Freund / eine Freundin von mir *(or anybody else you would like to write
    about).*

F.   Aussprache: f, v, ph, w   *(See also III. 1, 4, and 5 in the pronunciation section of
the Workbook.)*
1.   [f]   **f**ür, **f**ast, **f**rei, **f**rüh, **f**ertig, **f**it, **f**ühlen, **f**ehlen, **f**reundlich, **F**ilm, **F**ernsehen,
    ö**ff**nen, Brie**f**, el**f**, au**f**
2.   [f]   **v**erliebt, **v**erlobt, **v**erheiratet, **v**erständnisvoll, **v**ergessen, **v**erlieren, **v**er-
    suchen, **v**erschieden, **v**orbei, **v**ielleicht, **ph**antastisch, **ph**otographieren,
    Geogra**ph**ie, wie**v**iel
3.   [v]   **V**anille, **V**ision, **V**ideo, Kla**v**ier, reser**v**ieren, Sil**v**ester, Pullo**v**er, Uni**v**ersität
4.   [v]   **w**er, **w**en, **w**em, **w**essen, **w**arum, **w**erden, **w**ünschen, **W**aldweg, sch**w**im-
    men, sch**w**arz, sch**w**er, Sch**w**ester, z**w**ischen
5.   Wortpaare
    a.   *wine* / Wein   c.   *oven* / Ofen   e.   Vetter / Wetter
    b.   *when* / wenn   d.   *veal* / viel   f.   vier / wir

Hören Sie zu!

Leute sind verschieden.   *(Select three adjectives that best describe each of the four
people you hear discussed. Put their initials in front of the adjectives that apply to them:
K for Kirsten, **M** for Martin, **O** for Oliver, **S** for Sabine. Not all adjectives will be used.)*

ZUM ERKENNEN: das Krankenhaus, ¨er *(hospital)*; nächst- *(next)*; während *(while)*; die
Turnstunde *(P.E. class)*; die Katastrophe, -n; nicht einmal *(not even)*; verdienen *(to earn)*

Wie sind sie?

_____ arm	_____ attraktiv	_____ optimistisch
_____ reich	_____ freundlich	_____ selbstbewußt
_____ ruhig	_____ musikalisch	_____ gutaussehend
_____ fleißig	_____ sportlich	_____ verständnisvoll
_____ faul	_____ unsportlich	_____ temperamentvoll
_____ intelligent	_____ sympathisch	_____ unternehmungslustig

STRUKTUR

I. The Simple Past (Imperfect, Narrative Past)

The past tense is often referred to as the SIMPLE PAST because it is a single verb form in contrast to the perfect tenses (also called "compound past tenses"), which consist of two parts, an auxiliary and a past participle.

We spoke German.   Wir **sprachen** Deutsch.

In spoken German the present perfect is the preferred tense, especially in Southern Germany, Austria, and Switzerland. Only the simple past of **haben, sein,** and the modals is common everywhere.

The simple past is used primarily in continuous narratives such as novels, short stories, newspaper reports, and letters relating a sequence of events. Therefore, it is often also called the "narrative past."

Again, one German verb form corresponds to several in English.

Sie **sprachen** Deutsch. $\begin{cases} \textit{They spoke German.} \\ \textit{They were speaking German.} \\ \textit{They did speak German.} \\ \textit{They used to speak German.} \end{cases}$

1. t-Verbs *(weak verbs)*

    t-Verbs can be compared to such regular English verbs as *love / loved* and *work / worked,* which form the past tense by adding *-d* or *-ed* to the stem. To form the simple past of t-verbs, add **-te, -test, -te, -ten, -tet, -ten** to the STEM of the verb.

ich	lern**te**	wir	lern**ten**
du	lern**test**	ihr	lern**tet**
er	lern**te**	sie	lern**ten**

    Verbs that follow this pattern include: fragen, freuen, gratulieren, hören, interessieren, lachen, legen, machen, sagen, sammeln, setzen, spielen, suchen, stellen, stimmen, träumen, wandern, weinen, wohnen, wünschen.

    a. Verbs with stems ending in **-d, -t,** or certain consonant combinations add an **-e-** before the simple past ending.

ich	arbeit**ete**	wir	arbeit**eten**
du	arbeit**etest**	ihr	arbeit**etet**
er	arbeit**ete**	sie	arbeit**eten**

    Verbs that follow this pattern include: antworten, baden, bedeuten, heiraten, kosten, landen, mieten, öffnen, übernachten, warten.

b. Irregular t-verbs (sometimes called *mixed verbs*) usually have a stem change. Compare the English *bring / brought* and the German **bringen / brachte.**

ich	brachte	wir	brachten
du	brachtest	ihr	brachtet
er	brachte	sie	brachten

Here is a list of the PRINCIPAL PARTS of all the irregular t-verbs that you have used thus far. Irregular present-tense forms are also noted. You already know all the forms of these verbs except their simple past. Verbs with prefixes have the same forms as the corresponding simple verbs (**brachte mit**). If you know the principal parts of a verb, you can derive all the verb forms you need!

INFINITIVE	PRESENT	SIMPLE PAST	PAST PARTICIPLE
bringen		**brachte**	gebracht
denken		**dachte**	gedacht
haben	hat	**hatte**	gehabt
kennen		**kannte**	gekannt
wissen	weiß	**wußte**	gewußt

Modals also belong to this group. (The past participles of these verbs are rarely used.)

dürfen	darf	**durfte**	(gedurft)
können	kann	**konnte**	(gekonnt)
müssen	muß	**mußte**	(gemußt)
sollen	soll	**sollte**	(gesollt)
wollen	will	**wollte**	(gewollt)

NOTE: The simple past of irregular t-verbs has the same stem change as the past participle.

2. n-Verbs *(strong verbs)*

n-Verbs correspond to such English verbs as *write / wrote* and *speak / spoke*. They usually have a stem change in the simple past that is difficult to predict and must therefore be memorized. (Overall they fall into a number of groups with the same changes. For a listing by group, see Appendix.) To form the simple past, add **-, -st, -, -en, -t, -en** to the (IRREGULAR) STEM of the verb.

ich	sprach	wir	sprachen
du	sprachst	ihr	spracht
er	sprach	sie	sprachen

Below is a list of the PRINCIPAL PARTS of n-verbs that you have used up to now. You already know all the forms except the simple past. Irregular present-tense forms and the auxiliary **sein** are also noted.

INFINITIVE	PRESENT	SIMPLE PAST	PAST PARTICIPLE
an·fangen	fängt an	**fing an**	angefangen
an·ziehen		**zog an**	angezogen
beginnen		**begann**	begonnen

bleiben		**blieb**	ist geblieben
ein·laden	lädt ein	**lud ein**	eingeladen
empfehlen	empfiehlt	**empfahl**	empfohlen
essen	ißt	**aß**	gegessen
fahren	fährt	**fuhr**	ist gefahren
fallen	fällt	**fiel**	ist gefallen
finden		**fand**	gefunden
fliegen		**flog**	ist geflogen
geben	gibt	**gab**	gegeben
gefallen	gefällt	**gefiel**	gefallen
gehen		**ging**	ist gegangen
halten	hält	**hielt**	gehalten
hängen		**hing**	gehangen
heißen		**hieß**	geheißen
helfen	hilft	**half**	geholfen
kommen		**kam**	ist gekommen
lassen	läßt	**ließ**	gelassen
laufen	läuft	**lief**	ist gelaufen
lesen	liest	**las**	gelesen
liegen		**lag**	gelegen
nehmen	nimmt	**nahm**	genommen
rufen		**rief**	gerufen
schlafen	schläft	**schlief**	geschlafen
schreiben		**schrieb**	geschrieben
schwimmen		**schwamm**	ist geschwommen
sehen	sieht	**sah**	gesehen
sein	ist	**war**	ist gewesen
singen		**sang**	gesungen
sitzen		**saß**	gesessen
sprechen	spricht	**sprach**	gesprochen
stehen		**stand**	gestanden
steigen		**stieg**	ist gestiegen
tragen	trägt	**trug**	getragen
treiben		**trieb**	getrieben
trinken		**trank**	getrunken
tun	tut	**tat**	getan
vergessen	vergißt	**vergaß**	vergessen
verlieren		**verlor**	verloren
waschen	wäscht	**wusch**	gewaschen
werden	wird	**wurde**	ist geworden

3. Sentences in the simple past follow familiar word-order patterns.

Der Zug **kam** um acht.
Der Zug **kam** um acht **an.**
Der Zug <u>sollte</u> um acht <u>**ankommen.**</u>
V1   V2

Er wußte, daß der Zug um acht **kam.**
Er wußte, daß der Zug um acht **ankam.**
Er wußte, daß der Zug um acht <u>**ankommen**</u> <u>sollte.</u>
V2   V1

A.   **Geben Sie das Imperfekt** *(simple past)!*

BEISPIEL: feiern   **feierte**

1. fragen, fehlen, erzählen, klatschen, lachen, legen, bummeln, wechseln, photographieren, schicken, putzen, sich kämmen, sich rasieren, sich setzen, versuchen
2. arbeiten, baden, bedeuten, kosten, antworten, übernachten, öffnen
3. haben, müssen, denken, wissen, können, kennen
4. geben, nehmen, essen, sehen, lesen, finden, singen, sitzen, liegen, kommen, tun, sein, hängen, schreiben, treiben, heißen, einsteigen, schlafen, fallen, lassen, fahren, tragen, waschen, werden, einladen

B.   **Ersetzen Sie die Verben!**

BEISPIEL: Sie schickte das Paket. (mitbringen)
                     Sie brachte das Paket mit.

1. Sie schickten ein Taxi. (suchen, bestellen, mieten, warten auf)
2. Das hatte ich nicht. (wissen, kennen, denken, mitbringen)
3. Wann solltet ihr zurückkommen? (müssen, wollen, dürfen, können)
4. Wir fanden es dort. (sehen, lassen, verlieren, vergessen)
5. Er dankte seiner Mutter. (antworten, zuhören, helfen, schreiben)
6. Du empfahlst den Sauerbraten. (nehmen, wollen, bringen)

C.   **Wiederholen Sie die Texte im Imperfekt!**

1. **Weißt du noch?**   *(A brother and sister reminisce. Repeat in the simple past.)*

    BEISPIEL: Großvater erzählt stundenlang von seiner Kindheit *(childhood)*.
                     Großvater erzählte stundenlang von seiner Kindheit.

    a. Ich setze mich aufs Sofa und höre ihm zu.   **b.** Seine Geschichten interessieren mich.   **c.** Vater arbeitet im Garten.   **d.** Du telefonierst oder besuchst die Nachbarn.   **e.** Karin und Jörg spielen stundenlang Karten.   **f.** Mutter kauft ein oder bezahlt Rechnungen.   **g.** Großmutter legt sich nachmittags ein Stündchen hin und freut sich danach auf ihre Tasse Kaffee.   **h.** Das wiederholt sich oft am Wochenende. Richtig?

2. **Haben Sie das nicht gewußt?**   *(Two neighbors gossip about Lothar and Ute.)*

    BEISPIEL: Hat Ute ihren Mann schon lange gekannt?
                     Kannte Ute ihren Mann schon lange?

    a. Wie hat sie ihn kennengelernt?   **b.** Der Briefträger *(mail carrier)* hat ihr einen Brief von einem jungen Herrn gebracht.   **c.** Hast du nichts von ihrer Anzeige gewußt?   **d.** Sie hat Lothar durch die Zeitung kennengelernt.   **e.** Gestern haben sie Hochzeit gehabt.   **f.** Sie hat Glück gehabt.   **g.** Das habe ich mir auch gedacht.

3. **Schade!**   *(Bärbel talks to her friend about plans that didn't materialize.)*

BEISPIEL: Was willst du denn machen?
   Was wolltest du denn machen?

a. Ich will mit Karl-Heinz ins Kino gehen, aber ich kann nicht.   **b.** Warum, darfst du nicht?   **c.** Doch, aber meine Kopfschmerzen wollen einfach nicht weggehen.   **d.** Mußt du im Bett bleiben?   **e.** Nein, aber ich darf nicht schon wieder krank werden.   **f.** Leider kann ich nicht mit Karl-Heinz sprechen. **g.** Aber seine Mutter will es ihm sagen.   **h.** Er soll mich anrufen.

4. **Wo wart ihr?**   *(Caroline tells about a short trip to Switzerland.)*

BEISPIEL: Wir sind eine Woche in Saas Fee gewesen.
   Wir waren eine Woche in Saas Fee.

Von unserem Zimmer haben wir einen Blick auf *(view of)* die Alpen gehabt. Die Pension hat natürlich „Alpenblick" geheißen. Morgens haben wir lange geschlafen, dann haben wir gemütlich Frühstück gegessen. Später bin ich mit dem Sessellift auf einen Berg gefahren und bin den ganzen Nachmittag Ski laufen gegangen. Wolfgang ist unten geblieben, hat Bücher gelesen und Briefe geschrieben.

D. **Schriftliche Übung**   *(Write eight to ten sentences on one of the topics below. Write in the simple past without using any verb more than once.)*

1. **Als ich sechzehn war . . .**   *(Tell where you went to school, and how and why you liked or didn't like it. You may also pick any other age.)*

2. **Eine interessante Party**   *(Tell where the party was, who was there, what was so special about it, etc.)*

3. **Eine schöne Reise**   *(Tell where you went, who you traveled with, what you saw, etc.)*

II. The Conjunctions *als, wann, wenn*

Care must be taken to distinguish between **als, wann,** and **wenn,** all of which correspond to the English *when.* **Als** refers to a SINGLE EVENT IN THE PAST *(When I came home at 6 P.M., he wasn't back yet).* **Wann** introduces direct or indirect questions REFERRING TO TIME *(I wonder when he'll return).* **Wenn** covers all other situations, including repeated events in the past *(When he came, he always brought flowers. We'll call you when he comes in).*

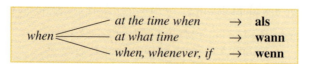

when
— *at the time when*   → **als**
— *at what time*   → **wann**
— *when, whenever, if*   → **wenn**

Als ich gestern abend nach Hause kam, war er noch nicht zurück.
When I came home last night (referring to a particular event in the past) . . .

Ich frage mich, **wann** er nach Hause kommt.
. . . when (at what time) he's going to come home.

Wenn du ankommst, ruf(e) mich an!
When you arrive, call me! (referring to a present or future event)

Wenn er kam, brachte er immer Blumen.
Whenever he came (referring to repeated events in the past) . . .

Remember that **wenn** *(if)* can also introduce a conditional clause:

Wenn es nicht regnet, gehen wir spazieren.
If it doesn't rain . . .

E. Was fehlt: als, wann oder wenn?

Übungen

1. _____ ihr kommt, zeigen wir euch die Bilder von unserer Reise.
2. Können Sie mir sagen, _____ der Zug aus Köln ankommt?
3. _____ wir letzte Woche im Theater waren, sahen wir Stephan und Sonja.
4. Sie freute sich immer sehr, _____ wir sie besuchten.
5. Sie bekommen diese Möbel, _____ sie heiraten. Wer weiß, _____ sie heiraten!
6. _____ ich ein Kind war, habe ich nur Deutsch gesprochen.

F. Verbinden Sie *(link)* **die Sätze mit als, wann oder wenn!**   *(If "when" stands at the beginning, make the first sentence the dependent clause. Watch the position of the verb.)*

BEISPIEL: Sie riefen an. Ich duschte mich. *(when)*
   Sie riefen an, als ich mich duschte.
   (when) Ich duschte mich. Sie riefen an.
   Als ich mich duschte, riefen sie an.

1. Wir sahen Frau Loth heute früh. Wir gingen einkaufen. *(when)*
2. *(when)* Sie spricht von Liebe. Er hört nicht zu.
3. Sie möchte (es) wissen. Die Weihnachtsferien fangen an. *(when)*
4. *(when)* Ich stand gestern auf. Es regnete.
5. *(when)* Das Wetter war schön. Die Kinder spielten immer im Park.
6. Er hat mir nicht geschrieben. Er kommt. *(when)*

III. **The Past Perfect**

1. Like the present perfect, the PAST PERFECT in both English and German is a compound form consisting of an auxiliary and a past participle. However, the AUXILIARY IS IN THE SIMPLE PAST.

Ich **hatte** das gut **gelernt.**   *I had learned that well.*
Er **war** um zehn Uhr nach Hause **gekommen.**   *He had come home at ten o'clock.*

ich	**hatte**	. . . gelernt	**war**	. . . gekommen
du	**hattest**	. . . gelernt	**warst**	. . . gekommen
er	**hatte**	. . . gelernt	**war**	. . . gekommen
wir	**hatten**	. . . gelernt	**waren**	. . . gekommen
ihr	**hattet**	. . . gelernt	**wart**	. . . gekommen
sie	**hatten**	. . . gelernt	**waren**	. . . gekommen

2. The past perfect is used to refer to events *preceding* other events in the past.

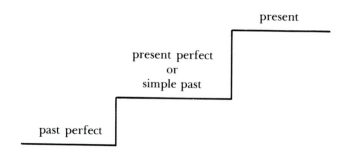

Er hat mich gestern angerufen.   He called me yesterday.
Ich **hatte** ihm gerade **geschrieben.**   I had just written to him.

Wir kamen zu spät am Bahnhof an.   We arrived too late at the station.
Der Zug **war** schon **abgefahren.**   The train had already left.

3. The conjunction **nachdem** *(after)* is usually followed by the past perfect in the subordinate clause, whereas the main clause is in the present perfect or simple past.

nachdem	*after*

Nachdem er mich **angerufen hatte,** schickte ich den Brief nicht mehr ab.
Nachdem der Zug **abgefahren war,** gingen wir ins Bahnhofsrestaurant.

Übungen

G.   Ersetzen Sie das Subjekt!

BEISPIEL: Sie hatten uns besucht. (du)
              Du hattest uns besucht.

1. Du hattest den Schlüssel gesucht. (ihr, Sie, sie / *sg.*)
2. Sie hatten das nicht gewußt. (wir, ihr, sie / *sg.*)
3. Ich war nach Dresden gereist. (sie / *pl.,* du, wir)
4. Sie waren auch in der Dresdener Oper gewesen. (er, du, ich)

H.   Auf englisch, bitte! *(Last night Stephan and Sonja looked at the video* Männer. *Now they are talking about when the movie first appeared.)*

1. Ich hatte den Film schon einmal gesehen.   **2.** Er war eine Sensation gewesen.
3. Man hatte den Film zur gleichen Zeit in sieben Kinos gezeigt.   **4.** Ich hatte
Glück gehabt.   **5.** Durch Walter hatte ich noch Karten für die Premiere bekommen.
6. Die Regisseurin Doris Dörrie war sogar da gewesen.   **7.** Ich hatte schon lange
nicht mehr so gelacht.

I.   Am Flughafen. Auf deutsch, bitte!

1. We got to the airport after the plane had landed.   **2.** When I arrived, they had already picked up **(holen)** their luggage.   **3.** After I had found them, we drove home.
4. My mother had been looking forward to this day.   **5.** When she had shown them the house, we sat down in the living room and talked about the family.

J. **Und dann?**

1. **Zu Hause** *(Mrs. Schneider recounts a typical day at home. Find out what happened next by asking **Und dann?** Note how she switches from the present perfect to the past perfect.)*

   BEISPIEL: Ich bin aufgestanden.—Und dann?
   Nachdem ich aufgestanden war, habe ich mir die Zähne geputzt.

   a. Ich bin aufgestanden.
   b. Ich habe mir die Zähne geputzt.
   c. Ich habe mich angezogen.
   d. Ich habe Frühstück gemacht.
   e. Alle haben sich an den Tisch gesetzt.
   f. Das Telefon hat geklingelt *(rang)*.
   g. Helmut hat die Zeitung gelesen.
   h. Er ist zur Arbeit gegangen.
   i. Ich habe mich an den Computer gesetzt.

2. **Was haben Sie am Wochenende gemacht?** *(Write five sentences in the simple past, then follow the pattern in exercise 1 [**Nachdem ich . . .**].)*

K. **Wiederholen Sie die Sätze im Imperfekt!**

1. Lothar denkt an Sabine. Er will ein paar Wochen segeln gehen. Aber sie hat keine Lust dazu. Er spricht mit Holger. Die beiden setzen eine Anzeige in die Zeitung. Ute liest die Anzeige und antwortet darauf. Durch die Anzeige finden sie sich. Danach hat Lothar für Sabine keine Zeit mehr. Er träumt nur noch von Ute. Am 24. Mai heiraten die beiden. Sie laden Holger zur Hochzeit ein. Die Trauung *(ceremony)* ist in der lutherischen Kirche. Ute heißt vorher *(before)* Kaiser. Jetzt wird sie Ute Müller.

2. Weil es im Fernsehen nichts Besonderes gibt, gehen Sonja und Stephan ins Theater. Sie haben keine Lust, einen Krimi zu sehen. Aber *Mutter Courage* gefällt ihnen gut. Sonja kennt das Stück schon, aber sie sieht es gern noch einmal. Während der Pause lädt Stephan sie zu einer Cola ein. Leider haben sie nur ein paar Minuten, weil die Pause kurz ist.

L.   Auf deutsch, bitte!   *(Use the simple past unless another tense is clearly required.)*

1. Arthur had been thinking of his daughter's wedding.   **2.** When we saw her in December, she was in love with a charming, well-to-do man.   **3.** They were supposed to get married in April.   **4.** I had already bought a beautiful present. **5.** Two weeks ago she got engaged to another man.   **6.** Michael is a poor student at (**an**) her university.   **7.** They didn't say when they wanted to get married.   **8.** On the weekend she called her parents.   **9.** She and Michael had just gotten married. **10.** They hadn't invited their parents to (**zu**) the wedding.   **11.** Arthur gets annoyed when he thinks about it.

Im Mai lernten sie sich kennen. Jetzt heiratete Michael seine blonde Schauspielerin

HALTET MIT HUMOR UND CHARME
EURE JUNGE LIEBE WARM!
MIT ALLEN GUTEN WÜNSCHEN

EINBLICKE

The brothers Grimm, Jacob (1785–1863) and Wilhelm (1786–1859), are well remembered for their collection of fairy tales, including **Hänsel und Gretel, Schneewittchen** (*Snow White*), **Rotkäppchen** (*Little Red Riding Hood*), **Aschenputtel** (*Cinderella*), **Dornröschen** (*Sleeping Beauty*), **Rumpelstilzchen, Rapunzel, König Drosselbart** (*King Thrushbeard*), **Die Bremer Stadtmusikanten**, and many others. Such stories had been transmitted orally from generation to generation and were long considered typically German. Modern research has shown, however, that some of these tales originated in other countries. The story of *Rapunzel,* for example, had already appeared in an Italian collection in 1634; there the heroine is called "Petrosinella." The next traceable reference is from France, where the girl's name is "Persinette." Researchers assume that the story travelled to Germany and Switzerland with Huguenots who left France after Louis XIV lifted the edict that granted them religious freedom. Jacob and Wilhelm Grimm heard many of the stories from women living in and around Kassel in northern Hesse, among them the sixteen-year-old Dorothea Wild, who later became Wilhelm's wife.

Jacob Grimm also wrote the first historical German grammar, in which he compared fifteen different Germanic languages and analyzed their stages of development; and the brothers' work on the **Deutsches Wörterbuch** was a pioneering effort that served as a model for later lexicographers. In 1840 the brothers became members of the German Academy of Sciences in Berlin.

WORTSCHATZ 2

der	König, -e	*king*
das	Gold	*gold*
	Stroh	*straw*
die	Königin, -nen	*queen*
	Welt	*world*

das erste (zweite . . .) Mal	*the first (second . . .) time*
zum ersten (dritten . . .) Mal	*for the first (third . . .) time*
froh	*glad, happy*
nächst-	*next*
niemand	*nobody, no one*
nun	*now*
plötzlich	*sudden(ly)*
voll	*full*
geschehen (geschieht), geschah, ist geschehen	*to happen*
herein·kommen, kam herein, ist hereingekommen	*to enter, come in*
nennen, nannte, genannt	*to name*
spinnen, spann, gesponnen	*to spin*
springen, sprang, ist gesprungen	*to jump*
versprechen (verspricht), versprach, versprochen	*to promise*

WAS IST DAS? der Müller, Ring, Rückweg, Sonnenaufgang; das Feuer, Männchen, Spinnrad; die Nachbarschaft; allein, golden

Rumpelstilzchen

once upon a time
vain
clever / she

talented
test
led / chamber / which

die / locked

necklace

was amazed
expected
greedy / more
ordered

Es war einmal° ein Müller. Er war arm, aber er hatte eine schöne Tochter. Eines Tages geschah es, daß er mit dem König sprach. Weil er eitel° war und dem König gefallen wollte, sagte er zu ihm: „Ich habe eine hübsche und kluge° Tochter. Die° kann Stroh zu Gold spinnen." Der König sprach zum Müller: „Das gefällt mir sehr. Wenn deine Tochter so geschickt° ist, wie du sagst, bring sie morgen in mein Schloß! Ich will sie auf die Probe stellen°." Am nächsten Tag brachte der Müller seine Tochter auf das Schloß. Der König führte° sie in eine Kammer°, die° ganz voll Stroh lag, und sagte: „Jetzt fang an zu arbeiten! Wenn du bis morgen früh nicht das ganze Stroh zu Gold gesponnen hast, mußt du sterben°." Dann schloß er die Kammer zu°, und die Müllerstochter blieb allein darin. 5

Da saß nun das arme Mädchen und weinte, denn sie wußte nicht, wie man Stroh zu 10 Gold spinnt. Da öffnete sich plötzlich die Tür. Ein kleines Männchen kam herein und sagte: „Guten Abend, schöne Müllerstochter! Warum weinst du denn?" „Ach", antwortete das Mädchen, „weil ich Stroh zu Gold spinnen soll, und ich weiß nicht wie." „Was gibst du mir, wenn ich dir helfe?" fragte das Männchen. „Meine goldene Kette°", antwortete das Mädchen. Das Männchen nahm die Goldkette, setzte sich an das Spinnrad und spann bis 15 zum Morgen das ganze Stroh zu Gold. Bei Sonnenaufgang kam der König. Er staunte° und freute sich, als er das viele Gold sah, denn das hatte er nicht erwartet°. Er wurde ganz gierig° und brachte die Müllerstochter in eine andere Kammer, wo noch sehr viel mehr° Stroh lag. Er befahl° ihr, auch das Stroh in einer Nacht zu Gold zu spinnen, wenn ihr das Leben lieb war. Wieder weinte das Mädchen, und wieder öffnete sich die Tür und das Männ- 20 chen kam herein. „Was gibst du mir, wenn ich dir das Stroh zu Gold spinne?" fragte es.

Schloß Neuschwanstein
von Ludwig II. stammt
aus *(dates back to)* dem
19. Jahrhundert.

„Meinen Ring vom Finger", antwortete das Mädchen. Wieder setzte sich das Männchen
ans Spinnrad und spann das Stroh zu Gold. Der König freute sich sehr, aber er hatte immer
noch nicht genug. Er brachte die Müllerstochter in eine dritte Kammer, wo noch mehr
25 Stroh lag und sprach: „Wenn du mir dieses Stroh auch noch zu Gold spinnst, heirate ich
dich morgen." Dabei dachte er sich: Wenn es auch nur eine Müllerstochter ist, eine so
reiche Frau finde ich in der ganzen Welt nicht. Als das Mädchen allein war, kam das
Männchen zum dritten Mal. Es sagte wieder: „Was gibst du mir, wenn ich dir noch einmal
das Stroh spinne?" Die Müllerstochter aber hatte nichts mehr, was sie ihm geben konnte.
30 „Dann versprich mir dein erstes Kind, wenn du Königin bist", sagte das Männchen. Die
Müllerstochter wußte nicht, was sie tun sollte, und sagte ja. Am nächsten Morgen heiratete
sie den König, und sie wurde Königin.

Nach einem Jahr brachte sie ein schönes Kind zur Welt. Sie hatte aber das Männchen
schon lange vergessen. Da stand es aber plötzlich in ihrer Kammer und sagte: „Gib mir das

became afraid
kingdom
living / more important than
grieve / pity
all right / then
keep

messenger

borders

hopped
screamed

brew

devil
stomped / hard on the floor
sank in / grabbed
ripped / in two

retold

Kind, wie du es mir versprochen hast!" Die Königin bekam Angst° und versprach dem 35
Männchen das ganze Gold im Königreich°, wenn es ihr das Kind lassen wollte. Aber das
Männchen sagte: „Nein, etwas Lebendes° ist mir wichtiger als° alles Gold in der Welt." Da
fing die Königin an, so zu jammern° und zu weinen, daß das Männchen Mitleid° bekam.
„Na gut°", sagte es, „du hast drei Tage Zeit. Wenn du bis dahin° meinen Namen weißt,
darfst du das Kind behalten°."   40

   Nun dachte die Königin die ganze Nacht an Namen, und sie schickte einen Boten° über
Land. Er sollte fragen, was es sonst noch für Namen gab. Am ersten Abend, als das Männchen kam, fing die Königin an mit „Kaspar, Melchior, Balthasar . . .", aber bei jedem
Namen lachte das Männchen und sagte: „Nein, so heiß' ich nicht." Am nächsten Tag fragte
man die Leute in der Nachbarschaft nach Namen. Am Abend sagte die Königin dem Männ- 45
chen viele komische Namen wie „Rippenbiest" und „Hammelbein", aber es antwortete
immer: „Nein, so heiß' ich nicht." Am dritten Tag kam der Bote zurück und erzählte: „Ich
bin bis an die Grenzen° des Königreiches gegangen, und niemand konnte mir neue Namen
nennen. Aber auf dem Rückweg kam ich in einen Wald. Da sah ich ein kleines Häuschen
mit einem Feuer davor. Um das Feuer sprang ein komisches Männchen. Es hüpfte° auf 50
einem Bein und schrie°:

   „Heute back ich, morgen brau° ich,
   übermorgen hol ich der Königin ihr Kind;
   ach, wie gut, daß niemand weiß,
   daß ich Rumpelstilzchen heiß!"   55

   Die Königin war natürlich sehr froh, als sie das hörte. Am Abend fragte sie das Männchen erst: „Heißt du vielleicht Kunz?" „Nein." „Heißt du vielleicht Heinz?" „Nein." „Heißt
du vielleicht Rumpelstilzchen?" „Das hat dir der Teufel° gesagt, das hat dir der Teufel
gesagt", schrie das Männchen und stampfte° mit dem rechten Fuß so fest auf den Boden°,
daß es bis zum Körper darin versank°. Dann packte° es den linken Fuß mit beiden Händen 60
riß° sich selbst entzwei°.

Märchen der Brüder Grimm (nacherzählt°)

Zum Text

A.   Erzählen Sie die Geschichte von Rumpelstilzchen noch einmal!   *(Retell the story
in your own words, using the simple past and the following key words.)*

Müller, Tochter, König, Stroh zu Gold spinnen, Kammer, sterben, weinen, Männchen,
Goldkette, Spinnrad, gierig, heiraten, Ring, Kind, Königin, nach einem Jahr, Angst,
Mitleid, behalten, einen Boten schicken, Häuschen, Feuer, springen, Teufel, auf den
Boden stampfen, im Boden versinken (versank), sich selbst in Stücke reißen (riß)

B.   Wußtest du das?   *(Read what the queen tells her son after the death of his father.
Underline the past perfect.)*

Jetzt, wo dein Vater gestorben ist, kann ich dir erzählen, wie es dazu kam, daß dein
Vater und ich heirateten. Er wollte nie, daß du weißt, daß dein Großvater nur Müller
war. Mein Vater brachte mich eines Tages auf das Schloß hier, weil er am Tag davor
dem König gesagte hatte, daß ich Stroh zu Gold spinnen kann. Der König brachte
mich in eine Kammer voll Stroh, und ich sollte es zu Gold spinnen. Ich wußte natürlich nicht, wie man das macht. Weil der König gesagt hatte, daß ich sterben sollte,
wenn das Stroh nicht am nächsten Morgen Gold geworden war, hatte ich große Angst
und fing an zu weinen. Da kam plötzlich ein Männchen in die Kammer. Für meine

Halskette wollte es mir helfen. Bevor es Morgen war, hatte es das ganze Stroh zu Gold gesponnen. Aber dein Vater brachte mich in eine andere Kammer voll Stroh. Wieder kam das Männchen und half mir, nachdem ich ihm meinen Ring gegeben hatte. Aber in der dritten Nacht hatte ich nichts mehr, was ich ihm geben konnte. Da mußte ich ihm mein erstes Kind versprechen. Am nächsten Tag heiratete dein Vater mich, und ich wurde Königin. Nach einem Jahr kamst du auf die Welt, und plötzlich stand das Männchen vor mir und wollte dich mitnehmen. Ich hatte es aber schon lange vergessen. Als ich jammerte und weinte, sagte es, daß ich dich behalten durfte, wenn ich in drei Tagen seinen Namen wußte. Am letzten Tag kam mein Bote zurück und sagte mir, daß er ein Männchen gesehen hatte, wie es um ein Feuer tanzte und schrie: „Ach, wie gut, daß niemand weiß, daß ich Rumpelstilzchen heiß'." Nachdem ich dem Männchen seinen Namen gesagte hatte, riß es sich selbst *(itself)* entzwei, und du durftest bei mir bleiben.

C. Als, wenn oder wann?

1. _____ die Müllerstochter das hörte, fing sie an zu weinen.
2. Immer, _____ die Königin nicht wußte, was sie tun sollte, weinte sie.
3. _____ du mir das Stroh auch noch zu Gold spinnst, heirate ich dich morgen.
4. Das Männchen lachte nur, _____ die Königin fragte, ob es Melchior hieß.
5. _____ die Königin den Namen Rumpelstilzchen nannte, ärgerte sich das Männchen furchtbar.
6. Wir wissen nicht genau, _____ sie geheiratet haben, aber _____ sie nicht gestorben sind *(have died)*, dann leben sie noch heute.

D. Fragen

1. Aus welcher Zeit kommen solche Märchen wie *Rumpelstilzchen?*
2. Warum ist *Rumpelstilzchen* ein typisches Märchen? Was ist charakteristisch für Märchen?
3. Was ist die Rolle der Frau in diesem Märchen? Sieht man die Frau auch heute noch so?
4. Was für Frauen findet man oft in Märchen? In welchen Märchen findet man starke *(strong)* Frauen? Was sind sie oft? Warum?
5. Warum heiratet der König die Müllerstochter? Gibt es das heute auch noch?
6. Wie endet die Geschichte in der englischen Version? Warum? Was für Geschichten hören (oder sehen) Kinder heute? Sind sie anders? Wenn ja, wie?

E. Mischmasch

(Following are three famous fairy tales all mixed together. In each numbered item, select one of the three phrases. Then connect them to one of these stories in its familiar form or, if you prefer, with a different twist. Alternatively, you can create an original fairy tale by supplying your own phrases.)

1. Es war einmal _____
   a. ein Müller. Der . . .
   b. ein kleines Mädchen. Das . . .
   c. ein kleiner Junge mit einer Schwester. Der . . .
   d. _____

2. a. hatte eine alte Großmutter.
   b. hatte eine hübsche Tochter.
   c. hatte immer Hunger.
   d. _____

3. Eines Tages _____ .
   a. rief *(called)* der König ihn / sie aufs Schloß
   b. wurde die Großmutter krank
   c. war wieder nichts im Kühlschrank
   d. _____

4. Da ging er / es / sie _____ ,
   a. in den dunklen Wald
   b. mit einem Kuchen und etwas Wein hin
   c. natürlich hin
   d. _____

5. a. um ihr zu helfen.
   b. um die Tochter zu zeigen.
   c. um etwas Essen zu bringen.
   d. _____

6. Aber er / es / sie _____ .
   a. war nur an Gold interessiert
   b. verlief sich *(got lost)* im Wald
   c. dachte nicht an den bösen *(bad)* Wolf.
   d. _____

7. Plötzlich _____
   a. sah er / sie ein paar schöne Blumen und sagte . . .
   b. kam ein Männchen und fragte . . .
   c. war da ein Häuschen aus Kuchen und Plätzchen und jemand sagte . . .
   d. _____

8. a. „Wer knuspert *(nibbles)* an meinen Häuschen?"
   b. „Sie freut sich bestimmt über ein paar Blumen."
   c. „Warum weinst du?"
   d. _____

9. Da _____
   a. ging er / es / sie zum Spinnrad und sagte . . .
   b. kam eine alte Frau und sagte . . .
   c. kam der böse Wolf und fragte . . .
   d. _____

10. a. „Bleib bei mir, . . .
    b. „Versprich mir dein erstes Kind, . . .
    c. „Wohin gehst du?" . . .
    d. _____

11. a. und ich will alles für dich tun."
    b. dann helfe ich dir."
    c. ich habe Hunger."
    d. _____

12. Später _____
    a. kam er / es / sie zurück und sagte . . .
    b. kam er / es / sie zurück und fragte . . .
    c. fragte er / es / sie . . .
    d. _____

13. a. „Gib mir das Kind, wenn du meinen Namen nicht weißt!"
    b. „Warum hast du so ein großes Maul *(mouth)*?"
    c. „Ich habe genug und möchte nach Hause."
    d. _____

14. Als er / es / sie das hörte, _____ .
    a. fraß er sie / ihn auf *(devoured)*
    b. wurde er / es / sie furchtbar böse
    c. freute er / es / sie sich und nannte ihn bei Namen
    d. _____

15. Da _____ .
    a. schubste *(shoved)* er sie in den Backofen
    b. riß er / sie sich entzwei
    c. kam ein Jäger *(hunter)* zur Hilfe
    d. _____

16. Die Moral von der Geschicht': _____ !
    a. Geh zu fremden Leuten *(strangers)* nicht
    b. Trau *(trust)* einem Wolf nicht
    c. Man muß sich nur zu helfen wissen
    d. _____

Hören Sie zu!

Erkennen Sie diese Märchen?   *(Can you recognize these excerpts from well-known fairy tales? Listen and match the number of the excerpt to the fairy tale listed below.)*

ZUM ERKENNEN: die Stimme *(voice);* wickelte *(wrapped);* der Haken *(hook);* gedeckt *(covered);* brachen ab *(broke off);* schütteten *(dumped);* die Linsen *(lentils);* die Asche; aus·lesen *(pick out);* deshalb *(therefore);* das Maul *(mouth of an animal);* kaum *(hardly);* verschlang *(gulped down);* drehte *(turned);* der Flachs *(flax);* die Spindel *(spindle);* erfüllte sich *(got fulfilled);* der Zauberspruch *(magic spell);* stach *(pricked);* endlich *(finally);* schlief ein *(fell asleep)*

_____ Dornröschen *(Sleeping Beauty)*

_____ Rapunzel

_____ Hänsel und Gretel

_____ Rotkäppchen

_____ Schneewittchen *(Snow White)*

_____ Aschenputtel *(Cinderella)*

HERZLICHEN GLÜCKWUNSCH ZUR VOLLJÄHRIGKEIT!   *coming of age*

UM SICH IN DIESER WELT DURCHZUSETZEN, MUSS MAN: *to succeed*

SCHLAU SEIN WIE EIN FUCHS...   *clever*

...TAPFER WIE EIN LÖWE...   *brave*

...GEDULDIG WIE EIN LAMM...

UND ARBEITSAM WIE EIN PFERD!   *hard working*

SPRECHSITUATIONEN

Expressing Admiration

You have now learned enough adjectives to express admiration for people as well as for objects. Remember that the flavoring particle (or intensifier) **aber** can also express admiration (see p. 203).

> Was für ein netter Mann / eine sympathische Frau!
> So ein interessantes Buch!
> Das ist aber nett!
> Wie nett! / Wie schön!
> Das gefällt mir aber!
> Das finde ich sehr schön!

Telling a Story

As you have seen in the reading text, many fairy tales start with the phrase **Es war einmal...** Here are some common expressions to catch a listener's attention when beginning to relate a story:

> Weißt du, was mir passiert ist *(happened)*?
> Du, mir ist heute / gestern 'was passiert!
> Ich muß dir 'was erzählen.
> Mensch, du glaubst nicht, was . . .
> Ich vergesse nie . . .
> Hast du gewußt, daß . . . ?
> Hast du schon gehört, daß . . . ?

Encouraging a Speaker

Wirklich?	Was hast du dann gemacht?
Natürlich! Klar!	Und wo warst du, als . . . ?
Und (dann)?	Und wie geht's weiter?

Übungen

A. **Was sagen Sie?** *(Express your admiration.)*

1. Sie haben einen besonders guten Film gesehen.
2. Sie haben einen sehr netten Mann / eine sehr nette Frau kennengelernt.
3. Sie haben ein besonders interessantes Museum besucht.
4. Sie sind auf den Turm *(tower)* eines großen Domes gestiegen und haben einen wunderbaren Blick.
5. Ein Freund hat ein sehr schönes, neues Sweatshirt.
6. Freunde haben Sie zum Essen eingeladen. Sie haben nicht gewußt, daß Ihre Freunde so gut kochen können.

7. Ihre Freunde haben ihre neue Wohnung sehr schick eingerichtet *(furnished)*.
8. Sie besuchen eine Professorin. Sie hat wunderschöne Blumen in ihrem Garten.
9. Eine junge Frau mit einem sehr hübschen und freundlichen Baby sitzt neben Ihnen im Flugzeug.
10. Sie sehen sich zusammen ein Photoalbum an. Dabei sehen Sie einige interessante Bilder. (Phantasieren Sie etwas!)

B. **Es tut mir leid, aber . . .**   *(Use your imagination to make excuses.)*

1. Sie sollten heute Ihrem Professor Ihren Aufsatz *(paper)* geben, aber Sie sind noch nicht damit fertig, weil . . .
2. Statt um elf zu Hause zu sein, kommen Sie erst nachts um eins zurück, weil . . .
3. Sie haben Ihren Eltern schon wochenlang nicht mehr geschrieben oder sie angerufen, weil . . .
4. Sie hatten versprochen, mit Ihrem Freund / Ihrer Freundin auszugehen, aber Sie haben es vergessen, weil . . .

C. **Ich muß dir 'was erzählen.**   *(Briefly tell a classmate something interesting that happened to you on your last vacation, during a plane trip, at work, or on a visit to your family. Your partner comments as you tell your story.)*

D. **Kurzgespräche**

1. Review the **Eigenschaften** on p. 299, then discuss with a classmate what kind of person your ideal partner should be.

   BEISPIEL: Er / sie muß viel lesen, Phantasie haben . . .

2. Describe yourself at an earlier age to a classmate. In some of your sentences use modals in the simple past to tell what you had to do or wanted to do.

   BEISPIEL: Als ich klein war, mußte / wollte ich zu Fuß zur Schule gehen . . .

Schick sein, reich sein, cool sein - und sonst nichts?

RÜCKBLICK   KAPITEL 8–11

I. Verbs

pp. 258–60

1. Reflexive Verbs

   If the subject and object of a sentence are the same person or thing, the object is a reflexive pronoun. The reflexive pronouns are as follows:

	ich	du	er / es / sie	wir	ihr	sie	Sie
acc.	mich	dich	**sich**	uns	euch	**sich**	**sich**
dat.	mir	dir	**sich**	uns	euch	**sich**	**sich**

   a. Many verbs can be used reflexively.

      Ich habe (mir) ein Auto gekauft.   *I bought (myself) a car.*

   b. Other verbs must be used reflexively, even though their English counterparts are often not reflexive.

      Ich habe mich erkältet.   *I caught a cold*

   c. With parts of the body, German normally uses the definite article together with a reflexive pronoun in the dative.

      Ich habe mir die Haare gewaschen.   *I washed my hair.*

      You are familiar with the following: sich anhören, sich ansehen, sich anziehen, sich ausruhen, sich ausziehen, sich baden, sich beeilen, sich duschen, sich erkälten, sich fit halten, sich (wohl)fühlen, sich (hin)legen, sich kämmen, sich langweilen, sich (die Nase / Zähne) putzen, sich rasieren, sich (hin)setzen, sich umziehen, sich waschen, sich wünschen (see also 2 below).

p. 279

2. Verbs with Prepositional Objects

   Combinations of verbs and prepositions often have a special idiomatic meaning. These patterns cannot be translated literally but must be learned.

   Er denkt an seine Reise.   *He's thinking of his trip.*

   You are familiar with the following: denken an, erzählen von, halten von, schreiben an, sprechen von, träumen von, warten auf; sich ärgern über, sich freuen auf, sich interessieren für.

3. Infinitive with **zu**

In German the use of the infinitive is much like that in English.

Ich habe viel zu tun.
Ich habe keine Zeit, eine Reise zu machen.
Vergiß nicht, uns zu schreiben!

p. 262

If the infinitive is combined with other sentence elements, a COMMA separates the infinitive phrase from the main clause. If a separable prefix is used, **zu** is inserted between the prefix and the verb.

Hast du Lust, heute nachmittag mit**zu**kommen?
Sie sind ins Kino gegangen, um sich einen neuen Film an**zu**sehen.

REMEMBER: Don't use **zu** with modals! (Möchtest du heute nachmittag **mitkommen**?)

4. Summary of Past Tenses

Be sure to learn the principal parts of verbs (infinitive, simple past, past participle). If you know that a verb is a regular t-verb, all its forms can be predicted; but the principal parts of irregular t-verbs and n-verbs must be memorized. You must also memorize those verbs that take **sein** as the auxiliary verb in the perfect tense.

a. The Perfect Tenses

pp. 124–27, 307–08

- Past participles:

t-verbs (weak verbs)	n-verbs (strong verbs)
(ge) + stem (change) + (e)t	(ge) + stem (change) + en
gekauft	gestanden
geheiratet	
gedacht	
eingekauft	aufgestanden
verkauft	verstanden
telefoniert	

- When used as auxiliaries in the PRESENT PERFECT, **haben** and **sein** are in the present tense. In the PAST PERFECT, **haben** and **sein** are in the simple past.

Er **hat** eine Flugkarte gekauft.   Er **ist** nach Kanada geflogen.
Er **hatte** eine Flugkarte gekauft.   Er **war** nach Kanada geflogen.

- In conversation, past events are usually reported in the present perfect. (The modals, **haben,** and **sein** may be used in the simple past.) The past perfect is used to refer to events happening BEFORE other past events.

Nachdem wir den Film gesehen hatten, haben wir eine Tasse Kaffee getrunken.

pp. 302–04

b. The Simple Past

• Forms:

t-verbs (weak verbs)		n-verbs (strong verbs)	
ich	(e)te		—
du	(e)test		st
er	(e)te		—
	stem (change) +	stem (change) +	
wir	(e)ten		en
ihr	(e)tet		t
sie	(e)ten		en
kaufte		stand	
heiratete			
dachte			
kaufte ein		stand auf	
verkaufte		verstand	
telefonierte			

• In writing, the simple past is used to describe past events. In dialogues within narration, however, the present perfect is correct.

5. Sentence Structure in the Past Tenses

Er **brachte** einen Freund.   . . . , weil er einen Freund **brachte.**
Er **brachte** einen Freund **mit.**   . . . , weil er einen Freund **mitbrachte.**
Er **wollte** einen Freund **mitbringen.**   . . . , weil er einen Freund **mitbringen wollte.**
Er **hat** einen Freund **mitgebracht.**   . . . , weil er einen Freund **mitgebracht hat.**
Er **hatte** einen Freund **mitgebracht.**   . . . , weil er einen Freund **mitgebracht hatte.**
   V1   V2   V2   V1

pp. 306–07

II. The Conjunctions *als, wann, wenn*

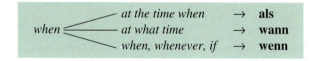

III. Cases

pp. 230–32

1. Genitive

   a. Masculine and neuter nouns have endings in the genitive singular.

   -es: for one-syllable nouns and nouns ending in **-s, -ß, -z, -tz, -zt** (des Kopfes, Halses, Fußes, Salzes, Platzes, Arztes [*physician's*]).

   -s: for nouns of more than one syllable and proper nouns (des Bahnhofs, Lothars, Lothar Müllers).

   b. n-Nouns usually end in **(-e)n; der Name** is an exception (des Herrn, Studenten; BUT des Namens).

2. Summary of the Four Cases

   a. Interrogative Pronouns

nom.	wer	was
acc.	wen	was
dat.	wem	—
gen.	wessen	—

   b. Use of the Four Cases and Forms of **der-** and **ein-**Words

	use	follows . . .	masc.	neut.	fem.	pl.
nom.	Subject, Predicate noun	**heißen, sein, werden**	der dieser ein mein	das dieses ein mein	die diese eine meine	die diese keine meine
acc.	Direct object	**durch, für, gegen, ohne, um**	den diesen einen meinen			
		an, auf, hinter, in, neben, über, unter, vor, zwischen				
dat.	Indirect object	**aus, außer, bei, mit, nach, seit, von, zu**	dem diesem einem meinem	dem diesem einem meinem	der dieser einer meiner	den diesen keinen meinen
		antworten, danken, gefallen, gehören, helfen, zuhören				
gen.	Possessive	**(an)statt, trotz, während, wegen**	des dieses eines meines	des dieses eines meines	der dieser keiner meiner	der dieser keiner meiner

IV. *Da-* and *wo-*Compounds

pp. 280–81

Pronouns following prepositions refer to people; **da-** and **wo-**compounds refer to objects and ideas. Most accusative and dative prepositions, and all two-way prepositions, can be part of such compounds. Prepositions beginning with a vowel are preceded by **dar-** and **wor-**.

Er wartet auf einen Brief.
Worauf wartet er? Er wartet **dar**auf.

V. Adjective Endings

1. Preceded Adjectives

pp. 255–56

Predicate adjectives and adverbs have no endings. Adjectives followed by nouns do have endings.

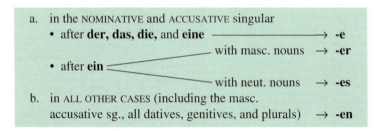

a.   in the NOMINATIVE and ACCUSATIVE singular
   • after **der, das, die,** and **eine** ⟶ **-e**
   • after **ein** ⟶ with masc. nouns → **-er**
      ⟶ with neut. nouns → **-es**
b.   in ALL OTHER CASES (including the masc.
      accusative sg., all datives, genitives, and plurals)   → **-en**

Der alt**e** Fernseher und das alt**e** Radio sind kaputt (*broken*).
Meine alt**er** Fernseher und mein alt**es** Radio sind kaputt.

p. 283

2. Unpreceded Adjectives

a.   Unpreceded adjectives have the endings that the definite article would have if it were used.

Heiß**e** Suppe und heiß**er** Tee schmecken bei kalt**em** Wetter prima.

b.   The following words are often used as unpreceded adjectives: **andere, einige, mehrere, viele,** and **wenige. Viel** and **wenig** in the singular, **mehr** and **ein paar,** numerals, some names of colors (**rosa, lila, beige**), and place names used as adjectives (**Frankfurter, Wiener**) have no endings.

Er hat mehrere interessante Theaterstücke und ein paar kurze Fernsehfilme geschrieben.

VI. Sentence Structure

pp. 236–37

1. Sequence of Adverbs

If two or more adverbs or adverbial phrases occur in one sentence, they usually follow the sequence time, manner, place. The negative **nicht** usually comes after the adverbs of time but before adverbs of manner or place.

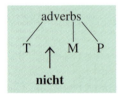

adverbs
T   M   P
nicht

Er fährt morgens gern mit dem Wagen zur Arbeit.
Er fährt morgens **nicht** gern mit dem Wagen zur Arbeit.

2. Summary Chart

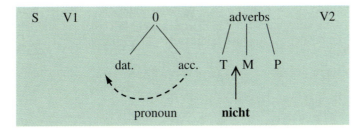

3. Time Expressions pp. 234–35

a. Specific time

To refer to specific time, a definite point in time, or length of time, German uses the ACCUSATIVE: **jeden Tag, nächstes Jahr, eine Woche, einen Monat.**

Other familiar phrases referring to specific time are:

- gerade, am Abend, am 1. Mai, im Mai, in einer Viertelstunde, um zwei Uhr, von Juni bis September, vor einer Woche

- vorgestern, gestern, heute, morgen, übermorgen, Montag, Dienstag, Mittwoch usw.

- früh (morgen), vormittag, mittag, nachmittag, abend, nacht; gestern früh, heute morgen, morgen vormittag, Montag nachmittag usw.

b. Indefinite and nonspecific time

- To refer to an indefinite point in time, the GENITIVE is used: **eines Tages.**

- Familiar time expressions referring to nonspecific times are: montags, dienstags, mittwochs usw.

  morgens, mittags, abends usw.

  bald, manchmal, meistens, monatlich, oft, stundenlang, täglich usw.

Wortschatzwiederholung

A. Fragen

1. **Welches Hauptwort** *(noun)* **kennen Sie dazu?**

   BEISPIEL: anfangen **der Anfang**

   fahren, fliegen, schenken, sprechen, amerikanisch, deutsch, freundlich, glücklich, monatlich, musikalisch, sportlich, verliebt

2. **Was ist ein Synonym dazu?**

   BEISPIEL: mit der Bahn **mit dem Zug**

   mit dem Auto, in 30 Minuten, in einer Viertelstunde, beginnen, laufen, telefonieren, schön

3. **Was ist das Gegenteil davon?**

abfliegen, sich anziehen, ausmachen, einsteigen, finden, gewinnen, weinen, dick, dumm, ehrlich, fleißig, freundlich, furchtbar, gesund, glücklich, hübsch, jung, leicht, lustig, nett, nie, privat, reich, selbständig, sympathisch, verheiratet

4. **Wann wurden** *(were)* **sie geboren?** Antworten Sie mündlich *(orally)*!

BEISPIEL: Hermann Hesse (1877)
   Hermann Hesse wurde 1877 geboren.

a. Johann Sebastian Bach (1685)   **b.** Johann Wolfgang von Goethe (1749)
c. Friedrich Schiller (1759)   **d.** Franz Liszt (1811)   **e.** Thomas Mann (1875)   **f.** Bertolt Brecht (1898)   **g.** Friedrich Dürrenmatt (1921)

B.   **Welches Wort paßt nicht?**

1. wandern, gewinnen, spazierengehen, laufen
2. häßlich, gemütlich, sympathisch, charmant
3. verheiratet, verschieden, ledig, geschieden
4. der Krimi, der Film, der Komponist, der Roman
5. täglich, wöchentlich, monatlich, gewöhnlich

C.   **Was kommt Ihnen dabei in den Sinn?**

BEISPIEL: Koffer   **packen, Reise, Ferien, . . .**

Wunsch, Hochzeit, Welt, Zeitung, Fernsehpause, Hobby, Nase, Auge, Bauch

D.   **Bilden Sie eine Worttreppe!**   *(Working in small groups, compete with other groups to make as long a word chain as possible.)*

BEISPIEL: charman**t**
            tre**u**
                ungemütlich

Strukturwiederholung

* **E.**   **Reflexivverben.** Variieren Sie die Sätze!

1. **Willi hält sich fit.**

   Do you *(formal)* keep fit? They're not keeping fit. How did she keep fit? Keep fit (3 ×). I'd like to keep fit. We must keep fit. We had to keep fit.

2. **Sie erkälten sich wieder.**

   We'll get a cold again. Don't catch a cold again (3 ×). They've caught a cold again. She doesn't want to get a cold again. We had caught a cold again. Why do you *(sg. fam.)* always get a cold? They always caught a cold.

* **F.**   **Am Morgen.** Auf deutsch, bitte!

1. You've *(sg. fam.)* got to get dressed.   **2.** First I want to take a shower and wash my hair.   **3.** And you *(sg. fam.)* need to shave.   **4.** Why don't you *(pl. fam.)* hurry up?   **5.** Listen *(pl. fam.)* to that.   **6.** He got annoyed and sat down.

G. **Verben mit Präpositionen.** Bilden Sie Sätze!

BEISPIEL: schreiben **Ich muß an meine Eltern schreiben.**

denken, erzählen, sich freuen, sich interessieren, sprechen, träumen, warten

H. **Infinitiv mit zu.** Bilden Sie Sätze!

1. **Es ist zu spät . . .**
   in die Oper gehen, ein Geschenk kaufen, an ihn schreiben, mit dem Krimi anfangen, alle einladen, das versuchen

2. **Es ist nicht leicht . . .**
   so früh aufstehen, immer aufpassen, Zeit zum Sport finden, moderne Musik verstehen, einen Roman schreiben, eine Sprache lernen, verlieren

I. **Sagen Sie es im Perfekt!**

1. Wohin geht ihr?—Wir besuchen Onkel Erich.
2. Was machst du heute?—Ich gehe schwimmen.
3. Wie gefällt Ihnen der Film?—Er ist wirklich ausgezeichnet.
4. Warum beeilt sie sich so?—Die Vorstellung fängt um acht an.
5. Weißt du, daß er ein sehr guter Schwimmer ist?—Nein, er spricht nicht viel von sich.
6. Wen ladet ihr ein?—Ein paar Freundinnen und Freunde kommen.

* **J.** **Bilden Sie Sätze im Plusquamperfekt** (past perfect)!

1. wir / nicht / denken / daran
2. Daniela und Yvonne / gehen / zum Schwimmbad
3. wir / sich anziehen / warm
4. er / versprechen / mir / das / schon zweimal
5. Auto / stehenbleiben / plötzlich
6. das / sein / nicht so lustig
7. aber / das / verdienen / er

* **K.** **Die Trappfamilie.** Was fehlt?

1. Gestern abend haben sie im zweit_____ deutsch_____ Fernsehen den bekannt_____ Film über die österreichisch_____ Familie Trapp gespielt. **2.** Erst ist es ein deutsch_____ Theaterstück gewesen, und dann ist daraus ein amerikanisch_____ Film geworden. **3.** Eigentlich kannte ich diesen interessant_____ Film schon von dem amerikanisch_____ Kino. **4.** Aber ich sehe mir gern amerikanisch_____ Stücke in deutsch_____ Sprache an. **5.** Der ganz_____ Film spielt rings um die hübsch_____ Stadt Salzburg. **6.** Am Anfang ist Maria in einem alt_____ Kloster (convent, n.), aber sie fühlt sich bei den streng_____ (strict) Nonnen (nuns, pl.) nicht richtig_____ wohl. **7.** Eines Tages schickt die verständnisvoll_____ Oberin (mother superior) sie zu der groß_____ Familie eines reich_____, verwitwet_____ Kapitäns (m.). **8.** Seine sieben_____ klein_____ Kinder sind anfangs nicht gerade nett_____, aber die temperamentvoll_____ Maria hat viel_____ gut_____ Ideen, wie sie die sieben Kinder unterhalten kann. **9.** Später heiratet der verwitwet_____ Kapitän das jung_____ Fräulein Maria. **10.** Kurz nach ihrer phantastisch_____ Hochzeit kommt das deutsch_____ Militär nach Österreich. **11.** Weil der österreichisch_____ Kapitän nicht zu der deutsch_____ Marine (f.) will, verlassen (leave) sie nach kurz_____ Zeit ihr schön_____ groß_____ Haus und fliehen (escape) über die hoh_____ (high) Berge

Blick auf Salzburg

in die neutral_____ Schweiz. **12.** Heute hat die bekannt_____ Trappfamilie ein neu_____ , groß_____ Haus in dem amerikanisch_____ Staat Vermont. **13.** Wie in viel_____ der sogenannt_____ *(so-called)* wahr_____ *(true)* Geschichten, ist in dem amerikanisch_____ Film *The Sound of Music* nicht alles wahr_____ .
14. Aber es ist ein nett_____ Film mit viel_____ schön_____ Musik.

L. **Ein Rendezvous.** Sagen Sie es im Imperfekt!

1. Sonja und Stephan gehen am Samstag abend aus. **2.** Zuerst versuchen sie, Opernkarten zu bekommen, aber alle Karten sind schon ausverkauft *(sold out)*.
3. Dann wollen sie mit einem Taxi zum Theater fahren, aber sie können kein Taxi finden. **4.** Als sie zum Theater kommen, gibt es auch keine Karten mehr.
5. Aber in der Nähe des Theaters ist ein Kino. **6.** Dort läuft ein neuer Film.
7. Der Film gefällt ihnen ausgezeichnet, weil er sehr komisch ist. **8.** Die Zuschauer lachen oft so laut, daß man nichts hören kann. **9.** Als sie aus dem Kino kommen, sehen sie plötzlich Jürgen und Barbara. **10.** In einem kleinen Restaurant essen sie ein paar Würstchen und trinken dazu ein Glas Bier.
11. Dann bummeln sie gemütlich durch die Stadt nach Hause.

* **M.** **Als, wann oder wenn?**

1. _____ das Stück zu Ende war, klatschten die Leute.
2. Weißt du, _____ die Party anfängt?
3. Könnt ihr mir die Zeitschrift geben, _____ ihr damit fertig seid?
4. _____ ich den Roman vor zwei Jahren las, gefiel er mir nicht so gut.
5. Ich muß immer an euch denken, _____ ich dieses Lied im Radio höre.
6. Er wußte auch nicht, _____ seine Nachbarn zurückkommen sollten.

N. **Der Genitiv.** Verbinden Sie die zwei Wörter wie in den Beispielen!

BEISPIEL: der Sender / der Brief   **der Sender des Briefes**
           der Brief / Annette   **Annettes Brief**

1. das Ende / der Krimi
2. der Genitiv / das Wort
3. die Farbe / unser Auto
4. der Flughafen / diese Stadt
5. der Sohn / mein Onkel
6. der Eingang / euer Haus
7. der Name / der Komponist
8. der Anfang / der Name
9. der Wunsch / alle Kinder
10. die Taschen / manche Frauen
11. die Musik / Beethoven
12. das Stück / Bertolt Brecht
13. die Geschichten / Herr Keuner

O. **wo- und da-Wörter**

1. **Kombinieren Sie!**

   BEISPIEL: mit   **womit? damit**

   durch, in, vor, zu, für, von, über, an, auf, bei

*2. **Was fehlt?**

   a. _____ denkst du? _____ Reise. *(of what, of my)*
   b. _____ spricht Professor Schulz heute? _____ spannenden Roman. *(about what, about a)*
   c. _____ hast du geträumt? _____ Ferien. *(about what, about my)*
   d. _____ wartest du? _____ Brief von Paul. Warte nicht _____ ! *(for what, for a, for that)*
   e. Trudi erzählt immer gern _____ Partys. _____ hat sie gerade erzählt. *(about her, about that)*
   f. Hast du schon _____ Eltern geschrieben? Ja, ich habe am Wochenende _____ geschrieben. *(to your, to them)*
   g. Er hat sich furchtbar _____ Brief geärgert, aber _____ ärgert er sich nicht? *(about the, about what)*
   h. Interessiert Jürgen sich _____ Sport? Nein, _____ interessiert er sich nicht. *(in, in that)*
   i. Interessiert Jürgen sich _____ Sabine? Nein, _____ interessiert er sich nicht. *(in, in her)*

P. **Wann und wie lange?**

1. **Er fährt morgen.**
   the day after tomorrow, after supper, Sundays, tomorrow morning, at 4:30, in 15 minutes, Monday morning, on Tuesday, in February, on the weekend, in the evening, in the fall, most of the time, sometimes, each year, now, never, one day

2. **Er bleibt zwei Tage.**
   from March to May, until Wednesday, until Friday afternoon, until 10:45, for months, one day

Q. **Die Musikschule**   *(Expand the sentences by including the phrases in parentheses.)*

BEISPIEL: Renate ging zur Musikschule in Dresden. (ein paar Jahre)
         Renate ging ein paar Jahre zur Musikschule in Dresden.

1. Ihr Eltern lebten in der Nähe von Meißen. (jahrelang)
2. Renate hat in einem Schülerheim in Dresden gewohnt. (mit vielen Mädchen)
3. Am Wochenende konnte sie einfach schnell nach Hause fahren. (nicht)
4. Sie hatte keine Zeit, jeden Tag mit der Bahn zu fahren. (stundenlang)
5. Dafür ist sie während der Ferien zu Hause gewesen. (gewöhnlich)
6. Ihre Schule soll leicht gewesen sein. (nicht)
7. Sie mußte jeden Tag arbeiten. (schwer)
8. Manchmal hat sie stundenlang Klavier gespielt. (mit ihrer Freundin)
9. Renate hatte sich schon immer für klassische Musik interessiert. (besonders)
10. Wir haben uns vor Jahren kennengelernt. (bei einem Musikwettbewerb in Weimar)

KAPITEL

12

Wege zum Beruf

Kontrolleurin bei der S-Bahn in Hamburg

LERNZIELE

Vorschau
- German schools and vocational training

Gespräche and Wortschatz
- Professions and work

Struktur
- Comparison of adjectives and adverbs
- Future tense
- Nouns with special features: certain predicate nouns and adjectival nouns

Einblicke
- Economic conditions and career decisions

Sprechsituationen
- Expressing agreement and disagreement
- Expressing hesitation

German Schools and Vocational Training

In Germany, education is the responsibility of the individual states. Every child attends the **Grundschule** for the first four years. After that, teachers, parents, and children choose the educational track that best suits a child's interests and abilities. About one third of German students go to a college preparatory school called **Gymnasium**, which runs from grades 5 through 13. During their final two years, students must pass a series of rigorous exams to earn their diploma (**das Abitur**), a prerequisite for university admission. All other students attend either a **Hauptschule** or **Realschule**. The **Hauptschule** runs through grade 9 and leads to some form of vocational training. The **Realschule** runs through grade 10, offering business subjects in addition to a regular academic curriculum, but one less demanding than that of a Gymnasium. Its diploma (**die mittlere Reife**) qualifies students to enter a business or technical college (**Fachschule** or **Fachoberschule**).

This three-tiered school system has often been criticized for forcing decisions about a child's future too early. Therefore a so-called orientation phase (**Orientierungsstufe**) has been introduced for grades 5 and 6 that gives parents more time to decide what school their child should attend. In another effort to increase flexibility, comprehensive schools (**Gesamtschulen**) have been established that combine the three different types of schools into one and offer a wide range of courses at various degrees of difficulty.

Since school attendance is compulsory from ages six to eighteen, most of those who end their general schooling at age fifteen or sixteen must continue in a program of practical, on-the-job training that combines apprenticeships (**Lehrstellen**) with eight to ten hours per week of theoretical instruction in a vocational school (**Berufsschule**). Apprenticeships usually take three years and are considered invaluable by German business and industry. They date back to the Middle Ages, when apprentices served for three years under one or several masters (**Meister**) in order to learn a trade. This principle extends today to all non-academic job training, and few young Germans enter the work force without such preparation for the job market. Apprenticeship training is carefully regulated in order to assure a highly skilled work force.

In 1990 Mecklenburg-Vorpommern, Saxony, Saxony-Anhalt, and Thuringia decided to retain the 12-year pattern of secondary education dating from GDR days, thus creating a discrepancy with the 13-year system in the West. Starting in 1997, the question of 12 vs. 13 years to the *Abitur* is supposed to be resolved. Opponents fear that the quality of education will be jeopardized. Advocates claim that a shortening of educational paths and an earlier entry into professional life will improve German chances in international competition and conform to most other European countries.

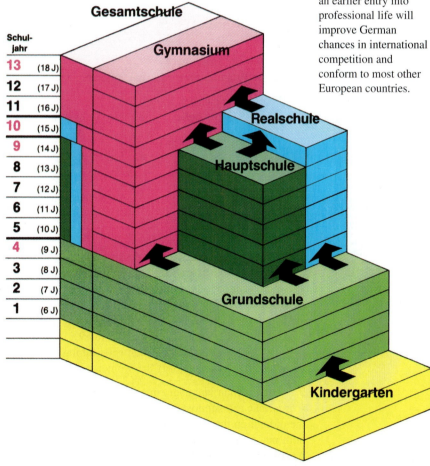

Gespräch   Weißt du, was du werden willst?

TRUDI   Sag mal Elke, weißt du schon, was du werden willst?

ELKE   Ja, Tischlerin.[1]

TRUDI   Ist das nicht viel Muskelarbeit?

ELKE   Ach, daran gewöhnt man sich. Ich möchte mich vielleicht mal selbständig machen.

TRUDI   Das sind große Pläne!

ELKE   Warum nicht? Ich habe keine Lust, immer nur im Büro zu sitzen und für andere Leute zu arbeiten.

TRUDI   Und wo willst du dich um eine Lehrstelle bewerben?

ELKE   Kein Problem. Meine Tante hat ihre eigene Firma und hat mir schon einen Platz angeboten.

TRUDI   Da hast du aber Glück.

ELKE   Und wie ist es denn mit dir? Weißt du, was du machen willst?

TRUDI   Vielleicht werde ich Zahnärztin. Gute Zahnärzte[2] braucht man immer, und außerdem verdient man sehr gut.

ELKE   Das stimmt, aber das ist ein langes Studium.

TRUDI   Ich weiß, aber ich freue mich eigentlich schon darauf.

Was stimmt?

1. Elke will ——— werden.
    a. Lehrerin   b. Sekretärin   c. Tischlerin

2. Sie möchte später gern ——— .
    a. selbständig sein   b. im Büro sitzen   c. für andere Leute arbeiten

3. Elkes Tante hat ——— .
    a. eine Lehrerstelle b. eine Lehrstelle   c. ein Möbelgeschäft

4. Trudi will ——— werden.
    a. Augenärztin   b. Fußärztin   c. Zahnärztin

5. Zahnärzte sollen gut ——— .
    a. dienen   b. verdienen   c. bedienen

Übrigens

1.   As in the United States and Canada, many jobs—especially blue-collar jobs—were until recently considered exclusively "men's work." Statistics show, however, that more and more occupations are now open to both sexes, and in some instances there has been a significant shift. For example, since 1977 the percentage of women being trained as travel agents has risen from 3% to 69%. During that same time period, the number of female typesetter trainees increased from 12% to 59%, and among postal workers 75% are women. There are, however, still more than 130 training fields in which men dominate, compared to 80 in which the vast majority are women.

2.   The German language, just like English, often works to the disadvantage of women; words that are supposedly inclusive (e.g., **Wissenschaftler, Ärzte, Lehrer**) reinforce the old notion that such professions are only for men. Today, official communications use both masculine and feminine forms in order to break out of this pattern (e.g., **Ärzte und Ärztinnen**).

Der Beruf, -e   *(profession, career)*

der	Arzt, ̈e	*physician, doctor*
	Beamte, -n (ein Beamter)[1]	*civil servant*
	Geschäftsmann, -leute	*businessman*
	Ingenieur, -e[2]	*engineer*
	Journalist, -en, -en	*journalist*
	Krankenpfleger, -	*(male) nurse*
	Lehrer, -	*teacher*
	Polizist, -en, -en	*policeman*
	Rechtsanwalt, ̈e	*lawyer*
	Verkäufer, -	*salesman*
	Wissenschaftler, -	*scientist*
	Zahnarzt, ̈e	*dentist*
die	Geschäftsfrau, -en	*businesswoman*
	Hausfrau, -en	*housewife*
	Krankenschwester, -n	*nurse*
	Sekretärin, -nen	*secretary*

[1] See *Struktur* III in this chapter, pp. 342–43.
[2] In most cases the feminine forms can be derived by adding **-in** (der Ingenieur / die Ingenieu**rin**; der Polizist / die Polizist**in**). Some require an umlaut in the feminine form (der Arzt / die **Ä**rztin; der Rechtsanwalt / die Rechtsanw**ä**ltin) or other small changes (der Beamte / die Beam**tin**).

Die Arbeit   *(work)*
Die Ausbildung   *(training, education)*

der	Arbeiter, -	*(blue-collar) worker*	*die*	Firma, Firmen	*company, business*
	Haushalt, -e	*household*		Stelle, -n	*position, job*
	Plan, ̈e	*plan*		Zukunft	*future*
das	Büro, -s	*office*		anstrengend	*strenuous*
	Einkommen, -	*income*		eigen-	*own*
	Geschäft, -e	*business; store*		gleich	*equal, same*
	Problem, -e	*problem*		hoch (hoh-)[3]	*high*
	Unternehmen, -	*large company*		(un)sicher	*(un)safe, (in)secure*

[3] **hoh-** is the adjective; **hoch** is the predicate adjective and adverb: die **hohen** Berge BUT Die Berge sind **hoch.**

Weiteres

an·bieten, bot an, angeboten	*to offer*
sich bewerben (bewirbt), bewarb, beworben (um)	*to apply (for)*
sich gewöhnen an (+ *acc.*)	*to get used to*
glauben (an + *acc.*)	*to believe (in)*
verdienen	*to earn, make money*
Ich will . . . werden.	*I want to be a(n) . . .*
Was willst du werden?	*What do you want to be?*

ZUM ERKENNEN: der Tischler, - *(cabinet maker);* die Muskelarbeit; die Lehrstelle, -n *(apprenticeship);* das Studium *(course of study)*

Zum Thema

A. Kurze Fragen

1. Was ist die feminine Form von Lehrer? Ingenieur? Arzt? Verkäufer? Arbeiter?
2. Was ist die maskuline Form von Rechtsanwältin? Sekretärin? Geschäftsfrau? Journalistin? Beamtin?
3. Wo arbeitet die Apothekerin? die Professorin? der Pfarrer? die Beamtin? der Bäcker? der Verkäufer?

B. Was sind das für Berufe? Sagen Sie's auf englisch, und erklären Sie dann auf deutsch, was die Leute tun!

Zahntechniker/in
Uhrmacher (Meister)
Gebrauchtwagenverkäufer Putzfrau
Fernfahrer   Koch
Chemie-Laboranten(innen)
Bankangestellter
Damen- und Herrenfriseur Telefonistin Sozialpädagogin
Phonotypistinnen
Arztsekretärin
Industriekaufmann
Rechtsanwaltsgehilfin
Diplom-Ingenieur Krankengymnast(in)
REISELEITER/-INNEN **Systemberater(in)** Repräsentanten Bäcker
Haushälterin Zahnarzthelferin
Kassiererin Buchhalter/in PSYCHOLOGE/IN
Fremdsprachenkorrespondentin Hausmeister

C. Zu welchem Arzt / welcher Ärztin geht man?

1. Wenn man Zahnschmerzen hat, geht man zu . . .
2. Wenn man schlechte Augen hat, geht man zu . . .
3. Mit kranken Kindern geht man zu . . .
4. Wenn man Hals-, Nasen- oder Ohrenprobleme hat, geht man zu . . .
5. Frauen gehen zu . . .

D. Männerberufe, Frauenberufe?   *(Working in groups, make a list of professions that in the past had gender preferences. Then decide how the picture looks today. You might like to include some of the vocabulary listed below.)*

ZUM ERKENNEN: Apotheker, -; Architekt, -en, -en; Berater, - *(counselor, adviser)*; Briefträger, -; Dirigent, -en, -en *(conductor)*; Elektriker, -; Fernfahrer, - *(truck driver)*; Friseur, -e / Friseuse, -n *(hairdresser)*; Kindergärtner, -; Klempner, - *(plumber)*; Künstler, - *(artist)*; Makler, - *(real estate agent)*; Maler, - *(painter)*; Maurer, - *(brick-layer)*; Mechaniker, -; Pilot, -en, -en; Psychiater, -; Steuerberater, - *(tax preparer)*; Taxi-fahrer, -; Wirtschaftsprüfer, - *(accountant)*

E.   Ein interessanter Beruf

1.   **Was ist Ihnen am Beruf wichtig?**   *(Poll each other as to the sequence of importance of the points below; then report to the class.)*

☐ viel Reisen
☐ viel Freizeit
☐ viel Prestige
☐ nette Kollegen
☐ saubere Arbeit
☐ Selbständigkeit
☐ ein Geschäftsauto
☐ hohes Einkommen
☐ interessante Arbeit
☐ gutes Arbeitsklima

☐ nicht zu viel Streß
☐ nicht zu viele Risiken *(risks)*
☐ nicht zu viel Fahrerei *(driving)*
☐ nicht zu viel Papierkrieg *(paper work)*
☐ Abwechslung *(variety)*
☐ Gleichberechtigung *(equality)*
☐ sicherer Arbeitsplatz *(job security)*
☐ geregelte Arbeitszeit *(regular work hours)*
☐ eigene Verantwortung *(responsibility)*
☐ die Chance, Karriere zu machen

2.   **In welchen Berufen findet man das?**   *(Tell which professions best meet the criteria mentioned above.)*

F.   **Berufspläne.** Was sagen Sie?

S1   Weißt du schon, was du werden willst?
S2   Ich werde _____ .
S1   Und warum?
S2   _____ . Und wie ist es denn mit dir? Weißt du, was du machen willst?
S1   _____ .
S2   Ist das nicht sehr _____ ?
S1   _____ .

G.   **Aussprache: b, d, g**   *(See also III.3 in the pronunciation section of the Workbook.)*

1.   [p]   A**b**fahrt, A**b**sender, O**b**st, Her**b**st, Er**b**se, hü**b**sch, o**b**, hal**b**, gel**b**
       BUT [p / b] verlie**b**t / verlie**b**en; blei**b**t / blei**b**en; ha**b**t / ha**b**en

2.   [t]   un**d**, gesun**d**, spannen**d**, anstrengen**d**, Gel**d**, Han**d**, währen**d**, sin**d**, sei**d**, abend**s**
       BUT [t / d] Freun**d** / Freun**d**e; Ba**d** / Bä**d**er; Kin**d** / Kin**d**er; wir**d** / wer**d**en

3.   [k]   mittag**s**, unterweg**s**, Ta**g**, Zu**g**, We**g**, Bahnstei**g**, Flugzeu**g**, Ber**g**
       BUT [k / g] fra**g**st / fra**g**en; flie**g**st / flie**g**en; trä**g**st / tra**g**en; le**g**st / le**g**en

Hören Sie zu!

Was bin ich?   *(You will hear five monologs, each describing someone's activities. Figure out what each person's job is and put the number of the description beside the appropriate job title.)*

ZUM ERKENNEN: korrigieren *(to correct)*; weg *(gone)*; hoffen *(to hope)*; die Köchin *(cook)*; schwierig *(difficult)*; Klienten; das Testament *(last will and testament)*

_____ Arzt / Ärztin
_____ Zahnarzt / -ärztin
_____ Krankenschwester / -pfleger
_____ Rechtsanwalt / -anwältin
_____ Hausfrau / -mann

_____ Journalist/in
_____ Sekretär/in
_____ Ingenieur/in
_____ Lehrer/in
_____ Polizist/in

STRUKTUR

I. The Comparison of Adjectives and Adverbs

In English and German adjectives have three degrees:

POSITIVE	COMPARATIVE	SUPERLATIVE
cheap	*cheaper*	*cheapest*
expensive	*more expensive*	*most expensive*

Whereas there are two ways to form the comparative and the superlative in English, there is only ONE WAY in German; it corresponds to the forms of *cheap* above.

NOTE: In German there is no equivalent of such forms as *more* and *most expensive.*

1. In the COMPARATIVE adjectives add **-er**; in the SUPERLATIVE they add **-(e)st**.

> **billig   billiger   billigst-**

a. Many one-syllable adjectives with the stem vowel **a, o,** or **u** have an umlaut in the comparative and superlative, which is shown in the end vocabulary as follows: warm **(ä),** groß **(ö),** jung **(ü).**

warm	**wärmer**	**wärmst-**
groß	**größer**	**größt-**
jung	**jünger**	**jüngst-**

Other adjectives that take an umlaut include: alt, arm, dumm, gesund, kalt, krank, kurz, lang, nah, rot, schwarz

b. Most adjectives ending in **-d** or **-t,** in an **s**-sound, or in vowels add **-est** in the superlative.

kalt	kälter	käl**test-**
heiß	heißer	heiß**est-**
neu	neuer	neu**est-**

Adjectives and adverbs that follow this pattern include: alt (ä), bekannt, charmant, gesund (ü), intelligent, interessant, laut, leicht, nett, oft (ö), rot (ö), schlecht, talentiert, verrückt; hübsch, weiß, kurz (ü), schwarz (ä), stolz; frei.

c. A few adjectives and adverbs have irregular forms in the comparative and / or superlative.

gern	**lieber**	**liebst-**
groß	**größer**	**größt-**
gut	**besser**	**best-**
hoch (hoh-)	**höher**	**höchst-**
nah	**näher**	**nächst-**
viel	**mehr**	**meist-**

2. The comparative of PREDICATE ADJECTIVES (after **sein, werden,** and **bleiben**) and of ADVERBS is formed as described above. The superlative, however, is preceded by **am** and ends in **-sten.**

> **billig   billiger   am billigsten**

Die Wurst ist billig.	*The sausage is cheap.*
Der Käse ist billig**er**.	*The cheese is cheaper.*
Das Brot ist **am** billig**sten**.	*The bread is cheapest.*
Ich fahre **gern** mit dem Bus.	*I like to go by bus.*
Ich fahre **lieber** mit dem Fahrrad.	*I prefer to (I'd rather) go by bike.*
Ich gehe **am liebsten** zu Fuß.	*Best of all I like (I like best) to walk.*
Ich laufe **viel.**	*I walk a lot.*
Theo läuft **mehr.**	*Theo walks more.*
Katrin läuft **am meisten.**	*Katrin walks the most (i.e., more than Theo and I).*

Caution: meisten in **die meisten Leute** is an adjective, **am meisten** is an adverb of manner, and **meistens** an adverb of time.

Die **meisten** Leute gehen gern spazieren.	*Most people love to walk.*
Mein Vater geht **am meisten** spazieren.	*My father walks the most.*
Mein Vater geht **meistens** in den Park.	*My father goes mostly to the park.*

3. As you know, adjectives preceding nouns are called ATTRIBUTIVE ADJECTIVES. In the comparative and superlative they have not only the appropriate comparative or superlative markers, but also the adjective endings they would have in the positive forms (see Chapters 9 and 10).

der gut**e** Käse	der besser**e** Käse	der best**e** Käse
Ihr gut**er** Käse	Ihr besser**er** Käse	Ihr best**er** Käse
gut**er** Käse	besser**er** Käse	best**er** Käse

Haben Sie keinen besser**en** Käse? Doch, aber besser**er** Käse ist teuer**er**.

4. There are four special phrases frequently used in comparisons:

a. When you want to say that one thing is like another or not quite like another, use **(genau)so . . . wie** or **nicht so . . . wie.**

Ich bin **(genau)so alt wie** sie.	*I'm (just) as old as she is.*
Sie ist **nicht so fit wie** ich.	*She is not as fit as I am.*

b. If you want to bring out a difference, use the **comparative + als.**

Ich bin **älter als** Helga.	*I'm older than Helga.*
Er ist **jünger als** sie.	*He is younger than she (is).*

c. If you want to express that something is getting continually more so, use **immer +
comparative.**

Die Tage werden **immer länger.**   *The days are getting longer and longer.*
Ich gehe **immer später** ins Bett.   *I'm getting to bed later and later.*
Autos werden **immer teuerer.**   *Cars are getting more and more expensive.*

d. If you are dealing with a pair of comparatives, use **je + comparative . . . desto +
comparative.**

Je länger, **desto** besser.   *The longer, the better.*
Je länger ich arbeite, **desto**   *The longer I work, the more tired I am.*
  müder bin ich.
Je früher ich ins Bett gehe, **desto**   *The earlier I go to bed, the earlier I get up*
  früher stehe ich morgens auf.   *in the morning.*

Note that **je** introduces a dependent clause. The **desto + comparative** phrase is
followed by a main clause in inverted word order.

Übungen

A. Komparativ und Superlativ. Geben Sie den Komparativ und den Superlativ, und
dann die Formen des Gegenteils!

BEISPIEL: schnell **schneller, am schnellsten**
            langsam **langsamer, am langsamsten**

billig, sauber, gesund, groß, gut, hübsch, intelligent, jung, kalt, lang, laut, nah, neu,
viel, glücklich

B. Ersetzen Sie die Adjektive!

BEISPIEL: Diese Zeitung ist so langweilig wie die andere Zeitung. (interessant)
            Diese Zeitung ist so interessant wie die andere Zeitung.

1. Axel ist so groß wie Horst. (alt, nett)
2. Hier ist es kühler als bei euch. (kalt, heiß)
3. Fernsehsendungen werden immer langweiliger. (verrückt, dumm)
4. Je länger das Buch ist, desto besser. (spannend, interessant)

C. Antworten Sie mit NEIN!   *(Respond negatively, using the adjective or adverb in
parentheses.)*

BEISPIEL: Ist dein Großvater auch so alt? (jung)
            Nein, er ist jünger.

1. Waren euere Schuhe auch so schmutzig? (sauber)
2. Verdient Jutta auch so wenig? (viel)
3. Ist seine Wohnung auch so toll? (einfach)
4. Sind die Geschäftsleute dort auch so unfreundlich? (freundlich)
5. Ist es bei Ihnen auch so laut? (ruhig)
6. Ist die Schule auch so weit weg? (nah)
7. Ist Ihre Arbeit auch so anstrengend? (leicht)

D. **Wie geht's weiter?** *(Complete each sentence, first with a comparative and then with a superlative.)*

BEISPIEL: Inge spricht schnell, aber . . .
Maria spricht schneller. Peter spricht am schnellsten.

1. Willi hat lange geschlafen, aber . . .
2. Brot zum Frühstück schmeckt gut, aber . . .
3. Ich trinke morgens gern Tee, aber . . .
4. Die Montagszeitung ist dick, aber . . .
5. Ich spreche viel am Telefon, aber . . .
6. Deutsch ist schwer, aber . . .
7. Hier ist es schön, aber . . .

E. **Ersetzen Sie die Adjektive!**

BEISPIEL: Peter ist der sportlichste Junge. (talentiert)
Peter ist der talentierteste Junge.

1. Da drüben ist ein moderneres Geschäft. (gut)
2. Mein jüngster Bruder ist nicht verheiratet. (alt)
3. Das ist die interessanteste Nachricht. (neu)
4. Zieh dir einen wärmeren Pullover an! (dick)
5. Die besten Autos sind sehr teuer. (viel)

F. **Vergleiche** *(Complete the following sentence fragments by comparing different professions.)*

BEISPIEL: . . . verdienen viel, aber . . .
Professoren und Professorinnen verdienen viel, aber Ärzte und Ärztinnen verdienen mehr.

1. . . . verdienen wenig, aber . . .
2. . . . haben viel Freizeit, aber . . .
3. . . . haben viel Papierkrieg *(paper work)*, aber . . .
4. . . . haben viel Fahrerei *(driving)*, aber . . .
5. . . . zu sein ist interessant, aber . . .
6. . . . zu sein ist anstrengend, aber . . .

G. **Eine bessere Stelle.** Was fehlt?

1. Möchtest du nicht _____ Postbeamtin werden? *(rather)*
2. Der Staat *(state)* bezahlt _____ deine Firma. *(better than)*
3. Da hast du _____ Sicherheit *(f.)*. *(the greatest)*
4. Bei der Post hast du _____ Freizeit _____ bei deiner Firma. *(just as . . . as)*
5. Vielleicht hast du sogar _____ Zeit _____ jetzt. *(more . . . than)*
6. Es ist auch nicht _____ anstrengend _____ jetzt. *(as . . . as)*
7. _____ Leute arbeiten für den Staat. *(more and more)*
8. Den _____ Leuten gefällt es. *(most)*
9. Ich finde es bei der Post _____ und _____ . *(the most interesting, the most secure)*
10. Eine _____ Stelle gibt es nicht. *(nicer)*
11. _____ du wirst, _____ ist es zu wechseln. *(the older . . . the harder)*

12.   Wenn du eine _____ Stelle haben willst, dann wechsele bald!
      _____ früher, _____ besser. *(better, the . . . the)*

13.   Beamter ist für mich _____ Beruf. *(the best)*

14.   Vielleicht verdienst du etwas _____ . *(less)*

15.   Aber dafür hast du _____ _____ Probleme. *(mostly, few)*

H.   Interview. Fragen Sie einen Nachbarn / eine Nachbarin, . . . !

1.   ob er / sie größer als die Eltern oder Großeltern ist

2.   ob er / sie jüngere Brüder oder Schwestern hat, und wer am jüngsten und wer am ältesten ist

3.   was er / sie am liebsten ißt und trinkt, und ob er / sie abends meistens warm oder kalt ißt

4.   wo er / sie am liebsten essen geht, und wo es am billigsten und am teuersten ist

5.   welche Fernsehsendung ihm / ihr am besten gefällt, und was er / sie am meisten sieht

6.   was er / sie am liebsten in der Freizeit macht, und was er / sie am nächsten Wochenende tut

7.   welche amerikanische Stadt er / sie am schönsten und am häßlichsten findet und warum

8.   wo er / sie jetzt am liebsten sein möchte und warum

PORSCHE
FAHREN IN SEINER SCHÖNSTEN FORM.

II. The Future

As you know, future events are often referred to in the present tense in both English and German, particularly when a time expression points to the future.

Wir **gehen** heute abend ins Kino.
$$\begin{cases} \textit{We're going to the movies tonight.} \\ \textit{We will go to the movies tonight.} \\ \textit{We shall go to the movies tonight.} \end{cases}$$

In German conversation this construction is the preferred form. German does have a future tense, however. It is used when there is no time expression and the circumstances are somewhat more formal.

1.   The FUTURE consists of **werden** as the auxiliary plus the infinitive of the main verb.

werden . . . + infinitive	
ich **werde** . . . gehen	wir **werden** . . . gehen
du **wirst** . . . gehen	ihr **werdet** . . . gehen
er **wird** . . . gehen	sie **werden** . . . gehen

Ich **werde** ins Büro **gehen.**   *I'll go to the office.*
Wirst du mich **anrufen**?   *Will you call me?*

2. If the future sentence also contains a modal, the modal appears as an infinitive at the very end.

> **werden** ... + verb infinitive + modal infinitive

Ich **werde** ins Büro **gehen müssen.**	*I'll have to go to the office.*
Wirst du mich **anrufen können?**	*Will you be able to call me?*

3. Sentences in the future follow familiar word-order rules.

Er **wird** auch **kommen.**

Er **wird** auch **mitkommen.**

Er <u>**wird**</u> auch <u>**mitkommen wollen.**</u>

V1   V2

Ich weiß, daß er auch **kommen wird.**

Ich weiß, daß er auch <u>**mitkommen**</u> <u>**wird.**</u>

V2   V1

4. The future form can also express PRESENT PROBABILITY, especially when used with the word **wohl.**

Er wird wohl auf dem Weg sein.	*He is probably on the way (now).*
Sie wird wohl krank sein.	*She is probably sick (now).*

5. Don't confuse the modal **wollen** with the future auxiliary **werden**!

Er **will** auch mitkommen.	*He wants to (intends to) come along, too.*
Er **wird** auch mitkommen.	*He will come along, too.*

Remember that **werden** is also a full verb in itself, meaning *to get, to become.*

Es **wird** kalt.	*It's getting cold.*

I.   Sagen Sie die Sätze in der Zukunft!   **Übungen**

BEISPIEL: Gute Zahnärzte braucht man immer.
Gute Zahnärzte wird man immer brauchen.

1. Dabei verdiene ich auch gut.   **2.** Aber du studierst einige Jahre auf der Universität.   **3.** Ich gehe nicht zur Uni.   **4.** Meine Tischlerarbeit ist anstrengend.
5. Aber daran gewöhnst du dich.   **6.** Fängst du bei deiner Tante an?   **7.** Dieser Beruf hat bestimmt Zukunft.   **8.** Ihr seht das schon.   **9.** Eines Tages mache ich mich selbständig.   **10.** Als Chefin *(boss)* in einem Männerberuf muß ich besonders gut sein.   **11.** Das darfst du nicht vergessen.   **12.** Aber ich kann vielen Leuten helfen.

J.   Beginnen Sie jeden Satz mit „Wissen Sie, ob ... ?"

BEISPIEL: Er wird bald zurückkommen.
Wissen Sie, ob er bald zurückkommen wird?

1.   Wir werden in Frankfurt umsteigen.
2.   Sie wird sich die Sendung ansehen.

3. Zimmermanns werden die Wohnung mieten.
4. Willi und Eva werden bald heiraten.
5. Müllers werden in Zürich bleiben.
6. Wir werden fahren oder fliegen.

K. Was bedeutet das auf englisch?

BEISPIEL: Martina wird Journalistin.
           Martina is going to be a journalist.

1. Walter will Polizist werden.   **2.** Die Kinder werden zu laut.   **3.** Ich werde am Bahnhof auf Sie warten.   **4.** Petra wird wohl nicht kommen.   **5.** Wir werden Sie gern mitnehmen.   **6.** Sie wird Informatik *(computer science)* studieren wollen.   **7.** Oskar wird wohl noch im Büro sein.   **8.** Wirst du wirklich Lehrer?

L. Eine moderne Familie. Auf deutsch, bitte!

1. Children, I want to tell you something.   **2.** Your mother is going to be a lawyer.   **3.** I'll have to stay home.   **4.** I'll (do the) cook(ing).   **5.** Helga, you will (do the) wash(ing).   **6.** Karl and Maria, you will (do the) clean(ing).   **7.** We'll (do the) shop(ping) together.   **8.** We'll have to work hard.   **9.** But we'll get used to it.   **10.** When we get tired, we'll take a break (**eine Pause machen**).   **11.** Your mother will make a lot of money (earn well).   **12.** And we will help her.

III. Nouns with Special Features

1. Certain predicate nouns

As you already know, German, unlike English, does NOT use the indefinite article before predicate nouns denoting professions, nationalities, religious preference, or political adherence.

Er ist **Amerikaner.**	*He is an American.*
Sie ist **Rechtsanwältin.**	*She's a lawyer.*

When an adjective precedes that noun, however, **ein** is used.

Er ist **ein** typischer Amerikaner.	*He's a typical American.*
Sie ist **eine** gute Rechtsanwältin.	*She's a good lawyer.*

2. Adjectival nouns

ADJECTIVAL NOUNS are nouns derived from adjectives, i.e., the original noun is dropped and the adjective itself becomes the noun. Adjectival nouns are used in English, but not very often. Plural forms usually refer to people, singular nouns to abstract concepts.

*Give me your **tired** (people), your **poor**.*
*The **best** is yet to come.*

German uses adjectival nouns quite frequently. They are capitalized to show that they are nouns, and they have the endings they would have had as attributive adjectives, depending on the preceding article, case, number, and gender. Use the same system you have already learned to put the correct endings on adjectival nouns (see below and Chapters 9 and 10). Masculine forms refer to males, feminine forms to females, and neuter forms to abstract concepts.

der Alte	the old man	mein Alter	my old man, my husband
die Alte	the old woman	meine Alte	my old woman, my wife
die Alten	the old people		
das Alte	the old, that which is old, old things		

Examples of common adjectival nouns are **der / die Bekannte, Deutsche, Kranke, Verlobte.**

Karin hat mich ihrem Verlobten vorgestellt.
Ich habe das Buch einer Bekannten von mir gegeben.

	singular		**plural**
	masc.	**fem.**	
nom.	der **Deutsche** ein **Deutscher**	die Deutsche eine Deutsche	die Deutschen keine Deutschen
acc.	den Deutschen einen Deutschen		
dat.	dem Deutschen einem Deutschen	der Deutschen einer Deutschen	den Deutschen keinen Deutschen
gen.	des Deutschen eines Deutschen	der Deutschen einer Deutschen	der Deutschen keiner Deutschen

Also: der Beamt**e** (ein Beamt**er**)   BUT   die Beamtin (eine Beamtin)

Karl ist Beamt**er**, und seine Frau ist Beamtin.
Ein Beamt**er** hat das gesagt. Wie heißt der Beamt**e**?
Hast du den Beamt**en** da drüben gefragt? Ich sehe keinen Beamt**en**.

M. Auf deutsch, bitte!   **Übungen**

1. He's a composer.
2. Is she a housewife?
3. She's a very good scientist.
4. He's going to be a policeman.
5. He was a bad teacher but a good car salesman.
6. She is Austrian.

N. Adjektive als Hauptwörter   *(Find the adjectival nouns, and give their English equivalents.)*

1. Dem Kranken geht es heute wieder besser.
2. Die Selbständigen werden es leichter haben.
3. Nicht alle Arbeitslosen werden Arbeit finden.
4. Das Dumme ist, daß Thomas morgen nicht kommen kann.
5. Ein Bekannter von uns will uns am Wochenende besuchen.
6. Verheirateten ist so etwas nicht wichtig.
7. Das ist etwas für Unternehmungslustige.
8. Du Glückliche!
9. Gute Gesundheit ist das Wichtigste.

O. Was fehlt?

1. Ein Deutsch_____ hat mir das erzählt.
2. Hast du den nett_____ Deutsch_____ kennengelernt?
3. Geben Sie dem Beamt_____ die Papiere!
4. Auch viele Deutsch_____ sind heute ohne Arbeit.
5. Der Deutsch_____ ist Journalist.
6. Zeigen Sie den Deutsch_____ die Büros!
7. Was hat der Beamt_____ Ihnen gesagt?
8. In Deutschland verdient ein Beamt_____ sehr gut.

Zusammen-fassung

P. Was ich einmal werden möchte / wollte. *(Write eight to ten sentences explaining what you would like to be, or once wanted to be, and why.)*

Q. Zukunftspläne. Auf deutsch, bitte!

1. Did you *(pl. fam.)* know that Volker wants to become a journalist?   **2.** He doesn't want to be a teacher.   **3.** There are only a few teaching positions (**Lehrerstellen**).   **4.** I've gotten used to it.   **5.** Trudi is as enterprising as he is.   **6.** She was my most talented student (**Schülerin**).   **7.** If she wants to become a dentist, she will become a dentist.   **8.** She's smarter, more independent, and nicer than her brother.   **9.** She says that she will work hard.   **10.** I know that she'll be self-employed one day.   **11.** I'll go to her rather than to another dentist.   **12.** The more I think of it, the better I like the idea.

Ohne Worte
Dick Lucas, Masters Agency

EINBLICKE

The worldwide trend toward industrial efficiency (high productivity and low labor costs), coupled with the enormous expenses of unification, have led to high unemployment (**Arbeitslosigkeit**) in Germany: 2.75 million unemployed (**Arbeitslose**) in the old federal states (a 9% jobless rate) and 1.27 million in the new federal states (16.5%) in 1994. In addition, some two million workers—1.4 million in eastern Germany alone—were in state-financed training and retraining programs or in early retirement. Rebuilding and privatizing the uncompetitive, formerly state-run industries of the new federal states in this era of increased international competition and recession has turned out to be much more difficult than anticipated.

Hard times are also forcing unions (**Gewerkschaften**) to compromise on their long-standing goals of ever higher pay, longer vacations, and more fringe benefits. In November 1993, for example, Volkswagen labor and management negotiated a four-day work week with reduced pay in order to save 30,000 jobs. Such concessions reflect the changing balance of power in German industry and mean a setback for labor, whose representatives—in accordance with the German law of co-determination—sit on the boards of directors in their respective industries. Unions are now finding it harder to flex their muscles, and high-tech industries and the growing service sector are less receptive to their efforts. Nonetheless, labor unions are still very important in Germany. Their flexibility and cooperative, non-confrontational partnership with management have contributed to four decades of relative industrial peace and one of the highest living standards in the world.

Lehrling *(apprentice)* und Meister

WORTSCHATZ 2

der	Bekannte (ein Bekannter)	*acquaintance*
das	Ding, -e	*thing*
die	Entscheidung, -en	*decision*
	Erfahrung, -en	*experience*
	Sicherheit	*safety, security*
	Umwelt	*environment*

deshalb	*therefore, that's why*
ins / im Ausland	*abroad*
sobald	*as soon as*
unbedingt	*definitely*
unter *(+ dat.)*	*among*
wahrscheinlich	*probably*
zuerst	*(at) first*
schwierig	*difficult*
aus·sehen (sieht aus), sah aus, ausgesehen	*to look (like), appear*
bitten, bat, gebeten	*to ask, request*
erwarten	*to expect*
hoffen	*to hope*
sich Sorgen machen (um)	*to be concerned, worry (about)*
sich vor·stellen	*to imagine*
ich stelle mir vor, daß . . .	*I imagine that . . .*

WAS IST DAS?   der Arbeitgeber, Auslandsaufenthalt, Bauboom, Bauingenieur, Biochemiker, Biologe, Briefsortierer, Computerkünstler, Küchenschrank, Physiker, Produzent, Telekommunikationsspezialist, Umweltexperte; das Filmstudio, Industrieunternehmen, Produkt; die Anwaltsfirma, Berufsentscheidung, Flexibilität, Hälfte, Mobilität, Umweltberaterin; eine Weile, in der Zwischenzeit; beruflich, chemisch, flexibel, geschäftlich, kreativ, ökologisch, praktisch, problematisch, umweltfreundlich, zukunftssicher; eröffnen, jobben, organisieren, reduzieren, transportieren

Berufsentscheidungen

(Eine öffentliche Diskussion an der Universität Göttingen)

Wie viele andere Studenten und Studentinnen, macht Lore Weber sich Sorgen um ihre berufliche Zukunft. Sie hat deshalb eine Diskussionsgruppe organisiert und eine Professorin und andere Studenten gebeten, Ideen beizutragen°.

to contribute

LORE WEBER: Eine der wichtigsten Fragen heute ist die Frage der Berufswahl°. Die Arbeitslosigkeit ist hoch, nicht nur unter den Arbeitern, sondern auch unter uns Akademikern°. In der Zeitung lesen wir zum Beispiel, daß die chemische Industrie immer mehr Stellen reduzieren und ganze Forschungszweige° ins Ausland verlegen° wird, wo gut ausgebildete Physiker, Chemiker oder Biologen billiger zu haben sind. Die Automobilbranche°, eine der wichtigsten Arbeitgeber für Ingenieure, ist auch unsicherer geworden. Mehr als die Hälfte der Industrieunternehmen werden in den nächsten Jahren Arbeitsplätze abbauen°, und im öffentlichen Dienst°, an Schulen und Universitäten wird es nicht besser aussehen. Mehrere meiner Freunde suchen schon lange Arbeit und jobben in der Zwi-

. . . choice

university graduates

fields of research / transfer

. . . industry

reduce / civil service

5

10

schenzeit als Kellner oder Verkäufer, Taxifahrer oder Briefsortierer bei der Post. Wir fragen
uns alle, wie unsere Zukunft aussehen wird, und hoffen, daß wir durch unsere Diskussion
15   eine bessere Vorstellung° davon bekommen.   *idea*

      Wir werden einfach der Reihe nach vorgehen°. Ich möchte Frau Professor Weigel   *proceed one after the other*
zuerst bitten, ihre Ansichten° über das Problem zusammenzufassen°. Frau Professor   *opinions / to summarize*
Weigel!

PROFESSOR WEIGEL: Vielen Dank, Frau Weber! Auf die Frage nach zukunftssicheren
20   Berufen kann man nur schwer eine Antwort geben. Die Berufswahl wird immer problema-
tischer. Zu den Berufen mit Zukunft zählen aber bestimmt Umweltexperten, Biochemiker,
Telekommunikations- und Computerspezialisten oder Rechtsanwälte.[1] Auch Architekten
und Bauingenieure haben gute Chancen, denn der Bauboom wird sicher noch eine ganze
Weile anhalten°: Bis zum Jahr 2005 sollen allein in den neuen Ländern Gebäude° für unge-   *continue / buildings*
25   fähr 2,4 Billionen Mark entstehen°. Selbständige in den verschiedenen Branchen werden   *be built*
auch genug Arbeit finden. Den Geisteswissenschaftlern° unter Ihnen empfehle ich, flexibel   *humanities scholars*
zu bleiben und auch außerhalb° Ihres Studiums praktische Erfahrungen zu sammeln, zum   *outside of*
Beispiel bei Verlagen° und anderen Firmen oder durch Auslandsaufenthalte. Was Sie auch   *publishing houses*
unbedingt brauchen, sind Informatikkenntnisse°. Eins ist klar, eine gute und breite° Ausbil-   *computer skills / broad*
30   dung ist und bleibt die beste Sicherheit. Neben guten Sprach- und Fachkenntnissen° wird   *special skills*
man Zusatzqualifikationen° suchen, wie zum Beispiel Flexibilität, Mobilität und die   *additional . . .*
Fähigkeit°, immer wieder Neues zu lernen und kreativ zu denken.   *ability*

BRIGITTE SCHINDLER: Ich habe Biologie studiert und werde ab° 1. Oktober an einem   *starting*
privaten Umweltforschungsinstitut in Berlin arbeiten. Als Umweltberaterin werde ich
35   ökologische Bilanzen für Unternehmen aufstellen°. Zum Beispiel werde ich Baustoffpro-   *make . . . evaluations*
duzenten° zeigen, wie sie die Umwelt belasten°, oder Tiefkühlkostproduzenten°, wie sie   *building materials . . . / pol-*
ihre Produkte umweltfreundlicher transportieren können. Als ich anfing zu studieren,   *lute / frozen foods . . .*
wollte ich eigentlich Lehrerin werden, aber so° finde ich meine Zukunft viel interessanter.   *in this way*

JÜRGEN SCHMIDT: Ich studiere Betriebswirtschaft°. Nach dem Studium möchte ich   *business administration*
40   mich selbständig machen. Mein Bruder und ich haben schon ein kleines Geschäft für
Kücheneinrichtungen° eröffnet. Zwei andere Studenten machen mit°, und wir haben sogar   *. . . furnishings and appli-*
eine Verkäuferin. Mein Bruder kümmert sich um° solche Dinge wie den Einbau° von   *ances / participate / takes*
Küchenschränken, und ich mache den geschäftlichen Teil. Sobald ich meine Prüfungen   *care of / installation*
hinter mir habe, werde ich mich in Dresden[2] oder Leipzig[3] umsehen°, um dort vielleicht ein   *look around*
45   Geschäft zu eröffnen. Unser Geschäft hier läuft ausgezeichnet, und ich erwarte, daß die
Nachfrage° dort noch größer sein wird.   *demand*

DETLEF GEERDS: Ich bin gerade mit meinem Jurastudium° fertig geworden. Auch ich   *study of law*
ziehe° in den Osten. Ein Bekannter von mir hat mir eine Stelle in seiner Anwaltsfirma in   *move*
Rostock[4] angeboten. Die Chancen für Rechtsanwälte sind in den neuen Ländern ausge-
50   zeichnet. Stellt euch vor, 1989 hat es in der ganzen DDR nur 400 Rechtsanwälte gegeben,
aber in Hamburg allein über 4000! Das Leben in Rostock wird am Anfang bestimmt
schwieriger sein als hier, aber auch interessanter. Außerdem wird mein Einkommen höher
sein, und ich werde wahrscheinlich schneller Partner werden.

KATRIN SCHNEIDER: Ich studiere Kunst und Informatik. Ich hoffe, daß ich eines Tages
55   als Computerkünstler für ein Filmstudio oder beim Fernsehen arbeiten werde. Ich finde es
wichtig, daß die Arbeit Spaß macht. Nur wenn man etwas gern tut, kann man wirklich gut
sein. Und weil die Arbeitslosigkeit unter uns Frauen größer ist als unter Männern, müssen
wir einfach besser sein. Ich versuche gerade, einen Platz für ein Praktikum° in Amerika zu   *practical training*
finden. Je mehr man gemacht hat, desto besser die Chancen. Die besten Jobs bekommen
60   nur die Besten.

Zum Text

A. Aussagen zum Text

1. Viele deutsche Firmen werden in den nächsten Jahren _____ .
   a. die meisten Physiker, Chemiker und Biologen ins Ausland schicken
   b. Arbeitsplätze reduzieren
   c. die billigsten Arbeiter haben

2. Frau Professor Weigel glaubt, daß Studenten vor allem _____ brauchen.
   a. Auslandsaufenthalte
   b. Rechtsanwälte
   c. Flexibilität, Mobilität und Kreativität

3. Brigitte Schindler wird ab 1. Oktober _____ .
   a. die Umwelt weniger belasten
   b. als Umweltberaterin arbeiten
   c. höchstwahrscheinlich als Lehrerin in Berlin arbeiten

4. Jürgen Schmidt möchte _____ .
   a. ein zweites Geschäft in einem der neuen Länder eröffnen
   b. seine Prüfungen so schnell wie möglich hinter sich haben
   c. Betriebswirtschaft studieren

5. Detlef Geerds erzählt, daß _____ .
   a. es in Ostdeutschland keine Rechtsanwälte gibt
   b. es in der DDR nur ungefähr 4000 Rechtsanwälte gegeben hat
   c. er in Rostock als neuer Rechtsanwalt besser verdienen wird als in Westdeutschland

6. Katrin Schneider stellt sich vor, daß _____ .
   a. Informatik für sie sehr schwierig sein wird
   b. Frauen beruflich besser sind als Männer
   c. die Chancen besser sind, wenn man auch praktische Erfahrungen in der Berufswelt hat

B. Wunschprofil von Arbeitgebern
(What employers are looking for. Working in groups, see how many statements you can make about this chart, using comparatives and superlatives.)

BEISPIEL: Flexibilität ist den Arbeitgebern am wichtigsten.

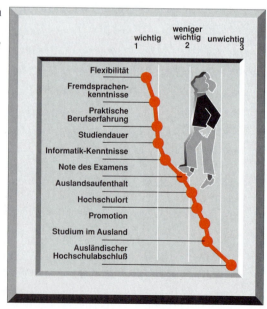

ZUM ERKENNEN: Hochschulort *(university location);* Hochschulabschluß *(university degree)*

C.   Blick auf den Arbeitsmarkt. Wiederholen Sie die Sätze in der Zukunft!

1. Die Berufswahl bleibt eine der wichtigsten Entscheidungen.   **2.** Gut ausgebildete Chemiker, Physiker und Biologen sind im Ausland billiger.   **3.** Deshalb verlegen immer mehr Unternehmen ganze Forschungszweige ins Ausland.   **4.** Das macht den Arbeitsmarkt für deutsche Wissenschaftler nicht leichter.   **5.** Ich denke, daß wirklich gute Leute immer Arbeit finden.   **6.** Ich weiß aber auch, daß man oft länger danach suchen muß.   **7.** Die besten Jobs bekommen nur die Besten.

D.   So wird's werden. Was fehlt?

1. _____ Leute müssen in der Zukunft wenigstens einmal ihren Beruf wechseln. *(most)*
2. Gute theoretische Kenntnisse werden _____ wichtig sein _____ praktische Erfahrungen. *(just as . . . as)*
3. _____ praktische Erfahrung man hat, _____ sind die Berufschancen. *(the more . . . the better)*
4. Man wird auch _____ Zusatzqualifikationen suchen. *(more and more)*
5. Detlef sagt, daß es 1989 in der ganzen DDR _____ 400 Rechtsanwälte gegeben hat. *(fewer than)*
6. Er hofft, in Rostock ein _____ Einkommen zu haben _____ in Göttingen. *(higher . . . than)*
7. _____ er seine Prüfungen hinter sich hat, wird er dorthin ziehen *(move)*. *(as soon as)*

E.   Stellenangebot   *(Write down a list of five to six questions you would ask during an interview for the advertised position.)*

F.   Was bin ich?   *(Using the **Hören Sie zu** section on p. 335 as a model, write your own "Who am I"-section, and let others in the class guess your occupation.)*

G.   In zehn / zwanzig Jahren   *(Write a paragraph of eight to ten sentences telling how you picture your life ten, twenty, or thirty years from now.)*

BEISPIEL: In zehn Jahren werde ich dreißig sein. Dann werde ich . . .
In zehn Jahren wird nichts mehr ohne den Computer gehen . . .

Hören Sie zu!

Drei Lebensläufe   *(Listen to the brief summaries of three young Germans' lives. You will find that they are quite unlike the résumés expected by employers in the U.S. and Canada. Then decide whether the statements below are true or false according to what you hear. It might be helpful to reread the **Vorschau** to this chapter before beginning this activity.)*

ZUM ERKENNEN: halbtags *(part-time);* verlassen *(to leave);* Schwerpunktfächer *(majors);* der Schreibmaschinenkurs *(typing course);* der Vorarbeiter *(foreman);* zum Militär *(to the army);* der Autounfall *(accident);* gestorben *(died);* bestanden *(passed)*

Richtig oder falsch?

—— 1.   Die Schmidts haben zwei Kinder, eine Tochter und einen Sohn.
—— 2.   Claudias Vater ist Ingenieur, ihre Mutter Sekretärin.
—— 3.   Claudias Schwerpunktfächer sind Deutsch und Mathematik.
—— 4.   Sie möchte am Abend Schreibmaschinenschreiben lernen.
—— 5.   In ihrer Freizeit liest und schwimmt sie.
—— 6.   Wolf Wicke ist am 23. 11. 1977 geboren.
—— 7.   Seine Eltern sind geschieden.
—— 8.   Er hat zwei jüngere Schwestern.
—— 9.   Wolf macht eine Lehre und geht zur Hauptschule.
—— 10. Wolf ist schon beim Militär gewesen.
—— 11. Christinas Mutter lebt nicht mehr.
—— 12. Christinas Bruder ist vier Jahre älter als sie.
—— 13. Nach dem Abitur hat sie zuerst ein Jahr gearbeitet.
—— 14. Jetzt ist sie Medizinstudentin in Heidelberg.
—— 15. Christina läuft gern Ski.

Übrigens

1.   The transition to a market economy in eastern Germany was facilitated by a government agency, called **die Treuhand[anstalt],** that was charged with privatizing, rehabilitating, or closing down state-owned enterprises from the days when the economy was centrally controlled. When the agency began operations in 1990, it assumed control of 8,000 combines (or "peoples' enterprises") that operated some 45,000 factories. In 1994 the Treuhand's unfinished business was turned over to the private business sector, a move that brought a bonanza to attorneys who specialize in property rights and employment law.

Der Dresdener Zwinger

2.   Dresden (pop. 519,000) experienced its "golden age" in the 18th century under the rule of Frederick August I of Saxony, who was also king of Poland. During his reign, the Frauenkirche and palace complex (**der Zwinger**), both masterpieces of European architecture, were constructed. The city became a major art center and was known throughout the world as the "Florence on the Elbe River." Reduced to rubble by Allied bombing just before the end of World War II, Dresden is now a center for trade and industry and for art and music. The Semper Opera House, where both Richard Wagner and Carl Maria von Weber conducted, was reopened in 1985. Reconstruction of the Frauenkirche, left in ruins since 1945, was begun in 1994.

3.   Leipzig (pop. 554,000) is known not only for its international industrial fair that began in the Middle Ages, but also for its printing and publishing industry that dates back to the 15th century. Johann Sebastian Bach spent many years in Leipzig. Goethe studied at the University of Leipzig, and Richard Wagner was born there. In the course of history, Leipzig was the scene of terrible battles several times, especially during the Thirty Years' War (1618–1648). In 1813 more than 300,000 soldiers fought there against 191,000 of Napoleon's troops, leaving some 90,000 casualties. The citizens of Leipzig played a major role in the toppling of the East German regime; in 1989 they demonstrated almost daily against the government. This action earned Leipzig the title "city of heroes."

4.   Rostock (pop. 239,000) lies on the Warnow River, which connects it with Warnemünde, its port on the Baltic. In the late Middle Ages the city was a powerful member of the Hanseatic League. Once proudly referred to as "East Germany's gateway to the world," today Rostock's industries—shipbuilding, fish processing, chemicals, and heavy manufacturing—are going through a painful transition.

SPRECHSITUATIONEN

When you participate in a discussion of a controversial topic, you need to be able to express agreement or disagreement.

Expressing Agreement

(Das ist) richtig.
Genau. *(Exactly.)*
Das stimmt (genau).
Das ist (leider) wahr.
Natürlich. / (Na) klar. / Sicher.
Sie haben recht. / Da hast du recht.
Das finde / glaube ich auch.
Das hoffe ich auch.

Expressing Disagreement

Das stimmt nicht.
(Das ist) gar nicht wahr.
Das finde ich (gar) nicht.
Das glaube ich (aber) nicht.
Das kann nicht sein.
Ach was! *(Oh, come on!)*
Unsinn! Quatsch! *(Nonsense!)*
Im Gegenteil. *(On the contrary.)*
Das ist doch lächerlich *(ridiculous)*.
Auf der einen Seite / auf der anderen Seite *(hand)* . . .

Expressing Hesitation

If you don't know how you feel about a topic or what to say—which might happen when conversing in a foreign language—you can use one of these phrases to bridge the gap or stall for time.

Ach so.   Gute Frage.
Nun / also / na ja / tja *(well)* . . .   Ich weiß nicht.
Das kommt darauf an.   (Ich habe) keine Ahnung.

Wir suchen lebensfrohe, selbstbewußte Frauen als Pflegemütter im SOS-Kinderdorf. Viele Kinder kennen kein intaktes Elternhaus. Im SOS-Kinderdorf finden sie eine neue Familie – ihre SOS-Kinderdorf-Familie.

SOS-Kinderdorf e.V.

Frau K. Wilhelms
Renatastr. 77
80639 München 19

A.   Was hältst du davon?   *(Working with a classmate, take turns expressing your feelings about the statements below.)*

1.   Die Schweiz ist keine Reise wert.
2.   Wir haben heute schon viel zu viel Freizeit.
3.   Wir leben heute gesünder als unsere Eltern und Großeltern.
4.   Es ist heute noch wichtiger als früher, Fremdsprachen zu lernen.
5.   Wir sitzen alle zu viel vor dem Fernseher.
6.   Fernsehen macht dumm.
7.   Kinder interessieren sich heute nicht mehr für Märchen.
8.   Die meisten Menschen verdienen lieber weniger Geld und haben mehr Freizeit.
9.   Wenn mehr Menschen weniger arbeiten, können mehr Menschen arbeiten.
10.   Je länger man im Ausland arbeitet, desto besser sind die Berufschancen.
11.   Weil immer mehr Leute Englisch lernen, wird es für Amerikaner und Kanadier immer uninteressanter, Deutsch zu lernen.
12.   Ich stelle mir vor, daß es nächstes Jahr in der Wirtschaft viel besser aussehen wird.

B.   Was denkst du?   *(Take turns with a classmate asking each other questions. Express hesitation before you answer.)*

1.   Was willst du einmal werden? Warum? (Warum bist du . . . geworden?)
2.   Wohin möchtest du am liebsten reisen? Warum?
3.   Möchtest du gern für den Staat arbeiten? Warum (nicht)?
4.   Was für Sendungen siehst du am liebsten im Fernsehen? Warum?
5.   Wie hältst du dich am liebsten fit? Warum?
6.   Welche Eigenschaft ist dir am wichtigsten bei einem Freund / einer Freundin oder einem Partner / einer Partnerin?
7.   Was ist dir in deinem Leben am wichtigsten?

C.   An wen denke ich?   *(Work in groups of four to five students. One thinks of a famous person, the others may ask up to twenty questions to figure out who it is.)*

D.   Kurzgespräche

1.   With a partner, discuss what <u>you</u> see as the advantages and disadvantages of the German school and job-training system in comparison with the American or Canadian system. Express your agreement or disagreement with your partner's opinion.

2.   With a partner, discuss the advantages and disadvantages of various job choices: which jobs you find interesting, lucrative, boring, too demanding, underpaid, etc. Take turns making statements, and express your agreement or disagreement with what your partner has said.

3.   You are discussing your job choice (**Photograph, Beamter, Krankenpfleger/in,** etc.) with your parents. They are not happy with your choice and express their disagreement. You agree or disagree with their objections

Das Studium

Studenten vor der Johann Wolfgang von Goethe Universität in Frankfurt am Main

LERNZIELE

Vorschau

- German universities

Gespräche and Wortschatz

- University study and student life

Struktur

- Subjunctive mood
- Present-time general subjunctive (Subjunctive II)
- Past-time general subjunctive

Einblicke

- The university system and a year abroad

Sprechsituationen

- Giving advice
- Asking for permission
- Granting or denying permission

German Universities

The first German universities were founded in the Middle Ages: Heidelberg in 1386, Cologne in 1388, Erfurt in 1392, Leipzig in 1409, and Rostock in 1419. In the beginning of the 19th century, Wilhelm von Humboldt redefined the purpose and mission of universities as institutions for pure research and independent studies by the nation's pre-eminent minds. In time, however, it became obvious that this ideal conflicted with the requirements of modern industrial society. In an effort to open opportunities to more students, many new universities and technical colleges (**Fachhochschulen**) have been founded, especially in the last twenty-five years.

There is no tradition of private universities in Germany. Practically all universities are state supported and require no tuition (**Studiengebühren**); students pay only certain activity fees and mandatory health insurance. If neither the students nor their parents are able to pay for their living expenses, the state helps out. Under the Federal Education Promotion Act (**Bundesausbildungsförderungsgesetz** = **BAföG**), students can obtain financial assistance, half of the amount as a grant and the other half as a loan to be repaid when the student enters a profession.

Although it is becoming increasingly difficult to find employment after graduation, students continue to go to universities in record numbers. Nearly every third young person prepares to attend the university. This enormous growth in the number of students has led to overcrowding and admissions restrictions (**Numerus clausus**) for some subjects. Openings are filled on the basis of high school grades and allocated by a central office in Dortmund, with a certain percentage of places reserved for foreign applicants.

Because German students spend an average of fourteen semesters (seven years!) at the university, and because many have completed basic military training or an apprenticeship before beginning their studies, most graduates are older than their international counterparts. When they finally enter the workforce, they usually have to compete with a younger international labor market. In an effort to address this issue and to reduce overcrowding and costs, discussions are underway to limit the number of semesters students may study and to require that they take their final comprehensive exams earlier.

Wie lange sie studieren
Durchschnittliche Studiendauer an den Hochschulen in Jahren

5,9 Jahre 7,5 Jahre 7 Jahre 7 Jahre unter 4 Jahre

Gespräche   Bei der Immatrikulation

PETRA   Hallo, David! Wie geht's?
DAVID   Danke, gut. Und dir?
PETRA   Prima. Was machst du denn da?
DAVID   Ich muß diese Einschreibungsformulare ausfüllen.
PETRA   Soll ich dir helfen?
DAVID   Wenn du Zeit hast. Ich kämpfe immer mit der Bürokratie.
PETRA   Hast du deinen Paß dabei?
DAVID   Nein, wieso?
PETRA   Darin ist deine Aufenthaltserlaubnis[1]; die brauchen wir.
DAVID   Ich kann ihn ja schnell holen.
PETRA   Mach das! Ich warte hier so lange auf dich.

Etwas später

DAVID   Hier ist mein Paß. Ich muß mich jetzt auch bald entscheiden, was ich belegen will. Kannst du mir da auch helfen?
PETRA   Na klar. Was ist denn dein Hauptfach? Wofür interessierst du dich?
DAVID   Mein Hauptfach ist moderne Geschichte. Ich möchte Kurse über deutsche Geschichte und Literatur belegen.
PETRA   Hier ist mein Vorlesungsverzeichnis. Mal sehen, was sie dieses Semester anbieten.

Was fehlt?   *(Complete the following sentences.)*

1. David füllt gerade ein . . . aus.   2. Leider hat er seinen . . . nicht dabei.   3. Er muß ihn erst . . .   4. Im Paß ist seine . . .   5. David weiß noch nicht, was er . . . soll.   6. Petra fragt ihn, wofür er . . .   7. Sein Hauptfach ist . . .   8. Petra kann ihm helfen, weil sie ihr . . . dabei hat.

Übrigens

1.   Everyone who establishes residence in Germany must register with the local registration office (**Einwohnermeldeamt**) within three to seven days of moving. Non-Germans who wish to reside in Germany longer than three months must get a residence permit (**Aufenthaltserlaubnis**). In addition, they are required to take a medical examination at the public health department (**Gesundheitsamt**). A work permit (**Arbeitserlaubnis**) is available to a non-German only if a German or other EU-citizen cannot fill the job.

WORTSCHATZ 1   Das Studium   *([course of] study)*

der			*das*		
	Hörsaal, -säle	*lecture hall*		Seminar, -e	*seminar*
	Kurs, -e	*course*		Stipendium, Stipendien	*scholarship*
	Professor, -en	*professor*			
	Zimmerkollege, -n, -n	*roommate*		System, -e	*system*

das	Fach, ⸚er	*subject*	die	Arbeit, -en	*here: (term) paper*
	Hauptfach, ⸚er	*major (field)*		Note, -n	*grade*
	Nebenfach, ⸚er	*minor (field)*		(Natur)wissen-	*science*
	Labor, -s	*lab*		schaft, -en	
	Quartal, -e	*quarter*		Zimmerkollegin,	*roommate*
	Semester, -	*semester*		-nen	

belegen	*to sign up for, take (a course)*
sich entscheiden, entschied, entschieden	*to decide*
holen	*to get (fetch)*
lehren	*to teach*
eine Prüfung machen	*to take an exam*
(eine Prüfung) bestehen, bestand, bestanden	*to pass (a test)*
(bei einer Prüfung) durch·fallen (fällt durch),	*to flunk (a test)*
fiel durch, ist durchgefallen	

Weiteres

Mal sehen.	*Let's see.*
Na klar.	*Of course.*
wieso?	*why? how come?*

ZUM ERKENNEN: das Einschreibungsformular, -e *(application for university registra-tion);* kämpfen *(to struggle, fight);* die Bürokratie *(here: red tape);* dabei haben *(to have with you);* das Vorlesungsverzeichnis, -se *(course catalog)*

A. Was sagt Ihnen der Schein? *(What does this certificate tell you about Miriam and her studies? Make five statements in German.)*

Zum Thema

```
Universität Regensburg
Deutsch als Fremdsprache



H̶e̶r̶r̶n̶
F̶r̶a̶u̶/Frl.      Miriam  B u r t o n ................................

aus            den USA
wird hiermit bescheinigt, daß e̶r̶/sie   an dem DEUTSCHKURS


            Landeskunde - Oberstufe I
...............................................

im   S̶o̶m̶m̶e̶r̶   Semester 19 93/94.......   teilgenommen hat.
     Winter

E̶r̶   hat die Abschlußprüfung mit       sehr gut
Sie                                .........................
bestanden.

                                    25.2.94
Regensburg, den .............                    (Dr. Armin Wolff, Akad. Direktor)

Bewertung: sehr gut (1); gut (2); befriedigend (3); ausreichend (4)
```

B.   Fragen übers Studium. Fragen Sie einen Nachbarn / eine Nachbarin, . . . !

1.   was er / sie studiert (hat) und warum
2.   wie viele Kurse er / sie dieses Semester belegt hat und welche
3.   welche Kurse er / sie besonders gut findet, und worin er / sie die besten Noten hat
4.   ob er / sie viele Arbeiten schreiben muß; wenn ja, in welchen Fächern
5.   ob er / sie außer Deutsch noch andere Sprachen spricht oder lernt
6.   wie lange er / sie noch studieren muß
7.   was er / sie danach macht
8.   wie die Chancen sind, in seinem / ihrem Beruf eine gute Stelle zu bekommen
9.   in welchen Berufen es momentan schwer ist, Arbeit zu finden
10. wo es noch bessere Möglichkeiten gibt

English / home economics / education	Anglistik°	Hauswirtschaft°	Pädagogik°
	Archäologie	Informatik	Pharmazie
law	Architektur	Jura°	Philologie
mining / nursing	Bergbau°	Krankenpflege°	Physik
business administration	Betriebswirtschaft°	Kunstgeschichte	Politik
agriculture	Biochemie	Landwirtschaft°	Psychologie
Romance languages	Biologie	Lebensmittelchemie	Romanistik°
	Chemie	Linguistik	Slawistik
mechanical engineering	Elektrotechnik	Maschinenbau°	Soziologie
forestry	Forstwirtschaft°	Mathematik	Sport
	Geographie	Medizin	Theologie
civil engineering	Geologie	Mineralogie	Tiefbau°
economics	Geschichte	Musik(wissenschaft)	Volkswirtschaft°
	Gesundheitswissenschaft	Naturwissenschaft	Zahnmedizin

C.   Aussprache: s, ß, st, sp   *(See also III. 6 and 12 in the pronunciation section of the Workbook.)*

1.   [z]   so, sauber, sicher, Semester, Seminar, Musik, Physik, Reise, Pause, lesen
2.   [s]   bis, eins, Ausweis, Kurs, Professor, Adresse, wissen, lassen, vergessen, interessant, außerdem, fleißig, häßlich, Fuß, Fluß, Grüße, Paß
3.   [št]   statt, Student, Studium, Stipendium, Stelle, Stück, Stunde, studieren, bestehen, vorstellen, bestimmt, anstrengend
4.   [st]   zuerst, meistens, desto, Semester, System, Journalist, Komponist, Kunst, Lust, Prost
5.   [šp]   spät, sportlich, spannend, spanisch, Spaß, Sprache, Beispiel, spinnen, springen

Hören Sie zu!

Wie wohnen deutsche Studenten?   *(Listen to the information and decide which of the answers below best reflects the meaning of the passage you hear.)*

ZUM ERKENNEN: ähnlich *(similar);* die Verwandten *(relatives);* teilen *(to share)*

Was stimmt?

1.   Die Wohnsituation für deutsche Studenten ist _____ für Studenten in den USA.
     a. genauso wie   b. sehr ähnlich wie   c. noch schwieriger als

2. 1992/93 waren _____ Studenten an deutschen Universitäten.
    a. 183.000   b. 1.830.000   c. 1.083.000

3. In den fünf neuen Ländern gibt es _____ .
    a. viel weniger Studenten als in den alten Ländern
    b. mehr Studenten als in den alten Ländern
    c. 1,69 Millionen Studenten

4. In den neuen Ländern wohnen _____ der Studenten in Studentenheimen.
    a. ungefähr 12%   b. ungefähr 62%   c. 141.000

5. Die meisten ausländischen Studenten wohnen _____ .
    a. bei ihren Eltern   b. in Wohnungen   c. in Studentenheimen

6. In den deutschen Studentenheimen sind _____ Ausländer.
    a. alle Studenten   b. sehr wenige   c. bis zu 50%

7. Die meisten deutschen Studenten wohnen _____ .
    a. bei ihren Eltern   b. in Wohngemeinschaften   c. nicht in Studentenheimen

Im Studentenheim

STRUKTUR

I. The Subjunctive Mood

Until now, almost all sentences in this book have been in the INDICATIVE MOOD. Sentences in the indicative mood are assumed to be based on reality. Sometimes, however, we want to speculate on matters that are unreal, uncertain, or unlikely; or we wish for something that cannot be; or we want to approach other people less directly, more discretely and politely. These things are done in the SUBJUNCTIVE MOOD.

1. Polite Requests or Questions

   Would you like a cup of coffee?
   Would you pass me the butter?
   Could you help me for a moment?

2. Hypothetical Statements and Questions

   He should be here any moment.
   What would you do?
   You should have been there.

3. Wishes

   If only I had more time.
   I wish you would hurry up.
   I wish I had known that.

4. Unreal Conditions

   If I had time, I'd go to the movies. (But I don't have time, so I'm not going.)
   If the weather were good, we'd go for a walk. (But it's raining, so we won't go.)
   If you had told me, I could have helped you. (But you didn't tell me, so I couldn't help you.)

   Contrast the sentences above with real conditions:

   If I have time, I'll go to the movies.
   If the weather is good, we'll go for a walk.

   In real conditions the possibility exists that the events will take place. In unreal conditions this possibility does not exist or is highly unlikely.

   NOTE: The forms of the present-time subjunctive are derived from the simple past: *If I told you (now) . . .* Those of the past-time subjunctive are derived from the past perfect: *If you had told me (yesterday) . . .* Another very common way to express the subjunctive mood is the form *would: I'd go; I would not stay home.*

 A. **Indikativ oder Konjunktiv (*subjunctive*)?**   *(Analyze whether these sentences are in the indicative or subjunctive mood, and whether they refer to the present, the future, or the past.)*

BEISPIEL: If you don't ask, you won't know.   **indicative: present / future**
              How would you know?   **subjunctive: present-time**
              What would you have done?   **subjunctive: past-time**

1.   If she can, she'll write.
2.   If only he'd study more.
3.   If only I had known that.
4.   They could be here any minute.
5.   Will you take the bike along?
6.   Would you please hold this?
7.   Could they help us for a minute?
8.   I had known that for a long time.
9.   We should really be going.
10. I wish you had told me that.
11. If you could stay over a Saturday, you could fly for a lower fare.
12. I wish I could buy that car.
13. Could you take the children along?
14. You shouldn't go barefoot in this weather.
15. What would they have done if you hadn't come along?
16. If it rains, we won't go.
17. If we had had the money, we'd have bought it.
18. I couldn't come yesterday because I was ill.
19. If she has the money, she'll give it to us.
20. You could have told me.

II. The Present-Time General Subjunctive

German has two subjunctives. The one most commonly used is often referred to in grammar books as the GENERAL SUBJUNCTIVE or SUBJUNCTIVE II. (The SPECIAL SUBJUNCTIVE or SUBJUNCTIVE I, primarily found in written German, is explained in Chapter 15.)

1.   Forms

The PRESENT-TIME SUBJUNCTIVE refers to the present *(now)* or the future *(later)*. As in English, its forms are derived from the forms of the <u>simple past</u>. You already know the verb endings from having used the **möchte**-forms of **mögen,** which are actually subjunctive forms. All verbs in the subjunctive have these endings:

Infinitive	Simple Past Indicative	Present-time Subjunctive
mögen	mochte	möch**te**
	mochtest	möch**test**
	mochte	möch**te**
	mochten	möch**ten**
	mochtet	möch**tet**
	mochten	möch**ten**

a.   t-Verbs *(weak verbs)*

The present-time subjunctive forms of regular t-verbs are identical to those of the simple past. Their use usually becomes clear from context.

Infinitive	Simple Past Indicative	Present-time Subjunctive
glauben	glaubte	**glaubte**
antworten	antwortete	**antwortete**

Wenn Sie mir nur **glaubten!**   *If only you would believe me!*
Wenn er mir nur **antwortete!**   *If only he would answer me!*

b.   Irregular t-Verbs *(mixed verbs)*

Most of the irregular t-verbs, which include the modals, have an umlaut in the present-time subjunctive. Exceptions are **sollen** and **wollen.**

Infinitive	Simple Past Indicative	Present-time Subjunctive
haben	hatte	**hätte**
bringen	brachte	**brächte**
denken	dachte	**dächte**
wissen	wußte	**wüßte**
müssen	mußte	**müßte**
dürfen	durfte	**dürfte**
können	konnte	**könnte**
mögen	mochte	**möchte**
wollen	wollte	**wollte**
sollen	sollte	**sollte**

haben	
ich hätte	wir hätten
du hättest	ihr hättet
er hätte	sie hätten

wissen	
ich wüßte	wir wüßten
du wüßtest	ihr wüßtet
er wüßte	sie wüßten

Hättest du Zeit?   *Would you have time?*
Könntest du kommen?   *Could you come?*

c.   n-Verbs *(strong verbs)*

The present-time subjunctive forms of n-verbs add the subjunctive endings to the past stem. If the past stem vowel is an **a, o,** or **u,** the subjunctive forms have an umlaut.

Infinitive	Simple Past Indicative	Present-time Subjunctive
sein	war	**wäre**
werden	wurde	**würde**
bleiben	blieb	**bliebe**
fahren	fuhr	**führe**
finden	fand	**fände**
fliegen	flog	**flöge**
geben	gab	**gäbe**
gehen	ging	**ginge**
laufen	lief	**liefe**
sehen	sah	**sähe**
tun	tat	**täte**

sein	
ich wäre	wir wären
du wärest	ihr wäret
er wäre	sie wären

gehen	
ich ginge	wir gingen
du gingest	ihr ginget
er ginge	sie gingen

Wenn ich du **wäre, ginge** ich nicht.   *If I were you, I wouldn't go.*
Wenn er **flöge, könnte** er morgen   *If he were to fly, he could be here*
   hier sein.   *tomorrow.*

d. **würde**-form

In conversation, speakers of German commonly use the subjunctive forms of **haben, sein, werden, wissen,** and the modals.

Hättest du Zeit?   *Would you have time?*
Das wäre schön.   *That would be nice.*
Was möchtest du tun?   *What would you like to do?*
Wenn ich das nur wüßte!   *If only I knew that!*

For the subjunctive forms of other verbs, however, German speakers frequently substitute a simpler verb phrase that closely corresponds to the English *would + infinitive*. It is <u>preferred</u> when the subjunctive form is identical to the indicative form, as is the case with t-verbs and with the plural forms of n-verbs whose sub-junctive forms don't have an umlaut (e.g., **gingen**). It is also frequently used in the conclusion clause of contrary-to-fact conditions (see section d. on p. 364).

Das täte ich nicht.
Das **würde** ich nicht **tun.**   } *I wouldn't do that.*

Wenn er mir nur glaubte!
Wenn er mir nur **glauben würde!**   } *If only he would believe me!*

Wir gingen lieber ins Kino.
Wir **würden** lieber ins Kino **gehen.** } *We would rather go to the movies.*

Wenn sie Zeit hätte, käme sie mit.
Wenn sie Zeit hätte, **würde** sie
   mitkommen.   } *If she had time, she would come with us.*

2. Uses

You are already familiar with the most common uses of the subjunctive in English. Here are examples of these uses in German.

a. Polite Requests or Questions

Möchtest du eine Tasse Kaffee?   *Would you like a cup of coffee?*
Würdest du mir die Butter geben?   *Would you pass me the butter?*
Könntest du mir einen Moment helfen?   *Could you help me for a minute?*

b. Hypothetical Statements and Questions

Er sollte jeden Moment hier sein.   *He should be here any minute.*
Das wäre schön.   *That would be nice.*
Was würdest du tun?   *What would you do?*
Ich würde spazierengehen.   *I'd go for a walk.*

c. Wishes

- Wishes starting with **Wenn** . . . usually add **nur** after the subject or any pronoun object.

  Wenn ich nur mehr Zeit hätte!   *If only I had more time!*
  Wenn er mir nur glauben würde!   *If only he'd believe me!*

- Wishes starting with **Ich wünschte,** . . . have BOTH CLAUSES in the subjunctive.

  Ich wünschte, ich hätte mehr Zeit.   *I wish I had more time.*
  Ich wünschte, du würdest dich beeilen. *I wish you'd hurry.*

d.   Unreal Conditions

Wenn ich morgen Zeit hätte, würde ich mit dir ins Kino gehen.	*If I had time tomorrow, I'd go to the movies with you.*
Wenn ihr mitkommen wolltet, müßtet ihr euch beeilen.	*If you wanted to come along, you'd have to hurry.*
Wenn wir euch helfen könnten, würden wir das tun.	*If we could help you, we would do it.*

Contrast the preceding sentences with real conditions.

Wenn ich morgen Zeit habe, gehe ich mit dir ins Kino.	*If I have time tomorrow, I'll go to the movies with you.*
Wenn ihr mitkommen wollt, müßt ihr euch beeilen.	*If you want to come along, you'll have to hurry.*
Wenn wir euch helfen können, tun wir es.	*If we can help you, we'll do it.*

Wenn ich ein Vöglein° wär',   *little bird*
und auch zwei Flügel° hätt',   *wings*
flög' ich zu dir.
Weil's aber nicht kann sein,
weil's aber nicht kann sein,
bleib' ich allhier°.   *right here*

Mein Hut°, der hat drei Ecken.   *hat*
Drei Ecken hat mein Hut.
Und hätt' er nicht drei Ecken,
dann wär' es nicht mein Hut.

Übungen

B.   Was tun? Auf englisch, bitte!

1.   Wohin möchtest du gehen?
2.   Wir könnten uns einen Film ansehen.
3.   Wir sollten in die Zeitung sehen.
4.   Ich würde lieber zu Hause bleiben.
5.   Ich wünschte, ich wäre nicht so müde.
6.   Hättest du morgen abend Zeit?
7.   Ich ginge heute lieber früh ins Bett.
8.   Morgen könnte ich länger schlafen.

Peter

Wenn ich meinen Eltern alles erzählen würde, na dann gute Nacht!

C.   Geben Sie das Imperfekt und die Konjunktivform!

BEISPIELE:	ich hole	**ich holte**	**ich holte**
	du bringst	**du brachtest**	**du brächtest**
	er kommt	**er kam**	**er käme**

1.   ich frage, mache, hoffe, belege, studiere, versuche
2.   du arbeitest, antwortest, erwartest, öffnest, heiratest
3.   er muß, kann, darf, soll, mag
4.   wir bringen, denken, wissen, haben
5.   ihr bleibt, schlaft, fliegt, seid, gebt, eßt, singt, sitzt, tut, seht, versprecht, werdet, fahrt

D.   Reisepläne. Was fehlt?

1.   **Bauers würden nach Wien fahren**   *(Use the **würde**-form.)*

S1   Dort _____ wir erst eine Stadtrundfahrt machen.

S2   Dann _____ Dieter sich sicher den Stephansdom ansehen. Und
du _____ dann durch die Kärntnerstraße bummeln. Natürlich
_____ ihr auch in die Hofburg gehen.

S1   Ja, und einen Abend _____ wir in Grinzing feiern.

S2   Das _____ euch bestimmt gefallen.

2.   **Ute führe in die Schweiz**   *(Use the suggested verb in the subjunctive.)*

a.   Ich _____ mit ein paar Freunden in die Schweiz fahren. (können)

b.   Erst _____ wir an den Bodensee. (fahren)

c.   Von dort _____ es weiter nach Zürich und Bern. (gehen)

d.   In Zürich _____ ich mir gern das Thomas-Mann-Archiv *(archives)*
_____ . (ansehen)

e.   Ihr _____ auch nach Genf fahren. (sollen)

f.   Dort _____ du Französisch sprechen. (müssen)

g.   Das _____ keine schlechte Idee! (sein)

E.   Sagen Sie es höflicher *(more politely)*!

1.   BEISPIEL: Können Sie uns die Mensa zeigen?
Könnten Sie uns die Mensa zeigen?

a. Darf ich kurz mit Ihnen sprechen?   **b.** Haben Sie Lust mitzukommen?
c. Können wir uns an einen Tisch setzen?   **d.** Haben Sie etwas Zeit?

2.   BEISPIEL: Rufen Sie mich morgen an!
Würden Sie mich morgen anrufen?

a. Erzählen Sie uns von der Reise!   **b.** Bringen Sie die Fotos mit!   **c.** Machen
Sie mir eine Tasse Kaffee!   **d.** Geben Sie mir die Milch!

F.   Wünsche

1.   **Beginnen Sie mit „Ich wünschte, . . .“**!   *(If you have trouble, do this exercise
in English first.)*

BEISPIEL: Der Kurs ist schwer.
*(**I wish the course were not so hard.**)*
Ich wünschte, der Kurs wäre nicht so schwer.

a. Ich muß viel lesen.   **b.** Das braucht viel Zeit.   **c.** Ich bin müde.   **d.** Ihr
seid faul.

2.   **Beginnen Sie mit „Wenn nur . . .“**!

BEISPIEL: Ich wünschte, ich könnte schlafen.
*(**If only I could sleep!**)*
Wenn ich nur schlafen könnte!

a.   Ich wünschte, wir hätten keine Prüfungen.

b.   Ich wünschte, ich könnte das verstehen.

c.   Ich wünschte, du könntest mir helfen.

d.   Ich wünschte, diese Woche wäre schon vorbei.

G.   Wiederholen Sie die Sätze im Konjunktiv!

BEISPIEL: Wenn das Wetter schön ist, kann man die Berge sehen.
             Wenn das Wetter schön wäre, könnte man die Berge sehen.

1. Wenn es möglich ist, zeige ich euch das Schloß.
2. Wenn du das Schloß sehen willst, mußt du dich beeilen.
3. Wenn ihr zu spät kommt, ärgert ihr euch.
4. Wenn das Schloß zu ist, können wir wenigstens in den Schloßpark gehen.
5. Wenn ihr mehr sehen wollt, müßt ihr länger hier bleiben.

H.   Persönliche Fragen

1. Was würden Sie gern lernen?
2. Wo würden Sie gern leben?
3. Würden Sie lieber in einem Haus oder in einer Wohnung wohnen?
4. Welchen Film würden Sie sich gern ansehen?
5. Was für ein Auto würden Sie sich am liebsten kaufen?
6. Was würden Sie jetzt am liebsten essen? trinken?

I.   Was wäre, wenn . . . ?

1. Wenn das Wetter heute schön wäre, . . .
2. Wenn ich jetzt in Florida (Alaska, usw.) wäre, . . .
3. Wenn ich morgen Geburtstag hätte, . . .
4. Wenn ich jetzt ein paar Tage frei hätte, . . .
5. Wenn ich eine Million Dollar hätte, . . .
6. Wenn ich Präsident (Professor, usw.) wäre, . . .

J.   Wie geht's weiter?

BEISPIEL: Ich wäre glücklich, wenn . . .
           Ich wäre glücklich, wenn ich gut Deutsch sprechen könnte.

1. Ich wäre froh, wenn . . .
2. Ich fände es prima, wenn . . .
3. Es wäre furchtbar, wenn . . .
4. Ich würde mich ärgern, wenn . . .
5. Ich würde sparen, wenn . . .
6. Ich wüßte, was ich täte, wenn . . .

K.   Wochenendpläne. Auf deutsch, bitte!

1. **a.** Would you like to come on Saturday?   **b.** It would be nice.   **c.** We could swim in the lake.   **d.** We wish we had time.   **e.** If Walter didn't have to work, we would come.   **f.** Could you come on Sunday?   **g.** Yes, I believe we can come.

2. **a.** Could you stay?   **b.** We could drive to the park.   **c.** We should go for a walk.   **d.** I was supposed to visit my grandfather last week.   **e.** We have to do it on Saturday.   **f.** I wish I knew why he has not called.   **g.** I know he would call me if he needed anything.   **h.** Would you like to go to a restaurant?   **i.** He wishes he didn't have to work on Sunday.

III. The Past-Time General Subjunctive

You already know that a simple-past form in English can express the present-time subjunctive (referring to *now* or *later*). The past-perfect form, or *would have* + participle, expresses the same thought in the PAST-TIME SUBJUNCTIVE (referring to *earlier*).

NOW OR LATER: If I *had* time, I *would* go with you.

EARLIER: If I *had had* time, I *would have* gone with you.

1. Forms

    a. In German the forms of the past-time subjunctive are based on the forms of the <u>past perfect</u>. The past-time subjunctive is very easy to learn because it simply consists of a form of **hätte** or **wäre** plus the past participle:

> **hätte . . .**
> } + past participle
> **wäre . . .**

Das **hätte** ich nicht **getan.**	*I wouldn't have done that.*
Hättest du das **getan?**	*Would you have done that?*
Ich **wäre** lieber ins Kino **gegangen.**	*I would have rather gone to the movies.*
Wärest du nicht lieber ins Kino **gegangen?**	*Wouldn't you have rather gone to the movies.*
Ich wünschte, du **hättest** mir das **gesagt!**	*I wish you had told me that!*
Wenn ich das **gewußt hätte, wären** wir ins Kino **gegangen.**	*If I had known that, we would have gone to the movies.*

    b. All modals follow this pattern in the past-time subjunctive:

> **hätte . . .** + verb infinitive + modal infinitive

Du **hättest** mir das **sagen sollen.**	*You should have told me that.*
Wir **hätten** noch ins Kino **gehen können.**	*We still could have gone to the movies.*

    For now, avoid using these forms in dependent clauses.

2. Uses

    The past-time subjunctive is used for the same purposes as the present-time subjunctive. Note that there are no polite requests in the past.

    a. Hypothetical Statements and Questions

Ich wäre zu Hause geblieben.	*I would have stayed home.*
Was hättet ihr gemacht?	*What would you have done?*
Hättet ihr mitkommen wollen?	*Would you have wanted to come along?*

b.   Wishes

Wenn ich das nur gewußt hätte!	*If only I had known that!*
Ich wünschte, du wärest da gewesen.	*I wish you had been there.*

c.   Unreal Conditions

Wenn du mich gefragt hättest, hätte ich es dir gesagt.	*If you had asked me, I would have told you.*
Wenn du da gewesen wärest, hättest du alles gehört.	*If you had been there, you would have heard everything.*

Übungen

L.   Sagen Sie die Sätze in der Vergangenheit!   *(Change the sentences from the present to the past, using the past-time subjunctive. If necessary, do the exercise in English first.)*

1.   BEISPIEL: Sie würde das tun.
                 (She would have done it.)
                 Sie hätte das getan.

   a. Sie würde euch anrufen.   **b.** Ihr würdet ihr helfen.   **c.** Ihr würdet sofort kommen.   **d.** Du würdest alles für sie tun.

2.   BEISPIEL: Hansi sollte nicht so viel Schokolade essen.
                 (Hansi shouldn't have eaten so much chocolate.)
                 Hansi hätte nicht so viel Schokolade essen sollen.

   a. Wir dürften ihm keine Schokolade geben.   **b.** Das sollten wir wissen.
   c. Er könnte auch Obst essen.   **d.** Wir müßten besser aufpassen.

M.   Was wäre gewesen, wenn . . . ?

1.   **Wiederholen Sie die Sätze in der Vergangenheit!**

   BEISPIEL: Wenn ich es wüßte, würde ich nicht fragen.
              (If I had known it, I wouldn't have asked.)
              Wenn ich es gewußt hätte, hätte ich nicht gefragt.

   a.   Wenn wir eine Theatergruppe hätten, würde ich mitmachen.
   b.   Wenn das Radio billiger wäre, würden wir es kaufen.
   c.   Wenn ich Hunger hätte, würde ich mir etwas kochen.
   d.   Wenn sie fleißiger arbeitete, würde es ihr besser gehen.

2.   **Und dann?**   *(Partner work. Say what you would have done or what might have been if . . . ! After your partner asks* **Und dann?***, you continue with additional hypothetical actions. Take turns.)*

   BEISPIEL: Ich hatte keinen Hunger. Wenn ich Hunger gehabt hätte, . . .
              . . . wäre ich in die Küche gegangen.
              Und dann?
              Dann hätte ich mir ein Wurstbrot gemacht.

   a. Gestern hat es geregnet. Wenn das Wetter schön gewesen wäre, . . .

   b. Ich bin nicht lange auf der Party gewesen. Wenn ich zu lange gefeiert hätte, . . .

   c. Natürlich hatten wir letzte Woche Vorlesungen. Wenn wir keine Vorlesungen gehabt hätten, . . .

N. Auf deutsch, bitte!

1. **a.** We should have stayed at home. **b.** If the weather had been better, we could have gone swimming in the lake. **c.** But it rained all day. **d.** I wish they hadn't invited us. **e.** If only we hadn't visited him.

2. **a.** If we had stayed home, we could have watched TV. **b.** We could have seen the new detective story. **c.** You should have gone out with her. **d.** If I had had time, I would have called her. **e.** If I have time, I will call her tomorrow. **f.** I had no time to call her yesterday. **g.** I could have called the day before yesterday, but I forgot to (it).

O. Indikativ oder Konjunktiv? Was bedeutet das auf englisch?

1. Wenn er uns besuchte, brachte er immer Blumen mit.
2. Können Sie mir Horsts Telefonnummer geben?
3. Wenn du früher ins Bett gegangen wärest, wärest du jetzt nicht so müde.
4. Gestern konnten sie nicht kommen, aber sie könnten uns morgen besuchen.
5. Er sollte gestern anrufen.
6. Ich möchte Architektur studieren.
7. Sie waren schon um 6 Uhr aufgestanden.
8. Ich wünschte, er ließe nicht immer alles auf dem Sofa liegen.

Zusammen-fassung

P. Guter Rat *(Good advice)*

1. **Was soll ich tun?** *(In small groups, give each other advice. One person mentions a problem, real or invented—e.g., having no money or energy, being hungry or thirsty, missing something—and the others advise him or her what to do.)*

   BEISPIEL: Ich bin immer so müde.
               Wenn ich du wäre, würde ich früher ins Bett gehen.

2. **Was hätte ich tun sollen?** *(This time give advice as to what one should have done or not done.)*

   BEISPIEL: Ich habe meine Schlüssel verloren.
               Du hättest besser aufpassen sollen.

Q. Kommst du mit? Auf deutsch, bitte!

1. Would you *(sg. fam.)* like to go (**fahren**) with us to Salzburg? **2.** We could go by train. **3.** It ought to be quieter now than in the summer. **4.** That would be nice. **5.** I'd come along, if I could find my passport. **6.** I wish you *(pl. fam.)* had thought of it earlier. **7.** Then I could have looked for it. **8.** If I only knew where it was. **9.** I'd like to see the churches, the Mozart house, and the castle (**die Burg**). **10.** The city is supposed to be wonderful. **11.** Without my passport I'd have to stay home.—Here it is! **12.** If you *(sg. fam.)* hadn't talked (**reden**) so much, you'd have found it more quickly.

EINBLICKE

Heidelberg am Neckar, Blick auf die Altstadt und das Schloß

German universities are academically self-governing and are headed by a president (**Rektor**) elected for several years. Purely administrative matters are handled by a permanent administrative staff of civil servants under the direction of a chancellor (**Kanzler**).

The system differs considerably from its counterparts in the United States. When entering a university, students come prepared with a broad general education and can therefore focus immediately on a major field of study. They are responsible for their own progress, taking only a few required courses. For participating in seminars, students receive a certificate (**Schein**) and a grade. After collecting a certain number of certificates, students are eligible to take an intermediate qualifying exam (**Zwischenprüfung**) and eventually a very comprehensive and rigorous final exam (**Abschlußprüfung**). They usually complete their studies with the equivalent of an M.A., called **Magister** in the arts and humanities, and **Diplom** in the natural or social sciences and in engineering. Some students continue their studies beyond these diplomas and obtain their doctorate. Those who wish to become teachers, doctors, or lawyers must pass a comprehensive state-administered, academic exam in their field (**erstes Staatsexamen**), followed by a second exam (**zweites Staatsexamen**) after a practical internship.

Ach was!	*Oh, come on.*
an deiner / seiner Stelle	*in your / his shoes; if I were you / he*
ausländisch	*foreign*
gar nicht	*not at all*
jedenfalls	*in any case*
so daß	*so that*
sowieso	*anyhow*
Angst haben (vor + *dat.*)	*to fear, be afraid (of)*
an·nehmen (nimmt an), nahm an, angenommen	*to suppose; to accept*
auf·hören	*to end; to stop doing something*
teilen	*to share*
teil·nehmen (nimmt teil), nahm teil, teilgenommen (an + *dat.*)	*to participate, take part (in)*
sich vor·bereiten (auf + *acc.*)	*to prepare (for)*

WAS IST DAS?   der Grammatikkurs, Intensivkurs, Lesesaal, Semesteranfang; das Archiv, Auslandsprogramm, Sommersemester; die Seminararbeit; Sprachprüfung; teilmöbliert

Ein Jahr drüben wäre super!

(Gespräch an einer amerikanischen Universität)

	TINA	Hallo, Margaret!
	MARGARET	Tag, Tina! Kennst du Bernd? Er ist aus Heidelberg und studiert ein Jahr bei
5		uns.
	TINA	Guten Tag! Wie gefällt's dir hier?
	BERND	Sehr gut. Meine Kurse und Professoren sind ausgezeichnet. Ich wünschte nur, es gäbe nicht so viele Prüfungen!
	TINA	Habt ihr keine Prüfungen?
10	BERND	Doch, aber weniger. Dafür° haben wir nach ungefähr vier Semestern eine große Zwischenprüfung und dann am Ende des Studiums das Staatsexamen.
	TINA	Ich würde gern einmal in Europa studieren.
	MARGARET	Ja, das solltest du unbedingt tun.
	TINA	Es ist bestimmt sehr teuer.
15	MARGARET	Ach was, so teuer ist es gar nicht. Mein Jahr in München hat auch nicht mehr gekostet als ein Jahr hier.
	TINA	Wirklich?
	BERND	Ja, unsere Studentenheime und die Mensa sind viel billiger als bei euch, und unsere Studiengebühren° sind viel niedriger°. Ohne mein Stipendium könnte
20		ich hier nicht studieren.
	TINA	Ist es schwer, dort drüben einen Studienplatz zu bekommen?
	BERND	Wenn du Deutsche wärest, wäre es wahrscheinlich nicht so einfach—je nach-dem°, was du studieren willst. Aber als Ausländerin in einem Auslandspro-gramm hättest du gar kein Problem.

instead

tuition / lower

depending on

TINA   Ich muß noch mal mit meinen Eltern sprechen. Sie haben Angst, daß ich ein 25
           Jahr verlieren würde.

MARGARET   Wieso denn? Wenn du mit einem Auslandsprogramm nach Deutschland gin-
           gest, würde das genauso wie ein Jahr hier zählen.

TINA   Ich weiß nicht, ob ich genug Deutsch kann.

MARGARET   Keine Angst! Viele Studenten können weniger Deutsch als du. Du lernst es ja 30
           schon seit vier Jahren. Außerdem haben die meisten Programme vor Seme-
           steranfang einen Intensivkurs für ausländische Studenten. Damit würdest du
           dich auch auf die Sprachprüfung am Anfang des Semesters vorbereiten.
           Wenn du die Prüfung wirklich nicht bestehen solltest—was ich mir nicht
just   vorstellen kann, denn dein Deutsch ist gut—, dann müßtest du eben° einen 35
           Grammatikkurs belegen und sie am Ende des Semesters wiederholen.

That's OK.   TINA   Das geht°. Vielleicht kann ich im Herbst ein Semester nach Deutschland.

MARGARET   Nur im Herbst ginge nicht, weil das Wintersemester erst Ende Februar
           aufhört.

TINA   Im Februar? Und wann ist das Frühlingssemester?   40

BERND   Bei uns gibt es ein Wintersemester und ein Sommersemester. Das Winter-
           semester geht von November bis März, das Sommersemester von April bis
           Ende Juli[1]. Du müßtest deshalb ein ganzes Jahr bleiben oder nur für das Som-
           mersemester kommen. Ein ganzes Jahr wäre sowieso besser, denn dann
           hättest du zwischen den Semestern Zeit zu reisen.   45

MARGARET   Stimmt. Da bin ich auch viel gereist. Ich war in Italien, Griechenland und
           danach noch in Ungarn.

TINA   Wunderbar! Was für Kurse sollte ich belegen?

BERND   Im ersten Semester würde ich nur Vorlesungen[2] belegen, keine Seminare. Da
takes notes   hört man nur zu und schreibt mit°. Im zweiten Semester solltest du dann auch 50
           ein Seminar belegen. Bis dann ist dein Deutsch jedenfalls gut genug, so daß
give a report du auch eine längere Seminararbeit schreiben oder ein Referat halten° könn-
           test.

TINA   Seminararbeiten und Referate auf deutsch?

MARGARET   Am Anfang geht's langsam, aber man lernt's.   55

BERND   Ich mach's ja auch auf englisch. Übrigens, was bei euch viel besser ist, sind
           die Bibliotheken. Wir müssen Bücher immer zuerst bestellen, was oft Tage
           dauert. Man kann nicht einfach in die Archive wie hier. Und die Fachbiblio-
lend out   theken[3] leihen keine Bücher aus°, außer am Wochenende.

TINA   Ich kann mir ja die Bücher kaufen.   60

BERND   Das wäre furchtbar teuer! Dann würde ich schon lieber im Lesesaal sitzen.

TINA   Und wie ist das mit Studentenheimen?

MARGARET   Wenn du an einem Auslandsprogramm teilnimmst, hast du keine Probleme.

BERND   An deiner Stelle würde ich versuchen, ein Zimmer im Studentenheim zu
           bekommen. Auf diese Weise würdest du leichter andere Studenten kennenler- 65
           nen. Die Zimmer sind oft sehr schön, teilmöbliert und mit Bad. Dazu müßtest
           du auf deinem Flur die Küche mit fünf oder sechs anderen Studenten teilen.

TINA   Da habe ich nichts dagegen. Findet ihr, Heidelberg wäre besser als Berlin
           oder München?

BERND   Ach, das ist schwer zu sagen.   70

MARGARET   Ich nehme an, wenn ich Berlin gekannt hätte, hätte ich dort studiert. Mir hat es
           da sehr gut gefallen. Aber erst mußt du wissen, ob du wirklich nach Deutsch-
           land willst. Wenn du das weißt, dann kann ich dir weiterhelfen.

TINA   Danke!

A.   Ein Jahr im Ausland. Was fehlt?

Angst haben, Europa, ein Jahr, eine Küche, München, Prüfungen, Sommersemester, Sprachprüfung, andere Studenten, Vorlesungen, Heidelberg, Wintersemester

1. Bernd ist aus _____ und studiert _____ in Amerika.
2. Ihm gefallen nur die vielen _____ nicht.
3. Tina möchte gern in _____ studieren.
4. Margarets Jahr in _____ hat nicht viel mehr gekostet als ein Jahr zu Hause.
5. Tinas Eltern _____ , daß ihre Tochter drüben ein Jahr verliert.
6. Ausländische Studenten müssen vor Semesteranfang eine _____ machen.
7. Das _____ geht von November bis Ende Februar, das _____ von April bis Ende Juli.
8. Im ersten Semester sollte Tina nur _____ belegen.
9. In einem Studentenheim kann man leichter _____ kennenlernen.
10. In einem deutschen Studentenheim muß man _____ mit anderen Studenten teilen.

B.   Das Studium hier und dort   *(In brief statements compare what Bernd says about studying in Heidelberg with what you know about studying here.)*

1. Prüfungen **2.** Studiengebühren **3.** Semesterkalender **4.** Kurse **5.** Bibliotheken

Staatsbibliothek in München

C.   An der Uni. Was fehlt?

1. Bernd _____ , es _____ nicht so viele Prüfungen. *(wishes, there were)*
2. Wenn Bernd kein Stipendium _____ _____ , _____ er nicht hier studieren können. *(had gotten, could have)*

3. Wenn Tina mit einem Austauschprogramm nach Deutschland _____ , _____ das wie ein Jahr hier zählen. *(would go, would)*

4. Tina _____ ein ganzes Jahr bleiben, oder sie _____ nur für das Sommersemester gehen. *(would have to, could)*

5. Ein ganzes Jahr drüben _____ besser. *(would be)*

6. Dann _____ Tina Zeit, zwischen den Semestern zu reisen. *(would have)*

7. In einem Studentenheim _____ Tina leichter deutsche Studenten kennenlernen. *(would)*

8. Wenn Margaret Berlin _____ _____ , _____ sie dort studiert. *(had known, would have)*

9. Wenn sie nicht an einer deutschen Uni _____ _____ , _____ sie nicht so gut Deutsch sprechen. *(had studied, could)*

10. Tina _____ , daß ihr Deutsch nicht gut genug _____ . Aber das _____ kein Problem _____ . *(is afraid, would be, shouldn't be)*

D. Aus dem Vorlesungsverzeichnis   *(Complete the statements by referring to the lectures listed below.)*

1. Die Vorlesungen sind alle über . . .   **2.** Mich würde besonders die Vorlesung über . . . interessieren. Sie wäre . . . von . . . bis . . .   **3.** Außerdem dürfte Professor . . .s Vorlesung über . . . interessant sein.   **4.** . . . würde mich nicht (weniger) interessieren, weil . . .

Geschichte der Stadt Rom in der Zeit der römischen Republik 3st., Mo 11 - 13, Mi 12 - 13	Lippold
Die sozialen und wirtschaftlichen Verhältnisse in der griechischen Welt von der Archaischen Zeit bis zum Beginn des Hellenismus 2st., Mo 14 - 15.30	Hennig
Kirche und Gesellschaft im früheren Mittelalter (5.-12. Jahrhundert) 3st., Do 12-13, Fr 11 - 13	Hartmann
Deutschland und Frankreich im 15. und 16. Jahrhundert. Der Beginn eines europäischen Gegensatzes 2st., Di, Mi 9 - 10	Schmid
Politik und Geschichte in Deutschland nach 1945 2st., Do 13 - 15	Haan
Demokratie oder Volksherrschaft? Zur Geschichte der Demokratie seit dem späten 18. Jahrhundert II 2st., Do 16 - 18	Lottes
Deutschland in der Industrialisierung 2st., Di 10 - 11, Mi 11 - 12	Bauer
Bayerische Geschichte zwischen 1800 und 1866 2st., Mi, Do 11 - 12	Volkert
Wirtschaft und Gesellschaft Bayerns im Industriezeitalter 2st., Mo, Di 11 - 12	Götschmann
Das Ostjudentum (19./20. Jahrhundert) 2st., Mi, Fr 8 - 9	Völkl
Rußland im "Mittelalter" 2st., Di, Do 8 - 9	Völkl
Europa zwischen den Weltkriegen (1919-1939) 2st., Mo 10 -12	Möller

E.   Am liebsten würde ich . . .

1.   Wenn ich könnte, würde ich einmal in . . . studieren.
2.   Am liebsten würde ich in . . . wohnen, weil . . .
3.   Am Anfang des Semesters . . .
4.   Am Ende des Semesters . . .
5.   Während der Semesterferien . . .

F.   Das wäre schön!   *(Write a paragraph of six to eight sentences on one of the topics below, using the subjunctive.)*

1.   Ein Jahr drüben wäre super!
2.   Mein Traumhaus.
3.   Meine Traumfamilie.

4.   Das würde mir gefallen.
5.   Das hätte mir gefallen.

Wir nutzen nur 10% unseres geistigen Potentials
A. Einstein

Hören Sie zu!

Wochenendpläne   *(Listen to the phone conversation between Clemens and Monika. Then decide whether the following statements are true or false according to what you hear.)*

ZUM ERKENNEN: nämlich *(namely, you see);* folgend *(following)*

Richtig oder falsch?

_____ 1.   Clemens fragt Monika, ob sie fürs Wochenende schon Pläne hat.
_____ 2.   Sie möchte eine Busfahrt machen.
_____ 3.   Sie möchte sich in die Sonne legen und ein bißchen schwimmen.
_____ 4.   Clemens hat am Wochenende leider keine Zeit.
_____ 5.   Er muß am Wochenende Geld verdienen.
_____ 6.   Am ersten muß er seine Miete zahlen.
_____ 7.   Clemens ist schon mit seiner Seminararbeit fertig.
_____ 8.   Wenn das Wetter schön wäre, würden sie dieses Wochenende an einen See fahren.
_____ 9.   Wenn das Wetter am nächsten Wochenende schön ist, werden sie an einen See fahren.

 # Übrigens

1.   The exact dates for the beginning and end of each semester differ in various parts of Germany, since each state is autonomous in regard to education.

2.   The registration process at German universities permits students to attend lectures and seminars for three weeks before making a final decision to enroll. That allows them to select only those courses that are suited to their needs and likes.

3.   Besides the large university library (**Universitätsbibliothek = UB**), there is a separate library (**Fachbibliothek**) with a reading room for each of the major disciplines, usually located in the building that houses these departments.

SPRECHSITUATIONEN

As you know, the subjunctive can express politeness. It is used therefore quite frequently when giving advice or asking for permission.

Giving Advice

Sie sollten / könnten . . .
Es wäre besser, wenn . . .
Wie wär's, wenn . . . ?
Ich würde . . .
An deiner / Ihrer Stelle, würde ich . . .
Wenn ich du / Sie wäre, würde ich . . .
Ich empfehle dir / Ihnen . . .
Du mußt unbedingt . . .
Du kannst / darfst nicht . . .
Ich rate dir / Ihnen . . . *(I advise you . . .)*

Asking for Permission

Darf / dürfte ich . . . ?
Kann / könnte ich . . . ?
Haben / hätten Sie etwas dagegen, wenn . . . ? *(Do / would you mind, if . . . ?)*
Ist es erlaubt, . . . (zu + *infinitive*)? *(Is it permitted, to . . . ?)*

Granting or Denying Permission

Ja, natürlich. Gern.
Es ist mir recht.
Ich habe nichts dagegen.

Es tut mir leid, aber . . .
Hier darf man nicht . . . *(It is not permitted . . .)*
Es ist nicht erlaubt . . . (zu + *infinitive*). *(You are not allowed to . . .)*
Es ist verboten . . . (zu + *infinitive*). *(It is forbidden to . . .)*
Es wäre mir lieber, wenn . . . *(I would prefer it if . . .)*

Übungen

 A. **Was tun?**   *(Take turns asking for or giving advice in the following situations.)*

1. Sie wissen nicht, was Sie werden wollen (oder welche Arbeitsmöglichkeiten es gibt).
2. Sie wissen nicht, was Sie als Hauptfach studieren wollen (oder was Sie tun müssen, um einen besseren Arbeitsplatz zu finden).
3. Sie möchten eigentlich gern Lehrer(in) werden, aber wenn Sie . . . studierten, könnten Sie bei Ihrem (Schwieger)vater arbeiten und mehr verdienen.
4. Sie möchten in Deutschland studieren / arbeiten, aber Ihre Familie ist dagegen.
5. Sie sollen heute abend mit einem Freund in ein Konzert gehen; er hat auch schon Karten. Aber Sie haben keine Lust dazu.

B. **Darf ich . . . ?** *(Working with a classmate, take turns asking for permission and granting or denying it.)*

1. mal kurz dein Buch haben
2. deine Hausaufgaben sehen / abschreiben *(copy)*
3. mein Radio anmachen / eine neue Kassette spielen
4. deinen Kuli / deinen Pullover . . . borgen *(borrow)*
5. für dich bezahlen / dir die Rechnung geben
6. deine Kreditkarte / dein Auto . . . borgen

C. **Schont die Parkanlagen!** *(Protect the park. You have just arrived in Germany and can't quite make out what the sign says. Your partner explains.)*

1. Im Park darf man nicht . . .
2. Es ist nicht erlaubt, . . .
3. Es ist verboten, . . .
4. Man soll . . .

SCHONT DIE PARKANLAGEN!

Es wird gebeten°:
Auf den Wegen zu bleiben
Blumen nicht abzupflücken°
Hunde an der Leine zu führen°
Denkmäler° sauber zu halten
Im Park nicht Fußball zu spielen
Fahrräder nicht in den Park mitzunehmen

please; lit. it is requested

pick

lead on a leash

monuments

D. **Kurzgespräch**

You call Margaret, who has been to Germany. Introduce yourself and ask whether you might ask her some questions. She says to go ahead, and you ask whether you should study in Germany. She replies that she would do it if she were you. You ask for how long you should go. She suggests that you go (for) a year. You would learn more German and see more of Europe. You ask whether you could have lunch together the next day. She says she would prefer it if you could have supper. You agree and say good-bye.

KAPITEL 14

Damals und jetzt

Kurfürstendamm mit Blick auf die Gedächtniskirche

LERNZIELE

Vorschau
- Chronicle of German history: 1945 to 1994

Gespräche and Wortschatz
- A visit to Berlin

Struktur
- Relative clauses
- Indirect speech

Einblicke
- Berlin yesterday and today

Sprechsituationen
- Expressing doubt and uncertainty
- Expressing probability and possibility
- Expressing concern
- Drawing conclusions

Chronicle of German History: 1945 to 1994

1945 Unconditional surrender of Germany (May 9). The Allies assume supreme power. Germany divided into four zones and Greater Berlin into 4 sectors (surrounded by the former East Germany). German territories east of the Oder and Neisse rivers ceded to Poland. Potsdam Conference concerning democratization, decentralization, and demilitarization of Germany.

1947 The American Marshall Plan provides comprehensive aid for the rebuilding of Europe, including Germany. Plan is rejected by the Soviet Union and Eastern Europe.

1948 Introduction of separate new currencies in Western and Eastern zones. Introduction of **D-Mark** into West Berlin leads to Berlin Blockade and Berlin Airlift (June 1948).

1949 Founding of the Federal Republic of Germany (FRG, May 23) and the German Democratic Republic (GDR, October 7).

1952 The GDR begins to seal the border with the FRG (May 27).

1953 Uprising in the GDR (June 17) is suppressed by Soviet military power.

1954 The FRG becomes a member of NATO.

1955 The GDR becomes a member of Warsaw Pact. The FRG becomes sovereign; the occupation is ended.

1961 Construction of the Berlin Wall and extensive fortification of East German borders.

1970 New **Ostpolitik**: FRG Chancellor Willy Brandt meets with GDR Minister-President Willi Stoph.

1971 Four-Power Agreement on Berlin guarantees unhindered traffic between West Berlin and the FRG. De facto recognition of the GDR.

1973 Bundestag approves Basic Treaty between the FRG and the GDR in which both states recognize each other's sovereignty and promise to keep "good neighborly" relations. The opposition party in Bonn rejects the treaty and refers to the constitutional mandate to reestablish German unity.

1989 Opening of Austro-Hungarian borders (September 10) brings streams of refugees from the GDR to the FRG. Demonstrations all across the GDR. Opening of the Berlin Wall (November 9) and the Brandenburg Gate (December 22).

1990 Economic union of both German states (July 2). German reunification (October 3). First joint elections (December 2).

1994 Final withdrawal of all Allied troops from Berlin.

EXTRABLATT

Berliner Zeitung

MITTWOCH, 3. OKTOBER 1990 ● EXTRABLATT ● 46. JAHRGANG ● KOSTENLOS ● 90 020 ● ISSN 0323–5793

Adé DDR — Willkommen Deutschland! Nach 45 Jahren sind wir wieder ein Volk in einem geeinten Land

Festakt im Schauspielhaus / Schwarzrotgoldene Fahne vor dem Reichstag / Berlin seit heute wieder deutsche Hauptstadt

Letzte Nachrichten aus der DDR

Gespräche   Hier ist immer etwas los

HEIKE   Und das ist die Gedächtniskirche[1] mit ihren drei Gebäuden. Wir nennen sie den „Hohlen Zahn", den „Lippenstift" und die „Puderdose."

MARTIN   Berliner haben doch für alles Spitznamen.[2]

HEIKE   Der alte Turm der Gedächtniskirche soll als Mahnmal so bleiben, wie er ist. Die neue Gedächtniskirche mit dem neuen Turm ist modern.

MARTIN   Und sie sehen wirklich ein bißchen aus wie ein Lippenstift und eine Puderdose. Sag mal, wohnst du gern hier in Berlin?

HEIKE   Eigentlich schon. Berlin hat wirklich viel zu bieten, nicht nur historisch, sondern auch kulturell.[3] Hier ist immer etwas los. Außerdem ist die Umgebung wunderschön.

MARTIN   Das stimmt. Du, warst du dabei, als sie die Mauer durchbrochen haben?[4]

HEIKE   Na klar! Das werde ich nie vergessen.

MARTIN   Ich auch nicht, obwohl ich's nur im Fernsehen gesehen habe.

HEIKE   Wir haben die ganze Nacht gewartet, obwohl es ganz schön kalt war. Als das erste Stück Mauer kippte, haben wir alle laut gesungen: „So ein Tag, so wunderschön wie heute, so ein Tag, der dürfte nie vergehen."

MARTIN   Ich sehe immer noch die Leute oben auf der Mauer tanzen und feiern.

HEIKE   Das war schon einmalig. Wer hätte gedacht, daß das alles so schnell gehen würde.

MARTIN   Und so friedlich.

HEIKE   Ja, Gott sei Dank. Daß da riesige Probleme waren, wurde uns erst später klar.

Richtig oder falsch?

_____   1. Martin ist Berliner.
_____   2. Der „Hohle Zahn" ist ein Teil der Gedächtniskirche.
_____   3. Er soll die Berliner an den Zahnarzt erinnern.
_____   4. Martin hat verschiedene Spitznamen für die Berliner.
_____   5. Heike findet Berlin sehr interessant.
_____   6. Heike war dabei, als sie die Mauer durchbrochen haben.
_____   7. Martin hat auch mitgefeiert.
_____   8. Das ganze geschah an einem schönen, warmen Nachmittag.
_____   9. Als das erste Stück Mauer kippte, haben die Leute die Polizei gerufen.
_____   10. Manche haben auf der Mauer getanzt.

Übrigens

1.   The **Gedächtniskirche** was built between 1891 and 1895 in memory of Emperor William I (1797–1888). Its ruined tower, kept as a reminder of the horror of war, has been incorporated in the modern group (1961) of a flat-roofed octagonal church and its separate bell tower. The blue-tone stained glass windows were made in Chartres.

2.   Berliners are known for their humor and "big mouth" (**Berliner Schnauze**), as seen in the amusing names they have given to various places. Besides the nicknames mentioned above, there are: the **Schwangere Auster** *(pregnant oyster),* a cultural center; the **Hungerkralle** *(hunger claw),* the monument to the Berlin Airlift of 1948–1949; the

Mauerdurchbruch am 9. 11. 1989

Palazzo Prozzo *(Braggarts' Palace)* or **Honeckers Lampenladen** *(Honecker's lamp-store)*, the parliament building of the former GDR; or the **Mauerspechte** *(wall [wood]peckers)*, the souvenir hunters who chipped away at the Berlin Wall after it was opened.

3.   Berlin is now returning to the cultural preeminence it had before World War II. It has around thirty major art museums, two important symphony orchestras, three opera houses, numerous theaters and cabarets, and well over one hundred educational institutions.

4.   During the first few years after the war, the open border between the Soviet and Western occupation zones was fairly easy to cross. By 1952, however, the increasing flight of the population had become so alarming that the GDR began to surround itself with a "protective strip" of barbed wire, armed guards, and a three-mile-deep "forbidden zone" along its border with the West. When the Berlin Wall was built in 1961, the entire border was massively reinforced with minefields, shrapnel-scattering guns, parallel steel fences, guard dogs, and watchtowers. Such devices were not designed to keep the enemy out, but to keep the people in. For twenty-eight years the Wall was the symbol of a "divided Berlin in a divided Germany in a divided Europe." On November 9, 1989, television viewers around the world witnessed the dramatic end to the artificial division of the city as hundreds of jubilant Berliners danced atop the breached Wall. On the following weekend three million East Germans (close to a fifth of the population) flooded through open checkpoints to the West. Suddenly Berlin was no longer an island. And that, said West Berlin's mayor, was "the nicest Christmas news for all Berliners."

Damals und jetzt   *(then [in those days] and now)*   **WORTSCHATZ 1**

der	Frieden	*peace*	*die*	Grenze, -n	*border*
	Krieg, -e	*war*		Mauer, -n	*wall*
	Spitzname, -ns, -n	*nickname*		Umgebung	*surrounding(s)*
	Turm, ¨e	*tower*			
das	Gebäude, -	*building*			
	Volk, ¨er	*people*			

Weiteres

aus·sehen (sieht aus), sah aus, ausgesehen wie (+ *nom.*)	*to look like (something or someone)*
erinnern (an + *acc.*)[1]	*to remind (of)*
sich erinnern (an + *acc.*)[1]	*to remember*
teilen	*to divide*
einmalig	*unique, incredible*
historisch	*historical(ly)*
kulturell	*cultural(ly)*
wunderschön	*beautiful*

[1] Ich werde **dich** an die Karten erinnern. *(I'll remind you of the tickets.)* BUT Ich kann **mich** nicht daran erinnern. *(I can't remember it.)*

ZUM ERKENNEN: hohl *(hollow);* der Lippenstift, -e *(lipstick);* die Puderdose, -n *(compact);* als Mahnmal *(as a memorial);* eigentlich schon *(actually yes);* bieten *(to offer);* durchbrochen *(broken through);* (um)kippen *(to tip over);* friedlich *(peacefully);* riesig *(enormous)*

Zum Thema

A.   Wie geht's weiter?   *(Use the phrases below in complete sentences. Use your imagination.)*

BEISPIEL: . . . sieht gut aus.
Heike sieht gut aus.

1.   . . . sieht . . . aus.
2.   . . . sieht aus wie ein(e) . . .
3.   . . . hat viel zu bieten.
4.   . . . ist immer etwas los.
5.   Ich erinnere mich gern an . . .
6.   Ich kann mich noch gut erinnern an die Zeit, als . . .
7.   Bitte erinnere mich nicht an . . . !
8.   Der Spitzname von . . . ist . . .

B.   Stadtbesichtigung   *(What would you say if you were taking a foreign visitor on a tour through your own city?)*

S1   Und das ist _____ .
S2   _____ .
S1   Ja, wir finden das auch _____ .
S2   Wie ist das Leben _____ ?
S1   _____ .
S2   Ist hier kulturell viel los?
S1   _____ .
S2   Die Umgebung ist _____ .
S1   Wie findest du / finden Sie _____ ?
S2   _____ .

C.   Stadtplan von Berlin   *(Map of Berlin. Complete these sentences with one of the words from the list below.)*

a.	Brandenburger	f.	Funkturm	k.	Schloß Charlottenburg
b.	Dom	g.	Gedächtniskirche	l.	Spree
c.	Europa	h.	Juni	m.	Stadtplan
d.	Fernsehturm	i.	Reichstagsgebäude	n.	Unter den Linden
e.	Flughafen	j.	Schloß Bellevue	o.	Zoo

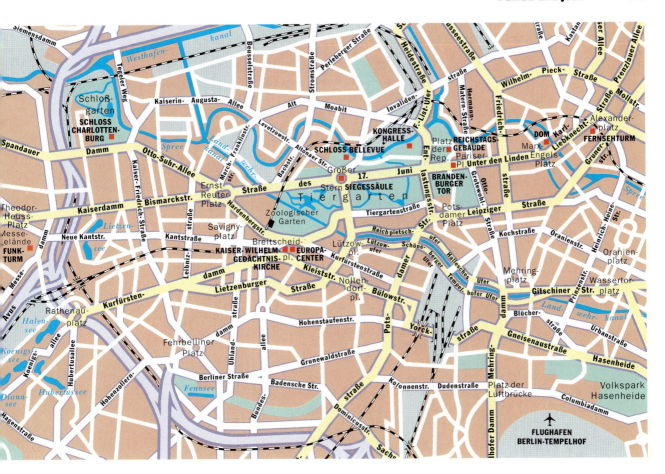

1. Dieser _____ von Berlin gibt einen kleinen Eindruck *(impression)* davon, wo die verschiedenen Straßen und wichtigen Gebäude sind.

2. Im Südwesten ist der Kurfürstendamm oder Ku'damm. Er führt zur _____ .

3. Gegenüber davon steht das _____ -Center.

4. In der Nähe ist auch der _____ .

5. Im Westen, nicht weit vom Theodor-Heuss-Platz, sind das Messegelände *(fairgrounds)* und der alte _____ .

6. Vom Theodor-Heuss-Platz geht eine lange Straße quer durch Berlin bis zum Alexanderplatz mit dem modernen _____ .

7. Sie führt vorbei am Großen Stern mit der Siegessäule *(Victory Column)* und weiter bis zum _____ Tor.

8. Diese lange Straße erinnert an den 17. _____ 1953, als die Ostberliner und die Deutschen in der DDR gegen die Sowjetunion rebellierten.

9. Sie hat verschiedene Namen. Östlich vom Brandenburger Tor heißt sie _____ .

10. Ganz in der Nähe vom Brandenburger Tor ist das alte _____ .

11. Die Straße Under den Linden führt ins alte Zentrum von Berlin, vorbei an der Humboldt Universität und bis auf eine Insel *(island)* mit dem Pergamonmuseum und dem alten _____ .

12. Auf beiden Seiten der Insel fließt *(flows)* die _____ .

13. Berlin hat viele schöne Parks und Seen. Oben links sieht man den Schloßgarten mit _____ .

14. Nicht weit vom Zoo ist _____ .

15. Der _____ Berlin-Tempelhof, der bei der Berliner Luftbrücke *(airlift)* eine so wichtige Rolle gespielt hat, liegt unten rechts auf der Karte.

D.   Aussprache: pf, ps, qu   *(See also III. 19, 21, and 22 in the pronunciation section of the Workbook.)*

1. [pf]   **Pf**arrer, **Pf**effer, **Pf**efferminz, **Pf**ennig, **Pf**und, A**pf**el, Ko**pf**, em**pf**ehlen
2. [ps]   **Ps**ychologe, **Ps**ychiater, **Ps**ychologie, **ps**ychologisch, **Ps**alm, **Ps**eudonym, Ka**ps**el
3. [kv]   **Qu**atsch, **Qu**alität, **Qu**antität, **Qu**artal, **Qu**ote, be**qu**em

Hören Sie zu!

Besuch in der DDR   *(Listen to Margaret tell about her experience in a summer study program in the former German Democratic Republic. Then decide which of the answers most closely reflects what she says.)*

ZUM ERKENNEN: der Kulturschock; die Tschechoslowakei; das Lehrmaterial; die Schreibmaschine, -n *(typewriter);* die Kopie, -n; der Anruf, -e *(phone call);* die Küste, -n *(coast);* der Kontrast, -e; extrem

1. Damals konnten amerikanische Studenten _____ in der DDR studieren.
    a.   in mehreren Programmen
    b.   nur im Sommer
    c.   nicht leicht

2. Im Sommer 1985 erwarteten die Menschen, daß die DDR _____ .
    a.   bald nicht mehr existieren würde
    b.   noch viele Jahre existieren würde
    c.   bald ein Teil der Bundesrepublik werden würde

3. Die anderen Studenten kamen _____ .
    a.   alle aus Polen
    b.   aus mehreren Ländern in Osteuropa
    c.   mit mehr Gepäck

4. Das Essen in der Mensa _____ .
    a.   schmeckte recht gut
    b.   war ausgezeichnet
    c.   war schlecht

5. Eine tschechische Studentin kaufte gern in der DDR ein, weil _____ .
    a.   es da mehr zu kaufen gab als in der Tschechoslowakei
    b.   es da mehr frisches Obst gab
    c.   sie zu Hause kein englisches Wörterbuch finden konnte

6. Man konnte in Rostock sehr leicht _____ .
    a.   mit Verwandten überall in der Welt telefonieren
    b.   überall hinfahren, wo man wollte
    c.   mit den Studenten über Politik sprechen

7. Die amerikanischen Studenten hatten einen zweiten Kulturschock, als sie _____ .
    a.   wieder in den USA ankamen
    b.   in Westberliner Geschäfte gingen
    c.   in Westberliner Restaurants aßen

STRUKTUR

I. Relative Clauses

RELATIVE CLAUSES supply additional information about a noun in a sentence.

There is the professor **who** *teaches the course.*
He taught the course **(that)** *I enjoyed so much.*
He teaches a subject **in which** *I'm very interested (I'm very interested in).*
He's the professor **whose** *course I took last semester.*

English relative clauses may be introduced by the relative pronouns *who, whom, whose, which,* or *that.* The noun to which the relative pronoun "relates" is called the ANTECEDENT. The choice of the relative pronoun depends on the antecedent (is it a person or a thing?) AND on its function in the relative clause. The relative pronoun may be the subject *(who, which, that),* an object or an object of a preposition *(whom, which, that),* or it may indicate possession *(whose).* German relative clauses work essentially the same way. However, while in English the relative pronouns are frequently omitted (especially in conversation), IN GERMAN THEY MUST ALWAYS BE USED.

Ist das der Roman, **den** ihr gelesen habt?   *Is that the novel you read?*

1. Forms and use

   The German relative pronouns have the same forms as the definite article, EXCEPT FOR THE GENITIVE FORMS AND THE DATIVE PLURAL.

	masc.	neut.	fem.	pl.
nom.	der	das	die	die
acc.	den	das	die	die
dat.	dem	dem	der	**denen**
gen.	**dessen**	**dessen**	**deren**	**deren**

   The form of the relative pronoun is determined by two factors:

   a. Its ANTECEDENT: is the antecedent masculine, neuter, feminine, or in the plural?

   Das ist **der Fluß, der** auf der Karte ist.
   Das ist **das Gebäude, das** auf der Karte ist.
   Das ist **die Kirche, die** auf der Karte ist.
   Das sind **die Plätze, die** auf der Karte sind.

b.   Its FUNCTION in the relative clause: is the relative pronoun the subject, an accusative or dative object, an object of a preposition, or does it indicate possession?

SUBJECT:	Ist das der Mann, **der** in Berlin wohnt?
ACCUSATIVE OBJECT:	Ist das der Mann, **den** du meinst?
DATIVE OBJECT:	Ist das der Mann, **dem** du geschrieben hast?
OBJECT OF PREP.:	Ist das der Mann, mit **dem** du gesprochen hast?
GENITIVE:	Ist das der Mann, **dessen** Tochter hier studiert?

The following examples indicate the ANTECEDENT and state the FUNCTION of the relative pronoun (RP) in each relative clause.

> . . . ANTECEDENT, (preposition) RP _____ V1.
> gender? number?   function?

Das ist der Professor. Er lehrt an meiner Universität.
Das ist **der Professor, der** an meiner Universität lehrt.
*That's **the professor who** teaches at my university.*
ANTECEDENT: der Professor; sg. / masc.
PRONOUN FUNCTION: subject → nom.

Wie heißt der Kurs? Du findest ihn so interessant.
Wie heißt **der Kurs, den** du so interessant findest?
*What's the name of **the course (that)** you find so interesting?*
ANTECEDENT: der Kurs; sg. / masc.
PRONOUN FUNCTION: object of **finden** → acc.

Da ist der Student. Ich habe ihm mein Buch gegeben.
Da ist **der Student, dem** ich mein Buch gegeben habe.
*There's **the student to whom** I gave my book (I gave my book to).*
ANTECEDENT: der Student; sg. / masc.
PRONOUN FUNCTION: object of **geben** → dat.

Kennst du den Professor? Erik hat sein Seminar belegt.
Kennst du **den Professor, dessen Seminar** Erik belegt hat?
*Do you know **the professor whose seminar** Erik has been taking?*
ANTECEDENT: den Professor; sg. / masc.
PRONOUN FUNCTION: related possessively to **Seminar** → gen.

Das Buch ist von einem Autor. Ich interessiere mich sehr für ihn.
Das Buch ist von **einem Autor, für den** ich mich sehr interessiere.
*The book is by **an author in whom** I'm very interested.*
ANTECEDENT: von einem Autor; sg. / masc.
PRONOUN FUNCTION: object of **für** → acc.

Die Autoren sind aus Leipzig. Der Professor hat von ihnen gesprochen.
Die Autoren, von denen der Professor gesprochen hat, sind aus Leipzig.
*The authors **of whom** the professor spoke are from Leipzig.*
ANTECEDENT: die Autoren; pl.
PRONOUN FUNCTION: object of **von** → dat.

Caution: Don't use the interrogative pronoun in place of the relative pronoun!

Wer hat das Seminar gegeben?
Das ist der Professor, **der** das Seminar gegeben hat.

Who gave the seminar?
That's the professor who gave the seminar.

2. Word order

   a. Relative pronouns can be the objects of prepositions. If that is the case, the preposition will always precede the relative pronoun.

     Das Buch ist von einem Autor, **für den** ich mich sehr interessiere.
     The book is by an author in whom I'm very interested.

   b. The word order in the RELATIVE CLAUSE is like that of all SUBORDINATE clauses: the inflected part of the verb (V1) comes last. Always separate the relative clause from the main clause by a COMMA.

$$\ldots, RP \underline{\hspace{3cm}} VI, \ldots$$

     Der Professor, **der** den Prosakurs **lehrt,** ist sehr nett.
             RP   V1

   c. Relative clauses immediately follow the antecedent unless the antecedent is followed by a prepositional phrase that modifies it, a genitive, or a verb complement (V2).

     Das Buch von Dürrenmatt, **das wir lesen sollen,** ist leider ausverkauft.
     Das Buch des Autors, **das wir lesen sollen,** ist teuer.
     Ich kann **das Buch** nicht bekommen, **das wir lesen sollen.**

A.   **Analysieren Sie die Sätze!**   *(Find the antecedent and state the function of the relative pronoun in each relative clause.)*   **Übungen**

BEISPIEL: Renate Berger ist eine Arbeiterin, die für gleiche Arbeit gleiches Einkommen möchte.
              ANTECEDENT: **eine Arbeiterin; sg. / fem.**
              PRONOUN FUNCTION: **subject → nom.**

1. Der Mann, der neben ihr arbeitet, verdient pro Stunde 1,80 DM mehr.
2. Es gibt leider noch viele Frauen, deren Kollegen ein höheres Einkommen bekommen.
3. Und es gibt Frauen, denen schlecht bezahlte Arbeit lieber ist als keine Arbeit.
4. Was denken die Männer, deren Frauen weniger Geld bekommen als ihre Kollegen?
5. Der Mann, mit dem Renate Berger verheiratet ist, findet das nicht so schlecht.
6. Aber die Frauen, die bei der gleichen Firma arbeiten, ärgern sich sehr darüber.
7. Es ist ein Problem, das die meisten Firmen haben.
8. Es gibt Berufe, in denen Männer für gleiche Arbeit mehr verdienen.
9. Und die Berufe, in denen fast nur Frauen arbeiten, sind am schlechtesten bezahlt.
10. Wir leben in einer Welt, in der Gleichberechtigung noch nicht überall Realität *(reality)* ist.

B.   Rundfahrt in Berlin   *(While Sepp shows slides from his visit to Berlin, his Austrian friends ask questions. Answer according to the model, using relative pronouns.)*

1.   BEISPIEL: Ist das der Alexanderplatz?
      Ja, das ist der Alexanderplatz, der so bekannt ist.

   a. Ist das der Dom?   **b.** Ist das das Operncafé?   **c.** Ist das die Staatsbibliothek?   **d.** Ist das der Fernsehturm?   **e.** Sind das die Museen?

2.   BEISPIEL: Ist das der Potsdamer Platz?
      Ja, das ist der Potsdamer Platz, den du da siehst.

   a. Ist das die Leipziger Straße?   **b.** Ist das der Landwehrkanal?   **c.** Ist das die Gedächtniskirche?   **d.** Ist das der Kurfürstendamm?   **e.** Ist das das Europa-Center?

3.   BEISPIEL: Ist das die Hochschule für Musik?
      Ja, das ist die Hochschule für Musik, zu der wir jetzt kommen.

   a. Ist das der Zoo?   **b.** Ist das die Siegessäule?   **c.** Ist das die Kongreßhalle?   **d.** Ist das das Reichstagsgebäude?   **e.** Sind das die Universitätsgebäude?

4.   BEISPIEL: Wo ist der Student? Sein Vater lehrt an der Universität.
      Da ist der Student, dessen Vater an der Universität lehrt.

   a. Wo ist die Studentin? Ihre Eltern wohnten früher *(formerly)* in Berlin.
   b. Wo ist das Mädchen? Ihr Bruder war so lustig.   **c.** Wo ist der Herr? Seine Frau sprach so gut Englisch.   **d.** Wo sind die alten Leute? Ihre Kinder sind jetzt in Amerika.

C.   Was gefällt Ihnen? Geben Sie Beispiele!

BEISPIEL: Stück
      Ein Stück, das mir gefällt, ist Goethes *Faust*.

1. Buch   **2.** Film   **3.** Fernsehsendung   **4.** Zeitschrift   **5.** Schlagersänger(in) *(pop singer)*   **6.** Komponist(in)   **7.** Restaurant   **8.** Auto   **9.** Stadt

EUROCARD. Für Leute, die auch sonst gute Karten haben.

D.   Kein Wiedersehen.   Geben Sie die fehlenden Relativpronomen!

1.   Der junge Mann, _____ da steht, heißt David.
2.   Das Mädchen, mit _____ er spricht, heißt Tina.
3.   Das andere Mädchen, _____ daneben steht, heißt Margaret.
4.   Sie sprechen über einen Film, _____ momentan im Kino läuft.
5.   Der Film, über _____ sie sprechen, spielt in Berlin.
6.   Die Geschichte spielt kurz vor dem Bau der Mauer, _____ Berlin von 1961 bis 1989 geteilt hat.

7. In den fünfziger Jahren sind viele mit der S-Bahn, _____ ja quer durch *(right through)* die Stadt fuhr, geflohen.

8. Ein junger Mann, _____ Freundin auch weg wollte, fuhr mit der S-Bahn nach West-Berlin und blieb dort.

9. Die Freundin, _____ Eltern in Weimar wohnten, wollte noch einmal ihre Eltern sehen.

10. Das war aber gerade an dem Tag, an _____ man die Mauer baute.

11. Das bedeutete, daß sie den Freund, _____ sie in West-Berlin zurückgelassen hatte und _____ dort auf sie wartete, nie wiedersehen würde.

12. Am Ende des Filmes, _____ sehr spannend war, blieb nur die Erinnerung an den Freund.

E. Verbinden Sie die Sätze! *(Combine these sentences with the help of a relative pronoun. If necessary, give the English version first.)*

BEISPIEL: Der Ku'damm ist eine bekannte Berliner <u>Straße</u>. Jeder kennt sie.
   (The Ku'damm is a famous Berlin street [that] everyone knows.)
   Der Ku'damm ist eine bekannte Berliner Straße, die jeder kennt.

1. <u>Die Gedächtniskirche</u> gefällt mir. Ihr habt schon von der Gedächtniskirche gehört.

2. <u>Der alte Turm</u> soll kaputt bleiben. Die Berliner nennen ihn den „Hohlen Zahn."

3. <u>Die Berliner</u> nennen den neuen Turm „Lippenstift." Die Berliner haben für alles einen Namen.

4. <u>Der Ku'damm</u> beginnt bei der Gedächtniskirche. Am Ku'damm gibt es viele schöne Geschäfte.

5. <u>Die Geschäfte</u> sind nicht billig. Sie sind sehr elegant.

6. Da gibt es auch <u>viele Cafés</u>. Man kann in den Cafés gemütlich sitzen.

7. <u>Das Café</u> war prima. Ich habe seinen Namen vergessen.

8. <u>Heike</u> hat mir alles gezeigt. Ihre Eltern wohnen in Berlin.

9. <u>Ihr Bruder</u> war auch sehr nett. Ich bin mit ihm am Abend in einen Jazzkeller gegangen.

10. In dem <u>Jazzkeller</u> konnte man auch tanzen. Ich fand den Jazzkeller übrigens einmalig.

F.   An der Uni. Auf deutsch, bitte!

1. Where's the lecture hall in which Professor Schulz is lecturing (reading)?
2. The course he teaches is modern German history.   **3.** The students who take his courses must work hard.   **4.** History is a subject that I find very interesting.
5. But I have a roommate who finds nothing interesting.   **6.** He's a person (**Mensch**) I don't understand.   **7.** He studies subjects he doesn't like.   **8.** The friends he goes out with (with whom he goes out) are boring.   **9.** He laughs at his father, whose money he gets every month.   **10.** But the girl he's engaged to (to whom he is engaged) is very nice.

II. Indirect Speech

When reporting what someone else has said, you can use DIRECT SPEECH with quotation marks, or INDIRECT SPEECH without quotation marks.

Heike said, "Berlin has a lot to offer."
Heike said (that) Berlin has a lot to offer.

Often, corresponding direct and indirect speech will require different personal pronouns and possessive adjectives, depending on who reports the conversation.

• If Heike says to Martin *"I'll bring my map,"* and she reports the conversation, she will say: *I told him I would bring my map.*

• If Martin reported the conversation, he would say: *She told me she would bring her map.*

• If a third person reported, he or she would say: *She told him she would bring her map.*

In spoken German such indirect reports are generally in the INDICATIVE when the opening verb is in the present (**Sie sagt, . . .**). However, when the opening verb is in the past (**Sie sagte, . . .**), the SUBJUNCTIVE usually follows. This section focuses on the latter.

Direct speech	„Ich bringe meinen Stadtplan mit."
Indirect speech	
Indicative	Sie sagt, sie **bringt** ihren Stadtplan mit.
Subjunctive	Sie sagte, sie **würde** ihren Stadtplan **mitbringen.**

NOTE: In German opening quotation marks are placed at the bottom of the line, especially in handwriting. Many publishers now use an alternative form of quotation marks: »Ich bringe meinen Stadtplan mit.«

1. Statements

    The tense of the indirect statement is determined by the tense of the direct statement.

    a. Direct statements in the present or future are reported indirectly in the present-time subjunctive or the **würde**-form.

    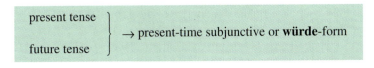

    „Ich komme später.“ ⎱   ⎰ Sie sagte, sie käme später.
    „Ich werde später kommen.“ ⎰   ⎱ Sie sagte, sie würde später kommen.

    b. Direct statements IN ANY PAST TENSE are reported indirectly in the past-time subjunctive.

    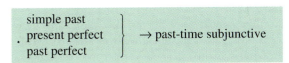

    „Sie hatte keine Zeit.“
    „Sie hat keine Zeit gehabt.“   Sie sagte, sie hätte keine Zeit gehabt.
    „Sie hatte keine Zeit gehabt.“

    c. The conjunction **daß** may or may not be used. If it is not used, the clause retains the original word order. If **daß** is used, the inflected part of the verb comes last.

    Sie sagte, sie **käme** morgen.
    Sie sagte, **daß** sie morgen **käme.**

    Sie sagte, sie **hätte** andere Pläne gehabt.
    Sie sagte, **daß** sie andere Pläne gehabt **hätte.**

2. Questions

    The tense of the indirect question is also determined by the tense of the direct question. Indirect YES / NO QUESTIONS are introduced by **ob**, and indirect INFORMATION QUESTIONS by the question word.

    Er fragte: „Hast du jetzt Zeit?“   *He asked, "Do you have time now?"*
    Er fragte, **ob** sie jetzt Zeit hätte.   *He asked whether she had time now.*

    Er fragte: „Wo warst du?“   *He asked, "Where were you?"*
    Er fragte, **wo** sie gewesen wäre.   *He asked where she had been.*

3. Imperatives

    Direct requests in the imperative are expressed indirectly with the auxiliary **sollen.**

    Sie sagte: „Frag(e) nicht so viel!“   *She said, "Don't ask so many questions."*
    Sie sagte, er **sollte** nicht so viel **fragen.**   *She said he shouldn't ask so many questions.*

Übungen

G. Stimmt das? *(Confirm that the different speakers really said what is mentioned below. Begin the indirect speech with **daß**.)*

BEISPIEL: Hat Phillip gesagt, er wäre im Theater gewesen?
            Ja, Phillip hat gesagt, daß er im Theater gewesen wäre.

1. Hat Phillip gesagt, er hätte das Stück sehr gut gefunden?
2. Hat Stephan gesagt, er wollte es sich auch ansehen?
3. Hat Sonja gesagt, sie würde mit Stephan ins Theater gehen?
4. Hat Sonja gesagt, sie würde heute nachmittag die Karten dafür kaufen?
5. Hat Stephan gesagt, er wollte das Stück erst lesen?

H. Verschiedene Leute im Gespräch   *(Give the English equivalents.)*

1. **Elke erzählt über Trudi**

    Trudi sagte, . . .
    a. Sie wollte Zahnärztin werden.   **b.** Gute Zahnärzte würde man immer brauchen.   **c.** Sie könnte leicht weniger arbeiten, wenn sie mal Kinder hätte. **d.** Als Zahnarzt würde man gut verdienen.   **e.** Man müßte natürlich lange studieren, aber darauf würde sie sich schon freuen.

2. **Bernd erzählt über Carolyn**

    Carolyn sagte, . . .
    a. Sie hätte letztes Jahr in Deutschland studiert.   **b.** Es hätte ihr gut gefallen. **c.** Sie hätte die Sprachprüfung leicht bestanden.   **d.** Während der Semesterferien wäre sie in die Schweiz gefahren.   **e.** Sie wäre erst vor drei Wochen zurückgekommen.

3. **Martin und Heike**

    Er hat sie gefragt, . . .
    a. ob ihr Berlin jetzt besser gefallen würde.   **b.** ob sie beim Mauerdurchbruch dabei gewesen wäre.   **c.** wie lange sie schon in Berlin wäre.   **d.** wo das Brandenburger Tor wäre.   **e.** wie man dorthin käme.   **f.** was es hier noch zu sehen gäbe.

    Sie hat ihm gesagt, . . .
    g. er sollte sich die Museen ansehen.   **h.** er sollte in ein Konzert gehen.   **i.** er sollte die Filmfestspiele besuchen.

4. **Katrin und Margaret**

    a. Katrin erzählte, daß sie 1987 mit ihrer Familie nach Berlin geflogen wäre. **b.** Sie hätte viel über Berlin gehört.   **c.** Sie hätte die Stadt einmal sehen wollen. **d.** Besonders interessant wäre natürlich die Mauer gewesen.   **e.** Viele Menschen hätten auf der Westseite bunte Bilder an die Mauer gemalt.   **f.** Man hätte auf eine Plattform steigen und über die Mauer sehen können.   **g.** Auch sehr interessant wäre eine Fahrt nach Ost-Berlin gewesen.   **h.** Ein Polizist hätte den Bus lange durchsucht, um zu sehen, ob vielleicht ein Ostberliner im Bus wäre, und hätte sich die Pässe sehr genau angesehen.   **i.** Die Museen in Ost- und West-Berlin hätten ihr und ihrer Familie besonders gut gefallen.   **j.** Als Katrin sagte, daß sie und ihr Mann im kommenden Jahr wahrscheinlich wieder nach Deutschland reisen würden, wollte ihre Tochter Margaret wissen, wie lange sie bleiben würden und ob sie wieder nach Berlin fahren würden.   **k.** Margaret fand, daß sie das unbedingt tun sollten.   **l.** Sie sollten aber auch andere Städte in den neuen Ländern besuchen.

I.   Was hat er / sie gesagt?   *(Ask your classmate five questions about himself/herself and then report to the class, using indirect speech.)*

BEISPIEL: **Er / sie hat mir erzählt, er / sie wäre aus Chicago, er / sie hätte zwei Brüder . . .**

J.   Ein toller Tag. Geben Sie das fehlende Relativpronomen!

1. Christa Grauer ist eine junge Frau, _____ mit einem Computer die Anzeigetafeln *(scoreboards)* in einem Kölner Fußballstadion bedient *(takes care of)*.
2. Sie erzählt von einem Tag, _____ sie nie vergessen wird.   **3.** Eine Woche nach dem 9. November, einem Tag, _____ Geschichte gemacht hat, spielte die deutsche Fußball-Nationalmannschaft *(. . . team)* gegen Wales.   **4.** Vor dem Spiel, zu _____ 60 000 Menschen gekommen waren, schrieb Christa wie immer die dritte Strophe *(stanza)* des Deutschlandliedes auf die Anzeigetafeln.   **5.** Das hatte sie schon 14 Jahre lang getan. Aber es gab wenige Spiele, bei _____ die Leute wirklich mitsangen.   **6.** Aber diesmal sangen Tausende mit, denn die Strophe, _____ Text ihnen bisher nicht viel bedeutet hatte, bedeutete ihnen plötzlich sehr viel.

K.   Kommentare über den Mauerdurchbruch

1.   **Heute**   *(Give the English equivalent. Then convert from indirect to direct speech. Be sure to change the pronouns accordingly.)*

a.   Andrea Bertram, Studentin

Andrea sagte, es wäre für sie wie ein Schock gewesen. Sie sei mit der Mauer groß geworden und hätte nicht gedacht, daß sich das mal ändern würde *(would change)*. Sie wäre am 10. November das erste Mal in West-Berlin gewesen. Das hätte ihr damals sehr gut gefallen. Aber jetzt fände sie es nicht mehr so toll. Es wäre alles irgendwie anders geworden. Früher wären die Westberliner netter zu ihnen gewesen.

b.   Joseph Schneider, Rentner

Als Rentner *(retired person)* wäre er öfter in West-Berlin gewesen. Da hätte er den Unterschied gesehen. Wer nicht unter dem System gelebt hätte, könnte sich gar nicht vorstellen, wie furchtbar es wäre, unfrei zu sein. Er hätte immer mit Angst gelebt. Jetzt könnte er wieder überall hin. Finanziell ginge es ihm nicht besonders gut, aber er wäre frei und hätte alles, was er brauchte.

Zusammen-fassung

Third stanza of the *Deutschlandlied:* Einigkeit und Recht und Freiheit für das deutsche Vaterland. Danach laßt uns alle streben, brüderlich mit Herz und Hand. Einigkeit und Recht und Freiheit sind des Glückes Unterpfand. Blüh im Glanze dieses Glückes, blühe deutsches Vaterland!

2. **Im November 1989**   *(Convert from direct to indirect speech. Be sure to change the pronouns accordingly.)*

BEISPIEL: Major der DDR-Grenztruppe: „Es ist eine verrückte Zeit."
Er sagte, es wäre eine verrückte Zeit.

NBC-Korrespondent: „Vor meinen Augen tanzte die Freiheit."
Er sagte, vor seinen Augen hätte die Freiheit getanzt.

a.   Ostberliner Taxifahrer: „So viel Fernsehen haben wir noch nie gesehen."
b.   Westberliner Polizist über seinen Kollegen in Ost-Berlin: „Wir haben uns jeden Tag gesehen. Jetzt will ich ihm mal die Hand schütteln *(shake)*."
c.   Afrikanischer Diplomat: „Ich dachte, die Deutschen können nur Fußball spielen oder Stechschritt *(goose-step)*, aber jetzt können sie sogar Revolutionen machen."
d.   Ronald Reagan: „Auf beiden Seiten sind Deutsche. Der Kommunismus hat seine Chance gehabt. Er funktioniert nicht."
e.   Ostdeutscher Autor Stephan Heym: „Die einzige *(only)* Chance, die wir haben, den Sozialismus zu retten *(save)*, ist richtiger Sozialismus."
f.   Ex-Bundeskanzler Willy Brandt: „Ich bin Gott dankbar, daß ich das noch erleben *(experience)* darf."
g.   Cellist Mstislaw Rostropowitsch: „Mauern sind nicht für ewig *(forever)* gebaut . . . In Berlin habe ich für mein Herz gespielt."
h.   Tschechischer Reformpräsident Alexander Dubček: „Wir haben zu lange im Dunkeln gelebt. Treten wir *(let's step)* ins Licht!"

Cellist Mstislaw
Rostropowitsch am
11. 11. 1989 an der
Berliner Mauer

L.   Bertolt Brecht. Auf deutsch, bitte!

1. Brecht, who was from Augsburg, studied medicine (**Medizin**) at first.   **2.** But it was the theater in which he was really interested.   **3.** Kurt Weill was a composer with whom Brecht often worked.   **4.** *Die Dreigroschenoper* is a play that Brecht and Weill wrote together.   **5.** *Mutter Courage* and *Der kaukasische Kreidekreis* are two plays he wrote in 1938.   **6.** The theater that Brecht directed (**leiten**) after 1948 is in Berlin.   **7.** Berlin is also the city in which he died (**starb**) in 1956.   **8.** *Der Augsburger Kreidekreis* is a story by Brecht that many students read.

EINBLICKE

Blick aufs
Brandenburger Tor

First mentioned in a document in 1237, Berlin became the seat of the electors (**Kurfürsten**) of Brandenburg in 1486 and later, after 1701, of the Prussian kings. After 1871 it gained political, economic, and cultural prominence as the capital of the German nation. At the beginning of World War II, Berlin was the sixth-largest city in the world, with over four million inhabitants. More than a third did not survive the war. In 1945, at the Yalta conference, Berlin was put under the four-power administration of the Allies: Great Britain, France, the United States, and the Soviet Union. Differences among the occupation powers, however, brought about the 1948 Soviet blockade and the division of the city. In 1949 East Berlin became the capital of the GDR. On August 13, 1961, the East German government began to build the Berlin Wall, a symbol for the division of Germany as a whole. Ironically, the Wall was opened for the same reason for which it had been built: to prevent a mass exodus of the population to the West, this time through an open border with Hungary. Once the Wall had been breached, the reunification of the city and the country could not be stopped. Today Berlin has a new future as the capital of Germany.

Berlin's return to its former position as the seat of German government and as the cultural and economic center of Germany has been very difficult. Five years after unification, unemployment was high, crime on the rise, traffic congested, and rents had skyrocketed. Despite increased tax revenues, Berlin's budget deficit was growing. The continued influx of asylum seekers further complicated the situation. On the positive side, the government and private investors were pumping billions into East Berlin for the modernization and development of that city's infrastructure. Construction and related industries thrived, and the arts were flourishing.

WORTSCHATZ 2

der	Gedanke, -ns, -n	*thought*
die	Heimat	*homeland, home*
	Insel	*island*
	Jugend	*youth*
	Macht, ⸚e	*power*
	Mitte	*middle*
	(Wieder)vereinigung	*(re)unification*

berühmt	*famous*
herrlich	*wonderful, great*
kaum	*hardly*
aus·tauschen	*to exchange*
behalten (behält), behielt, behalten	*to keep*
erkennen, erkannte, erkannt	*to recognize*
erleben	*to experience*
scheinen, schien, geschienen	*to seem, appear like*
schützen	*to protect*
verlassen (verläßt), verließ, verlassen	*to leave (a place)*

WAS IST DAS? der Bomber, Einmarsch, Jeep, Sonderstatus, Städteplaner; das Angebot, Gefühl, Medikament, Transportflugzeug, Turmcafé; die Blockade, Metropole, Olympiade, Paßkontrolle, Rote Armee, Teilung, Viereinhalbmillionenstadt; *(pl.)* die Westmächte; reagieren; britisch, enorm viel, grenzenlos, kapitalistisch, sowjetisch, sozialistisch, teils, total blockiert, ummauert, unbebaut, (un)freiwillig, vital

Berlin, damals und heute

Da saßen wir nun, Vater und Tochter, im Flugzeug auf dem Weg zu der Stadt, die er eigentlich nie vergessen konnte: Berlin. „Ich bin schon lange° in Amerika, aber Berlin . . . Nun, Berlin ist eben meine Heimat." Und dann wanderten seine Gedanken zurück zu den zwanziger bis vierziger Jahren, zu der Zeit, als er dort gelebt hatte. Die Viereinhalbmillionenstadt, von deren Charme und Esprit er heute noch schwärmt°, hätte seine Jugend 5 geprägt°. Und er erzählte mir von dem, was er dort so geliebt hatte: von den Wäldern und Seen in der Umgebung und von der berühmten Berliner Luft; von den Museen, der Oper und den Theatern, deren Angebot damals einmalig gewesen wäre; vom Kabarett mit seiner typischen „Berliner Schnauze"° und den Kaffeehäusern, in denen immer etwas los war. „In Berlin liefen eben alle Fäden° zusammen, nicht nur kulturell, sondern auch politisch und 10 wirtschaftlich°. Es war damals die größte Industriestadt Europas. Die Zentralverwaltung° fast aller wichtigen Industriefirmen war in Berlin. Und man kannte sich, tauschte Gedanken aus, auch mit Wissenschaftlern an der Universität. Einfach phantastisch! . . ."

   „Und dann kam 1933[1]. Viele verließen Berlin, teils freiwillig, teils unfreiwillig. Die Nazis beherrschten° das Straßenbild°. Bei der Olympiade 1936 sah die ganze Welt nicht 15 nur Berlins moderne S-Bahn und schöne Straßen, sondern auch Hitler. Und drei Jahre später war Krieg!" Nun sprach er von den schweren Luftangriffen° und den Trümmern°, die diese hinterlassen hätten, vom Einmarsch der Roten Armee, der Teilung Deutschlands unter den vier Siegermächten° (1945) und auch von der Luftbrücke[2], mit der die Westmächte auf die sowjetische Blockade reagiert hätten. „Plötzlich waren wir total blockiert, 20

for a long time

raves
shaped

big mouth
threads
economically / . . . administration

dominated / . . . scene

air raids / rubble

victorious Allies

Ein „Rosinenbomber"
während der Blockade

eine Insel. Es gab nichts zu essen, keine Kleidung, kein Heizmaterial°, keine Medikamente,   *fuel*
kaum Wasser und Strom°. An guten Tagen landeten in den nächsten zehn Monaten alle   *electricity*
paar Minuten britische und amerikanische Transportflugzeuge—wir nannten sie die Rosi-
nenbomber°—und brachten uns, was wir brauchten. Ohne die Westmächte hätten wir es nie   *raisin . . .*
25 geschafft°!"   *made*
     Dann kamen wir in West-Berlin an. Erst machten wir eine Stadtrundfahrt. „Es ist
wieder schön hier, und doch, die Weite° ist weg. Berlin schien früher grenzenlos, und jetzt   *wide-open space*
. . . überall diese Grenze." Immer wieder stand man vor der Mauer, die seit 1961 mitten
durch Berlin lief. Besonders traurig machte ihn der Blick auf das Brandenburger Tor[3], das
30 auf der anderen Seite der Mauer stand. Und doch gefiel mir diese ummauerte Insel. West-
Berlin war wieder eine vitale Metropole, die enorm viel zu bieten hatte.
     Der Besuch 1985 in Ost-Berlin, der Hauptstadt der DDR, war wie eine Reise in eine
andere Welt. Allein schon die Gesichter der Vopos° am Checkpoint Charlie[4] und das   *GDR police (Volkspolizei)*
komische Gefühl, das man bei der Paßkontrolle hatte! Berlin-Mitte war für meinen Vater
35 schwer wiederzuerkennen. Der Potsdamer Platz, der früher voller Leben gewesen war, war
leer. Leichter zu erkennen waren die historischen Gebäude entlang „Unter den Linden"[5]:
die Staatsbibliothek, die Humboldt-Universität[6] und die Staatsoper. Interessant waren auch
das Pergamonmuseum, der Dom und gegenüber der Palast der Republik, den die Berliner
„Palazzo Prozzo" nannten und in dem die Volkskammer° saß. Dann über allem der Fern-   *GDR house of representa-*
40 sehturm, dessen Turmcafé sich dreht°. Wir sahen auch einen britischen Jeep, der „Unter   *tives / turns*
den Linden" Streife fuhr°, was uns an den Sonderstatus Berlins erinnerte. Hier trafen die   *patrolled*
kapitalistische und die sozialistische Welt aufeinander°; und für beide Welten waren Ost-   *came together*
und West-Berlin Schaufenster° zweier gegensätzlicher° Systeme.   *shop windows / opposing*
     Heute ist das alles Geschichte. Die Berliner können wieder reisen, wohin sie wollen.
45 Berlin ist keine Insel mehr. Als mein Vater den Durchbruch° der Mauer im Fernsehen sah,   *breaching*
sagte er immer wieder: „Daß ich das noch erleben durfte!" Und unsere Gedanken gingen
zurück zu Präsident Kennedys Worten 1963 an der Mauer: „Alle freien Menschen sind
Bürger Berlins . . . Ich bin ein Berliner!"

John F. Kennedy in
Berlin am 26. 6. 1963

tasks   Seit der Wiedervereinigung steht Berlin vor schwierigen Aufgaben°. Man nimmt an,
                daß es als Hauptstadt in den nächsten paar Jahren wieder zur Vier- bis Fünfmillionenstadt 50
increase   anwachsen° wird. Politiker, Städteplaner, Architekten und Ökologen werden wichtige
make   Entscheidungen treffen° müssen. Wie kann man genug Wohnungen bauen, wo und in
be built / surrounding welcher Form sollten sie am besten entstehen°? Wie kann man die umliegenden° Wälder
green areas / keep und Seen schützen? Wo kann man Grünflächen° erhalten°? Wie kann man den unbebauten
strip of land   Streifen° am besten nutzen, auf dem einmal die Mauer stand? Man kann nur hoffen, daß 55
                das neue Berlin etwas von seinem alten Charme behält, und daß die Berliner ihren herr-
                lichen Humor nicht verlieren.

Zum Text   **A.   Richtig oder falsch?**

_____   1.   Der Vater und die Tochter fliegen nach Amerika.
_____   2.   Der Vater hatte 40 Jahre in Berlin gelebt.
_____   3.   Er hatte Berlin sehr geliebt.
_____   4.   In Berlin war damals nicht viel los gewesen.
_____   5.   1939 hatte der Krieg begonnen.
_____   6.   1945 teilten die Siegermächte Deutschland und Berlin.
_____   7.   Die Luftbrücke brachte den Berlinern nur Rosinen.
_____   8.   Von 1961 bis 1989 teilte die Mauer Berlin.
_____   9.   Ein Vopo war ein ostdeutsches Auto.
_____   10. Der Potsdamer Platz war der „Palazzo Prozzo" Ost-Berlins.
_____   11. „Unter den Linden" ist eine berühmte alte Straße in Berlin.
_____   12. Ost-Berlin war ein Schaufenster des Kapitalismus.
_____   13. Der Vater ist beim Öffnen der Mauer in Berlin gewesen.
_____   14. Präsident Nixon sagte 1963: „Ich bin ein Berliner."
_____   15. Seit der Wiedervereinigung ist Berlin wieder eine Sechsmillionenstadt.
_____   16. In den nächsten paar Jahren wird man in Berlin viele neue Wohnungen
                bauen müssen.
_____   17. Der ganze Streifen, auf dem einmal die Mauer stand, soll unbebaut
                bleiben.

B. **Suchen Sie die Relativpronomen im Text!** *(Working in groups of two to four stu-dents, underline all the relative pronouns and their antecedents that you can find in the text. Which group can find the greatest number?)*

C. **Bilden Sie Relativsätze!** *(Make up two relative clauses for each pronoun, then compare results with the rest of the class.)*

1. Berlin ist eine Stadt, die . . .
2. Berlin ist eine Stadt, in der . . .
3. Berlin ist eine Stadt, deren . . .
4. Berlin ist eine Stadt, von der . . .
5. Berlin ist eine Stadt, um die . . .

D. **Was fehlt?**

1. Mir gefällt diese Stadt, in _____ mehr als drei Millionen Menschen wohnen.
2. Es ist ein Kulturzentrum *(n.)*, _____ enorm viel zu bieten hat. **3.** Die Filmfestspiele, _____ Filme wirklich einmalig sind, muß man einmal gesehen haben. **4.** Der letzte Film, _____ ich mir angesehen habe, war herrlich. **5.** Ein anderer Film, an _____ Titel *(m.)* ich mich nicht erinnern kann, war etwas traurig. **6.** Es war ein Film, in _____ mehrere berühmte Schauspieler mitspielten. **7.** Der Hauptschauspieler, _____ am Ende seine Heimat verläßt, hieß Humphrey Bogart. **8.** Morgen abend gehe ich mit Heike, _____ Vater Extrakarten hat, ins Kabarett. **9.** Das Kabarett, _____ Name nicht nur in Berlin bekannt ist, heißt, „Die Stachelschweine" *(The Porcupines)*. **10.** Die Leute, über _____ sie lachen, sind meistens Politiker oder andere berühmte Persön-lichkeiten *(pl.)*, _____ jeder kennt.

E. **Vater und Tochter.** Lesen Sie das Gespräch, und erzählen Sie dann indirekt, was sie gesagt oder gefragt haben!

TOCHTER	Wie lange hast du dort gewohnt?
VATER	Ungefähr 25 Jahre.
TOCHTER	Wohnten deine Eltern damals auch in Berlin?
VATER	Nein, aber sie sind 1938 nachgekommen.
TOCHTER	Hast du dort studiert?
VATER	Ja, an der Humboldt-Universität.
TOCHTER	Hast du dort Mutti kennengelernt?
VATER	Ja, das waren schöne Jahre!
TOCHTER	Und wann seid ihr von dort weggegangen?
VATER	1949.
TOCHTER	Erzähl mir davon!
VATER	Ach, das ist eine lange Geschichte. Setzen wir uns in ein Café! Dann werde ich dir davon erzählen.

F. **Schriftliche Übung.** Wenn Sie die Wahl *(choice)* hätten, würden Sie in Berlin leben oder dort studieren wollen? Warum oder warum nicht? Schreiben Sie acht bis zehn Sätze!

Hören Sie zu!

Nach der Wiedervereinigung   *(Listen to the passage about reunification. Then decide whether the following statements are true or false.)*

ZUM ERKENNEN: kompliziert *(complicated);* viel geschafft *(accomplished a lot);* profitieren; garantieren; das Gefängnis *(prison);* existieren; die Direktorin *(principal);* klagen *(to complain)*

——— 1. Die Wiedervereinigung Deutschlands war nicht so leicht, wie man sich das vorgestellt hatte.

——— 2. Nach drei Jahren waren die Menschen im Westen nicht so optimistisch über die Zukunft wie die Menschen im Osten.

——— 3. Nach drei Jahren hatten mehr als 75 Prozent der Westdeutschen ein Auto und fast alle hatten Farbfernseher.

——— 4. Ein Arbeiter in Ostdeutschland verdiente so viel wie dreißig Menschen in Ungarn.

——— 5. In Altdöbern hat man in drei Jahren 164 neue Geschäfte und Firmen geöffnet.

——— 6. Jutta Laubach ist eine Altdöberner Geschäftsfrau, die ein Kleidergeschäft aufgemacht hat.

——— 7. Sie findet das neue System nicht so gut wie das alte, weil früher alles garantiert war.

——— 8. Helga Müller weinte, als sie hörte, daß die Berliner Mauer offen war.

——— 9. Sie glaubte, daß der Kommunismus ein gutes System war.

——— 10. Monika Bernhart findet ihr neues Leben zu schwer.

Übrigens

1. In 1933 Adolf Hitler became chancellor of Germany. This began a twelve-year dictatorship that culminated in World War II and ended in the total defeat and division of Germany in 1945, and cost the loss of millions of lives.

2. On June 24, 1948, at the height of the Cold War, Soviet troops tried to force the integration of West Berlin into the GDR by blocking all vital supply lines—roads, railroads, and canals leading into the city. The West then sustained the more than two million West Berliners through the famous airlift (**Luftbrücke**). The Russians finally ended their blockade on May 12, 1949.

3. When C. G. Langhans built the Brandenburg Gate 200 years ago (1788–1791), he intended it to be a "Gate of Peace." Instead it has witnessed two centuries of war and revolution. The Brandenburg Gate, inspired by the Propylaea of the Parthenon, is an arch crowned by the reconstructed Victory Quadriga (1793). In 1963 Communist soldiers dropped huge red drapes over the gate to prevent President Kennedy from looking into East Berlin during his visit to the western part of the city.

4. From 1945 to 1990, all of Berlin was officially governed by the four Allies, who patrolled it regularly. The one East-West crossing reserved exclusively for non-German visitors was "Checkpoint Charlie."

5.   Unter den Linden, a boulevard lined with imposing monuments, imperial palaces, and government buildings, has witnessed many pivotal moments in European history: parades of Prussian troops, Napoleon's triumphal march through Berlin, the erection of barricades by the revolutionaries of 1848 and 1918, Nazi book burnings in 1933, and Red Army soldiers fighting their way westward along the boulevard in the final days of World War II. More recently, the East German regime celebrated its achievements with organized marches along Unter den Linden, and the East German secret police (**Staatssicherheitsdienst = Stasi**) watched helplessly as demonstrators cheered Gorbachev for his liberalism in front of the Soviet Embassy. On the night of October 3, 1990, huge crowds celebrated German unification on this famous street.

6.   Humboldt University, named after the German linguist and philosopher Wilhelm von Humboldt (1767–1835), was founded in the mid-1770s. Its building complex includes the Old Palace, once the residence of Emperor William I. The philosophers Hegel and Schleiermacher, the linguists Wilhelm and Jacob Grimm, and the scientists Max Planck, Robert Koch, and Albert Einstein taught there. After the division of Germany following World War II, the university found itself in the eastern part of the city and became the academic showpiece of the GDR. Its Western counterpart, the Free University of Berlin, was founded in 1948. The collapse of East Germany left Humboldt University in upheaval. Its president was accused of having connections with the Stasi and was subsequently replaced by sociology professor Marlis Dürkop.

Blick auf die Spree und den Fernsehturm

SPRECHSITUATIONEN

Expressing Doubt and Uncertainty

If you are unsure of your response, you can use any of the following expressions:

Vielleicht . . .
Ich bin mir nicht sicher, aber . . .
Es ist möglich, daß . . .
Ich glaube (nicht), daß . . .
Soviel ich weiß *(as far as I know)*, . . .

If you don't know at all, use:

Ich weiß (es) nicht.
(Ich habe) keine Ahnung.

Expressing Probability and Possibility

You know that the future can be used to express probability. There are also other ways to express this.

Bestimmt.
Sicher.
Vielleicht.
Wahrscheinlich.
Es ist möglich, daß . . .
Ich bin sicher, daß . . .
Ich glaube, . . .
Ich nehme an, . . .

Expressing Concern

Here are several ways to say you are worried:

Ich mache mir Sorgen, daß . . .
Ich habe Angst, daß . . .
Ich (be)fürchte, daß . . . *(I fear that . . .)*
Ich mache mir Sorgen um . . .
Ich habe Angst vor (+ *dat.*) . . .

Drawing Conclusions

Darum / deshalb / . . .	*Therefore / That's why . . .*
Aus dem / diesem Grund . . .	*For that / this reason . . .*
Das (End)resultat ist . . .	*The (end) result is . . .*
Im großen und ganzen . . .	*On the whole . . .*

A.   **Was nun?**   *(Work in small groups of two to four students. Take turns asking a classmate many questions about his / her future plans. He / she is not at all certain about details and expresses this uncertainty in the responses. Choose one of the following situations, or invent your own.)*

1. He / she is going to study in one of the German-speaking countries.
2. He / she is about to graduate and has no definite plans for the future.
3. He / she has just applied to join the Peace Corps (**Entwicklungsdienst**).

B.   **Warum? Darum!**   *(Work in pairs. Your partner asks you questions about your future plans. This time you have a pretty good idea of what you are planning to do. Express the probability in your responses.)*

1. You are taking time off from your studies.
2. You are travelling in Europe for two and a half months.
3. During the summer you will be working as an intern for an American bank in Frankfurt.

C.   **Kurzgespräch**

You tell a fellow student, Gunther, that two mutual friends, Karin and Thomas, didn't return from a car trip to Italy yesterday, as they had said they would. You are worried that they might have had an accident (**einen Autounfall haben**) or bad weather as they crossed the mountains (**schlechtes Wetter / Schnee in den Bergen**), or that their car broke down (**eine Panne haben**). Gunther tries to reassure you. He comes up with various ideas as to why they might have been delayed: they wanted to stay a little longer, stopped to see another museum or town, are probably arriving any minute, etc.

Winter in St. Jakob, Österreich

Wo ein Wille ist, ist auch ein Weg

Das Schiller-Goethe Denkmal vor dem Nationaltheater in Weimar

LERNZIELE

Vorschau

■ The path to a united Europe: 1949 to 1994

Gespräche and Wortschatz

■ Environmental concerns

Struktur

■ Passive voice
■ Review of the uses of *werden*
■ Special subjunctive (Subjunctive I)

Einblicke

■ The question of German identity

Sprechsituationen

■ Describing objects

The Path to a United Europe: 1949 to 1994

1949   Establishment of the North Atlantic Treaty Organization (NATO) and the Council of Europe.

1950   France launches Schuman Plan, which proposed combining French and German coal and steel production under the authority of a single organization.

1951   Italy, Belgium, the Netherlands, and Luxembourg join in founding the European Coal and Steel Community (ECSC), known as Montanunion.

1957   The same six countries sign the agreements establishing the European Economic Community (EEC) and the European Atomic Energy Commission (EURATOM), known collectively as the Treaties of Rome. The EEC, EURATOM, and ECSC are called the "European Communities."

1960   Great Britain, Austria, Switzerland, Portugal, and the Scandinavian countries join in the European Free Trade Association (EFTA), an economically oriented alternative to the EEC.

1962   The European Communities (EC) Council of Ministers agrees on the principles of a common agricultural policy.

1968   Customs union abolishes remaining customs duties on industrial products between EC member states and establishes a common external tariff for non-EC countries.

1970   EC countries embark on a process of European Political Cooperation (i.e., a common foreign policy).

1973   Denmark, Ireland, and Great Britain become members of the EC.

1979   European Monetary System (EMS) comes into force. Creation of the European currency unit (ECU). First direct elections for the European Parliament—until then the national parliaments had chosen delegates.

1981   Greece joins the EC.

1986   Spain and Portugal join the EC.

1989   Fall of the Berlin Wall. Beginning of the reform process in Central and Eastern Europe.

1990   Reunification of West Germany and East Germany extends EC membership to the former East Germany. Hungary becomes a member of the Council of Europe.

1991   The EC and EFTA agree on the creation of a European Economic Area (EEA). Maastricht Agreement (December 9–11), which requires ratification by all twelve member states before going into effect, proposes an economic and monetary union by 1999 and a political union with a joint internal, judicial, foreign, and security policy.

1992   Germany, Belgium, France, Greece, Ireland, Italy, Luxembourg, the Netherlands, Portugal, and Spain approve Treaty of Maastricht; Denmark rejects it (but ratifies it in 1993). Strasbourg chosen as seat of the European Parliament; Brussels, of the Council and Commission; and Luxembourg, of the European Court of Justice and the Court of Auditors.

1993   European internal market becomes reality for the 345 million people in the twelve countries of the European Union.

1994   Fourth direct elections for the European Parliament.

Gespräche   **Zu Besuch in Weimar**

THOMAS Komisch. Dieses Denkmal von Goethe[1] und Schiller[2] kommt mir so bekannt vor. Ich glaube, ich habe es schon irgendwo gesehen.

DANIELA Warst du mal in San Francisco?

THOMAS Natürlich! Im Golden Gate Park!

DANIELA Genau! Vor ein paar Jahren war es noch leichter für uns, das Denkmal dort zu sehen, als hierher nach Weimar[3] zu kommen.

THOMAS Und dabei ist es nur etwa zwei Stunden von Göttingen entfernt.

DANIELA Hast du gewußt, daß Weimar für das Jahr 1999 zur Kulturhauptstadt Europas gewählt worden ist?

THOMAS Na klar. Dabei habe ich allerdings gemischte Gefühle.

DANIELA Wieso denn? Im 18. Jahrhundert haben hier doch viele berühmte Leute gelebt, und die Weimarer Republik ist danach genannt.

THOMAS Das stimmt, aber wenn man die Stadt oben vom Ettersberg[3] sieht, dann kommen alle möglichen Fragen auf.

DANIELA Da hast du natürlich recht.

DANIELA Du, die alten Häuser hier sind echt schön.

THOMAS Ja, sie sind erst vor ein paar Jahren restauriert worden. Das hat den Staat ganz schön viel Geld gekostet.

DANIELA Gut, daß hier keine Autos fahren dürfen.

THOMAS Gott sei Dank! Die Fassaden hätten die Abgase der Trabbis[4] nicht lange überlebt. Bei uns gibt es jetzt eine Bürgerinitiative, alle Autos in der Altstadt zu verbieten, um die alten Gebäude zu retten.[5]

DANIELA Das finde ich gut.

THOMAS Ja, wo ein Wille ist, ist auch ein Weg.

Richtig oder falsch?

_____ 1. Thomas und Daniela sind in Weimar.

_____ 2. Das Denkmal zeigt Goethe und Nietzsche.

_____ 3. Weimar soll 1999 Bundeshauptstadt werden.

_____ 4. Daniela geht gern auf den Ettersberg, denn sie findet den Blick von dort oben auf die Stadt wunderschön.

_____ 5. Leider sind die Gebäude, vor denen sie stehen, alle alt und grau.

_____ 6. Zum Glück gibt es im Zentrum von Weimar keine Autos.

_____ 7. Ein Trabbi ist—oder besser war—ein kleines Auto mit vielen Abgasen.

_____ 8. Thomas kommt aus einer Stadt, in deren Altstadt noch Autos fahren dürfen.

_____ 9. Eine Bürgerinitiative möchte, daß das so bleibt.

_____ 10. Man will die Altstadt, deren Gebäude sehr alt sind, retten.

Übrigens

1. Johann Wolfgang von Goethe (1749–1832) was one of Germany's greatest poets, novelists, and playwrights. He was also a leading thinker and scientist. Because of his vast

scope of knowledge and his comprehensive interest in the world of human experience, he is often referred to as "the last universal man." His works include *Die Leiden des jungen Werther, Wilhelm Meister,* and *Faust.*

2.   Friedrich von Schiller (1759–1805) ranks second only to Goethe among the leading figures of classical German literature. His dramas, often pleas for human freedom and dignity, inspired liberals in their fight for liberty during the early 1800s and during the Revolution of 1848. His works include *Don Carlos, Die Jungfrau von Orleans, Maria Stuart,* and *Wilhelm Tell.*

3.   The city of Weimar (pop. 64,000) boasts a proud cultural history. Johann Sebastian Bach was court organist there in the early 18th century. Goethe, who lived and worked in Weimar from 1775 until his death, drew Schiller, Gottfried Herder and many others to the town, which, nourished by genius, gave birth to "Weimar Classicism." Franz Liszt was musical director in Weimar in the mid-nineteenth century, and the philosopher and author Friedrich Nietzsche lived there for a time. In 1919 the National Assembly met in Weimar to draft a constitution for the new republic—henceforth known as the Weimar Republic. The assembly chose this site because of its popular associations with Germany's classical tradition. The new republic lasted only fourteen years, dissolved by Hitler soon after he was appointed chancellor in 1933. During the Nazi period, Weimar and its traditions were ignored and Goethe's works banned from schools. On the Ettersberg, a hill above the town, a memorial recalls the nearby Nazi concentration camp of Buchenwald.

4.   The old, smoke-belching East German Trabant (**Trabbi**) with its two-stroke engine emitted roughly nine times more hydrocarbons and five times more carbon dioxide than cars with four-stroke engines.

5.   German cities in both East and West have made a special effort to restore and protect historical buildings from the effects of acid rain and air pollution.

The Trabbi, nicknamed **Plastikbomber, Asphaltblase** *(Asphalt Bubble),* or **Rennpappe** *(Racing Cardboard),* was not inexpensive by GDR standards. People had to save the equivalent of 10–27 months' salary; credit did not exist. Delivery of the 26 HP car normally took at least 10 years; and its spare parts were one of the underground currencies of the former GDR.

Die Umwelt   *(environment, surroundings)*

ab·reißen, riß ab, abgerissen	*to tear down*
erklären	*to explain*
erlauben	*to allow, permit*
finanzieren	*to finance*
garantieren	*to guarantee*
gebrauchen[1]	*to use, utilize*
parken	*to park*
planen	*to plan*
reden (mit, über)	*to talk (to, about)*
renovieren	*to renovate*
restaurieren	*to restore*
retten	*to save, rescue*
(sich) verändern	*to change*
verbieten, verbot, verboten	*to forbid*
(wieder)auf·bauen	*to (re)build*
zerstören	*to destroy*

---

[1] Don't confuse **brauchen** *(to need)* with **gebrauchen** *(to use):* Ich **brauche** einen Kuli. BUT Ich kann diesen Kuli nicht **gebrauchen**, weil er kaputt ist.

Weiteres

der Staat, -en	*state*
das Denkmal, ⸚er	*monument*
allerdings	*however, to be sure*
echt	*real(ly); genuine(ly)*
etwa	*about, approximately*
Wo ein Wille ist, ist auch ein Weg.[2]	*Where there's a will, there's a way.*

[2] For other proverbs, see *Zum Thema,* exercise C.

ZUM ERKENNEN: Das kommt mir bekannt vor. *(That seems familiar to me.);* irgendwo *(somewhere);* dabei *(yet);* entfernt *(away);* wählen *(to select);* gemischte Gefühle *(mixed feelings);* alle möglich- *(all sorts of);* ganz schön viel *(quite a bit);* die Fassade, -n; die Abgase *(pl.) exhaust fumes;* überleben *(to survive);* die Bürgerinitiative, -n *(citizens' initiative)*

Zum Thema

A. **Reporter im Rathaus**   *(You're a radio reporter attending a meeting of the city-planning commission. Read what one man says, then report to YOUR listeners.)*
BEISPIEL: **Er hat gesagt, wir sollten nicht auf die Bürger hören, die immer . . .**

„Hören Sie nicht auf die Bürger, die immer wieder alles, ja die ganze Altstadt, retten wollen. Viele alte Innenhöfe *(inner courts)* sind dunkel und häßlich. Abreißen ist viel billiger und einfacher als renovieren! Wenn man die alten Gebäude abreißt und die Innenstadt schön modern aufbaut, dann kommt bestimmt wieder Leben in unser Zentrum. Auf diese Weise kann man auch die Straßen verbreitern *(widen)* und alles besser planen. Fußgängerzonen sind schön und gut, aber nicht im Zentrum, denn alle wollen ihr Auto in der Nähe haben. Das ist doch klar, weil's viel bequemer und sicherer ist! Ich kann Ihnen garantieren, wenn Sie aus dem Zentrum eine Einkaufszone machen, zu deren Geschäften man nur zu Fuß hinkommt *(gets to),* dann verlieren Sie alle, meine Damen und Herren, viel Geld!"

B. **Altbau oder Neubau?** Wo würden Sie lieber wohnen? Was spricht dafür und was dagegen? Stellen Sie eine Liste auf! Machen Sie eine Meinungsumfrage *(opinion poll)*!

C. **Ein paar Sprichwörter** *(proverbs)*
1. **Was bedeuten diese Sprichwörter?** Was ist die englische Version?

   a. Ohne Fleiß kein Preis.
   b. Es ist noch kein Meister° vom Himmel° gefallen.   *master / sky*
   c. Rom ist nicht an einem Tag gebaut worden.
   d. Morgen, morgen, nur nicht heute, sagen alle faulen Leute.
   e. Was Hänschen nicht lernt, lernt Hans nimmermehr°.   *nevermore*
   f. Viele Köche° verderben° den Brei°.   *cooks / spoil / porridge*
   g. Lügen° haben kurze Beine.   *lies*
   h. Morgenstund' hat Gold im Mund.
   i. Jeder ist seines Glückes Schmied°.   *blacksmith*
   j. Ende gut, alles gut.

2. **Schriftliche Übung**   *(Tell an anecdote or describe a situation demonstrating one of the proverbs. Write about eight to ten sentences.)*

D.   Aussprache: Glottal Stops   *(See also II. 42 in the pronunciation section of the Workbook.)*

1.   +Erich +arbeitet +am +alten Dom.
2.   Die +Abgase der +Autos machen +einfach +überall +alles kaputt.
3.   +Ulf +erinnert sich +an +ein +einmaliges +Abendkonzert +im +Ulmer Dom.
4.   +Otto sieht +aus wie +ein +alter +Opa.
5.   +Anneliese +ist +attraktiv +und +elegant.

Hören Sie zu!

Umweltprobleme   *(Listen to the passage about the environment, then decide whether the following statements are true or false.)*

ZUM ERKENNEN: die Tierart, -en *(animal species);* aus·sterben *(to become extinct);* das Ökosystem, -e; der Storch, ¨e *(stork);* das Paar, -e *(pair);* tot *(dead);* das Gift, -e *(poison);* die Finanzierung; produzieren; der Abfall, ¨e *(waste);* verbrannt *(burned);* die Wärme

Richtig oder falsch?

_____   1.   In Deutschland sind fast alle Wälder krank.
_____   2.   Die meisten Flüsse sind sehr schmutzig.
_____   3.   Man findet heute im Osten Deutschlands fast keine Störche mehr.
_____   4.   In Deutschland und Österreich tut man viel für die Umwelt.
_____   5.   Aus dem Rhein kommt das Trinkwasser für ungefähr 20 Millionen Deutsche.
_____   6.   Der Rhein ist heute voll von Chemikalien.
_____   7.   Es wird viel kosten, die Donau wieder sauberer zu machen und zu schützen.
_____   8.   Heute macht man in Deutschland alle Flaschen aus Altglas.
_____   9.   Auch manche Touristen denken heute ökologisch.
_____   10.   Nur durch eine gesunde Natur kann der Tourismus gesund bleiben.

Schloß Schwerin

STRUKTUR

I. The Passive Voice

English and German sentences are in one of two voices: the active or the passive. In the ACTIVE VOICE the subject of the sentence is doing something; it's "active."

The students ask the professor.

In the PASSIVE VOICE the subject is not doing anything, rather, something is being done to it; it's "passive."

The professor is asked by the students.

Note what happens when a sentence in the active voice is changed into the passive voice. The direct object of the active becomes the subject of the passive.

subj.   obj.

*The students ask **the professor.***

***The professor** is asked by the students.*

subj.   obj. of prep.

In both languages the active voice is used much more frequently than the passive voice, especially in everyday speech. The passive voice is used when the focus is on the person or thing at whom the action is directed, rather than on the agent who is acting.

Active Voice	**Die Studenten** fragen den Professor.
Passive Voice	**Der Professor** wird von den Studenten gefragt.

1. Forms

 a. In English the passive voice is formed with the auxiliary *to be* and the past participle of the verb. In German it is formed with the auxiliary **werden** and the past participle of the verb.

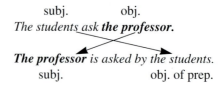

werden . . . + past participle			
ich	**werde**		*I am (being)*
du	**wirst**		*you are (being)*
er	**wird**	*gefragt*	*he is (being)*
wir	**werden**		*we are (being)*
ihr	**werdet**		*you are (being)*
sie	**werden**		*they are (being)*

(with *asked* applying to all on the right)

Der Professor **wird** von den Studenten **gefragt**.
Die Professoren **werden** von den Studenten **gefragt**.

b. The passive voice has the same <u>tenses</u> as the active voice. They are formed with the various tenses of **werden** + the past participle of the verb. Note, however, that in the perfect tenses of the passive voice, the past participle of **werden** is **worden!** When you see or hear **worden,** you know immediately that you are dealing with a sentence in the passive voice.

PRESENT	Er **wird**	. . . gefragt.	*He is being asked . . .*
SIMPLE PAST	Er **wurde**	. . . gefragt.	*He was asked . . .*
FUTURE	Er **wird**	. . . gefragt **werden**.	*He will be asked . . .*
PRES. PERF.	Er **ist**	. . . gefragt **worden**.	*He has been asked . . .*
PAST PERF.	Er **war**	. . . gefragt **worden**.	*He had been asked . . .*

Die Altstadt wird renoviert.	*The old part of town is being renovated.*
Die Pläne wurden letztes Jahr gemacht.	*The plans were made last year.*
Alles wird finanziert werden.	*Everything will be financed.*
Das ist entschieden worden.	*That has been decided.*
Manche Gebäude waren im Krieg zerstört worden.	*Some buildings had been destroyed during the war.*

In subordinate clauses, the pattern is:

Ich weiß, daß die Altstadt renoviert wird.
    , daß die Pläne letztes Jahr gemacht wurden.
    , daß alles finanziert werden wird.
    , daß alles schon entschieden worden ist.
    , daß manche Gebäude im Krieg zerstört worden sind.

c. Modals themselves are not put into the passive voice. Rather, they follow this pattern:

modal . . . + past participle + **werden**

In this book only the present and simple-past tense of the modals will be used.

PRESENT	Er **muß**	. . . gefragt **werden**.	*He must (has to) be asked . . .*
SIMPLE PAST	Er **mußte**	. . . gefragt **werden**.	*He had to be asked . . .*

Das Gebäude muß renoviert werden.	*The building must be renovated.*
Das Gebäude sollte letztes Jahr renoviert werden.	*The building was supposed to be renovated last year.*

In subordinate clauses the inflected verb stands at the end.

Ich weiß, daß das Gebäude renoviert werden muß.
    , daß das Gebäude letztes Jahr renoviert werden sollte.

2. Expression of the Agent

If the AGENT who performs the act is expressed, the preposition **von** is used.

Der Professor wird **von den Studenten** gefragt.	*The professor is being asked by the students.*
Alles ist **vom Staat** finanziert worden.	*Everything was financed by the state.*

3. Impersonal Use

In German the passive voice is frequently used without a subject or with **es** functioning as the subject.

Hier darf nicht gebaut werden. ⎫ *You can't build here. / Building is not*
Es darf hier nicht gebaut werden. ⎭   *permitted here.*

4. Alternative to the Passive Voice

One common substitute for the passive voice is a sentence in the active voice with **man** as the subject.

Hier darf nicht gebaut werden.   ⎫
                                                ⎬ → **Man** darf hier nicht bauen.
Es darf hier nicht gebaut werden.   ⎭

Übungen

A. Trier. Aktiv oder Passiv?   *(Decide whether statements are in the active or passive voice.)*

1. The city of Trier on the Moselle River recently celebrated its 2000th anniversary.
2. Trier was founded by the Romans in 15 B.C.
3. Its original name was *Augusta Treverorum.*
4. Under Roman occupation, *Germania* along the Rhine and Danube had been transformed into a series of Roman provinces.
5. The names of many towns are derived from Latin.
6. Remnants from Roman times can still be seen today.
7. New discoveries are made from time to time.
8. Beautiful Roman museums have been built.
9. One of them is located in the former *Colonia Agrippina* (**Köln**).

B. Köln. Was bedeutet das auf englisch?

1. a. Köln wurde während des Krieges schwer zerstört.
    b. Achtzig Prozent der Häuser in der Innenstadt waren zerbombt *(destroyed by bombs)* worden.
    c. Heute wird Köln wieder von vielen Touristen besucht.
    d. Vieles ist wieder aufgebaut und restauriert worden.
    e. Und vieles wird noch renoviert werden.

2. a. Erst sollten natürlich neue Wohnungen gebaut werden.
    b. Manche alten Gebäude konnten gerettet werden.
    c. Der Dom mußte restauriert werden.
    d. Aber die alten Kirchen aus dem zwölften Jahrhundert dürfen auch nicht vergessen werden.
    e. Das kann allerdings nicht ohne Geld gemacht werden.
    f. Durch Bürgerinitiativen soll genug Geld für die Restaurierung gesammelt werden.

3. a. In der Altstadt wird in Parkgaragen geparkt.
    b. Es wird viel mit dem Bus gefahren.
    c. In der Fußgängerzone wird nicht Auto gefahren.
    d. Dort wird zu Fuß gegangen.
    e. Dort wird gern eingekauft.

C. **Ein schönes altes Haus.** Sagen Sie die Sätze im Aktiv!

1. BEISPIEL: Nicht alle Gebäude waren vom Krieg zerstört worden.
    Der Krieg hatte nicht alle Gebäude zerstört.

    a. Viele Gebäude sind von Planierraupen *(bulldozers)* zerstört worden.
    b. Dieses Haus wurde von den Bürgern gerettet.
    c. Viele Unterschriften *(signatures)* wurden von Studenten gesammelt.
    d. Das Haus ist von der Uni gekauft worden.
    e. Die Fassade wird von Spezialisten renoviert werden.
    f. Die Hauspläne werden von Architekten gemacht.

2. BEISPIEL: Der Hausplan darf von den Architekten nicht sehr verändert
    werden.
    Die Architekten dürfen den Hausplan nicht sehr verändern.

    a. Ein Teil soll von der Stadt finanziert werden.
    b. Der Rest muß von der Uni bezahlt werden.
    c. Das Haus konnte von der Universität als Gästehaus ausgebaut werden.
    d. Das Parterre darf von den Studenten als Café gebraucht werden.

3. BEISPIEL: Das Gästehaus wird viel besucht.
    Man besucht das Gästehaus viel.

    a. Dort werden Gedanken ausgetauscht.
    b. Es wird auch Englisch und Französisch gesprochen.
    c. Heute abend wird ein Jazzkonzert gegeben.
    d. Letzte Woche wurde ein Film gezeigt.
    e. Hier werden auch Seminare gehalten werden.

D. **Ein alter Film.** Wiederholen Sie die Sätze im Passiv, aber in einer anderen
Zeitform!

BEISPIEL: Ein alter Film wird gespielt. *(simple past)*
    Ein alter Film wurde gespielt.

1. Er wird von den Studenten sehr empfohlen. *(present perfect)*
2. Während des Krieges wird er nicht gezeigt. *(simple past)*
3. Er wird verboten. *(past perfect)*
4. Es wird viel darüber geredet. *(future)*
5. Daraus kann viel gelernt werden. *(simple past)*
6. Er soll übrigens wiederholt werden. *(simple past)*

E. **Post und Geld.** Wiederholen Sie die Sätze im Passiv, aber mit einem Modalverb! Wie heißt das auf englisch?

BEISPIEL: Das Paket wird zur Post gebracht. (sollen)
Das Paket soll zur Post gebracht werden.
The package is supposed to be taken to the post office.

1. Die Paketkarte wird noch ausgefüllt. (müssen)
2. Dann wird es am ersten Schalter abgegeben. (können)
3. Auf der Post werden auch Telefongespräche gemacht. (dürfen)
4. Dollar werden auf der Bank umgetauscht. (sollen)
5. Nicht überall wird mit Reiseschecks bezahlt. (können)
6. Taxifahrer werden mit Bargeld bezahlt. (wollen)

F. **Im Restaurant.** Sagen Sie die Sätze im Passiv!

BEISPIEL: Hier spricht man Deutsch.
Hier wird Deutsch gesprochen.

1. Am anderen Tisch spricht man Französisch.
2. Mittags ißt man warm.
3. Dabei redet man gemütlich.
4. Natürlich redet man nicht mit vollem Mund.
5. Übrigens hält man die Gabel in der linken Hand.
6. Und vor dem Essen sagt man „Guten Appetit!"

G. **Wir geben eine Party**   *(Restate each sentence in the passive voice. Use the impersonal subject* **es**.*)*

1. **Was wird auf der Party gemacht?**

BEISPIEL: Man tanzt.
Es wird getanzt.

a. Man spielt Spiele. **b.** Man ißt Pizza. **c.** Man trinkt etwas dazu. **d.** Man erzählt Witze *(jokes).* **e.** Man lacht viel. **f.** Man hört CDs an. **g.** Man redet über Politik oder das Wetter.

2. **Was muß noch gemacht werden?**   *(Answer in the passive voice to say that things have already been done.)*

BEISPIEL: Fritz und Frieda müssen noch angerufen werden.
Fritz und Frieda sind schon angerufen worden!

a. Die Wohnung muß noch geputzt werden.   **b.** Der Tisch muß noch in die Ecke gestellt werden.   **c.** Die Gläser müssen noch gewaschen werden.   **d.** Das Bier muß noch kalt gestellt werden.   **e.** Die Kartoffelchips müssen noch in die Schüssel *(bowl)* getan werden.

> **„Je weniger die Leute darüber wissen, wie Würste und Gesetze gemacht werden, desto besser schlafen sie nachts."**
>
> Otto von Bismarck

II. Review of the Uses of *werden*

Distinguish carefully among the various uses of **werden.**

1. **werden** + predicate noun / adjective = a FULL VERB

    Er wird Arzt.   *He's going to be a doctor.*
    Es wird dunkel.   *It's getting dark.*

2. **werden** + infinitive = auxiliary of the FUTURE TENSE

    Ich werde ihn fragen.   *I'll ask him.*

3. **würde** + infinitive = auxiliary in the PRESENT-TIME SUBJUNCTIVE

    Ich würde ihn fragen.   *I would ask him.*

4. **werden** + past participle = auxiliary in the PASSIVE VOICE

    Er wird von uns gefragt.   *He's (being) asked by us.*
    Goethe wurde 1749 geboren.   *Goethe was born in 1749.*

H.   Analysieren Sie, wie *werden* gebraucht wird! Was bedeutet das auf englisch?   **Übung**

   BEISPIEL: Leonie ist nach Amerika eingeladen worden.
              werden + past participle = passive voice
              Leonie was invited (to go) to America.

1.   Leonie möchte Lehrerin werden.
2.   Das Studium dort mußte von ihr bezahlt werden.
3.   Es ist teuerer geworden, als sie dachte.
4.   Das wurde ihr nie erklärt.
5.   Was würdest du an ihrer Stelle tun?
6.   Ich würde ein Semester arbeiten.
7.   Das wird nicht erlaubt werden.
8.   Übrigens wird ihr Englisch schon viel besser.

III. The Special Subjunctive

German has another subjunctive, often called the SPECIAL SUBJUNCTIVE or SUBJUNCTIVE I.
English only has a few remnants of this subjunctive.

So be it. Long live the Queen. Be that as it may.

In German, the special subjunctive is used in similar expressions.

Gott sei Dank!   *Thanks be to God!*
Es lebe die Freiheit!   *Long live freedom!*
Wie dem auch sei.   *Be that as it may!*

Other than in such phrases, the Subjunctive I is rarely heard in conversation. It is primarily
used in formal writing and indirect speech, often to summarize another person's findings
or opinion. It is most frequently encountered in critical literary or scientific essays, in

literature, and in news articles, where it distances the author from his or her report and pre-serves a sense of objectivity.

In general, the forms of the third person singular are the ones used most often because they clearly differ from those of the indicative. When the forms of the special subjunctive are identical with those of the indicative, the general subjunctive is used. At this point, you need only to be able to recognize the forms of the special subjunctive and know why they are used.

1. PRESENT-TIME forms

The PRESENT-TIME forms of the special subjunctive have the same endings as the general subjunctive and are added to the stem of the INFINITIVE:

glauben	
ich glaube	wir glauben
du glaub**est**	ihr glaub**et**
er glaube	sie glaub**en**

Verbs that have a vowel change in the second and third person singular of the indicative don't have that vowel change in the special subjunctive. Note that the first and third person singular forms of **sein** are irregular in that they do not have an **-e** ending.

Infinitive	Special sub. er/es/sie	Indicative er/es/sie
haben	**habe**	hat
sein	**sei**	ist
tun	**tue**	tut
denken	**denke**	denkt
fahren	**fahre**	fährt
sehe	**sehe**	sieht
werden	**werde**	wird
wissen	**wisse**	weiß
dürfen	**dürfe**	darf
können	**könne**	kann
mögen	**möge**	mag
müssen	**müsse**	muß
wollen	**wolle**	will

ich habe	wir haben
du habest	ihr habet
er habe	sie haben

ich müsse	wir müssen
du müssest	ihr müsset
er müsse	sie müssen

ich sei	wir seien
du seiest	ihr seiet
er sei	sie seien

Er sagte, er **habe** keine Zeit.   *He said he had no time.*
Er sagte, sie **sei** nicht zu Hause.   *He said she wasn't home.*

2. To refer to the FUTURE *(to later),* combine the special subjunctive of **werden** with an infinitive.

> **werde . . .** + infinitive

Er sagte, er **werde** bald fertig **sein.**   *He said he'd be finished soon.*

3. To form the PAST-TIME special subjunctive, use the special subjunctive of **haben** or **sein** with a past participle.

habe . . . ⎫
         ⎬ + past participle
sei . . . ⎭

Er sagt, er **habe** keine Zeit **gehabt.**   *He says he didn't have time.*
Er sagte, sie **sei** nicht zu Hause **gewesen.**   *He said she hadn't been home.*

I. **Finden Sie den Konjunktiv!** *(Underline all subjunctive forms in the following texts.)*

1. **Ein Gedicht** *(poem)* **von Johann Wolfgang von Goethe (1828)**

Mir ist nicht bange°,
Daß Deutschland nicht eins werde,
Vor allem
Sei es eins in Liebe untereinander°—
Und immer sei es eins,
Daß der deutsche Thaler° und Groschen°
Im ganzen Reiche°
Gleichen Wert° habe—
Eins, daß mein Reisekoffer
Durch alle deutschen Länder ungeöffnet
Passieren° könnte.

I'm not afraid

among each other

"dollar" / "dime"
here: *country*
value

here: *travel*

2. **Städte deutscher Kultur**

Mein Onkel schrieb, daß Weimar, Leipzig, Halle, Wittenberg und Eisenach wichtige deutsche Kulturstädte seien. In Weimar sei Goethe Theaterdirektor und Staatsminister gewesen, und dort habe Schiller seine wichtigsten Dramen geschrieben. In Leipzig habe Bach 27 Jahre lang Kantaten und Oratorien für den

Die Wartburg bei Eisenach

Thomanerchor komponiert. Dieser Knabenchor *(boys choir)* sei heute noch sehr berühmt. Nicht weit von Leipzig liege Halle, wo Händel geboren worden sei. In Wittenberg, das man heute die Lutherstadt nenne, habe Luther mit seinen 95 Thesen die Reformation begonnen. Sein Zimmer auf der Wartburg bei Eisenach, wo er die Bibel ins Deutsche übersetzt hat, sei heute noch zu besichtigen. Man könne auch heute noch sehen, wo er dem Teufel ein Tintenfaß nachgeworfen habe *(had thrown an inkpot at the Devil)*. Er wisse nicht, woher diese Geschichte komme. Er glaube sie allerdings nicht.

3. **In der Vorlesung**

Der Professor erzählte von dem Archäologen Heinrich Schliemann. Schliemann habe sich schon als achtjähriges Kind für die Geschichte von dem Trojanischen Krieg interessiert und habe gesagt, er wollte später Troja *(Troy)* finden. Er sei als junger Mann sehr arm gewesen, aber er habe in Rußland und Amerika viel Geld verdient. Erst mit vierzig Jahren habe er angefangen, Archäologie zu studieren, und er habe später auch Troja gefunden. Besonders interessant sei, daß Schliemann etwa zwölf bis vierzehn Sprachen gelernt habe. Er habe eine besondere Methode entwickelt *(developed)*: z.B. habe er jeden Tag zwanzig Seiten vom *Vikar of Wakefield* und *Ivanhoe* gelernt und habe nach sechs Monaten gut Englisch gesprochen. Später habe er Fremdsprachen in etwa sechs Wochen gelernt!

Zusammen-fassung

J.   Wo ist mein Paß? Auf deutsch, bitte!

1. Yesterday was a bad day.   **2.** First I lost my passport.   **3.** Then my handbag and my money were stolen (**gestohlen**).   **4.** I tried to pay with traveler's checks. **5.** But without my passport, my checks weren't accepted.   **6.** It was good that Anne was there.   **7.** Anne paid the bill (The bill was paid by Anne).   **8.** This morning I was called by the police (**die Polizei**).   **9.** They had found my handbag. **10.** But my passport hasn't been found yet.   **11.** I wish I knew what I did with it. **12.** I hope it'll be found soon.

Das alte Leipziger Rathaus ist heute ein Museum.

EINBLICKE

„Möge diese Welt mit Gottes Hilfe eine Wiedergeburt der Freiheit erleben."

The political and economic collapse of the Communist bloc and the subsequent reunification of their country has forced Germans once more to consider what it means to be German. This search for a national identity goes back to a time well before Bismarck united the country in 1871. For centuries Germany had been divided into numerous small, autocratically ruled principalities. While this fragmentation contributed to the significant diversity among various parts of Germany, it also inhibited the development of a broadly based democratic consciousness. However, the failure of Germany's first democratic government, the Weimar Republic, must be attributed primarily to the economic depression in the early thirties which resulted in massive unemployment and provided the requisite conditions for Hitler's rise to power. After World War II, Germans on both sides of the Iron Curtain rejected the extreme nationalism and militarism that had resulted in two world wars. The East German government embraced the idea of international socialism, while West Germans sought prosperity through a market economy and fostered more of a united Europe. It remains to be seen what effect unification and the recent developments in Europe will have on the search for identity among the people of the reunited Germany.

"May this world under God have a rebirth of freedom." This text is written on the Liberty Bell of Berlin's *Schöneberger Rathaus,* a present of the American people to West Berlin after the 1950 blockade.

WORTSCHATZ 2

die	Landschaft	*landscape, scenery*
	Wirtschaft	*economy*

einzeln	*individual(ly)*
gefährlich	*dangerous*
gemeinsam	*common, joint*
stolz (auf + *acc.*)	*proud (of)*
typisch	*typical(ly)*
vereint	*united*
wirtschaftlich	*economic(ally)*
sich entwickeln	*to develop*
eine Frage stellen	*to ask (literally: pose) a question*
meinen	*to think (be of an opinion)*
zusammen·wachsen (wächst zusammen), wuchs zusammen, ist zusammengewachsen	*to grow together*

WAS IST DAS?   der Konflikt, Lebensstandard, Rechtsradikalismus, Umweltschutz; das Regime; die Demokratie, Freude, Lebensqualität, Nostalgie, Protestdemonstration, Souveränität; akzeptieren, identifizieren, plagen; absolut, arrogant, charakteristisch, dankbar, informiert, parlamentarisch, regional, skrupellos, weltoffen

Wer sind wir?

Constitutional Court
Constitution
federal state / loose confederation

Im Herbst 1993 entschied das Verfassungsgericht° in Karlsruhe, daß der Maastrichter Vertrag[1] nicht im Konflikt mit dem Grundgesetz° steht. Das Gericht machte aber auch klar, daß es Europa nicht als einen Bundesstaat° sehe, sondern als einen losen Staatenbund°, in dem die einzelnen Staaten ihre Souveränität behielten.

solutions
encouraged
introduced
prevented

founded

Das halten viele von uns für richtig. Natürlich fühlen wir uns als Europäer, aber wir 5 bleiben auch Deutsche. Was aber heißt das? Diese Frage wurde besonders nach 1945 in Deutschland immer wieder gestellt. Nach der furchtbaren Zeit des Krieges und des Nazi-Regimes suchte man neue Lösungen°. Das Land war in vier Zonen geteilt worden. Während in den drei westlichen Zonen von Anfang an eine parlamentarische Demokratie gefördert° wurde, wurde in der östlichen Zone das sowjetische System eingeführt°. Der kalte Krieg, 10 der sich nun schnell entwickelte, verhinderte° die Wiedervereinigung mit der sowjetischen Zone. 1949 wurden die Bundersrepublik und die Deutsche Demokratische Republik gegründet°, und wir waren plötzlich Ostdeutsche und Westdeutsche. Aber die Menschen auf beiden Seiten der Grenze fanden es schwer, sich mit diesen Staaten zu identifizieren. So setzte man große Hoffnungen auf internationale Ideen—im Westen auf die Idee eines 15 vereinten Europas und im Osten auf den Sozialismus—und beide Teile entwickelten sich getrennt°.

separately
circumstances
developed apart
East Germans / West Germans

poor devils without ambition

hence

ruthless
conditions

Durch die politischen und wirtschaftlichen Umstände° haben wir uns trotz gemeinsamer Sprache, Geschichte und Kultur auseinanderentwickelt°. Das wurde nach der Wiedervereinigung sehr schnell klar. Man sprach plötzlich von „Ossis"° und „Wessis"°. 20 Viele Westdeutsche meinten, daß die Ossis unselbständige und ehrgeizlose arme Teufel° seien, die finanziell zu früh zu viel erwarteten. Außerdem seien sie schlechte Autofahrer. Auf der anderen Seite meinten viele Ostdeutsche, daß die Wessis arrogant seien und dächten, ihnen gehöre die Welt. Sie würden immer alles besser wissen—daher° der Spitzname „Besserwessi." Als Geschäftsleute seien sie skrupellos und als Autofahrer absolut 25 rücksichtslos°. Manche wurden von „Ostalgie" geplagt, der Nostalgie im Osten nach den Zuständen° vor der Maueröffnung 1989.

Verallgemeinerungen° sind gefährlich. Da ist eigentlich wenig, was charakteristisch *generalizations*
wäre für uns alle. Vielleicht sind wir gesellig°, sitzen gern in Straßencafés oder in Garten- *social*
30 restaurants, organisieren uns in Vereinen° und lieben Fußball. Die Familie und die Freizeit *clubs*
bedeuten uns meistens mehr als der Staat. Vielleicht sind wir auch ein reiselustiges° Volk. *who love to travel*
Aber wir lieben auch unsere Heimat: die Landschaft, in der wir aufgewachsen sind°, die *grew up*
Stadt oder das Dorf. Viele sind wieder stolz auf ihre Herkunft°; regionale Dialekte werden *origin*
wieder mehr gesprochen und auch im Radio und im Theater gepflegt°. Das ist auch ver- *cultivated*
35 ständlich°, denn unsere Bevölkerung bestand schon immer aus° verschiedenen Volksstäm- *understandable / consisted*
men°. Wir waren nur kurze Zeit EIN Staat, nämlich von Bismarcks[2] Reichsgründung 1871 *of / ethnic groups*
bis zum Ende des Zweiten Weltkrieges 1945.

Wenn es schon schwer zu sagen ist, wie wir sind, so kann man doch sehen, daß wir uns
verändert haben. Wir sind weltoffener, informierter und kritischer geworden und sind nicht
40 mehr so autoritätsgläubig° wie am Anfang dieses Jahrhunderts. Das sogenannte typisch *believing in authority*
Deutsche ist nicht mehr so wichtig; das Ausländische ist interessanter geworden. Es werden Jeans statt Lederhosen° getragen. Man ißt besonders gern chinesisch oder italienisch; *leather pants*
und französischer Wein wird genauso gern getrunken wie deutsches Bier. Ja, und man en-
gagiert° sich wieder. Denken wir nur an die Protestdemonstrationen in der DDR, ohne die *gets involved*
45 die Grenze nicht so schnell geöffnet worden wäre, oder die Lichterketten° gegen den Rechts- *candlelight marches*
radikalismus. Der Kampf um° Umweltschutz und um unsere Lebensqualität ist auch sehr *struggle for*
wichtig geworden. Wir wollen natürlich unseren hohen Lebensstandard erhalten°, aber das *maintain*
dürfte auch mit weniger Energieverbrauch° und weniger Chemie möglich sein. *. . . consumption*

Wir sind dankbar, wieder ein Volk zu sein, wenn auch die Wiedervereinigung nicht
50 nur große Freude, sondern auch eine harte Nuß° ist. Es wird noch eine Weile dauern, bis *tough nut*
richtig „zusammengewachsen ist, was zusammengehört", wie Willy Brandt[3] es so schön
formuliert hat. Vielleicht wird das im vereinten Europa leichter werden, nämlich wenn wir
als Europäer lernen, Unterschiede zu akzeptieren und zu schätzen°. *appreciate*

A.   **Was paßt?**   **Zum Text**

1. Das Verfassungsgericht in _____ hat entschieden, daß der Maastrichter Vertrag
   nicht im Konflikt mit dem Grundgesetz steht.
   a. Bonn   b. Berlin   c. Karlsruhe

2. Das Gericht sagte, daß es Europa eigentlich als einen losen _____ sehe.
   a. Bundesstaat   b. Staatenbund   c. Bundesland

3. Nach dem 2. Weltkrieg ist Deutschland in _____ Zonen geteilt worden.
   a. zwei   b. drei   c. vier

4. Die Deutschen in Ost und West haben sich während dieser Zeit auseinanderent-
   wickelt, weil _____ haben.
   a. sie nichts gemeinsam   b. sie keine Zeit   c. die politischen Um-
                                                    stände sie getrennt

5. Manche Westdeutschen dachten, daß Ossis _____ seien.
   a. unselbständig   b. arrogant   c. skrupellos

6. Manche Ostdeutschen dachten, daß Wessis _____ .
   a. arme Teufel seien   b. alle arm wären   c. immer alles besser
                                                  wüßten

7. Vielleicht kann man allgemein *(in general)* von den Deutschen sagen, daß sie
    _____ .

   a. keine Fragen stellen   b. reiselustig sind   c. alle Dialekt sprechen

8. Sie lieben ihre _____ .
   a. Heimat   b. Spitznamen   c. Ausländer

9. Die Deutschen sind _____ geworden.
   a. autoritätsgläubiger   b. weltfremder   c. weltoffener

10. Deutschland war _____ EIN Staat.
   a. vor kurzer Zeit   b. nicht lange   c. von Bismarcks Reichs-
                                               gründung bis 1939

B. Was fehlt?

1. Die Frage nach der deutschen Identität _____ besonders nach 1945
    immer wieder _____ . *(was asked)*
2. 1945 _____ Deutschland _____ . *(was divided)*
3. 1989 _____ die Grenze wieder _____ . *(was opened)*
4. Ohne die Protestdemonstrationen _____ die Grenze nicht so schnell
    _____ _____ . *(would have been opened)*
5. Seit der Zeit _____ viel _____ _____ . *(has been done)*
6. Aber viel _____ noch _____ _____ . *(must be done)*
7. Umweltprobleme _____ ernst *(serious)* _____ . *(are taken)*
8. Die Deutschen _____ weltoffener _____ . *(have become)*
9. Französischer Wein _____ genauso gern wie deutsches Bier _____ .
    (is being drunk)
10. Zur gleichen Zeit _____ wieder mehr Dialekte _____ . *(are being
    spoken)*

C. Typisch deutsch!   *(Write a list of the points the author makes about "the Germans." How do they compare to your picture of them?)*

D. Typisch amerikanisch / kanadisch!

1. Was finden Sie typisch für die Amerikaner / Kanadier?
2. Was bedeutet uns viel?
3. Sind hier viele Menschen stolz auf ihre Herkunft?
4. Wie haben wir uns in diesem Jahrhundert verändert?
5. Gibt es hier auch regionale Dialekte? Wo?
6. Stellen Sie sich vor, Sie hätten in ein anderes Land geheiratet. Was würde Ihnen
    als typisch amerikanisch / kanadisch dort fehlen? Oder meinen Sie, daß Sie über-
    all gleich *(equally)* zu Hause wären?

Hören Sie zu!

Europäische Schulen   *(Listen to the passage, then decide which phrase best completes
the statements below.)*

ZUM ERKENNEN: erziehen *(to educate);* die Klassenkameradin *(classmate);* die Generation; objektiv; das Lehrbuch, ¨er; chauvinistisch; die Flotte *(fleet);* sich konzentrieren auf
(to concentrate on)

1. Internationale Schulen gibt es in _____ .
   a. jedem Land der EU
   b. den meisten europäischen Ländern
   c. mehreren europäischen Ländern

2. Die Schüler lernen _____ .
   a. keine Fächer in ihrer Muttersprache
   b. manche Fächer in ihrer Muttersprache
   c. nicht mehr als drei Sprachen

3. Sie lernen Geschichte _____ .
   a. immer in ihrer Muttersprache
   b. aus internationalen Lehrbüchern
   c. nie in ihrer Muttersprache

4. In französischen Lehrbüchern liest man _____ .
   a. nicht viel über solche Länder wie Belgien oder Luxemburg
   b. interessante Information über englische Kultur
   c. wie Nelson die spanische Flotte bei Trafalgar zerstört hat

5. Die Schüler lernen im Geschichtsunterricht, _____ .
   a. chauvinistischer zu werden
   b. die Geschichte ihres eigenen Landes objektiver zu sehen
   c. gutes Deutsch

6. Die erste Europa-Universität ist _____ .
   a. in Polen
   b. nicht nur für deutsche Studenten
   c. die Idee eines amerikanischen Professors

7. In den nächsten Jahren will man _____ .
   a. möglichst viele internationale Schulen eröffnen
   b. noch mehr internationale Universitäten eröffnen
   c. Schüler aus dem Osten in die europäischen Schulen einladen

Übrigens

1. The Maastricht Agreement of December 1991 included the following steps toward a united Europe: a single currency by 1999; eventually, a common defense under NATO; common EU citizenship that would confer the right to vote in local and European elections; joint decisions about foreign policy to be implemented by a majority of the member countries; greater law-making power for the European Parliament, with member countries retaining veto power in some matters; and a fund to help poorer member countries catch up to the others. Each country will set its own social policy.

2. Otto Graf von Bismarck (1815–1898) was instrumental in the founding of the Second German Empire in 1871, when the Prussian king was made emperor (**Kaiser Wilhelm I.**). Bismarck served as chancellor until 1890, when he was dismissed by the young **Kaiser Wilhelm II**.

3. Willy Brandt (1913–1992), one of Germany's best-known postwar statesmen, won the Nobel Peace Prize in 1971 for promoting better East-West relations during the Cold War. He was mayor of Berlin in 1960 when the Berlin Wall was built and stood next to President Kennedy when JFK made his famous speech in 1963. After serving as foreign minister from 1966 to 1969, he was elected chancellor of West Germany (1969–1974).

SPRECHSITUATIONEN

Describing Objects

When you are abroad, you may have to describe something you need or want to buy for which you don't know the appropriate German word. Here are some useful descriptive adjectives or phrases.

Wie ist es?

so groß wie	breit / eng *(wide / narrow)*
größer als	bunt / einfarbig *(colorful / all one color)*
dick / dünn	gepunktet / gestreift / kariert *(dotted / striped / plaid)*
groß / klein	hoch / niedrig *(high / low)*
kurz / lang	rund / viereckig *(round / square)*
leicht / schwer	süß / sauer / salzig *(sweet / sour / salty)*
hell[rot] / dunkel[rot]	weich / hart *(soft / hard)*

Woraus ist es?

das			*die*		
	Glas	*glass*		Baumwolle	*cotton*
	Holz	*wood*		Pappe	*cardboard*
	Leder	*leather*		Synthetik	*synthetics*
	Metall	*metal*		Wolle	*wool*
	Papier	*paper*			
	Plastik	*plastic*			
	Porzellan	*porcelain*			

Was macht man damit?	Man schreibt damit.
Wozu gebraucht *(uses)* man es?	Man gebraucht es, um besser zu sehen.

Often a sentence with a relative pronoun will be helpful in describing people or things.

Kennst du die Leute, die in dem neuen Gebäude an der Ecke wohnen?
Ist das nicht das Gebäude, in dem Alfred arbeitet?

Übungen

 A. **Woran denke ich?** *(Work in small groups. One person thinks of an object, the others have twenty questions to figure out what it is. The German word for the object should be one that has been used in the course.)*

B. **Beschreiben Sie!** *(Working with a partner, describe at least two of the following.)*

1. an item of clothing you can't part with
2. a favorite dish or snack
3. a painting or other piece of art you really like
4. a building (church, public building, museum, residence) you think is particularly interesting

C.   **Wie bitte?**   *(Pretend you are in a store and need to purchase something, but you don't know the German word for it. Describe it as best as you can, using gestures if necessary.†)*

1. towel
2. soap
3. deodorant stick
4. shampoo
5. suntan lotion

6. scissors
7. bandaids
8. needle
9. hair dryer
10. iron

11. umbrella
12. clothes hanger
13. checkered shirt
14. round tablecloth

D.   **Kurzgespräch**

You have lost your new book bag (billfold, key chain, designer sunglasses, etc.) and have gone to the university's lost-and-found office (**das Fundbüro**). Describe the items as best you can. The person on duty is writing down the information and is asking you for additional details (color, material, contents, value, special features, etc.)

---

†1. ein Handtuch 2. Seife 3. einen Deo-Stift 4. Shampoo 5. Sonnencreme 6. eine Schere 7. Pflaster 8. eine Nadel 9. einen Fön 10. ein Bügeleisen 11. einen Regenschirm 12. einen Kleiderbügel 13. ein kariertes Hemd 14. eine runde Tischdecke

RÜCKBLICK   KAPITEL 12–15

pp. 336–38

I. Comparison

1. The COMPARATIVE is formed by adding **-er** to an adjective, the SUPERLATIVE by adding **-(e)st.** Many one-syllable adjectives and adverbs with the stem vowel **a, o,** or **u** have an umlaut.

POSITIVE	COMPARATIVE	SUPERLATIVE
schnell	schneller	schnellst-
lang	länger	längst-
kurz	kürzer	kürzest-

    A few adjectives and adverbs have irregular forms in the comparative and superlative.

gern	lieber	liebst-
groß	größer	größt-
gut	besser	best-
hoch	höher	höchst-
nah	näher	nächst-
viel	mehr	meist-

2. The comparative of predicate adjectives and of adverbs ends in **-er**; the superlative is preceded by **am** and ends in **-sten.**

    Ich esse schnell. Du ißt schnell**er.** Er ißt **am** schnell**sten.**

3. In the comparative and superlative, adjectives preceding nouns have the same endings under the same conditions as adjectives in the positive form.

der gut**e** Wein	der besser**e** Wein	der best**e** Wein
Ihr gut**er** Wein	Ihr besser**er** Wein	Ihr best**er** Wein
gut**er** Wein	besser**er** Wein	best**er** Wein

4. Here are four important phrases used in comparisons:

    Gestern war es nicht **so heiß wie** heute. *(as hot as)*
    Heute ist es **heißer als** gestern. *(hotter than)*
    Es wird **immer heißer.** *(hotter and hotter)*
    Je länger du wartest, **desto heißer** wird es. *(the longer, the hotter)*
    Je heißer, desto besser. *(the hotter, the better)*

pp. 385–87

II. Relative Clauses

1. Relative clauses are introduced by RELATIVE PRONOUNS.

	masc.	neut.	fem.	plural
nom.	der	das	die	die
acc.	den	das	die	die
dat.	dem	dem	der	**denen**
gen.	**dessen**	**dessen**	**deren**	**deren**

The form of the relative pronoun depends on the NUMBER AND GENDER OF THE ANTECEDENT and on the FUNCTION of the relative pronoun WITHIN THE RELATIVE CLAUSE.

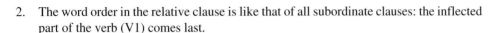

> ... ANTECEDENT, (preposition) RP _____ V1, ...
> gender? number?   function?

2. The word order in the relative clause is like that of all subordinate clauses: the inflected part of the verb (V1) comes last.

> ..., RP _____ V1, ...

Der junge Mann, **der** gerade hier **war,** studiert Theologie.
Die Universität, **an der** er **studiert,** ist schon sehr alt.

III. The Future

p. 340–41

1. The future consists of a present-tense form of **werden** plus an infinitive.

werden ... + infinitive	
ich werde . . . gehen	wir werden . . . gehen
du wirst . . . gehen	ihr werdet . . . gehen
er wird . . . gehen	sie werden . . . gehen

Er wird es dir erklären.

2. The future of a sentence with a modal follows this pattern:

> **werden** ... + verb infinitive + modal infinitive

Er wird es dir erklären können.

IV. The Subjunctive

pp. 360–61

English and German follow very similar patterns in the subjunctive:

If he came ...   Wenn er käme, ...
If he had come ...   Wenn er gekommen wäre, ...

German, however, has two subjunctives, the GENERAL SUBJUNCTIVE (SUBJUNCTIVE II) and the SPECIAL SUBJUNCTIVE (SUBJUNCTIVE I); the latter is primarily used in writing. The endings of both subjunctives are the same.

ich **-e**	wir **-en**
du **-est**	ihr **-et**
er **-e**	sie **-en**

**RÜCKBLICK
KAPITEL 12–15**

pp. 361–64, 367–68

1. Forms

   a.   GENERAL SUBJUNCTIVE (II)

present time or future time		past time
Based on the forms of the simple past; refers to *now / later*	Based on the forms of **werden** + infinitive; refers to *now / later*	Based on the forms of the past perfect; refers to *earlier*
er **lernte**	er **würde lernen**	er **hätte gelernt**
brächte	würde bringen	hätte gebracht
hätte	(würde haben)	hätte gehabt
wäre	(würde sein)	wäre gewesen
nähme	würde nehmen	hätte genommen
käme	würde kommen	wäre gekommen

* In conversation the **würde**-form is commonly used when referring to present time. However, avoid using the **würde**-form with **haben, sein, wissen,** and the modals. In past time, the **würde**-form is rarely used.

   Er **würde** es dir **erklären**.

* Modals in the past-time subjunctive follow this pattern:

   hätte . . . + verb infinitive + modal infinitive

   Er **hätte** es dir **erklären können**.

pp. 415–17

   b.   The SPECIAL SUBJUNCTIVE (I)

present time	future time	past time
Based on the forms of the infinitive; refers to *now / later*	Based on the forms of the future; refers to *later*	Based on the forms of the present perfect; refers to *earlier*
er **lerne**	er **werde lernen**	er **habe gelernt**
bringe	werde bringen	habe gebracht
habe	werde haben	habe gehabt
sei	werde sein	sei gewesen
nehme	werde nehmen	habe genommen
komme	werde kommen	sei gekommen

2. Use

   a.   The GENERAL SUBJUNCTIVE is quite common in everyday speech and is used in:

   * Polite Requests or Questions

Könnten Sie mir sagen, wo die Universität ist?	*Could you tell me where the university is?*

   * Hypothetical Statements or Questions

Er sollte bald hier sein.	*He should be here soon.*
Was würdest du tun?	*What would you do?*
Was hättest du getan?	*What would you have done?*

- Wishes

Wenn ich das nur wüßte!	*If only I knew that!*
Wenn ich das nur gewußt hätte!	*If only I had known that!*
Ich wünschte, ich hätte das gewußt!	*I wish I had known that!*

- Unreal Conditions

Wenn wir Geld hätten, würden wir fliegen.	*If we had the money, we'd fly.*
Wenn wir Geld gehabt hätten, wären wir geflogen.	*If we had had the money, we would have flown.*

- Indirect Speech (see below)

b. The SPECIAL SUBJUNCTIVE is used primarily in formal WRITING and in indirect speech, unless the form of the indicative is the same as the subjunctive, in which case the general subjunctive is used (ich komme = **ich komme** → **ich käme**; ich frage = **ich frage** → **ich würde fragen**).

V. Indirect Speech

The tense of the indirect statement is determined by the tense of the direct statement.

pp. 390–91

direct statement	indirect statement
present tense	→ present-time subjunctive or **würde**-form
future tense	→ **würde**-form or **werde**-form
simple past present perfect past perfect	→ past-time subjunctive

„Ich komme nicht."	Sie sagte, sie käme (komme) nicht.
	Sie sagte, sie würde nicht kommen.
„Ich werde nicht kommen."	Sie sagte, sie würde (werde) nicht kommen.
„Ich hatte keine Lust."	Sie sagte, sie hätte (habe) keine Lust gehabt.
„Ich bin nicht gegangen."	Sie sagte, sie wäre (sei) nicht gegangen.
„Ich hatte nichts davon gewußt."	Sie sagte, sie hätte (habe) nichts davon gewußt.

This is also true of questions. Remember to use **ob** when the question begins with the verb.

„Kommst du mit?"	Er fragte, ob ich mitkäme (mitkomme).
	Er fragte, ob ich mitkommen würde.
„Wirst du mitkommen?"	Er fragte, ob ich mitkommen würde (werde).
„Wo warst du?"	Er fragte, wo ich gewesen wäre (sei).
„Warum hast du mir nichts davon gesagt?"	Er fragte, warum ich ihm nichts davon gesagt hätte (habe).

Indirect requests require the use of **sollen.**

„Frag nicht so viel!"	Er sagte, sie sollte (solle) nicht so viel fragen.

RÜCKBLICK
KAPITEL 12–15

VI. The Passive Voice

In the active voice the subject of the sentence is doing something. In the passive voice the subject is not doing anything; rather, something is being done to it.

pp. 410–12

1. Forms

werden . . . + past participle	
ich werde . . . gefragt	wir werden . . . gefragt
du wirst . . . gefragt	ihr werdet . . . gefragt
er wird . . . gefragt	sie werden . . . gefragt

2. The tenses in the passive are formed with the various tenses of **werden** + past participle.

er **wird** . . . gefragt	er **ist** . . . gefragt **worden**
er **wurde** . . . gefragt	er **war** . . . gefragt **worden**
er **wird** . . . gefragt **werden**	

Das ist uns nicht erklärt worden.

3. Modals follow this pattern:

modal . . . + past participle + infinitive of **werden**

Das muß noch einmal erklärt werden.

4. In German the passive is often used without a subject or with **es** functioning as the subject.

Hier wird renoviert.
Es wird hier renoviert.

5. Instead of using the passive voice, the same idea may be expressed in the active voice with the subject **man.**

Man hat alles noch einmal erklärt.

p. 415

VII. Review of the Uses of *werden*

1.	FULL VERB	Er **wird** Arzt.	*He's going to be a doctor.*
2.	FUTURE	Ich **werde** danach **fragen.**	*I'll ask about it.*
3.	SUBJUNCTIVE	Ich **würde** danach **fragen.**	*I'd ask about it.*
4.	PASSIVE	Er **wird** danach **gefragt.**	*He's (being) asked about it.*

Wortschatzwiederholung

A. Fragen

1. **Verschiedene Berufe.** Wie viele Berufe kennen Sie auf deutsch? Sie haben eine Minute.

2. **Woran denken Sie dabei?**
   Zahnarzt, Hausfrau, Note, sich fühlen, parken, gewinnen, herrlich

3. **Was ist der Artikel dieser Wörter?** Was bedeuten sie auf englisch?
   Haushaltsgeld, Chemielabor, Weltkrieg, Zwischenprüfungsnote, Rechts- anwaltsfirma, Universitätsparkplatz, Liebesgeschichte, Berglandschaft, Hals- Nasen-Ohrenarzt, Berufsentscheidungsproblem, Lebenserfahrung

B. Was paßt?

1. **Nennen Sie das passende Verb!**
   der Gedanke, Plan, Traum, Verkäufer, Versuch, Wunsch; das Gebäude; die Erklärung, Entwicklung

2. **Nennen Sie das passende Hauptwort!**
   beruflich, frei, sportlich, verlobt; arbeiten, entscheiden, leben, lehren, studieren, teilen, trennen

C. Geben Sie das Gegenteil davon!

arm, dick, faul, furchtbar, gleich, häßlich, hell, langweilig, leicht, privat, schmutzig; damals, nie; aufhören, suchen, verbieten, vergessen, verlieren, zerstören; der Krieg, das Nebenfach, die Sicherheit

Strukturwiederholung

D. Vergleiche *(comparisons)*

1. **Geben Sie den Komparativ und den Superlativ!**

   BEISPIEL: lang **länger, am längsten**

   berühmt, dumm, faul, gern, gefährlich, groß, gut, heiß, hoch, hübsch, kalt, kurz, sauber, schwierig, typisch, viel, warm

2. **Ersetzen Sie das Adjektiv!**
   a. Rolf ist nicht so alt wie Heinz. (charmant, freundlich, bekannt, stolz)
   b. Carla ist älter als Erika. (sympathisch, nett, talentiert, ruhig)
   c. Die Stadt wird immer schöner. (groß, reich, interessant, international)

*3. **Was fehlt?**

    a. Wir wohnen jetzt in _____ Stadt. *(a prettier)*

    b. Die Umgebung ist noch _____ als vorher. *(more beautiful)*

    c. Es gibt keine _____ Umgebung. *(more interesting)*

    d. Peter hat _____ Arbeit. *(the most strenuous)*

    e. Aber er hat _____ Einkommen. *(the highest)*

    f. Er hat immer _____ Ideen. *(the most and the best)*

    g. Es gibt keinen _____ Kollegen. *(nicer)*

    h. Sie geben ihm _____ Freiheit *(freedom)*. *(the greatest)*

    i. _____ er hier ist, _____ gefällt es ihm. *(the longer, the better)*

    j. Die Lebensmittel kosten _____ bei euch. *(just as much as)*

    k. Aber die Häuser kosten _____ bei euch. *(less than)*

* **E.** **Bilden Sie Relativsätze!**

BEISPIEL: die Dame, _____ , . . . Sie wohnt im dritten Stock.
               Die Dame, die im dritten Stock wohnt, . . .

1. **der Freund, _____ , . . .**
    a. Er war gerade hier. **b.** Du hast ihn kennengelernt. **c.** Ihm gehört das Büchergeschäft in der Goethestraße. **d.** Seine Firma ist in Stuttgart.

2. **die Ärztin, _____ , . . .**
    a. Ihre Sekretärin hat uns angerufen. **b.** Sie ist hier neu. **c.** Wir haben durch sie von dem Programm gehört.

3. **das Gebäude, _____ , . . .**
    a. Ihr werdet es bald sehen. **b.** Du bist an dem Gebäude vorbeigefahren. **c.** Es steht auf der Insel. **d.** Man hat von dem Gebäude einen wunderschönen Blick *(m)*.

4. **die Leute, _____ , . . .**
    a. Sie sehen aus wie Amerikaner. **b.** Dort steht ihr Bus. **c.** Die Landschaft gefällt ihnen so gut. **d.** Du hast dich für sie interessiert. **e.** Du hast mit ihnen geredet.

F. **Sagen Sie die Sätze in der Zukunft!**

1. Ich nehme an einer Gruppenreise teil. **2.** Das ist billiger. **3.** Du mußt ihnen bald das Geld schicken. **4.** Meine Tante versucht, uns in Basel zu sehen. **5.** Wie kann sie uns finden? **6.** Das erklärst du ihr bestimmt.

* **G.** **Bilden Sie ganze Sätze im Konjunktiv!**

1. **Konjunktiv der Gegenwart oder würde-Form**

        a. ich / mich / fühlen / besser / / wenn / die / Arbeit / sein / fertig

        b. das / sein / wunderschön

        c. ihr / können / uns / dann / besuchen

        d. ich wünschte / / Rolf / haben / mehr Zeit

        e. wenn / ich / nur / können / sich gewöhnen / daran!

        f. erklären / du / mir / das?

        g. ich wünschte / / er / nicht / reden / so viel am Telefon

        h. was / du / tun?

2. **Konjunktiv der Vergangenheit**

    a. wir / nicht / sollen / in / Berge / fahren

    b. ich wünschte / / sie *(sg.)* / zu Hause / bleiben

    c. das / sein / einfacher

    d. wenn / wir / nur / nicht / wandern / so viel!

    e. wenn / du / mitnehmen / bessere Schuhe / / die Füße / weh tun / dir / nicht

    f. du / sollen / mich / erinnern / daran

    g. ich / es / finden / schöner / / bleiben / zu Hause

3. **Ich studiere dort.** Variieren Sie den Satz!

I'll study here. I'd study there. Would you *(sg. fam.)* like to study there? I wish I could study there. She could have studied there. If I study there, my German will get better. If I were to study there, I could visit you *(pl. fam.)*. I should have studied there.

H. **Indirekte Rede** *(indirect speech).* Ein Brief von David aus Amerika.

„Ich habe eine nette Wohnung. Mein Zimmerkollege ist aus New York. Ich lerne viel von ihm. Ich spreche nur Englisch. Manchmal gehe ich auch zu Partys. Ich lerne viele nette Studenten kennen. Die meisten wohnen im Studentenheim. Das ist mir zu teuer. Die Kurse und Professoren sind ausgezeichnet. Ich muß viel lesen, und es gibt viele Prüfungen. Aber eigentlich habe ich keine Probleme."

1. **Erzählen Sie, was David geschrieben hat!** *(Use the present-time subjunctive.)*

    BEISPIEL: David schrieb, er hätte eine nette Wohnung. Sein Zimmerkollege wäre aus New York . . .

2. **Was schrieb David damals über seine Zeit in Amerika?** *(Use the past-time subjunctive.)*

    BEISPIEL: David schrieb, er hätte eine nette Wohnung gehabt. Sein Zimmerkollege wäre aus New York gewesen . . .

I. **Sagen Sie die Sätze im Passiv!** *(Do not express pronoun agents.)*

1. Viele Studenten besuchen diese Universität.
2. Dieses Jahr renoviert man die Studentenheime.
3. Man baut ein neues Theater.
4. In dem alten Theater hat man viele schöne Theaterstücke gespielt.
5. Am Wochenende haben sie dort auch Filme gezeigt.
6. In der Mensa sprach man dann darüber.
7. Man wird das Theater am 1. Mai eröffnen.
8. Man muß diesen Tag feiern.

J. **Ein Jahr Deutsch!** Auf deutsch, bitte!

1. Now I have finished (**fertig werden mit**) my first year of German. **2.** I've really learned a lot. **3.** I never would have thought that it could be so much fun. **4.** Not everything has been easy. **5.** I had to learn many words. **6.** Many exercises had to be done. **7.** Soon we'll have our last exam. **8.** Because I've always prepared (myself) well, I don't have to work so much now. **9.** On the day after the exam there will be celebrating. **10.** I've been invited to a party by a couple of friends. **11.** If I had the money, I'd fly to Europe now. **12.** Then I could see many of the cities we read about, and I could use my German.

Appendix

1. Predicting the Gender of Certain Nouns

As a rule, nouns must be learned with their articles because their genders are not readily predictable. However, here are a few hints to help you determine the gender of some nouns in order to eliminate unnecessary memorizing.

a. Most nouns referring to males are MASCULINE.

   der Vater, der Bruder, der Junge

   • Days, months, and seasons are masculine.

      der Montag, der Juni, der Winter

b. Most nouns referring to females are FEMININE; BUT das Mädchen, das Fräulein (see c below).

   die Mutter, die Schwester, die Frau

   • Many feminine nouns can be derived from masculine nouns. Their plurals always end in **-nen**.

      sg.: der Schweizer / die Schweizerin; der Österreicher / die Österreicherin
      pl.: die Schweizerinnen, Österreicherinnen

   • All nouns ending in **-heit, -keit, -ie, -ik, -ion, -schaft, -tät,** and **-ung** are feminine. Their plurals end in **-en**.

      sg.: die Schönheit, Richtigkeit, Geographie, Musik, Religion, Nachbarschaft, Qualität, Rechnung
      pl. die Qualitäten, Rechnungen usw.

There are exceptions, e.g., **der Affe, der Löwe, der Neffe, der Name, das Ende,** etc.

   • Most nouns ending in **-e** are feminine. Their plurals end in **-n.**

      sg.: die Sprache, Woche, Hose, Kreide, Farbe, Seite
      pl.: die Sprachen, Wochen usw.

c. All nouns ending in **-chen** or **-lein** are NEUTER. These two suffixes make diminutives of nouns, i.e., they denote them as being small. In the case of people, the diminutive may indicate affection, or also belittling. Such nouns often have an umlaut, but there is no plural ending.

   sg.: der Bruder / das Brüderchen; die Schwester / das Schwesterlein
   pl. die Brüderchen, Schwesterlein

   • Because of these suffixes, two nouns referring to females are neuter.

      das Mädchen, das Fräulein

   • Most cities and countries are neuter.

      (das) Berlin, (das) Deutschland BUT die Schweiz, die Türkei

2. Summary Chart of the Four Cases

	use	follows . . .	singular masc.	singular neut.	singular fem.	plural
nom.	Subject, Predicate noun	**heißen, sein, werden**	der dieser[1] ein mein[2]	das dieses ein	die diese eine	die diese keine
acc.	Direct object	**durch, für, gegen, ohne, um**	den diesen einen meinen	mein	meine	meine
		an, auf, hinter, in, neben, über, unter, vor, zwischen				
dat.	Indirect object	**aus, bei, mit, nach, seit, von, zu**	dem diesem einem meinem	dem diesem einem meinem	der dieser einer meiner	den diesen keinen meinen
		antworten, danken, fehlen, gefallen, gehören, glauben,[3] gratulieren, helfen, schmecken usw.				
gen.	Possessive	**(an)statt, trotz, während, wegen**	des dieses eines meines	des dieses eines meines	der dieser keiner meiner	

NOTE:
1. The **der**-words are **dieser, jeder, welcher, alle, manche, solche.**
2. The **ein**-words are **kein, mein, dein, sein, ihr, unser, euer, ihr, Ihr.**
3. Ich glaube **ihm.** BUT Ich glaube **es.**

3. Pronouns

Interrogative Pronouns

nom.	wer?	was?
acc.	wen?	was?
dat.	wem?	
gen.	wessen?	

Personal Pronouns

nom.	ich	du	er	es	sie	wir	ihr	sie	Sie
acc.	mich	dich	ihn	es	sie	uns	euch	sie	Sie
dat.	mir	dir	ihm	ihm	ihr	uns	euch	ihnen	Ihnen

Reflexive Pronouns

	ich	du	er / es / sie	wir	ihr	sie	Sie
acc.	mich	dich	sich	uns	euch	sich	sich
dat.	mir	dir	sich	uns	euch	sich	sich

Relative Pronouns

	masc.	neut.	fem.	plural
nom.	der	das	die	die
acc.	den	das	die	die
dat.	dem	dem	der	denen
gen.	dessen	dessen	deren	deren

4. Adjective Endings

Preceded Adjectives

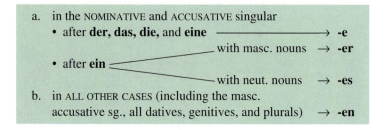

Unpreceded Adjectives

	masc.	neut.	fem.	plural
nom.	guter Käse	gutes Brot	gute Wurst	gute Säfte
acc.	guten Käse	gutes Brot	gute Wurst	gute Säfte
dat.	gutem Käse	gutem Brot	guter Wurst	guten Säften
gen.	guten Käses	guten Brotes	guter Wurst	guter Säfte

5. Comparison of Irregular Adjectives and Adverbs

	gern	groß	gut	hoch	nah	viel
Comparative	lieber	größer	besser	höher	näher	mehr
Superlative	liebst-	größt-	best-	höchst-	nächst-	meist-

6. Endings of Nouns

N-Nouns

	singular	plural
nom.	der Student	die Studenten
acc.	den Student**en**	die Studenten
dat.	dem Student**en**	den Studenten
gen.	des Student**en**	der Studenten

Other nouns are: Herr (-n, -en), Franzose, Gedanke (-ns, -n), Journalist, Junge, Komponist, Mensch, Nachbar, Name (-ns, -n), Polizist, Tourist, Zimmerkollege.

Adjectival Nouns

	masc.	fem.	plural
nom.	der Deutsche ein Deutscher	die Deutsche eine Deutsche	die Deutschen keine Deutschen
acc.	den Deutschen einen Deutschen		
dat.	dem Deutschen einem Deutschen	der Deutschen einer Deutschen	den Deutschen keinen Deutschen
gen.	des Deutschen eines Deutschen	der Deutschen einer Deutschen	der Deutschen keiner Deutschen

Other adjectival nouns are: der Beamte (BUT die Beamtin), der Angestellte, der Bekannte.

7. N-Verbs ("strong verbs") and Irregular T-Verbs ("weak verbs")

Principal Parts Listed Alphabetically

This list is limited to the active n-verbs and irregular t-verbs used in this text. Compound verbs like **ankommen** or **abfliegen** are not included, since their principal parts are the same as those of the basic verbs **kommen** and **fliegen**.

infinitive	present	simple past	past participle	meaning
anfangen	fängt an	fing an	angefangen	*to begin*
backen	bäckt	buk (backte)	gebacken	*to bake*
beginnen		begann	begonnen	*to begin*
bekommen		bekam	bekommen	*to receive*
bewerben	bewirbt	bewarb	beworben	*to apply*
bieten		bot	geboten	*to offer*
bitten		bat	gebeten	*to ask, request*
bleiben		blieb	ist geblieben	*to remain*
bringen		brachte	gebracht	*to bring*
denken		dachte	gedacht	*to think*
einladen	lädt ein	lud ein	eingeladen	*to invite*

infinitive	present	simple past	past participle	meaning
empfehlen	empfiehlt	empfahl	empfohlen	to recommend
entscheiden		entschied	entschieden	to decide
essen	ißt	aß	gegessen	to eat
fahren	fährt	fuhr	ist gefahren	to drive, go
fallen	fällt	fiel	ist gefallen	to fall
finden		fand	gefunden	to find
fliegen		flog	ist geflogen	to fly
geben	gibt	gab	gegeben	to give
gefallen	gefällt	gefiel	gefallen	to please
gehen		ging	ist gegangen	to go
geschehen	geschieht	geschah	ist geschehen	to happen
haben	hat	hatte	gehabt	to have
halten	hält	hielt	gehalten	to hold; stop
hängen		hing	gehangen	to be hanging
heißen		hieß	geheißen	to be called, named
helfen	hilft	half	geholfen	to help
kennen		kannte	gekannt	to know
klingen		klang	geklungen	to sound
kommen		kam	ist gekommen	to come
lassen	läßt	ließ	gelassen	to let; leave (behind)
laufen	läuft	lief	ist gelaufen	to run; walk
lesen	liest	las	gelesen	to read
liegen		lag	gelegen	to lie
nehmen	nimmt	nahm	genommen	to take
nennen		nannte	genannt	to name, call
rufen		rief	gerufen	to call
scheinen		schien	geschienen	to shine; seem
schlafen	schläft	schlief	geschlafen	to sleep
schreiben		schrieb	geschrieben	to write
schwimmen		schwamm	geschwommen	to swim
sehen	sieht	sah	gesehen	to see
sein	ist	war	ist gewesen	to be
singen		sang	gesungen	to sing
sitzen		saß	gesessen	to sit
spinnen		spann	gesponnen	to spin
sprechen	spricht	sprach	gesprochen	to speak
springen		sprang	ist gesprungen	to jump
stehen		stand	gestanden	to stand
steigen		stieg	ist gestiegen	to climb
tragen	trägt	trug	getragen	to carry; wear
treiben		trieb	getrieben	to engage in (sports)
trinken		trank	getrunken	to drink
tun	tut	tat	getan	to do
verlieren		verlor	verloren	to lose
wachsen	wächst	wuchs	ist gewachsen	to grow
waschen	wäscht	wusch	gewaschen	to wash
werden	wird	wurde	ist geworden	to become; get
wissen	weiß	wußte	gewußt	to know
ziehen	zieht	zog	(ist) gezogen	to pull; (move)

Principal Parts Listed by Stem-Changing Groups

This is the same list as the previous one, but this time it is divided in groups with the same stem changes.

I.	essen	(ißt)	**aß**	gegessen
	geben	(gibt)	gab	gegeben
	geschehen	(geschieht)	geschah	ist geschehen
	sehen	(sieht)	sah	gesehen
	lesen	(liest)	las	gelesen
	bitten		bat	gebeten
	liegen		lag	gelegen
	sitzen		saß	gesessen
II.	bewerben	(bewirbt)	bewarb	beworben
	empfehlen	(empfiehlt)	empfahl	empfohlen
	helfen	(hilft)	half	geholfen
	nehmen	(nimmt)	nahm	genommen
	sprechen	(spricht)	sprach	gesprochen
	beginnen		begann	begonnen
	schwimmen		schwamm	geschwommen
	spinnen		spann	gesponnen
	bekommen		bekam	bekommen
	kommen		kam	ist gekommen
III.	finden		fand	gefunden
	klingen		klang	geklungen
	singen		sang	gesungen
	springen		sprang	ist gesprungen
	trinken		trank	getrunken
IV.	bleiben		blieb	ist geblieben
	entscheiden		entschied	entschieden
	scheinen		schien	geschienen
	schreiben		schrieb	geschrieben
	steigen		stieg	ist gestiegen
	treiben		trieb	getrieben
V.	bieten		bot	geboten
	fliegen		flog	ist geflogen
	verlieren		verlor	verloren
	ziehen		zog	ist gezogen
VI.	einladen	(lädt ein)	lud ein	eingeladen
	fahren	(fährt)	fuhr	ist gefahren
	tragen	(trägt)	trug	getragen
	wachsen	(wächst)	wuchs	ist gewachsen
	waschen	(wäscht)	wusch	gewaschen
VII.	fallen	(fällt)	fiel	ist gefallen
	gefallen	(gefällt)	gefiel	gefallen
	halten	(hält)	hielt	gehalten
	lassen	(läßt)	ließ	gelassen
	schlafen	(schläft)	schlief	geschlafen
	laufen	(läuft)	lief	ist gelaufen
	heißen		hieß	geheißen
	rufen		rief	gerufen

VIII. n-verbs that do not belong to any of the groups above:

anfangen	(fängt an)	fing an	angefangen
backen	(bäckt)	buk (backte)	gebacken
gehen		ging	ist gegangen
hängen		hing	gehangen
sein	(ist)	war	ist gewesen
stehen		stand	gestanden
tun	(tut)	tat	getan
werden	(wird)	wurde	ist geworden

IX. irregular t-verbs

bringen	brachte	gebracht
denken	dachte	gedacht
haben	hatte	gehabt
kennen	kannte	gekannt
nennen	nannte	genannt
wissen (weiß)	wußte	gewußt

8. Sample Forms of the Subjunctive

General Subjunctive (Subjunctive II)

	können	haben	sein	werden	lernen	bringen	gehen
ich	könnte	hätte	wäre	würde	lernte	brächte	ginge
du	könntest	hättest	wärest	würdest	lerntest	brächtest	gingest
er	könnte	hätte	wäre	würde	lernte	brächte	ginge
wir	könnten	hätten	wären	würden	lernten	brächten	gingen
ihr	könntet	hättet	wäret	würdet	lerntet	brächtet	ginget
sie	könnten	hätten	wären	würden	lernten	brächten	gingen

Special Subjunctive (Subjunctive I)

	können	haben	sein	werden	lernen	bringen	gehen
ich	könne	habe	sei	werde	lerne	bringe	gehe
du	könnest	habest	seiest	werdest	lernest	bringest	gehest
er	könne	habe	sei	werde	lerne	bringe	gehe
wir	können	haben	seien	werden	lernen	bringen	gehen
ihr	könnet	habet	seiet	werdet	lernet	bringet	gehet
sie	können	haben	seien	werden	lernen	bringen	gehen

9. Table of Verb Forms in Different Tenses

• Indicative

	present		simple past		future	
ich	frage	fahre	fragte	fuhr	werde	
du	fragst	fährst	fragtest	fuhrst	wirst	
er	fragt	fährt	fragte	fuhr	wird	fragen / fahren
wir	fragen	fahren	fragten	fuhren	werden	
ihr	fragt	fahrt	fragtet	fuhrt	werdet	
sie	fragen	fahren	fragten	fuhren	werden	

present perfect

ich	habe			bin		
du	hast			bist		
er	hat		gefragt	ist		gefahren
wir	haben			sind		
ihr	habt			seid		
sie	haben			sind		

past perfect

	hatte			war		
	hattest			warst		
	hatte		gefragt	war		gefahren
	hatten			waren		
	hattet			wart		
	hatten			waren		

• Subjunctive

PRESENT-TIME

general subjunctive

ich	fragte	führe	würde	
du	fragtest	führest	würdest	
er	fragte	führe	würde	fragen / fahren
wir	fragten	führen	würden	
ihr	fragtet	führet	würdet	
sie	fragten	führen	würden	

special subjunctive

frage	fahre
fragest	fahrest
frage	fahre
fragen	fahren
fraget	fahret
fragen	fahren

PAST-TIME

general subjunctive

ich	hätte			wäre		
du	hättest			wärest		
er	hätte		gefragt	wäre		gefahren
wir	hätten			wären		
ihr	hättet			wäret		
sie	hätten			wären		

special subjunctive

habe			sei		
habest			seiest		
habe		gefragt	sei		gefahren
haben			seien		
habet			seiet		
haben			seien		

• Passive Voice

present

ich	werde	
du	wirst	
er	wird	gefragt
wir	werden	
ihr	werdet	
sie	werden	

simple past

wurde	
wurdest	
wurde	gefragt
wurden	
wurdet	
wurden	

future

werde	
wirst	
wird	gefragt werden
werden	
werdet	
werden	

present perfect

ich	bin	
du	bist	
er	ist	gefragt worden
wir	sind	
ihr	seid	
sie	sind	

past perfect

war	
warst	
war	gefragt worden
waren	
wart	
waren	

10. Translation of the *Gespräche*

p. 2

Schritt 1

How Are You?   MR. SANDERS: *Hello.* MS. LEHMANN: *Hello.* MR. SANDERS: *My name is Sanders, Willi Sanders. And what's your name?* MS. LEHMANN: *My name is Erika Lehmann.* MR. SANDERS: *I'm glad to meet you.*

MR. MEIER: *Good morning, Mrs. Fiedler. How are you?* MRS. FIEDLER: *Fine, thank you. And you?* MR. MEIER: *I'm fine too, thank you.*

HEIDI: *Hi, Ute! How are you?* UTE: *Hi, Heidi! Oh, I'm tired.* HEIDI: *Me too. Too much stress. See you later!* UTE: *Bye!*

p. 6

Schritt 2

What's That?   GERMAN PROFESSOR: *Now listen carefully and answer in German. What is that?* JIM MILLER: *That's the pencil.* GERMAN PROFESSOR: *What color is the pencil?* SUSAN SMITH: *Yellow.* GERMAN PROFESSOR: *Make a sentence, please.* SUSAN SMITH: *The pencil is yellow.* GERMAN PROFESSOR: *Is the notebook yellow too?* DAVID JENKINS: *No, the notebook isn't yellow. The notebook is light blue.* GERMAN PROFESSOR: *Good.* SUSAN SMITH: *Professor, what does* hellblau *mean?* GERMAN PROFESSOR: Hellblau *means* light blue *in English.* SUSAN SMITH: *And how does one say* dark blue? GERMAN PROFESSOR: Dunkelblau. SUSAN SMITH: *Oh, the pen is dark blue.* GERMAN PROFESSOR: *Correct. That's all for today. For tomorrow please read the dialogue again and learn the vocabulary, too.*

p. 11

Schritt 3

In the Clothing Store   SALESCLERK: *Well, how are the pants?* CHRISTIAN: *Too big and too long.* SALESCLERK: *And the sweater?* MAIKE: *Too expensive.* CHRISTIAN: *But the colors are great. Too bad!*

CHRISTIAN: *Hey, where's my jacket?* MAIKE: *I don't know.* SALESCLERK: *What color is the jacket?* CHRISTIAN: *Blue.* SALESCLERK: *Is that the jacket?* MAIKE: *Yes, thank you.*

p. 16

Schritt 4

How Much Is It?   SALESCLERK: *Hello. May I help you?* SILVIA: *I need some pencils, pens, and paper. How much are the pencils?* SALESCLERK: *95 pfennig.* SILVIA: *And the pen?* SALESCLERK: *2 marks 75.* SILVIA: *And how much is the paper over there?* SALESCLERK: *Only 6 marks 20.* SILVIA: *Fine. I'll take six pencils, two pens, and the paper.* SALESCLERK: *Is that all?* SILVIA: *Yes, thank you.* SALESCLERK: *17 marks 40, please.*

p. 22

Schritt 5

The Weather in April   NORBERT: *It's nice today, isn't it?* JULIA: *Yes, that's for sure. The sun is shining again.* RUDI: *But the wind is cool.* JULIA: *Oh, that doesn't matter.* NORBERT: *I think it's great.*

DOROTHEA: *The weather is awful, isn't it?* MATTHIAS: *I think so, too. It's raining and raining.* SONJA: *And it's so cold again.* MATTHIAS: *Yes, typical April.*

p. 27

Schritt 6

How Late Is It?   RITA: *Hi, Axel! What time is it?* AXEL: *Hi, Rita! It's ten to eight.* RITA: *Oh no, in ten minutes I have philosophy.* AXEL: *Take care, then. Bye!* RITA: *Yes, bye!*

PHILLIP: *Hi, Steffi! What time is it?* STEFFI: *Hi, Phillip! It's eleven thirty.* PHILLIP: *Shall we eat now?* STEFFI: *All right, the lecture doesn't start till a quarter past one.*

Kapitel 1

p. 42

At the Goethe Institute   SHARON: *Roberto, where are you from?* ROBERTO: *I'm from Rome. And you?* SHARON: *I'm from Sacramento, but now my family lives in Seattle.* ROBERTO: *Do you have (any) brothers or sisters?* SHARON: *Yes, I have two sisters and two brothers. How about you?* ROBERTO: *I have only one sister. She lives in Montreal, in Canada.* SHARON: *Really? What a coincidence! My uncle lives there, too.*

Later   ROBERTO: *Sharon, when is the test?* SHARON: *In ten minutes. Say, what are the names of some rivers in Germany?* ROBERTO: *In the north is the Elbe, in the east the Oder, in the south . . .* SHARON: *The Danube?* ROBERTO: *Right! And in the west the Rhine. Where is Düsseldorf?* SHARON: *Düsseldorf? Hm. Where's a map?* ROBERTO: *Oh, here. In the west of Germany, north of Bonn, on the Rhine.* SHARON: *Oh yes, right! Well, good luck!*

Kapitel 2

p. 64

At the Grocery Store   CLERK: *Hello. May I help you?* OLIVER: *I'd like some fruit. Don't you have any bananas?* CLERK: *Yes, over there.* OLIVER: *How much are they?* CLERK: *1 mark 80 a pound.* OLIVER: *And the oranges?* CLERK: *90 pfennig each.* OLIVER: *Fine, two pounds of bananas and six oranges, please.* CLERK: *Anything else?* OLIVER: *Yes, 2 kilos of apples, please.* CLERK: *16 marks 20, please. Thank you. Good-bye.*

In the Bakery   CLERK: *Good morning. May I help you?* SIMONE: *Good morning. One rye bread and six rolls, please.* CLERK: *Anything else?* SIMONE: *Yes, I need some cake. Is the apple strudel fresh?* CLERK: *Of course, very fresh.* SIMONE: *Fine, then I'll take four pieces.* CLERK: *Is that all?* SIMONE: *I'd also like some cookies. What kind of cookies do you have today?* CLERK: *Lemon cookies, chocolate cookies, butter cookies . . .* SIMONE: *Hm . . . I'll take 250 grams of chocolate cookies.* CLERK: *Anything else?* SIMONE: *No, thank you. That's all.* CLERK: *Then that comes to 18 marks 90, please.*

Kapitel 3

p. 88

In the Restaurant   AXEL: *Waiter, the menu, please.* WAITER: *Here you are.* AXEL: *What do you recommend today?* WAITER: *All of today's specials are very good.* AXEL: *Gabi, what are you having?* GABI: *I don't know. What are you going to have?* AXEL: *I think I'll take menu number one: veal cutlet and potato salad.* GABI: *And I'll take menu number two: stuffed beef rolls with potato dumplings.* WAITER: *Would you like something to drink?* GABI: *A glass of apple juice. And what about you?* AXEL: *Mineral water. (The waiter comes with the food.) Enjoy your meal!* GABI: *Thanks, you too. Mm, that tastes good.* AXEL: *The veal cutlet, too.*

Later   GABI: *We'd like to pay, please.* WAITER: *All right. All together?* GABI: *Yes. Please give me the bill.* AXEL: *No, no, no.* GABI: *Yes, Axel. Today I'm paying.* WAITER: *Well, one menu number one, one menu number two, one apple juice, one mineral water, two cups of coffee. Anything else?* AXEL: *Yes, one roll.* WAITER: *That comes to 60 marks 60, please.* GABI: *[Make it] 62 marks, please.* WAITER: *And eight marks change (back). Thank you very much.*

Kapitel 4

p. 118

On the Telephone   CHRISTA: *Hi, Michael!* MICHAEL: *Hi, Christa! How are you?* CHRISTA: *Not bad, thanks. What are you doing on the weekend?* MICHAEL: *Nothing special. Why?* CHRISTA: *It's Klaus's birthday the day after tomorrow, and we're giving a party.* MICHAEL: *Great. But are you sure that Klaus's birthday is the day after tomorrow? I think he already had his birthday.* CHRISTA: *Nonsense. Klaus's birthday is on May 3rd. And Saturday is the third.* MICHAEL: *OK. When and where is the party?* CHRISTA: *Saturday at seven at my place. But don't say anything. It's a surprise.* MICHAEL: *OK. Well, see you then.* CHRISTA: *Bye. Take care!*

Klaus Rings Christa's Doorbell   CHRISTA: *Hi, Klaus! Happy birthday!* KLAUS: *Hi! Thanks!* MICHAEL: *All the best on your birthday! (Many happy returns!)* KLAUS: *Hi, Michael! . . . Hello, Gerda! Kurt and Sabine, you too? What are you all doing here?* ALL: *We're wishing you a happy birthday!* KLAUS: *Thanks! What a surprise!*

p. 144

Kapitel 5

Excuse Me! Where Is . . . ?   TOURIST: *Excuse me! Can you tell me where the Sacher Hotel is?* VIENNESE: *First street on the left behind the opera.* TOURIST: *And how do I get from there to St. Stephen's Cathedral?* VIENNESE: *Straight ahead along Kärtnerstraße.* TOURIST: *How far is it to the cathedral?* VIENNESE: *Not far. You can walk there.* TOURIST: *Thank you.* VIENNESE: *You're welcome.*

Over There   TOURIST: *Excuse me. Where is the Burgtheater?* GENTLEMAN: *I'm sorry. I'm not from Vienna.* TOURIST: *Pardon me. Is that the Burgtheater?* LADY: *No, that's not the Burgtheater, but the opera house. Take the streetcar to city hall. The Burgtheater is across from city hall.* TOURIST: *And were does the streetcar stop?* LADY: *Over there on your left.* TOURIST: *Thank you very much.* LADY: *You're most welcome.*

p. 168

Kapitel 6

Apartment for Rent   INGE: *Hello, my name is Inge Moser. I've heard that you have a two-room apartment for rent. Is that right?* LANDLORD: *Yes, near the cathedral.* INGE: *How old is the apartment?* LANDLORD: *Fairly old, but it's been renovated and is quite big and light. It even has a balcony.* INGE: *What floor is it on?* LANDLORD: *On the fourth floor.* INGE: *Is it furnished or unfurnished?* LANDLORD: *Unfurnished.* INGE: *And how much is the rent?* LANDLORD: *1,100 marks.* INGE: *Is that with or without heat?* LANDLORD: *Without heat.* INGE: *Oh, that's a little too expensive. Thank you very much. Good-bye!* LANDLORD: *Good-bye!*

With a Group Sharing a House   INGE: *I like your house.* HORST: *We still have room for you. Come, I'll show it to you . . . Here on the left is our kitchen. It's small but practical.* INGE: *Who does the cooking?* HORST: *We all (do): Jens, Gisela, Renate, and I.* INGE: *And that's the living room?* HORST: *Yes. It's a bit dark, but that's all right.* INGE: *I like your chairs.* HORST: *They're old, but really comfortable. Upstairs there are four bedrooms and the bathroom.* INGE: *Only one bathroom?* HORST: *Yes, unfortunately. But down here there is another toilet.* INGE: *How much do you pay per month?* HORST: *400 marks each.* INGE: *Not bad. And how do you get to the university?* HORST: *I walk, of course. It's not far.* INGE: *That sounds good!*

p. 192

Kapitel 7

At the Bank   TOURIST: *Hello. Can you tell me where I can exchange money?* TELLER: *At counter 1.* TOURIST: *Thank you very much. (She goes to counter 1.) Hello. I'd like to change (some) dollars into schilling. Here are my traveler's checks.* TELLER: *May I please see your passport?* TOURIST: *Here you are.* TELLER: *Sign here, please.—Go to the cashier over there. There you'll get your money.* TOURIST: *Thank you. (She goes to the cashier.)* CASHIER: *324 schilling 63: one hundred, two hundred, three hundred, ten, twenty, twenty-four schilling and sixty-three groschen.* TOURIST: *Thank you. Good-bye.*

At the Hotel Reception Desk   RECEPTIONIST: *Good evening.* GUEST: *Good evening. Do you have a single room available?* RECEPTIONIST: *For how long?* GUEST: *For two or three nights; if possible, quiet and with a bath.* RECEPTIONIST: *Unfortunately we have only one double room, and that for only one night. But tomorrow there'll be a single room available. Would you like to see the double room?* GUEST: *Yes, I would.* RECEPTIONIST: *Room number 12, on the second floor to the right. Here's the key.* GUEST: *Say, can I leave my suitcase here for a minute?* RECEPTIONIST: *Yes, of course. Put it in the corner over there.* GUEST: *Thank you. One more thing, when do you close at night?* RECEPTIONIST: *At midnight. If you come later, you'll have to ring the bell.*

p. 224

Kapitel 8

At the Post Office in the Train Station   UTA: *I'd like to send this package to the United States.* CLERK: *By surface mail or by airmail?* UTA: *By airmail. How long will it take?* CLERK: *About ten days. Please fill out this parcel form.—Just a minute. Your return address is missing.* UTA: *Oh yes.—One more thing. I need a telephone card.* CLERK: *For 6, 12, or 50 marks?* UTA: *For 12 marks. Thank you very much.*

At the Ticket Counter   ANNEMARIE: *When does the next train for Interlaken leave?* CLERK: *In ten minutes. Departure at 11:28, track 2.* ANNEMARIE: *Good grief! And when will it arrive there?* CLERK: *Arrival in Interlaken at 2:16 P.M.* ANNEMARIE: *Do I have to change trains?* CLERK: *Yes, in Berne, but you have a connection to the InterCity Express with only a 24 minute stopover.* ANNEMARIE: *Fine. Give me a round-trip ticket to Interlaken, please.* CLERK: *First or second class?* ANNEMARIE: *Second class.*

Kapitel 9

p. 250

On the Telephone MRS. SCHMIDT: *This is Mrs. Schmidt.* BÄRBEL: *Hello, Mrs. Schmidt. It's me, Bärbel. Is Karl-Heinz there?* MRS. SCHMIDT: *No, I'm sorry. He just went to the post office.* BÄRBEL: *I see. Can you tell him that I can't go out with him tonight?* MRS. SCHMIDT: *Of course. What's the matter?* BÄRBEL: *I'm sick. My throat hurts and I have a headache.* MRS. SCHMIDT: *I'm sorry. I hope you get better soon.* BÄRBEL: *Thank you. Good-bye.* MRS. SCHMIDT: *Good-bye.*

See You in a Few Minutes YVONNE: *Mayer residence.* DANIELA: *Hi, Yvonne! It's me, Daniela.* YVONNE: *Hi, Daniela! What's up?* DANIELA: *Nothing special. Do you feel like playing squash or going swimming?* YVONNE: *Squash? No thanks. I'm still sore from the day before yesterday. I can hardly move. I hurt all over.* DANIELA: *Poor baby (lit.: lame duck)! How about chess?* YVONNE: *OK, that sounds fine. Are you coming to my place?* DANIELA: *Yes, see you in a few minutes.*

Kapitel 10

p. 274

A Glance at the Newspaper SONJA: *Say, what's on TV tonight?* STEPHAN: *I have no idea. Nothing special for sure.* SONJA: *Let me see.* Star Trek, *a documentary, and a detective story.* STEPHAN: *I don't feel like (watching) that.* SONJA: *Maybe there's something at the movies?* STEPHAN: *Yes,* The Firm *and* Sleepless in Seattle. SONJA: *I've already seen both.* STEPHAN: Mother Courage *is playing at the theater.* SONJA: *Not bad. Do you feel like going?* STEPHAN: *Yes, that sounds good. Let's go.*

At the Ticket Window SONJA: *Do you still have tickets for tonight?* YOUNG LADY: *Yes, in the first row of the first balcony on the left and on the right in the orchestra.* STEPHAN: *Two seats in the orchestra. Here are our student ID's.* YOUNG LADY: *28 marks, please.* SONJA: *When does the performance start?* YOUNG LADY: *At 8:15 PM.*

During the Intermission STEPHAN: *Would you like a coke?* SONJA: *Yes, I'd love one. But let me pay. You've already bought the programs.* STEPHAN: *OK. How did you like the first act?* SONJA: *Great. I once read* Mother Courage *in school, but I've never seen it on stage.* STEPHAN: *I haven't either.*

Kapitel 11

p. 298

Wanted: *charming, adventurous, affectionate ADAM. Reward: pretty, dynamic EVE, mid 20s, likes antiques, old houses, fast cars, animals, (and) children.*

What I'm looking for Exists. *But how to find it? Woman with university degree, late 20s/ 1 meter 53 (5 feet), slim, musical, is looking for congenial, well-educated, honest man with a sense of humor.*

Which Man with Feelings, *up to 45 years young, likes traveling, dancing, swimming, skiing and (likes) me? I (am): attractive, dark-haired, adventurous, and chic. Divorced, early 30s, two nice boys.*

I'm Not a Millionaire. *I don't want to buy my happiness, but earn it. I (am): 28, 1 meter 70 (5 feet 7), am not looking for a fashion doll or disco queen, but a nice, natural girl, who may also be pretty.*

Dancing, Sailing, *and traveling are my three great passions. What congenial woman with imagination wants to join me? I'm a journalist (Aquarius), optimistic and unconventional.*

To Experience Love Together ... at home, in a concert, while dancing, in the mountains, on the tennis court or golf course, in or on the water, wherever, for all this I wish for a good-looking, professional woman in her 30s with a lot of charm and esprit, who also likes to read and write.

Kapitel 12

p. 332

Do You Know What You Want to Be? TRUDI: *Say, Elke, do you already know what you want to be?* ELKE: *Yes, a cabinet-maker.* TRUDI: *Isn't that very strenuous?* ELKE: *Oh, you get used to it. Perhaps someday I'll open my own business.* TRUDI: *Those are big plans.* ELKE: *Why not? I don't feel like always sitting in an office and working for other people.* TRUDI: *And where do you want to apply for an apprenticeship?* ELKE: *No problem. My aunt has her own business and has already offered me a place (as an apprentice).* TRUDI: *You're lucky.* ELKE: *And how about you? Do you know what you want to do?* TRUDI: *Perhaps I'll be a dentist. Good dentists are always needed and, besides, it pays* *very well.* ELKE: *That's true, but you have to study for a long time.* TRUDI: *I know, but I'm actually looking forward to it.*

p. 356

Kapitel 13

During Registration   PETRA: *Hi, David. How are you?* DAVID: *Fine thanks. And you?* PETRA: *Fine. What are you doing there?* DAVID: *I've got to fill out these registration forms.* PETRA: *Shall I help you?* DAVID: *If you have time. I'm always struggling with red tape.* PETRA: *Do you have your passport with you?* DAVID: *No, why?* PETRA: *Your residence permit is in it; we need it.* DAVID: *I can get it quickly.* PETRA: *Do that. I'll wait for you here.*

A Little Later   DAVID: *Here is my passport. I'll also have to decide soon what to take. Can you help me with that, too?* PETRA: *Sure. What's your major? What are you interested in?* DAVID: *My major is modern history. I'd like to take some courses in German history and literature.* PETRA: *Here's my course catalog. Let's see what they're offering this semester.*

p. 380

Kapitel 14

There's Always Something Going On Here   HEIKE: *And that's the Memorial Church with its three buildings. We call them the "Hollow Tooth," the "Lipstick," and the "Compact."* MARTIN: *Berliners have nicknames for everything, don't they?* HEIKE: *The old tower of the Memorial Church is to stay the way it is, as a memorial (to the war). The new Memorial Church with the new tower is modern.* MARTIN: *And they really look a little like a lipstick and a compact. Tell me, do you like living here in Berlin?* HEIKE: *Actually, yes. Berlin really has a lot to offer, not only historically but also culturally. There's always something going on here. Besides, the surroundings are beautiful.* MARTIN: *That's true. Say, were you there when they broke through the Wall?* HEIKE: *Of course. I'll never forget that.* MARTIN: *I won't either, although I only saw it on TV.* HEIKE: *We waited all night, even though it was really cold. When the first piece of wall tipped over, we all sang loudly: "A beautiful day like today, a day like this should never end."* MARTIN: *I (can) still see the people dancing and celebrating on top of the Wall.* HEIKE: *That was really incredible (lit. unique). Who would have thought that it all would happen so fast.* MARTIN: *And so peacefully.* HEIKE: *Yes, thank God. Only later did we realize the enormous problems (ahead).*

p. 406

Kapitel 15

A Visit to Weimar   THOMAS: *It's funny. This monument of Goethe and Schiller seems so familiar to me. I think I've seen it somewhere before.* DANIELA: *Have you (ever) been to San Francisco?* THOMAS: *Of course! In the Golden Gate Park!* DANIELA: *Exactly. A few years ago it was still easier for us to see the monument there than to come here to Weimar.* THOMAS: *And yet it's only two hours away from Göttingen.* DANIELA: *Did you know that Weimar was selected as cultural capital of Europe for the year 1999?* THOMAS: *Sure. But I have some mixed feelings about that.* DANIELA: *How come? During the 18th century a lot of famous people lived here, and the Weimar Republic is named for that.* THOMAS: *That's true, but when you see the town from up there on the Ettersberg, all sorts of questions come up.* DANIELA: *Yes, there you have a point (lit. you're right).*

DANIELA: *The old houses here are really pretty.* THOMAS: *Yes, they were renovated only a few years ago. That cost the state quite a bit of money.* DANIELA: *It's good that no cars are allowed here.* THOMAS: *Thank God. The façades wouldn't have survived the exhaust fumes of the Trabbis for long. In our city they now have a citizens' initiative to prohibit all cars in the old part of town in order to save the old buildings.* DANIELA: *I think that's good.* THOMAS: *Yes, where there's a will, there's a way.*

11. Answer Key to Selected Exercises in *Rückblicke*

Kapitel 1–3

pp. 114–15

E.
1. Wir trinken Saft. Trinken Sie/trinkt ihr/trinkst du Saft? Sie trinkt keinen Saft.
2. Ich antworte den Leuten. Sie antworten den Leuten. Antwortet sie den Leuten? Antworten Sie den Leuten! Antworten Sie den Leuten nicht! Warum antworten Sie/antwortet ihr/antwortest du den Leuten nicht?
3. Sie fahren nach Berlin. Warum fährt sie nach Berlin? Ich fahre nicht nach Berlin. Fahren Sie/fahrt ihr/fährst du nach Berlin? Fahren Sie nach Berlin! Fahren Sie nicht nach Berlin!
4. Wer ißt Fisch? Essen Sie/eßt ihr/ißt du Fisch? Sie essen keinen Fisch. Essen Sie Fisch!
5. Ich werde müde. Sie wird nicht müde. Werden Sie nicht müde! Wer wird müde? Wir werden auch müde.
6. Ich habe Hunger. Haben Sie/habt ihr/hast du Hunger? Wer hat Hunger? Sie haben Hunger. Sie haben keinen Hunger. Wir haben keinen Hunger.
7. Sie sind/ihr seid/du bist sehr groß. Sie sind nicht sehr groß. Ich bin sehr groß. Ist er nicht groß?

F.
1. Herr Schmidt ist Österreicher. Nein, er ist/kommt aus der Schweiz. Ist Frau Bayer Österreicherin? Sie ist auch nicht/keine Österreicherin. Man sagt/sie sagen, Frau Klein ist Amerikanerin. Joe ist auch Amerikaner.
2. Hier gibt es einen Fluß (ein Restaurant, keine Mensa, keinen See). Es gibt hier Berge (Bäckereien, Seen, keine Geschäfte/Läden, keine Cafés).
3. Wem gehört das Geschäft/der Laden? Was gehört dem Großvater? Sie sagt, es gehört dem Bruder nicht. Es gehört der Tante nicht.
4. Was bringt er der Freundin? Wem bringt er Blumen? Wer bringt die Blumen? Warum bringt er Blumen? Bringt er der Freundin keine Blumen? Sie bringen den Kindern ein paar Plätzchen. Bringt sie den Freunden eine Flasche Wein? Er bringt den Nachbarn Äpfel. Ich bringe den Schwestern ein paar Bücher.

H.
1. . . . keinen Schokoladenpudding.   2. . . . dem Vater nicht.   3. . . . den Ober nicht?
4. . . . kein Messer.   5. . . . keine Milch.   6. . . . nicht nach Hause?   7. . . . keine Rindsrouladen?   8. . . . keinen Kaffee.   9. . . . nicht gern Eis.   10. . . . nicht mein Freund.
11. . . . keinen Durst?   12. . . . nicht sehr kalt.

Kapitel 4–7

pp. 219–21

F.
1. a. wissen   b. Kennst   c. Kennt   d. kenne, weiß   e. Weißt
4. a. Dürfen wir das Geschenk aufmachen? Wir wollen (möchten) es aufmachen. Ich kann es nicht aufmachen. Er muß es aufmachen. Warum soll ich es nicht aufmachen? Möchten Sie/möchtet ihr/möchtest du es aufmachen?
   b. Ich bin gestern angekommen. Sie kommt heute an. Wann kommen sie an? Wann ist er angekommen? Kommt er auch an? Ich weiß, daß sie morgen nicht ankommen. Sie sollen übermorgen ankommen. Ist sie schon angekommen?

G.
1. Er fragt Sie. Sie fragt ihn. Fragen sie uns? Ja, sie fragen dich. Wir fragen euch. Fragt sie nicht! Hast du sie gefragt? Haben sie dich nicht gefragt? Habt ihr mich gefragt?
2. Ihm gefällt unser Museum. (Unser Museum gefällt ihm.) Gefällt ihnen dieses Museum? Ihnen gefällt ihr Museum nicht. (Ihr Museum gefällt ihnen nicht.) Welches Museum gefällt dir? Mir gefällt so ein Museum. (So ein Museum gefällt mir.) Gefällt euch kein Museum? Museen gefallen mir nicht. (Mir gefallen Museen nicht.) Solche Museen haben mir nie gefallen. (Mir haben solche Museen nie gefallen.) Ihm gefällt jedes Museum. (Jedes Museum gefällt ihm.)
3. Das tut ihr leid. Tut das Ihnen/euch/dir leid? Das tut ihm nicht leid. Das hat mir leid getan. Das hat ihnen leid getan.

I.
2. a. aber   b. aber   c. sondern   d. aber   e. sondern

pp. 326–29

Kapitel 8–11

 E.

1. Halten Sie sich fit? Sie halten sich nicht fit. Wie hat sie sich fit gehalten (hielt sie sich fit)? Halten Sie sich/haltet euch/halte dich fit! Ich möchte mich fit halten. Wir müssen uns fit halten. Wir mußten uns fit halten.

2. Wir erkälten uns wieder. Erkälten Sie sich/erkältet euch/erkälte dich nicht wieder! Sie haben sich wieder erkältet. Sie will sich nicht wieder erkälten. Wir hatten uns wieder erkältet. Warum erkältest du dich immer? Sie haben sich immer erkältet (erkälteten sich immer).

F. 1. Du mußt dich anziehen. 2. Erst will / möchte ich mich duschen und mir die Haare waschen. 3. Und du mußt dich rasieren. 4. Warum beeilt ihr euch nicht? 5. Hört euch das an! 6. Er ärgerte sich und setzte sich hin (hat sich geärgert und sich hingesetzt).

J. 1. Wir hatten nicht daran gedacht. 2. Daniela und Yvonne waren zum Schwimmbad gegangen. 3. Wir hatten uns warm angezogen. 4. Er hatte mir das schon zweimal versprochen. 5. Das Auto war plötzlich stehengeblieben. 6. Das war nicht so lustig gewesen. 7. Aber das hatte er verdient.

K. 1. zweiten, deutschen, bekannten, österreichische 2. deutsches, amerikanischer 3. interessanten, amerikanischen 4. amerikanische, deutscher 5. ganze, hübsche 6. alten, strengen, richtig 7. verständnisvolle, großen, reichen, verwitweten 8. sieben kleinen, nett, temperamentvolle, viele gute 9. verwitwete, junge 10. phantastischen, deutsche 11. österreichische, deutschen, kurzer, schönes, großes, hohen, neutrale 12. bekannte, neues, großes, amerikanischen 13. vielen, sogenannten wahren, amerikanischen, wahr 14. netter, viel schöner

M. 1. Als 2. wann 3. wenn 4. Als 5. wenn 6. wann

O. 2. a. Woran, An meine b. Worüber, Über einen c. Wovon, Von meinen d. Worauf, Auf einen, darauf e. von ihren, Davon f. an deine, an sie g. über den, worüber h. für, dafür i. für, für sie

pp. 432–33

Kapitel 12–15

D. 3. a. einer hübscheren b. schöner c. interessantere d. die anstrengendste e. das höchste f. die meisten und beßten g. netteren h. die größte i. Je länger, desto besser j. genauso viel wie k. weniger als

E.
1. a. der gerade hier war b. den du kennengelernt hast c. dem das Büchergeschäft in der Goethestraße gehört d. dessen Firma in Stuttgart ist
2. a. deren Sekretärin uns angerufen hat b. die hier neu ist c. durch die wir von dem Programm gehört haben
3. a. das ihr bald sehen werdet b. an dem du vorbeigefahren bist c. das auf einer Insel steht d. von dem man einen wunderschönen Blick hat
4. a. die wie Amerikaner aussehen b. deren Bus dort steht c. denen die Landschaft so gut gefällt d. für die du dich interessiert hast e. mit denen du geredet hast

G.
1. a. Ich würde mich besser fühlen (fühlte mich besser), wenn die Arbeit fertig wäre. b. Das wäre wunderschön. c. Ihr könntet uns dann besuchen. d. Ich wünschte, Rolf hätte mehr Zeit. e. Wenn ich mich nur daran gewöhnen könnte! f. Würdest du mir das erklären? g. Ich wünschte, er redete nicht so viel am Telefon (würde nicht . . . reden). h. Was würdest du tun?/Was tätest du?
2. a. Wir hätten nicht in die Berge fahren sollen. b. Ich wünschte, sie wäre zu Hause geblieben. c. Das wäre einfacher gewesen. d. Wenn wir nur nicht so viel gewandert wären! e. Wenn du bessere Schuhe mitgenommen hättest, hätten dir die Füße nicht so weh getan. f. Du hättest mich daran erinnern sollen. g. Ich hätte es schöner gefunden, zu Hause zu bleiben.

3. Ich werde hier studieren. Ich würde da/dort studieren. Würdest du da gern studieren (Möchtest du . . . studieren)? Ich wünschte, ich könnte da studieren. Sie hätte da studieren können. Wenn ich da studiere, wird mein Deutsch besser (werden). Wenn ich da studieren würde, könnte ich euch besuchen. Ich hätte da/dort studieren sollen.

H.

1. David schrieb, er hätte eine nette Wohnung. Sein Zimmerkollege wäre aus New York. Er lernte viel von ihm (würde . . . lernen). Er spräche nur Englisch (würde . . . sprechen). Manchmal ginge er auch zu Partys (würde . . . gehen). Er lernte viele nette Studenten kennen (würde . . . kennenlernen). Die meisten wohnten im Studentenheim (würden . . . wohnen). Das wäre ihm zu teuer. Die Kurse und Professoren wären ausgezeichnet. Er müßte viel lesen, und es gäbe viele Prüfungen (würde . . . geben). Aber eigentlich hätte er keine Probleme.

2. David schrieb, er hätte eine nette Wohnung gehabt. Sein Zimmerkollege wäre aus New York gewesen. Er hätte viel von ihm gelernt. Er hätte nur Englisch gesprochen. Manchmal wäre er auch zu Partys gegangen. Er hätte viele nette Studenten kennengelernt. Die meisten hätten im Studentenheim gewohnt. Das wäre ihm zu teuer gewesen. Die Kurse und Professoren wären ausgezeichnet gewesen. Er hätte viel lesen müssen, und es hätte viele Prüfungen gegeben. Aber eigentlich hätte er keine Probleme gehabt.

I.

1. Diese Universität wird von vielen Studenten besucht.   2. Dieses Jahr werden die Studentenheime renoviert.   3. Ein neues Theater wird gebaut.   4. In dem alten Theater sind viele schöne Theaterstücke gespielt worden.   5. Am Wochenende sind dort auch Filme gezeigt worden.   6. In der Mensa wurde dann darüber gesprochen.   7. Das Theater wird am 1. Mai eröffnet (werden).   8. Dieser Tag muß gefeiert werden.

J.

1. Jetzt bin ich mit meinem ersten Jahr Deutsch fertig geworden.   2. Ich habe wirklich viel gelernt.   3. Ich hätte nie gedacht, daß es soviel Spaß machen könnte.   4. Nicht alles ist leicht gewesen.   5. Ich mußte viele Wörter lernen.   6. Viele Übungen mußten gemacht werden.   7. Bald machen wir unsere letzte Prüfung (werden . . . machen).   8. Weil ich mich immer gut vorbereitet habe, muß ich jetzt nicht so viel arbeiten/lernen.   9. Am Tag nach der Prüfung wird gefeiert (werden).   10. Ich bin von ein paar Freunden zu einer (auf eine) Party eingeladen worden.   11. Wenn ich das Geld hätte, würde ich jetzt nach Europa fliegen.   12. Dann könnte ich viele der Städte sehen, über die wir gelesen haben, und ich könnte mein Deutsch gebrauchen.

Vocabularies

GERMAN-ENGLISH

The vocabulary includes all the ACTIVE AND PASSIVE vocabulary used in *Wie geht's?* The English definitions of the words are limited to their use in the text. Each active vocabulary item is followed by a number and a letter indicating the chapter and section where it first occurs.

NOUNS   Nouns are followed by their plural endings unless the plural is rare or nonexistent. In the case of n-nouns the singular genitive ending is also given: **der Herr, -n, -en.** Nouns that require adjective endings appear with two endings: **der Angestellte (ein Angestellter).** Female forms of masculine nouns are not listed if only **-in** needs to be added: **der Apotheker.**

VERBS   For regular t-verbs ("weak verbs"), only the infinitive is listed. All irregular t-verbs ("irregular weak verbs") and basic n-verbs ("strong verbs") are given with their principal parts: **bringen, brachte, gebracht; schreiben, schrieb, geschrieben.** Separable-prefix verbs are identified by a dot between the prefix and the verb: **mit·bringen.** Compound mixed and n-verbs are printed with an asterisk to indicate that the principal parts can be found under the listing of the basic verb: **mit·bringen*, beschreiben*.** When **sein** is used as the auxiliary of the perfect tenses, the form **ist** is given: **wandern (ist); kommen, kam, ist gekommen.**

ADJECTIVES and ADVERBS   Adjectives and adverbs that have an umlaut in the comparative and superlative are identified by an umlauted vowel in parentheses: **arm (ä) = arm, ärmer, am ärmsten.**

ACCENTUATION   Stress marks are provided for all words that do not follow the typical stress pattern. The accent follows the stressed syllable: **Balkon′, Amerika′ner, wiederho′len.** The stress is not indicated when the word begins with an unstressed prefix, such as **be-, er-, ge-.**

ABBREVIATIONS

~	repetition of th*e key word*	*nom.*	nominative
abbrev.	abbreviation	*o.s.*	oneself
acc.	accusative	*pl.*	plural
adj.	adjective	*refl. pron.*	reflexive pronoun
adv.	adverb	*rel. pron.*	relative pronoun
comp.	comparative	*S*	Schritt
conj.	subordinate conjunction	*sg.*	singular
dat.	dative	*s.th.*	something
fam.	familiar	*W*	Wortschatz 1
gen.	genitive	*G*	Grammatik, Struktur
inf.	infinitive	*E*	Einblicke (Wortschatz 2)
lit.	literally		

A

der **Aal, -e** eel
ab- away, off
ab starting, as of
ab·bauen to reduce
ab·brechen* to break off
der **Abend, -e** evening; **am ~** in the evening (6E); **(Guten) ~!** (Good) evening. (S1)
abend: gestern ~ yesterday evening (8G); **heute ~** this evening (8G)
das **Abendessen, -** supper, evening meal (3W); **zum ~** for supper (3W)
abends in the evening, every evening (S6)
aber but, however (S3,2G,5G); *flavoring particle expressing admiration* (7G)
ab·fahren* (von) to depart, leave (from) (8W)
die **Abfahrt, -en** departure (8W)
der **Abfall, ⸚e** waste, garbage
ab·fliegen* (von) to take off, fly (from) (8W)
die **Abgase** *(pl.)* exhaust fumes
ab·geben* to give away, hand in
abhängig (von) dependent (on)
die **Abhängigkeit** dependence
ab·holen to pick up
das **Abitur, -e** final comprehensive exam (at the end of the Gymnasium)
ab·nehmen* to take s.th. from, take off
abonnieren to subscribe
ab·pflücken to pick, break off
ab·reißen* to tear down (15W)
der **Abschluß, ⸚sse** diploma, degree
die **Abschlußparty, -s** graduation party
die **Abschlußprüfung, -en** final exam
der **Absender, -** return address (8W)
absolut' absolute(ly)
die **Abwechslung, -en** distraction, variety
ach oh; **~ so!** Oh, I see! (9W); **~ was!** Oh, come on! (13W)
die **Achtung** respect; **~!** Watch out! Be careful!

ade (*or* **adé**) good-bye, farewell
das **Adjektiv, -e** adjective
der **Adler, -** eagle
die **Adresse, -n** address (8W)
der **Adventskranz, ⸚e** Advent wreath
die **Adventszeit** Advent season
das **Adverb', -ien** adverb
der **Affe, -n, -n** monkey; **Du ~!** You nut!
(das) **Ägypten** Egypt
der **Ägypter, -** the Egyptian
ägyptisch Egyptian
Aha'! There, you see. Oh, I see.
ähnlich similar; **Das sieht dir ~.** That's typical of you.
die **Ahnung: Keine ~!** I've no idea. (10W)
die **Akademie', -n** academy
der **Akademiker, -** (university) graduate
akademisch academic
der **Akkusativ, -e** accusative
der **Akt, -e** act (play)
das **Aktiv** active voice
aktiv' active
die **Aktivität', -en** activity
aktuell' up to date, current
der **Akzent', -e** accent
akzeptieren to accept
all- all (7G); **vor ~em** above all, mainly (10E); **~e drei Jahre** every three years
allein' alone
allerdings however (15W)
allerlei all sorts of
alles everything all (2W); **Das ist ~.** That's all. (2W)
allgemein (in) general; **im allgemeinen** in general
der **Alltag** everyday life
die **Alpen** *(pl.)* Alps
die **Alpenblume, -n** Alpine flower
das **Alphabet'** alphabet
als as; *(conj.)* (at the time) when (11G); *(after comp.)* than (12G)
also therefore, thus, so; well
alt (ä) old (S3); **ur~** ancient
der **Alte (ein Alter)** old man (12G); **die ~** old lady (12G); **das ~** old things (12G)
das **Alter** age
die **Altstadt, ⸚e** old part of town

der **Amateur', -e** amateur
die **Ameise, -n** ant
(das) **Amerika** America (1W)
der **Amerikaner, -** the American (1W)
amerikanisch American (1W)
die **Ampel, -n** traffic light
an- to, up to
an (+ *acc. / dat.*) to, at (the side of), on (vertical surface) (6G)
analysieren to analyze
an·bieten to offer (12W)
ander- other (9E)
andererseits on the other hand
anders different(ly), in other ways (9E); **etwas anderes** something different (9E)
anerkannt recognized, credited
die **Anerkennung, -en** recognition
der **Anfang, ⸚e** beginning, start (10W): **am ~** in the beginning (10W)
an·fangen* to begin, start (10W)
der **Anfänger, -** beginner
die **Angabe, -n** information
das **Angebot, -e** offering, offer
angeln to fish; **~ gehen*** to go fishing
angepaßt geared to
angeschlagen posted
der **Angestellte (ein Angestellter)** employee, clerk
die **Angestellte (ein Angestellter)** employee, clerk
die **Anglistik** study of English
der **Angriff, -e** attack
die **Angst, ⸚e** fear, anxiety; **~ haben* (vor** + *dat.*) to fear, be afraid (of) (13E); **~ bekommen*** to become afraid, get scared
an·halten* to continue
sich **an·hören** to listen to (9G); **Hör dir das an!** Listen to that.
an·kommen* (in + *dat.*) to arrive (in) (7E); **Das kommt darauf an.** That depends. (7E)
die **Ankunft** arrival (8W)
an·machen to turn on (a radio, etc.) (10W)
die **Anmeldung** reception desk
die **Annahme, -n** hypothetical statement *or* question

an·nehmen* to accept (7E, 13E); to suppose (13E)
der **Anorak, -s** parka
an·reden to address
an·richten to do (damage)
der **Anruf, -e** (phone) call
an·rufen* to call up, phone (7G)
an·schlagen* to post
der **Anschluß, ¨sse** connection
die **Anschrift, -en** address
(sich) **an·sehen*** to look at (9G)
die **Ansicht, -en** opinion, attitude; view
die **Ansichtskarte, -n** (picture) postcard (8W)
an·sprechen* to address, speak to
(an)statt (+ *gen.*) instead of (8G)
anstrengend strenuous (12W)
die **Antiquität′, -en** antique
der **Antrag, ¨e** application
die **Antwort, -en** answer
antworten to answer (S2)
an·wachsen* to increase
die **Anwaltsfirma, -firmen** law firm
die **Anzahl** number, amount
die **Anzeige, -n** ad
die **Anzeigetafel, -n** scoreboard
(sich) **an·ziehen*** to put on (clothing), get dressed (9G)
an·zünden to light
der **Apfel, ¨** apple (2W)
der **Apfelstrudel, -** apple strudel
die **Apothe′ke, -n** pharmacy (2E)
der **Apothe′ker, -** pharmacist
der **Appetit′** appetite; **Guten ~!** Enjoy your meal. (3W)
der **April′** April (S5); **im ~** in April (S5)
der **Äqua′tor** equator
das **Äquivalent′** equivalent
die **Arbeit, -en** work (12W); ~ (term) paper (13W); **bei der ~** at work; **Tag der ~** Labor Day
arbeiten to work (3W)
der **Arbeiter, -** (blue-collar) worker (12W); **Vor~** foreman
der **Arbeitgeber, -** employer
die **Arbeitserlaubnis** work permit
der **Arbeitnehmer, -** employee
das **Arbeitsklima** work climate
arbeitslos unemployed
der **Arbeitslose (ein Arbeitsloser)** unemployed person
die **Arbeitslosigkeit** unemployment
der **Arbeitsplatz, ¨e** job; place of employment
das **Arbeitszimmer, -** study (6W)
archa′isch archaic
die **Archäologie′** archeology
der **Architekt′, -en, -en** architect
die **Architektur′** architecture
das **Archiv, -e** archive
ärgerlich annoying
sich **ärgern über** (+ *acc.*) to get annoyed (upset) about (10G); **Das ärgert mich.** That makes me mad.
die **Arka′de, -n** arcade
arm (ä) poor (11W)
der **Arm, -e** arm (9W)
die **Armbanduhr, -en** wristwatch
die **Armut** poverty
das **Arsenal′, -e** arsenal
die **Art, -en** kind, type
der **Arti′kel, - (von)** article (of)
der **Arzt, ¨e / die Ärztin, -nen** physician, doctor (12W)
die **Asche** ashes
ästhe′tisch aesthetic
die **Atmosphä′re** atmosphere
die **Attraktion′, -en** attraction
attraktiv′ attractive (11W)
auch also, too (S1)
auf (+ *acc. / dat.*) on (top of) (6G); open (7W)
auf- up, open
auf·bauen to build up (15W)
aufeinan′der·treffen* to come together
der **Aufenthalt, -e** stay, stopover (8W); **Auslands~** stay abroad
die **Aufenthaltserlaubnis** residence permit
auf·essen* to eat up
die **Aufgabe, -n** assignment; task, challenge
auf·geben* to give up
auf·halten* to hold open
auf·hören (zu + *inf.*) to stop (doing s.th.) (13E)
auf·machen to open (7G)
die **Aufnahme** acceptance, reception
auf·nehmen* to take (a picture)
auf·passen to pay attention, watch out (7G); **Passen Sie auf!** Pay attention.
der **Aufsatz, ¨e** essay, composition, paper
auf·schreiben* to write down (7G)
auf·stehen* to get up (7G)
auf·stellen to put up, set up
auf·wachsen* to grow up
der **Aufzug, ¨e** elevator
das **Auge, -n** eye (9W)
der **Augenblick, -e** moment; **(Einen) ~!** Just a minute!
der **August′** August (S5); **im ~** in August (S5)
aus (+ *dat.*) out of, from (a place of origin) (3G); **Ich bin ~ . . .** I'm from (a native of) . . . (1W)
aus- out, out of
aus·arbeiten to work out
aus·(be)zahlen to pay out
die **Ausbildung** training, education (12W)
sich **auseinan′der·entwickeln** to develop apart
aus·füllen to fill out (8W)
der **Ausgang, ¨e** exit (7W)
aus·geben* to spend (money) (8E)
aus·gehen* to go out (7G)
ausgezeichnet excellent (6E)
aus·helfen* to help out
das **Ausland** foreign country; **im / ins ~** abroad (12E)
der **Ausländer, -** foreigner (10E)
ausländisch foreign (13E)
das **Auslandsprogramm, -e** foreign-study program
aus·leihen* to loan, lend out
aus·lesen* to pick out
aus·machen turn off (a radio etc.) (10W)
aus·packen to unpack
aus·richten to tell; **Kann ich etwas ~?** Can I take a message?
(sich) **aus·ruhen** to relax (9E)
die **Aussage, -n** statement
aus·sehen* to look, appear (12E); ~ **(wie** + *nom.*) to look (like) (14W)
außer (+ *dat.*) besides, except for (3G)
äußer- outer
außerdem (*adv.*) besides (6E)

außerhalb (+ *gen.*) outside (of)

die **Aussprache** pronunciation

aus·steigen* to get off (8W)

aus·sterben* to become extinct

der **Austausch** exchange; **das ~programm, -e** exchange program

aus·tauschen to exchange (14E)

die **Auster, -n** oyster

ausverkauft sold out

die **Auswahl (an** + *dat.*) choice, selection (of)

der **Ausweis, -e** ID, identification (7W)

aus·zahlen to pay out

(sich) **aus·ziehen*** to take off (clothing), get undressed (9G)

authen'tisch authentic

das **Auto, -s** car (5W)

die **Autobahn, -en** freeway

autofrei free of cars

automatisiert' automated

die **Automobil'branche** car industry

der **Autor, -en** author (10W)

autoritäts'gläubig believing in authority

B

backen (bäckt), buk (backte), gebacken to bake

das **Backblech. -e** cookie sheet

der **Bäcker, -** baker

die **Bäckerei', -en** bakery (2W)

das **Bad, -er** bath(room) (6W)

der **Badeanzug, -e** swimsuit

die **Badehose, -n** swimming trunks

baden to bathe, swim (6W); **sich ~** to take a bath (9G)

die **Badewanne, -n** bathtub

das **Badezimmer, -** bathroom

die **Bahn, -en** railway, train (8W); **~übergang, -e** railroad crossing

der **Bahnhof, -e** train station (5W)

der **Bahnsteig, -e** platform (8W)

bald soon (7W); **so~'** as soon as (12E)

der **Balkon', -s** balcony (6W)

der **Ball, -e** ball

die **Bana'ne, -n** banana (2W)

bange worried

die **Bank, -en** bank (7W)

die **Bank, -e** bench

der **Bankier', -s** banker

der **Bann** ban

die **Bar, -s** bar, pub

der **Bär, -en** bear; **Du bist ein Brumm~.** You're a grouch.

barfuß barefoot

das **Bargeld** cash (7W)

der **Bart, -e** beard

basteln to do crafts

der **Bau, -ten** building, construction

der **Bauch, -e** stomach, belly (9W)

bauen to build (6E)

der **Bauer, -n, -n** farmer

der **Bauernhof, -e** farm

das **Baugesetz, -e** building code

der **Bauingenieur, -e** civil engineer

das **Bauland** building lots

der **Baum, -e** tree (6W)

die **Baumwolle** cotton

der **Baustoff, -e** building material

der **Bayer, -n, -n** the Bavarian

(das) **Bayern** Bavaria (in southeast Germany)

bayrisch Bavarian

der **Beamte (ein Beamter) / die Beamtin, -nen** civil servant (12W)

beantworten to answer

bedeuten to mean, signify (S2)

die **Bedeutung, -en** meaning, significance

bedienen to take care of, serve

die **Bedienung** service, service charge

sich **beeilen** to hurry (9G)

beeindrucken to impress

beeinflussen to influence

beenden to finish

der **Befehl, -e** instruction, request, command

befehlen (befiehlt), befahl, befohlen to order

befriedigend satisfactory

befürchten to fear

beginnen, begann, begonnen to begin (S6)

die **Begrenzung, -en** limitation, limit

begrüßen to greet, welcome

die **Begrüßung, -en** greeting; **zur ~** as greeting

behalten* to keep (14E)

die **Behandlung, -en** treatment

beherrschen to dominate, rule

bei (+ *dat.*) at, near, at the home of (3G); **Hier ~.** This is __'s office / residence.

beid- both (11W)

das **Bein, -e** leg (9W); **auf den Beinen** on the go

das **Beispiel, -e** example; **zum ~ (z.B.)** for example (e.g.)

bei·tragen* (zu) to contribute (to)

bekannt well known (5E); **Das kommt mir ~ vor.** That seems familiar to me.

der **Bekannte (ein Bekannter)** acquaintance (12E)

die **Bekannte (eine Bekannte)** acquaintance (12E)

bekommen* (hat) to get, receive (4W)

belasten to burden; pollute

belegen to sign up for, take (a course) (13W)

beliebt popular

die **Belohnung, -en** reward

benutzen to use

das **Benzin'** gas(oline)

beo'bachten to watch, observe

die **Beo'bachtung, -en** observation

bequem' comfortable, convenient (6W)

der **Berater, -** counselor, adviser, consultant

berauben to rob

der **Berg, -e** mountain (1W)

die **Bergbahn, -en** mountain train

der **Bergbau** mining

bergsteigen gehen* to go mountain climbing

der **Bericht, -e** report

berieseln *here:* to shower with

der **Beruf, -e** profession (12W)

beruflich professional(ly); **~ engagiert'** professionally active

die **Berufsschule, -n** vocational school

der **Berufstätige (ein Berufstätiger)** someone who has a job

berühmt famous (14E)

bescheinigen to verify, document

beschreiben* to describe

die **Beschreibung, -en** description

beschriftet labeled

besichtigen to visit (an attraction), tour (5W)

der **Besitz** property

besitzen* to own
besonders especially (3E);
nichts Besonderes nothing special (9W)
besser better (12G)
die **Besserung** improvement; **Gute ~!** Get well soon. I hope you get better.
best- best (12G); **am besten** it's best (12G)
bestätigen to verify
bestehen* to pass (an exam) (13W); **~ aus** (+ *dat.*) to consist of; **es besteht** there is
bestellen to order (3W)
die **Bestellung, -en** order
bestimmt surely, for sure, certain(ly) (11W)
der **Besuch, -e** visit, visitor
besuchen to visit (8W); attend
der **Besucher, -** visitor
beten to pray
der **Beton′** concrete
betonen to stress, emphasize
betreten* to enter, step on
die **Betriebswirtschaft** business administration
das **Bett, -en** bed (6W); **ins ~** to bed
betteln to beg
der **Bettler, -** beggar
die **Bevölkerung** population
bevor *(conj.)* before (4G)
sich bewerben (um) to apply (for) (12W)
die **Bewertung, -en** evaluation, grading
bewußt conscious(ly)
bezahlen to pay (for) (3W)
der **Bezirk, -e** district
die **Bibel, -n** Bible
die **Bibliothek′, -en** library (5W)
die **Biene, -n** bee
das **Bier, -e** beer (2W)
bieten, bot, geboten to offer
der **Biki′ni, -s** bikini
die **Bilanz′, -en: eine ~ auf·stellen** to make an evaluation
das **Bild, -er** picture (S2)
bilden to form; **~ Sie einen Satz!** Make a sentence.
die **Bildung** education
billig cheap, inexpensive (S3)
die **Billion, -e′n** *(American)* trillion (S4)
die **Biochemie′** biochemistry

der **Bioche′miker, -** biochemist
der **Bio-Laden, ∷** health-food store
der **Biolo′ge, -n**, die **Biolo′gin, -nen** biologist
die **Biologie′** biology
bis to, until (S4); **~ gleich!** See you in a few minutes; **~ später!** See you later! So long! (S6)
bisher′ until now
bißchen: ein ~ some, a little bit (4E); **Ach du liebes ~!** Good grief!, My goodness!, Oh dear! (2E)
bitte please (S1); **~! / ~ bitte!** You're welcome. (S6, 2E); **~ schön!** You're welcome.; **Hier ~ !** Here you are.; **~ schön?** May I help you?; **Wie ~?** What did you say? Could you say that again? (S3)
die **Bitte, -n** request
bitten, bat, gebeten to ask, request (12E); **um etwas ~** to request s.th.
das **Blatt, ∷er** leaf; sheet
blau blue (S2)
das **Blei** lead
bleiben, blieb, ist geblieben to stay, remain (3W)
der **Bleistift, -e** pencil (S2)
der **Blick (auf + acc.)** view (of), glance at
der **Blickpunkt, -e** focus
blind blind
blitzen to sparkle
der **Block, ∷e** block
die **Blocka′de, -n** blockade
die **Blockflöte, -n** recorder (musical instrument)
blockiert′ blocked
blond blond
blühen to flourish
die **Blume, -n** flower (2E)
die **Bluse, -n** blouse (S3)
der **Boden** ground, floor
die **Bohne, -n** bean (2W)
der **Bomber, -** bomber
der **Bonus, -se** bonus
das **Boot, -e** boat
borgen to borrow
böse angry, mad, upset
der **Bote, -n, -n** messenger
die **Bouti′que, -n** boutique
die **Bowle, -n** alcoholic punch
boxen to box

der **Braten, -** roast
die **Bratwurst, ∷e** fried sausage
der **Brauch, ∷e** custom
brauchen to need (S4)
brauen to brew
braun brown (S2); **~ gebrannt** tanned
die **Braut, ∷e** bride
der **Bräutigam, -e** bridegroom
das **Brautkleid, -er** wedding dress
die **BRD (Bundesrepublik Deutschland)** FRG (Federal Republic of Germany)
brechen (bricht), brach, gebrochen to break
der **Brei, -e** porridge
breit broad, wide
das **Brett, -er** board; **Schwarze ~** bulletin board
die **Brezel, -n** pretzel
der **Brief, -e** letter (8W)
der **Briefkasten, ∷** mailbox (8W)
brieflich by letter
die **Briefmarke, -n** stamp (8W)
der **Briefsortierer, -** mail sorter
der **Briefträger, -** mailman
die **Brille, -n** glasses
bringen, brachte, gebracht to bring (3W)
die **Broschü′re, -n** brochure
das **Brot, -e** bread (2W)
das **Brötchen, -** roll (2W); **belegte ~** sandwich
der **Brotwürfel, -** small piece of bread, cube
die **Brücke, -n** bridge (5W)
der **Bruder, ∷** brother (1W)
das **Brüderchen, -** little brother
brummig grouchy
der **Brunnen, -** fountain
das **Buch, ∷er** book (S2)
der **Bücherwurm, ∷er** bookworm
die **Buchführung** bookkeeping
der **Buchhalter, -** bookkeeper
die **Buchhandlung, -en** bookstore (2W)
das **Büchlein, -** booklet, little book
buchstabie′ren to spell
die **Bude, -n** booth, stand; **Schieß~** shooting gallery
das **Büfett′, -s** dining room cabinet; buffet
das **Bügeleisen, -** iron (for clothes)
die **Bühne, -n** stage; **auf der ~** on stage
bummeln (ist) to stroll (5E)

der **Bund, ⸚e** confederation; federal government

der **Bundesbürger, -** citizen of the Federal Republic

die **Bundesfeier, -n** Swiss national holiday

das **Bundesland, ⸚er** state, province

die **Bundespost** federal postal service

die **Bundesrepublik (BRD)** Federal Republic of Germany (FRG)

der **Bundesstaat, -en** federal state

bunt colorful; multicolored

die **Burg, -en** castle

der **Bürger, -** citizen (10E)

der **Bürgersteig, -e** sidewalk

das **Bürgertum** citizenry

das **Büro', -s** office (12W)

die **Bürokratie'** bureaucracy, red tape

die **Bürste, -n** brush

der **Bus, -se** bus (5W); **mit dem ~ fahren*** to take the bus (5W)

der **Busbahnhof, ⸚e** bus depot

der **Busch, ⸚e** bush

die **Butter** butter (2W)

C

das **Café', -s** café (3W)

campen gehen* to go camping

der **Campingplatz, ⸚e** campground

die **CD, -s** CD, compact disc (9W)

der **Cellist, -en, -en** cello player

das **Cello, -s** cello

das **Chaos** chaos

die **Charakterisie'rung, -en** characterization

charakteri'stisch characteristic

charmant' charming (11W)

der **Charme** charm

der **Chauffeur', -e** chauffeur

chauvini'stisch chauvinist

der **Chef, -s** boss

die **Chemie'** chemistry

chemisch chemical(ly)

der **Chor, ⸚e** choir (10W)

der **Christkindlmarkt, ⸚e** Christmas fair

der **Clown, -s** clown

der **Club, -s** club

die **Cola** Coke (2W)

das **College, -s** college

die **Combo, -s** (musical) band

der **Compu'ter, -** computer

computerisiert' computerized

die **Cornflakes** (*pl.*) Cornflakes, cereal

cremig creamy, smooth

D

da there (S2); **~ drüben** over there (5W)

dabei' along; there; yet; **~ haben*** to have with you

das **Dach, ⸚er** roof

der **Dachboden, ⸚** attic

der **Dachdecker, -** roofer

der **Dachshund, -e** dachshund

dafür for it; instead

dagegen against it; **Hast du etwas ~, wenn . . . ?** Do you mind, if . . . ?

daher' therefore; from there

dahin': bis ~ until then

die **Dahlie, -n** dahlia

damals then, in those days (14W)

die **Dame, -n** lady (5W); **~ spielen** to play checkers (9W)

der **Däne, -n, -n**/die **Dänin, -nen** the Dane

(das) **Dänemark** Denmark

dänisch Danish

der **Dank: Vielen ~!** Thank you very much. (5W)

dankbar grateful, thankful

danke thank you (S1); **~ schön!** Thank you very much; **~ gleichfalls!** Thanks, the same to you. (3W)

danken (+ *dat.*) to thank (3G); **Nichts zu ~!** You're welcome. My pleasure.

dann then (2W)

dar·stellen to portray

darum therefore (12E)

das that (S2)

daß (*conj.*) that (4G); **so ~** (*conj.*) so that (13E)

der **Dativ, -e** dative

das **Datum, Daten** (calendar) date (4W)

die **Dauer** length, duration

dauern to last (duration) (4W); **Wie lange dauert das?** How long does that take? (4W)

die **DDR (Deutsche Demokratische Republik)** German Democratic Republic (GDR)

dein (*sg. fam.*) your (1W)

die **Dekoration', -en** decoration

dekorie'ren to decorate

der **Demokrat', -en, -en** democrat

die **Demokratie'** democracy

demokra'tisch democratic

der **Demonstrant', -en, -en** demonstrator

die **Demonstration', -en** demonstration

demonstrie'ren to demonstrate

denken, dachte, gedacht to think (4W); **~ an** (+ *acc.*) to think of / about (10G)

der **Denker, -** thinker

das **Denkmal, ⸚er** monument (15W)

denn because, for (2G); *flavoring particle expressing curiosity, interest* (7G)

der **Deostift, -e** deodorant stick

die **Depression', -en** (mental) depression

deshalb therefore (12E)

deswegen therefore

deutsch: auf ~ in German (S2)

(das) **Deutsch: Sprechen Sie ~?** Do you speak German? (1W)

der **Deutsche (ein Deutscher)** the German (1W, 12G)

die **Deutsche (eine Deutsche)** the German (1W)

die **Deutsche Demokratische Republik (DDR)** German Democratic Republic (GDR)

(das) **Deutschland** Germany (1W)

deutschsprachig German-speaking

der **Dezem'ber** December (S5); **im ~** in December (S5)

d.h. (das heißt) that is (i.e.)

das **Dia, -s** slide (photograph)

der **Dialekt', -e** dialect

der **Dialog', -e** dialogue

dick thick, fat (S3); **~ machen** to be fattening

dienen to serve

der **Dienst, -e** service; **öffentliche ~** civil service

der **Dienstag** Tuesday (S5); **am ~** on Tuesday

dienstags on Tuesdays (2E)

dies- this, these (7G)

das **Diktat', -e** dictation

die **Dimension', -en** dimension

das **Ding, -e** thing (12E)

der **Dinosau'rier, -** dinosaur

das **Diplom', -e** diploma (e.g., in natural and social sciences, engineering), M.A.; **der ~ingenieur', -e** academically trained engineer

der **Diplomat', -en, -en** diplomat

direkt' direct(ly)

die **Direkto'rin, -nen** (school), principal, manager

der **Dirigent', -en, -en** (music) conductor

die **Diskothek', -en** discotheque

die **Diskussion', -en** discussion

diskutie'ren to discuss

sich **distanzie'ren** to keep apart

die **Disziplin'** discipline

die **DM (Deutsche Mark)** German mark

doch yes (I do), indeed, sure (2W); yet, however, but; on the contrary; *flavoring particle expressing concern, impatience, assurance* (7G)

der **Dokumentar'film, -e** documentary

der **Dollar, -** dollar (7W)

der **Dolmetscher, -** interpreter

der **Dom, -e** cathedral (5W)

dominie'ren to dominate

der **Donnerstag** Thursday (S5); **am ~** on Thursday

donnerstags on Thursdays (2E)

doppelt double

das **Doppelzimmer, -** double room (7W)

das **Dorf, ̈er** village (8E)

dort (over) there (4E)

draußen outside, outdoors; **hier ~** out here; **weit ~** far out

die **Dreißigerin, -nen** woman in her 30s

die **Droge, -n** drug

die **Drogerie', -n** drugstore (2E)

duften to smell good

dumm (ü) stupid, silly (10W,11W); **Das ist zu ~.** That's too bad.

die **Dummheit, -en** stupidity

der **Dummkopf, ̈e** dummy

dunkel dark (6W); **~haarig** dark-haired

dünn thin, skinny (S3)

durch (+ *acc.*) through (2G); **mitten ~** right through

durchbre'chen* to break through, penetrate

der **Durchbruch** breaching

durcheinander mixed up, confused

durch·fallen* to flunk (an exam) (13W)

der **Durchschnitt** average; **im ~** on the average

dürfen (darf), durfte, gedurft to be allowed to, may (5W); **Was darf's sein?** May I help you?

der **Durst** thirst (2E); **Ich habe ~.** I'm thirsty. (2E)

die **Dusche, -n** shower

der **Duschvorhang, ̈e** shower curtain

(sich) **duschen** to take a shower (9G)

das **Dutzend, -e** dozen

E

eben after all, just (*flavoring particle*)

die **Ebene, -n** plain

echt authentic; real(ly), genuine(ly) (15W)

die **Ecke, -n** corner (6W)

egal' the same; **Es ist mir ~.** It doesn't matter. It's all the same to me.; **~ wie / wo** no matter how / where

die **Ehe, -n** marriage (11W)

ehemalig former

das **Ehepaar, -e** married couple

eher rather

die **Ehre** honor

ehrgeizlos without ambition

ehrlich honest (11W)

die **Ehrlichkeit** honesty

das **Ei, -er** egg (2W); **ein gekochtes ~** boiled egg; **Rührei** scrambled eggs; **Spiegel~** fried egg

die **Eidgenossenschaft** Swiss Confederation

das **Eigelb** egg yolk

eigen- own (12W)

die **Eigenschaft, -en** characteristic (11W)

eigentlich actual(ly) (4E); **~ schon** actually, yes

die **Eigentumswohnung, -en** condo(minium)

eilig hurried; **es ~ haben*** to be in a hurry

ein a, an (16G,7G); **die einen** the ones; **einer** one

ein- into

einan'der each other

die **Einbahnstraße, -n** one-way street

der **Einbau** installation

der **Einblick, -e** insight

der **Eindruck, ̈e** impression

einfach simple, simply (7E)

die **Einfahrt, -en** driveway; **Keine ~!** Do not enter.

der **Einfluß, ̈sse** influence

ein·führen to introduce

die **Einführung, -en** introduction

der **Eingang, ̈e** entrance (7W)

einig- (*pl. only*) some, a few (10G); **so einiges** all sorts of things

ein'kaufen to shop; **~ gehen*** to go shopping (2E,7G)

die **Einkaufsliste, -n** shopping list

die **Einkaufstasche, -n** shopping bag

das **Einkommen,** income (12W)

ein·laden* (zu) to invite (to) (11W)

die **Einladung, -en** invitation

ein·lösen to cash (in) (7G); **einen Scheck ~** to cash a check (7W)

einmal once, (at) one time; one order of; (5E); **auch ~** for once; **nicht ~** not even; **noch ~** once more, again (S3); **es war ~** once upon a time

einmalig unique (14W)

der **Einmarsch, ̈e** marching in

ein·packen to pack (in a suitcase)

ein·richten to furnish

die **Einrichtung, -en** furnishings and appliances

einsam lonely

ein·schlafen* to fall asleep

sich **ein·schreiben*** to register

das **Einschreibungsformular', -e** application for university registration

sich **ein·setzen (für)** to support actively

ein·steigen* to get on *or* in (8W)

der **Eintritt** entrance fee

der **Einwohner, -** inhabitant

das **Einwohnermeldeamt, ̈er** resident registration office

einzeln individual(ly) (15E)

das **Einzelzimmer, -** single room (7W)

einzig- only

das **Eis** ice, ice cream (3W)
eisern (made of) iron
eisig icy
eiskalt ice-cold
eitel vain
der **Elefant′, -en, -en** elephant
elegant′ elegant
der **Elek′triker, -** electrician
elek′trisch electric
die **Elektrizität′** electricity
der **Elek′tromecha′niker, -** electrical mechanic
die **Elek′trotech′nik** electrical engineering
das **Element′, -e** element
der **Ellbogen, -** elbow
die **Eltern** *(pl.)* parents (1W); **Groß~** grandparents (1 W); **Stief~** step-parents; **Ur-groß~** great-grandparents
die **Emanzipation′** emancipation
emanzipiert′ emancipated
emotional′ emotional(ly)
empfangen* to receive
die **Empfangsdame, -n** receptionist
empfehlen (empfiehlt), empfahl, empfohlen to recommend (3W)
die **Empfehlung, -en** recommendation
das **Ende** end (10W); **am ~** in the end (10W); **zu ~ sein*** to be finished
enden to end
endlich finally
die **Energie′** energy
eng narrow
sich **engagie′ren** to get involved
der **Engel, -** angel
(das) **England** England (1W)
der **Engländer, -** the Englishman (1W)
englisch: auf ~ in English (S2)
(das) **Englisch: Sprechen Sie ~?** Do you speak English? (1W)
enorm′ enormous
die **Ente, -n** duck; **Lahme ~!** Poor baby!
entfernt away
enthalten* to contain
der **Enthusias′mus** enthusiasm
entlang along; **die Straße ~** along the street
sich **entscheiden, entschied, entschieden** to decide (13W)

die **Entscheidung, -en** decision (12E); **eine ~ treffen*** to make a decision
entschuldigen to excuse; **~ Sie bitte!** Excuse me, please. (5W)
die **Entschuldigung, -en** excuse; **~!** Excuse me! Pardon me! (5W)
entsprechen* to correspond to
entstehen* (ist) to develop, be built
(sich) **entwickeln** to develop (15E)
die **Entwicklung, -en** development
(sich) **entzwei·reißen*** to tear (oneself) apart
die **Erbse, -n** pea (2W)
die **Erdbeere, -n** strawberry (2W)
die **Erde** earth (12E); **unter der ~** underground
die **Erfahrung, -en** experience (12E)
der **Erfolg, -e** success
sich **erfüllen** to be fulfilled, come true
ergänzen to supply, complete
ergreifen, ergriff, ergriffen to grab
erhalten* to keep up, preserve, maintain
die **Erholung** recuperation, relaxation
erinnern (an + *acc.*) to remind (of) (14W)
sich **erinnern (an + *acc.*)** to remember (14W)
die **Erinnerung, -en (an + *acc.*)** reminder, memory of
sich **erkälten** to catch a cold (9G)
die **Erkältung, -en** cold
erkennen* to recognize (14E); **Zum ~** for recognition (only)
erklären to explain (15W)
die **Erklärung, -en** explanation
erlauben to permit, allow (15W)
die **Erlaubnis** permit, permission
erleben to experience (14E)
das **Erlebnis, -se** experience
die **Ermäßigung, -en** discount
die **Ernährung** nutrition
ernst serious(ly)
die **Ernte, -n** harvest
das **Erntedankfest** (Harvest) Thanksgiving
eröffnen to open up, establish

erreichen to reach
erscheinen* (ist) to appear
erschrecken (erschrickt), erschrak, ist erschrocken to be frightened
ersetzen to replace
erst- first
erst only, not until
erwärmen to heat (up)
erwarten to expect (12E)
erzählen (von + *dat.*) to tell (about) (8E,10G)
erziehen* to educate
die **Erziehung** education
der **Esel, -** donkey; **Du ~!** You dummy!
der **Esprit′** esprit
eßbar edible
essen (ißt), aß, gegessen to eat (S6)
das **Essen, -** food, meal (2W); **beim ~** while eating
das **Eßzimmer, -** dining room (5W)
etwa about, approximately (15W)
etwas some, a little (2W); something (3W); **so ~ wie** s.th. like; **noch ~** one more thing, s.th. else; **Sonst noch ~?** Anything else?
euer *(pl. fam.)* your (7G)
(das) **Euro′pa** Europe
der **Europä′er, -** the European
europä′isch European
der **Evangelist′, -en, -en** evangelist
ewig eternal(ly); **für ~** forever
exakt exact(ly)
das **Exa′men, -** exam
existie′ren to exist
experimentell′ experimental
extra extra
das **Extrablatt, ̈er** special publication

F

das **Fach, ̈er** subject (13W); **Haupt~** major (field) (13W); **Neben~** minor (field) (13W); **Schwerpunkt~** major (field)
der **Fachbereich, -e** field (of study)
die **Fachkenntnis, -se** special skill
die **Fach(ober)schule, -n** business or technical school

die **Fachrichtung, -en** specialization

das **Fachwerkhaus, ¨er** half-timbered house

der **Faden, ¨** thread

die **Fähigkeit, -en** ability

die **Fähre, -n** ferry

fahren (fährt), fuhr, ist gefahren to drive, go (by car, etc.) (3G)

die **Fahrerei'** (incessant) driving

die **Fahrkarte, -n** ticket (8W)

der **Fahrplan, ¨e** schedule (of trains, etc.) (8W)

das **(Fahr)rad, ¨er** bicycle (6E); **mit dem ~ fahren*** to bicycle

der **(Fahr)radweg, -e** bike path

die **Fahrt, -en** trip, drive (8W)

fair fair

der **Fall, ¨e** case; **auf jeden ~** in any case

fallen (fällt), fiel, ist gefallen to fall (4E); **~ lassen*** to drop

falsch wrong, false (S2)

die **Fami'lie, -en** family (1W)

fangen (fängt), fing, gefangen to catch

die **Farbe, -n** color (S2); **Welche ~ hat . . . ?** What color is . . . ? (S2)

der **Farbstoff, -e** dye, (artificial) color

der **Fasching** carnival; **zum ~** for carnival (Mardi Gras)

die **Fassa'de, -n** façade

fast almost (7E)

die **Fastenzeit** Lent

die **Faszination'** fascination

faszinie'ren to fascinate

faul lazy

die **Faulheit** laziness

der **Februar** February (S5); **im ~** in February (S5)

fechten (ficht), focht, gefochten to fence

der **Federball, ¨e** badminton (ball)

fehlen to be missing, lacking

fehlend missing

der **Fehler, -** mistake

feierlich festive

feiern to celebrate (4W)

der **Feiertag, -e** holiday (4W)

die **Feind, -e** enemy

feindlich hostile

das **Feld, -er** field

das **Fenster, -** window (S2)

die **Ferien** *(pl.)* vacation (4W)

der **Ferienplatz, ¨e** vacation spot

fern far, distant

die **Ferne** distance

der **Fernfahrer, -** truck driver

das **Ferngespräch, -e** long-distance call

fern·sehen* to watch TV (9W)

das **Fernsehen** TV (the medium) (10W); **im ~** on TV (10W)

der **Fernseher, -** TV set (6W)

fertig finished, done (S6)

fertig·machen to finish

das **Fest, -e** celebration (4W); **~spiel, -e** festival

festgesetzt fixed

festlich festive

das **Feuer, -** fire

das **Feuerwerk, -e** firework(s)

die **Figur', -en** figure

der **Film, -e** film (10W)

die **Finan'zen** *(pl.)* finances

finanziell' financial(ly)

finanzie'ren to finance (15W)

die **Finanzie'rung** financing

finden, fand, gefunden to find (S5); **Ich finde es . . .** I think it's . . . (S5); **Das finde ich auch.** I think so, too. (S5)

der **Finger, -** finger (9W)

der **Finne, -n, -n**/die **Finnin, -nen** the Finn

finnisch Finnish

die **Firma, Firmen** company, business (12W)

der **Fisch, -e** fish (2W); **ein kalter ~** a cold-hearted person

fit: sich ~ halten* to keep in shape (9E)

der **Flachs** flax

die **Flasche, -n** bottle (3E); **eine ~ Wein** a bottle of wine (3E)

das **Fleisch** *(sg.)* meat (2W)

der **Fleischer, -** butcher

die **Fleischerei', -en** butcher shop

fleißig industrious(ly), hardworking (13W)

flexi'bel flexible

die **Flexibilität'** flexibility

fliegen, flog, ist geflogen to fly (8W); **mit dem Flugzeug ~** to go by plane (8W)

fliehen, floh, ist geflohen to flee, escape

fließen, floß, ist geflossen to flow

fließend fluent(ly)

das **Floß, -e** raft

die **Flöte, -n** flute, recorder

die **Flotte** fleet

die **Flucht** escape

der **Flüchtling, -e** refugee

der **Flug, ¨e** flight (8W)

der **Flügel, -** wing

der **Flughafen, ¨** airport (8W)

die **Flugkarte, -n** plane ticket

der **Flugsteig, -e** gate

das **Flugzeug, -e** airplane (8W)

der **Flur** hallway, entrance foyer (6W)

der **Fluß, ¨sse** river (1W)

folgen (ist) (+ *dat.*) to follow

folgend following

der **Fön, -e** hair dryer

das **Fondue', -s** fondue

fördern to encourage

die **Forel'le, -n** trout

die **Form, -en** form, shape

das **Formular', -e** form

formulie'ren to formulate

der **Forschungszweig, -e** field of research

der **Förster, -** forest ranger

die **Forstwirtschaft** forestry

die **Frage, -n** question (1W); **eine ~ stellen** to ask a question (15E); **Ich habe eine ~.** I have a question. (S6)

fragen to ask (S2); **sich ~** to wonder (9G)

fraglich questionable

(der) **Frankfurter Kranz** rich cake ring with whipped cream and nuts

(das) **Frankreich** France (1W)

der **Franzo'se, -n, -n** / die **Franzö'sin, -nen** French person (1W, 2G)

franzö'sisch French (1W)

(das) **Franzö'sisch; Ich spreche ~.** I speak French. (1W)

die **Frau, -en** Mrs., Ms. (S1); woman; wife (1W)

die **Frauenbewegung** women's movement

das **Fräulein, -** Miss, Ms.; young lady (S1)

frech impudent, sassy, fresh

die **Frechheit** impertinence

frei free, available (7W)

freigiebig generous

die **Freiheit** freedom

das **Freilichtspiel, -e** outdoor performance

frei·nehmen* to take time off

der **Freitag** Friday (S5); **am ~** on Friday (S5); **Kar~** Good Friday

freitags on Fridays (2E)

freiwillig voluntary

die **Freizeit** leisure time (9W)

fremd foreign

die **Fremd′sprache, -n** foreign language

die **Fremd′sprachenkorrespon-den′tin, -nen** bilingual secretary

fressen (frißt), fraß, gefressen to eat (like a glutton or an animal); **auf·~** to devour

die **Freude, -n** joy

sich **freuen auf** (+ acc.) to look forward to (10G); **Freut mich.** I'm glad to meet you. (S1); **(Es) freut mich auch.** Likewise, Glad to meet you, too; **Das freut mich für dich.** I'm happy for you.

der **Freund, -e** (boy)friend (3E)

die **Freundin, -nen** (girl)friend (3E)

freundlich friendly (11W)

die **Freundlichkeit** friendliness

die **Freundschaft, -en** friendship

der **Frieden** peace (14W)

friedlich peaceful(ly)

frieren, fror, gefroren to freeze

frisch fresh (2W)

der **Friseur′, -e** barber, hairdresser

die **Friseu′se, -n** beautician, hairdresser

froh glad, happy (11E)

fröhlich cheerful, merry

der **Fronleich′nam(stag)** Corpus Christi (holiday)

der **Frosch, ¨e** frog

früh early, morning (8G)

früher earlier, once, former(ly) (12E)

der **Frühling, -e** spring (S5)

das **Frühstück** breakfast (3W); **(Was gibt's) zum ~?** (What's) for breakfast? (3W)

frustriert′ frustrated

die **Frustrie′rung** frustration

der **Fuchs, ¨e** fox; **ein alter ~** a sly person

sich **fühlen** to feel (a certain way) (9W)

führen to lead

die **Führung, -en** guided tour

füllen to fill

die **Funktion′, -en** function

für (+ acc.) for (S2,2G); **was ~ ein . . . ?** what kind of a . . . ? (2W)

die **Furcht** fear, awe

furchtbar terrible, awful (S5)

sich **fürchten (vor)** to be afraid (of)

der **Fürst, -en, -en** sovereign, prince

der **Fuß, ¨e** foot (9W); **zu ~ gehen*** to walk (5W)

der **Fußball, ¨e** soccer (ball) (9W)

der **Fußgänger, -** pedestrian; **~überweg, -e** pedestrian crossing; **~weg, -e** pedestrian walkway; **~zone, -n** pedestrian area

G

die **Gabel, -n** fork (3W)

die **Galerie′, -n** gallery

die **Gans, ¨-e** goose; **eine dumme ~** a silly person *(fem.)*

ganz whole, entire(ly) (9E); very; **im großen und ~en** on the whole; **~ meinerseits.** The pleasure is all mine; **~ schön** quite (nice)

die **Gara′ge, -n** garage (6W)

garantie′ren to guarantee (15W)

gar nicht not at all (13E)

der **Garten, ¨** garden (6W)

das **Gartenstück, -e** garden plot

die **Gasse, -n** narrow street

der **Gast, ¨e** guest (7W)

der **Gastarbeiter, -** foreign (guest) worker

das **Gästezimmer, -** guest room

das **Gasthaus, ¨er** restaurant, inn

der **Gasthof, ¨e** small hotel (7E)

die **Gaststätte, -n** restaurant, inn

das **Gebäck** pastry

das **Gebäude, -** building (14W)

geben (gibt), gab, gegeben to give (3G); **es gibt** there is, there are (2W); **Was gibt's?** What's up?; **Was gibt's Neues?** What's new? (9W); **Was gibt's im . . . ?** What's (playing) on . . . ? (10W); **Das gibt's doch nicht!** That's not possible!

das **Gebiet, -e** area, region

gebildet well educated (11W)

geboren: Ich bin . . . ~ I was born . . . (S5); **Wann sind Sie ~?** When were you born? (S5); **Wann wurde . . . geboren?** When was . . . born?

gebrauchen to use, utilize (15W)

der **Gebrauchtwagen, -** used car

die **Gebühr, -en** fee

der **Geburtstag, -e** birthday (4W); **Wann haben Sie ~?** When is your birthday? (4W); **Ich habe am . . .(s)ten ~.** My birthday is on the . . . *(date)* (4W); **Ich habe im . . . ~.** My birthday is in . . . *(month)*. (4W); **Herzlichen Glückwunsch zum ~!** Happy birthday!; **zum ~** at the / for the birthday (4W)

der **Gedanke, -ns, -n** thought (14E)

das **Gedeck, -e** complete dinner

geduldig patient (11W)

die **Gefahr, -en** danger (12E)

gefährlich dangerous (15E)

das **Gefälle, -** decline

gefallen (gefällt), gefiel, gefallen (+ dat.) to like, be pleasing to (3G); **Es gefällt mir.** I like it. (3G)

das **Gefängnis, -se** prison

gefettet greased

der **Gefrierschrank, ¨e** freezer

das **Gefühl, -e** feeling

gegen (+ acc.) against (2G); toward (time), around

die **Gegend, -en** area, region (8E)

der **Gegensatz, ¨e** contrast, opposite

gegensätzlich opposing

das **Gegenteil, -e** opposite (S3); **im ~** on the contrary

gegenüber (**von** + dat.) across (from) (5W)

die **Gegenwart** present (tense)

das **Gehalt, ¨er** salary

gehen, ging, ist gegangen to go, walk (S3); **Es geht mir . . .** I am (feeling) . . . (S1); **Das geht nicht.** That's impossible. That doesn't work. You can't.; **Es geht.** That's all right.; **So geht's.** That's the way it goes.; **Wie**

geht's? Wie geht es Ihnen?
How are you? (S1); **zu Fuß**
~ to walk (5W)

gehören (+ *dat.*) to belong to
(3G)

die **Geige, -n** violin

der **Geisteswissenschaftler, -** humanities scholar

geistig mentally, intellectual(ly)

geizig stingy

das **Geländer, -** railing

gelb yellow (S2)

das **Geld** money (7W); ~ **aus·geben*** to spend money
(8E); **Bar~** cash (7W);
Klein~ change (7W);
Erziehungs~ government
stipend for child care

die **Gelegenheit, -en** opportunity,
chance

gelten (gilt), galt, gegolten to
apply to, be valid for, be true

gemeinsam together, shared,
joint(ly); (in) common (15E)

die **Gemeinschaft, -en** community

gemischt mixed

die **Gemse, -n** mountain goat

das **Gemüse, -** vegetable(s) (2W)

gemütlich cozy, pleasant, comfortable, convivial (5E)

die **Gemütlichkeit** nice atmosphere, coziness

genau exact(ly); ~**so** the same;
~ **wie** just like (9E)

die **Generation', -en** generation

generös' generous

genießen, genoß, genossen to
enjoy

der **Genitiv, -e** genitive

genug enough (5E); **Jetzt habe
ich aber ~.** That's enough.
I've had it.

geöffnet open (7W)

die **Geographie'** geography

die **Geologie'** geology

das **Gepäck** baggage, luggage (7W)

gerade just, right now (4W); ~
als just when; **(immer) geradeaus'** (keep) straight
ahead (5W)

germa'nisch Germanic

die **Germani'stik** study of German
language and literature

gern (lieber, liebst-) gladly
(2W); **furchtbar ~** very

much; ~ **geschehen!** Glad to
. . . ; **Ich hätte ~** . . . I'd like
to have . . . (2W)

die **Gesamtschule, -n** comprehensive high school

das **Geschäft, -e** store (2W); business (12W)

geschäftlich concerning business

die **Geschäftsfrau, -en** businesswoman (12W)

der **Geschäftsmann, -leute** businessman (12W)

**geschehen (geschieht),
geschah, ist geschehen** to
happen (11E); **Das
geschieht dir recht.** That
serves you right.

das **Geschenk, -e** present (4W)

die **Geschichte, -n** story (10W);
history (10E)

geschickt talented, skilful

geschieden divorced (11W)

das **Geschlecht, -er** gender, sex

geschlossen closed (7W)

die **Geschwindigkeit, -en** speed

die **Geschwister** *(pl.)* brothers
and/or sisters, siblings

gesellig sociable

die **Gesellschaft, -en** society

das **Gesetz, -e** law

gesetzlich legal(ly)

gesichert secure

das **Gesicht, -er** face (9W)

das **Gespräch, -e** conversation, dialogue

gestern yesterday (4W,8G)

gestreift striped

gesucht wird wanted

gesund (ü) healthy (9W)

die **Gesundheit** health

das **Gesundheitsamt** health department

geteilt divided; shared

das **Getränk, -e** beverage

getrennt separated, separately

die **Gewalt** violence

die **Gewerkschaft, -en** trade union

gewinnen, gewann, gewonnen
to win (12E)

das **Gewitter, -** thunderstorm

sich **gewöhnen an** (+ *dat.*) to get
used to (12W)

gewöhnlich usual(ly) (3E)

gierig greedy

gießen, goß, gegossen to pour

das **Gift, -e** poison

die **Giraf'fe, -n** giraffe

die **Gitar're, -n** guitar (9W)

die **Gladio'le, -n** gladiola

das **Glas, ¨er** glass (2E); **ein ~** a
glass of (2E)

glauben to believe, think (2W);
**Ich glaube es. Ich glaube
ihm.** I believe it. I believe
him.; ~ **an** (+ *acc.*) to believe (in) (12W)

gleich equal, same (12W); right
away; **Bis ~!** See you in a
few minutes! (9W)

gleichberechtigt with equal
rights

die **Gleichberechtigung** equality,
equal rights

gleichfalls: Danke ~! Thank
you, the same to you. (3W)

das **Gleis, -e** track (8W)

der **Gletscher, -** glacier

die **Glocke, -n** bell

glorreich glorious

das **Glück** luck; ~ **haben*** to be
lucky (4E) **Viel ~!** Good
luck!; **Du ~spilz!** You lucky
thing!

glücklich happy (11W)

der **Glückwunsch, ¨e** congratulation; **Herzliche Glückwünsche!** Congratulations! Best
wishes! (4W)

der **Glühwein** mulled wine

der **Gnom, -e** gnome, goblin

das **Gold** gold (11E)

golden golden

der **Goldfisch, -e** gold fish

(das) **Golf** golf; **Mini~** miniature
golf

der **Gott** God; ~ **sei Dank!** Thank
God!; **Um ~es willen!** For
Heaven's sake! My goodness!

der **Grad, -e** degree

die **Gramma'tik** grammar

gramma'tisch grammatical(ly)

gratulie'ren (+ *dat.*) to congratulate (4W); **Wir ~!** Congratulations.

grau gray (S2)

die **Grenze, -n** border (14W)

grenzenlos unlimited

der **Grieche, -n, -n** / die **Griechin,
-nen** the Greek

(das) **Griechenland** Greece

griechisch Greek

die **Grippe** flu

groß (größer, größt-) large, big, tall (S3)

die **Größe, -n** size, height

die **Großeltern** *(pl.)* grandparents (1W); **Ur~** great-grand-parents

die **Großmutter, ⸚** grandmother (1W); **Ur~** great-grand-mother

der **Großvater, ⸚** grandfather (1W); **Ur~** great-grandfather

Gruezi! Hi! *(in Switzerland)*

grün green (S2); **ins Grüne / im Grünen** out in(to) nature

der **Grund, ⸚e** reason; **aus dem ~** for that reason

gründen to found

das **Grundgesetz** Constitution, Basic Law

die **Grundschule, -n** elementary school, grades 1–4

die **Gründung, -en** founding

die **Grünfläche, -n** green area

die **Gruppe, -n** group

der **Gruß, ⸚e** greeting; **Viele Grüße (an + acc.) . . .!** Greetings (to . . .)!

grüßen to greet; **Grüß dich!** Hi!; **Grüß Gott!** Hello! Hi! *(in southern Germany)*

der **Gummi** rubber

gurgeln to gargle

die **Gurke, -n** cucumber (2W); **saure ~** pickle

gut (besser, best-) good, fine (S1); **~aussehend** good-looking (11W); **Das ist noch mal ~ gegangen.** Things worked out all right (again); **na ~** well, all right; **Mach's ~!** Take care. (4W)

das **Gute: Alles ~!** All the best.

die **Güte** goodness; **Ach du meine ~!** My goodness! (8W)

das **Gymna′sium, Gymna′sien** academic high school (grades 5–13)

H

das **Haar, -e** hair (9W)

haben (hat), hatte, gehabt to have (S6,2G); **Ich hätte gern . . .** I'd like (to have) . . . (2W)

der **Hafen, ⸚** port

der **Haken, -** hook

halb half (to the next hour) (S6); **~tags** part-time; **in einer ~en Stunde** in half an hour (8W)

die **Hälfte, -n** half

die **Halle, -n** large room for work, recreation, or assembly

Hallo! Hello! Hi!

der **Hals, ⸚e** neck, throat (9W); **Das hängt mir zum ~ heraus.** I'm fed up (with it).

halten (hält), hielt, gehalten to hold, stop (a vehicle) (5W); **~ von** to think of, be of an opinion (10G)

die **Haltestelle, -n** (bus, etc.) stop (5W)

das **Halteverbot, -e** no stopping *or* parking

der **Hamster, -** hamster

die **Hand, ⸚e** hand (3E,9W)

die **Handarbeit, -en** needlework

der **Handball, ⸚e** handball

der **Handel** trade

der **Handschuh, -e** glove

das **Handtuch, ⸚er** towel

der **Handwerker, -** craftsman

hängen to hang (up) (6W)

hängen, hing, gehangen to hang (be hanging) (6W)

harmo′nisch harmonious

hart (ä) hard; tough

hassen to hate

häßlich ugly (11W)

die **Häßlichkeit** ugliness

das **Hauptfach, ⸚er** major (field of study) (13W)

die **Hauptrolle, -n** leading role

hauptsächlich mainly

die **Hauptsaison** (high) season

die **Hauptschule, -n** basic high school, grades 5–9

die **Hauptstadt, ⸚e** capital (1W)

die **Hauptstraße, -n** main street

das **Hauptwort, ⸚er** noun

das **Haus, ⸚er** house (6W); **nach ~e** (toward) home (3W); **zu ~e** at home (3W); **das Zuhause** home

das **Häuschen, -** little house

die **Hausfrau, -en** housewife (12W)

der **Haushalt, -e** household (12W)

die **Haushälterin, -nen** house-keeper

häuslich home-loving, domestic

die **Hauswirtschaft** home economics

das **Heft, -e** notebook (S2)

heilig holy; **Aller~en** All Saints' Day; **~e Drei Könige** Epiphany

der **Heiligabend** Christmas Eve; **am ~** on Christmas Eve

der **Heimcomputer, -** home computer

die **Heimat** homeland, home (14E)

heiraten to marry, get married (11W)

heiratslustig eager to marry

heiß hot (S5)

heißen, hieß, geheißen to be called; **Ich heiße . . .** My name is . . . (S1); **Wie ~ Sie?** What's your name? (S1)

die **Heizung** heating (system)

das **Heiz′material′** heating material, fuel

helfen (hilft), half, geholfen (+ *dat.*) to help (3G)

hell light, bright (6W)

das **Hemd, -en** shirt (S3)

die **Henne, -n** hen

heran′- up to

der **Herbst, -e** fall, autumn (S5)

der **Herd, -e** (kitchen) range

herein′- in(to)

herein′·kommen* to come in, enter (11E)

herein′·lassen* to let in

die **Herkunft** origin

der **Herr, -n, -en** Mr., gentleman (S1,2G); Lord

herrlich wonderful, great (14E)

herum′- around

herum′·laufen* to run around

herum′·reisen (ist) to travel around

das **Herz, -ens, -en** heart; **mit ~** with feelings

der **Heurige, -n** *(sg.)* new wine

die **Heurigenschänke, -n** Viennese wine-tasting inn

heute today (S4); **für ~** for today (S2); **~ morgen** this morning (8G)

heutig- of today

hier here (S2)

die **Hilfe, -n** help (15E)

der **Himmel** sky; heaven; **~fahrt(stag)** Ascension (Day)

hin und her back and forth

hinauf'·fahren* to go or drive up (to)

hinein'·gehen* to go in(to), enter

hin·legen to lay or put down; **sich ~** to lie down (9G)

sich **(hin·)setzen** to sit down (9G)

hinter (+ *acc./dat.*) behind (6G)

hinterlassen* to leave behind

die **(Hin- und) Rückfahrkarte, -n** round trip ticket (8W)

hinun'ter down

histo'risch historical(ly) (14W)

das **Hobby, -s** hobby (9W)

hoch (hoh-) (höher, höchst-) high(ly) (12W)

das **Hochhaus, ¨er** high-rise building

hoch·legen to put up (high)

die **Hochschule, -n** university, college

die **Hochzeit, -en** wedding (11W)

(das) **Hockey** hockey

der **Hof, ¨e** court, courtyard

hoffen to hope (12E)

die **Hoffnung, -en** hope

höflich polite(ly)

die **Höhe, -n** height, altitude; **Das ist doch die ~!** That's the limit!

der **Höhepunkt, -e** climax

hohl hollow

die **Höhle, -n** cave

holen (go and) get, pick up, fetch (13W)

der **Holländer, -** the Dutchman

holländisch Dutch

die **Hölle** hell

das **Holz** wood

hörbar audible

hören to hear (S2)

der **Hörer, -** listener; receiver

der **Hörsaal, -säle** lecture hall (13W)

das **Hörspiel, -e** radio play

die **Hose, -n** slacks, pants (S3)

das **Hotel', -s** hotel (5W,7W)

hübsch pretty (11W)

der **Hügel, -** hill

das **Hühnchen, -** chicken

der **Humor'** (sense of) humor

der **Hund, -e** dog; **Fauler ~!** Lazy bum!

Hunderte von hundreds of

der **Hunger** hunger (2E); **Ich habe ~.** I'm hungry. (2E)

hungrig hungry

hüpfen (ist) to hop

der **Hut, ¨e** hat

die **Hütte, -n** hut, cottage

I

ideal' ideal

das **Ideal', -e** ideal

der **Idealis'mus** idealism

die **Idee', -n** idea (9W)

sich **identifizie'ren** to identify oneself

idyl'lisch idyllic

ignorie'ren to ignore

ihr her, its, their (7G)

Ihr (*formal*) your (1W,7G)

die **Imbißbude, -n** snack bar, fast-food stand

die **Immatrikulation'** enrollment (at university)

immer always (4E); **~ geradeaus** always straight ahead (5W); **~ länger** longer and longer (12G); **~ noch** still; **~ wieder** again and again (12G)

der **Imperativ, -e** imperative

das **Imperfekt** imperfect, simple past

in (+ *acc./dat.*) in, into, inside of (6G)

inbegriffen in (+ *dat.*) included in

der **India'ner, -** the Native American

der **In'dikativ** indicative

in'direkt indirect(ly)

die **Individualität'** individuality

individuell' individual(ly)

die **Industrie', -n** industry

der **Industrie'kaufmann, -leute** industrial manager

industriell' industrial

der **Infinitiv, -e** infinitive

die **Informa'tik** computer science

die **Information', -en** information

informativ' informative

(sich) **informie'ren** to inform, get informed

der **Ingenieur', -e** engineer (12W)

die **Initiati've, -n** initiative

innen (*adv.*) inside

der **Innenhof, ¨e** inner court

die **Innenstadt, ¨e** center (of town), downtown

inner- inner

innerhalb within

die **Insel, -n** island (14E)

das **Institut', -e** institute

das **Instrument', -e** instrument

die **Inszenie'rung, -en** production

intellektuell' intellectual(ly)

intelligent' intelligent (11W)

die **Intelligenz'** intelligence

intensiv' intensive

interessant' interesting (5E); **etwas Interessantes** s.th. interesting

das **Interes'se, -n (an** + *dat.*) interest (in)

sich **interessie'ren für** to be interested in (10G)

international' international

interpretie'ren to interpret

das **Interview, -s** interview

interviewen to interview

in'tolerant intolerant

das **Inventar', -e** inventory

inzwi'schen in the meantime

irgendwo somewhere

(das) **Ita'lien** Italy (1W)

der **Italie'ner, -** the Italian (1W)

italie'nisch Italian (1W)

J

ja yes (S1); *flavoring particle expressing emphasis* (7G)

die **Jacke, -n** jacket, cardigan (S3)

der **Jäger, -** hunter

das **Jahr, -e** year (S5)

jahrelang for years

die **Jahreszeit, -en** season

das **Jahrhun'dert, -e** century

-jährig years old; years long

jammern to complain, grieve

der **Januar** January (S5); **im ~** in January (S5)

je (+ *comp.*) . . . **desto** (+ *comp.*) . . . the . . . the . . . (12G); **~ nachdem** depending on

die **Jeans, -** jeans (S3)

jed- (*sg.*) each, every (7G)

jedenfalls in any case (13E)

jeder everyone, everybody

jederzeit any time

der **Jeep, -s** jeep

jemand someone, somebody (11W)

jetzt now (S6)

der **Job, -s** job

jobben to have a job that is not one's career

joggen gehen* to go jogging

das **Joghurt** yogurt

(das) **Judo: ~ kämpfen** to do judo

der **Journalist', -en, -en** journalist (12W)

das **Jubilä'um, Jubiläen** anniversary

das **Judentum** Jewry

die **Jugend** youth (14E)

die **Jugendherberge, -n** youth hostel (7E)

der **Juli** July (S5); **im ~** in July (S5)

jung (ü) young (11W)

der **Junge, -n, -n** boy (1W,2G)

der **Junggeselle, -n, -n** bachelor

der **Juni** June (S5); **im ~** in June (S5)

Jura: Er studiert ~. He's studying law.

K

das **Kabarett', -e** (*or* **-s**) cabaret

das **Kabelfernsehen** cable TV

der **Kaffee** coffee (2W); **~ mit Schlag** coffee with whipped cream

der **Kaffeeklatsch** chatting over a cup of coffee (and cake)

der **Kaiser, -** emperor

der **Kaka'o** hot chocolate

das **Kalb, ̈er** calf: **Kalbsleber** calves' liver

der **Kalen'der, -** calendar

kalt (ä) cold (S5); **~ oder warm?** with or without heat?

die **Kälte** cold(ness)

die **Kamera, -s** camera

der **Kamin', -e** fireplace

der **Kamm, ̈e** comb

(sich) **kämmen** to comb (o.s.) (9G)

die **Kammer, -n** chamber

der **Kampf, ̈e (um)** fight, struggle (for)

kämpfen to fight, struggle

(das) **Kanada** Canada (1W)

der **Kana'dier, -** the Canadian (1W)

kana'disch Canadian (1W)

der **Kanal', ̈e** channel

die **Kanti'ne, -n** cafeteria (at a workplace)

das **Kanu', -s** canoe

der **Kanzler, -** chancellor

kapitali'stisch capitalist

das **Kapi'tel, -** chapter

kaputt' broken

kaputt'·gehen* to get broken, break

kariert' checkered

der **Karneval** carnival

die **Karot'te, -n** carrot (2W)

die **Karrie're, -n** career

die **Karte, -n** ticket (8W); card (9W); **~n spielen** to play cards (9W)

die **Kartof'fel, -n** potato (3W); **der ~brei** (*sg.*) mashed potatoes; **das ~mehl** potato flour, starch; **der ~salat** potato salad

der **Käse** cheese (2W); **Das ist (doch) ~!** That's nonsense.

die **Kasse, -n** cash register, cashier's window (7W)

das **Kasseler Rippchen, -** smoked loin of pork

die **Kasset'te, -n** cassette (9W)

die **Kassie'rerin, -nen** cashier; clerk, teller

die **Katze, -n** cat; **(Das ist) alles für die Katz'!** (That's) all for nothing!

kaufen to buy (2W)

das **Kaufhaus, ̈er** department store (2W)

der **Kaufmann, -leute** merchant

kaum hardly (14E)

kein no, not a, not any (1G)

der **Keller, -** basement

der **Kellner, -** waiter (3W)

die **Kellnerin, -nen** waitress (3W)

kennen, kannte, gekannt to know, be acquainted with (6G)

kennen·lernen to get to know, meet (7E)

der **Kenner, -** connoisseur

die **Kenntnis, -se** knowledge, skill

der **Kerl, -e** guy

der **Kern, -e** core

die **Kerze, -n** candle (4E)

die **Kette, -n** chain, necklace

die **Ket'tenreaktion', -en** chain reaction

das **Kilo, -s (kg)** kilogram

der **Kilome'ter, - (km)** kilometer

das **Kind, -er** child (1W)

der **Kindergarten, ̈** kindergarten

der **Kindergärtner, -** kindergarten teacher

kinderlieb loves children

das **Kinn, -e** chin

das **Kino, -s** movie theater (5W)

die **Kirche, -n** church (5W)

die **Kirsche, -n** cherry

klagen to complain

klappen to work out

klar clear; **(na) ~!** Sure! Of course! (13W)

die **Klasse, -n** class

die **Klas'senkamera'din, -nen** classmate

das **Klassentreffen, -** class reunion

das **Klassenzimmer, -** classroom

klassisch classical

klatschen to clap (10W)

das **Klavier', -e** piano (9W)

das **Kleid, -er** dress (S3)

der **Kleiderbügel, -** clothes hanger

der **Kleiderschrank, ̈e** closet

die **Kleidung** clothing (S3)

der **Klei'dungsarti'kel, -** article of clothing

klein small, little, short (S3)

das **Kleingeld** change (7W)

der **Klient', -en, -en** [Kli:ent'] client

das **Klima, -s** climate

die **Klimaanlage, -n** air conditioning

klingeln to ring a bell

klingen, klang, geklungen to sound; **(Das) klingt gut.** (That) sounds good. (6W)

das **Klo, -s** toilet

klopfen to knock

der **Kloß, ̈e** dumpling

das **Kloster, ̈** monastery; convent

klug (ü) smart, clever

die **Knappheit** shortage

die **Kneipe, -n** pub

das **Knie, -** knee (9W)

der **Knirps, -e** little fellow, dwarf

der **Knoblauch** garlic

der **Knöd(e)l, -** dumpling (*in southern Germany*)

der **Knopf, ̈e** button

der **Knoten, -** knot

knuspern to nibble

der **Koch, ̈e / die Köchin, -nen** cook

kochen to cook (6W)

der **Koffer, -** suitcase (7W)

der **Kolle′ge, -n, -n** / die **Kolle′gin, -nen** colleague; **Zimmer~** roommate (13W)

die **Kolonialisie′rung** colonization

kombinie′ren to combine

der **Komfort′** comfort

ko′misch funny (strange, comical) (10W)

kommen, kam, ist gekommen to come (1W); **Komm rüber!** Come on over!

der **Kommentar′, -e** commentary

kommerziell′ commercial

die **Kommo′de, -n** dresser (6W)

kommunis′tisch communist

der **Kom′parativ, -e** comparative

kompliziert′ complicated

komponie′ren to compose

der **Komponist′, -en, -en** composer (10W)

die **Konditorei′, -en** pastry shop

der **Konflikt′, -e** conflict

der **Kongreß′, -sse** conference

der **König, -e** king (11E); **Heilige Drei ~e** Epiphany (Jan. 6)

die **Königin, -nen** queen (11E)

das **Königreich, -e** kingdom

die **Konjunktion′, -en** conjunction

der **Kon′junktiv** subjunctive

können (kann), konnte, gekonnt to be able to, can (5G)

die **Konsequenz′, -en** consequence

das **Konservie′rungsmittel, -** preservative

das **Konsulat′, -e** consulate

die **Kontakt′linse, -n** contact lense

das **Konto, -s** (*or* **Konten**) account

der **Kontrast′, -e** contrast

kontrollie′ren to control, check

die **Konversation′, -en** conversation

sich **konzentrie′ren (auf** + *acc.*) to concentrate (on)

das **Konzert′, -e** concert (10W)

der **Kopf, ̈e** head (9W)

kopf·stehen* to stand on one's head

die **Kopie′, -n** copy

der **Korb, ̈e** basket

der **Korbball, ̈e** basketball

der **Körper, -** body (9W)

körperlich physical(ly)

der **Korrespondent′, -en, -en** correspondent

korrigie′ren to correct

kosten to cost; **Was ~ . . . ?** How much are . . . ? (S4); **Das kostet (zusammen) . . .** That comes to . . . (S4)

die **Kosten** (*pl.*) cost

das **Kostüm′, -e** costume; woman's suit

der **Kracher, -** firecracker

die **Kraft, ̈e** strength, power

die **Kralle, -n** claw

krank (ä) sick, ill (9W)

die **Kran′kengymna′stin, -nen** physical therapist

das **Krankenhaus, ̈er** hospital

die **Krankenkasse, -n** health insurance

die **Krankenpflege** nursing

der **Krankenpfleger, -** male nurse (12W)

die **Krankenschwester, -n** nurse (12W)

die **Krankheit, -en** sickness

der **Kranz, ̈e** wreath

der **Krapfen, -** doughnut

der **Kratzer, -** scratch

die **Krawatte, -n** tie

kreativ′ creative

die **Kreativität′** creativity

die **Kredit′karte, -n** credit card

die **Kreide** chalk (S2)

der **Kreis, -e** circle; county

die **Kreuzung, -en** intersection

das **Kreuzworträtsel, -** crossword puzzle

der **Krieg, -e** war (14W)

der **Kri′tiker, -** critic

der **Krimi, -s** detective story (10W)

der **Krimskrams** old junk

kritisch critical(ly)

kritisie′ren to criticize

die **Krone, -n** crown

krönen to crown

die **Küche, -n** kitchen (6W); cuisine

der **Kuchen, -** cake (2W)

die **Kugel, -n** ball, sphere

kühl cool (S5)

der **Kühlschrank, ̈e** refrigerator (6W)

der **Kuli, -s** pen (S2)

die **Kultur′, -en** culture

kulturell′ cultural(ly) (14W)

sich **kümmern (um)** to take care (of)

die **Kunst, ̈e** art

der **Künstler, -** artist

der **Kurfürst, -en, -en** elector

der **Kurort, -e** health resort, spa

der **Kurs, -e** course (13W)

kurz (ü) short (S3); **~ vor** shortly before; **vor ~em** recently

die **Kürze** shortness, brevity

das **Kurzgespräch, -e** brief conversation

die **Kusi′ne, -n** (female) cousin (1W)

küssen to kiss

die **Küste, -n** coast

L

das **Labor′, -s** (*or* **-e**) lab (13W)

die **Laboran′tin, -nen** lab assistant

lachen to laugh (10W)

lächerlich ridiculous

laden (lädt), lud, geladen to load

der **Laden, ̈** store; **grüne ~** environmental store; **Tante-Emma-~** small grocery store

die **Lage, -n** location

lahm lame

das **Lamm, ̈er** lamb

die **Lampe, -n** lamp (6W); **Hänge~** hanging lamp; **Steh~** floor lamp

das **Land, ̈er** country, state (1W); **auf dem ~** in the country (6E); **aufs ~** in(to) the country(side) (6E)

landen (ist) to land (8W)

die **Landeskunde** cultural and geographical study of a country

die **Landkarte, -n** map (1W)

die **Landschaft, -en** landscape, scenery (15E)

die **Landung, -en** landing

der **Landwirt, -e** farmer

die **Landwirtschaft** agriculture

landwirtschaftlich agricultural

lang (ä) (*adj.*) long (S3)

lange (*adv.*) long; **noch ~ nicht** not by far; **schon ~ (nicht mehr)** (not) for a long time; **wie ~?** how long? (4W)

langsam slow(ly) (S3)

sich **langweilen** to get (or be) bored (9E)

langweilig boring, dull (10W)

lassen (läßt), ließ, gelassen to leave (behind) (7W)

(das) **Latein'** Latin

laufen (läuft), lief, ist gelaufen to run, walk (3G)

laut loud(ly), noisy (4E); **Sprechen Sie ~er!** Speak up. (S3)

läuten to ring

der **Lautsprecher, -** loudspeaker

leben to live (6E)

das **Leben** life (9E)

lebend living; **etwas Lebendes** something living

die **Lebensfreude** joy of living

lebensfroh cheerful, full of life

die **Lebensmittel** (pl.) groceries (2W)

der **Lebensstandard** standard of living

die **Leber, -n** liver

der **Leberkäse** (Bavarian) meat loaf made from minced pork

der **Lebkuchen, -** gingerbread

das **Leder** leather

die **Lederhose, -n** leather pants

ledig single (11W)

leer empty

legen to lay, put (flat) (6W); **sich ~** to lie down (9G)

die **Lehre, -n** apprenticeship

lehren to teach (13W)

der **Lehrer, -** teacher (12W)

der **Lehrling, -e** apprentice

die **Lehrstelle, -n** apprenticeship (position)

leicht light, easy (10E)

leid: Es tut mir ~. I'm sorry. (5W)

die **Leidenschaft, -en** passion

leider unfortunately (5E)

leihen, lieh, geliehen to lend

die **Leine, -n** leash

leise quiet(ly), soft(ly)

leiten to direct

die **Leiter, -n** ladder

das **Leitungswasser** tap water

lernen to learn, study (S2)

der **Lerntip, -s** study suggestion

das **Lernziel, -e** learning objective

lesbar legible

lesen (liest), las, gelesen to read (S2)

der **Leser, -** reader

die **Leseratte, -n** bookworm

der **Lesesaal, -säle** reading room

letzt- last (10E)

(das) **Letzeburgisch** Luxembourg dialect

die **Leute** (pl.) people (1W)

das **Licht, -er** light

die **Lichterkette, -n** candlelight march

lieb- dear (5E)

die **Liebe** love (11W)

lieben to love (6E)

lieber rather (12G); **Es wäre mir ~, wenn . . .** I would prefer it, if . . .

der **Liebling, -e** darling, favorite; **~sdichter** favorite poet; **~sfach** favorite subject

liebst-: am liebsten best of all (12G)

das **Lied, -er** song (4E); **Volks~** folk song

liegen, lag, gelegen to lie, be (located) (1W); be lying (flat) (6W)

der **Liegestuhl, -̈e** lounge chair

lila purple

die **Lilie, -n** lily, iris

die **Limona'de, -n** soft drink, lemonade (2W)

die **Lingui'stik** linguistics

link- left; **auf der ~en Seite** on the left

links left (5W); **erste Straße ~** first street to the left (5W)

die **Linse, -n** lentil; lense

die **Lippe, -n** lip

der **Lippenstift, -e** lipstick

der **Liter, -** liter

das **Loch, -̈er** hole

der **Löffel, -** spoon (3W); **ein Eß~** one tablespoon (of)

logisch logical

lokal' local(ly)

los: ~·werden* to get rid of; **etwas ~ sein*** to be happening, going on; **Was ist ~?** What's the matter? (9W)

lösen to solve

die **Lösung, -en** solution

der **Löwe, -n, -n** lion

die **Luft** air (12W); **~brücke** airlift

die **Luftpost** airmail; **der ~leichtbrief, -e** aerogram; **per ~** by airmail

die **Lüge, -n** lie

die **Lust** inclination, desire, fun; **Ich habe (keine)~(zu) . . .** I (don't) feel like (doing s.th.) . . . (9W)

lustig funny (4E); **reise~** eager to travel

luxuriös' luxurious

der **Luxus** luxury

M

machen to make, do (2W); **Spaß ~** to be fun (4E); **Mach's gut!** Take care! (4W); **Was machst du Schönes?** What are you doing?; **(Das) macht nichts.** (That) doesn't matter. That's OK. (5E); **das macht zusammen** that comes to

die **Macht, -̈e** power (14E)

das **Mädchen, -** girl (1W)

das **Magazin', -e** magazine; feature (e.g., on TV)

die **Magd, -̈e** maid

der **Magi'ster, -** M.A.

die **Mahlzeit, -en** meal; **~!** Enjoy your meal (food)!

das **Mahnmal, -e** memorial (of admonishment)

der **Mai** May (S5); **im ~** in May (S5)

der **Mais** corn

der **Makler, -** (real-estate) agent, broker

mal times, multiplied by

das **Mal, -e: das erste ~** the first time (11E); **zum ersten ~** for the first time (11E); **~ sehen!** Let's see. (13W)

malen to paint

der **Maler, -** painter

man one (they, people, you) (3E)

das **Management** management

manch- many a, several, some (7G)

manchmal sometimes (3E)

manipuliert' manipulated

der **Mann, -̈er** man, husband (1W)

männlich masculine, male

die **Mannschaft, -en** team

der **Mantel, -̈** coat (S3)

das **Manuskript', -e** manuscript

das **Märchen, -** fairy tale

die **Margari'ne, -n** margarine

die **Mari'ne, -n** navy

die **Mark (DM)** mark (S4); **zwei Mark** two marks (S4)

der **Markt, -̈e** market (2W)

die **Marmela′de, -n** marmalade, jam (2W)

der **März** March (S5); **im ~** in March (S5)

die **Maschi′ne, -n** machine

der **Maschi′nenbau** mechanical engineering

die **Maske, -n** mask

die **Massa′ge, -n** massage

die **Masse, -n** mass

die **Massenmedien** *(pl.)* mass media

das **Material′** material

die **Mathematik′** mathematics

die **Mauer, -n** wall (14W)

das **Maul, ¨er** big mouth (of animal)

der **Maurer, -** bricklayer

die **Maus, ¨e** mouse; **~efalle, -n** mousetrap

das **Mecha′niker, -** mechanic

die **Medien** *(pl.)* media

das **Medikament′, -e** medicine, prescription

die **Medizin′** (the field of) medicine

das **Mehl** flour

mehr more (12G); **immer ~** more and more (12G)

mehrer- *(pl.)* several (10G)

die **Mehrwertsteuer, -n** value-added tax

meiden, mied, gemieden to avoid

mein my (1W,7G)

meinen to mean, think (be of an opinion) (15E)

die **Meinung, -en** opinion; **meiner ~ nach** in my opinion

die **Meinungsumfrage, -n** opinion poll

meist-: am meisten most (12G)

meistens mostly, usually (7E)

der **Meister, -** master

die **Mensa** student cafeteria (3W)

der **Mensch, -en, -en** human being, person; people *(pl.)* (1E,2G); **~!** Man! Boy! Hey!; **Mit~** fellow man

die **Menschheit** humankind

das **Menü′, -s** dinner, daily special

merken to notice

die **Messe, -n** (trade) fair

das **Messegelände, -** fairgrounds

das **Messer, -** knife (3E); **Taschen~** pocket knife

das **Metall′, -e** metal

der **Meter, -** meter

die **Metropo′le, -n** metropolis

der **Metzger, -** butcher

die **Metzgerei′, -en** butcher shop

mies miserable

die **Miete, -n** rent

mieten to rent (6W)

der **Mieter, -** renter, tenant

die **Mietwohnung, -en** apartment

der **Mikrowellenherd, -e** microwave oven

die **Milch** milk (2W)

das **Militär′** military, army

militä′risch military

die **Milliar′de, -n** *(American)* billion (S4)

der **Million′, -en** million

der **Millionär′, -e** millionaire

mindestens at least

die **Mineralogie′** mineralogy

das **Mineral′wasser** mineral water

minus minus (S4)

die **Minu′te, -n** minute (S6)

mischen to mix; **darunter ~ to** blend in

der **Mischmasch** mishmash, hodgepodge

die **Mischung, -en** mixture

misera′bel miserable

die **Mission′, -en** mission

mit *(+ dat.)* with (3G); along

mit·bringen* to bring along (7G)

mit·fahren* to drive along

mit·feiern to join in the celebration

mit·gehen* to go along (7G)

mit·kommen* to come along (7G)

das **Mitleid** pity

mit·machen to participate

mit·nehmen* to take along (7G)

mit·schicken to send along

mit·singen* to sing along

der **Mittag, -e** noon

mittag: heute ~ today at noon (8G)

das **Mittagessen, -** lunch, midday meal (3W); **beim ~** at lunch; **zum ~** for lunch (3W)

mittags at noon (S6)

die **Mitte** middle, center (14E); mid

das **Mittel, -** means (of)

das **Mittelalter** Middle Ages; **im ~** in the Middle Ages (14W)

mittelalterlich medieval

(das) **Mitteleuropa** Central Europe

mittelgroß average size

mitten: ~ durch right through; **~ in** in the middle of (6E)

die **Mitternacht: um ~** at midnight

der **Mittwoch** Wednesday (S5); **am ~** on Wednesday; **Ascher~** Ash Wednesday

mittwochs on Wednesdays (2E)

die **Möbel** *(pl.)* furniture (6W)

die **Mobilität′** mobility

möbliert′ furnished

möchten *or* **möchte** (*see* **mögen**)

das **Modal′verb, -en** modal auxiliary

die **Mode** fashion; **~puppe, -n** fashion doll

modern′ modern

mögen (mag), mochte, gemocht to like (5G); **Ich möchte . . .** I would like (to have) . . . (2W)

möglich possible (7W); **alle ~en** all sorts of

die **Möglichkeit, -en** possibility

der **Mohnkuchen** poppy-seed cake

der **Moment′, -e** moment; **(Einen) ~!** One moment. Just a minute. (7W)

momentan′ at the moment, right now

der **Monat, -e** month (S5); **im ~** a month, per month (6W)

monatelang for months

monatlich monthly (10E)

der **Mond, -e** moon

der **Montag** Monday (S5); **am ~** on Monday

montags on Mondays (2E)

die **Moral′** moral

der **Mörder, -** murderer

morgen tomorrow (S4,4W); **Bis ~!** See you tomorrow; **für ~** for tomorrow (S2)

der **Morgen** morning: **Guten ~!** Good morning. (S1)

morgen: heute ~ this morning (8G)

morgens in the morning (S6), every morning

müde tired (S1); **tod~** dead tired

die **Müdigkeit** fatigue

der **Müll** garbage

der **Müller, -** miller
der **Müllschlucker, -** garbage dis-
posal
der **Mund, ¨er** mouth (9W)
die **Mundharmonika, -s** harmon-
ica
mündlich oral(ly)
das **Muse′um, Muse′en** museum
(5W)
die **Musik′** music (9E)
musika′lisch musical (11W)
die **Musik′wissenschaft** musicol-
ogy
(der) **Muskat′** nutmeg
der **Muskelkater** charley horse;
Ich habe ~. My muscles are
sore.
das **Müsli** whole-grain granola
müssen (muß), mußte, gemußt
to have to, must (5G)
das **Muster, -** example, model; pattern
der **Mustersatz, ¨e** sample sentence
die **Mutter, ¨** mother (1W); **Groß~**
grandmother (1W); **Ur-
groß~** great-grandmother
mütterlich motherly
die **Mutti, -s** Mom

N

na well; **~ also** well; **~ gut**
well, all right; **~ ja** well; **~
klar** of course (13W) **~ und!**
So what?
nach (+ *dat.*) after (time), to
(cities, countries, continents)
(3G); **je ~** depending on
der **Nachbar, -n, -n** neighbor
(1E,2G)
die **Nachbarschaft, -en** neighborhood; neighborly relations
nachdem′ *(conj.)* after (11G)
nacherzählt retold, adapted
die **Nachfrage** demand
nachher afterwards
nach·kommen* to follow
nach·laufen* to run after
nach·machen to imitate
der **Nachmittag, -e** afternoon; **am
~** in the afternoon
nachmittag: heute ~ this afternoon (8G)
nachmittags in the afternoon
(S6), every afternoon
der **Nachname, -ns, -n** last name
die **Nachricht, -en** news (10E)

nächst- next (11E)
die **Nacht, ¨e** night (7W); **Gute ~!**
Good night!
nacht: heute ~ tonight (8G)
der **Nachteil, -e** disadvantage
die **Nachteule, -n** night owl
der **Nachtisch** dessert (3W); **zum ~**
for dessert (3W)
nachts during the night, every
night (8G)
der **Nachttisch, -e** nightstand
nach·werfen* to throw after
die **Nadel, -n** needle
nah (näher, nächst-) near
(5W,12G)
die **Nähe** nearness, vicinity; **in der
~** nearby; **in der ~ von** (+
dat.) near (5W)
nähen to sew
der **Name, -ns, -n** name (8G);
Mein ~ ist . . . My name is
. . . (S1); **Mädchen~** maiden
name; **Vor~** first name;
Nach~ last name; **Spitz~**
nickname (14W)
nämlich namely, you know
die **Nase, -n** nose (9W); **Ich habe
die ~ voll.** I'm fed up (with
it).
national′ national
der **Nationalis′mus** nationalism
die **Nationalität′, -en** nationality
die **Natur′** nature
natür′lich natural(ly), of
course (2W)
die **Natur′wissenschaft, -en** natural science (13W)
natur′wissenschaftlich scientific
neben (+ *acc. / dat.*) beside,
next to (6G)
nebeneinander next to each
other
das **Nebenfach, ¨er** minor (field of
study) (14W)
der **Nebensatz, ¨e** subordinate
clause
negativ negative(ly)
**nehmen (nimmt), nahm,
genommen** to take (S4); to
have (food) (3G)
nein no (S1)
nennen, nannte, genannt to
name, call (11E); **ich nenne
das** that's what I call
nett nice (11W)

neu new (S3); **Was gibt's
Neues . . . ?** What's new?
(9W)
neugierig curious
der **Neujahrstag** New Year's Day
nicht not (S1); **gar ~** not at all
(13E); **~ nur . . . sondern
auch** not only . . . but also
(3E); **~ wahr?** isn't it? (S5)
nichts nothing (3W); **~ Besonderes** nothing special (9W)
nie never (4E); **noch ~** never
before, not ever (4E)
niedrig low
niemand nobody, no one (11E)
nimmermehr never again
nobel noble
noch still (4W); **~ ein** another
(3W); **~ einmal** once more,
again (S2); **~ lange nicht** not
by far; **~ nicht** not yet (6E);
~ nie never (before), not
ever (4E); **Sonst ~ etwas?**
Anything else?; **weder . . . ~**
neither . . . nor (10E)
der **Nominativ, -e** nominative
die **Nonne, -n** nun
der **Norden: im ~** in the north (1W)
nördlich (von) to the north,
north (of) (1W)
normal′ normal; by regular
(surface) mail
(das) **Nor′wegen** Norway
der **Nor′weger, -** the Norwegian
nor′wegisch Norwegian
die **Note, -n** grade (13W)
nötig necessary, needed
die **Notiz′, -en** note; **~en machen**
to take notes
der **Novem′ber** November (S5);
im ~ in November (S5)
nüchtern sober
die **Nudel, -n** noodle (3W)
null zero (S4)
der **Numerus clausus** admissions
restriction at a university
die **Nummer, -n** number (7W)
nun now (11E)
nur only (S4)
die **Nuß, ¨sse** nut
der **Nußknacker,-** nutcracker
nutzen to use

O

ob *(conj.)* if, whether (4G)
oben upstairs (6W); up; **~
genannt** above mentioned

der **Ober, -** waiter (3W); **Herr ~!** Waiter! (3W)

die **Oberin, -nen** mother superior

die **Oberstufe, -n** upper level

das **Objekt', -e** object

objektiv' objective(ly)

das **Obst** *(sg.)* fruit (2W)

obwohl *(conj.)* although (4G)

oder or (S3,2G)

der **Ofen, :** oven

offen open (2E)

öffnen to open (S4)

öffentlich public

oft often (2E)

ohne (+ *acc.*) without (2G)

das **Ohr, -en** ear (9W)

Oje'! Oops! Oh no!

ökolo'gisch ecologic(ally)

das **Ö'kosystem', -e** ecological system

der **Okto'ber** October (S5); **im ~** in October (S5)

das **Öl, -e** oil, lotion

die **Olympia'de, -n** Olympics

die **Oma, -s** grandma

das **Omelett', -s** omelet

der **Onkel, -** uncle (1W)

die **Oper, -n** opera (10W); **die Seifen~** soap opera

das **Opfer, -** victim

oran'ge (color) orange (S2)

die **Oran'ge, -n** orange (2W)

das **Orche'ster, -** orchestra (10W)

ordentlich orderly; regular

die **Ordnungszahl, -en** ordinal number

die **Organisation', -en** organization

(sich) **organisie'ren** to organize

das **Original', -e** original

der **Ort, -e** place, town; location

der **Osten: im ~** in the east (1W)

(das) **Ostern: zu ~** at / for Easter (4W); **Frohe ~!** Happy Easter.

(das) **Österreich** Austria (1W)

der **Österreicher, -** the Austrian (1W)

österreichisch Austrian

östlich (von) east (of), to the east (of) (1W)

der **Ozean, -e** ocean

P

paar: ein ~ a couple of, some (2E)

das **Paar, -e** couple, pair

pachten to lease

packen to pack (7E); to grab

die **Pädago'gik** education

das **Paddelboot, -e** canoe

paddeln to paddle

das **Paket', -e** package, parcel (8W)

die **Paket'karte, -n** parcel form

die **Palatschinken** *(pl.)* crêpes

das **Panora'ma** panorama

die **Panne, -n** mishap

der **Panzer, -** tank

das **Papier', -e** paper (S2)

der **Papier'krieg** paper work, red tape

das **Papier'warengeschäft, -e** office supply store

die **Pappe** cardboard

der **Park, -s** park (5W)

parken to park (15W)

das **Parkett': im ~** (seating) in the orchestra

der **Parkplatz, -e** parking lot

parlamenta'risch parliamentary

die **Partei', -en** (political) party

das **Parter're: im ~** on the first floor (ground level) (6W)

das **Partizip', -ien** participle

der **Partner, -** partner (11W)

die **Party, Partys** party (4W)

der **Paß, -sse** passport (7W)

passen to fit; **Das paßt mir nicht.** That doesn't suit me.

passend appropriate, suitable

passie'ren (ist) to happen

das **Passiv** passive voice

die **Pause, -n** intermission, break (10W); **eine ~ machen** to take a break

das **Pech** tough luck; **~ haben*** to be unlucky (4W); **~ gehabt!** Tough luck!

pendeln (ist) to commute

die **Pension', -en** boarding house; hotel (7E)

das **Perfekt** present perfect

permanent' permanent

die **Person', -en** person; **pro ~** per person

persön'lich personal(ly)

die **Persön'lichkeit, -en** personality

der **Pfannkuchen, -** pancake

der **Pfarrer, -** minister, cleric

der **Pfeffer** pepper (3W)

die **Pfefferminze** peppermint

die **Pfeife, -n** pipe

der **Pfennig, -e** German penny, pfennig (S4); **zwei ~** two pennies (S4)

das **Pferd, -e** horse

(das) **Pfingsten** Pentecost

das **Pflaster, -** bandaid

die **Pflegemutter, :** foster mother

das **Pflichtfach, -er** required subject

das **Pfund** pound (2W); **zwei ~** two pounds (of) (2W)

die **Phantasie', -n** fantasy, imagination

phantas'tisch fantastic (9W)

die **Pharmazie'** pharmaceutics, pharmacy

die **Philologie'** philology

der **Philosoph', -en, -en** philosopher

die **Philosophie'** philosophy

die **Phonotypi'stin, -nen** dictaphone-typist

die **Photographie'** photography

photographie'ren to take pictures (9W)

die **Physik'** physics

der **Physiker, -** physicist

physisch physical(ly)

das **Picknick, -s** picnic

picknicken gehen* to go picnicking

piepen to peep, chirp; **Bei dir piept's!** You're cuckoo. You must be kidding.

der **Pilot', -en, -en** pilot

die **Pizza, -s** pizza (3W)

der **Plan, -e** plan (12W)

planen to plan (15W)

die **Planier'raupe, -n** bulldozer

das **Plastik** plastic

die **Plastiktüte, -n** plastic bag

die **Platte, -n** record; platter

der **Plattenspieler, -** record player

der **Platz, -e** (town) square, place (5W); seat

die **Platzanweiserin, -nen** usher

das **Plätzchen, -** cookie (2W)

plötzlich suddenly (11E)

der **Plural, -e (von)** plural of (S2)

plus plus (S4)

das **Plusquamperfekt** past perfect

der **Pole, -n, -n** / die **Polin, -nen** native of Poland

(das) **Polen** Poland

polnisch Polish

die **Politik'** politics

die **Politik′(wissenschaft)** political science, politics

poli′tisch political(ly)

die **Polizei′** *(sg.)* police

der **Polizi′st, -en, -en** policeman (12W)

die **Pommes frites** *(pl.)* French fries (3W)

der **Pool, -s** swimming pool

populär′ popular

das **Portemonnaie, -s** wallet

der **Portier′, -s** desk clerk

das **Porto** postage

(das) **Portugal** Portugal

der **Portugie′se, -n, -n** / die **Portugiesin, -nen** the Portuguese

portugie′sisch Portuguese

das **Porzellan′** porcelain

die **Post** post office (5W); mail (8W)

der **Postdienst** postal service

das **Postfach, ¨er** P.O. box (8W)

das **Posthorn, ¨er** bugle

die **Postkarte, -n** postcard (8W)

die **Postleitzahl, -en** zip code

prägen to shape

das **Praktikum, Praktika** practical training

praktisch practical(ly) (6W)

die **Präposition′, -en** preposition

der **Präsident′, -en, -en** president

die **Praxis** practical experience

der **Preis, -e** price; prize

die **Presse** press

das **Presti′ge** prestige

prima great, wonderful (S6)

der **Prinz, -en, -en** prince

die **Prinzes′sin, -nen** princess

privat′ private

das **Privat′gefühl, -e** feeling for privacy

das **Privileg′, Privilegien** privilege

pro per

die **Probe, -n** test; **auf die ~ stellen** to test

probie′ren to try

das **Problem′, -e** problem (12W)

problema′tisch problematic

das **Produkt′, -e** product

die **Produktion′** production

der **Produzent′, -en, -en** producer

produzie′ren to produce

der **Profes′sor, -en** professor (13W)

profitie′ren to profit

das **Programm′, -e** program, channel (10W)

der **Programmie′rer, -** programmer

das **Prono′men, -** pronoun

proportional′ proportional(ly)

Prost! Cheers!; **~ Neujahr!** Happy New Year!

der **Protest′, -e** protest

protestie′ren to protest

protzen to brag

das **Proviso′rium** provisional state

das **Prozent′, -e** percent

die **Prüfung, -en** test, exam (1W); **eine ~ bestehen*** to pass an exam (13W); **bei einer ~ durch·fallen*** to flunk an exam (13W); **eine ~ machen** to take an exam (13W)

der **Psalm, -e** psalm

das **Pseudonym′, -e** pseudonym

der **Psychia′ter, -** psychiatrist

die **Psy′choanaly′se** psychoanalysis

der **Psycholo′ge, -n, -n** / die **Psycholo′gin, -nen** psychologist

die **Psychologie′** psychology

psycholo′gisch psychological(ly)

das **Publikum** audience

die **Puderdose, -n** compact

der **Pudding, -s** pudding (3W)

die **Pulle, -n** *(colloquial)* bottle: **volle ~** with the pedal to the metal

der **Pulli, -s** sweater (S3)

der **Pullo′ver, -** pullover, sweater (S3)

pünktlich on time

die **Puppe, -n** doll

putzen to clean; **sich die Zähne ~** to brush one's teeth (9G)

die **Putzfrau, -en** cleaning lady

Q

die **Qualifikation′, -en** qualification

die **Qualität′** quality

die **Quantität′** quantity

das **Quartal′, -e** quarter (university) (13W)

das **Quartett′, -e** quartet

das **Quartier′, -s** *(or* **-e***)* lodging

der **Quatsch** nonsense

die **Quelle, -n** source

quer durch all across

die **Querflöte, -n** flute

das **Quintett′, -s** quintet

die **Quote, -n** quota

R

rad·fahren (fährt Rad), fuhr Rad, ist radgefahren to bicycle

das **Radio, -s** radio (6W)

der **Rand, ¨er** edge

der **Rang, ¨e** theater balcony; **im ersten ~** in the first balcony

der **Rasen, -** lawn

sich **rasie′ren** to shave o.s. (9G)

der **Rat** advice, counsel

raten (rät), riet, geraten to advise, guess

das **Rathaus, ¨er** city hall (5W)

rätoromanisch Romansh

die **Ratte, -n** rat

rauchen to smoke

der **Raum** space

das **Raumschiff, -e** spaceship

reagie′ren to react

die **Reaktion′, -en** reaction

die **Real′schule, -n** high school, grades 5–10

rebellie′ren to rebel

rechnen to calculate

die **Rechnung, -en** check, bill (3W)

recht: Du hast ~. You're right. (11W); **Das geschieht dir ~.** That serves you right.

recht-: auf der ~en Seite on the right side

das **Recht, -e** right

rechts right (5W); **erste Straße ~** first street to the right (5W)

der **Rechtsanwalt, ¨e** lawyer (12W)

die **Rechtsanwältin, -nen** lawyer (12W)

der **Rechts′radikalis′mus** right-wing radicalism

die **Rechtswissenschaft** study of law

die **Rede, -n** speech

reden (mit / über) to talk (to / about), chat (15W)

die **Redewendung, -en** idiom, saying

reduzie′ren to reduce

das **Referat′, -e** report; **ein ~ halten*** to give a report

reflexiv′ reflexive

das **Reform'haus, ˝-er** healthfood store

das **Regal', -e** shelf (6E)

regeln to regulate

der **Regen** rain

der **Regenschirm, -e** umbrella

die **Regie'rung, -en** government

das **Regi'me, -s** regime

die **Region', -en** region

regional' regional(ly)

der **Regisseur', -e** director (film)

regnen to rain; **Es regnet.** It's raining. (S5).

regulie'ren to regulate

reiben, rieb, gerieben to rub

reich rich (11W)

das **Reich, -e** empire, kingdom

der **Reichtum, ˝-er** wealth

reif ripe; mature

die **Reife** maturity; **mittlere ~** diploma of a Realschule

die **Reihe, -n** row

der **Reis** rice (3W)

die **Reise, -n** trip (7E); **eine ~ machen** to take a trip, travel

das **Reisebüro, -s** travel agency

der **Reiseführer, -** tour guide

der **Reiseleiter, -** travel guide

reiselustig fond of traveling

reisen (ist) to travel (7E)

der **Reisescheck, -s** traveler's check

reißen, riß, ist gerissen to tear

reiten, ritt, ist geritten to ride (on horseback)

die **Reitschule, -n** riding academy

der **Rektor, -en** university president

relativ' relative(ly)

das **Relativ'pronomen, -** relative pronoun

der **Relativ'satz, ˝-e** relative clause

die **Religion', -en** religion

das **Rendezvous, -** date

rennen, rannte, ist gerannt to run

renovie'ren to renovate (15W)

der **Repräsentant', -en, -en** representative

repräsentativ' representative

reservie'ren to reserve (7E)

die **Reservie'rung, -en** reservation

die **Residenz', -en** residence

resignie'ren to resign, give up

der **Rest, -e** rest

das **Restaurant', -s** restaurant (3E)

restaurie'ren to restore (15W)

die **Restaurie'rung** restoration

das **Resultat', -e** result

retten to save, rescue (15W)

das **Rezept', -e** recipe

die **Rezeption', -en** reception (desk)

das **R-Gespräch, -e** collect call

richtig right, correct (S2); **Das ist genau das Richtige.** That's exactly the right thing.

die **Richtigkeit** correctness

die **Richtung, -en** direction; **in ~** in the direction of

riechen, roch, gerochen to smell

das **Riesenrad, ˝-er** ferris wheel

riesig huge, enormous

die **Rindsroulade, -n** stuffed beef roll

der **Ring, -e** ring

rings um (+ *acc.*) all around

das **Risiko, Risiken** risk

der **Ritter, -** knight

der **Rock, ˝-e** skirt (S3)

die **Rolle, -n** role; **Haupt~** leading role

der **Roman', -e** novel (10W)

die **Romani'stik** study of Romance languages

die **Roman'tik** romanticism

roman'tisch romantic

römisch Roman

rosa pink (S2)

die **Rose, -n** rose

die **Rosi'ne, -n** raisin

rot (ö) red (S2); **bei Rot** at a red light

die **rote Grütze** berry sauce thickened with cornstarch

das **Rotkäppchen** Little Red Riding Hood

das **Rotkraut** red cabbage

rötlich reddish

die **Roula'de, -n** stuffed beef roll

der **Rückblick, -e** review

die **(Hin- und) Rückfahrkarte, -n** round-trip ticket (8W)

der **Rückgang** decline

der **Rucksack, ˝-e** backpack

der **Rückweg, -e** return trip, way back

ruck zuck quickly, in a jiffy

das **Ruderboot, -e** rowboat

rudern to row

rufen, rief, gerufen to call

die **Ruhe** peace and quiet

der **Ruhetag, -e** holiday, day off

ruhig quiet (7W)

der **Ruhm** fame

rühren to stir; **sich ~** to move; **Ich kann mich kaum ~.** I can hardly move.

der **Rum** rum

rund round

die **Rundfahrt, -en** sightseeing trip

der **Rundfunk** radio, broadcasting

der **Russe, -n, -n** / die **Russin, -nen** the Russian

russisch Russian

(das) **Rußland** Russia

S

der **Saal, Säle** large room, hall

die **Sache, -n** thing, matter

der **Saft, ˝-e** juice (2W)

sagen to say, tell (S2), **Sag mal!** Say. Tell me (us etc.); **wie gesagt** as I (you etc.) said

die **Saison', -s** season

der **Salat', -e** salad, lettuce (2W)

das **Salz** salt (3W)

salzig salty

die **Salzstange, -n** pretzel stick

sammeln to collect (9W)

der **Sammler, -** collector

der **Samstag** Saturday (S5); **am ~** on Saturday (S5)

samstags on Saturdays (2E)

der **Samt** velvet

der **Sand** sand

der **Sängerknabe, -n, -n** choir boy

der **Satellit', -en** satellite

der **Satz, ˝-e** sentence (1W); **Bilden Sie einen ~!** Make a sentence.

sauber clean, neat (S3)

die **Sauberkeit** cleanliness

sauber·machen to clean

sauer sour; acid

der **Sauerbraten** marinated pot roast

das **Sauerkraut** sauerkraut

die **Säule, -n** column

die **S-Bahn, -en** commuter train

das **Schach: ~ spielen** to play chess (9W)

schade too bad (5W)

das **Schaf, -e** sheep

schaffen to work hard, accomplish

schaffen, schuf, geschaffen to create

der **Schaffner, -** conductor

die **Schale, -n** shell, peel

die **(Schall)platte, -n** record

der **Schalter, -** ticket window, counter (7W)

der **Schaschlik, -s** shish kebab

schätzen to appreciate

das **Schaufenster, -** display window; **in die ~ sehen*** to go window-shopping

das **Schaumbad, ¨er** bubble bath

der **Schauspieler, -** actor (10W)

der **Scheck, -s** check (7W)

die **Scheidung, -en** divorce (11W)

der **Schein, -e** certificate

scheinen, schien, geschienen to shine (S5); to seem (like), appear (to be) (14E)

schenken to give (as a present) (4W)

die **Schere, -n** scissors

schick chic, neat (11W)

schicken to send (8W)

die **Schießbude, -n** shooting gallery

das **Schiff, -e** ship, boat; **mit dem ~ fahren*** to go by boat

das **Schild, -er** sign

der **Schinken, -** ham

der **Schlachter, -** butcher

schlafen (schläft), schlief, geschlafen to sleep (3E)

schlaflos sleepless

der **Schlafsack, ¨e** sleeping bag

die **Schlafstadt, ¨e** bedroom community

das **Schlafzimmer, -** bedroom (6W)

schlagen (schlägt), schlug, geschlagen to hit

der **Schlager, -** popular song, hit

der **Schlagersänger, -** pop singer

die **Schlagsahne** whipped cream

die **Schlange, -n** snake

schlank slim, slender (11W)

schlecht bad(ly) (S1)

schließen, schloß, geschlossen to lock, close

schließlich after all, in the end

schlimm bad, awful

das **Schloß, ¨sser** palace (5W)

der **Schlüssel, -** key (7W)

schmecken to taste (good); **Das schmeckt (gut).** That tastes good. (3W)

schmelzen (schmilzt), schmolz, geschmolzen to melt

der **Schmerz, -en** pain, ache; **Ich habe (Kopf)schmerzen.** I have a (head)ache. (9W)

der **Schmied, -e** blacksmith

der **Schmutz** dirt

schmutzig dirty (S3)

der **Schnee** snow

schneiden, schnitt, geschnitten to cut

schneien to snow; **es schneit** it's snowing (S5)

schnell quick(ly), fast (S3)

der **Schnellweg, -e** express route

das **Schnitzel, -** veal cutlet

der **Schock, -s** shock

die **Schokola′de** chocolate

schon already (1E)

schön fine, nice, beautiful (S5)

die **Schönheit** beauty

der **Schrank, ¨e** closet, cupboard (6W); **Gefrier~** freezer; **Kleider~** closet; **Küchen~** kitchen cabinet; **Kühl~** refrigerator

der **Schrebergarten, ¨** leased garden

der **Schreck** shock; **Auch du ~!** My goodness!

schrecklich terrible

schreiben, schrieb, geschrieben to write (S3); **~ an (+ acc.)** to write to (10G)

die **Schreibmaschine, -n** typewriter

der **Schreibtisch, -e** desk (6W)

schreien, schrie, geschrien to scream

schriftlich written; in writing

der **Schriftsteller, -** writer, author

der **Schritt, -e** step; pre-unit

schubsen to shove

der **Schuh, -e** shoe (S3); **Sport~** gym shoe, sneaker

die **Schule, -n** school (5W)

der **Schüler, -** pupil, student

die **Schüssel, -n** bowl

schütteln to shake

schütten (in + acc.) to dump, pour (into)

der **Schutz** protection

der **Schütze, -n, -n** rifleman, marksman, Sagittarius

schützen to protect (14E)

der **Schwabe, -n, -n** / die **Schwäbin, -nen** the Swabian

(das) **Schwaben(land)** Swabia

schwäbisch Swabian

die **Schwäche, -n** weakness

schwanger pregnant

schwärmen (von + dat.) to rave (about)

schwarz (ä) black (S2); **~·fahren*** to ride [on a bus or subway] without paying

das **Schwarzbrot, -e** rye bread

der **Schwede, -n, -n** / die **Schwedin, -nen** the Swede

(das) **Schweden** Sweden

schwedisch Swedish

das **Schwein, -e** pig, pork; scoundrel; **~ haben*** to be lucky; **~ gehabt!** You were lucky!

die **Schweinshaxe, -n** pigs' knuckles

die **Schweiz** Switzerland (1W)

der **Schweizer, -** the Swiss (1W)

Schweizer/schweizerisch Swiss

schwer heavy; difficult, hard (10E)

die **Schwester, -n** sister (1W)

das **Schwesterchen, -** little sister

schwierig difficult (12E)

schwimmen, schwamm, geschwommen to swim (9W); **~ gehen*** to go swimming (9W)

das **Schwimmbad, ¨er** swimming pool

der **Schwimmer, -** swimmer

ein Sechstel one sixth

der **See, -n** lake (1W)

die **See** sea, ocean

das **Segelboot, -e** sailboat

segelfliegen gehen* to go gliding

segeln to sail; **~ gehen*** to go sailing

sehen (sieht), sah, gesehen to see, look (3G); **Mal ~!** Let's see! (13W)

die **Sehenswürdigkeit, -en** sight (worth seeing), attraction

sehr very (S5)

die **Seide, -n** silk

die **Seife, -n** soap

die **Seifenoper, -n** soap opera

die **Seilbahn, -en** cable car

sein his, its (7G)

sein (ist), war, ist gewesen to be (S1, S2, 2G); **Ich bin's.** It's me; **So bin ich.** That's the way I am.

seit (+ *dat.*) since, for (time) (3G)

die **Seite, -n** page; **auf ~** on page, to page (S4); **auf der einen/anderen ~** on the one/other hand

die **Sekretä'rin, -nen** secretary (12W)

der **Sekt** champagne (4W)

die **Sekun'de, -n** second (S6)

selbst -self; **~ wenn** even if

selbständig self-employed, independent (11W)

die **Selbständigkeit** independence

selbstbewußt self-confident (11W)

das **Selbstbewußtsein** self-confidence

selten seldom

das **Seme'ster, -** semester (13W)

das **Seminar', -e** seminar (13W)

die **Seminar'arbeit, -en** term paper

der **Sender, -** (radio or TV) station

die **Sendung, -en** (part of) TV or radio program (10E)

das **Sendungsbewußtsein** sense of mission

der **Senf** mustard

der **Septem'ber** September (S5); **im ~** in September (S5)

die **Serie, -n** series

servie'ren to serve (food)

die **Serviet'te, -n** napkin (3W)

Servus! Hi! (*Bavaria, Austria*)

die **Sesamstraße** Sesame Street

der **Sessel, -** armchair (6W)

der **Sessellift, -e** chairlift

setzen to set (down), put (6W); **sich ~** to sit down (9G)

das **Shampoo', -s** shampoo

die **Show, -s** show

sicher sure, certain (4W); safe, secure (12W)

die **Sicherheit** safety, security (12E)

sicherlich surely, certainly, undoubtedly

sichern to secure

sichtbar visible

die **Siedlung, -en** settlement, subdivision

der **Sieg, -e** victory

der **Sieger, -** victor

das **Silber** silver

(das) **Silve'ster: zu ~** at / for New Year's Eve (4W)

singen, sang, gesungen to sing (4W)

sinken, sank, ist gesunken to sink

der **Sinn, -e** mind, sense, meaning; **in den ~ kommen*** to come to mind

die **Situation', -en** situation

sitzen, saß, gesessen to sit (be sitting) (6W)

Ski laufen gehen* to go skiing (9W); **Wasserski laufen gehen*** to go waterskiing

der **Skiläufer, -** skier

der **Skilift, -e** skilift

skrupellos unscrupulous

die **Slawi'stik** study of Slavic language and literature

die **Slowa'kische Republik'** = die **Slowakei'** Slovac Republic

so so, like that; in this way; **~ daß** (*conj.*) so that (13E); **~ ein** such a (7G); **~ so** fair; **~ . . . wie** as . . . as (12G)

sobald' as soon as

die **Socke, -n** sock

das **Sofa, -s** sofa, couch (6W)

sofort' immediately, right away (8E)

sogar' even (6W)

sogenannt so-called

der **Sohn, ⸚e** son (1W)

solch- such (7G)

der **Soldat', -en, -en** soldier

sollen (soll), sollte, gesollt to be supposed to (5G)

der **Sommer, -** summer (S5); **im ~** in the summer (S5)

das **Sonderangebot, -e: im ~** on sale, special

sondern but (on the contrary) (5W,5G); **nicht nur . . . ~ auch** not only . . . but also (3E)

der **Sonderstatus** special status

die **Sonne** sun; **Die ~ scheint.** The sun is shining. (S5)

der **Sonnenaufgang, ⸚e** sunrise

die **Sonnenbrille, -n** sunglasses

die **Sonnencreme, -s** suntan lotion

das **Sonnenöl** suntan lotion

der **Sonnenuntergang, ⸚e** sunset

der **Sonntag** Sunday (S5); **am ~** on Sunday (S5); **Toten~** Memorial Day

sonntags on Sundays (2E)

sonst otherwise; **~ noch etwas?** Anything else?

die **Sorge, -n** worry, concern; **sich ~en machen (um)** to be concerned, worry (about) (12E)

die **Soße, -n** sauce, gravy

sowieso' anyway, anyhow (13E)

sowje'tisch Soviet

sowohl . . . als auch as well as

der **Sozialis'mus** socialism

die **Sozial'kunde** social studies

die **Sozial'pädago'gin, -nen** social worker

die **Souveränität'** sovereignty

die **Soziologie'** social studies, sociology

(das) **Spanien** Spain (1W)

der **Spanier, -** the Spaniard (1W)

spanisch Spanish (1W)

spannend exciting, suspenseful (10W)

sparen to save (money or time) (6E)

sparsam thrifty

sparta'nisch Spartan, frugal

der **Spaß, ⸚e** fun; **~ machen** to be fun (4E)

spät late; **Wie ~ ist es?** How late is it? What time is it? (S6)

später later; **Bis ~!** See you later! (S6)

spazie'ren·gehen* to go for a walk (9W)

der **Spazier'gang, ⸚e** walk

der **Speck** bacon

die **Speise, -n** food, dish

die **Speisekarte, -n** menu (3W)

die **Spekulation', -en** speculation

das **Spezial'geschäft, -e** specialty shop

die **Spezialisie'rung** specialization

der **Spezialist', -en, -en** specialist

die **Spezialität', -en** specialty

der **Spiegel, -** mirror

das **Spiel, -e** game, play (9W)

spielen to play; **Tennis ~** to play tennis (S6); **Dame ~** to play checkers (9W); **Schach ~** to play chess (9W)

der **Spielplan, ⸚e** program, performance schedule

der **Spielplatz, ⸚e** playground

das **Spielzeug** toys

der **Spieß, -e** spit; spear

die **Spindel, -n** spindle

spinnen, spann, gesponnen to spin (yarn) (11E); **Du spinnst wohl!** You're crazy!

das **Spinnrad, ¨er** spinning-wheel

der **Spitzname, -ns, -n** nickname (14W)

spontan' spontaneous

der **Sport** sport(s) (9W); ~ **treiben*** to engage in sports (9W)

der **Sportler, -** athlete

sportlich athletic, sporty (11W)

die **Sprache, -n** language (1W)

-sprachig -speaking

sprechen (spricht), sprach, gesprochen to speak (S3); ~ **Sie lauter!** Speak louder (S3); **Man spricht . . .** They (people) speak . . .; ~ **von** to speak about (10G); **Ist . . . zu ~?** May I speak to . . . ?

der **Sprecher, -** speaker

die **Sprech'situation, -en** (situation for) communication

das **Sprichwort, ¨er** saying, proverb

springen, sprang, ist gesprungen to jump (11E)

das **Spritzgebäck** cookies shaped with a cookie press

der **Spruch, ¨e** saying

die **Spülmaschine, -n** dishwasher

der **Staat, -en** state (15W)

der **Staatenbund** confederation

staatlich public

die **Staatsangehörigkeit** citizenship

der **Staatssicherheitsdienst = die Stasi** GDR secret police

die **Staatsbürger, -** citizen

die **Stadt, ¨e** city, town (1W)

das **Stadtbild, -er** overall appearance of a city

das **Städtchen, -** small town

der **Stadtplan, ¨e** city map (5W)

der **Stammbaum, ¨e** family tree

stammen (aus + dat.) to stem (from), originate

stampfen to stomp

der **Standard, -s** standard

das **Standesamt, ¨er** marriage registrar

stark (ä) strong

die **Station', -en** (bus) stop

die **Stati'stik, -en** statistic

statt (+ gen.) instead of (8G)

der **Stau, -s** traffic jam

staunen to be amazed

stechen (sticht), stach, gestochen to prick

der **Stechschritt** goosestep

stehen, stand, gestanden to stand (or be standing) (6W); **Wie steht der Dollar?** What's the exchange rate of the dollar? (7W)

stehen·bleiben* to come to a stop, remain standing

stehlen (stiehlt), stahl, gestohlen to steal

steif stiff

steigen, stieg, ist gestiegen to go up, rise, climb

steigern to increase

steil steep

der **Stein, -e** stone

die **Stelle, n** job, position, place (12W); **an deiner ~** in your shoes, if I were you (13E)

stellen to stand (upright), put (6W); **eine Frage ~** to ask a question (15E)

sterben (stirbt), starb, ist gestorben to die

der **Stern, -e** star

die **Stereoanlage, -n** stereo set

die **Steuer, -n** tax

der **Steuerberater, -** tax preparer

Stief-: die ~eltern stepparents; **die ~mutter** stepmother; **der ~vater** stepfather

der **Stier, -e** bull

der **Stil, -e** style

still quiet

die **Stimme, -n** voice

stimmen: (Das) stimmt. (That's) true. (That's) right. (6W)

das **Stipen'dium, Stipen'dien** scholarship (13W)

der **Stock, -werke: im ersten ~** on the second floor (6W)

der **Stollen, -** Christmas cake/bread with almonds, raisins, and candied peel

stolz (auf + acc.) proud (of) (15E)

das **Stopschild, -er** stop sign

der **Storch, ¨e** stork

stören to bother, disturb

der **Strafzettel, -** (traffic violation) ticket

die **Straße, -n** street (5W)

die **Straßenbahn, -en** streetcar (5W)

strate'gisch strategic

der **Strauch, ¨er** bush

der **Stre'ber, -** one who studies excessively, grind

der **Streifen, -** strip of land

streng strict(ly)

der **Streß** stress; **zu viel ~** too much stress

das **Stroh** straw (11E)

der **Strom** electricity

die **Strophe, -n** stanza

die **Struktur', -en** structure; *here:* grammar

der **Strumpf, ¨e** stocking

das **Stück, -e,** piece; **ein ~** a piece of (2W); **zwei ~** two pieces of (2W); (theater) play (10W)

der **Student', -en, -en / die Studen'tin, -nen** student (S6)

das **Studentenheim, -e** dorm (6W)

die **Studiengebühr, -en** tuition

der **Studienplatz, ¨e** opening to study at the university

studie'ren to study a particular field; ~ **(an + dat.)** to be a student at a university (4E)

der **Studie'rende (ein Studierender)** student

das **Studium, Studien** course of study (13W)

der **Stuhl, ¨e** chair (S2,5W)

die **Stunde, -n** hour, class lesson (S6); **in einer halben ~** in half an hour (8W); **in einer Viertel~** in 15 minutes (8W); **in einer Dreiviertel~** in 45 minutes (8W)

stundenlang for hours (5E)

der **Stundenplan, ¨e** schedule (of classes)

das **Subjekt', -e** subject

die **Suche** search

suchen to look for (2W); **gesucht wird** wanted

der **Süden: im ~** in the south (1W)

südlich (von) south (of), to the south (of) (1W)

super superb, terrific (S5)

der **Su'perlativ, -e** superlative

der **Supermarkt, ¨e** supermarket (2W)

su'permodern' very modern

die **Suppe, -n** soup (3W)
süß sweet
das **Sweatshirt, -s** sweatshirt (S3)
das **Symbol', -e** symbol
die **Sympathie'** congeniality
sympa'thisch congenial, likable (11W)
die **Symphonie', -n** symphony
synchronisiert' dubbed
die **Synthe'tik** synthetics
das **System', -e** system (13W)
die **Szene, -n** scene

T

die **Tablet'te, -n** pill
die **Tafel, -n** (black)board (S2);
Gehen Sie an die ~! Go to the (black)board. (S3)
der **Tag, -e** day (S5); **~!** Hi (informal)! **am ~** during the day (6E); **eines Tages** (gen.) one day (8G); **Guten ~!** Hello. (S1); **jeden ~** every day (8G); **~ der Arbeit** Labor Day
tagelang for days
-tägig days long
täglich daily (10E)
das **Tal, ⸚er** valley
das **Talent', -e** talent
talentiert' talented (11W)
die **Tante, -n** aunt (1W)
der **Tanz, ⸚e** dance
tanzen to dance (4W)
die **Tasche, -n** bag, pocket (7W); handbag
die **Tasse, -n** cup (2E); **eine ~** a cup of (2E)
die **Tatsache, -n** fact
tauchen (in + acc.) to dip (into)
tauschen to trade
das **Taxi, -s** taxi (5W)
der **Techniker, -** technician
technisch technical
der **Tee, -s** tea (2W)
der **Teenager, -** teenager
der **Teil, -e** part (1E)
teilen to share (13E); to divide (14W)
teilmöbliert partly furnished
die **Teilnahme** participation
teil·nehmen* (**an** + dat.) to participate (in), take part (in) (13E)
teils partly

die **Teilung, -en** division
das **Telefon', -e** telephone (6W); **die ~karte, -n** telephone card (8W); **die ~nummer, -n** telephone number (8W); **die ~zelle, -n** telephone booth
telefonie'ren to call up, phone (8W)
der **Teller, -** plate (3W)
das **Temperament', -e** temperament
temperament'voll dynamic (11W)
die **Temperatur', -en** temperature
das **Tennis: ~ spielen** to play tennis (S6)
der **Teppich, -e** carpet (6W)
die **Terras'se, -n** terrace
das **Testament', -e** last will and testament
teuer expensive (S3)
der **Teufel, -** devil
der **Text, -e** text
das **Thea'ter, -** theater (5W)
das **Thema, Themen** topic
der **Theolo'ge, -n, -n** theologian
die **Theologie'** theology
die **Theorie', -n** theory
das **Thermome'ter, -** thermometer
der **Tiefbau** civil engineering
die **Tiefkühlkost** frozen foods
das **Tier, -e** animal; **die ~art, -en** animal species
tierlieb fond of animals
das **Tierkreiszeichen, -** sign of the zodiac
der **Tiger, -** tiger
das **Tintenfaß, ⸚sser** inkwell
der **Tip, -s** hint
der **Tisch, -e** table (S2,5W); **Nacht~** nightstand
die **Tischdecke, -n** tablecloth
der **Tischler, -** cabinet-maker
das **Tischtennis: ~ spielen** to play ping-pong
der **Titel, -** title
tja well
der **Toast, -s** toast
die **Tochter, ⸚** daughter (1W)
der **Tod** death
Toi, toi, toi! Good luck!
die **Toilet'te, -n** toilet (6W)
tolerant' tolerant
toll great, terrific (S5)
die **Toma'te, -n** tomato (2W)
der **Ton, ⸚e** tone, note, pitch
der **Topf, ⸚e** pot

das **Tor, -e** gate
die **Torte, -n** (fancy) cake
tot dead
total' total
der **Total'schaden, ⸚** total wreck
töten to kill
die **Tour, -en** tour
der **Touris'mus** tourism
der **Tourist', -en, -en** tourist (5W)
der **Touri'stikumsatz** spending on travel
das **Tournier, -e** tournament
die **Tracht, -en** (folk) costume
traditionell' traditional(ly)
tragen (trägt), trug, getragen to carry (3G); to wear (3G)
die **Tragetasche, -n** tote bag
der **Trainer, -** coach
das **Training** training
das **Transport'flugzeug, -e** transport plane
transportie'ren to transport
trauen to trust
der **Traum, ⸚e** dream
träumen (von) to dream (of) (11W)
der **Träumer, -** dreamer
traurig sad (10W)
die **Traurigkeit** sadness
die **Trauung, -en** wedding ceremony
(sich) **treffen (trifft), traf, getroffen** to meet
das **Treffen, -** meeting, reunion
treiben, trieb, getrieben to push
die **Treppe, -n** stairs, stairway
treten (tritt), trat, ist getreten to step
treu faithful, true, loyal
sich trimmen to keep fit
trinken, trank, getrunken to drink (2W)
das **Trinkgeld, -er** tip
der **Trockner, -** dryer
die **Trommel, -n** drum
die **Trompe'te, -n** trumpet
trotz (+ gen.) in spite of (8G)
trotzdem nevertheless, in spite of that (6E)
der **Tscheche, -n, -n** / die **Tschechin, -nen** the Czech
die **Tschechische Republik'** = **Tschechei'** (or [das] **Tschechien**) Czech Republic
die **Tschechoslowakei'** (former) Czechoslovakia

tschechisch Czech

Tschüß! So long; (Good-)bye! (S1)

das **T-Shirt, -s** T-shirt (S3)

tun (tut), tat, getan to do (4W)

die **Tür, -en** door (S2)

der **Türke, -n, -n / die Türkin, -nen** the Turk

die **Türkei'** Turkey

türkisch Turkish

der **Turm, ˸e** tower (14W); steeple

turnen to do sports *or* gymnastics

typisch typical(ly) (15E)

U

die **U-Bahn, -en** subway (5W)

über (+ *acc. / dat.*) over, above (6G); about (10G)

überall everywhere (3E)

überein'·stimmen to agree

überfüllt' overcrowded

das **Überhol'verbot, -e** no passing

überle'ben to survive

übermorgen the day after tomorrow (4W)

übernach'ten to spend the night (7E)

überra'schen to surprise (4W)

die **Überra'schung, -en** surprise (4W)

überset'zen to translate

die **Überset'zung, -en** translation

üblich usual, customary

übrigens by the way; **die übrigen** the rest

die **Übung, -en** exercise, practice

das **Ufer, -** riverbank

die **Uhr, -en** watch, clock; o'clock (S6); **Wieviel ~ ist es?** What time is it? (S6); **~zeit** time of the day (7W)

der **Uhrmacher, -** watchmaker

um (+ *acc.*) around (the circumference) (2G); at . . . o'clock (S6); **~ . . . zu** in order to (9G); **fast ~** almost over

umge'ben (von) surrounded by

die **Umge'bung** (*sg.*) surroundings (14W)

umgekehrt vice versa

(um·)kippen (ist) to tip over

umliegend surrounding

ummau'ert surrounded by a wall

der **Umsatz** sales, spending

sich **um·sehen*** to look around

der **Umstand, ˸e** circumstance

um·steigen* (ist) to change (trains etc.) (8W)

der **Umtausch** exchange

um·tauschen to exchange

die **Umwelt** environment, surroundings (15W)

sich **um·ziehen*** to change (clothing), get changed (9G)

der **Umzug, ˸e** parade; move, moving

unabhängig (von) independent (of)

un'attraktiv' unattractive

unbebaut vacant, empty

unbedingt definitely (12E)

unbegrenzt unlimited

unbequem uncomfortable, inconvenient (6W)

und and (S1,2G)

und so weiter (usw.) and so on (etc.)

unehrlich dishonest (11W)

der **Unfall, ˸e** accident

unfreiwillig involuntary

unfreundlich unfriendly (11W)

der **Ungar, -n, -n** the Hungarian

ungarisch Hungarian

(das) **Ungarn** Hungary

ungebildet uneducated (11W)

ungeduldig impatient (11W)

ungefähr about, approximately (1E)

ungemütlich unpleasant, uncomfortable

ungestört unhindered

unglaublich inbelievable, incredible

das **Unglück** bad luck

unglücklich unhappy (11W)

die **Uni, -s** (*abbrev.*) university (5W)

die **Universität', -en** university (5W)

unmöbliert unfurnished

unmöglich impossible

unmusikalisch unmusical (11W)

unrecht haben* to be wrong (11W)

uns us, to us (5G); **bei ~** at our place (3G); in our city/country

unselbständig dependent (11W)

unser our (7G)

unsicher insecure, unsafe (12W)

der **Unsinn** nonsense

unsportlich unathletic (11W)

unsympathisch uncongenial, unlikable (11W)

untalentiert untalented (11W)

unten downstairs (6W)

unter (+ *acc. / dat.*) under, below (6G); among (12E); **~einander** among each other

der **Untergang** fall, downfall

die **Unterhal'tung** entertainment (10W)

das **Unterneh'men, -** large company (12W)

unterneh'mungslustig enterprising (11W)

der **Unterricht** instruction, lesson, class

der **Unterschied, -e** difference

unterschrei'ben* to sign (7W)

die **Unterschrift, -en** signature

unterstüt'zen to support

unterwegs' on the go, on the road

untreu unfaithful

unverheiratet unmarried, single (11W)

die **Unwahrscheinlichkeit** *here:* unreal condition

unzerstört intact

unzufrieden discontent

Urgroß-: die ~eltern great-grandparents; **die ~mutter** great-grandmother; **der ~vater** great-grandfather

der **Urlaub** paid vacation; **der Mutterschafts~** maternity leave

ursprünglich original(ly)

die **USA (Vereinigten Staaten von Amerika)** (*pl.*) USA

u.s.w. (und so weiter) etc. (and so on)

V

der **Vampir', -e** vampire

die **Vanil'le** vanilla

die **Variation', -en** variation

variie'ren to vary

die **Vase, -n** vase

der **Vater, ˸** father (1W); **Groß~** grandfather (1W); **Urgroß~** great-grandfather; **Stief~** step-father

der **Vati, -s** Dad

verallgemei'nern to generalize

die **Verallgemei'nerung, -en** generalization

(sich) **verändern** to change (15W)
verantwortlich responsible
die **Verantwortung, -en** responsibility
verantwortungsvoll responsible
das **Verb, -en** verb
verbannen to ban
verbessern to improve
verbieten, verbot, verboten to forbid, prohibit (15W)
verbinden, verband, verbunden to link, connect, combine, tie together
das **Verbot, -e** restriction
verboten forbidden (15W)
der **Verbrauch** consumption
der **Verbraucher, -** consumer
verbreiten to distribute, spread
die **Verbreitung, -en** distribution
verbrennen, verbrannte, verbrannt to burn
verbunden in touch, close
die **Verbundenheit** closeness
verdammen to curse
verderben (verdirbt), verdarb, verdorben to spoil
verdienen to deserve; earn; make money (12W)
der **Verein, -e** club, association; **Turn~** athletic club
die **Vereinigten Staaten (U.S.A.)** (pl.) United States (U.S.)
die **Vereinigung** unification (15E)
vereint united (15E)
das **Verfassungsgericht** Constitutional Court
Verflix! Darn it!
die **Vergangenheit** past; simple past
vergehen* (ist) to pass (time), end
vergessen (vergißt), vergaß, vergessen to forget (11W)
der **Vergleich, -e** comparison
vergleichen, verglich, verglichen to compare
das **Verhältnis, -se** relationship, condition
verheiratet married (11W)
verhindern to prevent
die **Verkabelung** connecting by cable
verkaufen to sell (2W)
der **Verkäufer, -** salesman, sales clerk (12W)
der **Verkehr** traffic
das **Verkehrsmittel, -** means of transportation

der **Verlag, -e** publishing house
verlassen (verläßt), verließ, verlassen to leave (behind) (14E)
sich **verlaufen*** to get lost
verlegen to transfer, relocate
sich **verlieben (in + acc.)** to fall in love (with) (11W)
verliebt (in + acc.) in love (with) (11W)
verlieren, verlor, verloren (an + dat.) to lose (in) (11W)
sich **verloben (mit)** to get engaged (to)
verlobt (mit) engaged (to) (11W)
die **Verlobung, -en** engagement
verlockend tempting
vermieten to rent out (6W)
der **Vermieter, -** landlord
verneinen to negate
die **Vernichtung** destruction
verrückt crazy (4E)
verschenken to give away
verschieden various, different (kinds of) (10E)
verschlechtern to deteriorate
verschlingen, verschlang, verschlungen to gulp down, devour
die **Verschmutzung** pollution
verschönern to beautify
versinken* to sink (in)
die **Verspätung** delay; **Der Zug hat ~.** The train is late.
versprechen* to promise (11E)
der **Verstand** reasoning, logic
verständlich understandable
verständnisvoll understanding (11W)
verstecken to hide
verstehen* (hat) to understand (S3)
versuchen to try (11W)
die **Verteidigung** defense
der **Vertrag, ⸚e** contract
vertraulich confidential
die **Verwaltung, -en** administration
der **Verwandte (ein Verwandter)** relative
verwitwet widowed
verwöhnen to indulge, spoil
das **Verzeichnis, -se** index, catalog
verzeihen, verzieh, verziehen to forgive; **~ Sie (mir)!** Forgive me. Pardon (me)!

die **Verzeihung** pardon; **~!** Excuse me! Pardon me! (5W)
der **Vetter, -n** cousin (1W)
der **Videorecorder, -** VCR
viel- (mehr, meist-) much, many (3W,10G,12G); **ganz schön ~** quite at bit
vielleicht' perhaps (3E)
vielseitig versatile (11W)
viereckig square
das **Viertel, -:** **(um) ~ nach** (at) a quarter past (S6); **(um) ~ vor** (at) a quarter to (S6); **in einer ~stunde** in a quarter of an hour (8W); **in einer Dreiviertelstunde** in three quarters of an hour (8W)
die **Vision', -en** vision
vital' vital
der **Vogel, ⸚** bird; **Du hast einen ~.** You're crazy.
die **Voka'bel, -n** (vocabulary) word
das **Vokabular'** vocabulary
das **Volk, ⸚er** folk; people, nation (14W)
die **Völkerkunde** ethnology
die **Volksherrschaft** here: domination by the people
das **Volkslied, -er** folk song
der **Volksstamm, ⸚e** ethnic group
der **Volkswagen, -** VW
die **Volkswirtschaft** (macro)economics
voll full (11E)
der **Volleyball, ⸚e** volleyball
von (+ dat.) of, from, by (3G); **~ ... bis** from ... until (S4); **vom ... bis zum** from the ... to the (4W)
vor (+ acc. / dat.) in front of, before (6G); **~ einer Woche** a week ago (4W); **~ allem** above all, mainly (10E)
voran'·kommen* to advance
vorbei'·bringen* to bring over
vorbei'·fahren* to drive by, pass
vorbei'·gehen* (bei + dat.) to pass by (7G)
vorbei·kommen* to come by, pass by
vorbei sein* to be over, finished
(sich) **vor·bereiten (auf + acc.)** to prepare (for) (13E)
die **Vorbereitung, -en** preparation
die **Vorbeugung, -en** prevention

die **Vorfahrt** right of way

vor·gehen* to proceed; **der Reihe nach ~** to proceed one after the other

vorgestern the day before yesterday (4W)

vor·haben* to plan (to), intend (to)

der **Vorhang, ⁔e** curtain (6W)

vorher ahead (of time), in advance, before

vor·kommen* (in) to appear (in); **Das kommt mir ... vor.** That seems ... to me.

die **Vorlesung, -en** lecture, class (university) (S6); **~sverzeichnis, -se** course catalog

vormittag: heute ~ this (mid)-morning (8G)

der **Vorname, -ns, -n** first name

die **Vorschau** preview

die **Vorsicht: ~!** Careful! (7E)

vor·stellen: Darf ich ~? May I introduce?

sich **vor·stellen** to imagine (12E); **ich stelle mir vor, daß** I imagine that (12E)

die **Vorstellung, -en** performance (10W); idea

der **Vorteil, -e** advantage

der **Vortrag, ⁔e** talk, speech, lecture

vorüb′ergehend temporary

vor·wärmen to preheat

vor·ziehen* to prefer (9E)

W

das **Wachs** wax

wachsen (wächst), wuchs, ist gewachsen to grow; **zusammen·~** to grow together (15W)

die **Waffe, -n** weapon

die **Waffel,-n** waffel

wagen to dare

der **Wagen, -** car (8W); railroad car (8W)

die **Wahl** choice, selection

wählen to choose; elect; select

das **Wahlfach, ⁔er** elective (subject)

der **Wahnsinn** insanity; **Das ist ja ~!** That's crazy.

wahnsinnig crazy

während (+ *gen.*) during (8G); while *(conj.)*

wahr true; **nicht ~?** isn't it? (S5)

wahrschein′lich probably (12E)

die **Währung, -en** currency

der **Wald, ⁔er** forest, woods (6E)

der **Walzer, -** waltz

die **Wand, ⁔e** wall (S2)

der **Wanderer, -** hiker

wandern (ist) to hike (9W)

der **Wanderweg, -e** hiking trail

wann? when?, at what time? (S5,11G)

wäre: Wie wär's mit ... ? How about ... ?

die **Ware, -n** goods, wares, merchandise

warm (ä) warm (S5)

die **Wärme** warmth

warnen (vor) to warn (against)

warten to wait; **~ auf** (+ *acc.*) to wait for (10G)

warum? why? (2E)

was? what? (S2,2G); **~ für (ein)?** what kind of (a)? (2W)

das **Waschbecken, -** sink

die **Wäsche** laundry

die **Waschecke, -n** corner reserved for washing

(sich) **waschen (wäscht), wusch, gewaschen** to wash (o.s.) (9G)

der **Waschlappen, -** washcloth (*fig.* wimp)

die **Waschmaschi′ne, -n** washing machine

das **Wasser** water (2W)

der **Wassermann, ⁔er** Aquarius

Wasserski laufen* to water ski

der **Wechsel** change

der **Wechselkurs, -e** exchange rate

wechseln to (ex)change (7W)

die **Wechselstube, -n** exchange office

weder ... noch neither ... nor (10E)

weg away, gone

der **Weg, -e** way, path, trail (5W); route; **nach dem ~ fragen** to ask for directions

wegen (+ *gen.*) because of (8G)

weh tun* to hurt; **Mir tut (der Hals) weh.** My (throat) hurts. I have a sore throat. (9W)

weich soft

die **Weide, -n** willow

(das) **Weihnachten: zu ~** at / for Christmas (4W); **Fröhliche ~!** Merry Christmas!

der **Weihnachtsbaum, ⁔e** Christmas tree

das **Weihnachtslied, -er** Christmas carol

der **Weihnachtsmann, ⁔er** Santa Claus

weil *(conj.)* because (4G)

die **Weile: eine ~** for a while

der **Wein, -e** wine (2W); **Tafel~** table wine; **Qualitäts~** quality wine; **Qualitäts~ mit Prädikat** superior wine

der **Weinberg, -e** vineyard

weinen to cry (10W)

die **Weinstube, -n** wine cellar, tavern

weise wise

die **Weise: auf diese ~** (in) this way (11W)

weiß white (S2)

weit far (5W)

die **Weite** distance; wide-open spaces

weiter: und so ~ (usw.) and so on (etc.): **~ draußen** farther out; **Wie geht's ~?** How does it go on?

Weiteres additional words and phrases

weiter·fahren* (ist) to drive on (8E); continue the trip

weiter·geben* to pass on

weiter·gehen* (ist) to continue, go on

welch- which (7G); **Welche Farbe hat ... ?** What color is ... ? (S2)

die **Welle, -n** wave

die **Welt, -en** world (11E)

weltoffen cosmopolitan

wem? (to) whom? (3G)

wen? whom? (2G)

wenig- little (not much), few (10G)

wenigstens at least

wenn *(conj.)* if, (when)ever (4G,11G); **selbst ~** even if

wer? who? (1G); who(so)ever

die **Werbung** advertisement (10W)

werden (wird), wurde, ist geworden to become, get (3G); **Was willst du ~?**

What do you want to be?
(12W); **Ich will . . . ~.** I want
to be a . . . (12W)

**werfen, (wirft), warf, gewor-
fen** to throw

der **Wert, -e** value

wertvoll valuable

wessen? (+ *gen.*) whose? (8G)

der **Westen: im ~** in the west (1W)

westlich von west of

der **Wettbewerb, -e** contest

das **Wetter** weather (S5)

wichtig important (1E)

wickeln to wrap

widersteh′en* (+ *dat.*) to
withstand

wie? how? (S1); like, as; **~
bitte?** What did you say?
Could you say that again?
(S3); **so . . . ~** as . . . as (1E);
~ lange? how long? (4W);
~ gesagt as I (you, etc.) said

wieder again (S5); **immer ~**
again and again, time and
again (12G); **Da sieht man's
mal ~!** That just goes to
show you. (15W)

der **Wiederaufbau** rebuilding

wieder·erkennen* to recognize again

wiederho′len to repeat (S2)

die **Wiederho′lung, -en** repetition,
review

**wieder·hören: Auf Wieder-
hören!** Good-bye. *(on the
phone)* (6W)

**wieder·sehen*: Auf Wiederse-
hen!** Good-bye (S1)

die **Wiedervereinigung** reunification (14E)

wiegen, wog, gewogen to
weigh; **Laß es ~!** Have it
weighed.

der **Wiener, -** the Viennese

die **Wiese, -n** meadow

Wieso′ (denn)? How come?
Why? (13W)

wieviel? how much? (3W);
**Den wievielten haben wir
. . . ?** What is the date . . . ?
(4W)

wie viele? how many? (3W)

wild wild

der **Wille, -ns, -n** will; **Wo ein ~
ist, ist auch ein Weg.**
Where there's a will, there's
a way. (15W)

der **Wind, -e** wind

---

der **Winter, -** winter (S5); **im ~** in
(the) winter (S5)

das **Winzerfest, -e** vintage festival

wirken to appear

wirklich really, indeed (S5)

die **Wirklichkeit** reality

die **Wirtschaft** economy (15E)

wirtschaftlich economical(ly)
(15E)

der **Wirtschaftsprüfer, -** accountant

das **Wirtschaftswunder** economic
boom (literally: miracle)

wissen (weiß), wußte, gewußt
to know (a fact) (6G); **Ich
weiß nicht.** I don't know.
(S3); **soviel ich weiß** as far
as I know

die **Wissenschaft, -en** science, academic discipline (13W);
Natur~ natural science(s)
(13W)

der **Wissenschaftler, -** scientist
(12W)

der **Witz, -e** joke; **Mach (doch)
keine Witze!** Stop joking!

witzig witty, funny

wo? where? (S2,6G)

die **Woche, -n** week (S5)

das **Wochenende, -n** weekend;
am ~ on the weekend
(4W)

wochenlang for weeks

wöchentlich weekly (10E)

-wöchig weeks long

woher′? from where? (1W)

wohin′? where to? (6G)

wohl *flavoring particle expressing probability*

wohlriechend fragrant

die **Wohngemeinschaft, -en** group
sharing a place to live

wohnen to live, reside (1E)

das **Wohnsilo, -s** (high-rise) apartment (cluster)

der **Wohnsitz, -e** residence

die **Wohnung, -en** apartment (6W)

der **Wohnwagen, -** camper

das **Wohnzimmer, -** living room
(6W)

der **Wolf, ¨e** wolf

die **Wolke, -n** cloud

die **Wolle** wool

wollen (will), wollte, gewollt
to want to (5G)

das **Wort, -e** (connected) word;
mit anderen Worten in
other words

---

das **Wort, ¨er** (individual) word

das **Wörtchen. -** little word

das **Wörterbuch, ¨er** dictionary

der **Wortschatz** vocabulary

das **Wunder, -** wonder, miracle

wunderbar wonderful(ly) (S1)

sich **wundern: ~ Sie sich nicht!**
Don't be surprised.

wunderschön beautiful (14W)

der **Wunsch, ¨e** wish (11W);
~traum, ¨e ideal dream

(sich) **wünschen** to wish (4W)

die **Wunschwelt** ideal world

die **Wurst, ¨e** sausage (2W); **Das
ist doch ~!** It doesn't matter.

das **Würstchen, -** wiener, hot dog
(2E)

würzen to season

Z

die **Zahl, -en** number (S4)

zählen to count (S4)

der **Zahn, ¨e** tooth (9W); **sich die
Zähne putzen** to brush
one's teeth (9G)

der **Zahnarzt, ¨e / die Zahnärztin,
-nen** dentist (12W)

die **Zahnbürste, -n** toothbrush

die **Zahn′medizin′** dentistry

die **Zahnpaste, -n** toothpaste

die **Zahnradbahn, -en** cog railway

der **Zahntechniker,-** dental technician

zart tender

zärtlich affectionate (11W)

die **Zärtlichkeit** affection

der **Zauberspruch, ¨e** magic spell

z.B. (zum Beispiel) e.g. (for
example)

das **Zeichen, -** signal, sign

der **Zeichentrickfilm, -e** cartoon,
animated film

die **Zeichnung, -en** drawing

zeigen to show (5W); **Zeig
mal!** Show me (us, etc.)!

die **Zeit, -en** time (S6); tense; **die
gute alte ~** the good old
days

die **Zeitschrift, -en** magazine
(10W)

die **Zeitung, -en** newspaper
(10W); **Wochen~** weekly
newspaper

die **Zelle, -n** cell, booth

das **Zelt, -e** tent

zentral′ central(ly)

das **Zentrum, Zentren** center; **im
~** downtown

zerbomben to destroy by bombs

zerstören to destroy (15W)

die **Zerstörung** destruction

ziehen, zog, gezogen to pull (11E); to raise (vegetables, etc.); to move

ziehen, zog, ist gezogen to move (relocate)

das **Ziel, -e** goal, objective; destination

ziemlich quite, fairly (6W)

die **Zigeu'nerin, -nen** gypsy

das **Zimmer, -** room (S2)

der **Zim'merkolle'ge, -n, -n** / die **Zimmerkolle'gin, -nen** roommate (13W)

der **Zimmernachweis, -e** room-referral service

das **Zitat', -e** quote

die **Zitro'ne, -n** lemon (2W)

der **Zoll** customs; toll

die **Zone, -n** zone, area

der **Zoo, -s** zoo

zu (+ *dat.*) to, in the direction of, at, for (purpose) (3G); too (S3); closed (2); (+ *inf.*) to (9G)

zu·bleiben* (ist) to stay closed

der **Zucker** sugar (3W)

zuerst' (at) first (12E)

der **Zufall, ⁻e** coincidence; **So ein ~!** What a coincidence!

zufrie'den satisfied, content

der **Zug, ⁻e** train (8W); **mit dem ~ fahren*** to go by train (8W)

zu·halten* to hold closed

zu·hören to listen (7G); **Hören Sie gut zu!** Listen well.

die **Zukunft** future (12W)

zu·machen to close (7G)

zurück'- back

zurück'·bleiben* (ist) to stay behind

zurück'·bringen* to bring back

zurück'·fliegen* (ist) to fly back

zurück'·geben* to give back, return

zurück'·halten* to hold back

zurück'·kommen* (ist) to come back, return (7G)

zurück'·nehmen* to take back

zurück'·sehen* to look back

sich **zurück'·ziehen*** to withdraw

zusam'men together (2W); **alle ~** all together; **~gewürfelt** thrown together

zusam'men·fassen to summarize

die **Zusam'menfassung, -en** summary

die **Zusam'mengehörigkeit** affiliation; solidarity

zusammen·wachsen* to grow together (15E)

zu·schließen* to lock

zu·sehen* to watch; see to it

der **Zustand, ⁻e** conditions

zu·stimmen to agree

zuvor' previously; **wie nie ~** as never before

zwischen (+ *acc. / dat.*) between (6G); **~durch** in between

die **Zwischenlandung, -en** stopover

die **Zwischenzeit** time in between

ENGLISH-GERMAN

Except for numbers, pronouns, **da-** and **wo**-compounds, this vocabulary includes all active words used in this book. If you are looking for certain idioms, feminine equivalents, or other closely related words, look at the key word given and then check it in the German-English vocabulary. Irregular t-verbs ("irregular weak verbs") and n-verbs ("strong verbs") are indicated by an asterisk (*); check their forms and auxiliaries in the list of principal parts in the Appendix, Part 7.

A

able; to be ~ können*
about (approximately) ungefähr
above über (+ *dat. / acc.*); **~ all** vor allem
abroad im/ins Ausland
academic discipline die Wissenschaft, -en
to **accept** an·nehmen*
ache: I have a (head)~. Ich habe (Kopf)schmerzen.
acquaintance der Bekannte (ein Bekannter)
across (from) gegenüber (von + *dat.*)
actor der Schauspieler, -
actual(ly) eigentlich
address die Adresse, -n; **return ~** der Absender, -
advertising die Werbung
affectionate zärtlich
afraid: to be ~ (of) Angst haben* (vor)
after (time) nach (+ *dat.*); **~ (+ *past perf.*)** nachdem
afternoon der Nachmittag, nachmittag; **in the ~** nachmittags
afterward danach
again wieder, noch einmal; **Could you say that ~?** Wie bitte?; **~ and ~** immer wieder
against gegen (+ *acc.*)
ago vor (+ *dat.*); **a week ~** vor einer Woche
ahead: straight ~ geradeaus
aid die Hilfe
air die Luft
airplane das Flugzeug, -e
airport der Flughafen, ⸚
all all-, alles *(sg.)*; **That's ~.** Das ist alles.
to **allow** erlauben
allowed: to be ~ to dürfen*

almost fast
already schon
also auch
although *(conj.)* obwohl
always immer
America (das) Amerika
American *(adj.)* amerikanisch; **(person)** der Amerikaner, -
among unter (+ *acc. / dat.*)
and und
angry: to get ~ about sich ärgern über (+ *acc.*)
another noch ein
to **answer** antworten
answer die Antwort, -en
anyhow sowieso
anyway sowieso
apart auseinander
apartment die Wohnung, -en
to **appear (to be)** scheinen*
to **applaud** klatschen
apple der Apfel, ⸚
to **apply** sich bewerben (um)
approximately ungefähr
April der April; **in ~** im April
area die Gegend, -en
arm der Arm,-e
armchair der Sessel, -
around um (+ *acc.*)
arrival die Ankunft
to **arrive (in)** an·kommen* (in + *dat.*)
art die Kunst, ⸚e
as wie; **~ . . . ~** so . . . wie
to **ask** fragen, bitten*; **to ~ a question** eine Frage stellen
at an (+ *dat.*); **(o'clock)** um . . . (Uhr); **(the place of)** bei (+ *dat.*)
athletic sportlich; **un~** unsportlich
attention: to pay ~ auf·passen
attractive attraktiv, hübsch
August der August; **in ~** im August
aunt die Tante, -n
Austria (das) Österreich

Austrian (person) der Österreicher, -
author der Autor, -en
available frei

B

bad(ly) schlecht; schlimm; **too ~** schade
bag die Tasche, -n
baggage das Gepäck
bakery die Bäckerei, -en
balcony der Balkon, -e (*or* -s)
banana die Banane, -n
bank die Bank, -en
bath(room) das Bad, ⸚er; **to take a ~** sich baden
to **be** sein*; **(become)** werden*; **Be . . . !** Sei (Seid, Seien Sie) . . . !
bean die Bohne, -n
beautiful (wunder)schön
because *(conj.)* weil, denn; **~ of** wegen (+ *gen.*)
to **become** werden*
bed das Bett, -en; **~room** das Schlafzimmer, -
beer das Bier
before vor (+ *acc. / dat.*); *(conj.)* bevor; **not ~ (time)** erst; *(adv.)* vorher
to **begin** beginnen*, an·fangen*
beginning der Anfang, ⸚e; **in the ~** am Anfang
behind hinter (+ *acc. / dat.*)
to **believe (in)** glauben (an + *acc.*); **(things)** Ich glaube es.; **(persons)** Ich glaube ihm / ihr.
belly der Bauch, ⸚e
to **belong to** gehören (+ *dat.*)
below unter (+ *acc. / dat.*)
beside neben (+ *acc. / dat.*)
besides *(adv.)* außerdem
best best-, am besten
better besser
between zwischen (+ *acc. / dat.*)

bicycle das Fahrrad, ⸚er

to **bicycle** mit dem Fahrrad fahren*

big groß (ö)

bill die Rechnung, -en

billion (American) die Milliarde, -n

birthday der Geburtstag, -e; **on / for** ~ zum Geburtstag

bit: a little ~ ein bißchen

black schwarz (ä)

blackboard die Tafel, -n

blouse die Bluse, -n

blue blau

boarding house die Pension, -en

body der Körper, -

book das Buch, ⸚er

bookstore die Buchhandlung, -en

border die Grenze, -n

bored; to get (or be) ~ sich langweilen

boring langweilig

born geboren (ist); **I was** ~ **May 3, 1968, in Munich.** Ich bin am 3.5.68 in München geboren.

both (things, sg.) beides; (pl.) beide

bottle die Flasche, -n; **a** ~ **of . . .** eine Flasche . . .

boy der Junge, -n, -n

bread das Brot,- e

break (intermission) die Pause, -n

breakfast das Frühstück; **(What's) for ~?** (Was gibt's) zum Frühstück?

bridge die Brücke, -n

bright (light) hell

to **bring** bringen*; **to ~ along** mit·bringen*

brother der Bruder, ⸚

brown braun

to **brush (one's teeth)** sich (die Zähne) putzen

to **build** bauen; **to re~** wieder-auf·bauen; **to be built** entstehen*

building das Gebäude, -

bus der Bus, -se

business das Geschäft, -e

businessman der Geschäftsmann, -leute

businesswoman die Geschäftsfrau, -en

but aber; doch; **not only . . . ~ also** nicht nur . . . sondern auch

butter die Butter

to **buy** kaufen

by von (+ dat.)

C

café das Café, -s

cafeteria (student) die Mensa

cake der Kuchen, -

to **call** rufen*; **to ~ (up)** an·rufen*, telefonieren; **to ~ (name)** nennen*; **to be called** heißen*

campground der Campingplatz, ⸚e

can können*

Canada (das) Kanada

Canadian (adj.) kanadisch; **(person)** der Kanadier, -

candle die Kerze, -n

capital die Hauptstadt, ⸚e

car das Auto, -s, der Wagen,-; **(railroad ~)** der Wagen, -

card die Karte, -n; **post~** die Postkarte, -n

cardigan die Jacke, -n

to **care: Take ~!** Mach's gut!

Careful! Vorsicht!

carpet der Teppich, -e

carrot die Karotte, -n

to **carry** tragen*

case: in any ~ jedenfalls

cash das Bargeld; ~ **register** die Kasse, -n

to **cash (in) (a check)** ein·lösen

cassette die Kassette, -n

cathedral der Dom, -e

to **celebrate** feiern

celebration das Fest, -e

center die Mitte

certain(ly) bestimmt

chair der Stuhl, ⸚e; **arm~** der Sessel, -

chalk die Kreide

champagne der Sekt

change das Kleingeld

to **change** (sich) verändern; **(clothing)** sich um·ziehen*; **(money, etc.)** wechseln, um·tauschen; **(trains)** um·steigen*

channel das Programm, -e

charming charmant

cheap billig

check der Scheck, -s; **traveler's** ~ der Reisescheck, -s

cheese der Käse

chic schick

child das Kind, -er

choir der Chor, ⸚e

Christmas (das) Weihnachten; **at / for** ~ zu Weihnachten

church die Kirche, -n

citizen der Bürger, -

city die Stadt ⸚e; ~ **hall** das Rathaus, ⸚er; ~ **map** der Stadtplan, ⸚e

civil servant der Beamte (ein Beamter)

to **clap** klatschen

class (group) die Klasse, -n; **(time)** die Stunde, -n; **(instruction, school)** der Unterricht; **(instruction, university)** die Vorlesung, -en

clean sauber

to **clean** putzen

clerk: (civil servant) der Beamte (ein Beamter); **(salesman)** der Verkäufer, -

clock die Uhr, -en; **o'clock** Uhr

to **close** zu·machen

closed zu, geschlossen

closet der Schrank, ⸚e

clothing die Kleidung

coat der Mantel, ⸚

coffee der Kaffee

Coke die Cola

cold kalt (ä)

cold: to catch a ~ sich erkälten

to **collect** sammeln

color die Farbe, -n; **What** ~ **is . . . ?** Welche Farbe hat . . . ?

colorful bunt

to **comb** (sich) kämmen

to **come** kommen*; **to ~ along** mit·kommen*; **to ~ back** zurück·kommen*; **to ~ in** herein·kommen*; **That comes to . . . (altogether).** Das kostet (zusammen) . . .; **Oh, ~ on!** Ach was!

comfortable bequem

comical komisch

common gemeinsam

compact disc, CD die CD,-s

company die Firma, Firmen; **large** ~ das Unternehmen,-

composer der Komponist, -en, -en

concern die Sorge,-n
to **be concerned (about)** sich Sorgen machen (um)
concert das Konzert, -e
congenial sympathisch; **un~** unsympathisch
to **congratulate** gratulieren
to **continue** weiter·gehen*, weiter·machen
convenient bequem
to **cook** kochen
cookie das Plätzchen, -
cool kühl
corner die Ecke, -n
correct richtig
to **cost** kosten
to **count** zählen
counter der Schalter, -
country das Land, ⸚er; **in(to) the ~(side)** auf dem / aufs Land
couple: a ~ of ein paar
course der Kurs, -e; **of ~** natürlich; (na) klar
cousin der Vetter, -n / die Kusine,-n
cozy gemütlich
crazy verrückt
to **cry** weinen
cucumber die Gurke, -n
cup die Tasse, -n; **a ~ of . . .** eine Tasse . . .
cupboard der Schrank, ⸚e
cultural(ly) kulturell
curtain der Vorhang, ⸚e

D

daily täglich
to **dance** tanzen
danger die Gefahr, -en
dangerous gefährlich
dark dunkel
date (calendar) das Datum, Daten; **What's the ~ today?** Den wievielten haben wir heute?
daughter die Tochter, ⸚
day der Tag, -e; **during the ~** am Tag; **one ~** eines Tages; **all ~ long, the whole ~** den ganzen Tag; **each ~** jeden Tag; **in those days** damals
dear lieb-; **Oh ~!** Ach du liebes bißchen!
December der Dezember; **in ~** im Dezember
to **decide** sich entscheiden*

definitely unbedingt
dentist der Zahnarzt, ⸚e / die Zahnärztin, -nen
departure die Abfahrt,-en
to **depend: That depends.** Das kommt darauf an.
dependent unselbständig
desk der Schreibtisch, -e
dessert der Nachtisch
to **destroy** zerstören
to **develop** (sich) entwickeln; **~ apart** sich auseinander·entwickeln
difference der Unterschied, -e
different(ly) verschieden, anders; **something ~** etwas anderes
difficult schwer, schwierig
dining room das Eßzimmer, -
dinner das Mittagessen, das Abendessen
dirty schmutzig
dishonest unehrlich
to **divide** teilen
divorce die Scheidung, -en
divorced geschieden
to **do** tun*, machen
doctor der Arzt, ⸚e / die Ärztin, -nen
dollar der Dollar, -
door die Tür, -en
dorm das Studentenheim, -e
downstairs unten
to **dream (of)** träumen (von)
dress das Kleid, -er
dressed: to get ~ (sich) an·ziehen*; **to get un~** (sich) aus·ziehen*
dresser die Kommode, -n
to **drink** trinken*
to **drive** fahren*; **to ~ on (keep on driving)** weiter-fahren*; **to ~ up** hinauf·fahren*
drugstore die Drogerie, -n
dull langweilig
during während (+ *gen.*)
dynamic temperamentvoll

E

each jed-
ear das Ohr, -en
earlier früher
early früh
to **earn** verdienen
earth die Erde
east der Osten; **~ of** östlich von

Easter Ostern; **at / for ~** zu Ostern
easy leicht
to **eat** essen*
economy die Wirtschaft
educated gebildet
egg das Ei, -er
employee der Angestellte (ein Angestellter)
end das Ende; **in the ~** am Ende
engaged verlobt; **to get ~ (to)** sich verloben (mit)
engineer der Ingenieur, -e
England (das) England
English (*adj.*) englisch; **in ~** auf englisch; **(language)** Englisch; **Do you speak ~?** Sprechen Sie Englisch?; **(person)** der Engländer, -
enough genug
to **enter** herein·kommen*
entertainment die Unterhaltung
entire(ly) ganz
entrance der Eingang, ⸚e
environment die Umwelt
equal gleich
especially besonders
etc. usw., und so weiter
even sogar
evening der Abend, -e, abend; **Good ~.** Guten Abend! **in the ~** abends, am Abend
every jed-
everything alles
everywhere überall
exact(ly) genau
exam die Prüfung, -en; **to pass an ~** eine Prüfung bestehen*; **to flunk an ~** bei einer Prüfung durch·fallen*; **take an ~** eine Prüfung machen
excellent ausgezeichnet
exchange der Umtausch
to **exchange** um·tauschen, wechseln; **What's the ~ rate of the dollar?** Wie steht der Dollar?
exciting spannend
to **excuse** sich entschuldigen; **~ me!** Entschuldigen Sie! Entschuldigung! Verzeihung!
exit der Ausgang, ⸚e
to **expect** erwarten
expensive teuer

to **experience** erleben
to **explain** erklären
   eye das Auge, -n

F

face das Gesicht, -er
fairly ziemlich
to **fall** fallen*; **to ~ in love (with)** sich verlieben (in + *acc.*)
fall der Herbst, -e; **in (the) ~** im Herbst
false falsch
family die Familie, -n
famous berühmt
fantastic phantastisch, toll
far weit
fast schnell
fat dick
father der Vater, ⸚
fear die Angst, ⸚e
to **fear** Angst haben* (vor)
February der Februar; **in ~** im Februar
to **feel (a certain way)** sich fühlen; **How are you (feeling)?** Wie geht es Ihnen? Wie geht's?; **I'm (feeling) . . .** Es geht mir . . .; **to ~ like (doing something)** Lust haben* (zu + *inf.*)
few wenig-; ein paar
to **fill out** aus·füllen
film der Film, -e
to **finance** finanzieren
to **find** finden*
fine gut (besser, best-), schön
finger der Finger, -
finished fertig
firm die Firma, Firmen
first erst-; **~ of all, at ~** (zu)erst
fish der Fisch, -e
flight (plane) der Flug, ⸚e
to **fly** fliegen*
floor; on the first ~ im Parterre; **on the second ~** im ersten Stock
flower die Blume, -n
to **follow** folgen (ist) (+ *dat.*)
food das Essen; **Enjoy your ~.** Guten Appetit!
foot der Fuß, ⸚e
for für (+ *acc.*); **(since)** seit (+ *dat.*)
to **forbid** verbieten*
forbidden verboten
foreign ausländisch

foreigner der Ausländer, -
forest der Wald, ⸚er
to **forget** vergessen*
fork die Gabel, -n
foyer der Flur
France (das) Frankreich
free frei
French *(adj.)* französisch; **in ~** auf französisch; **(language)** Französisch; **Do you speak ~?** Sprechen Sie Französisch?; **(person)** der Franzose, -n, -n / die Französin, -nen
fresh frisch
Friday (der) Freitag; **on Fridays** freitags
friend der Freund, -e
friendly freundlich; **un~** unfreundlich
from von (+ *dat.*); **(a native of)** aus (+ *dat.*); **I'm ~ . . .** Ich bin aus. . . , Ich komme aus . . .; **(numbers) ~ . . . to** von . . . bis; **(place) ~ . . . to** von . . . zu / nach
front: in ~ of vor (+ *acc.* / *dat.*)
fruit das Obst
full voll
fun der Spaß; **to be ~** Spaß machen
funny lustig, witzig; komisch
furniture die Möbel *(pl.)*
future die Zukunft

G

game das Spiel, -e
garage die Garage, -n
garden der Garten, ⸚
gentleman der Herr, -n, -en
genuine(ly) echt
German *(adj.)* deutsch; **in ~** auf deutsch; **(language)** Deutsch; **Do you speak ~?** Sprechen Sie Deutsch?; **(person)** der Deutsche (ein Deutscher) / die Deutsche (eine Deutsche)
Germany (das) Deutschland
to **get (become)** werden*; **(fetch)** holen; **(receive)** bekommen*; **to ~ off** aus·steigen*; **to ~ on** *or* **in** ein·steigen*; **to ~ up** auf·stehen*; **to ~ to know** kennen·lernen; **to ~ used to** sich gewöhnen an

girl das Mädchen, -
to **give** geben*; **(as a present)** schenken
glad froh
gladly gern (lieber, liebst-)
Glad to meet you. Freut mich.
glass das Glas, ⸚er; **a ~ of . . .** ein Glas . . .
to **go** gehen*; **to ~ by (e.g., bus)** fahren* mit; **to ~ by plane** fliegen*; **to ~ out** aus·gehen*; **to ~ up** hinauf·fahren*
good gut (besser, best-); **~-looking** gutaussehend
Good-bye! Auf Wiedersehen! Tschüß!; **(on the phone)** Auf Wiederhören!
goodness: My ~! Ach du liebes bißchen!
grade die Note, -n
grandfather der Großvater, ⸚
grandmother die Großmutter, ⸚
grandparents die Großeltern *(pl.)*
gray grau
great (size) groß; **(terrific)** prima, toll
green grün
greeting der Gruß, ⸚e
grief: Good ~! Ach du liebes bißchen!
groceries die Lebensmittel *(pl.)*
to **grow** wachsen*; **to ~ together** zusammen·wachsen*
to **guarantee** garantieren
guest der Gast, ⸚e
guitar die Gitarre, -n

H

hair das Haar, -e
half halb; **in ~ an hour** in einer halben Stunde
hallway der Flur
hand die Hand, ⸚e
to **hang (up)** hängen
to **hang (be hanging)** hängen*
to **happen** geschehen*
happy glücklich, froh
hard (difficult) schwer
hardly kaum
to **have** haben*; **to ~ to** müssen*
head der Kopf, ⸚e
healthy gesund (ü)
to **hear** hören

heavy schwer
Hello! Guten Tag!
help die Hilfe
to **help** helfen* (+ *dat.*)
her ihr
here hier
Hi! Guten Tag! Hallo!
high hoch (hoh-) (höher, höchst)
to **hike** wandern (ist)
his sein
historical(ly) historisch
history die Geschichte
hobby das Hobby, -s
to **hold** halten*
holiday der Feiertag, -e
home: at ~ zu Hause; **(toward) ~** nach Hause; **at the ~ of** bei (+ *dat.*); **(homeland)** die Heimat
honest ehrlich
to **hope** hoffen
hot heiß
hotel das Hotel, -s, der Gasthof, ¨e, die Pension, -en
hour die Stunde, -n; **for hours** stundenlang
house das Haus, ¨er
household der Haushalt
housewife die Hausfrau, -en
how wie; **~ much?** wieviel?; **~ many?** wie viele?; **~ much is . . . ?** Was kostet . . . ?; **~ much are . . . ?** Was kosten . . . ? **~ are you?** Wie geht's?, Wie geht es Ihnen?; **~ come?** Wieso?
however aber, allerdings; doch
human being der Mensch, -en, -en
hunger der Hunger
hungry: I'm ~. Ich habe Hunger.
to **hurry** sich beeilen
to **hurt** weh tun*; **My (throat) hurts.** Mir tut (der Hals) weh.
husband der Mann, ¨er

I

ice, ice cream das Eis
idea die Idee,-n; **I've no ~!** Keine Ahnung!
identification der Ausweis, -e
if *(conj.)* wenn; ob
ill krank (ä)

to **imagine** sich vor·stellen; **I ~ (that)** ich stelle mir vor
immediately sofort
impatient ungeduldig
important wichtig
in in (+ *dat. / acc.*)
income das Einkommen, -
independent selbständig
individual(ly) einzeln
inexpensive billig
indeed wirklich, doch
industrious(ly) fleißig
inn der Gasthof, ¨e
insecure unsicher
inside in (+ *dat. / acc.*)
in spite of trotz (+ *gen.*)
instead of (an)statt (+ *gen.*)
intelligent intelligent
interest (in) das Interesse (an + *dat.*)
interested: to be ~ in sich interessieren für
interesting interessant
intermission die Pause, -n
to **invite (to)** ein·laden* (zu)
island die Insel, -n
isn't it? nicht wahr?
Italian *(adj.)* italienisch; **in ~** auf italienisch; **(language)** Italienisch; **Do you speak ~?** Sprechen Sie Italienisch?; **(person)** der Italiener, -
Italy (das) Italien
its sein, ihr

J

jacket die Jacke, -n
jam die Marmelade, -n
January der Januar; **in ~** im Januar
Jeans die Jeans, -
job die Arbeit; **(position)** die Stelle, -n
joint(ly) gemeinsam
juice der Saft, ¨e
July der Juli; **in ~** im Juli
to **jump** springen*
June der Juni; **in ~** im Juni
just gerade; **~ like** genau(so) wie; **~ when** gerade als

K

to **keep** behalten*; **to ~ in shape** sich fit halten*
key der Schlüssel, -

kind nett; **what ~ of (a)?** was für (ein)?
king der König, -e
kitchen die Küche, -n
knee das Knie, -
knife das Messer, -
to **know (be acquainted with)** kennen*; **(a fact)** wissen*; **(a skill)** können*
known bekannt

L

lab das Labor, -s (*or* -e)
lady die Dame, -n
lake der See, -n
lamp die Lampe, -n
to **land** landen (ist)
landscape die Landschaft
language die Sprache, -n
large groß (ö)
last letzt-
late spät; **How ~ is it?** Wie spät ist es?, Wieviel Uhr ist es?
later später; **See you ~.** Bis später!
to **laugh** lachen
lawyer der Rechtsanwalt, ¨e / die Rechtsanwältin, -nen
to **lay (down)** legen
lazy faul
to **learn** lernen
to **leave (behind)** lassen*; **~ from** ab·fahren* von, ab·fliegen* von; **(~ a place)** verlassen*
lecture die Vorlesung, -en; **~ hall** der Hörsaal, -säle
left links; link-
leg das Bein, -e
leisure time die Freizeit
lemonade die Limonade, -n
to **let** lassen*
letter der Brief, -e
lettuce der Salat
library die Bibliothek, -en
to **lie (to be located)** liegen*; **to ~ down** sich (hin·)legen
life das Leben
light leicht; **(bright)** hell
likable sympathisch; **un~** unsympathisch
like wie; **just ~** genau(so) wie; **s.th. ~** so etwas wie
to **like** gefallen*; **I would ~ (to have)** ich möchte, ich hätte gern

to **listen** zu·hören (+ *dat.*); **to ~ to** sich an·hören

little klein; (**amount**) wenig, ein bißchen; (**some**) etwas

to **live** leben; (**reside**) wohnen

living room das Wohnzimmer, -

long (*adj.*) lang (ä); (*adv.*) lange; **how ~?**; wie lange?; **So ~!** Tschüß!

to **look** sehen*; **to ~ (like)** aus·sehen* (wie + *nom.*); **to ~ at** sich an·sehen*; **to ~ for** suchen; **to ~ forward to** sich freuen auf (+ *acc.*)

to **lose** verlieren*

loud(ly) laut

love die Liebe; **to be in ~ (with)** verliebt sein* (in + *acc.*); **to fall in ~ (with)** sich verlieben (in + *acc.*)

to **love** lieben

luck das Glück; **to be lucky** Glück haben*; **to be unlucky** Pech haben*

luggage das Gepäck

lunch das Mittagessen, -; **for ~** zum Mittagessen

M

magazine die Zeitschrift, -en

mail die Post; **~box** der Briefkasten, ⁻

mainly vor allem

major (field of study) das Hauptfach, ⁻er

to **make** machen

man der Mann, ⁻er; (**human being**) der Mensch, -en, -en; **gentle~** der Herr, -n, -en

many viele; **how ~?** wie viele?; **~ a** manch-

map die Landkarte, -n; **city ~** der Stadtplan, ⁻e

March der März; **in ~** im März

mark (German) die Mark (DM)

market der Markt, ⁻e

marmalade die Marmelade, -n

marriage die Ehe, -n

married verheiratet

to **marry, get married** heiraten

matter: (That) doesn't ~. (Das) macht nichts. **What's the ~?** Was ist los?

may dürfen*

May der Mai; **in ~** im Mai

meal das Essen, -; **Enjoy your ~.** Guten Appetit!

to **mean (signify)** bedeuten; (**think**) meinen

meanwhile inzwischen

meat das Fleisch

to **meet (get to know)** kennen·lernen; **Glad to ~ you.** Freut mich (sehr, Sie kennenzulernen).

menu die Speisekarte, -n

middle die Mitte; **in the ~ of** mitten in / auf (+ *dat.*)

milk die Milch

minor (field of study) das Nebenfach, ⁻er

minute die Minute, -n; **See you in a few ~s!** Bis gleich!

Miss (das) Fräulein, -

Monday (der) Montag; **on Mondays** montags

money das Geld; **to earn ~** Geld verdienen; **to spend ~** Geld aus·geben*

month der Monat, -e; **per ~** im Monat, pro Monat; **for one ~** einen Monat

monthly monatlich

monument das Denkmal, ⁻er

more mehr; **once ~** noch einmal

morning der Morgen; **Good ~.** Guten Morgen!; **in the ~** morgens; (**early**) **~** früh, morgen; **mid~** der Vormittag, vormittag

most meist-; **am meisten**

mostly meistens

mother die Mutter, ⁻

mountain der Berg, -e

mouth der Mund, ⁻er

movie (film) der Film, -e; (**theater**) das Kino, -s

Mr. Herr

Mrs. Frau

Ms. Frau

much viel (mehr, meist-); **how ~?** wieviel?

museum das Museum, Museen

music die Musik

musical musikalisch; **un~** unmusikalisch

must müssen*

my mein

N

name der Name, -ns; -n; **What's your ~?** Wie heißen Sie?; **My ~ is . . .** Ich heiße . . . , Mein Name ist . . .

to **name** nennen*

napkin die Serviette, -n

nation das Volk, ⁻er

near (distance) nah (näher, nächst-); (**vicinity**) bei (+ *dat.*), in der Nähe von (+ *dat.*)

neat prima; schick

neck der Hals, ⁻e

to **need** brauchen

neighbor der Nachbar, -n, -n

neither . . . nor weder . . . noch

never nie

nevertheless trotzdem

new neu; **s.th. ~** etwas Neues; **nothing ~** nichts Neues; **What's ~?** Was gibt's Neues?

New Year's Eve Silvester; **at / for ~** zu Silvester

news die Nachricht, -en

newspaper die Zeitung, -en

next nächst-; **~ to** neben (+ *dat. / acc.*)

nice schön, nett

nickname der Spitzname, -ns, -n

night die Nacht, ⁻e, nacht; **at ~** nachts; **to spend the ~** übernachten

no nein

nobody niemand

noisy laut

no one niemand

noodle die Nudel, -n

noon der Mittag, -e, mittag; **at ~** mittags; **after~** der Nachmittag, nachmittag

north der Norden; **in the ~** im Norden; **~ of** nördlich von

nose die Nase, -n

not nicht; **~ any** kein; **~ only . . . but also** nicht nur . . . sondern auch; **~ yet** noch nicht; **~ at all** gar nicht

notebook das Heft, -e

nothing (to) nichts (zu); **~ special** nichts Besonderes

novel der Roman, -e

November der November; **in ~** im November

now jetzt, nun; **just ~** gerade

number die Nummer; -n, die Zahl, -en

nurse die Krankenschwester, -n; *(male)* der Kranken-pfleger, -

O

o'clock Uhr

October der Oktober; **in ~** im Oktober

of course natürlich; doch

to **offer** an·bieten*

office das Büro, -s

often oft

old alt (ä)

on auf (+ *acc. / dat.*); **~ the first of July** am ersten Juli

once einmal; **~ more** noch ein-mal; **~ in a while** manchmal; **(formerly)** früher

one **(people, they)** man

only nur; **(not before)** erst; **not ~ ... but also** nicht nur . . . sondern auch

open auf, offen, geöffnet

to **open** öffnen, auf·machen

opposite das Gegenteil, -e

or oder

orange die Orange, -n; **(color)** orange

orchestra das Orchester, -

order: in ~ to um . . . zu (+ *inf.*)

to **order** bestellen

other ander-

our unser

out of aus (+ *dat.*)

over (location) über (+ *acc. / dat.*); **(finished)** vorbei; **~ there** da drüben

own *(adj.)* eigen-

P

to pack packen

package das Paket, -e

page die Seite, -n; **on / to ~ . . .** auf Seite . . .

to **paint** malen

palace das Schloß, ¨sser

pants die Hose, -n

paper das Papier, -e; **(term paper)** die Arbeit, -en

parcel das Paket, -e

parents die Eltern *(pl.)*

to **pardon: ~ me!** Entschuldigung! Entschuldigen Sie! Verzei-hung!

park der Park, -s

to **park** parken

part der Teil, -e; **to take ~ (in)** teil·nehmen* (an + *dat.*)

to **participate (in)** teil·nehmen* (an + *dat*)

party die Party, -s

to **pass (an exam)** bestehen*; **to ~ by** vorbei·gehen*, vorbei-kommen*, vorbei·fahren*

passport der Paß, ¨sse

past: in the ~ früher

patient geduldig

to **pay** bezahlen

pea die Erbse, -n

peace der Frieden

pen der Kuli, -s

pencil der Bleistift, -e

penny der Pfennig, -e; **two pennies** zwei Pfennig

people die Leute *(pl.)*; **(human being)** der Mensch, -en, -en; **(nation)** das Volk, ¨er

pepper der Pfeffer

per pro

performance die Vorstel-lung, -en

perhaps vielleicht

person der Mensch, -en, -en

pharmacy die Apotheke, -n

to **phone** an·rufen*, telefonieren

physician der Arzt, ¨e / die Ärztin, -nen

piano das Klavier, -e; **to play the ~** Klavier spielen

picture das Bild, -er; **to take ~s** photographieren

piece das Stück, -e

pink rosa

place (location) der Platz, ¨e; **at our ~** bei uns; **in your ~** an deiner Stelle

plan der Plan, ¨e

to **plan** planen, vor·haben*

plane das Flugzeug, -e

plate der Teller, -

platform der Bahnsteig, -e

play das Stück, ¨e

to **play** spielen; **to ~ checkers** Dame spielen; **to ~ chess** Schach spielen; **to ~ tennis** Tennis spielen

pleasant gemütlich; **un~** un-gemütlich

to **please** gefallen*

please bitte

pocket die Tasche, -n

policeman der Polizist, -en, -en

policewoman die Polizistin, -nen

poor arm (ä)

position die Stelle, -n

possible möglich; **im~** un-möglich

postcard Ansichtskarte, -n

post office die Post

P.O. box das Postfach, ¨er

potato die Kartoffel, -n

pound das Pfund, -e

power die Macht, ¨e

practical(ly) praktisch

to **prefer** lieber tun*; vor·ziehen*

present (gift) das Geschenk, -e

pretty hübsch

probably wahrscheinlich

problem das Problem, -e

profession der Beruf, -e

professor der Professor, -en

program das Programm, -e; die Sendung, -en

to **promise** versprechen*

to **protect** schützen

proud (of) stolz (auf + *acc.*)

pudding der Pudding, -s

to **pull** ziehen*

pullover der Pullover, -, Pulli, -s

purple lila

to **put (set down)** setzen; **(stand upright)** (hin·)stellen; **(lay down)** (hin·)legen; **(hang up)** (hin·)hängen; **to ~ on (clothing)** (sich) an·ziehen*

Q

quarter das Viertel; **a ~ to** Viertel vor; **a ~ past** Viertel nach; **in a ~ of an hour** in einer Viertelstunde; **(university) quarter** das Quartal, -e

question die Frage, -n; **to ask a ~** eine Frage stellen

quick(ly) schnell

quite ziemlich

R

radio das Radio, -s

railway die Bahn, -en

to **rain** regnen; **It's raining.** Es regnet.

rather lieber

to **read** lesen*

ready fertig

really wirklich; echt

to **rebuild** wiederauf·bauen

to **receive** bekommen*

to **recognize** erkennen*

to **recommend** empfehlen*

red rot (ö)

refrigerator der Kühl-
schrank, ⸚e

region die Gegend, -en; das
Gebiet, -e

regular normal

to relax sich aus·ruhen

to remain bleiben*

to remember sich erinnern (an +
acc.)

to remind (of) erinnern (an +
acc.)

to renovate renovieren

to rent mieten; to ~ out vermieten

to repeat wiederholen

reporter der Journalist,
-en, -en

to request bitten*

to rescue retten

to reserve reservieren

to reside wohnen

responsible verantwor-
tungsvoll

restaurant das Restaurant, -s

to restore restaurieren

to return zurück·kommen*

return address der Absender, -

reunification die Wiedervereinigung

rice der Reis

rich reich

right rechts, recht-; (correct)
richtig; You're ~. Du hast
recht.; isn't it (right)? nicht
wahr?; (That's) ~. (Das)
stimmt.; ~ away sofort

river der Fluß, ⸚sse

roll das Brötchen, -

room das Zimmer, -;
bed~ das Schlafzimmer, -;
bath~ das Bad, ⸚er (Badezimmer, -); dining ~ das Eßzimmer, -; living ~ das
Wohnzimmer, -; guest ~ das
Gästezimmer, -; single ~ das
Einzelzimmer, -; double ~
das Doppelzimmer, -

roommate der Zimmerkollege,
-n, -n, die Zimmerkollegin,
-nen

round-trip ticket die Hin- und
Rückfahrkarte, -n

to run laufen*

S

sad traurig

safe sicher

safety die Sicherheit

salad der Salat, -e

salt das Salz

same gleich; the ~ to you
gleichfalls

Saturday (der) Samstag; on
Saturdays samstags

sausage die Wurst; ⸚e

to save (money or time) sparen;
(rescue) retten

to say sagen; Could you ~ that
again? What did you ~?
Wie bitte?

scared: to be ~ (of) Angst
haben* (vor)

scenery die Landschaft

schedule (transportation) der
Fahrplan, ⸚e

scholarship das Stipendium,
Stipendien

school die Schule, -n

science die Wissenschaft, -en;
natural ~ die Naturwis-
senschaft, -en

scientist der Wissenschaftler, -

second die Sekunde, -n

secretary die Sekretärin, -nen

secure sicher

security die Sicherheit

to see sehen*; Let's ~. Mal
sehen.; Oh, I ~. Ach so!

to seem scheinen*

self-confident selbstbewußt

self-employed selbständig

to sell verkaufen

semester das Semester, -

seminar das Seminar, -e

to send schicken

sentence der Satz, ⸚e

September der September; in
~ im September

to set (down) setzen

several mehrer- (pl.)

to share teilen

shared gemeinsam

to shave sich rasieren

shelf das Regal, -e

to shine scheinen*

shirt das Hemd, -en

shoe der Schuh, -e

shop das Geschäft, -e

to shop ein·kaufen; to go ~ing
einkaufen gehen*

short klein; kurz (ü)

to show zeigen

shower die Dusche, -n; to take
a ~ (sich) duschen

sick krank (ä)

to sign up for belegen

to signify bedeuten

silly dumm (ü)

simple, simply einfach

since (time) seit (+ dat.)

to sing singen*

single (unmarried) unverheiratet, ledig

sister die Schwester, -n

to sit (be sitting) sitzen*; to ~
down sich (hin·)setzen

to ski Ski laufen*; to go ~ing Ski
laufen gehen*

skinny dünn

skirt der Rock, ⸚e

slacks die Hose, -n

slender schlank

to sleep schlafen*

slim schlank

slow(ly) langsam

small klein

to snow schneien

soccer: to play ~ Fußball spielen

sofa das Sofa, -s

some etwas (sg.); einig- (pl.);
(many a) manch-; (a couple
of) ein paar

somebody jemand

something (to) etwas (zu)

sometimes manchmal

son der Sohn, ⸚e

song das Lied, -er

soon bald; See you ~! Bis bald!

sorry: I'm ~. Es tut mir leid.

so that (conj.) so daß

soup die Suppe, -n

south der Süden; in the ~ im
Süden; ~ of südlich von

Spain (das) Spanien

Spanish (adj.) spanisch; in ~
auf spanisch; (language)
Spanisch; Do you speak ~?
Sprechen Sie Spanisch?;
(person) der Spanier, -

to speak sprechen*; ~ up
(louder)! Sprechen Sie
lauter!

special : something ~ etwas
Besonderes; nothing ~
nichts Besonderes

spectator der Zuschauer, -

to spend (money) aus·geben*

spoon der Löffel, -

sport(s) der Sport; to engage
in ~ Sport treiben*

spring der Frühling, -e; in
(the) ~ im Frühling

square der Platz, ¨e
stamp die Briefmarke, -n
to stand (upright), be standing
   stehen*
start der Anfang, ¨e
state der Staat, -en
to stay bleiben*
still noch
stomach der Bauch, ¨e
stop (for buses etc.) die Haltestelle, -n
to stop (doing s.th.) auf·hören (zu
   + inf.)
to stop (in a vehicle) halten*
stopover der Aufenthalt, -e
store das Geschäft, -e; department ~ das Kaufhaus, ¨er
story die Geschichte, -n; detective ~ der Krimi, -s
straight gerade; ~ ahead
   geradeaus
strange komisch
strawberry die Erdbeere, -n
street die Straße, -n; main ~
   die Hauptstraße, -n
streetcar die Straßenbahn, -en
strenuous anstrengend
strict(ly) streng
to stroll bummeln (ist)
student der Student, -en, -en /
   die Studentin, -nen
study das Studium, Studien;
   (room) das Arbeitszimmer, -
to study lernen; (a particular
   field, be a student at a university) studieren (an +
   dat.)
stupid dumm (ü)
subject das Fach, ¨er
subway die U-Bahn
such so ein (sg.); solch (pl.)
sudden(ly) plötzlich
sugar der Zucker
suitcase der Koffer, -
summer der Sommer, -; in
   (the) ~ im Sommer
sun die Sonne; The ~ is shining. Die Sonne scheint.
Sunday (der) Sonntag; on
   Sundays sonntags
superb super
supermarket der Super-
   markt, ¨e
supper das Abendessen; for ~
   zum Abendessen
to suppose an·nehmen*
sure sicher; doch (na) klar; for
   ~ bestimmt

surely bestimmt, sicher
surprise die Überraschung, -en
to surprise überraschen
surroundings die Umgebung;
   (ecology) die Umwelt
suspenseful spannend
sweater der Pullover, -, der
   Pulli, -s
sweatshirt das Sweatshirt, -s
to swim schwimmen*, baden
Swiss (person) der Schweizer, -; (adj.) Schweizer
Switzerland die Schweiz

T

table der Tisch, -e
to take nehmen*; to ~ along
   mit·nehmen*; to ~ off
   (clothing) (sich)
   aus·ziehen*; to ~ off
   (plane) ab·fliegen*; (last)
   dauern; to ~ (a course)
   belegen; to ~ an exam eine
   Prüfung machen; ~ care!
   Mach's gut!
talented talentiert; un~ untalentiert
to talk reden, sprechen*; to ~ to
   reden mit, sprechen* mit; to
   ~ about reden über (+ acc.),
   sprechen* (von)
to taste schmecken; That tastes
   good. Das schmeckt (gut).
taxi das Taxi, -s
tea der Tee, -s
to teach lehren
teacher der Lehrer, -
to tear down ab·reißen*
telephone das Telefon, -e
tell sagen, erzählen (von +
   dat.)
tennis Tennis
terrible, terribly furchtbar
terrific toll, super
test die Prüfung, -en; to take a
   ~ eine Prüfung machen
than (after comp.) als
to thank danken (+ dat.)
Thank you. Danke!; ~ very
   much. Vielen Dank!
that das; (conj.) daß; so ~
   (conj.) so daß
the . . . the je (+ comp.) . . .
   desto (+ comp.)
theater das Theater, -; movie ~
   das Kino, -s
their ihr

then dann; (in those days)
   damals
there da, dort; over ~ da
   drüben; ~ is (are) es gibt
therefore deshalb
thick dick
thin dünn
things: all sorts of ~ so einiges
to think (of) denken* (an +
   acc.); (be of an opinion)
   glauben, meinen; I ~ it's . . .
   Ich finde es . . . ; I ~ so, too.
   Das finde ich auch.
thinker der Denker, -
thirst der Durst
thirsty: I'm ~. Ich habe Durst.
this dies-
thought der Gedanke, -ns, -n
throat der Hals, ¨e
through durch (+ acc.)
Thursday (der) Donnerstag;
   on Thursdays donnerstags
ticket die Karte, -n; (bus, etc.)
   die Fahrkarte, -n; (return
   ticket) die (Hin- und) Rückfahrkarte, -n ~ window der
   Schalter, -
time die Zeit, -en; What ~ is it?
   Wie spät ist es? Wieviel Uhr
   ist es?; at what ~? wann?;
   in the mean~ inzwischen;
   one ~ einmal; the first ~ das
   erste Mal; for the first ~
   zum ersten Mal
tired müde
to zu (+ dat.); an (+ acc.); (a
   country, etc.) nach
today heute
together gemeinsam, zusammen; ~ with mit (+ dat.)
toilet die Toilette, -n
tomato die Tomate, -n
tomorrow morgen; the day
   after ~ übermorgen
too (also) auch; (too much) zu
   viel
tooth der Zahn, ¨e
tourist der Tourist, -en, -en
tower der Turm, ¨e
town die Stadt, ¨e
track das Gleis, -e
traffic der Verkehr
trail der Weg, -e
train der Zug, ¨e, die Bahn, -en;
   ~ station der Bahnhof, ¨e
training die Ausbildung
to travel reisen (ist)
tree der Baum, ¨e

trillion *(American)* die Billion, -en

trip die Reise, -n, die Fahrt, -en; **to take a ~** eine Reise machen

true richtig, wahr; **(That's) ~.** (Das) stimmt.

to **try** versuchen

T-shirt das T-Shirt, -s

Tuesday (der) Dienstag; **on Tuesdays** dienstags

to **turn: to ~ off** (radio, etc.) aus·machen; **to ~ on** (radio, etc.) an·machen

TV (medium) das Fernsehen; **(set)** der Fernseher, -; **to watch ~** fern·sehen*

typical(ly) typisch

U

ugly häßlich

unathletic unsportlich

uncle der Onkel, -

under unter (+ *acc.* / *dat.*)

to **understand** verstehen*

understanding verständnisvoll

uneducated ungebildet

unfortunately leider

unfriendly unfreundlich

unification die Vereinigung

United States (U.S.) die Vereinigten Staaten (U.S.A.) *(pl.)*

university die Universität, -en (die Uni, -s)

unlucky: to be ~ Pech haben*

unmarried unverheiratet

unmusical unmusikalisch

unique einmalig

unsafe unsicher

untalented untalentiert

until bis; **not ~** erst

upset: to get ~ about sich ärgern über (+ *acc.*)

upstairs oben

usual(ly) gewöhnlich, meistens

to **use** gebrauchen

to **utilize** gebrauchen

V

vacation die Ferien *(pl.)*

various verschieden-

vegetable(s) das Gemüse, -

versatile vielseitig

very sehr; ganz

viewer der Zuschauer, -

village das Dorf, ¨er

to **visit** besuchen; **(sightseeing)** besichtigen

W

to **wait (for)** warten (auf + *acc.*)

waiter der Kellner, -, der Ober, -; Herr Ober!

waitress die Kellnerin, -nen

to **walk** zu Fuß gehen*, laufen*; **to go for a ~** spazieren·gehen*

wall die Wand, ¨e; **(thick)** die Mauer, -n

to **want to** wollen*, möchten*

war der Krieg, -e

warm warm (ä)

to **wash (o.s.)** (sich) waschen*

watch (clock) die Uhr, -en

to **watch: (TV)** fern·sehen*; **(pay attention)** auf·passen; **~ out!** Passen Sie auf!

water das Wasser

way der Weg, -e; **this ~** auf diese Weise

to **wear** tragen*

weather das Wetter

wedding die Hochzeit, -en

Wednesday (der) Mittwoch; **on Wednesdays** mittwochs

week die Woche, -n; **all ~ long** die ganze Woche; **this ~** diese Woche

weekend das Wochenende, -n; **on the ~** am Wochenende

weekly wöchentlich

welcome: You're ~. Bitte (bitte)! Nichts zu danken!

well *(adv.)* gut

west der Westen; **in the ~** im Westen; **~ of** westlich von

what? was?; **~ did you say?** Wie bitte?; **~'s new?** Was gibt's (Neues)?; **~'s on . . . ?** Was gibt's im . . . ?; **So ~!** Na und!; **~ kind of (a)?** was für (ein)?

when (at what time) wann?; **(whenever)** *(conj.)* wenn; *(conj., single action in past)* als; **just ~** *(conj.)* gerade als

where? wo?; **from ~?** woher?; **~ to?** wohin?

whether *(conj.)* ob

which? welch-?

while *(conj.)* während

white weiß

who? wer?

whole ganz

whom? wen?, wem?

whose wessen?

why? warum?, wieso?

wife die Frau, -en

wild wild

to **win** gewinnen*

window das Fenster, -; **ticket ~** der Schalter, -

wine der Wein, -e

winter der Winter; **in (the) ~** im Winter

to **wish** (sich) wünschen

with mit (+ *dat.*); **(at the home of)** bei (+ *dat.*); **~ me (us . . .)** bei mir (uns . . .)

without ohne (+ *acc.*)

woman (Mrs., Ms.) die Frau, -en

wonderful(ly) wunderbar, prima

woods der Wald, ¨er

work die Arbeit

to **work** arbeiten

worker der Arbeiter, -

world die Welt, -en

worry die Sorge, -n

to **worry (about)** sich Sorgen machen (um)

to **write** schreiben*; **to ~ to** schreiben an (+ *acc.*); **to ~ about** schreiben über (+ *acc.*); **to ~ down** auf·schreiben*

wrong falsch; **You are ~.** Du hast unrecht.

Y

year das Jahr, -e; **all ~ long** das ganze Jahr; **next ~** nächstes Jahr

yellow gelb

yes ja; doch

yesterday gestern; **the day before ~** vorgestern

yet doch; **not ~** noch nicht

young jung (ü)

your dein, euer, Ihr

youth die Jugend

youth hostel die Jugendherberge, -n

Photo and Illustrations Credits

355   Scala
359   Ulrike Welsch
370   Masa Uemura/Leo de Wys Inc.
373   Peter Menzel
378   Kerth/Leo de Wys Inc.
381   Rene Burri/MAGNUM
383   ADAC SPECIAL BERLIN/Kartendesign
          Hamburg
389   Emmet Lewis/Wide World Photos
394   Inter Nationes

395   Inter Nationes
397   German Information Center
398   German Information Center
401   Inter Nationes
403   Paul Conklin/Monkmeyer Press Photo
404   ADN-ZB/Hirndorf
409   Ulrike Welsch
417   Inter Nationes
418   Inter Nationes
425   Inter Nationes

Index

This index is limited to grammatical entries. Topical vocabulary (e.g., days of the week, food, hobbies, etc.) and material from the Sprechsituationen can be found in the table of contents. Entries appearing in the Rückblicke are indicated by parentheses.